A READER, RHETORIC AND HANDBOOK

FROM READING TO *Writing*

Laurence Steven • Douglas H. Parker • Jack Lewis

Prentice-Hall Canada Inc., Scarborough, Ontario

Canadian Cataloguing in Publication Data
Steven, Laurence
From reading to writing

Bibliography: p.
Includes index.
ISBN 0-13-332016-2

1. English language—Rhetoric. 2. College readers.
I. Parker, Douglas H. (Douglas Harold), 1942-
II. Lewis, Jack, 1929- . III. Title.

PE1408.S88 1988 808'.0427 C88-093667-3

Prentice-Hall, Inc., Englewood Cliffs, New Jersey
Prentice-Hall International, Inc., London
Prentice-Hall of Australia, Pty., Ltd., Sydney
Prentice-Hall of India Pvt., Ltd., New Delhi
Prentice-Hall of Japan, Inc., Tokyo
Prentice-Hall of Southeast Asia (Pte.) Ltd., Singapore
Editora Prentice-Hall do Brasil Ltda., Rio de Janeiro
Prentice-Hall Hispanoamericana, S.A., Mexico

ISBN 0-13-332016-2

Production Editor: Katherine Mototsune
Copy Editor: Lois Rock
Production Coordinator: Matt Lumsdon
Typesetting: Keystrokes Plus

5 WC 95

Printed and bound in Canada by Webcom Limited

The following pages constitute an extension of the copyright page. Every reasonable effort has been made to find copyright holders. The publishers would be pleased to have any errors or omissions brought to their attention.

Robert Thomas Allen: "Where Women Feared to Tread" *The Canadian,* August 1976. By permission of the author.

Barbara Amiel: "Anyone who supports censorship be warned: this may make you upchuck" *Maclean's,* May 1978. By permission of the publisher. "The Chaos of Criminal Justice in Canada. Or: in defence of vengeance" *Saturday Night,* September 1975. By permission of the author.

Margaret Atwood: from *Survival: Thematic Guide to Canadian Literature.* By permission of the House of Anansi Press.

Kerry Banks: from "Diagnosing Dracula" *Equinox: The Magazine of Canadian Discovery,* November/December 1983. By permission of the author.

Pierre Berton: "Floating Down the Yukon" *Maclean's,* December 1972. "Legends in the Rough" *The Canadian,* September 11, 1976. Both by permission of the author.

Clark Blaise: from *A North American Education.* Copyright © 1973 by Clarke Blaise. By permission. From "To Begin, To Begin" *The Narrative Voice,* John Metcalf, ed. By permission of the author.

Barry Broadfoot: "Grand Beach Then and Now" *My Own Years.* Copyright © 1983 by Barry Broadfoot. Reprinted by permission of Doubleday Publishing Group.

Harry Bruce: "The Alchemy of Sailing" *Maclean's,* July 1973. By permission of the publisher.

Ted Byfield: from *Just Think, Mr. Berton . . . A Little Harder.* By permission of the author.

Morley Callaghan: "Morley Callaghan Remembers Foster Hewitt" *Saturday Night,* September 1985. By permission of the author.

June Callwood: "June Callwood's Canada: Crying Broken-hearted Over You" *Maclean's,* January 1972. By permission of the author.

Dalton Camp: from *An Eclectic Eel* (Deneau, 1981). "The Decline in Public Morality" *Saturday Night,* January 1981. By permission of the author.

Emily Carr: from *Growing Pains.* By permission.

Dr. Cynthia Carver: from *Patient Beware: Dealing with Doctors and other Medical Dilemmas.* By permission of the author.

Anne Charney: "The Monument" *Saturday Night,* January 1981. By permission of the author.

Nancy Miller Chenier: from *Reproductive Hazards at Work: Men, Women and the Fertility Gamble.* By permission of the Canadian Advisory Council on the Status of Women.

David Coburn: from "Patient's Rights: A New Deal in Health Care" *Canadian Forum,* May 1980. By permission of the author.

Anne Collins: "On Commitment" *Toronto Life,* September 1985. By permission of the author.

John Robert Colombo: "Recipe for a Canadian Novel" *Abracadabra.* Used by permission of the Canadian Publishers, McClelland and Stewart, Toronto.

Commissioner of Official Languages: from *Annual Report, 1985.* By permission of the author.

Gerald M. Craig: "Northern Miracle?" *The United States and Canada* © 1968 by the President and Fellows of Harvard College.

Robertson Davies: from *A Voice from the Attic.* Used by permission of the Canadian Publishers, McClelland and Stewart, Toronto.

Ken Dryden: from *The Game.* Reprinted by permission of MacMillan of Canada, A Division of Canadian Publishing Corporation.

Valmai Howe Elkins: from *The Rights of the Pregnant Parent,* © 1985. Reprinted by permission of Lester & Orpen Dennys Publishers, Ltd., Canada.

Howard Engel: from *The Suicide Murders.* By permission of the author and his agent.

T.E. Farley: from *Exiles and Pioneers: Two Visions of Canada's Future, 1825-1975.* By permission of Borealis Press.

Timothy Findley: "Better Dead than Read? An Opposing View" *Books in Canada,* December 1978. By permission of the author.

Allan Fotheringham: "Dan George's Last Stand" *Maclean's,* July 1971. By permission of the author.

Graham Fraser: "A Sense of Being" *Notes for a Native Land,* Andy Wainwright, ed. Reprinted by permission of Oberon Press.

Trent Frayne: "As French-Canadian as Baseball" *Maclean's,* August 1971. By permission of the author.

Barbara Freeman: "Every Stroke Upward: Women Journalists in Canada, 1880-1906" *Canadian Women's Studies,* Fall 1986. By permission of the author and the publisher.

Northrop Frye: from *The Educated Imagination.* By permission of the author.

Robert Fulford: "Beware: the Censors are Marching Again" *Saturday Night,* September 1978. "Charter of Wrongs" *Saturday Night,* December 1976. Both by permission of the author.

John Gault: from "Politics: The Bawdy Politic" *Toronto Life,* April 1984. By permission of the author.

Globe and Mail: Anonymous article, 7 August 1987. By permission of The Globe and Mail, Toronto.

George Grant: from *Lament for a Nation.* Used by permission of the Canadian Publishers, McClelland and Stewart, Toronto.

Sandra Gwyn: "Over Home" *Saturday Night,* January 1987. By permission of the author.

Peter Gzowski: from *The Morningside Papers.* Used by permission of the Canadian Publishers, McClelland and Stewart, Toronto.

Roderick Haig-Brown: from "The Nature of Estuaries" *Fisherman's Fall.* By permission.

Robert H. Haynes: "What is the Biological Revolution?" *Man and the Biological Revolution,* Robert H. Haynes, ed. By permission of the author and York University.

Ralph Heintzman: "Liberalism and Censorship" editorial for *Journal of Canadian Studies,* Vol.13 No.4. By permission of the publisher.

Abby Hoffman: "Running for Gold" *Maclean's,* February 1975. By permission of the author.

Helen Hoffman: from *Mind Tricks for Parents* (with Janet Rosenstock). By permission of Paper Jacks Ltd.

A.Y. Jackson: from *A Painter's Country.* Courtesy of Dr. Naomi Jackson Groves.

Belva Kalbfleisch: "My Mother is a Taxidermist" *Chinook Expressways I* by Thorn & Irwin. Copyright © 1980, Gage Publishing Limited. Reproduced by permission of Gage Educational Publishing Company.

William Kilbourn: from "The Quest for the Peaceable Kingdom" *Canada: A Guide to the Peaceable Kingdom.* By permission of the author.

Margaret Laurence: "The Greater Evil" *Toronto Life,* September 1984. By permission of the Estate of Margaret Laurence. "Where the World Began" *Heart of a Stranger.* Used by permission of the Estate of Margaret Laurence and the Canadian Publishers, McClelland and Stewart, Toronto.

Irving Layton: from "What Canadians Don't Know About Love" *Engagements.* Used by permission of the Canadian Publishers, McClelland and Stewart, Toronto.

Stephen Leacock: from "The Rival Churches of St. Asaph and St. Osoph" *Arcadian Adventures with the Idle Rich.* Used by permission of the Canadian Publishers, McClelland and Stewart, Toronto.

René Lévesque: "Heartbreak" *Memoirs,* Philip Stratford, trans. Used by permission of the Canadian Publishers, McClelland and Stewart, Toronto.

Jack Ludwig: from "The Calgary Stampede" which appeared as "Get an Outfit, Be a Cowboy" in *Maclean's,* July 1975. © Jack Ludwig 1975, reprinted by permission of the author.

Hugh MacLennan: from "By Their Foods..." *Scotchman's Return and Other Essays.* By permission of Russell and Volkening, Inc. as agents for the author. Copyright under the Berne Convention.

George Radwanski: from *Trudeau.* By permission of the author.

Mordecai Richler: from "Going Home" *Notes on an Endangered Species.* Reprinted by permission of International Creative Management.

Sir Charles G.D. Roberts: "In the Deep of the Grass" *The Watchers of the Trails.* Used by permission of the Canadian Publishers, McClelland and Stewart, Toronto.

Spider Robinson: from *Mindkiller.* By permission of Holt, Rinehart and Winston.

Colin Ross: "The Story of Grey Owl" *The Compass,* Winter, 1979. By permission of the author and the publisher.

Lionel Rubinoff: from "National Purpose and Ideology" *Notes for a Native Land,* Andy Wainwright, ed. Reprinted by permission of Oberon Press.

R. Murray Schafer: "Canadian Culture: Colonial Culture" *Canadian Forum,* March 1984. By permission of the author.

G.B. Sinclair: "Grounds for Concern" *Saturday Night,* September 1982. By permission of the author.

Robin Skelton: from "O Canada" *Notes on a Native Land,* Andy Wainwright, ed. Reprinted by permission of Oberon Press.

Patricia Smart: From "La Nuit de la Poésie 80" *Canadian Forum,* June/July 1980. By permission of the author.

Victor C. Smith: from "Lumber, Pulp & Paper and Forestry" *A Vast and Magnificent Land,* Matt Bray and Ernie Epp, eds. By permission of the Ontario Ministry of Northern Affairs.

Sam Solecki: "Anansi, Oberon, Press Porcepic, Lester and Orpen Dennys, Hurtig, Turnstone, . . . The State of the Canadian Publishing Industry" *Canadian Forum,* October 1980. By permission of the author.

Edna Staebler: from *Food that Really Schmecks.* By permission of McGraw-Hill Ryerson.

Paul Stuewe: "Better Dead than Read?" *Books in Canada,* October 1978. By permission of the author.

Antonine Maillet: "Aunt Evangeline's Treasure" Wayne Grady, trans. *Saturday Night* January 1987. Originally published in *Par Dernière Chez Mon Père,* Leméac, 1987. By permission of the publisher and translator.

Marci McDonald: "Out of the Rough" *Maclean's,* June 1975. By permission of the publisher.

Liz McKee: "A Woman's View of Liberation" *Canada and the World,* December 1974. By permission of the publisher.

Marshall McLuhan: "The Violence of the Media" *Canadian Forum,* September 1976. By permission .

Brian Moore: from "The Tragic Vein of the Ordinary" *Conversations with Canadian Novelists,* [Silver] Donald Cameron, ed. Reprinted by permission of Curtis Brown Ltd. Copyright © 1973 by Brian Moore.

W.L. Morton: from "Canadian Nationhood and American World Power" *The Canadian Identity.* Copyright © W.L. Morton 1961. By permission of The University of Wisconsin Press.

Farley Mowat: from *And No Birds Sang.* By permission. "The Coming of the Deer" *The People of the Deer.* Used by permission of the Canadian Publishers, McClelland and Stewart, Toronto.

H.V. Nelles: from "Creighton's Seminar" *Canadian Forum,* September 1980. By permission of the author.

Peter C. Newman: from *Renegade in Power.* Used by permission of the Canadian Publisher, McClelland and Stewart, Toronto.

Toni Onley: "The Longest Night" *Saturday Night,* February 1985. By permission of the author.

Jacques Plante: "How to Watch the Stanley Cup" *Maclean's,* May 1971. By permission of the publisher.

Al Purdy: "Boozy Saddles" *Maclean's,* May 1975. By permission of, and with additions by, the author.

David Suzuki: "A Planet for the Taking" *Canadian Forum,* February 1985. By permission of the author.

Scott Symons: from *Place d'Armes.* Used by permission of the Canadian Publishers, McClelland and Stewart, Toronto.

Kent Thompson: from "Academy Stuff" *The Narrative Voice,* John Metcalf, ed. By permission of the author.

Marq de Villiers: from "Too Many Guns" *Toronto Life,* August 1975. By permission of the author.

George Whalley: "Introduction" *Death in the Barren Ground: The Diary of Edgar Christian,* George Whalley, ed. Reprinted by permission of Oberon Press. From *The Legend of John Hornby.* By permission of John Murray Publishers, London.

Richard B. Wright: from *The Weekend Man.* By permission.

Table of Contents

PART THREE The Research Paper / *455*

PART FOUR Supporting Material / *501*

Preface

From Reading to Writing: A Reader, Rhetoric and Handbook sprang from a constellation of factors: our desire for a one-volume text for our multi-sectioned first year course English 1500, Introductory Composition; our desire for an all *Canadian* book; our wish to consider the course readings as occasions for thought rather than primarily as models; our inability to discover a book that stressed "reading into writing" adequately for our needs; and our conviction that we had something good to offer teachers of composition.

Our experience teaching Introductory Composition often included a common frustration that arose from readers and rhetorics that did not mesh, or that seemed (because each had its own pedagogy) to contradict each other. The rhetorics often did not give reading the attention we felt it deserved, while the readers shirked on the options available in the process of writing, often presenting an approach to essay writing that offered the readings only as models. Being teachers of literature as well as composition, we were aware of the latent power of literature (in the broad sense) to evoke thought in the students who encounter it. Further, we knew that the most engaged thinkers usually wrote the best essays for us. We speculated that if we could make the implicit process of our literature courses explicit in the composition course, we would have for our students a more coherent offering than the traditional fare. Gradually, we transformed our composition course from a bottom-up approach (through punctuation, grammar, sentence structure, paragraphing, to the whole essay) using a similarly arranged handbook and a "model approach" reader, to a top-down approach that stressed the rhetorical context of Subject, Audience, and Purpose inherent in any writing occasion, working down through outline to paragraphs, and dealing with sentence structure and mechanics in the revision stage. But we went further. We pushed back beyond the invention stage (normally first in the process) to see reading as the primary impetus for the thought which results in the student's essay.

Such a transformation in our course necessitated new texts; thus began the search that ended, a few years later, with the publication of this text. Along the way we encountered two recurrent stumbling blocks in the many books we sampled: the lack of a thorough-going "reading into writing" approach, and the lack of sufficient Canadian content. While we could improvise the pedagogy, we could not turn an American author into a Canadian one. The composition course is often taken by students who will never take a literature course; our belief is that it provides a splendid opportunity for students to encounter Canadian writers, and therefore Canadian ideas.

Many people aided us in our search and in the preparation of the book itself. We would like to thank a few of them: Professor Pat Aitken, the current English Department Language Programme Coordinator, was an invaluable source of ideas and criticism, most of which originated in the crucible of the classroom. She is also the author of the Instructor's Manual, which so ably supports this text. Another colleague, Professor John Riddell, wrote the original version of what ultimately became our chapter on Scholarly Format. Mr. Ashley Thomson, of the Laurentian University Library, allowed us to adapt library assignments which he has used with our classes over the years. Ms. Elizabeth Dornbush and Ms. Lise Smulders rendered yeoman service: the first as research assistant; the second as word processor and scrawl decipherer. Our department secretary, Ms. Helen Curlook, helped us in a myriad of ways and we thank her. We want especially to thank Ms. Melanie Beach, whose writing plays so integral a role in the book. We appreciated, also, the constructive comments of reviewers who read the book in various stages of its development: Professor Paul Bidwell, University of Saskatchewan; Professor Lillian Falk, Saint Mary's University; Professor Kenneth F. Long, University of Windsor; Sheila Trant, Centennial College. Laurentian University made the project easier for us with two grants from the Laurentian University Research Fund. Our editors at Prentice-Hall, David Jolliffe and Katherine Mototsune, brought order out of chaos, and kept us on schedule. . . . Finally, we wish to thank our families, who provide for each of us a personal subject, audience, and purpose.

L.S., D.H.P., J.L.

To the students of English 1500
Introductory Composition:
past, present, and to come

Introduction

Reading: A Discipline for the Intellect

No matter what you are studying at the post-secondary level—from the most esoteric of philosophy courses to the most practical of commerce offerings—there is one thing you can count on: your years of higher learning will require you to discipline your thought. Why else would the various branches of learning be called disciplines? Each has its own body of knowledge and/or method of proceeding, most of which is contained in books. Though lectures will provide you with information, and though laboratory sessions, practicums, and examinations will test your learning, the *act* of reading will be a vital part of your studies, whatever the discipline. We stress the word "act" because fruitful reading demands active, rather than passive readers. Third- and fourth-year students have not simply absorbed more information than their counterparts in first year; upper-year students have learned to *think* more independently. Reading seriously *teaches* us how to think. If we do not succumb to boredom or frustration (understandable responses to new and difficult reading) but persevere, we are forcing our minds to explore new landscapes.

The present text will help you discipline your reading. And disciplined reading will not only take you beyond your initial reactions and so enable you to *understand* a piece of writing; it will also encourage you consciously to *evaluate* that writing. An analogous situation may illustrate the point more vividly. Imagine you are a rather traditional person beginning a two-hour bus trip. Just as you settle yourself into your seat an apparition wearing battle fatigues and sporting wildly cropped, purple hair, sits down beside you. Your immediate reactions may involve panic, disgust, or curiosity. If you yield to the first two, you effectively prevent any relationship from developing and deny yourself an opportunity to learn something new. If, however, you act on your curiosity and ask, ever so inoffensively, why that person wants to wear purple hair, you open the door to a relationship. You are inviting your travelling companion to convey something of the meaning of his or her life to you. That meaning may confirm your fears or may correct misconceptions you may have harboured. Whatever the outcome, the experience is a spur to thought and therefore to intelligent evaluation. Similarly, disciplined reading leads you to establish an informed perspective on your chosen subject. And this perspective is the natural basis for your own writing.

About This Text

Most university or college composition courses have at least two texts: a rhetoric that presents the writing process and an anthology of readings that serve as models. Some others add a third text: a handbook of grammar and style. This text combines aspects of all three to show how good writing arises out of good reading. Part One (the first three chapters) deals with the reading and writing process; Part Two (the next five chapters) constitutes an anthology of readings; Part Three (the ninth and tenth chapters) offers a step-by-step consideration of the university research paper; and Part Four (the appendices) provides supporting materials to which writers may refer on a regular basis.

The chapters on process in Part One take you step-by-step through a *reading occasion,* indicating what good readers do regularly, though often unconsciously. Here we encourage you to read actively, to see reading as an activity whose quality depends on how engaged with the piece you are. We then move to the *writing occasion*—the place where most process rhetorics begin and end. This text differs in that when you turn from the reading to the writing occasion, you take with you the raw material for your writing in the form of written responses to your reading. Too often, in our opinion, rhetorics aimed at post-secondary students ignore the fact that reading is the most obvious source of raw material for writing.

Consequently, the anthology chapters provide a substantial number of readings to which you can respond. The arrangement of essays in chapters 4, 5, 6, and 7 is two-fold. First, they are grouped broadly by mode: narration, description, exposition, argumentation. Such grouping is the standard format followed by most composition readers and it allows the readings to function as models of the mode of writing in question. The second method of arrangement, however, is of greater significance to this text: readings, all of them Canadian, are grouped according to subject matter—for example, censorship, nostalgia, action/adventure, and sports. We expect that you will read and respond to the various essays with a specific goal in mind: writing your own essays on the same general subject. This approach enables you to produce your essays in the same way you do for most other university and college courses: by reading, interpreting, and responding. Chapter 8 provides supplementary essays arranged alphabetically, but with notations on mode and subject added.

The remaining chapters are adjuncts to the central parts on reading and writing. The chapters on the research paper give you the additional background and direction needed for an actual research paper: using the library, documenting format, quoting and paraphrasing, and so on. The first of two appendices enables you to further your understanding of common developmental strategies: comparison and contrast; cause and effect; classification and division; illustration; definition; and process analysis. We have placed these strategies in an appendix so as not to confuse them with the fundamental purposes (or modes) of writing: narration, description, exposition, argumentation. Any strategy can be put to work in the service of any mode. To suggest, for example, as many composition texts do, that comparison and contrast is strictly an expository strategy is to limit the usefulness of the strategy and to disregard much good writing. The second appendix, on grammar and usage, enables you to find quick instruction on the nuts and bolts of English style. It does not pretend to be comprehensive but stresses recurrent errors and problem areas.

How to Use This Book

As teachers of composition, we developed this book because we felt that we were not spending enough time on reading with our students. We provided readings for study because they were good models of some particular writing feature and not because of their subjects as such. We found ourselves either curtailing class discussion on the general questions a reading raised in order to spend enough time on the basic requirements of our course or allowing the discussion to develop at the expense of the more formal presentation of rhetorical principles. In neither case was the intimate connection between good reading and good writing demonstrated. The present text is our attempt to supply the deficiency and to show that good writing is born of good reading.

Part One: The Process Chapters *(Chapters 1 - 3)*

The process chapters provide a detailed, step-by-step procedure that guides you from your initial encounter with a selection of paragraphs through to a revised version of an essay you write in response. Chapter 2, "The Reading Occasion," offers you a method for handling your reading in a systematic fashion. We do not offer the approach as a straitjacket but as a framework that may prove helpful. You can easily adapt it to suit your own needs. For each reading we recommend the following steps:

Step 1: Begin with *active reading*
Step 2: Make brief notes on *subject, audience,* and *purpose*
Step 3: Identify the *thesis statement, topic sentence* or, if neither of these appears, the *controlling idea*
Step 4: Identify *developmental strategies*
Step 5: Prepare a two-level *outline:* main and subsidiary points only
Step 6: Prepare a *summary* of the main points, in a radically abbreviated form
Step 7: Write a *response* of at least one hundred words to the piece

Chapter 3, "The Writing Occasion," carries on directly from the reading occasion. In traditional process rhetorics, the first stage is "invention," in which students are introduced to various strategies for engendering raw material for their writing. When we consider writing's intimate connection with reading, however, we see that much of our invention is implicit in active reading. Following the seven-point framework for reading outlined above draws into consciousness many of the concerns you must face in your own writing as a student. Your responses, in great measure, are the raw material out of which you will fashion your own essays.

Consequently, once you have arrived at responses for each of the readings under consideration, we ask you to do the following:

Step 1: Make an *examination of the responses* to discover your personal stance toward the issue (or issues) presented in the readings as a whole
Step 2: Consider your own *subject, audience,* and *purpose* to refine that personal stance into a workable *topic*
Step 3: Determine effective *developmental strategies*
Step 4: Develop a *thesis statement*
Step 5: Develop an *outline*
Step 6: Complete a *planning checklist* and proceed to write a *first draft*
Step 7: Conduct a *revision* from large items to small.

You will have noticed that the reading and writing frameworks parallel each other to a high degree. The parallel formats are our way of acknowledging and stressing the similarities between the processes of good reading and good writing. Chapter 1, "Why Stress Reading into Writing?" presents these processes as mirror images that have their roots in interpretation.

In chapters 2 and 3 we offer three complementary avenues to facilitate your assimilation of the processes of reading and writing which this text employs:

1. Demonstration
First of all, we demonstrate the procedure by reading and responding to paragraphs by Northrop Frye and Irving Layton. Then we write a short essay that arises from our responses to those paragraphs. At each stage of the process we provide both a general discussion and a specific illustration of the principle involved.

2. Student examples
Next, we illustrate the reading and writing procedure by presenting the results of a student's encounter with two different paragraphs.

3. Hands on
Finally, we present a third pair of paragraphs for you to work on. For each step in the process we ask leading questions designed to focus your attention and help you get under way.

Although your instructor may want to proceed in another fashion, our initial suggestion is that you read and work on our demonstration of a particular step, the student example of it, and your own exercise on it, in a parallel fashion. You will probably get a better grasp of active reading, for example, if you (1) read what we have to say about it generally; (2) examine how we put theory into practice when we actively read two paragraphs; (3) compare our work with what a student does to two different paragraphs; (4) try it on your own.

Part Two: The Anthology Chapters (*Chapters 4 - 8*)

Readings in this text will normally be assigned as part of an essay assignment. The process initiated with two paragraphs in chapters 2 and 3 is repeated in the anthology chapters but with readings anywhere from two to ten pages in length. Twenty of the thirty-nine essays in the anthology are grouped according to subject and dominant mode. Each of chapters 4, 5, 6, and 7—"Narration," "Description," "Exposition," and "Argumentation"—contains an introductory discussion of its respective mode, an exercise on recognizing the principles, a reading-and-writing essay assignment, and a group of essays on a specific subject. In each chapter, you complete the seven-step active reading process for all essays, as well as answering the questions appended to each one. The responses thus generated form the basis of the essay that should be written predominantly in the mode of the chapter. In chapter 7, "Argumentation," for example, you are expected to write an argumentative piece on censorship after actively reading and responding to six essays on the subject. In chapter 4, "Narration," on the other hand, you will write a predominantly narrative piece on the general subject of action and adventure after reacting to a group of four pieces on this theme. Chapter 5, "Description," also presents only four pieces, this time on the subject of nostalgia. Chapter 6, "Exposition," like "Argumentation" offers a group of six essays, but the subject here is sports. "Exposition" and "Argumentation" warrant six essays each because these modes are most commonly the ones you must read and write in during your post-secondary school years.

Chapter 8, "Supplementary Readings," collects nineteen additional essays. The essays are presented alphabetically by author, but notations on subject and dominant mode are included. Consequently, it is possible to use the groups we have constructed or to construct others. We provide a list of possible subject groupings. These hypothetical groups are made up of both the supplementary essays and the ones more formally attached to chapters.

Part Three: The Research Paper (*Chapters 9 - 10*)

The research paper is the longest single assignment in this text. Obviously, it is not tied to any of the readings in the anthology. The reading-into-writing process, however, is as applicable here as anywhere else, if not more so. Research involves reading; you cannot get round that fact. Consequently, the earlier chapters of this text should stand you in good stead if your course incorporates a research paper. In fact, it is possible that one of your shorter, earlier papers could act as a catalyst for a research topic. In that case, the readings in this text might very well contribute to the project.

Part Four: Supporting Material (*Appendices 1 - 2*)

Appendix 1: The Developmental Strategies

In separating the developmental strategies from the traditional modes we hope to stress their place as supporting materials or techniques that are used in the service of one of the larger modes of writing. Doing so, however, assumes that you will familiarize yourself with the techniques and will dip into the appendix as carpenters reach into their toolboxes for the correct tool for the job at hand. Our discussions of developmental strategies—whether those discussions occur at regular steps in the reading and writing processes or incidentally in passing—will assume you have a basic knowledge of the technique. Your instructor may assign the appendix material formally and spend class time on the strategies that way. If not, be sure you devote some time to the introductions to comparison and contrast, cause and effect, classification and division, illustration, definition, and process analysis in the appendix. Without some awareness of how these strategies function, you will be limited in what you can discern in your reading and what you can accomplish in your writing.

Appendix 2: Glossary of Usage and Guide to Revision

The grammar and usage appendix is also something for you to dip into as you have need. The entries are arranged alphabetically and are tied to a list of common correction symbols printed inside the back cover of the book. When, for example, you find the *agr* symbol on your essay, you can locate the symbol on the inside back cover and you will find a reference to the proper pages in the appendix. There you will find a concise discussion of the problem, examples of it, and a brief exercise for practice. The appendix is not exhaustive but aims to address common problems.

PART ONE

THE PROCESS: FROM READING TO WRITING

1 *Why Stress Reading Into Writing?*

People who read only as a diversion from watching television often encourage us to believe—by example as well as precept—that reading is passive. They view it as something that one does at the end of a hard working day in a semi-somnolent state, or during periods of leisure, or on one's holidays, or as an aid to sleeping. Reading is, in fact, a true activity, an endeavour that calls for the reader's complete intellectual and emotional engagement. Whether we are aware of it or not, reading involves an unspoken agreement between writer and reader. The writer writes to communicate a view, to make a point, to win an argument, to show a position. The mere fact of doing so, however, demonstrates the writer's assumption that an appropriate reader will give time to the work and make a genuine effort to understand what is written. The reader, on the other hand, gives the necessary time and attention to reading with the assumption that the writer is actually saying something worthwhile.

Whenever we write we are going public, putting our reputations as clear thinkers on the line for all to read and assess, now, tomorrow, and, perhaps, forever. Hence it is important for us, as both writers and readers, to remember that most writers design sentences to mean something, to have a content that the perceptive reader can come to understand and appreciate. Here, however, is one place where the unwritten agreement between writer and reader is often thwarted. For although it is difficult to write a sentence that does not have at least some meaning, it is all too easy to turn out sentences that are simplistic or banal. The writer's job is to say something *effectively;* the reader's job is to understand what is being said and, beyond this, to judge its value.

The good writer knows it is possible to communicate a view, make a point, win an argument, or show a position either well or badly depending upon how much care is taken in shaping the writing to suit the purpose. Writing, then, is an amalgam of content and form: the content—the *what* of the writing process—can be reinforced or undermined by the form—the *how* of the writing process. In return, the active reader must assess critically the success a writer has had in communicating ideas by examining both the content and the form—the *what* and the *how.*

This relationship between writer and reader—this struggle to communicate on the one hand and to understand and assess the communication on the other—is one of the most significant intellectual activities. It is also one of the most solitary. Writing, after all is said and done, is a confrontation between the writer and the page. The active reader must also confront the text, armed only with intelligence, emotional make-up, common sense, and past reading experience. Marshalling these forces is no mean feat. The British novelist D.H. Lawrence defined the proper critic as "a man in his wholeness, wholly attending." Lawrence sets a high standard; but high standards stretch us—we grow toward them. A critic, after all, is simply a reader who is more attentive than most of us. If we set out to become fully engaged, wholly attentive readers, we soon encounter the many distractions our world throws in our path. Hacking our way through their insinuating tendrils makes us appreciate Lawrence's assertion that his ideal readers are "rare as phoenixes." Though few of us will become phoenixes, all of us can discipline ourselves enough to become good readers. The basic requirements are peace and quiet, adequate time, and perseverance. A reader must confront a text alone and make sense of a number of linguistic symbols on a page in order to understand exactly and to evaluate appropriately what it is a writer wants to communicate. Reading, therefore, demands as much serious attention as we would devote to any skill or sport we were determined to learn.

Though active and critical reading is best cultivated in the proper environment, the rudiments of it are apparent in the most mundane reading we do. To exemplify this point, think of an experience that is as close to universal as any other: reading a personal letter. Suppose that, as a student living away from home, you receive a letter from one of your parents. Recall how easy it is not to understand or, worse still, to misunderstand something that is said in that letter. With only the letter before you, you try to understand what the symbols on the page really mean: "Does this sentence show that Mom is angry?" "Why does that sentence sound humorous?" "Do I detect a note of disappointment in this phrase?" When you start thinking about what is being said in a letter from home and how it is being said, you see that the *what* cannot really be separated from the *how*. At this point you are at the initial stages of critical, active reading. You have engaged your mind to answer questions that arise because of the symbols on the page. You try to sort out ambiguities and tones; you come to grips with generalizations and contradictions; you wonder why sentence 4 precedes sentence 5 when, in fact, it might make more sense following it. In short, you are involved in the important task of *interpretation*, which Canadian novelist Robertson Davies describes as an activity in which we get "the words off the page and into [our] head[s] in the most effective way." Reading a letter from home may not strike you as a very sophisticated activity, but it is, for all that, an act of critical reading.

Interpretation

Though it *is* an act of critical reading, perusing a letter from home is not an act in which you find yourself thrown entirely upon your own resources, as you may be with reading scholarly material in the classroom or the library. For, in reading a letter from home, you are often unconsciously assisted in the task of interpretation by a personal knowledge of the writer. Your knowledge of the writer's personality, idiosyncracies, sense of humour, values, and needs helps you interpret what is written. And, of course, if you are totally confused by what is being said in a letter from home, you can always abdicate your role as an active reader and telephone home for further clarification.

Unfortunately, reading something written by an author who is unknown to you is a far more lonely and demanding job. It is also a job that you will be called upon to do on a regular basis in your college or university career. More often than not, without any knowledge of the writer's personality and perhaps even without any knowledge of who the author of a particular work is, you will be called upon in your reading to interpret—to determine what is being said in a written passage through how it is being said. When you are thrown upon your own resources of intelligence, common sense, and critical acumen in this manner, each job of interpreting you do tests your skills as an active reader.

Nevertheless, the example of the family letter proves that active reading or interpretation is something you already do. The *activity* of interpretation is so central to all parts of our lives and so unconscious a part of them that we are likely to take it for granted, much as we do breathing. Unless you are a complete and utter misanthrope and live on an uninhabited island, you engage in the activity of interpretation and critical assessment every day of your life.

Let us take another example: suppose you are invited to a friend's house to watch an important championship hockey game. Even before you leave home, you begin, probably largely subconsciously, to interpret the situation, focusing on such matters as the occasion for the visit, who will be there, and why you were invited. Your consideration of these three factors will in large measure determine the following: when you arrive, how you dress, what you bring with you, the type of language you use at the event, even your general behaviour. If the other people who are coming are your peers, you are more likely to wear your team's colours and come prepared to cheer noisily than you would if you knew the other guests were your friend's grandparents. In either case, wearing evening dress and sending a formal RSVP would be as inappropriate as wearing blue jeans to the Governor General's ball and arriving without a formal invitation. Knowing what is *meant* by an invitation to a social event is a crucial interpretative decision upon which your reputation might very well depend. Interpretation, in short, is part and parcel of our daily lives—an activity at which we must become adept for the sake of our social survival.

The three factors that you regularly interpret in social situations relate to the writing and reading process as well. The circumstances of the visit can be thought of as the *subject,* the other guests as the *audience,* and the reason for your being invited as the *purpose.* The writer must make clear the *subject* on which he or she is writing, the *audience* for whom the work is intended, and the *purpose* of the writing. The critical and active reader, in order to participate fully in the unspoken bond between reader and writer, must pick up the clues that the writer provides about *subject, audience,* and *purpose.* In short, critical reading mirrors careful writing; what the writer has in mind when writing, the reader has in mind when reading. The inevitable conclusion is that learning how to become a true critical and active reader can help you become a better writer: reader and writer ask the same questions.

Subject, Audience, and Purpose: Mirror Images

Whenever you undertake to read or write something you enter the experience with certain assumptions, expectations, and intentions. Taken together, these characteristics of your endeavour can be called your reading or writing *occasion.* By focusing on its subject, audience, and purpose you are able to break down this occasion into its component parts. The procedure allows you to become conscious of your reading and writing as activities subject to your direction. We need to stress here, however, that the breakdown into subject, audience, and purpose, though useful, is arbitrary. The occasion itself is seamless—no one aspect can be neatly separated from the rest. Each one of these three components entails the other two in its full elucidation. Remember, then, that breaking down the occasion into its parts simply facilitates analysis of the processes. Your goal is to employ this analysis in your quest for a greater synthesis, which may take one of two forms: a deeper understanding of your reading or an informed piece of writing.

Subject

Subject and the Reader

No matter what the occasion, everything you read must be about something: it must have a subject. In large measure, your understanding of the subject of a reading will be determined by your recognition of its audience and purpose, but in all cases you must search for a central and specific focus that is appropriate to the length of the piece you are reading. If you are asked to read and assess a three-page essay on Canadian culture, you will have to decide, first of all, what aspect of the general subject the piece of writing deals with. Clearly, you cannot expect much of an essay if the writer has chosen to talk about Canadian culture in general in three pages: inevitably you would be faced with vague generalities rather than substantial content. The reader confronted with such material would have a better chance of discovering what the essay was about if one of the first sentences read as follows: "If we can judge from the declining subscriptions to the O'Keefe Centre over the last three years, Canadian culture is in a sad state." The virtue of this sentence is that it narrows the general subject to a specific topic that can be dealt with in three pages. As a critical reader, you should always ask yourself what the central focus of any piece of writing is. Search for the sentence that most clearly answers this question for you; this sentence is generally known as the *thesis statement* and is the one that should guide your reading. If you cannot isolate a specific thesis statement, try to identify the cluster of sentences that embodies the controlling idea of the piece. Keep coming back to the thesis statement or controlling idea in order to determine whether or not the author is still on topic and making sense. If you find that you repeatedly get lost in the material, one of two things is wrong: either you are not reading carefully enough (remember peace, quiet, and concentration) or the author of the piece is not adhering to the central focus. Keep in mind that it is not good enough for writers merely to have a subject; they must also offer the reader a perspective on that subject, a main idea, usually in the form of a thesis statement.

Subject and the Writer

The writer must, of course, begin somewhere. When you are writing, your subject will often be determined by the audience for whom you are writing and the purpose you have in mind. For example, your treatment of a subject such as Canadian culture would very much depend on whether you were writing to convince business people to invest in Canadian art or to explain to schoolchildren the importance of the Group of Seven painters. But merely announcing such a basic intention—persuading business people or teaching schoolchildren—would not complete your search for a subject. You would have to guide your reader by supplying a specific focus, which you would normally present in a thesis statement. In general, such a statement not only helps the reader but also allows the writer to select appropriate materials and to organize ideas more clearly.

Audience

Audience and the Reader

For any piece of writing, the reader must ask who is being addressed. The need to do so emphasizes the importance of audience as a central component in the reading occasion. If you are reading a letter from your Member of Parliament, you will—or should—detect a particular tone that is radically different from the tone in a letter from your mother. Similarly, knowing for whom something is written helps any reader clarify what is being said. If you were reading a speech on skiing that was prepared for a group of people from a South Sea island, you would expect to read something entirely different from a talk on skiing given to a group of Canadian sports broadcasters. The former piece of writing could take very little for granted about skiing; the latter, a good deal. The reader must at all times be conscious of who is writing, and for whom. A clear recognition of the author's intended audience goes a long way in helping the reader to determine the content and effectiveness of the writing under consideration.

Audience and the Writer

All writing occasions imply an audience. Failure to decide on and consistently address a kind of reader will almost certainly mar your writing. For instance, such failure may lead to inappropriate diction, lack of clarity, and even to a breakdown in the unity of your subject. Using such specialized terms as *slalom* and *herringboning* without explanation to an audience of people who know very little about skiing invites the dangers indicated above: you will have your audience wishing for an interpreter. Clear understanding of your audience can help you narrow your subject and formulate an effective thesis statement.

Purpose

Purpose and the Reader

Coming to understand why a piece was written is likely to involve the reader in a consideration not only of the subject matter but also of the writer's attitude towards the subject and of the writer's choice of audience. For instance, the purpose of a store owner worried about legislation on Sunday opening may be to convince the public that the opportunity to shop seven days a week is a great convenience. Having recognized what the owner is up to, the reader can make an appropriate response, whether that be a defence of the owner's case, an attack upon it, or a general observation concerning it. You must be a vigilant reader if you are to recognize the clues that reveal an author's purpose. While purely descriptive or narrative purposes are more easily identifiable, argumentative and expository purposes often blur into each other. Passages that appear in most respects to be expository—wanting only to show or explain—may betray an argumentative stance simply through the author's choice of diction. Compare the following sentences:

1. Small investors sold off numerous holdings today.
2. Small investors unloaded numerous holdings today.

In the first sentence we have an observation, pure and simple. In the second sentence the word *unloaded* exerts a certain pressure on us to interpret the information in a designated way; the implication of panic selling is calculated to evoke a more emotional response that the non-committal *sold off* of the first sentence. The one word *unloaded* introduces an argumentative tone into what may very well be a largely expository context. Do not expect your reading to have one single purpose. Identify, rather, what seems to be the author's *dominant* purpose.

Purpose and the Writer

The writer must not only identify subject and audience; the purpose of the writing must also be clear in the writer's mind. This may seem an obvious point, but obvious things often do not get the attention they deserve, just *because* of their obviousness. Be sure you spend time considering why you are writing. As you do so, of course, the purpose will shade over into both subject and audience. If, for example, you are a conservationist writing to other conservationists about industrial pollution, there is a good chance that you do not need to convince anyone of anything. You may simply be explaining the implications of the latest industrial accident. If, on the other hand, your audience is a group of industrialists, you may have to argue quite strenuously to convince them that the accident is as serious as you believe. Whatever decision you make about purpose (whether you write predominantly in an expository, argumentative, descriptive, or narrative mode) will have a profound effect on the nature of your writing: its range of reference, its organization, its tone, its diction, and so on. Making a thoughtful decision about purpose early on will make your writing easier, and keep your readers on track: *the track you want them on.*

2 *The Reading Occasion*

Demonstration

In the introduction we outlined seven steps that we feel will help you get maximum value from your reading. They were as follows:

Step 1: Begin with *active reading*
Step 2: Make brief notes on *subject, audience* and *purpose*
Step 3: Identify the *thesis statement, topic sentence,* or *controlling idea*
Step 4: Identify *developmental strategies*
Step 5: Prepare an *outline*
Step 6: Prepare a *summary*
Step 7: Write a *response*

Step 1 is done with a pencil on the piece of reading itself. To facilitate regular practice of the other steps we suggest that you maintain a reading workbook in which you do the note-taking for Steps 2 through 7 for each reading you encounter in the course. The notes need not be extensive, but even brief notes will help to fix your active reading in your mind. Referring to the reading workbook will serve to bring a piece of writing and your reactions to it back to your consciousness quickly; it will also give you substance for class discussions of your reading.

In the following pages we will demonstrate the principles of active reading by going through each step of the reading occasion for two paragraphs: one by Canadian critic Northrop Frye, the other by Canadian poet Irving Layton. After a discussion of each step, we will give our version of a reading workbook entry.

READING ONE

Step 1: Active Reading

Whenever possible, read with a pencil in your hand. Making brief notations in the margins or underlining significant words or shifts of thought adds another dimension to your reading: the dimension of engaged thought. As English professors, we can attest to the importance of the scrawling we have done in the books we use as class texts. Publishers' representatives have a hard time convincing professors to switch to new editions of Charles Dickens or William Shakespeare when the margins of the current copies are full of pearls of professorial wisdom. Indeed, the marginalia of the nineteenth-century poet-critic-philosopher Samuel Taylor Coleridge is being collected in multi-volumes by Princeton University Press precisely because these jottings contain much of his most lively thought! Don't underestimate your reactions *as you read.* Keep a pencil at the ready so you can take full advantage of the reading experience.

Marginalia

Use your margins to record thoughts, observations, disagreements, confusions—anything that might contribute to your better understanding of the piece or your responding to it. If you see distinct changes in thought that signal shifts in the argument or exposition, take note of these. You might want to use letters or numbers; in that way your observations become preliminary notes on *outline.*

Underlining and Circling

When we read inactively words have a tendency to fade quickly from our minds. We seldom take the time to perambulate around a word. We slipped perambulate in there on purpose, because many of you will not know what it means. The inactive reader would probably skim over it, barely registering any lack of awareness. But, as active readers, you know this is a place to put on the brakes and grab your dictionary! It is also the place to underline, circle, or otherwise mark the word out as deserving further attention. Doing so makes review far easier by bringing to mind main points, figures of speech, the author's tone, and so on. And these features, combined with your marginalia, set you well on your way to an informed consideration of subject, audience, purpose and the other aspects of the reading occasion.

Linking

Use your pencil to link main points, or points that repeat with variation. Often a parallel structure will reveal the author's thought more readily if you actually circle and link the parallel items. At least the connections will be apparent when you review the material later.

Further Comments on Marking Texts

Ideally, you should use a pencil to mark up a page, writing legibly but lightly. The process we recommend is intended to stir up your ideas as well as to have you record them; you may find yourself changing ideas as you go.

For dealing with library books or other material that must not be marked up, a good plan is to make photocopies—once you have decided on what is of interest to you—and write on the photocopy. If photocopying is not possible, you can do an imitation of our active reading process by jotting down notes on an extra pad of paper, circling and joining words there, writing out brief judgments, and otherwise bringing the original under the control of your active responses.

You should readily mark up your textbook itself at any point that stirs your interest. What follows is our active reading of a paragraph by Northrop Frye:

illustrative transition

tone → informal → audience

A – general illustrative supposition

Let us suppose that some intelligent man has been chasing status symbols all his life, until suddenly the bottom falls out of his world and he sees no reason for going on.

targets particular audience

B – specific illustrations of supposition

He can't make his solid gold cadillac represent his success or his reputation or his sexual potency any more: now it seems to him only absurd and a little pathetic. No psychiatrist or clergyman can do him any good, because his state of mind is neither sick nor sinful: he's wrestling with his angel.

Diction ↓ Purpose ↓ convince or persuade

allusion ↓ audience

C – recognition of need

He discovers immediately that he wants more education, and he wants it in the same way that a starving man wants food. But he wants education of a particular kind.

shift in thought

I – the need defined – topic sentence

His intelligence and emotions may quite well be in fine shape. It's his imagination that's been starved and fed on shadows, and it's education in that he specifically wants and needs.

Northrop Frye, *The Educated Imagination*, (Toronto: CBC Enterprises, 1963), p.65

Step 2(a): Subject

The question we most commonly ask when someone recommends a new book to us is "What is it about?" And it is this question that initially guides any new reading we do. We are searching for the proverbial hook to hang our hat on, some clue to the subject that will allow the supporting details to fall into place.

Looking for the subject is often the first task the reader undertakes. Sometimes this clue can be gathered quickly, simply by skimming the writing. At other times determining subject requires a good deal more work and thinking. The latter would seem to be the case in the passage by Northrop Frye. Notice how the paragraph begins. The "Let us suppose" indicates that the author is presenting an illustration of something—and that *something* is the subject we are looking for. The intelligent man whose world has fallen apart is *not* the subject; he is only an illustration of it. To find the subject we need to keep reading. Sentences 2 and 3 give more specific details about this man and his predicament—but they do not state what the predicament is. In sentence 4, however, we get a shift in direction: the man "discovers" something. Sentences 5 and 6 define the limits of the discovery, and in so doing they gradually bring the subject into focus. As the paragraph moves toward its conclusion, it moves further away from illustration and closer to generalization until in sentence 7—the topic sentence—the subject is finally found. Although it is tempting to locate the topic sentence in sentence 4 where the notion of education is first mentioned, this would be a hasty judgment since it is not until sentence 7 that we learn that the man in the passage is longing for a particular type of education, namely, of the imagination.

Once you have found the *topic sentence* (if you are reading a paragraph) or the *thesis statement* (if your reading is longer than a paragraph) or the *controlling idea* (if an unequivocal topic sentence or thesis statement is not apparent) you should expect to recognize supporting details for it throughout either the remaining or (in this case) the earlier parts of the piece. You should be able to see the logic and coherence in the writing even though you may not agree with what the author is saying. In the paragraph under examination we can see how sentences 1 and 7 (the first and last of the paragraph) sandwich between them the particular details that each calls for. We hear in sentence 1 in a general way of what happens to "some intelligent man" who "has been chasing status symbols all his life." Sentence 7 concludes the passage by indicating that such symbols are only "shadows" that starve the imagination. What falls between these two general statements is illustration: a reference to a particular status symbol, the "solid gold cadillac," and references to what the symbol stands for: "success," "reputation," and "sexual potency." The starvation that the man now feels (sentence 7) is illustrated in his pathetic feelings (sentence 2) and in the fact that a psychiatrist and a clergyman cannot help him (sentence 3). The notion of starvation in sentence 7 finds an echo in the simile of a starving man wanting food in sentence 4. (Notice how we have linked these items in our active reading.) In short, the passage is a fine example of how the subject or the *what* is articulated and illustrated throughout. There is a sense of orderly and coherent interplay between general statement and detail. The former frames the passage; the latter is found between the two framing sentences.

Reading workbook notes
Step 2(a): Subject

The need for an educated imagination to give meaning to a materially full but imaginatively empty life.

Practice Reading: Subject

Actively read the following paragraphs, focusing on clues to subject. After you have completed your textual notations and marginalia, prepare reading workbook notes on subject for each one comparable in length to ours just above.

> As far as our unscientific observation goes, the loons in the [Algonquin] Park have three calls. One of the three Tom likes best; the second he regards as my favourite; the third both of us consider unworthy of loons. This third we have heard most frequently on Dickson Lake. It is an irregular sort of wild and noisy medley, and there is a barbaric, unrestrained quality to it which makes us suspect the baneful influence of white civilisation. It is, of course, musical, as any sound made by a loon is bound to be, and I imagine sometimes that it resembles one or two short passages in the first movement of Stravinsky's "Rite of Spring,"

but when I hear the loons my memory of the Stravinsky is too dim, and when I hear the Stravinsky my memory of the third cry is far too attenuated.

J.D. Robins, *The Incomplete Anglers* (Toronto: Collins, 1943), pp. 176-177.

Looking at the evolution of politics and culture in Quebec, it's clear that the poets have always been in the avant-garde of political change. It's well known that the nationalist poets of the 1950's and 60's—Gaston Miron, Gatien Lapointe, Michele Lalonde and many others—articulated a vision that was later to find its political expression through the Parti Québécois. But one could go back even earlier, and see in the alienation and premature silence of the two great poets of traditional Quebec, Emile Nelligan and Hector de Saint-Denys Garneau, a powerful statement about the repressive society in which they were trying to find a language. If poetry has any one common subject that subject is freedom, and thus the poet—whether or not he perceives himself as political—is always to some degree at odds with the status quo.

Patricia Smart, "La Nuit de la Poésie 80," *Canadian Forum*, June-July, 1980, p. 18.

So if, as a society, we cannot stamp out prostitution, then we should learn to make the best of it. Let's start by making each and every sexual act by *consenting adults,* whether it involves money or whether it doesn't, free-and-clear legal. I realize that morality *can* be legislated, but I contend that once you've reached the age of majority, you should have the right to go to hell (or wherever) in your own way. Instead of squandering time on prostitution, which is rarely more than a straight business deal, we could be concentrating our resources on crimes that really matter—or on changing the brutal milieu that breeds most criminals. If some prostitution is inextricably tied to the criminal element, it is because our collective hypocrisy has driven it in that direction. If Prohibition has taught us nothing else, it has taught us that if people want something bad enough, they'll get it; and if honest businesspersons are prevented from supplying the sought-after goods or services, dishonest businesspersons will move in and fill the gap. When we drive a "sin" such as prostitution underground, we drive it into the arms of organized crime, which grows and prospers from our moralistic efforts.

John Gault, "Politics: The Bawdy Politic," *Toronto Life,* April, 1984, p. 18.

Step 2(b): Audience

All writing, of course, is addressed to a literate audience, but having said this we have to acknowledge that there are various degrees of literacy and various audiences to whom authors can address themselves. One of the most reliable clues to audience is the diction of the piece under scrutiny. A careful examination of our passage from Northrop Frye reveals that the author eschews colloquialisms, street talk, slang, and dialect. He opens by saying "Let us suppose," not "Y'all give a listen now to this here example." Frye designated the man's materialism as "absurd and a little pathetic" rather than as "dumb and a little silly." Frye speaks of "psychiatrists," not "shrinks," and "cadillacs," not "caddies"; the central figure of the illustration is an "intelligent man," not a "smart guy." At the other extreme, Frye makes no use of diction belonging to a particular, specialized discipline or of language requiring special knowledge. His intelligent man *has* been "chasing status symbols all his life, until suddenly the bottom falls out of his world. . . ;" he *has not* been "conspicuously consuming all his life, until suddenly his purview undergoes a radical negative transformation. . . ." Frye uses the concrete image of the "solid gold cadillac" rather than a vague phrase such as "proliferating acquisitions." The man is said to be "wrestling with his angel" rather than "engaged in a psychological debate between his id and superego."

Because Frye is careful to pitch his diction in the middle of the range from informal to highly formal, there is no reason to believe that the general reader could not understand what is being said. But general audiences are made up of individuals, and though the audience may generally understand, there will be some readers who will not know what Frye means by "status symbols" or by "wrestling with his angel." Others may not realize that the "solid gold cadillac" is a figurative way of summing up all the man's material wealth—his status symbols. Some people may just not be able to afford the luxury of Frye's educated imagination; they may be too busy struggling to pay the rent to find time to chase status symbols or wrestle with angels. These people would not form part of Frye's audience. The target audience for his piece needs to be in a position to comprehend the crisis the "intelligent man" is going through; they need, probably, at least a middle-class income, if not a higher one. They need a certain level of "intelligence" themselves. The paragraph might easily have come from such magazines as *Canadian Forum* or *Saturday Night;* it would come less easily from *Maclean's* or *Atlantic Insight,* and with difficulty from *Canadian Living* or *Leisureways.*

Beyond these characteristics for Frye's ideal reader, we should ask ourselves about another one brought about through the changing social movements of recent years. In discussing the passage we have followed Frye's lead in speaking of the intelligent "man," rather than "person" or other alternative. Although we feel sure that Frye had people in general in mind and intended nothing invidious by his masculine references, his language (and ours in so far as we followed his lead) may alienate some readers sensitive to feminist issues who otherwise meet the criteria of income and intelligence that we have spoken of. In brief, Frye may have limited the number of receptive readers of his passage more than he wanted to do. The point is worth generalizing: in addressing yourself to an audience, keep in mind the human sensitivities (whether of sex or of race or of religion or social class) that may have a bearing on the language you use.

Reading workbook notes
Step 2(b): Audience

Intelligent middle- or high-income people who either are or have the potential to be chasers after status symbols, and who, consequently, can comprehend - if not appreciate - the predicament Frye has outlined.

Practice Reading: Audience

Actively read the following paragraphs, focusing on clues to audience. After you have completed your textual notations and marginalia, prepare reading workbook notes on audience for each one comparable in length to ours just above.

> Feast your eyes on the star of the show! You'd love to slip behind the wheel right now, wouldn't you? This hand-built, street-ready reproduction of Chevrolet's legendary Corvette Grand Sport—valued at more than $40,000—is the grand prize in a contest sponsored by B.F. Goodrich. It will go to a lucky new owner—perhaps even a *Leisureways* reader—in a draw to be held during the Automotive Day festivities, sponsored by CAA-Toronto, at the Canadian National Exhibition in Toronto on

Thursday, Aug. 28. Make a note of the date. Plan to be at the CNE then. It's an outing you shouldn't miss.

Bill McLaughlan, "A Dream in Motion," *Leisureways*, July, 1986, p. 21.

There are 8 or 10 different types of porphyrias known to modern science. In a form of the disease that has been associated with the werewolf legend, the body makes porphyrin but cannot properly insert the iron, leading to an excess of useless skin. This in itself poses no problem, but exposure to sunlight produces disastrous effects: porphyrins become chemically active and in turn excite oxygen, transforming it from its normally benign state into a form of extreme toxicity that destroys skin cells en masse. Lesions occur. "In extreme cases, the fingers and nose fall off," says Dolphin. "If you have this condition, you soon learn to venture out only at night." Other side effects include tightening of the lips and gums, which brings the teeth into prominence, and an excessive growth of hair. Because porphyrins will reemit the sunlight originally absorbed, a person suffering from the disease may glow in the dark.

Taken together, the gruesome symptoms paint a picture remarkably similar to the mediaeval descriptions of werewolfs.

Kerry Banks, "Diagnosing Dracula," *Equinox: The Magazine of Canadian Discovery*, November/December, 1983, p. 18.

Step 2(c): Purpose

Every author has a purpose in mind when writing. Successful writing communicates that purpose; unsuccessful writing does not. We are not here speaking of the effectiveness of the communication, but of whether the purpose is communicated at all. Before we can evaluate an author's purpose, we must know what it is. Authors may want to tell a story (narrative mode—see chapter 4), describe an event, phenomenon, or person (descriptive mode—see chapter 5), explain something (expository mode—see chapter 6), or convince someone of something (argumentative mode—see chapter 7). Or they may want to do a little of each. Whatever choice they finally make carries certain implications for the presentation of their writing: its tone, its diction, its range of reference, its audience. For example, an author who begins an article on the safety of nuclear power with a detailed, specialized exposition of how the Pickering, Ontario, reactor functions has misconceived the primary purpose of such an article, which is to convince an uneasy populace. Though the expository account of the workings of the reactor will have to be included to make the argument a convincing one, it should not usurp the role of dominant purpose. Further, the author should adjust its diction and range of reference to that which can reasonably be expected of the audience implied by the dominant purpose.

Whether consciously or unconsciously, perceptive readers pick up the clues to purpose that careful writers provide for them, explicitly and/or implicitly. The opening of the Frye passage—"Let us suppose"—signals an illustration of some point; it is *showing* us something. We are right to detect an expository element in Frye's purpose. But exposition is not all there is to it. The first sentence supposes "that some intelligent man has been chasing status symbols all his life...." Though Frye is not explicit about his purpose, he has deliberately chosen a phrase—"chasing status symbols"—calculated to make middle-and upper-income readers in western capitalist society reflect on their material pursuits. The phrase carries connotations of triviality, banality, and self-interest that a more neutral phrase like "acquiring material possessions" does not carry to nearly the same extent. Without explicitly doing so, Frye has introduced an argumentative element into the passage. Readers will feel the need—even if slightly—to defend themselves against the charge of being status-symbol chasers. And this is exactly where Frye wants them. He can go on to *explain* the need for an educated imagination through illustration and definition while at the same time his choice of diction and range of reference brings one set of standards—status symbols, solid gold cadillacs, success, reputation, sexual potency—into an implicitly *argumentative* conflict with another—wrestling with angels, educated imagination.

Frye, then, is concerned both to explain and convince. The expository aspect may be the one we identify more immediately, as Frye explains the phenomenon that is intriguing him, but finally it is the argumentative aspect that determines the tone and range of intellectual and emotional reference and that induces readers to reflect on the state of their imaginations.

This overlap of purposes, or modes, is what you will find in most writing. Though writers will have dominant purposes, the routes they travel to express them will often seem to carry you away from the goal. Do not be too quick to nail down an author's purpose or to condemn the author for the lack of a firm one. Authors deserve the benefit of the doubt about purpose—for a while.

Reading workbook notes
Step 2(c): Purpose

To induce his audience to reflect on their possible need for an educated imagination by implicitly convincing them of their predicament, while explicitly explaining the phenomenon to them.

Practice Reading: Purpose

Actively read the following paragraph focusing on clues to purpose. After you have completed your textual notations and marginalia, prepare reading workbook notes on purpose comparable in length to ours just above.

> John Diefenbaker was at once sentimental and distinctly clear-eyed. There was in him an attitude of urgent morbid reluctance to make decisions. He was the most approachable Canadian ever to

occupy the office of prime minister. Yet he had few intimate friends. His outward bearing was one of easy confidence. Yet he continually suspected dark plots were being planned against him and once spent an hour explaining to a casual acquaintance that he would probably be the first Canadian prime minister assassinated in office. He was a stickler for protocol and at times insatiably vain. Yet he could be genuinely humble in exercising the privileges of his office. He flew into a rage at the 1961 convocation of Memorial University in Newfoundland, where he was receiving an honourary degree, because Eleanor Roosevelt, representing the President of the United States, was accidentally given precedence over him. Yet in 1958 when he unexpectedly brought Prime Minister Harold Macmillan of Britain and Chancellor of the Exchequer Selwyn Lloyd to his official residence following a formal function at Government House, instead of summoning one of his four servants, he called up to his wife: "Olive, these boys down here are hungry. What have we got in the refrigerator?"

Peter C. Newman, *Renegade in Power* (Toronto: McClelland and Stewart Ltd., 1963), pp. 3-4.

Step 3: Thesis Statement, Topic Sentence, or Controlling Idea

All effective writing has a central idea that unifies and organizes the details surrounding it. No matter whether the piece of writing is a paragraph, an essay, or a book, there will be a point at which the author encapsulates the subject, often the purpose, and sometimes even indications of audience as well, in a strategic sentence or group of sentences. If we are dealing with paragraphs we traditionally call this central idea the *topic sentence.* In longer pieces of writing it is referred to as the *thesis statement.* In both these cases, only one sentence is involved. Writers, however, are not nearly as systematic as composition teachers would like them to be. Often the central idea consists of two or three sentences, occasionally more. We suggest that to avoid confusion you call this cluster of sentences the *controlling idea.* Do not feel that you must designate one of them as a topic sentence or thesis statement; often you just cannot do it.

In our "Practice Reading: Subject" exercises above there is a paragraph about loon calls. While you probably had little trouble commenting on its subject, you may have run into difficulty if you tried to pin down a topic sentence for the paragraph because this paragraph does not have one; it has a controlling idea instead. The last clause in the first sentence, combined with the third sentence, gives us the central idea for the paragraph as a whole.

Though it is usual for expository and argumentative writing to have a topic sentence, thesis statement, or controlling idea that either is apparent or surfaces readily enough in active reading, often narrative and descriptive writing will not have an explicit central idea. Of course, this does not mean it is not there: it just means the author is relying on the reader to recognize implications and draw conclusions more actively than otherwise. In fiction especially, the central idea hovers behind the scenes waiting for the perceptive reader to take the critical leap that will reveal it. Readers, however, see different things; nowhere is this clearer than in reading fiction. While most readers' interpretations will share a family resemblance, they will not normally be identical.

In expository and argumentative writing, where the central idea is more often explicitly stated, identity is achievable. In paragraphs, the topic sentence is normally the first sentence and acts both as an introduction to the paragraph and often as a transition from the previous one. But this is by no means a law of composition. Frye's topic sentence is the last one in his paragraph; it acts as a conclusion, as a fully explicit statement of an idea that has been building throughout the paragraph. Do not be too hasty to identify a topic sentence. The third paragraph in the "Practice Reading: Subject" exercise, for example, places its topic sentence at the end, though on a cursory glance the first sentence seems to fill this function. Similarly, though longer pieces often locate their thesis statements as the last sentence in the introductory paragraph, this is, again, not a rule. You will find many writers in the anthology section of this book who do otherwise to good purpose. Finally, though these are hints to help locate a central idea, there is no substitute for vigilance—*active* reading.

Reading workbook notes
Step 3: Thesis Statement, Topic Sentence, or Controlling Idea

The last sentence in Frye's paragraph is the Topic Sentence - "It's his imagination that's been starved and fed on shadows, and it's education in that he specifically wants and needs."

Step 4: Developmental Strategies

Developmental strategies are techniques that authors use to help them express their purposes. Whether the mode of writing is narration, description, exposition, or argumentation, certain techniques are used again and again to develop the thought. In appendix 1 (pp. 502 - 534) we introduce you to six of the most common strategies: comparison and contrast, cause and effect, classification and division, illustration, definition, and process analysis. As we said in the introduction, you need to familiarize yourself with these brief discussions to enable you to identify the strategies in your reading and utilize them in your writing. If you rely solely on the comments we make here on the strategies Frye uses, you will learn something about illustration, definition, and cause and effect (though hardly all you need to know), but you will not learn anything about comparison and contrast, classification and division, and process analysis. So read appendix 1!

Frye's most obvious strategy is illustration. The whole passage is one large illustration or example of the need for an educated imagination. The piece begins with "Let us suppose," clearly signalling that an illustration is forthcoming, and the opening sentence sets the scene. Sentences 2 and 3 are specific illustrations of the more general opening supposition. The status symbols are identified: solid gold cadillac, success, reputation, sexual potency. The intelligent man's seeing no reason for going on is given credence when we learn that psychiatrists and clergymen can do nothing for him.

Sentence 4 shifts the strategy from specific illustrations to definition. For the rest of the piece, Frye gradually defines the need for an educated imagination by narrowing the possibilities of what the need is. It is a need for education, but education of a particular kind, and so on. This strategy of definition began earlier but worked in a negative fashion. Frye defined the need by what it was not. It was not something that status symbols could satisfy; nor was it something that professionals could cure. In sentence 4 we simply get a shift from negative to positive definition. And it is not until sentence 7 that the full definition comes.

Although illustration and definition are the clearest strategies employed by Frye, the passage also embodies an implicit cause-and-effect structure. Because the man chases status symbols, Frye implies, "the bottom falls out of his world and he sees no reason for going on." That is one cause-and-effect relationship (though not developed). A second one arises out of the first: Because he sees no reason for going on in his conventional lifestyle, he casts about for other avenues to meaning. The effect of this searching is that he "discovers immediately that he wants more education. . . ."

Again we must stress that the overlap of strategies is natural and common. Frye's piece is an amalgam of illustration, definition, and cause and effect; all three intertwine and yet add their own distinctive qualities to the reading. Do not feel you must subordinate some strategies to find one that colours the whole piece. Often one does, but it need not be the case. Strategies, unlike purposes (which can also overlap), are more clearly tools—writers use them where they are appropriate. Carpenters do not limit themselves to screwdrivers if the job at hand calls for hammers and drills as well.

Reading workbook notes
Step 4: Developmental Strategies

1: Illustration: The whole paragraph is an illustration but it embodies more specific illustrations within it.

2: Definition: The illustrations define what the man's malaise is not. They are followed by more positive statements which work to define what the malaise is.

3: Cause and effect: The passage carries an underlying implication that chasing status symbols caused the bottom to fall out of the man's life. A major effect of such a change was that the man began to recognize his need for education.

Step 5: Outline

Though a thesis statement unifies a piece of writing, and though developmental strategies add dimension to an author's points, these points must still be organized in a coherent manner. As a reader you are concerned to recognize that coherency because it contributes to the author's meaning or lack of meaning. A passage that switches points in mid-discussion, or that wanders off on pointless digressions that began as brief illustrations, or that fails to discuss points promised by a thesis statement, reflects poorly on its author. Take time to register your author's shifts in thought consciously. We suggest that you use the standard outline format in your reading workbook, though your active reading need not be so systematic.

The standard outline format (which we go into in more detail in Chapter 3, "The Writing Occasion") employs Roman numerals for main points, and letters and Arabic numbers for subsidiary points. A skeleton outline format could run as follows:

I. ____________________

  A. ____________________

  B. ____________________

II. ____________________

  A. ____________________

  B. ____________________

  C. ____________________

III. ____________________

  A. ____________________

  B. ____________________

    1. ____________________

    2. ____________________

We recommend that you limit your outlining to two levels only in your active reading. Indentifying main and subsidiary points will soon give you an idea of how coherent your author is being. When you are dealing with a paragraph only, the main point will be the topic sentence and the subsidiary points the various details that support it. In larger pieces, however, a main point can encompass numerous paragraphs. Do not equate main points with topic sentences; they are frequently not the same thing.

In Frye's paragraph we first encounter a general supposition about an intelligent man. Next come some specific illustrations that develop the supposition. Following the illustrations the thought shifts to a recognition of a general need for education. Finally, in the topic sentence, the need is defined. In the following reading workbook notes we have completed a formal outline in standard format for Frye's piece.

Reading workbook notes
Step 5: Outline

A. General illustrative supposition: intelligent man's life falls apart

B. Specific illustrations of the suppositions

1. Solid gold cadillac is now meaningless

2. Psychiatrist and clergyman cannot help

C Recognition of need for more education

I. The need defined: education of the imagination

Step 6: Summary

Learning to summarize your reading will give you practice in recognizing what is essential and what is peripheral in a piece of writing. Seldom is every point of equal weight; main points are developed by subsidiary points, and subsidiary points may be fleshed out with illustrative details. In summarizing you are concerned with the essential subject of the piece, and not so much with the audience and purpose. You are not commenting on the author's attitude but trying to capture the essence of the piece as concisely as possible in your own words. Of course, if it is present, the thesis statement, topic sentence, or controlling idea will provide a focus for your summary, though you will have to recognize as well the main points of the author's development of that thesis.

As we discovered earlier, the topic sentence of Frye's paragraph is the final one; the development of his thesis is found in what precedes the final sentence. An appropriate summary of the paragraph as a whole might read as follows: "After suddenly awakening to the fact that his materially successful life is meaningless, an intelligent man finds that he 'wants and needs' to educate his imagination." As you can see, this summary is a lot shorter than the original (one sentence as compared to seven), but it captures, nevertheless, the essence of the original. Notice how Frye's precise illustrations have been omitted; it is not the business of the summary to say everything that the original has said. Furthermore—and this is important—notice how our summary uses words *other* than the ones found in the source. Using your own words is a good test of whether or not you really understand the passage you have read. If you find yourself constantly resorting in your summary to the diction of the source, there is a good chance that you have not fully digested the meaning of the passage. If, however, you do use occasional important words or phrases from the original, be sure to put them within quotation marks. Notice how "wants and needs" are treated in our summary.

The length of a summary will vary with the length and complexity of the source: from a brief sentence for a paragraph or so, to a sentence or two for a short essay, to a well-honed paragraph for a longer essay. The rule of thumb is that a summary is *radically* shorter than the original and is in your own words.

Reading workbook notes
Step 6: Summary

After suddenly awakening to the fact that his materially successful life is meaningless, an intelligent man finds that he "wants and needs" to educate his imagination.

Step 7: Response

Having completed steps 1 through 6 conscientiously, you will in all likelihood have a solid understanding of the reading in question. You can now make an informed response to the piece. This response is what university and college reading is all about. Whether you agree, disagree, or are neutral to Frye's passage probably will not even be an issue if you are not confident that you understand it. If you have this confidence, however, you have a basis from which to defend your response, whatever it may be.

Do not feel you must make a sentence-by-sentence critique of your source. Your response should reflect the thinking to which the reading has incited you. If Frye's reference to status symbols irritates you, say why; if you know of another illustration that bears out Frye's contentions, outline it. Allow the reading to be a spur to your thought on the subject; do not allow it to channel that thought too precisely if you want to go elsewhere. Your response is *yours;* the only stipulations are that it should relate at least tangentially to the subject of the source and that it should be *informed.* Note that an informed response can only occur after steps 1 through 6 are complete.

Make your response at least one hundred words long; give yourself some room to think. You will often find that once you have begun the response will grow even longer. Do not stifle this growth; it is the raw material out of which you will build your essay—the more you have the better. Do not worry about impeccable logic or exquisite style at this point. You will have plenty of time to see to these things later on. If your response contains questions that do not yet have answers, so be it. Just get the ideas down quickly before you lose them.

Reading workbook notes
Step 7: Response

It seems all too clear when we look around us that Frye is correct in his feeling that we are materially successful but spiritually poverty-stricken. Increasingly in Canada we seem to be importing our values from the U.S. We are avid consumers, but the more we consume of U.S. culture the less Canadian we become. Is our problem that we are a young country? We need to develop our imaginations, as Frye says, but how can we do this when T.V. culture deadens them? Even the C.B.C. has fallen on tough times, and it has traditionally been the promoter and protector of Canadian culture. Frye may imply that we need to wrestle with our angels, but how soon will it be before we cannot be awakened to that need?

READING TWO

What follows is a second reading passage related in part at least to the first one. The author is the Canadian poet Irving Layton. In our reading of Layton's paragraph we will follow essentially the same pattern that we used with Frye's; however, there will be far less editorial and explanatory commentary on the method of reading. We will move more directly to the reading workbook notes in the earlier steps, and in the later ones there will be no intervening commentary.

Step 1: Active Reading

Diction → Audience → Purpose → Persuasion

When Canadians are done with the excitements of professionalized sports and alcohol, a voice in their miserable nightmarish souls tells them that contact, abandonment, passion, and the understanding heart are what matter most in our lives. Isolated from one another by the fears and repressions engendered in a materialistic society almost wholly given up to the worship of money and status; hoodwinked by egomaniacal poltroons among politicos and business executives; and robbed of their birthright of joy and intensity by any prude or long-faced puritan that can shake a finger at them, Canadians plead for compassion as no other people on earth. This is a cold country in more ways than one. The drag of middle-class mores is strongest here, for the mitigating forces of population, culture, heterogeneity are not sufficiently present to free the individual from the entangling coils of life-denying creeds and the inhibiting ideologies and customs of the dominant ethnic groups. He's caught early and stays trapped till the end of his days.

I - Topic sentence; shift! → point of view unsure?; II A, II B, II C - illustrations of victimization; Diction → Antagonistic; II - Cry of victims; Diction → Commiserating; III; A; B

Irving Layton, "What Canadians Don't Know about Love," *Engagements* (Toronto: McClelland and Stewart Ltd., 1972), p.99.

Step 2(a): Subject

Layton's general concern in this paragraph is that Canadians are coerced by their milieu to place secondary matters ahead of primary ones, even though within their own beings they are aware of the foolishness of their choice. He voices his concern in sentence 1, which serves as the topic sentence of the paragraph. The rest of the piece delineates other examples of these secondary matters and emphasizes their life-destroying qualities. Sentence 2 targets a range of forces the author regards as anti-life, including materialism, politics, business, and puritanism. Sentence 3 picks up the notion of Canada's traditionally cold winter climate and uses it as a metaphor for our chilling and anti-life "middle-class mores"—a phrase that seems to summarize all that the author despises about certain values found in our country. The final sentence suggests a certain hopelessness by indicating that the anti-life forces capture people early and stay with them until their deaths.

Reading workbook notes
Step 2(a): Subject

Layton comes out in support of "contact," "abandonment," and "passion" in our lives and rails against the "middle-class mores" of contemporary Canadian society which attack and undermine these life-affirming notions.

Step 2(b): Audience

Layton takes something of a scattergun approach to audience in this paragraph, cutting a swathe across the whole spectrum of Canadian society and never truly focusing on a defined audience. To say his audience is a general Canadian one might be true, but it tells us very little. Analyzing audience more closely gives us clues to Layton's approach and purpose. The Canadians mentioned in the topic sentence (sentence 1) appear initially to be typical "Canucks," watching hockey and drinking beer; other Canadians might resent Layton's including them in this group. When we look closer, though, we wonder if Layton himself is clear about who these Canadians are, for the pronouns designating them shift significantly from "their" and "them" when referring to the voice in their "miserable" souls, to "our" after listing the healthy qualities we lack. Though he begins in a posture critical of Canuckishness, by the end of the sentence he is sympathizing with "our" plight as victims of a lack of vitality. This sympathy continues in sentence 2 and concludes in the main clause: "Canadians plead for compassion as no other people on earth." But by whom are we victimized? Is it the people who isolate, hoodwink, and rob us, the worshippers of money and status, the politicos and business executives, the prudes and long-faced puritans? These victimizers are the purveyors of "life-denying creeds," "inhibiting ideologies," and "customs of dominant ethnic groups"—in brief, of "middle-class mores." But, we ask, are not these victimizers also Canadians, and therefore also victims, "trapped till the end of [their] days" as the rest of us supposedly are? And what of Layton? Is he outside the "entangling coils"? Significantly the pronouns in the last sentence are "he" and "his," not "we" and "our."

Reading workbook notes
Step 2(b): Audience

Layton's audience is not designated specifically. A general middle-class Canadian audience could read the piece with interest, but would probably be unsure whether it was the subject of commiseration or attack.

Step 2(c): Purpose

The tone of anger and distrust in the face of "middle-class mores" suggests that the principal mode is argumentation. Notice how Layton sets one set of standards against another in the opening sentence and then proceeds to attack what he regards as "life-denying" aspects of Canadian life while commiserating with the victims. There is a good deal of emotion generated in this passage by the use of strong diction. Words and phrases like "miserable," "nightmarish," "egomaniacal poltroons," "hoodwinked," "politicos," "prude," "long-faced puritan," "entangling coils," and "life-denying" all signal that the author is writing in anything but a dispassionate manner. Notice also the length, energy, and breathlessness of sentence 2, where Layton piles up a series of attacks on certain manifestations of the Canadian soul. The paragraph is deliberately polemical, intended to provoke sympathy, anger, thought, and a response. As the scattergun technique we outlined in the section on audience indicates, the passage appeals more to emotion than to reason. Layton is assuming an almost prophetic voice, of one "crying in the wilderness." And we all know, Layton seems to imply, that reason must defer to inspiration and vision.

Reading workbook notes
Step 2(c): Purpose

Layton undertakes an emotional, polemical argument to incite a passionate response in his readers. Such a response might rekindle life in our "nightmarish" souls.

Step 3: Thesis Statement, Topic Sentence, or Controlling Idea

Layton's topic sentence, unlike Frye's, comes at the beginning. There he sets up the opposition he will develop throughout the remainder of the paragraph.

Reading workbook notes
Step 3: Thesis Statement, Topic Sentence, or Controlling Idea

Layton's first sentence is the topic sentence of the paragraph:

"When Canadians are done with the excitements of professionalized sports and alcohol, a voice in their miserable, nightmarish souls tells them that contact, abandonment, passion, and the understanding heart are what matter most in our lives."

Step 4: Developmental Strategies

Layton develops his paragraph through a combination of *illustration* and *cause and effect*. Sentence 2 establishes a parallel series of illustrations—"isolated... by," "hoodwinked by," "robbed... by"— which act simultaneously as the cause of our pleading "for compassion as no other people on earth." The fourth sentence again employs illustration and cause and effect. The lack of "population, culture, heterogeneity" is the cause of our continued imprisonment within the "entangling coils of life-denying creeds and the inhibiting ideologies and customs of the dominant ethnic groups."

Reading workbook notes
Step 4: Developmental Strategies

Layton uses a combination of illustration and cause and effect. He initially illustrates the various causes of our victimization, then he outlines the cultural environment that engenders these causes, which he then illustrates further.

Steps 5 - 7

Reading workbook notes
Step 5: Outline

I. Topic Sentence: Opposing standards set up—passion vs sterility
  A. Isolation through materialism
  B. Hoodwinking by politics and business
  C. Robbery at hands of prudery and puritanism

II. Canadians plead for compassion

III. Drag of middle-class mores is strong
  A. No cultural milieu to counteract it
  B. Canadians are trapped

Step 6: Summary

Materialism, politics, business, and puritanism, combined with the lack of a healthy cultural milieu, trap Canadians in the web of "middle-class mores" where we "plead for compassion" because our souls tell us that "passion" is what we need.

Step 7: Response

While we may find it easy to agree with Layton that the drag of "middle-class mores" is strong in Canada, surely we should demand more specifics from him with regard to the "contact, abandonment, passion, and the understanding heart" which he advocates. All but the last of these terms (and even it too with some stretching) could describe a typical McDonald's advertisement on TV. Doesn't this give us pause? Just where are we to find the healthy cultural milieu which will nurture what Layton wants when the whole drive of our culture is following the US in the opposite direction? Layton feels that our "miserable" souls still sense what they need, somewhere deep inside. Can we be so sure? Is hoping so enough? Layton's emotional scattergun approach may raise hackles, or elicit self-satisfied nods, or both; it is also sure to perpetuate Layton's image as Canada's self-proclaimed voice crying in the wilderness. But until Layton comes in from the cold he enjoys so much he is unlikely to make a tangible difference to our predicament.

Student Examples

In this section we present the active reading and reading workbook entries completed by one of our students, Melanie Beach, for paragraphs by Cynthia Carver and Valmai Howe Elkins that address the general subject of patient care. While Beach adheres to the seven-step reading occasion format for each piece, we are not presenting her entries simply as models. As you will see, Beach's work is clearly "in process," and as such is open to discussion. We hope you will take the opportunity to question her work, to see alternatives to her observations, to further points she initiates. While we obviously feel our student's work is sound, it is by no means the final word on either passage, or on how to complete effectively a reading workbook entry. We have asked leading questions at places where we believe discussion would be especially profitable.

READING ONE

Step 1: Active Reading

I often hear complaints about unfriendly, hostile or rude hospital staff. There is no reason why this should be the case. Any store or business that received several complaints about the unpleasantness of one of its salespeople would promptly investigate the matter and fire the employee if the complaints were valid. The same should be true in the hospital. People who come into hospital are scared and ill. They do not need to spend their time fending off rudeness or hostility; such efforts are not going to promote well being. Obviously some patients are cranky and likely to find any staff they are in contact with unsatisfactory; but by and large, patients are grateful for service and reasonably tolerant. Any staff member about whom several patients have made complaints should be observed carefully. Perhaps change to another function might be the answer for that employee. Workers should not be where they are obviously unhappy and making their charges unhappy.

Cynthia Carver, *Patient Beware: Dealing with Doctors and Other Medical Dilemmas* (Scarborough: Prentice-Hall Canada Inc., 1984), p. 162.

Steps 2 - 7

Reading workbook notes

Article

Excerpt from Dr. Cynthia Carver's Patient Beware: Dealing with Doctors and Other Dilemmas (1984)

Step 2(a): Subject

The author has proposed the argument that there are those in the medical profession who are not personable in communicating with their patients and that the patients are suffering because of this. The paragraph indicates, primarily, bed-side manner or staff-patient interactions, their negative aspects and the result.

Step 2(b): Audience

The author is writing to the hospital administration in order that they might become aware of and take action to alleviate this problem with staff who do not conduct themselves properly in their patient-care techniques. The author offers some solutions to this problem in acknowledgment of her audience. The author may also be writing to the audience who will be in agreement with her ideas in hopes, perhaps, that they will aid her in her plea for action against these hospital staff.

1. Beach seems more tentative in her second note on audience than her first. Is this tentativeness traceable to ambiguity in Carver's paragraph?
2. If Carver's piece is directed to hospital administration, then is her book title misleading?

Step 2(c): Purpose

The author is supporting the position of the hospital patients. She complains about the staff. Carver's main purpose is to convince the hospital staff that there indeed is a problem that they must become aware of, and to persuade these people that they must take action to rectify this problem. She does this persuading by convincing these health professionals that the unhealthy attitudes and atmosphere they are presenting are detrimental to the well-being of their clientele.

Step 3: Topic Sentence

The thesis comes about at the conclusion of this paragraph as Carver says, "workers should not be where they are obviously unhappy and making their charges unhappy." She has not taken an altogether negative attitude against hospital staff and has even offered suggestions to alleviate the problem.

Step 4: Developmental Strategy

The main strategy by which Carver develops her paragraph is cause and effect. She lays out the problem and indicates the detrimental effects in her plea to resolve the problem. For example, Carver says that the hospital staff are being "unfriendly, hostile or rude" toward their patients and that these fearful and sick people should not have to defend themselves against such behaviour in their weakened state. Carver also uses an element of comparison and contrast in her use of analogy comparing the expected behaviour of the hospital staff to that of salespeople who might be faced with the same situation, and the effect of management on these particular salespeople.

1. Do you agree with the choice of topic sentence? Does it reflect Carver's overall point?
2. Is there another sentence, or cluster of them (don't forget our discussion of "controlling idea," p. 28) that captures Carver's concern more completely?

Step 5: Outline

I. Complaints about hospital staff, the effect of negative patient care, and the solution to the problem
   A. Complaints
      1. Unfriendly
      2. Hostile
      3. Rude
   B. Analogy of salespeople's conduct in a business and their management's solution

C. Defence for patients
  1. Their feelings
  2. Effect of such behaviour by staff on the patients
D. Defence for staff: negative attitudes of some patients
E. Strong defence for the patients
F. Solution offered to remedy the problem
  1. Observation
  2. Change of positions to satisfy both staff member and patient

Step 6: Summary

Carver has stated that there is a problem within the hospital, between patient and staff member. The problem is that staff members are not conducting themselves in a personable and healthy manner. She offers several suggestions such as observation of staff or change of positions in order to offer patients the best atmosphere for their well-being.

Step 7: Response

Everyone who works in a patient care setting —mainly hospitals and nursing homes— must contend with many people each day. All of these people are individuals with various personalities, wants, and needs. All of the staff have their own unique mannerisms as well, and in contending with their many patients must learn to deal with these different kinds of people. They must learn to adapt themselves to all situations. These employees realize the many natures of the patients but it seems that they must be reminded that patients are ill or feeble and that many of them, consequently, may be short tempered. The ill tempers of staff, on the other hand, may arise from understaffing. It sometimes happens that single employees are overburdened with an unreasonable number of charges. Such a workload may not facilitate adequate personal attention to patients. An ultimate result might be misunderstandings between staff and their patients. This ends in an unhealthy work atmosphere and of course an unhealthy atmosphere for collective recovery from illness or depression.

By mentioning understaffing and workload is Beach challenging Carver's contention that there "is no reason why" there should be unmannerly hospital staff?

READING TWO

Step 1: Active Reading

Childbirth with dignity means being treated with sensitivity and kindness; it means being free to choose positions which are most comfortable; it's assessing the need for any obstetrical procedure on an individual basis, rather than because of "policy"; it's doing everything possible to help a woman work with her labor without interventions, and where intervention is deemed necessary, never allowing the needs of the woman to become secondary to the equipment used. It's respecting parents' wishes and providing reasonable choice in the way their child is born. It's, as one wonderful head nurse once said to me, the right to give birth as you choose: "If the couple want to chant and sing and burn incense and have the baby squatting, that's fine with me!" A rare and compassionate nurse who was as good as her word.

Valmai Howe Elkins, *The Rights of the Pregnant Parent* (Toronto: Lester & Orpen Dennys Ltd., 1985), p. 228.

Steps 2 - 7

Reading workbook notes

Article

Excerpt from The Rights of the Pregnant Parent by Valmai Howe Elkins

Step 2(a): Subject

The author, who obviously has gone through the pains of childbirth, has written an article explaining that the woman giving birth has a right to the most comfortable atmosphere in which to have her child.

Step 2(b): Audience

The author has written (it seems) to those in the medical profession, who are actively involved with expectant mothers at the birth of their children. She seems to be reminding these people that the woman giving birth already feels very awkward and perhaps apprehensive or afraid and that she must be treated with kindness and sympathy at this time. The author may also be writing to expectant mothers who may be reassured by the fact that they really do have a say in what goes on at the birth of her child.

Are both speculations about audience equally valid? If not, why not? Which is more appropriate for the piece? Why?

Step 2(c): Purpose

The author seems to be redefining requirements for a comforting childbirth. She is letting health professionals know that the medical technology should not interfere with human compassion at this time when a woman is very sensitive. She is also saying that although childbirth may be a routine process for the medical people, it is not for the expectant mother and that these professionals must not get caught up in their routine so much that they neglect to be compassionate and so on. Through definition, the author persuades her audience to consider her stance.

Is Elkins's purpose purely persuasive?

Step 3: Topic Sentence

The thesis is immediately indicated in the opening line. "Childbirth with dignity means being treated with sensitivity and kindness." This sentence also indicates the structure of the piece as each point is made by definition.

Do you agree with the choice of topic sentence? If not, where do you place it? Why?

Step 4: Developmental Strategy

This particular argument has been developed by a definition approach.

Are there no other strategies that could have been identified? Does not Beach's active reading marginalia suggest at least one other?

Step 5: Outline

I. Meaning of childbirth with dignity
   A. Freedom to choose most comfortable position
   B. Individual needs for most effective procedure
   C. Give adequate aid to mother, encouragement, but let her control the situation
   D. Be always concerned with the progress and make certain the woman is not in any difficulty or danger
   E. Allow parents to make reasonable decisions
   F. Example: Parents must have the right to give birth to their child whichever way they want within reason

What does point (D) reflect from the original?

Step 6: Summary

The author tries to make those involved with the delivery of a child recognize that each woman has specific individual needs at this delicate period and must be treated with concern and compassion.

What important point from the piece, and from her subject notes, has Beach left out here?

Step 7: Response

We often hear that childbirth is a very delicate and sensitive time. Emotions are said to be readily displayed, especially by expectant mothers. Though it is an emotional time, the mother not only has to contend with her flighty feelings, but she must also bear with the pains she may be feeling at this time. Before the birth of her child, she spends hours sometimes preparing and waiting, and all the while she is expending physical energy. This tiring process can result in unleashed emotions, sometimes good, sometimes not so good. It is likely that the expectant mother will become anxious and restless. It is up to the hospital staff to be prepared for the different needs of each individual mother and to make her feel as much at ease as they possibly can by offering her encouragement, sympathy, understanding and compassion.

How might Beach's response have changed if she had responded directly to Elkins's contention that parents have a "right" to choose how they will give birth?

Hands On: Reading

In this section *you* put theory into practice by completing reading workbook notes for complementary passages by Pierre Berton and Ted Byfield on the place of the church in society. Pierre Berton's book *The Comfortable Pew* caused a stir in religious circles in 1964. Ted Byfield published his response to it, *Just Think, Mr. Berton . . . A Little Harder,* in 1965. As we recommended in the Introduction, you should do each step here in conjunction with your reading of the same step in the "Demonstration" and "Student Examples" sections of this chapter. Proceeding in this manner will keep you refreshed on theory, and will offer you Beach's work and ours as varying possibilities on how to approach the readings. In any event, this is your first hands-on writing assignment in this text. By the time you have finished the "Hands On: Writing" section of chapter 3, the work you are about to do now will have blossomed into your first essay prepared wholly according to principles presented in this text. Take the time to answer our leading questions conscientiously. They will guide you into fuller observations of the reading passages and thereby into fuller responses. The fuller your responses are, the more solid will be the foundation of your writing occasion. The questions in the anthology chapter assignments are not so systematic or thorough; consequently it is in your best interest to pay close attention to the questions here.

READING ONE

In the great issues of our time, the voice of the Church, when it has been heard at all, has been weak, tardy, equivocal, and irrelevant. In those basic conflicts that ought to be tormenting every Christian conscience—questions of war and peace, of racial brotherhood, of justice versus revenge, to name three—the Church has trailed far behind the atheists, the agnostics, the free thinkers, the journalists, the scientists, the social workers, and even, on occasion, the politicians. In other areas, the Church has simply stood aloof. It has, for instance, virtually ignored the whole contemporary question of business morals, the tensions within industry and labour, the sexual revolution that has changed the attitudes of the Western world.

Pierre Berton, *The Comfortable Pew* (New York: J.B. Lippincott, 1965), p. 16.

Step 1: Active Reading

1. How many words indicate Berton's non-neutral stance? Circle them.
2. What stylistic feature is present in three out of four sentences and appears twice in one of them?
3. Which word is most significant in sentence 3, and how does it further develop items in sentence 1?
4. Where should you be marking a slight change in direction of thought?
5. What marginal notation should accompany the phrase "for instance" in sentence 4?

Step 2(a): Subject

1. What is Berton's perception of the place of the church in "the great issues of our time"?
2. How does Berton's title, *The Comfortable Pew,* contribute to his subject?

Step 2(b): Audience

1. Who is Berton's audience? On what evidence in the passage do you base your answer?
2. What audience assumptions does Berton make? Can you draw an audience profile based on these assumptions?

Step 2(c): Purpose

1. Is Berton's purpose primarily expository or argumentative? On what do you base your answer?
2. On the basis of the opening section of sentence 2 (prior to the first dash), what can you determine about Berton's purpose?

Step 3: Thesis Statement, Topic Sentence, or Controlling Idea

1. Which of the above three items embodies the main idea in Berton's paragraph?
2. How is the rest of the paragraph seen to be only a development of the main idea?

Step 4: Developmental Strategies

1. Which items, in sentences 2 and 4, indicate Berton's method, or methods, of development?
2. How does sentence 3 act as an organizational pivot?
3. What role does sentence 1 play in Berton's organization?

Step 5: Outline

1. How do sentences 2 and 4 present different aspects of Berton's subject?

Step 6: Summary

1. When you remove the detail, which three or four points remain to be summarized?

Step 7: Response

1. Do you support or oppose Berton's position? Why?
2. Do you have personal information or experience that bears on this issue?

READING TWO

The Christian rule on sex has never, of course, been popular. It has been flouted to varying degrees ever since it was proclaimed by both Christian and secular societies. Neither are sexual revolutions particularly novel. Third- and fourth-century Rome witnessed a "sexual revolution," but historians are not inclined to look upon the period as a broadening or awakening of the human spirit. They are more apt to say, instead, that the popular rejection of moral principle inevitably precedes and contributes to the fall of a civilization. I suppose it could have been argued that if the fourth-century church expected to make itself really popular with the Romans it would have to relax its morality and catch up with the times. But the church did not compromise and, strangely, the church did not collapse. It was the Roman civilization that collapsed.

Ted Byfield, *Just Think, Mr. Berton* (New York: Morehouse-Barlow Co., 1965) [1st American Ed.], pp. 72-73.

Step 1: Active Reading

1. How do "of course" in sentence 1, "particularly novel" in sentence 3, " 'sexual revolution' " in sentence 4, "I suppose" in sentence 6, and "strangely" in sentence 7 contribute to Byfield's slightly ironic tone?
2. What effect does Byfield's repetition of "collapse" and "collapsed" in the last two sentences have?
3. Which terms in sentences 1, 5, and 6 tie together?
4. Which terms or phrases in sentences 5, 6, and 7 indicate the "varying degrees" to which people have "flouted" the "Christian rule on sex"?
5. Where should you be marking slight shifts in the direction of thought?

Step 2(a): Subject

1. What is Byfield's perception of the place of the church in relation to society's view of sex?
2. How is Byfield's piece an answer to Berton's?

Step 2(b): Audience

1. Who is Byfield's audience? On what evidence in the passage do you base your answer?
2. What audience assumptions does Byfield make? Can you draw an audience profile based on these assumptions?

Step 2(c): Purpose

1. Is Byfield's purpose primarily expository or argumentative? On what do you base your answer?
2. Taking into account your answer to question 1 of "Step 1: Active Reading," what does Byfield's slightly ironic tone indicate about his purpose?

Step 3: Thesis Statement, Topic Sentence, or Controlling Idea

1. Which of the above three items embodies the main idea in Byfield's paragraph?
2. Does Byfield unify his main idea adequately for this paragraph?

Step 4: Developmental Strategies

1. How do sentences 2 and 4 indicate one strategy, and sentences 5 and 6 another?

Step 5: Outline

1. How does sentence 2 relate to sentence 1?
2. How do sentences 4 and 5 relate to sentence 3?
3. How do sentences 6, 7, and 8 represent a shift in thought from what precedes them?

Step 6: Summary

1. When you remove the detail, which four points remain to be summarized?

Step 7: Response

1. Do you support or oppose Byfield's position? Why?
2. Do you have personal information or experience that bears on this issue?

3 *The Writing Occasion*

Demonstration

Although there are often times when your reading and writing occasions will be quite separate, in most college and university assignments they will be one continuous process. We have broken them into two chapters for ease of discussion, but you shouldn't assume from this that one process stops when you've written your response, and that another begins when you change your focus to your own writing occasion. Steps 1 through 7 of the reading occasion are ways to help you become informed about the general subject of the readings; Steps 1 through 7 of the writing occasion continue that informing process to the point at which you feel ready to impart your knowledge to others. The writing occasion steps are as follows:

Step 1: Make an *examination of the responses* you made to the readings to determine your personal stance to the broad subject of the readings

Step 2: Consider your own *subject, audience,* and *purpose* to refine that personal stance into a workable *topic*

Step 3: Determine effective *developmental strategies*

Step 4: Develop a *thesis statement*

Step 5: Develop an *outline*

Step 6: Complete a *planning checklist* and proceed to write a *first draft*

Step 7: Conduct a *revision* from large items to small.

We suggest that you keep a writing journal for materials you accumulate during the writing occasions. The journal notes we offer in the following pages show what we came up with when working toward our demonstration essay at the particular time we did it. They are not rigid directives; a writing journal demands freedom and flexibility. Each time you write you may find yourself adjusting to a unique set of circumstances.

Step 1: Examination of the Responses

Traditional process rhetorics speak of the *invention* stage in the writing process in which you use various techniques to help you generate raw material for your writing. Given a broad subject area you might try *brainstorming:* freely jotting down whatever comes into your mind as you consider the subject. The purpose of brainstorming is to write quickly and without concern for quality of ideas: you just want to accumulate material for later perusal. Another technique is to use the *basic journalist's questions—who? what? when? where?* and *why?*—as a means of addressing your general subject from different angles and so again generating material that your conventional perspective might have missed.

We find both these techniques helpful, but, on their own, we feel they often disregard what is one of the most common sources of information for your writing: the reading you have done. The seven-step reading occasion presented in chapter 2 is actually a sustained invention technique for your writing. Your informed responses are valuable pieces of thought on the general subject of the readings; they should be the logical starting place when you change focus from reading to writing and begin to determine the subject, audience, and purpose for your own essay. Consequently, in this step of the writing occasion we ask you to make an *examination of your responses* to see just what your interests are in the area under study. The best way to begin this examination is by *actively reading* those responses. Once you have ascertained what your main responses are, you can do some brainstorming and ask some questions to generate even more material if necessary. What follows, then, is our brief active reading of our responses to the passages by Frye and Layton, followed by a list of items generated from those responses.

Response to Northrop Frye

It seems all too clear when we look around us that Frye is correct in his feeling that we are materially successful but spiritually poverty-stricken. Increasingly in Canada we seem to be importing our values from the US. We are avid consumers but the more we consume of US culture the less Canadian we become. Is our problem that we are a young country? We need to develop our imaginations as Frye says, but how can we do this when TV culture deadens them? Even the CBC has fallen on tough times, and it has traditionally been the promoter and protector of Canadian culture. Frye may imply that we need to wrestle with our angels, but how soon will it be before we cannot be awakened to that need?

1 a) and b)
2
3
4
5
6
7

1. Material success / spiritual poverty
2. Importing values from US
3. Losing our Canadianness
4. Canada's youth as a country a problem?

5. TV culture deadens imagination
6. CBC cutbacks
7. Complacency increasing: can we be awakened?

Response to Irving Layton

While we may find it easy to agree with Layton that the drag of "middle-class mores" is strong in Canada, surely we should demand more specifics from him with regard to the "contact, abandonment, passion, and the understanding heart" which he advocates. All but the last of these terms (and even it too with some stretching) could describe a typical McDonald's advertisement on TV. Doesn't this give us pause? Just where are we to find the healthy cultural milieu which will nurture what Layton wants when the whole drive of our culture is following the US in the opposite direction? Layton feels that our "miserable" souls still sense what they need, somewhere deep inside. Can we be so sure? Is hoping so enough? Layton's emotional scattergun approach may raise hackles, or elicit self-satisfied nods, or both; it is also sure to perpetuate Layton's image as Canada's self-proclaimed voice crying in the wilderness. But until Layton comes in from the cold he enjoys so much, he is unlikely to make a tangible difference to our predicament.

1. Need specifics about passion
2. His language like McDonald's
3. Our culture follows US
4. Can we turn around?
5. Is raising hackles enough?
6. Is Layton role playing?
7. Can he effect a change in this mode?

The amount of raw material you generate from your responses will, of course, depend on the size of those responses. While we recommend a minimum of a hundred words for a response, you can be sure that the fuller your response is, the more raw material it will generate. In our case the responses were little more than the minimum hundred words; consequently we probably need to do some brainstorming and questioning of our items to bring more potential considerations into consciousness. If the length of your assignment suggests that you may be able to deal with eight to ten points in some fashion, then you would be wise to have a pool of up to fifty items to choose from. It is always easier to cull good points from mediocre ones, or trim fat from a flabby first draft than it is to generate new material at a later date. Too often we find ourselves trying to wring another thin paragraph out of an exhausted point because we have not generated enough ideas in the beginning. Take the time you need at this stage: it will prevent real problems later.

To illustrate just what brainstorming can do we have reproduced here the results of *one minute's worth* of non-stop jottings on only one of the items on Frye given above—"TV culture deadens imagination":

- Canadian TV primarily American
- Even CBC TV 50% American
- Since 1950 s North America a TV culture
- Less reading - about ourselves as Canadians
  - about our past
- TV teaches us American culture and values
- We learn about - acquisitiveness
  - competition
  - superficiality
  - rugged individualism
- TV cannot sustain serious thought
- Reality is turned into a commodity
- As a commodity Canadian reality cannot compete - not glossy enough

The basic journalist's questions, when applied to another of the response items—"Material success/spiritual poverty"—evoked the following thoughts:

Who?

- Middle and upper income status seekers

- People who accumulate electronic and technical "toys"
- Those who seek constant entertainment
    - at malls
    - on TV
    - on video
- Those who lack purpose outside of materialism
- Baby boomers

What?

- Reality lies in things – commodities – rather than values
- Life is a commodity to be "used" and "discarded"
- We are what we <u>have</u>
- Sharing affluence with the US carries a cost
- Canada is seen as real estate, not our home, so we neglect past

When?

- increasingly since the advent of TV brought American culture into our livingrooms
- When we are negotiating a free-trade deal with the US
- When our economy is determined by the American economy

Where?

- In Québec, with a James Bay Hydro Project undertaken on the strength of economic considerations only

- In our media generally, which takes its cue from American commercialism
- In Rome, just before the fall of the Roman empire—Nero fiddled
- In the mid Atlantic, where a New York garbage barge tries to pay a third world country to take its 4000 tons of trash

Why?

- Because we are a young country without solid traditions
- Because we are therefore easily influenced
- Because we are attracted by material wealth, glitter, and ease—the Pinocchio syndrome

As you can see from even this preliminary examination of our responses, there are numerous avenues waiting to be explored. Of course we cannot follow all the intriguing signposts; that was never the intention. Having options, though, is the basis of freedom of choice. Generate more material at the outset and you have a broader range from which to choose; consequently, the substance of your essay will be more informed and more thorough than that of the person who slaps down the first four or five ideas that emerge from the depths of the unconscious.

Step 2: Subject, Audience, and Purpose into Topic

As you examine your responses to your reading and employ invention techniques, you will probably recognize recurrent interests; the same idea may appear in different aspects in different contexts. These recurrent ideas become important now because you are beginning to determine the boundaries of your writing occasion—your subject, audience, and purpose. To this point you have been generating ideas out of your responses to a group of readings that share a common, general subject; now you want to pull back and ask yourself just *what* you want to say, *who* your reader is, and *why* you are writing. When you make concrete decisions about this triad you are establishing your specific *rhetorical context* for this writing occasion. Once you know the basics of the context you can give it focus in a concise topic. Often process rhetorics suggest that you should determine subject, narrow it to a topic, and then consider audience and purpose in a cursory fashion once the topic is down in black and white. Other process rhetorics often stress the recursiveness of the writing process—the overlapping and doubling back which occurs while you are in the planning stages—and imply that audience and purpose will make themselves felt in these re-perusals of subject. We prefer to stress subject, audience, and purpose equally *before* topic selection. This way you can be confident that your rhetorical context is solid before you get too far along in your planning.

Step 2(a): Subject

For any writing project that involves prior reading a *general subject area* is a given. If the project deals with the women's movement, it is not likely that you will go off to read material on environmental pollution; the reading you do and the writing that finally results from your study will in some way relate to the broad subject of the women's movement. This does *not* mean, however, that the subject of your essay is the women's movement, except in the vaguest of senses. Your subject will be a narrower, more clearly defined concept or experience, or a group of them. It will depend on your responses to your reading and on your personal experience. It will be shaped by the constraints of the assignment or writing occasion and by the pressures your audience and purpose exert. It will manifest itself most tangibly in your essay's topic, title, and thesis statement.

In our demonstration case, for example, the Frye and Layton passages, despite their differences in specific subject, audience, and purpose, share essentially the same general subject: the proliferation of shallow and material values at the expense of the inner life. This can be expressed more simply as spiritual bankruptcy. The broad limits of any essay we write, then, are determined by this general subject. To strike out into the wonders of genetic engineering or freshwater fishing, however enticing we find these subjects, would be to disregard the reading we have done. So, given the broad subject of spiritual bankruptcy, what are we going to write about? When we look over our responses, and the material generated through invention techniques, we see some recurrent interests:

The Canadian Situation

- Losing ourselves in materialism
- American influence on Canada
- The role of TV
- Our youth as a country
- Life as a commodity

Obviously our concern is with the Canadian situation; we seem to be sacrificing our distinctiveness as a nation for the material success so evident south of the border. The subject we will want to develop, then, is spiritual bankruptcy in an affluent Canada.

Step 2(b): Audience

Determining who your reader is, is an essential decision in your process: it contributes to a strong focus, a definite diction, and a consistent tone and range of reference. At all costs, avoid falling into the trap of writing for a vaguely "general" audience. As our discussion of Frye's audience in the last chapter indicated, general audiences are made up of individuals with distinguishing characteristics. You do not always have to identify a specific person or group explicitly, but if your writing implicitly recognizes and addresses a well-defined audience, it will convey the authority of experience, whereas the essay with an ill-defined audience will often appear general and nondescript.

Compare the following two opening paragraphs from student essays. Which makes the more effective appeal to audience? Why?

> The recent "drug scene" among teenagers has been the subject of discussion ever since it became a matter of concern in the mid 1960s. Although students in their adolescent years are tempted every day by sex, alcohol, and drugs, the dominant temptation for many is marijuana. I will discuss the types of students who use marijuana, the reasons for their doing so, and the effects of the drug on them, in hopes of discouraging users of marijuana.

> It's Friday night, and as usual it's party time around the city. Guys and gals, friends and sweethearts, begin to plan the night's events. They'll probably stop by the liquor store if they're old enough, and even if they're not they can probably find someone to get the alcohol for them. Tonight, though, the odds are that one of them will become impaired, and that others will suffer because of one person's stupidity. Today's teenager is tomorrow's future, and there is growing concern that the future will be an alcoholic nightmare.

Try drawing a profile of the audience for your essay. Consider such things as age, sex, financial status, level of education, ethnic background, occupation, religion, and location. Any supposedly "general" audience will have certain distinctive characteristics. To be an effective writer you will have to identify those characteristics and make allowances for them. Of course, any audience you target will be determined to some degree by your purpose—but the reverse is just as true. An environmentalist pamphlet soliciting donations to help fight acid rain would be well advised to tailor its appeal differently for audiences in Vancouver and Sudbury. The distinctive characteristics of your audience should be at least suggested by your responses to your reading and any subsequent inventing you have done. If you have taken some notes on your subject, these will help you as well. In our subject—spiritual bankruptcy in an affluent Canada—a number of audience pointers are apparent:

- Canadian
- Affluent, or with the potential to be so
- Relatively well-educated

If we consider the responses and inventing we did we can add other possibilities:

- The generations that have grown up with TV
- Somewhat complacent
- Lacking substantial awareness of Canadian culture
- Regularly exposed to American media

Given these pointers to audience—pointers that indicate our areas of concern (though we may not have been conscious of them as such previously)—we can now identify three possible audiences which the pointers describe:

- Entrepreneurs in their twenties or thirties
- University students
- Young professionals

Because of our own bias as university professors writing a textbook, the most natural target audience for us will be university students. This does not mean that we will *explicitly* address university students; our decision simply means that as we are writing we will need to keep in mind that a university student reader (possibly a reader of a university paper) should be able to follow and respond to our essay.

Step 2(c): Purpose

As we said in the sections "Purpose and the Reader" and "Purpose and the Writer" in chapter 1 (pp. 13 - 14), knowing *what* you want to write about and *who* your reader is, will help you articulate *why* you want to write—what your purpose is. Writing to university students will mean that we need to explain certain pieces of information but can assume that other types of information will be readily understood. Consequently, we can ascertain, in part, the degree to which our purpose will be expository rather than argumentative by considering audience. Our decision to write about spiritual bankruptcy in an affluent Canada, however, reveals a negative evaluation of our spiritual state and thus a (possibly implicit) argumentative aspect of our subject.

To firm up your purpose, which may have its origins in unfocused anger, or curiosity, or the simple desire to impart information, examine your responses to your reading and the inventing you have done. There you will find not only subject matter but an attitude toward that subject matter. You need to ask yourself what that attitude implies. In our responses to Frye and Layton, for example, we express a concern about increasing complacency among Canadians and wonder whether we can be awakened to our spiritual poverty. Do we even recognize a problem? Surely here we are revealing a purpose: we feel Canadians should be awakened. To awaken will involve more than simply showing and explaining—we imply that Canadians need a sound shake to wake them. In writing, that shake becomes argument or persuasion. Yet we also wonder, in response to Layton's piece, whether raising hackles is enough. Our response to Layton generally is somewhat ambivalent. While we can support some of what he says, we question his method. Consequently, if his purpose is to persuade through frontal attack, ours will be more restrained. We want to explain what spiritual bankruptcy means in Canada and how it comes about, but we also want to convince our audience that we need to change directions.

Expository - explain what spiritual bankruptcy means in Canada

Argumentative - convince audience of need to change direction

Step 2(d): Topic

Your topic provides a focus for your rhetorical context of subject, audience, and purpose. It will reflect, either explicitly or implicitly, the subject area, the level of audience, and the considered purpose. In our case, our subject—spiritual bankruptcy in an affluent Canada—needs to be narrowed down to a workable size. As it stands, our essay could be about anything from declining church attendance, to exploitation of native sacred homelands, to loss of political idealism, to all of these and more. When we examine our responses, however, and when we consider audience and purpose, we see that we are more concerned with causes of spiritual bankruptcy than with effects (though of course they go hand in hand). Audience and purpose indicate that we want to explain the causes of the situation to an audience including university students and, in so doing, convince them that the problem must be addressed.

Your topic must also reflect the limitations imposed by the writing occasion. If you are in first-year university physics, you are probably not going to set out to explain quantum mechanics to your peers—you simply do not have the expertise. You must gauge your own ability to handle a topic; by all means explore things that interest you and about which you know nothing, but be realistic about your capabilities. Also be realistic about constraints of length. In five pages you simply cannot do everything; judicious pruning of your topic is in order. Conversely, you may have to make a topic expand to fill arbitrary requirements provided by the occasion.

When we consider the limitations of our writing occasion—preparing a demonstration essay for university students—certain strictures become apparent: the essay should not be too long if it is to be accessible for student perusal; we cannot, therefore, provide in-depth coverage of our subject. We need to choose which of the causes of spiritual bankruptcy we feel may best introduce the problem to our readers. A suitably narrowed topic for the essay we propose to write, then, might be the following:

The major causes of spiritual bank-ruptcy in an affluent, complacent Canada

Step 3: Developmental Strategies

Effective writing is planned writing. In the reading process discussed in chapter 2, you could ascertain the developmental strategies after finding the thesis statement. When you are writing, however, *now* is the time to address the "how" of your essay. Consequently, we have moved the step on developmental strategies from its earlier fourth place position to third. The developmental strategies will help you determine the claim you want to make in your thesis statement. Further, in considering developmental strategies, you are addressing the *how* of your essay. Before you embark on an outline for a draft, you need to take some time to speculate on what might be the best way to package your material. An essay that presents a distinct form to its readers often has the advantage of clarity and directness over the essay that cobbles its ideas together just as they pour from the writer's head. What form your writing assumes will depend on the concerns you expressed in your responses, inventing, and rhetorical context. Often your topic itself will indicate a method of development, as ours does: the major *causes* of spiritual bankruptcy in an affluent, complacent Canada. But, of course, a quick look at our responses and inventing shows an interest in a cause-and-effect relationship in a number of items. Causes of spiritual bankruptcy are as follows: (1) sharing affluence with the United States; (2) treating Canada as real estate, not our home, so we neglect our past; (3) being a youthful country; (4) allowing TV culture to deaden the imagination.

Cause and effect is not the only developmental strategy available. Appendix 1 contains concise discussions of comparison and contrast, classification and division, illustration, definition, and process analysis, as well as cause and effect. We urge you to familiarize yourself with these strategies: without the options they can offer you, your range may be severely limited.

All this step in the process actually does is make you stop and consider consciously something you will probably already have dealt with. When we consider developmental strategies and come up with cause and effect, it is because our preliminary work recurrently touched on cause-and-effect relationships. If your topic were violence in children's sports, for example, and you neglected this stage, you might be neglecting crucial pointers to development that were embodied in your preliminary work. The pointers might involve causes of such violence; they might implicitly compare different sports; they might challenge current definitions of violence; they probably would list examples of such violence. Stopping to look over your earlier work, with developmental strategies in mind, makes good practical sense: you do not want to waste work you have already done.

Main developmental strategy will be cause and effect.

Step 4: Thesis Statement

Your topic becomes a thesis when you make some sort of claim about it. It is this claim or attitude or point of view or position that will control the direction of your essay and that your readers will rely on to keep them oriented. Take the topic of chemical insecticide spraying in urban areas. Though this may seem fairly well defined, it is the thesis which truly tells us the author's concern. Notice how the addition of a *claim* to this topic promises a different essay in each of the following examples:

1. The benefits of chemical insecticide spraying in urban areas far outweigh the disadvantages.
2. Chemical insecticide spraying in urban areas is the result of a failure of imagination on the part of city councils.
3. Chemical insecticide spraying in urban areas is a necessary evil.

Each of these thesis statements is a bill of lading promising the delivery of certain goods. If you tell your readers at the outset that such spraying is a necessary evil, they will be understandably confused if they encounter, in paragraph 5, a recommendation to ban the practice. Their opinion of you as a thinker, if not as a writer, will probably fall.

Besides being sure that your thesis statement and the ensuing essay are consistent, you must be sure your thesis statement *says something.* Many writers editorialize in a thesis statement rather than make a claim. If, for example, we were to make the following thesis statement out of our topic— "In this essay we will examine the major causes of spiritual bankruptcy in an affluent, complacent Canada"—we would be essentially only repeating the topic. Though some direction is given to the reader, it is vague and has little impact. There is no authorial presence in the thesis, because there *is* no thesis. The most logical thing for us to do, given that our topic deals with major causes, is to give an indication of what those causes are. We should also be sure to put them in the form of an assertion, and thus avoid editorializing—talking *about* what we will do.

After another examination of all the work we have done so far, we come up with four causes that have clearly been evident at earlier stages of our process. Having identified them, we prepare the thesis statement for our draft:

> Although Canada is one of the most affluent countries in the world, its very affluence, as well as its youth, its lack of culture, and its proximity to the United States, make it a potential victim of spiritual bankruptcy.

This version says what the causes are, and what *they* do, rather than what *we* are going to do. The reader's attention is drawn in the right direction.

A final word about thesis statements concerns rigidity. At this stage of your process, do not allow the thesis statement to become a straitjacket; assume it will change as you write and revise your draft. (Ours does, as you will see.) While your final thesis statement is a guide for your reader, this preliminary version is equally a guide for you—but *only* a guide. It will get you into a draft, but other pressures may force a change of direction. Do not rule out these changes. You have a revision process to handle just these eventualities.

Step 5: Outline

Your outline represents a preliminary walk through your paper, making sure that your developmental strategy will enable you to say what you want to say. Because you have a number of things to say, an order is inevitable; outlining your essay can help you in putting together a piece of writing that is clear, precise, and logical. Outlines themselves need not be, and generally are not, things of beauty that stand on their own to be admired. Rather, they are a means to an end, that end being a carefully constructed piece of work.

The plan you come up with, finally, will depend on your purpose and choice of developmental strategies; a paper arguing against capital punishment by unfavourably comparing the retentionist position to the abolitionist view will order its paper differently from a neutral exposition comparing the two views. Be sure to read carefully the chapters on narration, description, exposition, and argumentation, as well as Appendix 1 on developmental strategies. Here we are only showing you how to make the actual outline; those chapters will give you a greater sense of how to order what goes into it.

There are two basic kinds of outline: the point outline and the sentence outline. Both employ the standard system of numbers and letters we ran through in chapter 2 (p. 31): Roman numerals for main headings, and letters and Arabic numerals for sub-headings. This system is arbitrary but effective; it gives you a simple method of keeping your ideas in their proper places.

Point Outline

The point outline (often called the topic outline) is, as its title suggests, written in point form. It is the format you will most likely use for the majority of your writing occasions. It gives you a quick view of your essay as a whole, without the detail. Some people find the lack of detail a problem and so opt for the fuller sentence outline, but most feel the point format gives enough information to keep them on track. Another advantage of the point outline is that, because it looks less formal, it is easy to tinker with as you draft and revise. You should consider any outline as tentative, and point outlines look more tentative; in fact, some writers refer to them as preliminary outlines. Here is a point outline for our paper on spiritual bankruptcy in an affluent, complacent Canada:

The Major Causes of Spiritual Bankruptcy in Canada

Thesis Statement

Although Canada is one of the most affluent countries in the world, its very affluence, as well as its youth, its lack of culture, and its proximity to the United States, make it a potential victim of spiritual bankruptcy.

I. Introduction: Canada's ease in a troubled world

II. Canada's affluence

A. Accumulation of wealth at odds with a country's life

B. Little time for anything but acquisition

III. Canada's youth

A. Analogy with children; no historical vision

B. No developed identity; therefore no concern for spiritual welfare

IV. Canada's lack of culture

A. Apparent lack of concern with national culture

B. Neglect of native Indian and Inuit cultures

V. Canada's proximity to the US

A. Anti-spiritual influence of US on Canada

B. US material success is Canada's role model

VI. Conclusion: Wealthy but soulless?

Sentence Outline

By using full sentences, authors are able to put more of their detail and tone into the outline. Consequently the outline provides a great deal of guidance to the drafting author. This, of course, can work well, if you have anticipated the twists and turns of the paper adequately. If you have not, however, you may feel less inclined to deviate from a sentence outline when a tantalizing new idea emerges as you draft. Sentence outlines have a degree of formality that offers security to the writer but can make the outline a straitjacket. A straitjacket is the last thing you need as you embark on your draft. Many writers only use a sentence outline after they have written a draft and have found the new things that were waiting to be discovered. The formal sentence outline then guides them through the revised version, where surprises are less likely. We recommend that you use a point outline for your draft and a sentence outline for your revised version, but because some people write more effectively by using the sentence outline to guide the draft, we have provided an example, again using our demonstration topic:

The Major Causes of Spiritual Bankruptcy in Canada

Thesis Statement

Although Canada is one of the most affluent countries in the world, its very affluence, as well as its youth, its lack of culture, and its proximity to the United States, make it a potential victim of spiritual bankruptcy.

I. Introduction: Relative to the pain and suffering in the world, Canadians have it easy.

II. Canada's affluence threatens its spiritual development.

A. The accumulation of money and material benefits has traditionally been at odds with the development of a country's inner life.

B. Canadians intent upon increasing their standard of living seem to have little time for their own inner selves.

III. Canada's youth as a country threatens its spiritual development.

A. Like children themselves, young countries seem not to worry about the past or future, but live only for today.

B. A young country like Canada, with little sense of its own identity, seems not to have to worry about its past and its spiritual welfare.

IV. Canada's lack of culture threatens its spiritual development.

A. If culture is, in some sense, the repository of spiritual values, Canada's apparent unconcern with culture suggests spiritual impoverishment.

B. Those forces within our country with a cultural heritage—Indians and Inuit—are largely ignored by the rest of us.

V. Canada's proximity to the United States threatens its spiritual development.

A. The US exerts a depressingly anti-spiritual parental influence over Canada.

B. In looking for role models, Canada, by virtue of its closeness to the US, has turned toward it and sees only its material success.

VI. Conclusion: Of what real worth is a wealthy but soulless nation?

Overlap and repetition of points

One of the advantages of preparing an outline is that it will let the vigilant author recognize potential trouble spots before writing headlong into them. If, in an outline on the harmful effects of acid rain, you have a main heading entitled "Effects on Business" with a sub-heading "The Maple Syrup Industry," and you have another main heading entitled "Effects on Nature" with a sub-heading "Maple Trees," you might consider rearranging your outline to avoid the overlap of points and inevitable repetition. If change is not feasible, then you can at least make sure the points are largely distinct and that repetition is kept to a minimum.

Keeping points distinct

Another trouble spot is the clotting that can occur when points that are distinct are placed together through superficial similarity. In the same outline on the harmful effects of acid rain you might have a main heading entitled "Physical effects." If "Disagreeable Odours" and "Respiratory Diseases" are both included as sub-headings here, you have some reconsidering to do; possibly a division into short-term and long-term physical effects would suffice. Preparing the outline gives you the opportunity to work out these knots before you have committed too many words to paper.

Titles

A word or two about effective titles is pertinent at this point. In our experience, students often do not recognize the importance of the titles they give their essays—many do not attach titles at all, especially to drafts or outlines. You should. The title is the first thing your reader encounters; consequently it is your initial chance to hook that reader. This does not mean a title should be flashy or esoteric (such titles carry their own problems), but there is no reason why it should be dull, and every reason why it should be *informative.* The title should reflect the topic and ideally the thesis of the essay in miniature; it should enable readers to tell at a glance generally what they can expect from the time you are asking them to spend reading your work. The problem of titles that do not carry enough information becomes clear when you read indexes. Here are three entries on E.J. Pratt's poetry from Michael Gnarowski's *A Concise Bibliography of English-Canadian Literature.* As a researcher, and assuming the names of the authors are unfamiliar to you, consider which entry helps you the most, and which the least.

Northrop Frye, "Silence upon the Earth," *Canadian Poetry* 27:71-3 Aug '64.

Vincent Sharman, "E.J. Pratt and Christianity," *Canadian Literature* 19:21-32 Winter '64.

F. Davey, "E.J. Pratt: Rationalist Technician," *Canadian Literature* 61:65-78 Summer '74.

Exercises

1. Here are point outlines written by two students for ten-page research papers. Comment on the titles, thesis statements, overlap of points and distinctiveness of points:

Marijuana

Thesis Statement

Although students in their adolescent years are tempted every day by sex, alcohol, and drugs, the dominant temptation for many is marijuana.

I. Types of students
   A. Rich and poor
   B. Nonusers and users

II. Reasons for smoking marijuana
   A. Society
   B. Being ignored
   C. Challenge
   D. Curiosity
   E. Peer pressure

III. Effects
   A. Short-term and long-term

The Abortion Issue: Pro-Choice versus Pro-Life

Thesis Statement

Not only has the abortion issue been a long, heated argument, but it also has many strong points for and against it.

I. Types of abortions.
   A. Clandestine abortions.
   B. Therapeutic abortions.

II. Effects -- pros and cons
   A. Psychological.
   B. Physical.
   C. Social.
   D. Financial.
   E. Religious.

III. Debate -- pros and cons
   A. Moral issue?
   B. Religious issue?
   C. Social issue?

2. In the following section you will read a draft of our essay on spiritual bankruptcy. It contains numerous problems, some of which are structural and can be traced back to problems in our outline. Before you read any of the section, examine the point and sentence outlines we included for it. By looking for the types of problems we discussed earlier in this section, try to anticipate what the problems with the draft will be.

Step 6: First Draft

One of the most difficult parts of the writing process is the point at which you actually start to put words on paper. A natural temptation that all writers face is to avoid the actual business of writing by convincing themselves that their topic needs more thought or research. There comes a time, however, when the writing must begin; in fact, if you have done your preliminary work thoroughly, the drafting stage is a necessary next step to give shape to your work. Without it, any amount of further thinking on your topic is not going to clarify the project. One can always introduce new issues, directions, or items into a topic in the revision stage.

Step 6(a): Planning Checklist

In order to reassure you that your preliminary work has, in fact, generated sufficient material for your draft, we suggest (as do many writing instructors and texts) that you complete a planning checklist. If you have followed the process conscientiously to this point in the book, you should have no trouble responding to these questions. If you do have trouble responding, the checklist will indicate specific areas for review by referring you to appropriate pages in this chapter. In any event, completing the checklist, though a somewhat artificial act, will force you to distance yourself from your material, and to take stock of your project, and will in all likelihood convince you that you are ready to proceed.

Step 1: Responses and Invention

1. Have you examined your responses to the assigned readings to determine your concerns? (pp. 57 - 59)
2. Have you fleshed out these concerns with invention techniques such as brainstorming and the basic journalist's questions? (pp. 59 - 62)

Step 2: Rhetorical Context

Step 2(a): Subject

1. Is your subject related, tangentially at least, to the general subject of your readings? (pp. 63 - 64)
2. Does your subject reflect the concerns you identified in your responding and inventing? (pp. 63 - 64)
3. Does your subject take into account your audience and purpose? (pp. 62 - 63)

Step 2(b): Audience

1. Does your audience reflect the concerns you identified in your responding and inventing? (pp. 65)
2. Have you drawn up a profile for your audience? (pp. 64 - 65)

Step 2(c): Purpose

1. Does your purpose reflect the concerns you identified in your responding and inventing? (pp. 66)
2. Does your purpose take into account your subject and audience? (pp. 62 - 63, 66)

Step 2(d): Topic

1. Does your topic reflect, either explicitly or implicitly, the subject area, level of audience, and considered purpose of your rhetorical context? (pp. 66 - 67)
2. Does your topic reflect the limitations imposed by the writing occasion: your capabilities and your length constraints? (pp. 67)

Step 3: Developmental Strategies

1. Have you chosen one or more developmental strategies that reflect the concerns you identified in the earlier stages? (pp. 67 - 68)
2. Have you read the appropriate material in Appendix 1 "The Developmental Strategies"? (pp. 502 - 534)

Step 4: Thesis Statement

1. Does your thesis statement make a claim about your topic (pp. 68 - 69)
2. Does your thesis statement avoid editorializing? (pp. 69)
3. Does your thesis statement reflect the concerns you identified in the earlier stages? (pp. 69)

Step 5: Outline

1. Does your outline employ the standard format for main headings and sub-headings? (pp. 31, 70)
2. Does the order of ideas in your outline reflect any necessary further reading on your chosen purpose and developmental strategies? (pp. 70)
3. Have you examined your outline for overlap of points and distinctiveness of points? (pp. 74)
4. Have you attached an appropriate title to your outline? (pp. 74)

Step 6(b): First Draft

Once you are satisfied that your planning is sound, you need to get your draft down as quickly as possible. Pin your outline up on the wall in front of you and proceed to write your way through it. If a particular section seems thorny or otherwise will not come clear, leave it and move on to the next section or to one you feel confident about. The beauty of an outline is that you can always come back to an earlier section later; you are not going to forget about it. Try writing each section on a separate sheet of paper; doing so will help break down the conception, shared by most writers, that you must proceed from A to Z. The separate sheets, done in whatever order most suits you, can always be appropriately ordered later. Using separate sheets will also give you more freedom to jot down notes for new ideas as they occur. Later you can see whether or not they will fit.

Always write in complete sentences and complete paragraphs; only in this way can you be sure you are getting everything in and meeting requirements you have got to face eventually. If anything, put in more than you need. Do not worry here about some wordiness and repetition slipping in if it helps you get the thoughts down. Keep in mind that the revision stage will force you to focus on both the large and small matters of your paper; you will have time for pruning and reshaping then.

What follows is the draft of our paper on spiritual bankruptcy. As you can see, we have also included our active reading and marginalia on the draft itself. This is the work that provides the basis of Step 7, which is revision, and you will need to flip back to this worked-over draft quite often for demonstration of points under discussion there.

The Major Causes of Spiritual Bankruptcy in Canada

- not relevant to topic

I. As we look around us in the latter half of the twentieth century, it is not difficult to see that society is in a state of dreadful confusion and instability. War and rumors of war threaten us every day; terrorism and political instability are commonplace; entire countries are being threatened by starvation while others luxuriate in seemingly endless wealth and resources; one country's god is another's devil as religious conflict abounds across the globe. The world seems full of strife, doubt, uncertainty, and hardship. Relative to the pain and suffering in the world, Canadians have it easy, and no doubt find a great deal of satisfaction when they contemplate the fortunate state of their country. Yet social critics of our own country tell us that we are at a stage in our development where we need to take stock of what we consider (valuable and important.) wdy Northrop Frye, for example, warns us of placing too much faith in material possessions at the expense of our inner life; similarly, Irving Layton argues that "cold" Canadians think too much of themselves and of what they possess and too little of others. What both of these critics seem to be suggesting is that acquisitiveness is a habit of mind dangerous to the spiritual life not only of individuals but of whole countries. In our opinion, though Canada is one of the most affluent countries in the world, its very affluence, as well as its youth, its lack of culture, and its proximity to the United States, make it a potential victim of spiritual bankruptcy.

- does audience know these people?

unsure

II. History seems to make it very clear that countries that take their wealth for granted eventually suffer and crumble as a result of an undue emphasis on material well-being. The most notorious example of this principle is, of course, the Roman Empire. The notion of Nero fiddling while Rome burned is a fine metaphor for the final destructive influences of the pleasure principle. History tells us that the Roman Empire was one of the most advanced and developed empires of any age. And yet it fell, almost overnight. In its final days we are told that religious values declined, social programmes decayed and individual fulfillment and political corruption became the order of the day. With the loss of its civic sense and the increase in self-advancement came the gradual decay of the entire society. Although Canadians are not Romans and Canada

wdy

unsure?

-by whom?

- good coherency provided by reference to Rome

is not Rome, there is a clear message here for us. Daily we are bombarded through the media with images of what the good life is. All of these images seem to have one thing in common, that is the importance of acquisitions and possessions. We are regularly told that we can buy happiness and contentment, and buy we do. Canadians are among the world's greatest spenders and consumers. They are also among the world's greatest contributors to the pollution and garbage problems we all face. In other words, Canadians buy things, use them as best they can, and then discard them. This depressing cycle of use and discarding should indicate to us how fruitless it is to try and purchase happiness. This type of "fulfillment" is as disposable and temporary as the various goods that we jettison onto a growing heap of detritus, a heap of useless commodities that in future may stand as a monument to our own dissatisfaction with life. There is a good deal to be said for increasing the standard of living of any country, but if with this increase comes a decline in the importance of spiritual values and inner development, we should worry about the excessively high price we are paying for our own material welfare.

wdy · *pass* · *unsure?* · *shift in pronoun use* · *weak repetition* · *good rep.*

need better transition for greater coherency

III. As the adage has it, youth is a time of life that is all too often wasted on the young. In order to become aware of who or what one really is, it is necessary to learn something about one's past so as to be able to determine one's future. Although we should be careful about using adages and

coherency problem in opening sentences: adage → past →

adage youth roots

especially careful when we try to use them to wdy "solve" complex situations, it is, nevertheless, true that young countries often seem to show a lack of judgment and consideration that we often wdy regard as characteristic of young people themselves. In Canada, we have only recently begun to consider our roots and because our roots do not go very deep, we are often in the position of trying to determine from whom or from what traditions we have sprung. Although it may strike some as a needless waste of time to examine our past, such an examination is central to discovering a sense of who we are and, as a consequence, developing a sense of spiritual awareness. Canada needs to know about its heroes, its struggles to become, its origins. Such photographs of our country's past do very much the same for a nation as an individual photo album does for a family: it tells us about our ancestry, it teaches us to respect our roots, it encourages us to think about those whom we will one day leave behind. A young country like Canada cannot afford to live only for today if it expects to have a spiritual dimension of its collective life and a vision of the future. To live for the present, to "go for it" as the current philosophy would have it, is to accept only the contemporary mythologies. And those, like our disposable commodities, do not have much depth or substance to them. For the sake of its spiritual survival, Canada must not let its youth coerce it into becoming merely a part of the "Pepsi generation."

good par.

- transition to new point clear but lacks strong coherency

IV. Another threat to Canada's spiritual well-being is its apparent lack of concern with (nurturing and supporting) what culture it does possess and its reluctance to encourage the development of new cultural endeavors. The increasing study of Canadian literature in our schools is a hopeful sign, which has put pressure on our publishing industry to back Canadian authors. Yet if culture is, in some sense at least, the repository of a country's soul and spiritual values, then Canada's reticence about cultural activity is a good indication of how it feels about things of the spirit. Canadians regularly ignore their artists, witness the financial difficulties that both the Stratford Festival and O'Keefe Centre have recently suffered through. Although we have a National Arts Council that awards grants to struggling artists to help them survive while they practise their craft, it is badly underfunded. The recent financial cutbacks inflicted on the CBC -- traditionally seen as the only disseminator of truly Canadian thoughts, ideas, and culture -- suggest the present government's attitudes toward culture as well. All around us we seem to see the indicators that suggest that culture doesn't pay. Perhaps the two most outstanding examples of this fact are found in our Indian and Inuit peoples. Most Canadians choose to ignore these two ancient groups largely because they are different from the rest of us and live by a different code. But by ignoring them and letting them suffer in poverty and neglect we are also ignoring the significant cultural achievements that they have made to this country.

good trans. signal

wdy

off topic

why is this neglect occurring? ↓ because we live in a throwaway society influenced by U.S. individualism and materialism

unsure?

unsure and wdy

- transition clear but argument would be tighter if points rose logically and irresistably out of prior paragraphs.

ref.

V. The final detrimental influence on Canada's development of a spiritual dimension is its proximity to the United States. In our opinion, the US exerts a depressingly anti-spiritual influence over Canada which we, as Canadians, are all too ready to bow to. Perhaps we are intimidated by its size or perhaps by its success as one of the world's two great superpowers. Whatever the reason, we are prepared to unquestioningly accept its many mindless magazines and television and radio broadcasts. But we suspect the real reason we are prepared and even willing to model ourselves on the United States is because, as we have already suggested, Canadians are enchanted and enthralled by the idea of material wealth. The US is undoubtedly the richest country in the world with the highest standard of living. As we also suggested earlier, there seems to be a correlation between wealth and cultural decadence. And this is as true for the United States as it is for Canada. Where else can we find so many activities meant to fill a spiritual void as in the United States? Fast-food restaurants, fun cities, pleasure palaces and Disney universes abound. Where else but on American airwaves can one watch so many situation comedies, game shows, sports programmes, and cartoons. Canada impressed by what the United States has achieved is an all-too-willing consumer and emulator of this cultural mush. As a result the country becomes increasingly interested in and finally addicted to wealth and the joys it apparently brings. Such joys, temporarily at least, win out over more legitimate concerns such as the country's need for a profound inner life.

wdy

rep. of point in par. 2

- need to avoid this repetition somehow

rep. again

? c

? c

ref. unsure? redundant wdy

VI. We have not presented an altogether pleasant picture of Canada's spiritual situation, but we think it reflects, nevertheless, the reality of the situation in this country. It may very well be that for Canada to come to grips with its soul, it may have to deprive itself of many things that it now considers important. (The question that Canadians must ask themselves, finally,) is of what real worth is a wealthy but soulless nation?

Step 7: Revision

Too often students feel that their first draft is the final one. You have to break this habit. The effective writer sees the draft as an opportunity to begin honing the work, crafting the overall conception into the shape desired. Revision is not simply the correction of errors or the smoothing out of stylistic wrinkles; revision is also re-vision—re-seeing your work now that it is stretched out in front of you. On reading through your draft you may recognize, for the first time, an obvious weakness in structure that your planning simply had not shown. Or you may see implications in ideas that did not reveal themselves until complete paragraphs were read side by side. Give yourself the time to take revision seriously. Some texts recommend that 50 percent of the time devoted to any writing occasion be given to revision. Half your time may not be practical in many instances, but you can be sure that *if* you spend 50 percent of your time revising you *will* improve your writing.

Step 7(a): Revision Process

Effective revision demands a method, otherwise you will waste a lot of energy. You need to concentrate your attention on one aspect of your essay at a time. A common practice, which we heartily endorse, is the top-down approach, which breaks revision into five stages. Our version is as follows:

1. Large items
(a) Beginning
(b) Closing
(c) Overall coherence

2. Paragraphs
(a) Units of thought
(b) Transitions
(c) Topic sentence
(d) Coherence
(e) Development

3. Sentences
(a) Variety
(b) Passive and active voice
(c) Wordiness

4. Diction
(a) Clichés
(b) Repetition as an asset and liability
(c) Jargon

5. Effective Punctuation—A Matter of Choice

If you follow this top-down approach, moving from large to small items, you avoid the problem of the fully revised paragraph that you have to throw out because it turns out not to be relevant to the final essay. Why revise sentences, diction, and punctuation if there is a chance you will not use the revised material? Start with the large items, which encompass the breadth of the essay, and once you have settled them to your satisfaction, move down to a concentrated look at paragraphs, and further, down to the nuts and bolts of grammar and punctuation. And remember, revising is *not* proofreading, which comes after the revision is complete and you have prepared the manuscript. Revision deals with substantive matters as well as grammar, punctuation, and spelling; proofreading deals only with cosmetic matters: largely spelling, though considerations of punctuation and manuscript format may arise.

What follows is a careful analysis of the first draft of our essay on spiritual bankruptcy.

1. Large Items

(a) Beginning

Unity of subject. Let us look at the content of this opening paragraph to see where it might be improved. Is it not possible that there is a unity problem in this paragraph? The opening three sentences are irrelevant to the thesis statement. Sentence 1 introduces the notion of the world's general instability. Sentence 2 lists some examples, and sentence 3 sums up the point that the world is in a sorry state. But what do all of these points have to do with spiritual bankruptcy? If we, as authors, are trying to suggest that *Canada,* while affluent, is spiritually poverty-stricken, we should say so without leading our readers to believe that what we might be writing is an essay on the sorry state of the world. In other words, rather than building to the thesis statement, the first three sentences are in competition with it. As such, we should excise them, and so reach our point more quickly.

Audience. Another possible criticism one can make about the opening paragraph is that a clear sense of audience is not provided. We refer to "us" in the paragraph, thereby suggesting that the audience is Canadian, but beyond that reference there is no indication of what type or category of

Canadian is being addressed. Readers should ask themselves questions such as the following: "Could a group of public school students understand this essay?" "Is it addressed to university students, manual labourers, or computer programmers?" "In what type of magazine might it appear?" We should have given a clearer sense of the audience for whom this essay was intended. In our section on audience earlier in this chapter (pp. 64 - 65) we targeted university students. We should take this into account in our final version of the paper by recognizing that certain students will likely not know who Irving Layton and Northrop Frye are.

(b) Closing

The final paragraph has some good points in it. It does not merely repeat the thesis statement nor does it simply sum up what the major paragraphs have said. But in the context of the entire essay, with its long paragraphs and sentences, it may strike some as very short. In fact, the end of the essay seems to be upon the reader before he or she is aware of it. A reader who had the benefit of the outline might not feel that the end of the essay came too quickly, being able to anticipate it from the outline itself. A reader without the outline, however, might be taken by surprise by the brevity of the conclusion and the quick ending. What the conclusion needs to overcome this sense of disjunction is a clinching point or image that rises out of or sums up the earlier argument.

(c) Overall coherence

If overall coherence refers to the way in which the essay in general hangs together and the way in which it develops the thesis statement, then we can find at least one problem in overall coherence. Although the outline *looks* orderly enough with its clear initial headings (I, II, III, IV, V, VI) indicating the major parts of the thesis statement to be developed and its sub-headings (two for each major heading for a total of eight), plus an introduction and conclusion, one has to wonder about possible repetition in the essay as a result of overlapping material cropping up in apparently distinct parts of the outline and essay. The clearest example can be found by examining points II A and V B of the outline. Section II deals with Canada's affluence and Section V with Canada's proximity to the United States. But within each of these sections, in the outline at least, wealth and acquisitiveness seem to be major components. A careful examination of the essay proves that the repetition finds its way into the draft. Paragraphs 2 and 5 contain essentially the same argument, namely that the accumulation of wealth is antagonistic to the development of an inner life. Nothing works against the overall coherence of a paper as much as unnecessary repetition. Since this weakness is evident in this paper, we may have to consider revising the outline by developing a legitimate variation on the notion of affluence as it is affected by Canada's proximity to the United States. This necessitates stronger links (coherence) with paragraph 2 (affluence), paragraph 3 (loss of the past, and youth), and paragraph 4 (neglect of culture). In order to provide these links in logic and argument, we must shift the order of the items in the essay. What seems to be emerging is an awareness that these causes of spiritual bankruptcy in Canada are linked and reinforce each other in the fashion of a vicious circle. Possibly this is the image we want for our conclusion.

Audience. Our discussion of audience in the paragraph on the beginning of the essay needs to be extended to the entire essay. An essay must have a consistent view of its audience throughout. The present draft is not consistent; for example, while the references to Frye and Layton, as well as Nero and Rome, appeal to a certain level of education, the photograph album analogy in paragraph 3 is much more general. And what about the reference to the Book of Matthew in paragraph 1, sentence 2? How many readers would catch it? In our revision we must constantly keep our student audience in mind. While stretching readers is good, losing them is not.

Purpose. Although argument is ostensibly the mode of the essay, the repeated qualifiers—"it seems," "it suggests," "in our opinion," "we think"—take away from the force of the argument. The paper needs more obviously argumentative transitional signals. (See pp. 273 for a discussion of such signals.)

2. Paragraphs

(a) Units of thought

Just as an essay has a topic and thesis to which it adheres throughout its course, so a paragraph should be a distinct unit of thought. All its sentences should contribute to the development of the topic of the paragraph as expressed in the topic sentence. This does not mean that different points cannot be expressed in the same paragraph: you need only look at our outline to see that this is not so. What it means is that these differing points must serve as supporting evidence for the controlling idea—usually, again, in the form of a topic sentence. If a point does not offer such support it is irrelevant not only to the particular paragraph in which it appears but quite likely to the thesis of the essay as a whole. As examples we can briefly point again to the first three sentences of paragraph 1, which have nothing to do with either Canada or spiritual bankruptcy, and as such detract from the unity of the paragraph. Paragraphs that lack unity can derail the reading process. In paragraph 4, for example, sentence 2 appears to represent the author's attempt to present all sides of the case by balancing the pessimistic view; actually, however, the sentence is simply off topic and creates a lack of unity in the paragraph.

(b) Transitions

Transitions between paragraphs refer to the smooth movement from one paragraph to the next in an essay. The opening sentence of paragraph 2, which is the first paragraph devoted to the development of the thesis statement, seems to be clearly developed from the final sentence of paragraph 1. As the thesis statement makes clear, the detrimental effect of affluence on a country's spiritual development is going to be the first point we develop. Sentence 1 of paragraph 2 mentions "wealth" in its second line, "material well-being" in its third and the effects of an under-emphasis on both between these two references. This links the opening of paragraph 2 to the end of paragraph 1 and provides a smooth transition between the two.

The transition between paragraphs 3 and 2 is not as clear as the transition between 1 and 2. Opening paragraph 3 with a reference to an adage might immediately strike one as an irrelevance. In order to see its significance we must return to the thesis statement to see that Canada's youth is the next point we want to discuss. A good transitional sentence should remind the reader of the thesis and should not assume the reader can call it to mind.

The transition for paragraph 4 is much clearer and is made so by its two initial words, "Another threat." These words immediately suggest that we are moving to a different point and that it has some connection with the claim made in the thesis statement. Indeed, the rest of sentence 1 in paragraph 4 makes it clear what the threat is and immediately reminds us of the point made in the thesis statement. Good things can also be said about the opening of paragraph 5. Once again the opening words indicate that we are moving to a new point, a point that is a movement beyond the previous one. From a certain perspective, transitional signals in paragraphs 4 and 5 work because they suggest a break and a change in thought, and this reflects adequately that the points are separate elements. If, however, we want to revise to create greater coherence between the points in the various paragraphs, the transitional signals must be revised accordingly.

(c) Topic sentence

As stated earlier, the thesis statement in paragraph 1 is that paragraph's topic sentence. Our intention is to build towards it, and in this, as we have seen, we are not altogether successful, perhaps because the opening sentence is a competing topic sentence in this paragraph.

The opening sentence of paragraph 2 is that paragraph's topic sentence. The *general* maxim it contains is used to demonstrate how it applies to a *particular* case, namely, Canada. The topic sentence in paragraph 3 is not altogether clear. It could be sentence 1 or 2 or perhaps even 3, 5, 9, or 10. The reason why all of these sentences compete for the position of topic sentence is that all of them make general claims that need detailed illustration but none of them receives it. In fact, one of the major problems with this paragraph is that it exists only on the level of generality. As a result we have a number of general sentences vying with each other for top billing. Unfortunately, none of them is sufficiently well-developed to make it clear which is the paragraph's topic sentence.

The topic sentences in paragraphs 4, 5, and 6 are clear as they stand. All are the opening sentence in each paragraph.

(d) Coherence

Just as an essay must have overall coherence (linkages between main points) so paragraphs must demonstrate a similar coherence. Notice our active reading notations on paragraph 2 of the draft. You can easily see how each sentence coheres to the ones around it through the repetition of key words, or pronouns, or concepts. Such links, or transitions, assist the reader's understanding. Notice the notations we make on paragraph 3. Although the ideas of youthfulness and the past are present and repeated, the sentences do not cohere. Sentence 1 refers to the adage; sentence 2 refers to the past; sentence 3 returns to the adage, then adds the idea of youth; and sentence 4 speaks of roots. Clearer linkages are in order.

(e) Development

Paragraphs without development are like cream-filled doughnuts without the cream. One begins them with anticipation but arrives at the end without a sense of fulfillment. A paragraph's topic sentence needs to be fleshed out with supporting details, like the reference to Nero in paragraph 2, or the analogy to the photograph album in paragraph 3, or the litany of trash items in sentences 10 and 11 of paragraph 5. But when we look more closely at paragraph 3 we recognize that, with the exception of the photo album analogy, the rest of the paragraph is undeveloped, as the number of sentences that could function as topic sentences indicates. Development, therefore, means detail. But it also means effective order. A paragraph may have unity, coherence, and detail and still be undeveloped because it lacks an order or an arrangement or pattern for its sentences. A number of common patterns are as follows:

1. Order of importance: from least to most, such as paragraph 4 of our sample draft.
2. Order of generality: from abstract to concrete or vice versa.
3. Order of time: from past to present to future or vice versa (or any part of this pattern).
4. Order of space: geographical arrangement; east to west or north to south, etc.
5. Causal order: from cause to effect (see Appendix 1 for more).
6. Comparison and contrast order (see Appendix 1 for more).

3. Sentences

As we have mentioned on a number of occasions already, the subject of a piece of writing is inextricably bound up with the choice of developmental strategy. The more engaging your writing, the more your reader responds positively to your subject. Writing demonstrates a writer's personality; you want your reader to find you a person worth spending time with. One of the best ways to turn people off, whether they are your readers or the people you meet in life, is to bore them. A series of plodding, monotone paragraphs—whether or not their content has intrinsic value—will lose your reader's attention as surely as yours is lost by the bore who imposes upon you in the cafeteria. And paragraphs are composed of sentences.

(a) Variety

When we speak of sentence variety, what we are referring to is not only a judicious mix of sentences that are distinguished from each other by clausal structures (simple, compound, complex, and compound-complex) but also the use of sentences of different length. Using only sentences of the same length—long or short—creates a prosaic paragraph with a boring rhythm. And failing to use a blend of different clausal structures often masks where you want the emphasis to fall in your sentences, paragraphs, and essays.

Exercise

Using your dictionary (we recommend the *Gage Canadian Dictionary*, but any good *college* dictionary will do), determine the meaning of simple, compound, complex, and compound-complex sentences. Once you have done so, find examples of each type in our draft on spiritual bankruptcy.

• • •

A sentence analysis of a couple of paragraphs of the draft may help clarify the importance of sentence variety. Of the eight sentences in the first paragraph, only one is made up of ten words or less. All of the other sentences are very long, running from thirty to forty-four words. This, by itself, might strike some as a classic case of a paragraph made up of far too many long sentences. And yet the paragraph's sentences do not *read* excessively long. There are a couple of good reasons for this. Look, for instance, at sentence 2. Although by word count it is the longest sentence in the paragraph (forty-four words), it is not cumbersome or excessively long because it is a nicely constructed compound-complex sentence that uses parallelism and the semicolon to good effect. Although, strictly speaking, it is one sentence, it is made up of a number of easily digestible and parallel independent clauses. As such, despite its length, its rhythm is pleasing and not breathless. Similarly, sentence 6 (forty-three words) has a strong break (indicated by the semicolon) at about its mid point; this too helps divide the sentence into two digestible halves. The conclusion seems to be that a series of long sentences in and of itself is not necessarily a bad thing, if the *construction* of the sentence does not offend the reader's sense of rhythm.

Let us look at the first seven sentences of paragraph 2 to see how sentence variety can be put to good effect. The longest sentence in this group is the first one made up of thirty words. Sentence 2 has thirteen words; sentence 3, twenty-one; sentence 4, nineteen; sentence 5, six; sentence 6, twenty-six; and sentence 7, twenty-one. Notice as well how we have struck a balance and found a pleasing enough rhythm by using only two of the clausal sentence structures and by judiciously mixing their use. Sentence 1 is complex; sentence 2, simple; sentence 3, simple; sentence 4, complex; sentence 5, complex; sentence 6, complex; and sentence 7, simple. A final point about this section of the second paragraph is how the author uses a strikingly short sentence to attain emphasis. Sentence 5 is made up only of six words, and pulls the reader up short. Quite appropriately, as it turns out, since our point here—that wealthy countries can crumble—is one of the most important in the whole paragraph.

Seven of the ten remaining sentences in this paragraph fall into the medium range for sentence length (fifteen to twenty words). This consistency might suggest that this section of the paragraph has a boring sameness; however, in the centre of these sentences comes an eleven-word sentence which provides a change of pace, and the paragraph concludes with two long sentences (forty-one and fifty words) which, rather than leaving one breathless, encapsulate the core of this long paragraph.

Two other sentence forms that will vary your sentence rhythm and help you achieve a certain emphasis are loose and periodic sentences:

1. *Loose sentences* are made up of a main idea followed by a number of clauses or phrases which create the effect of further thought adhering to the original idea. An example is the thesis statement of the draft under study.
2. *Periodic sentences* withhold their meaning until the reader reaches the end because the main verb or activity is held in reserve and thus emphasized through anticipation. An example is sentence 4 in paragraph 4.

Finally, four common sentence types found in most writing are the declarative, interrogative, imperative, and exclamatory:

1. *Declarative sentences* or basic statements are the ones we most commonly use. The topic sentences of each paragraph in the draft are declarative, as are the majority of all the sentences.
2. *Interrogative sentences* ask questions. They may be used for rhetorical effect as in the final sentence of the draft. Do not overuse rhetorical questions. Such overuse gives an artificial flavour to your writing.
3. *Imperative sentences* issue commands, as in the final sentence of paragraph 3. Used sparingly they can give an effect of urgency and intensity to your writing. Overused they simply irritate the reader, who does not appreciate being bludgeoned.

4. *Exclamatory sentences* indicate shock, surprise, disgust, discomfort, or any heightened emotional reaction. Purely emotional reactions should not play a large part in your writing since they tend to unduly overshadow discursive thought. There are no exclamatory sentences in the draft because the writing occasion does not warrant them—the occasional imperative sentence is enough.

(b) Passive and active voice

Excessive use of the passive voice saps energy from your writing. As a general rule, activity is better than passivity in writing; it keeps the reader moving forward on the crest of the thought. Paragraph 2, sentence 9 uses the passive construction, "we are bombarded through the media", which defuses the power of the word "bombard." Notice how much more powerful, because active, a possible revised version is: "Daily the media bombard us with images. . . . " On the whole the rest of the essay makes use of the active voice to good effect.

(c) Wordiness

Wordiness works against clarity and precision in writing. In our draft we fell into the habit of using doublings when one word would suffice. Notice the following examples throughout the paper: "valuable and important" (paragraph 1; sentence 5); "advanced and developed" (paragraph 2, sentence 4); "acquisitions and possessions" (paragraph 2, sentence 10); "happiness and contentment" (paragraph 2, sentence 11); "spenders and consumers" (paragraph 2, sentence 12); "disposable and temporary" (paragraph 2, sentence 16); "nurturing and supporting" (paragraph 4, sentence 1).

Another example of wordiness is unnecessary qualification. Phrases such as "it seems to us" and "seems to be suggesting" merely add words rather than meaning to the essay and may also suggest to the reader that the authors are unsure of their position.

4. Diction

(a) Clichés

Clichés are evident in the essay but they are used in such a way as to point to their cliché status, for example, "go for it" (paragraph 3, sentence 9) and "Pepsi generation" (paragraph 3, sentence 11). Generally you should eschew clichés or use them as we do in our draft, namely, to illustrate their linguistic emptiness.

(b) Repetition as an asset and liability

As we have already stated in the section of this discussion on coherence within paragraphs, repetition is a necessary and vital part of good writing.

In order to make sentences and paragraphs cohere you have to make use of repetition of words, phrases, and structures; one of the most effective forms of the latter is parallelism. Notice how the repetition of the single word "heap" in paragraph 2, sentence 16 provides coherence in this long sentence. You may be more familiar, however, with repetition as a negative feature of writing. Remember when we mentioned the needless repetition of the idea of affluence in paragraphs 2 and 5? Notice how we are forced to use the phrases "As we have already suggested," and "As we also suggested earlier." These phrases indicate potential problems with repetition. Notice also the needless repetition of "This" as an opening word in sentences 15 and 16 of paragraph 2.

(c) Jargon

On the whole the draft is jargon free. If we had written sentence 5, paragraph 1 as, "Social critics of our own country tell us that we are at a paradigmatic stage of socializing development and we need to interface with our significant others and prioritize our values," we would have been well and truly "jargonizing."

5. Effective Punctuation

Writers often consider punctuation a mundane matter and so do not come to appreciate its potential for shaping the meaning of a piece. Though there are many punctuation rules that you must simply master, other aspects of punctuation are open to the writer's choice depending on the desired effect. We will only look at one example here in any detail—the usage appendix discusses punctuation in greater depth.

Sentence 5 of paragraph 2 contains an interrupter—a phrase or clause interrupting the main sentence—which is set off by dashes (—). The dashes indicate that the reader is to *emphasize* what comes between them, namely the idea that the CBC is the only true disseminator of Canadian culture. The interrupter could, however, have been enclosed in parentheses. In terms of punctuation the sentence would still be perfectly fine, but the emphasis would have changed. The parentheses signal to the reader to *de*-emphasize what is between them, and to see that material as of supplementary interest but not as anything to divert attention from the main sentence. Finally, the author could have enclosed the interrupter with simple commas—thus indicating that the enclosed material is to be read with the *same* emphasis as that given to what precedes and follows it. Commas are the most common choice, but style and purpose may warrant one of the other alternatives. It is good to know your options.

Now that you have seen our comments on the large through small items for our draft we want you to actively read the following revised sentence outline and essay and then answer the questions that follow.

Step 7(b): Revised Outline

A Vicious Circle: The Major Causes of Spiritual Bankruptcy in Canada

Canada's material affluence—a direct result of American economic and, in turn, cultural influence on a young, impressionable country—precipitates Canada's spiritual bankruptcy.

I. Canada cannot afford complacency.

   A. We think we have it made.

   B. Cultural critics tell us otherwise.

II. Canada's affluence threatens its spiritual development.

   A. The Roman Empire is an object lesson for Canada.

   B. Canada has a depressing cycle of influence: buy, use, and discard.

III. Two factors contribute to Canada's devotion to material affluence.

   A. Canada's youth leaves her vulnerable to external influence.

   B. Canada's location means the greatest external influence will be the US.

IV. Canada's adherence to the American way—the "throwaway society"—inevitably leads us to neglect our past and culture.

   A. Knowing Canada's past does for the nation what having a photo album does for a family.

B. Our culture – the repository of our national soul – is being ignored.

V. Canadian affluence, on the American model, generates a vicious circle that can only culminate in spiritual bankruptcy.

Questions on Step 7(b): Revised Outline

1. Does the revised title add to or detract from the essay? Explain your answer.
2. How does the revised outline solve the repetition problem of the original?
3. What other structural changes have been made?

Step 7(c): Revised Essay

A Vicious Circle: The Major Causes of Spiritual Bankruptcy in Canada

I. It is easy for Canadians to be complacent: we have one of the world's highest standards of living; we have vast natural resources; and we have the military and economic might of the richest and most powerful nation on earth on our side -- the lap of luxury has never felt so good. Yet even here, in the best of all possible worlds, there are occasional gnats -- gadflies reminding us that while material affluence may gorge the stomach, it starves the soul. University of Toronto Professor of English and cultural critic Northrop Frye, for one, suggests that educating the imagination might help fill the void that faces an intelligent western person when, after "chasing status symbols all his life . . . the bottom falls out of his world and he sees no reason for going on." The outspoken poet Irving Layton -- Canada's self-styled gadfly if there ever was one -- brings the argument home to roost; for him, the souls of Canadians are "miserable, nightmarish"; we are "isolated from one another by the fears and repressions engendered in a materialistic society almost wholly given up to the worship of money and status." Hard words, but true. Canada's material affluence -- a direct result of American economic and, in turn, cultural influence on a young, impressionable country -- precipitates Canada's spiritual bankruptcy.

II. History makes it clear that countries which take their wealth for granted eventually crumble. The image of Nero fiddling while Rome burned is a fine metaphor for the final destructive influence of the pleasure principle. Rome was one of the most advanced empires of any age. And yet it fell, almost overnight. Although Canada is not Rome, there is surely a message here for us. Daily the media bombard us with images of the good life, all of which have one thing in common: the importance of possessions. We are regularly told that we can buy happiness -- and buy we do. Canadians are among the world's greatest consumers. We are also among the world's greatest polluters. In other words, Canadians buy things, use them, and discard them. Such a depressing cycle should indicate to us how fruitless it is to try to purchase happiness. This type of "fulfillment" is as temporary as the goods that we jettison onto a growing heap of detritus, a heap that in future may stand as a monument to our dissatisfaction with life. There is a good deal to be said for increasing the standard of living of any country, but if this increase comes at the expense of spiritual values and inner development, we should worry about the excessively high price we are paying for our material welfare.

III. Canada's devotion to material affluence has been accelerated by two intertwined factors: her relative youth as a country and her location next door to the world's capitalistic dynamo. Young countries often show a lack of judgment that is characteristic of many young people, and Canada is no exception. Lacking the solid sense of national vision which rises out of rooted historical traditions, Canada finds herself vulnerable to economic and cultural influence from outside. And for us, outside means the US. America exerts a depressingly anti-spiritual influence over Canada which we, enchanted and enthralled by the idea of material wealth -- so manifest south of the border -- are all too ready to bow to. Yet the cultural decadence that was attendent on Rome's wealth also plagues the US. Where else can we find so many activities meant to fill a spiritual void: fast-food restaurants, fun cities, Disney universes, and Crystal Cathedrals abound. Where else but on American airwaves -- which is what Canadian TV largely consists of -- can one watch so many situation comedies, game shows, sports programmes, and cartoons -- and all of them punctuated by advertisements? Canada, impressed by what the US has achieved, and lacking its own -- and different -- standards of value, is an all-too-willing consumer and emulator of this cultural mush. As a result, the country becomes increasingly interested in, and finally addicted to, wealth and the joys it apparently brings. Such joys increasingly win out over the country's need for a profound inner life.

IV. Canada's adherence to the American materialist vision of success -- the "throwaway society" -- inevitably leads us to neglect our own past and our own culture. Such neglect is potentially tragic, since for people to be aware of who or what they really are, it is necessary for them to know something about their past. Canada needs to know about its heroes, its struggles to become, its origins. Such photographs of our country's past do very much the same for a nation as an individual photograph album does for a family: it tells us about our ancestry, it teaches us to respect our roots, it encourages us to think about those people we will one day leave behind. To live for the present, to "go for it" as the current philosophy would have it, is to accept only the contemporary mythologies. And those, like our disposable commodities, do not have much substance. If culture is, in some sense at least, the repository of a country's soul and spiritual values, then Canada's adherence to the superficial contemporary mythologies is indicative of how it feels about things of the spirit. To take the clearest example, the 1986 financial cut-backs on the CBC -- traditionally seen as the only disseminator of truly Canadian thought and culture -- betray the government's attitude toward the world of value.

V. Canadian affluence, on the American model, generates a vicious circle which can only culminate in spiritual bankruptcy. Our neglect of our past and our culture leaves a vacuum in Canadian life which American commercialism rushes to fill. And this commercialism encourages further neglect. It may very well be that for Canada to come to grips with its soul, it will have to deprive itself of many things it now considers important. Yet of what real worth is a wealthy but soulless nation?

Questions

1. Large Items

(a) Beginning

i. How does the revised opening solve the *unity* problem found in the draft opening?
ii. How and why has the appeal to authority changed?
iii. How and why has the thesis statement changed?
iv. Is the audience any clearer in this opening?

(b) Closing

i. How does the image of the vicious circle rise out of the argument that precedes it to act as a clinching point?

(c) Overall coherence

i. Subject.
- (a) How does the revised essay solve the repetition problem of the original? (Draw on your answer to the outline question.)
- (b) Demonstrate how each paragraph now seems to flow from the one preceding it.
- (c) Which sentence in paragraph 3 provides a coherency link with paragraph 2?

ii. Audience.
- (a) Is the audience any clearer in the revised essay as a whole?
- (b) Are there any references, names, or allusions that are unclear?

iii. Purpose.
- (a) How has the argumentative structure been strengthened in the revised version?
- (b) List five argumentative transitional signals.

2. Paragraphs

(a) Units of thought

i. Can anything in the revised version be said to be irrelevant or off topic?

(b) Transitions

i. Why does sentence 1 of paragraph 3 provide a good transition from paragraph 2 to 3?

ii. How does the final sentence of paragraph 3 act as a transition to paragraph 4?

iii. Using your answers to Questions 1 and 2, demonstrate how we have revised the draft to provide greater coherence between points.

(c) Topic sentence

i. Identify the topic sentence in each paragraph.

ii. Using examples from the essay, demonstrate the effects gained by having the topic sentence come at the beginning of the paragraph and end of the paragraph.

iii. How has the problem of numerous topic sentences in paragraph 3 of the draft been solved?

(d) Coherence

i. Analyze paragraph 4 of the revised version for coherence. There are at least 14 coherency linkages.

(e) Development

i. How can paragraph 4 of the revised version be said to embody both a general to specific pattern of development and a cause and effect pattern of development?

3. Sentences

(a) Variety

i. Figure 1 plots the sentences of paragraph 1 on a graph according to number of words. Is the length of the opening sentences justified? Why or why not?

ii. After counting the words in each sentence of paragraph 2 of the revised version, plot the totals on a graph like that in Figure 1. How does visualizing the pattern of sentence variety help you account for the effect of the paragraph?

(Try graphing some of your own paragraphs; you might be surprised at what you discover.)

(b) Passive and active voice

i. Is the passive overused?

(c) Wordiness

i. Is there unnecessary repetition?

ii. Is there unnecessary qualification?

iii. Demonstrate how parallelism within and between sentences contributes to variety.

4. Diction

(a) Clichés

i. Are there clichés you could eliminate?

(b) Repetition as an asset and liability

i. Find examples of positive repetition within each paragraph of the revised version.

ii. Find examples of positive repetition between paragraphs.

(c) Jargon

i. Does any jargon remain? Should it be replaced?

5. Effective Punctuation

i. Analyze the effect of the punctuation in sentence 1 of paragraph 1 of the revised version.

ii. Why does the author use dashes (--) around the interrupter in sentence 4 of paragraph 1?

iii. Why does the author use a colon before the final phrase in sentence 6 of paragraph 2, and a dash before the final phrase in sentence 7?

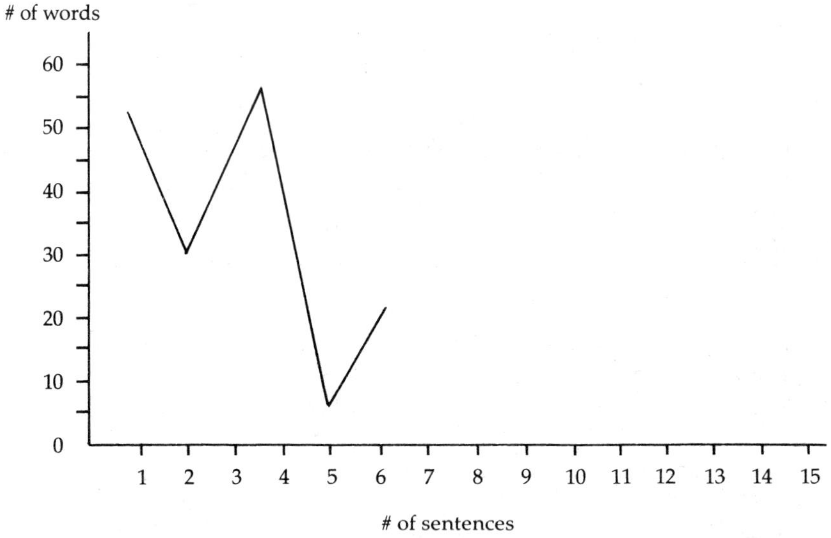

Figure 1. Graph representation of sentences of paragraph one of revised version of essay on spiritual bankruptcy.

Student Examples

In this section we rejoin our student, Melanie Beach, in mid-process. In chapter 2 we read her completed responses to readings by Dr. Cynthia Carver and Valmai Howe Elkins on the general subject of patient care. In what follows, we have presented the work Beach did for her writing occasion. Though we make occasional comments on her process, we generally let that work speak for itself. If you need further clarification on the step-by-step procedure, review the appropriate step in the preceding section of this chapter.

Steps 1 - 5

Step 1: Examination of the Responses:

Carver article

- workers have many patients to care for
- patients have individual needs
- staff must adapt
- staff need reminding
- understaffing ↓
- leads to lack of adequate attention to individual needs

Everyone who works in a patient care setting -- mainly hospitals and nursing homes -- must contend with many people each day. All of these people are individuals with various personalities, wants, and needs. All of the staff have their own unique mannerisms as well, and in contending with their many patients must learn to deal with these different kinds of people. They must learn to adapt themselves to all situations. These employees realize the many natures of the patients but it seems that they must be reminded that patients are ill or feeble and that many of them, consequently, may be short tempered. The ill tempers of staff, on the other hand, may arise from understaffing. It sometimes happens that single employees are overburdened with an unreasonable number of charges. Such a workload may not facilitate adequate personal attention to patients. An ultimate result might be misunderstandings between staff and

- creates unhealthy atmosphere

patients. This ends in an unhealthy work atmosphere and of course an unhealthy atmosphere for effective recovery from illness or depression.

1. Hospital and nursing home workers have many patients
2. Patients have individual needs
3. Staff must adapt
4. Staff need reminding of duties
5. Understaffing
6. Lack of attention to individual needs
7. Unhealthy atmosphere

Step 1: Examination of the Responses: Elkins article

- emotions

- complex situation for mother

- mothers anxious and restless

We often hear that childbirth is a very delicate and sensitive time. Emotions are said to be readily displayed, especially by expectant mothers. Though it is an emotional time, the mother not only has to contend with her flighty feelings, but she must also bear with the pains she may be feeling at this time. Before the birth of her child, she spends hours sometimes, preparing and waiting and all the while she is expending physical energy. This tiring process can result in unleashed emotions, sometimes good, sometimes not so good. It is likely that the expectant mother will become anxious and restless. It is up to the

-staff must be prepared to meet individual needs

hospital staff to be prepared for the different needs of each mother, and to make her feel as much at ease as they possibly can by offering her encouragement, sympathy, understanding and compassion.

-staff must meet emotional and psychological needs as well as physical, especially in times of stress or change

1. Emotions
2. Complex situation for mother
   - flighty feelings
   - pains
   - exertion of energy
   - tiring process
3. Mothers anxious and restless
4. Staff must meet individual needs
5. Staff must meet emotional and psychological as well as physical needs
   - especially in times of stress and change

Having identified a number of her concerns, Beach can now go on to discover what more she knows in this area by using invention techniques. In the following dated sequence we present material drawn from her journal. In our classes we recommend that the journals be completely unstructured. We recommend that students do their prewriting—brainstorming, questioning, subject, audience and purpose analysis, outline, etc.—in the journals, but we also stress the importance of the journal as a place for *any* writing they want to do. Our only requirement is that students keep the journal—regularly. Beach uses mainly a combination of brainstorming and short paragraphs; the one tends to lead her into the other. You will see that she also tries narrative at one point to give a different perspective to her jottings. Also notice that though she clearly has certain persistent concerns, her formulated subject, audience, and purpose come after Beach has generated substantial material.

Friday January 9

- Hospital staff must be prepared to meet the needs of their patients
- Hospitals must deal with patients of varying ages
- Many of the patients in a nursing home are elderly; therefore the staff of nursing homes must be suited to deal with this age of patients. If they are unsuited to interacting with the elderly, the staff decrease their ability to meet the needs—especially psychological needs—of their patients
- Elderly people require care in varying degrees
- Some incapacitated; some ambulatory
- Self-help
- Great number of old people in society
- Nursing homes seem understaffed
- Cannot keep track of individual's belongings
- Cannot cater to individual needs
- Like watching children; one never knows what they will do
- People in nursing homes are sometimes lonely if they have no regular visitors

Monday January 12

There is a constantly growing number of elderly people in our society. Of these, an increasing proportion require nursing-care facilities to partake in everyday activities. Nursing homes are filled to the seams. No sooner does one individual die than another person requiring assistance in carrying out everyday activities fills the newly made vacancy.

Individuals in nursing homes require varying degrees of assistance. They range from totally disabled to mildly impaired in their performance of daily functions. In any case, all those in a nursing home require a certain amount of assistance.

There is a very significant problem however. The individual nurses must take care of a great many patients. These medical facilities are grossly understaffed. The nurses and their assistants have so many charges to care for that they have no time for adequate individual attention.

- More health professionals needed
- More money
- More time spent with individuals
- More attention to individual needs
- More encouragement for staff-patient, patient-patient communication and interaction
- Nursing staff just mechanical, not humane — should be more compassionate

- Take care of critical elements necessary for daily function, e.g. pills, but forget psychological needs, which are just as critical

Tuesday January 13

In the nursing home the foul odour of urine lingers heavily in the corridors and follows visitors up elevators, reluctant to leave the range of their nostrils. Finally, as all senses eventually do, our noses adapt and we forget about the stench. Slumped pitifully in an old faded armchair is a demented old man. He has smoked a cigarette down through the filter, and his fingers are charred at the tips, evidence that he has done this before. Suddenly, from out of hiding, appears a disgruntled nurse. "Stop that, Mr. So-and-So," she bellows into his ear. He seems oblivious to the pain. Taking the remnants of the cigarette, she retreats again.

What is happening here? Has humanity lost its feel for sensitivity and understanding?

Wednesday January 14

- Patients in hospitals and nursing homes have various needs, both physical and psychological – they are individuals
- Patients must be given the attention they need in order to alleviate anxiety,

loneliness, fear, or any other disturbing emotion

- The excuse of understaffing cannot be used since these facilities are in the business of serving the health needs of the individuals in them and should be staffed adequately to cover these needs
- Staff must create and maintain an atmosphere that will be stimulating for physical and mental health. They must be patient, understanding, and sympathetic, and must be prepared to interact with the elderly
- Nursing homes seem to have greater difficulty maintaining an atmosphere that is most beneficial for their patients' total health. Staff in these homes often complain of understaffing and over-population, yet the patients in a nursing home are often people who require the most attention. They are often incapable of providing for their own emotional needs and end their days in lonely solitude
- Staff in these homes need to be reminded of their duty to deal with a patient's psychological as well as physical needs
- Understaffing complaints often reflect personnel too caught up in their routines for getting chores done

- Patients have differing needs; some can't use stimulation; others it can make self-sufficient — which in turn reduces the workload for the staff

Step 2(a): Subject

Patient care in nursing homes

Step 2(b): Audience

Nursing home administration

Step 2(c): Purpose

To persuade the administration to modify staff skills to show a more effective response to both psychological and daily physical needs of their patients

Step 2(d): Topic

Inadequate care of the needs of the elderly in nursing homes

Do the subject, audience, purpose and topic adequately reflect the material Beach generated in step 1? Do other purposes suggest themselves?

Step 3: Developmental Strategy

Cause and effect

Does not Beach's journal entry for Tuesday, January 13, suggest another extremely effective development strategy?

Step 4: Thesis Statement

Not only must nursing home staff members satisfy the basic needs of the elderly, such as feeding, clothing, and bathing, but they must also be able to fulfill the psychological needs of their charges as well.

Step 5: Outline

The Needs of the Elderly

Thesis Statement

Not only must nursing home staff members satisfy the basic needs of the elderly, such as feeding, clothing, and bathing, but they must also be able to fulfill the psychological needs of their charges as well.

I. Introduction
   A. Elderly are like children and need care
   B. Thesis statement
II. Routine as a problem
   A. Staff, in their routine, forget humane approach
   B. Staff must remember that all their patients are individuals with individual wants and needs
      1. Sympathy
      2. Empathy
      3. Compassion

III. Understaffing
  A. Not enough staff to take care of many individual needs of patients
  B. Not all patients require, or can benefit from, stimulation
IV. Importance of Stimulation
  A. Busy nurses often can't give needed attention
    1. Verbal communication
    2. Kindly gestures
    3. Inspiration
  B. Family members may neglect to visit
  C. Without stimulation the brain cannot perform adequately
    1. Elderly patients need external stimulation
    2. Stimulation can lead to regression of symptoms and revelation of skills, talents, and knowledge
V. Interaction
  A. Encourage patient-patient, patient-nurse interaction and socialization
  B. Interaction could be encouraged by non-regular staff
    1. Volunteer workers
    2. Nurses in training
    3. Sociologists
    4. Psychologists

Exercise

1. Using the questions in the planning checklist (pp. 76 - 77) assess whether or not Beach was adequately prepared to write the draft that follows.

Step 6(b): First Draft

In our classes we encourage vigorous revision in two ways: through peer comment and instructor comment. Each student distributes copies of his or her draft to a small group of peers who actively read it, starting with large items and moving to small. The instructor does the same. We find that the peer readers concentrate on the large matters of subject, audience, purpose, and overall coherence and organization, and that the student writer finds this response most helpful. Though students are often initially leery of comments their fellow students make, and want the instructor to give the final word, as the course progresses the writers grow to appreciate this peer input and often come to consider the instructor as just another helpfully critical voice.

On the draft reproduced below you will find both peer and instructor comments. For the smaller matters—style, grammar, and punctuation—you should use the marking symbols in conjunction with the directions inside the cover of the text to determine what the problem is, and, for practice, to correct it. For the larger matters—subject, audience, purpose, and organization—you should compare the draft with the revised version to assess the degree to which Beach has taken the comments and suggestions into account.

The Needs of the Elderly

I. Old age is analogous to childhood in certain respects. Like the young, whose cognitive and physical processes necessary for self-care are not yet mature, the elderly, though mature, lose their ability to perform such functions. *(Do they all?)* Like children, the elderly require special care and attention though for them it is often found in nursing homes. *(C)* If they are placed in the care of a nursing facility, it is because they have either mental or physical disabilities that hinder them from providing for their own needs. Thus, they must rely on the patience and consideration of the special people who work in these geriatric institutions to perform such duties for them. Not only must nursing home staff members satisfy the basic needs of the elderly, such as feeding, clothing, and bathing, but they must also be able to fulfill the psychological needs of their charges as well.

Thesis Statement

II. Providing for the psychological well-being of the aging individuals in a nursing home is of prime importance to their total health though it is an area that is often not dealt with adequately. Of course there are a great many items which must be taken care of in order to satisfy the needs of individuals and a systematic routine has to be followed in order to get these things done. Nevertheless, the process must not become too mechanical. The nursing staff must be reminded that they are not dealing just with floors of people as a whole, but with individuals who have unique wants and needs. The nurses must remember that a certain amount of sympathy, compassion, and understanding specific to the needs of each patient must be given.

Good topic sentence

Purpose clearer by second paragraph

C

pass.

pass.

By whom?

pass.

III. The nursing staff may argue that there are too few staff members to provide for all of the individual demands that the elderly place on them, and that time plays a factor in the completion of their work. However, not all areas of a nursing home require that staff provide for all of these needs. It may be that only in certain areas where the patients are comprehensive and show lesser signs of dementia that the nurses must

Such as?

What needs? Vague

Jargon?

care for psychological as well as the basic needs. Therefore staff who may be able to provide intimate socialization with their patients may be more concentrated in these areas for specified periods each day.

How do you know these points?

IV. Granted there is an awful lot of work that the nursing home staff must deal with, still in carrying out these duties they should not neglect the fact that their elderly patients require stimulation in order to have adequate mental health care. Whether it is by verbal communication or by simple gestures, such basic tactics will show beneficial results in the regression of withdrawal symptoms, unveiling of skills or talents or knowledge, or new hope may be found, for example. The staff must encourage their patients to communicate not only their simple conversations, but their feelings and ideas. This mental stimulation may deter further dementia of patients and may effectively lessen the workload of the staff. If the nurses show a little extra concern for these particular needs, loneliness and anxiety may be eliminated.

CS

Faulty par.

Reference to family needed? It was mentioned in the outline.

...not only... but

incomplete comparison

pass.

V. Not only must there be patient-nurse interaction, but similarily, patient interaction with other patients must be encouraged. So often it is the case that patients in nursing homes withdraw into their own spheres, seemingly oblivious to their external environments. With the promotion of communication with others in their same situation the need for further stimulation by the professionals could be lessened or eliminated.

Slip an example in here: shuffle-board, bake-offs, etc.

pass.

Had potential for examples in outline, but none here

pass.

pass. **VI.** For the benefit of the total health of nursing home residents nurses must be reminded of their full responsibility for maintaining the most advantageous atmosphere (in which these people must live) Not only must the physical health of the individual be of priority, but the mental hygiene must be just as adequately cared for. wdy pass.

Step 7: Final Version

Step 7(b): Revised Outline

More Than Basic: Satisfying the Needs of the Elderly in Nursing Homes

Thesis Statement

This nursing home, while apparently taking care of the basic needs of the elderly, such as feeding, clothing, and bathing, has not, I feel, provided so well for the psychological needs of these individuals.

Introduction

Basic needs are cared for adequately, but not psychological ones.

I. The atmosphere is not conducive to stimulating mental hygiene.

II. Routine is the staff's response to their many jobs.

A. There are many needs for the staff to contend with.

B. Routine should never override the needs of the elderly.

III. Staffing is a major concern.
   A. There are real needs for more staff to satisfy.
   B. Because the needs of patients differ, staff should be focused on those who need stimulation.

IV. A greater personal response is needed.
   A. An anecdote shows the importance of the personal response.
   B. Fancy tactics are not necessary.
   C. Personal interaction can lead patients to great self-sufficiency.

V. Conclusion
   The staff needs to be reminded of its duty to the psychological as well as the physical needs of the elderly.

Step 7(c): Revised Essay

More Than Basic: Satisfying the Needs of the Elderly in Nursing Homes

To the Board of Directors of the __________ Nursing Home:

Though I am by no means a professional in the care of the elderly, I am, nevertheless, human. From this perspective, I have made some observations while visiting in your facility. This nursing home, while apparently taking care of the basic needs of the elderly, such as feeding, clothing, and bathing, has not, I feel, provided so well for the psychological needs of these individuals. Maintaining the psychological well-being of aging people is of prime importance to their total health. The elderly require sympathy and understanding, as well as an environment in which to keep their minds active. This particular area is one that does not seem to be dealt with adequately.

As I visit with my grandfather, I watch in utter dismay the poor souls in the nursing home. Some meticulously pick cigarette butts out of ash trays, others shuffle from place to place seemingly oblivious to their environments, others still, aimlessly rock and stare far beyond me. On the whole they are silent, though now and again I hear someone holler down the hall for a nurse. The atmosphere is quite somber and not conducive to stimulating mental hygiene, in my estimation. Furthermore, it is not necessary.

I realize that the nursing staff must deal with many individual needs each day and that this is laborious and time-consuming work. But, like many jobs, the work becomes routine after a while. It is one thing to follow a systematic schedule in order to organize oneself, yet it is another to let this flow of duties become so patterned that the nurses neglect the psychological needs of the elderly. This is a health care facility and must maintain total health care of the elderly.

But, you might argue, it takes time and people to provide for all of the individual demands of these aging people. I agree. However, their demands for proper care, and this includes the nurturing of their psychological needs, must be met. Not all of the patients in a nursing home will require that all of these needs be satisfied since there is a great variance in their degrees of disability and in their mental capabilities. In areas where the tenants comprehend their surroundings and show less signs of senile dementia, staff should be channelled in order to spend more time in therapy with these individuals.

A more mind-stimulating environment is needed for some of the patients in this nursing home. All too often they seem to sit in a semi-conscious state, many of them silent even though they may be able to speak. Simple conversation alone can draw the patients out of their shells. I recall one woman who sat alone whimpering and uttering something inaudible. I walked over and asked her what was wrong but she did not answer me. I began talking to her and before too long her speech became discernible, and her face held a contented little smirk by the time I excused myself. She just needed someone to talk to, and to hear her.

How many more require treatment like this? Apparently we do not have to use fancy tactics with these old people. A little prompting may be all that is needed. An atmosphere that promotes communication with the elderly, and amongst them, where there is sincere understanding and care for all of their needs, may be all that these people require. Eventually they may become self-sufficient in providing for their own, or their peers', psychological demands.

For the benefit of the complete health of the nursing home residents, the staff must be reminded of its responsibility to maintain the most advantageous atmosphere possible. Not only must the physical health of these individuals be of priority, but the mental hygiene must be just as adequately cared for. It is up to the nursing home staff and you, the directors, to provide this service since you are the ones who control the environment in which these patients must live.

Hands On: Writing

As you move from reading to writing in this first essay assignment, take advantage of the questions we ask below. They will serve to remind you of the process you have read through in the preceding sections of this chapter, and will ensure that you do not neglect any significant observations.

Complete the planning checklist presented on pages 76 to 77 as the most effective way to put a check on your own writing process in its first five steps:

Step 1: Examination of the Responses
Step 2: Subject, Audience, and Purpose into Topic
Step 3: Developmental Strategies
Step 4: Thesis Statement
Step 5: Outline

As well as acting as a check on work already completed, the checklist questions can give you guidance on what you need to do as you begin.

Once you have completed Step 6, your draft, answer the following questions to make sure your revision is thorough.

1. Large Items

(a) Does your essay have a thesis or controlling idea which you make clear at the beginning unless another placement is fully justified?
(b) Have you provided a sense of ending? Does your conclusion point back in some way to the beginning?
(c) Is your overall organization apparent? Have you employed appropriate developmental strategies?
(d) Are all your paragraphs related to your thesis?

2. Paragraphs

(a) Is the thought of each paragraph united?
(b) Are there clear transitions between paragraphs?
(c) Does each paragraph have a clear topic sentence?
(d) Are there clear links between sentences within paragraphs?
(e) Is each paragraph developed thoroughly with examples, illustrations, and details?

3. Sentences

(a) Are your sentences varied in form and length?
(b) Have you avoided excessive use of the passive voice?
(c) Have you avoided wordiness by cutting away anything in your sentence which does not add directly to your paper?
(d) Have you avoided basic sentence errors: unjustified comma splices, fused sentences, and fragments?

4. Diction

(a) Have you avoided ineffective clichés?
(b) Have you avoided unnecessary repetition? Have you strengthened coherence through judicious repetition?
(c) Have you avoided unnecessary jargon?
(d) Is your diction appropriate for your audience?

5. Punctuation

(a) Have you considered how your punctuation shapes your meaning?
(b) Is all your punctuation appropriate?

Before you hand in your revised version (Step 7) answer the following questions:

1. Have you proofread thoroughly for spelling, punctuation, and typographical errors?
2. Have you adhered to proper format for presentation: cover page if necessary, margins, spacing?

PART TWO

THE ANTHOLOGY

4 *Narration*

Introduction to the Mode

Narration is, put simply, story-telling, and as such it is one of the oldest pastimes of humankind. Human beings, no matter what age they are, love telling and listening to stories. Well-constructed narratives appeal to our imagination and to our desire to know what happened. This urge to read on, to come to know more of the story, depends largely on the ability of the story-teller to capture our attention. One Canadian author argues that the beginning of the story is what makes or breaks it. He puts it this way:

> The most interesting thing about a story is not its climax or dénouement—both dated terms—nor even its style and characterization. It is its beginning, its first paragraph, often its first sentence. More decisions are made on the basis of the first few sentences of a story than on any other part, and it would seem to me after having read thousands of stories, and beginning hundreds of my own (completing, I should add, only about fifty), that something more than luck accounts for the occasional success of the operation. What I propose is theoretical, yet rooted in the practice of writing and of reading-as-a-writer; good stories *can* start unpromisingly, and well-begun stories can obviously degenerate, but the observation generally holds: the story seeks its beginning, the story many times is its beginning, amplified.
>
> The first sentence of a story is an act of faith—or astonishing bravado. A story screams for attention, as it must, for it breaks a silence. It removes the reader from the everyday.... It is an act of perfect rhythmic balance, the single crisp gesture, the drop of the baton that gathers a hundred disparate forces into a single note.

Clark Blaise, "To Begin, To Begin," in *The Narrative Voice,* ed. John Metcalf (Toronto: McGraw-Hill Ryerson, 1972), p.22.

In light of the foregoing quotation and keeping in mind that an author's intent is to capture our imaginations and interest early in a narrative, comment on how the following two passages from Canadian narratives do or do not succeed as examples of good story-telling:

> 1994 Halifax Harbor at night is a beautiful sight, and June usually finds the Macdonald Bridge lined with lovers and other appreciators. But in Halifax even June can turn on one with icy claws.
>
> A thermometer sheltered from the brisk wind would have shown a little below Centigrade zero. Norman Kent had the magnificent scenery all to himself.
>
> He was aware of the view; it was before his face, and his eyes were not closed. He was aware of the cold too, because occasionally when he worked his face frozen tears would break and fall from his cheeks. Neither meant anything to him. He was even vaguely aware of the sound of steady traffic behind him, successive dopplers like the rhythmic moaning of some wounded giant. That meant nothing to him either. On careful reflection Norman could think of nothing that *did* mean anything to him, and so he put one leg over the outer rail.
>
> Spider Robinson, *Mindkiller* (New York: Berkley Books, 1983; Holt Rinehart, 1982), p. 1.

> I was looking for a four-letter word for "narrow path", when I heard high heels on the stairs. High heels usually means business for me rather than for Dr. Bushmill, the chiropodist. With men on the stairs, it was only guessing. I put away the newspaper in time to see a fuzzy silhouette through the frosted glass of the door hesitate for a moment before knocking. I called "Come in already!" and she did.
>
> She was the sort of woman that made you wish you'd stayed in the shower for an extra minute or taken another three minutes shaving. I felt a little underdressed in my own office. She had what you could call a tailored look. Everything was so understated it screamed. I could hear the echo bouncing off the bank across the street.
>
> She took a chair on the other side of my bleached oak desk and played around with her handbag. It matched her shoes, and I thought that the car outside probably matched the rest of the outfit. Sitting in the sunlight, with the shadow of the letters of my sign caressing her trim figure, she looked about thirty, but I put part of that down to decent treatment, regular meals, baths and trips to Miami, things like that. When she raised her eyes to look at me, they were gray.

"You're Mr. Cooperman?" she asked.

"Would I lie to you?" I said, trying to help her over the awkward stage. The sign on the door told the truth too: ***BENJAMIN COOPERMAN LICENCED PRIVATE INVESTIGATOR.*** "What can I do for you, Miss...?" Her lips smiled suddenly, like a puppeteer pulled the right string and then released it. Her eyes didn't change.

Howard Engel, *The Suicide Murders* (Markham: Penguin, 1985), pp. 1-2. First published by Clarke, Irwin, 1980.

The appeal to the reader's imagination that narrative fictional writing holds can be equally strong in non-fictional narrative. The most obvious difference between these two types of narrative, though by no means a hard and fast distinction, is that while fictional narrative is primarily concerned with telling a story, non-fictional narrative usually has a point to make. In other words, non-fictional narrative does more than simply tell a good story; it uses the story as the medium for further authorial commentary. This commentary coupled with the narrative might be used, for instance, to inform or convince or persuade the reader.

Types of Narrative

Three types of non-fictional narrative that are very much a part of our daily lives are the personal narrative, the reportorial narratives, and the analytical narrative.

Personal Narrative

Personal narrative usually consists of a combination of event and commentary. Notice, for instance, the following passage from Farley Mowat's account of his reaction to the Second World War:

On the second day of September, 1939, I was painting the porch of our clapboard house in the rural Ontario town of Richmond Hill when my father pulled into the driveway at the helm of his red convertible. He looked as if he might have had a drink or two—high-colored and exhilarated.

"Farley, my lad, there's bloody big news! *The war is on!* Nothing official yet, but the Regiment's been ordered to mobilize, and I'm to go back in with the rank of major, bum arm and all. There'll be a place for you too. You have to sweat a bit for it, of course, but if you keep your nose clean and work like hell there'll be the King's Commission."

He spoke as if he were offering me a knighthood or, at the very least, membership in some exceedingly exclusive order.

> My father's news excited me tremendously, for I had long been inflamed by his fulminations against the Russophobe French, British and U.S. politicians and industrialists who had connived at the growth and spread of fascism, concealing their real admiration for it beneath the public explanation that it was the only trustworthy "bulwark against communism." I shared my father's conviction that these men had betrayed democracy, and I took the debacle of Munich and the sellout of Czechoslovakia as proof of this. I believed that every healthy young man in the freedom-espousing countries was duty-bound to take up arms against the fascist plague and, in particular, the singularly bestial German brand.
>
> Farley Mowat, *And No Birds Sang* (Toronto: McClelland and Stewart-Bantam, 1979), pp. 3-4.

In this passage, Mowat begins with a narrative reminiscence of a certain day in 1939. He tells us what he was doing on this particular day and he quickly introduces dialogue to give the anecdote immediacy and a sense of drama. But the event soon gives way to a passage of extended commentary in which the author thinks about the effects that his father's news has on him. This personal narrative, then, is made up of story *per se* plus commentary in the form of the author's reaction to the scene he has just presented. Both elements are central to this particular type of narrative since the story without the commentary would seem to have no point, and the commentary without the story would have no meaningful context.

Not all personal narratives, however, include commentary as explicit as that found in the foregoing excerpt. Notice the following passage:

> I will close on a memory, an important one. A different Florida when Venice was still underwater. There was a day years earlier in Fort Lauderdale. As usual, a Sunday, shortly after we had moved there from Hartley. A hurricane was a hundred miles off-shore and due to strike Fort Lauderdale in the next six hours. We drove from our house down Las Olas to the beach (Fort Lauderdale was still an inland city then), and parked a half mile away safe from the paint-blasting sand. We could hear the breakers under the shriek of the wind shaking the wooden bridge we walked on. Then we watched them crash, brown with weeds and suspended sand. And we could see them miles off-shore rolling in forty feet high and flashing their foam like icebergs. A few men in swimming suits and woolen sweaters were standing in the crater pools pulling out the deep-sea fish that had been stunned by the trip and waves. Other fish littered the beach, their bellies

> blasted by the change in pressure. My mother's face was raw and her glasses webbed with salt. She went back to the car on her own. My father and I sat on the bench for another hour and I could see behind his crusty sunglasses. His eyes were moist and dancing, his hair stiff and matted. We sat on the bench until we were soaked and the municipal guards rounded us up. Then they barricaded the boulevards and we went back to the car, the best day of fishing we'd ever had, and we walked hand in hand for the last time, talking excitedly, dodging coconuts, power lines, and shattered glass, feeling brave and united in the face of the storm. My father and me. What a day it was, what a once-in-a-lifetime day it was.
>
> Clark Blaise, "A North American Education," in *The Narrative Voice,* ed. John Metcalf (Toronto: McGraw-Hill Ryerson, 1972), p. 16.

In this long passage, the author clearly places the emphasis on the story itself. It is not until we reach the very end of it that we begin to see the commentary emerging. Until that point it is difficult to know exactly how the speaker feels about the experience he is living through. But in the second last sentence we begin to sense that it was an exhilarating experience for him. The final sentence makes the speaker's reaction very clear: the experience was so unusual and so charged with energy (a view that we can find within the narrative section itself) that he regards it as a "once-in-a-lifetime day."

Personal narratives are almost always written from the first-person point of view, where the narrator refers to himself as "I" or "me." The greatest effect of the first-person viewpoint is immediacy and authenticity. We are generally more likely to believe someone who says "I was there, I saw it," or "It happened to me!" On the other hand, if a more distanced approach is called for, the third person point of view (he-him-she-her) is appropriate. While the third person is rare in personal narratives, it is the most common choice in both reportorial and analytical narratives.

Reportorial Narrative

Reportorial narrative offers information. Medical case studies are a good example of the reportorial type. They present events in the third person without additional commentary. The doctors involved use the case study as raw material from which they arrive at their own conclusions. Notice the following case study:

> Pierre and Marie, married four years, with a new house and savings in the bank, are eager to have children. Since Marie has already experienced two miscarriages, they are apprehensive when she becomes pregnant again, and they exercise great care to promote a

full-term pregnancy. However, Marie miscarries for the third time. After unsatisfactory consultations with various health professionals, they hear of a physician noted for her success in fertility problems. She draws their attention to one precaution they failed to observe. They both continued to work at their regular jobs—Pierre as an anaesthetist spending many of his working hours in a poorly-ventilated hospital operating room, and Marie as a scientist engaged in viral research in a government laboratory. Both jobs involve potential reproductive hazards for men and women. Can these two workers continue at their jobs without further damaging their ability to produce healthy offspring?

Nancy Miller Chenier, *Reproductive Hazards at Work: Men, Women and the Fertility Gamble* (Ottawa: Canadian Advisory Council on the Status of Women, 1982), pp. 1-2.

What we learn about in this passage are the details of a married couple's childless life together. The author tells us who they are, how long they have been married, what they work at, and some details concerning the wife's pregnancies. The problem (apparently involving the reproductive system of one or the other partner or perhaps of both of them) may be related to their jobs. The question with which the passage closes suggests a possible explanation for the problem, but clearly the entire situation is going to require far more investigation. The case study, then, gives the professional experts enough details to allow them to investigate the situation further and perhaps find an answer to the question that concludes the paragraph.

Factual news reporting provides other occasions for reportorial narrative:

Japan car sales

Foreign car sales in Japan rose 59 per cent from the previous year's levels to a record 9,597 in July, a spokesman for the Japan Automobile Importers Association says.

West German car sales, which accounted for nearly three-quarters of July's import sales, were up 56 per cent from last year's levels. Although sales of U.S.-made cars also rose sharply, they accounted for only 3.7 per cent of the total.

The monthly sales rise, which surpassed the previous record of 9,504 sales set in June, reflected narrower price gaps between imported and Japanese cars and lower loan rates offered by foreign car makers, the spokesman said.

Sales of foreign cars in Japan in the first seven months of this year came to 54,053, a 42 per cent increase from last year's levels.

The Globe and Mail, August 7, 1987, p. B13

This news report is devoid of authorial opinion or judgment. Its main concern is to present a disinterested and objective picture of an event. What we get, in short, are just the facts.

Plot summaries are also good examples of reportorial narrative. Normally we are told the events as they appear, with no additional commentary. Pick up any copy of Coles Notes to see how plot summaries work as reportorial narratives.

Writers of reportorial narratives are aiming for a certain objectivity; they do not want personal opinions clouding the issue or the facts. However, you should remember that complete objectivity is an unattainable ideal—simply our status as individual human beings means each of us will express personal, cultural, or political biases unconsciously, in the very style of our lives, despite our desire for impartiality. We must be wary of accepting blindly the reportorial narratives we read.

Analytical Narrative

In analytical narrative the author is more concerned to present an interpretation of events than to present the events themselves. In other words, the story serves as a point of departure for extended *commentary;* the events serve as the occasion for a discussion of wider issues. Notice the following excerpt:

> Peaceful Toronto, Toronto the Good: I am on my way to the beer store near the corner when a small red Volkswagen cuts through the College and Bathurst intersection on a red light. It bounces off another car, swerves, skids, comes to rest pointing the way it had come! Another car follows it through the light, stops. Two men jump out. The teenage driver of the Volks sees the two men, pulls a gun from his pocket and begins to shoot. My journalistic integrity in shreds, I turn to run into an alley. But before I can move, the two men jump back into their car and drive straight at the kid, who gets off one more shot before he is flung into the gutter. The two men leap out again, seize him, throw him down over the hood of his car, and hold him there. I look around for the cameras. There aren't any. Those bullets were real. That accident was real. The screams of the people waiting at the streetcar stop were real.
>
> . . . .
>
> The argument about gun control yields up the same emotional quotient as abortion or capital punishment. Defenders of the private ownership of guns occasionally declare that the "disarming of the citizenry" is part of the Communist conspiracy; whereas people who

> have never shot a gun in their lives (but who have seen *Godfather I* and *Godfather II* and will probably see *Godfather III* when it comes out) are convinced only depraved criminals or right-wing fanatics would ever want to do so. Amiable discourse, as you might expect, is absent. Everyone agrees on the hard facts, the statistics. But even in the moderate middle there is no agreement on how to interpret them.
>
> Marq de Villiers, "Too Many Guns," *Toronto Life* (August, 1975), p. 6.

The piece goes on in this vein looking at the issue of guns and gun control in Canada. Clearly, the introduction to this piece is written as narrative. It has the advantage of capturing and holding our attention as every good introduction should. But its purpose goes beyond this: it serves to bring to the reader's attention through anecdote the issue that the rest of the essay will analyse and comment on in great detail. Interpretive biography and history work much the same way. They begin by introducing stories but quickly move on to the analyses of these stories; however, it is important to remember that even when the author's principal task is to analyse events or happenings, he or she must always maintain a secure hold on the narrative events that engender their respective analyses. To forget to answer the reader's "What happened?" can be fatal to a work of biography or history, or any other analytical narrative.

Before moving on, it may be worth noting that though chronological order is probably the most common principle of narrative organization, this is not a hard-and-fast rule. Your organization depends on what will create the best effect in your writing. Do not adhere slavishly to chronological order if your piece suggests that another method will yield better results.

Though narrative, as we have seen, is an independent mode with various classifications, it is often used in college and university writing as an aid to other kinds of writing. You will probably not often be asked to write narrative pure and simple. Rather, you will probably be asked to produce expository and argumentative writing to which narrative can be brought as an aid. Look back at the Marq de Villiers passage on guns that was quoted in part above. De Villiers is clearly more interested in the moral debate surrounding gun control than he is in the narrative events that introduce the analysis. However, he wins reader attention by beginning the analysis with a poignant and gripping story that leads naturally into the analysis itself. A clear understanding of how narrative works can help you write more effective non-narrative essays. The great beauty of narrative writing is that it brings into action more aspects of our human make-up than the discursive modes of exposition and argumentation. While narrative involves our usual reasoning faculties, it also makes appeals to the imagination, the emotions, the memory. These appeals make our reading a more complete experience. Writers have not been slow to recognize this; just as authors know that robust diction carries more weight than cliché and commonplace, so they know that using narrative anecdotes and illustrations will give weight to their argument or exposition.

When you are writing narrative, either as the dominant mode of composition or in the service of some other mode, you will inevitably be faced with a decision about the degree of detail you want to include. In certain contexts too much narrative detail will only divert attention from the main issue. Notice the following passage:

> Changing a tire can be a simple enough task if you have the proper equipment and go at the job in a methodical way. One bright sunny morning at about 6:30 a.m. I decided that I would get up early and go golfing in order to beat the crowds of people who normally congregate at golf courses in good weather. I jumped into my car and proceeded in a carefree, breezy manner towards the golf course which is about six miles from my house. After having driven about three miles, I noticed that the road had suddenly become very bumpy and my car's steering very difficult to manage. Imagine my surprise when I realized that I had a flat right rear tire. After spending about forty five minutes changing the tire, and another fifteen cleaning my hands, I arrived at the golf course only to have to stand in a long line of other eager golfers who had got out of bed after me, but who had, nevertheless, a better journey to the golf course than I had.

Although this small essay begins by suggesting that it is going to outline the steps one should take in changing a tire, it never fulfills its promise. Rather it gets sidetracked and talks more about the incidents leading up to the flat tire and the consequences of it than the process itself. In other words, the narrative that is meant to lead into the process takes on a life of its own and abandons the essay's main goal.

In other contexts, however, a thorough presentation of narrative detail is necessary in order to make the analysis that follows comprehensible. Often writers move back and forth between summary and detailed presentation in an essay, and even in a single paragraph. If you were assigned a process essay on how to change a tire, you might choose to begin with a paragraph-long anecdote from personal experience. In two or three sentences you could summarize the pleasurable events of a particular trip up to the fateful moment the tire burst. Then you could switch into a more detailed presentation to describe your handling of the blow-out itself, which would include the process part of the assignment. Vivid detail is a great asset to any writing, but remember that it needs a context to give it significance. Notice in the following paragraph how the author judiciously combines both the process and the narrative. Notice, as well, how the narrative segments do not compete with the process but rather enhance and personalize it:

> The ideal rising temperature for bread dough is between 80 and 90 degrees Fahrenheit; if it is much cooler the rising is sluggish, if very much hotter the yeast might burn itself out. If the thermostat in your home is set at 80 you can put your bowl of dough anywhere. If your temperature is normal, a warm spot or high shelf in your kitchen might do, or you could turn on the heat in your oven at its lowest setting for 5 minutes, then turn it *off* and put the dough in. A friend of mine puts hers in the warming oven, set at its lowest. My mother puts her bowl of coffee-cake dough on a board on top of a radiator. I put mine on a sunny window ledge. In winter I put it on a shelf above an electric heating unit.
>
> While visiting at a summer cottage I found a perfect rising-place on a cool day was the seat of my car parked in the sun. And one shivery morning in September I mixed my bread dough at dawn and went back to my warm welcome bed. Like the slap of a frosty wet fish the thought struck me that dough won't rise well in the cold. I got up, brought the covered bowl to my bed and tucked it under the electric blanket. Of course I slept again. Of course the dough rose. Very quickly.
>
> Edna Staebler, *Food that Really Schmecks* (Scarborough: McGraw-Hill Ryerson, 1968), p. 137.

When using paragraphs of narrative material in expository or argumentative essays, two methods of keeping a proper proportion of context and detail are deductive and inductive narration. In deductive narration the writer begins the paragraph by stating his or her main point. This statement is often called the topic sentence. The paragraph then develops the point through narrative event and detail. Inductive narration works in reverse. The narrative events and detail build up to a concluding topic sentence that expresses the main point of the whole. A good example of deductive development can be found in the Staebler passage; an example of the latter is the following:

> When I received word that my first job interview would take place Monday morning at 9:30 I was ecstatic and found it extremely difficult to sleep for the whole preceding weekend. When Monday dawned at about 5:00 a.m. I jumped out of bed, showered for what seemed an endless period, and ate a very sparse breakfast, not wanting to have

too much on my stomach. I then proceeded to get dressed in my very best clothes, certain in this case of the wisdom of the adage that clothes make the person. Even after this seemingly endless period of time I spent properly preparing myself, I discovered that it was still only 8:00 and that I still had an hour and a half to wait for my interview. In order to help pass the time I decided to walk to the office where the interview was to be held. However, I had not taken into account the fickleness of mother nature. No sooner had I reached the half-way point—the point of no return as it were—than it began to pour rain. I arrived at my interview sodden and sullen, my new dress looking very much as if it had just been thrown into a lake with me in it. Obviously even the best-prepared people must finally realize that there are certain factors which will always remain beyond their control.

Hands On: Reading

Exercise

Actively read the following passage paying particular attention to the subject, audience, and purpose of the piece. As you consider the essay, think about the many aspects and strategies of narration outlined in this chapter and relate them to the essay's subject, audience, and purpose. Once you have actively read the essay, write a summary of it and a response to it.

GRAHAM FRASER

A SENSE OF BEING

Dear Andy,

I have been sitting agonizing for some time about the contribution you asked for. I sat down two or three times and started typing; to my dismay, I never seemed to get farther than all the old chestnuts and clichés: elaborating on "Mon pays, ce n'est pas un pays, c'est l'hiver"; the nearness of the "cleansing wild"; what Fernand Dumont called the "quality of small nations"—all of which is valid, quite true, and, in fact, at the root of why I love this country. Even so, it sounds pretty trite and superficial when I put it down.

Part of the reason I ultimately couldn't write a nice gutsy Manifesto, I suppose, on My Love For My Country, is just that triteness. The only time Canadians talk to each other as Canadians is when they are trying to convince each other that their country **EXISTS.** The whole exercise begins to resemble Descartes' arguments for the existence of God.

It all comes down to feeling. I grew up believing in the intangible existence of Canada, and I still do—in a very powerful and irrational way. My father came to his strong belief in Canada's identity when he began making two- and three-week canoe trips along the routes of the explorers and fur traders. He established an almost mystic bond with Canada's past, present and future—and I grew up with this bond. It's almost true to say that I have had my strongest spiritual sensations in a canoe, watching the Northern Lights.

I guess I realized this most clearly when I was 18 and working at a summer camp in North Carolina. The camp was in hill country, in the Smoky part of the Appalachian chain. The same chain of mountains as that in Quebec's Eastern Townships, only, if anything, more beautiful. What at first exhilarated me about the area was how many towns and villages there were in every direction. But then I began to get almost claustrophobic. Over every hill there was a valley—with a highway in it, and a village or a town. For the first time, the most obvious fact about Canada really hit me. If you drive north from Ottawa, where I was born, up Highway II, after about two hours, you reach Mont Laurier. The road stops going north. You can drive south-east to St. Jovite, and, eventually, Montreal, or north-west to Val d'Or, but north, there is nothing. There are two railway tracks, cutting through the remoter parts of Northern Quebec between you and the Arctic.

That sounds like a pretty trivial observation, but I thought about it quite a bit in North Carolina. But powerful as that geographic fact may be as a psychic truth for those Canadians who spent their boyhood summers in canoes, it isn't much to hang a national identity on. Personal nationalism, yes—collective nationalism in this increasingly urbanized branch-plant conglomerate, no.

In fact, our collective feeling for the North is pretty unimpressive. From Diefenbaker's Northern Vision through Arthur Laing's Operation Northland to that Arctic loss-leader Ookpik, all the whipped-up attempts to get us to Think North just haven't worked.

When you think about it, two years later, the Centennial attempts to get us to Think History didn't have much effect either. As a nation, we have systematically and in an organized fashion discredited all of our national leaders. I'm not saying that they don't deserve it—but the process of intellectual cannibalism that has gone on seems to indicate some kind of serious inability to come to terms with Canadian politics as it is, on the part of anyone who writes about politics in Canada.

I was particularly struck by this while watching how Americans have banded together to canonize Lyndon Johnson, and place him in History. Any American president, no matter how bad, acquires something of the stature of his office. In contrast, any Canadian Prime Minister, no matter how honest (or successful in walking the tightrope of Canadian federalism), is systematically discredited in the public mind.

In Quebec, it is very different on both counts. There is a psychic concern for the wilderness to the extent that people write very beautiful (and very popular) songs about power dams. The concern for the past, the common culture, the language is so obvious that there isn't much point in continuing the comparison.

A large part of my personal agonizing about Canadian national identity has been concerned with Quebec. I learned French—principally out of some sort of sense of national duty and some kind of belief in a bilingual Canada. But in fact, being a bilingual Canadian is rather pointless and a bit of a pain in the neck. After innumerable student conferences, debates, interviews, earnest conversations in French with federal politicians from Quebec, and three summers working in French in student groups whose underlying aim was to prove that bilingualism is a good thing, I've decided the hell with it. I can decide to live in Quebec, in French, or in Toronto, say, in English.

Perhaps that rather bitter conclusion is at the root of why I couldn't face the idea of writing something earnest for you, Andy. Aside from whatever personal satisfaction each of us gets from being two hours from pre-Cambrian solitude, I'm not sure that English Canadians have much interest in each other as Canadians. Quebec stands now as the lynch-pin of our potentially bilingual identity—and Quebec is not enough. Marchand, Pelletier and Trudeau to the contrary, I think it's too late for Quebec to opt into Confederation, and too late for us to identify ourselves as a nation without our picturesque French-speaking colony.

Recently, I spent six days travelling with René Levesque as he spoke to English-Canadian students on six campuses. I had thought I'd come to terms with separatism some time before, at least to the extent that I realized the decision wasn't mine, and that I was prepared to accept the idea intellectually.

But one evening, at Trent University, I sat listening to Levesque quiety, calmly, almost sadly explain that we would have to decide whether or not we would deal with an independent Quebec in good faith, and, as if for the first time, I realized the extent to which my idea of Canada depended on Quebec. I sat and quietly wept.

For a long time I really believed in a new Canada... a kind of potential pan-Canadian Expo, inspired with Pierre Trudeau's urbanity and grace. But that kind of excitement hasn't so much failed (I'm not one of those who feels bitter and betrayed by the Prime Minister) as just proved to be irrelevant. The legalism of constitutional debate is simply insufficient to provoke this country into a sense of being.

But possibly, if we did sustain the kind of collective pride, self-interest, self-protection and self-promotion that a vigorous nationalism needs to survive the anti-national effects of North American technology, we would effectively destroy the charm that Canada has. We have very little folk culture or pop culture of our own; giving Canada Council grants to Bobby Gimby will not give us what we think we need.

But, as I say, what renewed nationalism we have had in the last few years has bloomed with things like Expo and the Bi-and-Bi report. Bilingualism is proffered as the answer to the crippling contradictions in Canadian history, and I'm afraid it won't do. We, in English Canada, are going to have to rationalize our existence by ourselves, because Quebec won't be doing it for us much longer.

Good luck with the book, Andy. Perhaps someone will be able to strike a more optimistic note than I.

Graham Fraser

Graham Fraser, "A Sense of Being," from Andy Wainwright, ed., *Notes for a Native Land* (Ottawa: Oberon Press, 1969), pp. 13-16.

Hands On: Reading into Writing

The following assignment deals with writing in the narrative mode. The subject is action/adventure.

Assignment

1. Actively read the following four narrative essays on various aspects of action/adventure.

2. Answer the questions appended to each essay. Your careful responses to these questions should act as a spur to your thought and so should assist you when you complete the reading workbook entry.
3. Complete a reading workbook entry for each essay:
   (a) Comment on subject, audience, and purpose.
   (b) Identify thesis statement, topic sentence, or controlling idea.
   (c) Comment on developmental strategies.
   (d) Prepare an outline.
   (e) Write a summary.
   (f) Write a response of at least one hundred words.
4. Once you have finished dealing with the readings on an individual basis, you will have at least four hundred words of informed response on the subject of action/adventure. This body of material will serve as the basis for your own *narrative* essay on the subject, which should consist of three or four double-spaced typewritten pages. Remember what has been mentioned time and again in this book: the techniques that you learn as you actively read will be the ones that you put to good use when you write your own essay.
   (a) Examine your responses.
   (b) Develop a workable topic in view of your subject, audience, and purpose.
   (c) Determine effective developmental strategies.
   (d) Develop a thesis statement.
   (e) Develop an outline.
   (f) Write a first draft.
   (g) Revise.

PIERRE BERTON

LEGENDS IN THE ROUGH

1 *He was tough, bold, colorful and dashing—a swarthy bullet-headed rapscallion, blessed with the traditional pirate's flair for eluding his clumsier pursuers. Again and again, Bill Johnston was able to evade capture. No jail, it seemed, could hold him....*

2 As I wrote those words (for a book called *My Country*) I pulled up short: they sounded so, well, *American*. This was a Canadian I was writing about! And scarcely anybody has heard of him.

3 *...Moreover, to add a touch of spice to his legend, there is a beautiful daughter lurking offstage. She aids him in his escapes. She watches out for his enemies through a telescope from her home in French Creek. She sends him signals in a specially designed Morse-style code. She secretly dispatches food*

and provisions when he hides out in the watery labyrinth of the Thousand Islands. Small wonder, then, that the saga of Bill Johnston inspired at least two novels, a stage play and a sheaf of folk songs. . . .

4 Needless to say, the novels, the play and the songs were all written by Americans. We did not have a History Industry in the 19th century and we scarcely have one now. Save for a learned article in a scholarly journal and a plaque near Ganonoque, the Buccaneer of the St. Lawrence remains, to us, an obscure figure. Surely our one and only pirate deserves better than this.

5 The problem is that most Canadians don't believe we have any history and until they do, these larger-than-life figures—the heroes, saints, charlatans and blackguards who crowd our past—will be condemned to lurk in the shadows.

6 I know this because the attitude—that we have no history worth talking about—was expressed forcibly to me when I began a television program, also called *My Country,* in which I proposed to tell, each week, a true story from the Canadian past. At the outset, however, hardly anybody was prepared to believe that the Canadian heritage included enough stories of that kind to flesh out a weekly show.

7 Well, I've made 52 such shows. They're still being seen in major Canadian cities from Halifax to Vancouver. I've gathered some of them into a book (including the saga of Bill Johnston the pirate). And there's no doubt in my mind that I could find hundreds more.

8 I'm not thinking only of heroes, though we've had our share of those. (During the recent Olympic Games, my mind kept harking back to the Golden Age of Sculling in the 1870s when Ned Hanlan, of Toronto, the world's fastest oarsman, set records that have yet to be broken, long before the modern Games were created.) I'm thinking also of such magnificent mountebanks as Edward Arthur Wilson, that strange Eurasian mystic who called himself The Brother, XII and who literally ran a slave colony on three islets near Nanaimo, B.C. in the early Thirties. I'm thinking of Charles Bedaux, the international mystery man, who mounted an incredible safari through the wilds of northern British Columbia in 1934 (one packhorse groaning under a load of ladies' shoes; another under a hundredweight of French novels) and who was later captured in North Africa as a Nazi spy. I'm thinking of Charles Blondin, the tightrope walker who carried a man on his back across the gorge of Niagara in 1858, to the gasps of 300,000 onlookers.

9 I'm thinking, especially, of that most controversial of all Canadian zealots in the 19th century, Charles Chiniquy. In the 1840s Chiniquy

was perhaps the best-known Roman Catholic priest in the country. In the 1880s he was, probably, the best-known Protestant. As a young Abbé in Quebec his oratory was so spell-binding that he was able in a single month to persuade 20,000 tipplers to sign a pledge of total abstinence. After his row with the Church—a row that involved both sexual and financial peccadillos—Chiniquy became a Presbyterian minister and an Orangeman with an undimmed personal charisma. In one year he persuaded 7,000 staunch Quebec Catholics to embrace Protestantism. He was a world figure, and a contentious one. In Australia, which he toured at the age of 70, one town required four days of martial law to calm it down after his appearance.

10 But who, even in Quebec, knows much about Chiniquy today? I confess, I did not even recognize his name until I launched the *My Country* series.

11 The trouble is that, to a Canadian, history is something other nations—notably the Americans—have and we don't. This is because the Americans have always been able to exploit their past through the mass media—through motion pictures, Tin Pan Alley songs, bestselling novels, books of popular history and even musical comedies. Until very recently, we haven't done that. I've often thought that the National Film Board might have been better employed making widescreen adventure stories about this country rather than sensitive, award-winning documentaries about the wheatfields and the fishing villages.

12 It is films like *Red River,* novels like A.B. Guthrie's *The Way West,* popular histories like Jim Bishop's *The Day Lincoln Was Shot,* tuneful ditties such as Frank Loesser's *Praise the Lord and Pass the Ammunition,* stage plays like *Inherit the Wind,* musicals like *Oklahoma!* or *Carousel,* that help give the Americans their sense of identity.

13 We Canadians know more about the siege of the Alamo, the gunfight at the O.K. Corral or the battle of the Little Big Horn than we do about the search for Gun-an-noot or the commando raid that the Chevalier de Troyes made against the British on James Bay. Yet both these Canadian stories and scores of others, have an epic quality to them.

14 Of the former I have written:

15 *There are no sad songs for Gun-an-noot the invisible Indian. No banjos or electric guitars twang out the tale of his long exile in the mountains of British Columbia. Ira Hayes had his Johnny Cash but Gun-an-noot, who vanished for 13 years, eluding all efforts to capture him, has yet to find his balladeer. . . . Yet this is the stuff from which folk songs are fashioned: the story*

of a man who shadowed his own pursuers, who regularly managed to visit his wife and family, who sired five children when he was on the run from the police. No one ever captured Gun-an-noot; when the time came, he gave himself up, voluntarily."

16 As for De Troyes' astonishing guerrilla attack, again I confess that until I dug into it for the TV program, and later at more length for the book, I had never heard of it. Here is a story in which 100 men set off in 1686, on a 12-week canoe trip into totally unknown country with the object of capturing three supposedly impregnable forts, bristling with cannon. No riskier or more reckless venture can be imagined. Seventy of them, half starved, living on weeds part of the time, armed only with muskets, pikes and swords, formed an attack force that subdued all three strongholds and captured an armed naval vessel without losing a man in battle. Does anyone believe that, had this adventure occurred south of the border, it would not now be firmly fixed as legend in the minds of the Americans?

17 What we lack in Canada is a History Industry. Now that television has matured, we may get one. But we cannot, apparently, make or distribute big-screen movies and we have never had a Tin Pan Alley to celebrate past triumphs.

18 I'm always struck, for instance, by the extraordinary number of songs the Americans have to celebrate wartime victories, such as the battle of Iwo Jima. The Artillery, the Air Force, the Navy and the Marines sing of the caissons rolling along, the wild blue yonder, anchors away and deeds of valor from the halls of Montezuma to the shores of Tripoli. But we don't even have a *Ballad of Vimy Ridge,* while our military ditties are hand-me-downs from the British Army.

19 I have a dark suspicion that more Canadians are familiar with the name of Eddie Rickenbaker than they are with that of Billy Bishop, largely because of the History Industry south of the border. Yet it was Bishop, not Rickenbaker, who emerged as the greatest living Allied ace of the First World War: in just four weeks he shot down more planes than Rickenbaker did in his entire tour of duty. If it hadn't been for the super-caution of the British in confirming kills, he would have been credited with more planes shot down than Manfred von Richthofen, the German Red Baron. Shortly after I did a *My Country* program about Bishop, a viewer sent me an article from *Argosy* magazine, June, 1975, dealing, allegedly, with all the leading aces of two world wars. The magazine gave Rickenbaker a full column. To my amazement and fury Bishop's name was not even mentioned.

20 When people say that Canadian history is dull what they're *really* saying is that they'd like it to be like American history, which is really the only history the media provide us with. American history is different, certainly; but not any more interesting than ours. It's quite true that we did not revolt violently against George III, that we didn't attempt to massacre each other in the bloodiest of civil wars and that we did not dispatch troops of cavalry to our own West to exterminate the Indians. But we fail to recognize our own epics. When I first began my researches into the story of the building of the Canadian Pacific, a number of friends, some of them writers, could not understand the project. Why bother to write about anything so prosaic as a *railway?* was the general attitude.

21 It is only recently that popular writers in Canada have found it practical to explore our heritage. That task was, for decades, left to the academics writing for a small coterie of scholars. The best book about Louis Riel was written by an American, Joseph Kinsey Howard. (George Stanley's biography is impeccable in its scholarship but is certainly not designed for a mass market.) In the Thirties and Forties, when the American History Industry reached a kind of peak and the big historical novel became the rage, no Canadian writer produced an epic of the past to compete with *Anthony Adverse* or *Gone with the Wind.* Kenneth Roberts, an American, wrote *Northwest Passage.* Thomas B. Costain, a Canadian, churned out a series of bestselling costume dramas, but none of them was set in his native land.

22 This put-down of our own past is reinforced by some of the evidence in *Survival,* Margaret Atwood's intriguing exploration of Canadian literature. Canadian novelists and poets, she says, tend to write more about losers than about winners: "Canadian authors spend a disproportionate amount of time making sure their heroes die or fail." Peter Pearson, a distinguished Canadian film director, recently said much the same thing about the subject matter of Canadian motion pictures. This preoccupation with failure has helped put a curse on our past because it has fostered a general feeling that there is not much in our history worth applauding.

23 The opposite is true. Novelists and poets may see us as losers, as Atwood suggests; the literary emphasis may be on the victims of adversity. But that is not the way the ordinary Canadian, faced with adversity, has seen himself. I call as evidence a large if obscure body of literature that deals in plain, unsentimental language with the business of winning. These are the stories of everyday Canadians,

amateur writers all, who have struggled, triumphed and lived to write about it.

24 To a very large extent it has been these stories that have made *My Country* work. I am thinking, for example, of Thomas McMicking's account of his 141-day trek across Canada with the Overlanders of '62; of Jennie Dill's newspaper stories of the now forgotten cross-Canada hike of 1921; of Joshua Slocum's magnificent memoir of his 42,000-mile voyage alone around the world on the little sloop, *Spray.*

25 These true adventure tales and scores more like them—the memoirs of prairie settlers, bush pilots, prospectors, surveyors and wilderness wives—all ring with a kind of superb confidence that seems to be missing from the literature that Atwood studied. Here, for instance, is Jennie Dill, writing from Bassano, Alberta, on May 22, 1921:

26 *"Race well in hand. Few will ever know what the struggle meant to me, although I feel fine. . . . Frank will never forgive me for the manner in which I have made him walk. When he wanted to rest I wanted to keep going, and while I do not think that Frank is a quitter, I pride myself with the thought that I have kept him going. . . . This wonderful hike has taught me a great lesson, which I shall endeavor to teach my sex when the contest is over. The subject is not what men can do women can do, but what men have done women CAN MORE THAN DO."*

27 At that point Mrs. Dill and her husband had walked some 2,500 miles from Halifax, through waist-high snows, Ontario gumbo and prairie dust, following the railway line across the nation, sleeping sometimes in cold so chilling that frost formed on their comforter, attacked in northern Ontario by a timber wolf, which Jennie dispatched with a single revolver shot, and moving at an ever-increasing pace—as much as 35 miles in a single day—in the hope of setting a record. They still had more than 1,000 miles ahead of them and no hope of any reward. They did it for the hell of it and, in the end, they triumphed over their rivals, covering 3,700 miles in a record 134 days.

28 Thomas McMicking's description of his arrival at Fort Edmonton on July 21, 1862, is in the same vein. Since leaving Fort Pitt, he and his party of 143 Overlanders, heading for the goldfields of the Cariboo, had suffered appalling hardships, struggling through a torrential deluge that did not let up for 11 days. The rivers became torrents, the smallest creeks were too dangerous to ford and there wasn't a bridge between the Red and the Rockies. Between July 18 and 20, the party built eight bridges, some of them more than 100 feet in length. Once,

when no trees were available, McMicking ordered a swollen creek filled with carts to form a passage. On July 19, the worst day of all, the party was neck-deep in water, every stitch of clothing, worn or packed, dripping wet. A final obstacle presented itself: a 200-foot ravine with a foaming torrent at the bottom, its sides so steep that no man or animal could keep his feet while sliding downward. Trees had to be felled for a bridge, a trail opened up and carts and cattle let down the flanks by ropes. In the distance, the men could dimly see the palisades of the fort.

29 *"During the preceding 11 days* [McMicking wrote] *our clothing had never been dry, we had just passed through what we considered a pretty tough time, and the toil-worn, jaded, forlorn and tattered appearance of the company was in striking and amusing contrast with our appearance a few months before; so marked, indeed, was the change that our most intimate friends at home would scarcely have recognized us. But our courage was still unbroken and, although we had been much longer on the road than we anticipated, we had yet full confidence in our ability to reach the El Dorado of our hopes."*

30 Reach it they did; and when they discovered that the gold in the Cariboo was long gone, they did not whine nor whimper but set about the business of making a place for themselves in a new environment. It is no coincidence that some of British Columbia's solidest citizens were former Overlanders.

31 In *Survival,* Margaret Atwood points out that "the poems Canadians tend to make out of the settler motifs are likely to end with the abondonment of the farm" and "that you could make a whole anthology of Canadian poems about tumbledown houses and deserted farms." Yet the real story of the settlement of the Prairies is one of triumph over hardship. I must have read 20 such accounts, many of them by women, told matter-of-factly without boasting, self-pity or over-dramatization: the ghastly trip on the immigrant ships, the weary journey in the colonist cars and then the first view of the plains, empty of timber, the sod so tough that, though it defies the plow, it can be used as building blocks for the first home. Here again is one of the great epics of Canadian history and it is not the story of losers.

32 A kind of Canadian style emerges from this unknown body of literature—a style conveyed by François Xavier Prieur in the foreword to his own account of his part in the Lower Canada Rebellion of 1838 and his subsequent exile to the penal colony of Australia.

33 "I do not propose to write history," says Prieur. "I wish to provide, for those who do, my share of the exact information concerning the things that I have seen with my own eyes, touched with my own hands, and suffered in my own person."

34 Again there is no self-pity in Prieur's extraordinary account of his tribulations and no bitterness, either. "It is . . . in a spirit of calm I write," he tells us. All during his exile, even in the Quebec prison "when over me hung the weight of the death sentence; when the dead bodies of some of the companions of my captivity hung suspended from the gibbet," this remarkable youth recorded his experiences on scraps of notepaper. Eight years of imprisonment and exile—not a single word from his family in all that dark period—did not crush him. He not only survived his experience; he prospered from it. I find it marvelously apt that, in 1875, this ex-convict was named superintendent of all prisons in Canada.

35 Yet his story is scarcely known. I myself had not heard it until I began the *My Country* series. It was the first story I told on television but in the book I have saved it for the last because it seems to me to be the most Canadian of tales. It is impossible to read Prieur without being moved by the intensity of longing that he and his fellow convicts from Quebec felt for their homeland. Hideous in its details, his is essentially a love story—love of family, love of country, love of God.

36 Alas, few Canadians can read it in full. The book has been out of print in Canada for more than a century. It is available in a few libraries, ironically enough, in a recent edition published in Australia. Only when we get a History Industry of our own, can we do justice to François Xavier Prieur and all the other unknowns who have so much to tell us about our country.

Pierre Berton, "Legends in the Rough," *The Canadian*, 11 Sept 1976, pp. 4-6, 8.

Questions

1. Subject

It would be fair to say that part of Pierre Berton's subject in this essay is the long-lost heroes of Canada's past. But to say this would be to state only a small part of the subject. At least as important as the delineation of the heroes is the attitude that the author brings to the subject. What is the attitude? Point to those places in the essay where it is found.

2. **Audience**
   Obviously the audience that this essay is directed to is an everyday Canadian one. But explain how everyday Canadians are meant to feel about their knowledge of their country's heroes. Do we as an audience resent the author's tone toward us or does he point the finger at himself as much as at us? Illustrate.
3. **Purpose**
   Is the author's purpose merely to narrate snippets from a series of stories or does he use narrative to serve another end? If so, what is it?
4. **Structure and Style**
   (a) Comment on the effectiveness of the repetition in paragraph 8 and the quick shifts from one example to another.
   (b) Explain how the opening four paragraphs of this essay are appropriate to the author's subject. In what way might they be seen as a summary of the entire essay?
   (c) Comment on the effective placement of examples and illustrations to support general statements.
   (d) How does the second last sentence's use of the word "ironically" remind us of much that has come before in this essay? Explain how using this word at this point in the essay helps reinforce the author's purpose.

PETER GZOWSKI

from THE MORNINGSIDE PAPERS

1 At one time or another during the past few days I have done, at least once, each of the following things:

2 I have had Chinese food delivered to my house. Barbecued chicken wings, honey-and-garlic spare ribs, beef and snow peas and an order of steamed rice, with extra mustard and plum sauce. Not very good, as it turned out, too bready and tasting of rewarmed cardboard—but delivered right to my door.

3 I have played with the converter on my rented cable TV, flicking and jumping between *Hollywood Squares* and a panel discussion on the nuclear holocaust, intercutting a young cable reporter's guide to the traffic courts with a concert of the Boston Pops, simultaneously watching a soccer game and the provincial news, checking up on the prices of stocks I cannot afford, the departure times of airplanes I'll never ride and the fluctuations in the costs of foods I do not care for,

and never once, because of the magic control at my fingers, having to watch a commercial.

4 I have lurched to the door in the mornings and found my local paper lying soggy on my doorstep. I have summoned a taxi to the same door. I have shooed away someone who wanted to park his Volvo on the bricks that cover what once was the front lawn of the house I live in, bought a package of cigarettes at two in the morning, gone to a movie within three blocks of where I live, shovelled up the junk mail in my foyer, been wakened by the sound of breaking glass at four AM, worried if the neighbours can see me stride naked to the bathroom, locked my door at night, ridden the subway, bought a morning newspaper the night before, seen a major-league baseball game in a real—well, since it was in Toronto, almost real—major-league park and walked to work. And every day, my list of new adventures grows.

5 I have, you see, recently moved back to the big city. I was born here, and raised nearby, and after all the other places I've lived and worked I've always come back to it. But for the past five years I've really been away. During those years I made new friends and found new pleasures, and yet now I've come back again. This time, the city seems to have changed. Or maybe I have. I see it now through new eyes. In five years the city mouse has become a country mouse and now he sees his old turf differently. metaphor

6 In the country, I couldn't get Chinese food delivered, or watch the cable, or get the paper brought to my home. To go to a move theatre has been a major excursion. What I needed to buy (or read) I bought by travelling, usually by car and always by daylight. Now, I'm having some difficulty adjusting to my new conveniences, and during the next few days I thought I'd ruminate out loud about some of the things I'm learning—as well as some of the things about my life as country mouse I'm already beginning to miss.

II

7 On the morning of the first Saturday I moved back to the city, I went shopping. In itself, this was not a new experience for me, for in the past five years, while I have lived as a country mouse, I have often spent Saturday mornings shopping. I have jumped in my car and driven to the local bakery for a dozen sticky Chelsea buns and a copy of the morning paper, which lacked, because of my distance from its printing presses, the previous evening's sports scores. Later, if I have

needed stuff, I have cruised the local merchants, chequebook in hand, and driven twenty kilometres to the nearest bookstore, where I have kept a charge account, or the provincial liquor outlet for another jug or two of the wine I know goes well with fresh sweet corn.

8 In the city, though, I needed no car, and my chequebook would have been only slightly less useful than a walletful of *zlotys* or a necklace of wampum. In the city you need hard, cold cash—or the 1980s equivalent of cash: hard, cold plastic.

9 In the city, I live downtown, on the edge of what my friend Harry Bruce, who has since moved to Halifax, christened the land of the white-painters. There are more BMWs on the street where I walk than there are trees. The houses are closer together than seats on a subway train. As evening falls you can hear the Jacuzzis flush as if in unison, and right around the corner there are more stores than there were in all of Rome. Without crossing the street I could buy, if I had the money, a Cuisinart or the *New York Times*, vitamin B_{12} or a quiche to go. There are three kinds of orange drink in my neighbourhood convenience store, and twenty-four kinds of doughnuts next door. I could have my suede cleaned, my fuel pump tuned, my walls hung or my aquarium stocked. If I did cross the street I could buy a silken kite or a Stilton cheese, a German knife, a Danish peppermill, a Swedish bar stool, a Hungarian table wine or a Mandarin orange. I could get egg bread or bread rolls, breaded veal or a well-bred parakeet. I could buy a marinated leg of lamb, a chocolate-coated cherry, Kiwi fruit, canned artichoke hearts, fresh lobsters, hot croissants and cold Heineken. I could take home a live Dieffenbachia or ice cubes made of glass, a wicker end table, the latest issue of a magazine I would not like my children to see me reading or a copy of the kind of book I used to carry under my arm at university, title-side out.

10 I could live my life in the neighbourhood I have moved to, I think, and never sample all its wares.

11 And yet, as Mordecai Richler says, and yet.

12 On Saturday morning I went to see if I could buy something that would make me a cup of cappuccino before I came to work. Cappuccino in the morning is one of my fantasies, although the only person I have met yet who can afford to drink it is Peter Pocklington. I went to my neighbourhood kitchenware store. (In the village I have just moved from, the equivalent is one corner of the Home Hardware, just behind the fertilizer.) A lady with a German accent came to help me.

First she asked me how many cups I wanted to make, and when I just said one or two she gave me a one-sentence lecture about the need to entertain my friends. Then she showed me a machine that looked as if, were I to pull the right levers in the right order, it would leave in eight minutes for Brandon. When I said that was too complicated she showed me something automatic that, I think, would not only have made me a cappuccino but have served as the centrepiece for next week's exhibition on shapes of the future. When I demurred, my helpful storefrau led me to something that appeared to have been made for filling the gas tanks of model airplanes.

13 Nothing I saw cost less than $198.50.

14 And all I wanted was a cup of coffee.

15 I felt as my first-born son must have felt on the second Christmas of his life when, surrounded by half-opened packages and urged on by his loving parents to open more, more and more again, he burst into tears of sadness and being overwhelmed.

16 I went back to my rented house, past the parked BMWs, past the silent Jacuzzis, past the white-painted bricks, to my white-painted townhouse.

17 I had been gone for an hour and a half, window shopping in the casbah of the trendies, and I had bought . . . nothing. My plastic was intact.

III

18 On the first turn you take if you drive toward the city from the house I have been living in for the past five years is a pond. I'm not sure why it lies there; on a golf course it would be casual water, and you could move your ball from it, and on the prairies it would be a slough (a word unknown in the east). But beside Highway 7 in rural Ontario it is a pond; no river runs in, no stream out. A willow tree droops over one corner, and in the summer and early fall there are cat tails and bull rushes at its edges. Even when the wind is high, it is quiet and still. On the last morning I drove in from the country, a tall blue heron posed a dozen feet from its shore.

19 I stopped my car to stare; the heron did not move.

20 If I had dared to predict, when I moved to the country five years ago, how much I would become intrigued by birds, my friends would have laughed at me. I was a total city mouse then; I rode taxis and ordered meals in, and for adventure took my kids to the zoo. In the

country, blue jays jabber at me outside my kitchen window, and I jabber back, and run out with a handful of Thompson's wild bird food, $1.39 the four-pound bag, to pacify them. I am their servant. My mornings are better when they start with a brilliant male cardinal, tiptoeing in to get food for his lady. In the afternoons, an oriole pipes from the black walnut and I stop work. One summer evening as I sat with the latest P.D. James in the garden a hummingbird hovered over my teacup. I have seen grackles and juncos, bluebirds and warblers, woodpeckers and flickers, jays, buntings, larks and nuthatches, chickadees, thrushes, whippoorwills and enough sparrows to start my own cathedral—all outside my windows, or just over the first rolling hill. I do not always know what they are, for I am not always quick enough to find the right page in Roger Tory Peterson, my copy of which is now as well-thumbed as a family Bible. One magic morning I watched in wonder as a college of mourning doves waddled up through the early mists.

21 I am a sucker for all of this, and during the years I lived in the country my books, binoculars and birdseed have become as much a part of my life as backgammon once was, or Beefeater gin.

22 And now, I think I'm going to miss it.

23 There are compensations for all this, I know. Better shopping and faster taxis—or, in my case, taxis at all. Strangely, I can walk to work in the city, where I had to drive for anything in the country—or anything except work, most of which I did at home, next to the chattering blue jays. The snow won't shut me in this winter, and I don't have to worry about the well freezing or the door blowing off the barn.

24 The country surprised me when I moved there, and the city is surprising me again. This morning on my way to it I saw four sparrows, a starling and one of the last robins of the fall. But what I thought about was the blue heron, standing still near his private pond.

IV

25 One of the things I have not yet had to do in the first days of living back in the city is fill the gas tank of my car. This is not a part of country living that I miss. In the country, I have had to buy gasoline almost as often—or so it has seemed—as I have had to change my socks, and the habit has come close to breaking me.

26 I don't know what gasoline cost when I used to live here. They sold it by the gallon then, and every couple of weeks I'd notice the tank

was low and cruise in for a top-up. It cost ten dollars, or thereabouts, if I was empty. A nuisance. Now they sell it by the litre, and I know *exactly* what it costs. The car I drive is fuel-efficient, and I read the prices on the pumps before I buy, but it's twenty bucks minimum when I'm close to empty and I seem to be in gas stations more often than I'm in my kitchen. The nuisance has become a real factor in my fiscal affairs, and I am having no more luck with my budget than Allan MacEachen has had with his.

27 That's only one part of what, I've come to realize, my flight to the country has cost me in dollars. Another part is the phone. I know I talk on the phone a lot, and that phone calls are part of my work, but I never before realized that the rest of the world has lived in a place called long distance. If you had asked me my phone number any time over the past five years I would have begun my answer with my area code, and even my kids, now grown and living in the city, think my number begins with a one. While this has some advantages—one of them is that I know, when someone wants to interrupt my solitude, he has been willing to spend a dollar to do so—it makes my monthly letter from the Bell look like the stock-market columns in the Friday Report on Business.

28 I had not thought of any of this when I left. I thought of the country as a retreat, a quiet place, where life would be simple and pleasant and cheap, and where I could cut down on the need I have felt most of my adult life to make as much money as I could just to stay even. Well, quiet and simple and pleasant it has been, I assure you, but cheap? I might as well have bought a racehorse. I pay rent on my mailbox and a tax on my trees. Fertilizer costs money so the grass will grow long, and the local university student charges me to keep it, occasionally, short. The tomatoes I have tried to grow have been more expensive—if better—than those I could buy in a city supermarket, and I have not been able to put up the capital to buy equipment to do my own preserves. Even my daily newspaper, which I have to use gasoline to go to buy, costs me more than it would have cost in the city. At times I have looked at my city friends the way the have provinces have looked at the have-nots in a federal conference, as if I were subsidizing them and they didn't realize it.

29 Look, I know I've done lots of things wrong. I ought to have bought a sheep for the lawn and started making my own soap instead of driving four miles to buy it at inflated rural prices. In the winters, I ought to have huddled over an oil stove rather than watching the fireplace

cheerfully crackling away with the last of my paperback royalties. I have not, I promise you, lived extravagantly, and the old stone house where I've been hiding out—once the home of a working quarry-master—is more cottage than estate, even though it burns more fuel than Premier Davis's private jet. But one of the strongest lessons I have learned in my time away from the life I grew up with is that being a country mouse is at least as expensive as being a city mouse, and I don't think city mice realize it.

30 Am I wrong about this? I don't think so. I don't think the city slickers know what it costs us hayseeds to stay where we want to stay. You may want to add to what I've discovered. Or argue with my conclusions. Or tell me what you know about saving money in the country that—short of trying to ride my sheep to the store on Saturdays—I didn't think of when I was there. If you do, please drop me a line. I'd ask you to call me, but I know the cost of long distance. Boy, do I know the cost of long distance.

Peter Gzowski, *The Morningside Papers* (Toronto: McClelland & Stewart Ltd., 1985), pp. 16-22.

Questions

1. **Subject**
   Explain exactly what Peter Gzowski is attempting to outline in this essay and comment on his attitude towards his narration.
2. **Audience**
   To whom does Gzowski direct his essay? Does the audience need to experience *exactly* what Gzowski experiences about city and country life to appreciate the point or is there enough general mythological material present about these contrasting sides of existence to help us understand the distinctions he is drawing? The antiquity of the city mouse/country mouse notion might help you in your response to this latter point.
3. **Purpose**
   Explain how the use of the narrative mode in this essay helps to convey the author's main point.
4. **Structure and Style**
   (a) By focusing on paragraphs 2, 3, and 4 of this essay, comment on the effectiveness of Gzowski's use of detail. Does this detail and the way in which it is presented convey the author's attitude towards city living? In what sense is the phrase "new adventures" (last sentence, paragraph 4) ironic? Justify the author's use of a sentence fragment in sentence 2, paragraph 2.

(b) In what sense is paragraph 9 an encapsulation of the author's entire attitude toward city life?
(c) Compare the contrasting attitudes found in paragraphs 12 and 20.
(d) Comment on the effectiveness and appropriateness of some single-sentence paragraphs in this essay.

TONI ONLEY

THE LONGEST NIGHT

1 Nothing is inevitable, they say, but death and taxes. In a recent twelve-month period, however, I have stared both in the face and survived. In September, 1983, I came within hours of burning my inventory of paintings and prints to escape the harassment of Revenue Canada, but I won the dispute. In September, 1984, I came within seconds of losing my life when my skiplane crashed on a glacier in Garibaldi Provincial Park, 120 kilometres north of Vancouver, but I lived to tell the tale.

2 I've been flying for more than eighteen years. In 1966 I was teaching at the University of Victoria and living near the airport. I had done only art-related jobs and I wondered if I could do something that required mechanical finesse. I took flying lessons, got my licence, and in 1967 bought a used Champion Skytrack with the $5,000 I had made from an exhibition in Montreal. I flew it for eight years, across Canada, to Mexico, landing it on beaches on the West Coast, rarely stopping at airports except to fuel. Then I wanted to get to the eastern Arctic. I bought an amphibious Lake Buccaneer, which I still have for exploring mountain lakes. But once on the lakes I would look up at the glaciers and yearn to be in their pristine environment. In 1981 I sold all the watercolours from my book, *Silent Thunder,* for nearly $100,000 and put it into a Polish-built Wilga 80, which I equipped with skis.

3 I couldn't have painted the glaciers unless I had been on them. Above the timber line the painting was often painted for me. Surrounded by sky, rock, and ice, I was able to concentrate on the things that were essential, to spend hours looking for the particular elements that would describe the whole atmosphere. The mind became uncluttered, perception cleared, and I seemed to flow with nature. The painting just rolled off the brush like a song, and there were days when I could do no wrong.

4 Some of the most enjoyable times of my life have been up in the mountains. The silence enveloped me, punctuated occasionally by the sound of a distant waterfall or the rumble of a far-off avalanche. The ringing in my ears was the sound of my own blood circulating. I was where few people, maybe no-one, had ever been, in a private universe far above the crowded, smoky valleys. All that stood between me and my return to those valleys was a fragile piece of technology, my skiplane, with the call letters C-FLUF—after my mother's nickname, "Fluff."

5 I can remember when I first landed on a glacier, on Powder Mountain on September 17, 1982. I had an animal fear of being out of my environment, in a world I was unprepared for. It was as if I had been thrust into the ice age from the lush green gardens of Vancouver thirty minutes away. I had felt godlike while flying around the mountain peaks, but on the glacier I felt small and powerless. I walked with unsure feet and thoughts of impending avalanches and crevasses ready to swallow me up.

• • •

6 John Reeves, the Toronto photographer renowned for his portraits of artists and writers, had been commissioned by CP Air's in-flight magazine to do a photo essay about me—"The Flying Artist" or some such thing. Later, when we were stranded together in the wreckage of my plane, he said, "I suppose you realize this scotches our story. CP Air won't want to publish something that ends in an aircraft disaster."

7 On September 6 we went up to the Bishop Glacier on the shoulder of Mount Garibaldi, but we had got a late start and the weather was poor so we stayed only half an hour. The next day would be better, I promised. Our plan was to go up to the highest glacier in the area, the Cheakamus, at 8,000 feet; to land on it, do some painting and photography; and then go down 1,000 feet to a spectacular glacier on Mamquam Mountain, after which we would return to the Bishop, down at 5,000 feet, so that John could see the peaks of Garibaldi that had been clouded-in the first day.

8 The next morning we got onto the Cheakamus without trouble, but it was not so easy to get off. The winds were gusting—one minute calm, the next up to forty knots, not unusual in the mountains—and the snow was wet and sticky, which slowed the takeoff down the face of the glacier. I waited for the winds to die, then started my first run, but I couldn't get a good speed because of the snow. So halfway down I chopped the power and taxied back up the steep knoll for a second

try. My first tracks were packed ice now, so I shouldn't have had another problem with speed. I waited for the winds to drop, then I fired off again, holding in the tracks. When I reached the end of them I had enough speed to take off. I pulled on full flaps, which is usually sufficient to "pop" the plane off the ground by moving the weight from the skis to the wings. But nothing happened. It felt as if I had no flaps, that the wings were flat. I looked out and saw that the flaps were in position. I also saw that the gusting winds had caught up with us. Fine snow was blowing on the surface of the glacier in the direction we were going. That meant my wings had no lift. Essentially, though we were going fifty miles per hour, we were standing still.

9 It was too late to stop or turn. My options were to chop power, slow, and drop into the horizontal crevasse that stretched ahead, fifty feet wide and two hundred feet deep; or maintain power, try to leap the crevasse, and hope we wouldn't smash into the crevasse's ice wall or slide across the other side and drop into the next wide crevasse that loomed ahead. In retrospect, I made the right decision. I held power and we leaped the first crevasse. Then, by the greatest good fortune, the plane nestled into a narrow, perpendicular crevasse. It was the only one on the mile-wide glacier that ran in the direction of our descent; it formed the stubby stem of a T immediately across from where we jumped the broad crevasse; and it was just wide enough to accommodate the body of the plane while supporting the wings. It minimized the impact of the crash yet prevented us from sliding on toward the next fall. Six feet to the right or left and we would have smashed into the ice.

10 I would like to say that this was a magnificent piece of flying, but the truth is that I had lost control. Some other hand had pushed us into the only place that could have stopped our fall and cradled us through the long night. We hung suspended there from two o'clock in the afternoon until our rescue at eight the next morning.

11 I have no memory of the impact, no sight or sound. My first recollection was that my legs were pinned behind the controls and twisted, jagged metal. The engine had been pushed back into the cabin and my seat had been uprooted and pushed sideways. It was a wonder I hadn't been cut in half. Meanwhile my seat had pushed John's almost out of the plane to the right. John was unconscious. His head was hanging down and blood was dripping from his mouth. I had felt no fear before the crash, because I had been too busy, but now I was filled with a raw terror. I was on the edge of panic. For an hour, as I tried to free my trapped legs by working my feet out of my shoes, I kept shouting at him, "John, are you all right?" He flinched at the sound of my voice, but I thought I had lost him, that I would have to live with that for the rest of my life.

12 Metal ripped into my legs as I struggled to unpin them, but the pain was diminished by my adrenaline and my concern for John. I was also afraid that at any moment we would burst into flames, because I could see gasoline pouring onto the hot engine and live wires. That fear subsided after fifteen minutes or so as the engine cooled. Finally I got free. The floor beneath John had been ripped open when the engine had pulled to the left. I remember thinking how lucky John was that his seat belt and shoulder harness hadn't sprung open, as mine had, or he might have followed his cameras out of the plane and dropped 200 feet into the crevasse below. He was still unconscious. I slapped his face and his eyes opened wide immediately. His memory had gone, but the blood running from the corner of his mouth was only from a tooth having gone into his lip.

13 "What kind of place is this?" he asked. "I hope they have a good wine cellar."

14 I unbuckled him and got him into the back seat. It was 3:15. I wondered if my emergency locator transmitter (ELT) had gone off on impact. I turned it on manually. Later I learned that the search-and-rescue unit at Comox had picked up my signal by satellite at that time. My radio was dangling through the hole in the floor. I reached down and pulled up the headset and microphone. I could confirm on the emergency frequency that my ELT was transmitting, but I couldn't call out a Mayday because the cable to the antenna was severed.

15 I crawled back into the luggage compartment to stretch out my broken leg and bind up my left ring finger, which had been opened to the bone. John put on my parka and tried to make himself comfortable in the left back seat. I was lying beside him, and I spread out my one sleeping bag to cover me and cover John's feet and legs. There was nothing to do but wait. At 4:30 we heard the unmistakable drone of an armed forces Buffalo and then it came into view through the six-inch gap where the windshield had been. It circled over the valley, probably 500 feet above us, getting closer but not too close because Mount Davidson and Castle Towers Mountain were near and the weather was worsening. When it flew away we at least knew we had been spotted. It was only a matter of time before help arrived.

• • •

16 A half-hour passed, then we heard the sound of a big Chinook Rescue Helicopter working its way up the face of the glacier into what must have been whiteout conditions because of the snow that had started to fall. It was searching for us. I wanted to contact the pilot on the radio and say, "Please go back. We're O.K." We could see its grey outline and yellow searchlights. It was maybe 300 yards away, but between us and it lay many great crevasses. The helicopter put down on a shelf of ice and appeared to be looking for signs of life. We were down in the crevasse and couldn't wave, and our shouts wouldn't have been heard above the wind and the engines. I was tempted to push out the rear window, climb out, and wave, but that window provided the only shelter we would have for the cold night. After ten minutes, the helicopter backed into the gloom and the drifting snow. All was quiet except for the wind that gusted up to sixty miles per hour, driving snow in through every opening. Soon it was dark.

• • •

17 It must have struck me at some point during the night that I was with one of the most entertaining, voluble men in Canada. But John was not talking. He had a fractured cheekbone, which would have made talking painful, and we preferred to be quiet. John was later to describe his looks as "asymmetrical chipmunk." He suggested that in future I should pack a chessboard or at least Trivial Pursuit in my survival kit. He was so nonchalant about things that no-one would have guessed that we were in a desperate situation. "Another fine mess you've got us in, Ollie," he said. But John Reeves on the surface is very different from John Reeves underneath. Later, the doctors discovered that his heart rate was almost off the chart, so there had been an enormous amount of inner turmoil and shock.

18 We were like cavemen, our language reduced to the most basic. I would say, "Cheese? For strength," and he would answer, "No, not hungry." At one point, before the sun had gone, I asked him if he wanted to shoot some photographs for the record with the one camera that had been saved. He said something like, "No, I'm not a crash photographer."

19 Our only difference occurred when he said, "Toni, I think maybe we should get out of this bloody wreck and bivouac out on the snow."

20 "John," I said, "with that wind, we'd freeze to death. We've got the only shelter between here and Vancouver, and we can't walk out of this."

21 Most of the time we were too deep in our own thoughts for conversation. I often thought of my wife, Yukiko. By eight in the evening she would have phoned the number I had given her for the rescue coordination centre in Victoria. They would have told her that my skiplane had been spotted but that there was no sign of life. I felt so helpless being out of contact. I knew she would have phoned our friends, George and Inge Woodcock. I pictured them together. At ten I made an image of them and repeated in my mind, "I am alive, I am alive." Yukiko was to tell me later that she didn't get the message but that Inge had called at that time to say she had a strong feeling that John and I were all right. One never knows how one will behave in an emergency. Yukiko was very calm. She didn't fall apart or phone my family and get everyone tied in knots. She asked the RCMP not to release my name. And she spent much of the long night tidying the house.

22 Meanwhile, John and I tried to sleep. I nodded off and had a strange dream. I dreamed that a Revenue Canada ski patrol had found us. Their leader asked if I intended to declare a loss with the crash of my plane and would I fill out a form. I tried but had difficulty in my cramped position; besides, it was dark. I protested and asked for help, but the leader said, "That is not the responsibility of this department." I asked him to contact search-and-rescue, and he said, "We do not communicate with that department or any other government department." I awoke and there was only the wind and the snow.

23 The gusting wind kept moving the plane, which creaked and groaned like a ship, then settled a little deeper into the crevasse. My fear was that the tail would drop down and the plane would be supported only by the flaps and ailerons of the wings. I would be head down in the luggage compartment; John would fall on me; and we might both be carried out the rear window into the crevasse. Once during the night the plane's tail did fall suddenly.

24 "Oh my God," I thought. "We're going to drop."

25 Despite my broken leg, I leaped into the front as the plane lurched. I grabbed hold of the structure to receive John's weight if he fell back on me. But the tail had dropped only a few feet and the elevator had lodged on the edge of the crevasse. We were safer now, so I crawled back.

26 I was wet to the skin. The snow had melted in the aircraft and soaked me. John was dry but somewhat uncomfortable in his

cramped lotus position. I was shaking uncontrollably and said to John, "I might not get through another night like this." I knew from a survival course how dangerous it is to be wet. My main worry was that the ceiling would stay down and we would be in the clouds through the next day so that a helicopter could not get in. John and I intertwined our feet to keep warm, and three or four times in the night he tucked the sleeping bag tightly around our legs.

• • •

27 Dawn came slowly, then suddenly I was blinded by a flash of yellow light as the sun rose over the black mountains. The snow melted off the rear window and soon the inside of the plane grew warm. I was impatient for our rescue and kept imagining that I heard helicopters, but it was only the wind. At eight, however, I definitely heard the chop-chop-chop and a Bell Jet Ranger passed overhead. But it went out into the valley again. John described the scene as from a movie: "They're coming, they're coming, they're coming. They're going, they're going, they're gone." Minutes passed before the helicopter came back, heading straight for us. I pushed on the rear window and it popped out, making a slow pirouette before plunging into the crevasse. I stood up on my good leg and frantically waved a yellow stuffbag. The helicopter came in and hovered off our left wing. It couldn't land on the sloping ice, so a paramedic hopped out and crawled along our wing. I held John's legs as the paramedic grabbed his arm and pulled him out, and the two of them inched their way back across the wing. Then I crawled across it, pushing myself with my good leg while the paramedic pulled my arm. I couldn't stand, so he dragged me to the helicopter. John pulled me in, and soon we were off.

28 In Squamish, I was placed on a stretcher and wheeled to a waiting ambulance. A young reporter from the Vancouver *Province* was taking notes on a folded pad and I asked her to phone my wife and tell her we were safe. That's how the reporter found out that I was the infamous artist who had defied Revenue Canada. She stuck to me and eventually had to be ejected by a strong nurse as I was being prepared for an x-ray at the hospital. Her determination seemed an incredible affirmation of life, I thought, even if I was the victim of it.

29 In the aftermath it was hard to get back to ordinary living. I'm not a religious person in the sense that I don't belong to an organized group, but I believe there's a power at work. I don't understand it and I wish I did. There are things I can't put words to but am always

thinking about. Was I saved for some reason? Is there a divine plan? Do I have unfinished work?

30 As to whether I'll fly again, I'll have to discuss that with my wife and family. Flying has become such an integral part of my art that I can't imagine painting without the fresh, mysterious images I bring home from the coastal islands, glaciers, and mountain lakes. I'll miss my mountains and snowfields, and I'll not be able to bring myself to paint them until I can wander among them again.

Toni Onley, "The Longest Night," *Saturday Night* (February 1985), pp. 24, 26-27.

Questions

1. **Subject**
   In the essay, the author is telling a story about a near brush with death that he and a friend had. But the subject of the essay clearly involves more than this. The subject, in fact, is very much bound up with spiritual notions of both a non-religious and a near-religious nature. Explain.
2. **Audience**
   The author seems to know that the vast majority of humankind is primarily interested in an adventure story. Discuss the ways in which he builds his story into an exciting adventure.
3. **Purpose**
   Look up "memoir" in your dictionary. Does the meaning of this word help explain the essay's narrative purpose?
4. **Structure and Style**
   (a) Although we are regularly warned not to use clichés, the author makes use of one in his opening sentence. Does the cliché help make the opening effective?
   (b) Explain why the subject about which the author dreams in paragraph 22 is appropriate and helps contribute to the unity of the essay.
   (c) Comment on why you feel the dialogue throughout the essay is appropriate.

AL PURDY
BOOZY SADDLES

1 My friend Tom Howe and I left Vancouver for Anahim Lake in the Chilcotin in early June, driving his father's nearly-new, three-quarter ton, pickup truck. Tom is a writer and photographer who worked on a Chilcotin ranch two years ago. He was returning there, as I was, to write about the annual three-day rodeo.

2 The 400 miles or so to Williams Lake is good highway despite the loops and twists of Hell's Gate and the Fraser Canyon. Some 200 miles from Vancouver the monster snowcapped mountains become mere giants, almost barren of trees, and brown from lack of rain in the near-desert BC interior. After Cache Creek comes Cariboo country, with cattle ranges reaching all the way north to Prince George. We stop for gas at 100 Mile House; I once wrote a poem about this town which certainly nobody in the community has heard of.

3 We reach Williams Lake on the evening of the first day. Next morning we buy some beer, and then we drive west into the Chilcotin. The first 30 miles are paved as a come-on for tourists; the remainder, a mythical distance to Anahim, varies according to whom you ask for directions. (Reminds me of the Khyber Pass or maybe just a place where road builders moved all rocks into the middle of the road.) Tom drives around 30 mph, then down to 20; even 10 sometimes.

4 "Migawd, Tom, if it's really 200 miles we won't get there till snow falls at this rate."

5 "You wanta drive?"

6 "Tom, you know you wouldn't trust me to drive your dad's truck."

7 "Then shaddup!" So we have a beer, but it's getting a little flat now because the beer bubbles were burst by bumps in the road. "Hold on," Tom says, and hits the truck up to 50. All I can feel at that speed is soothing rhythm, like some six-foot gal was giving my spine a hard rub-down in a Yonge Street massage joint. Since crossing Fraser for the umpteenth and last time, we have entered an empire—cattle country—remote from even the remote Cariboo. No towns, only clusters of six or a dozen houses; the clusters have names but they all look alike. High mountains are returning, shawled with snow; the Coast Range. Blue lakes spring up with every curve in the road; occasional cowboys clop around in the increasing grassland areas. I want

to open the window and yell "Hi podner," but refrain because of the dust. Fifty miles ahead is Anahim Lake (named for a Chilcotin Indian chief). A hundred miles farther or through a pass in the Coast Range is the Pacific Ocean, and the town of Bella Coola, and the rock where the explorer Mackenzie scribbled: "Alexander Mackenzie, from Canada by land . . ."

8 The beer is flat by Anahim—definitely and conclusively. But we can't waste it, being unsure of where to get a further supply. I check into Anahim's one motel, and Tom takes his tent and camping equipment to the rodeo grounds and sets up shop. Then both of us go our separate, exploring ways.

9 Anahim is a village of fewer than 200 people. The stampede grounds and jackpine jungle around it are thronged with jalopies, trucks, campers, pickups and trailers. White tents glimmer in green clearings, campfires crackle at night. More than 1,000 people are encamped. The entire Chilcotin Indian tribe has arrived for its annual birthday party of booze and laughter. Carrier Indians, called "Sticks" derisively by the warlike Chilcotins, are also in attendance. Everyone is being primed or already primed with scotch, vodka, gin, rum, wine and beer, and/or the local variety of poison called "Itcha Mountain Fog" (said to have occasioned more fatalities than the last Indian war). Carl, the grocer at nearby Nimpo Lake, has 300 cases of beer.

10 The rodeo at Anahim is more than a game. It's a honing of necessary, but everyday skills; the players are reenacting the daily events of their lives. Calf- and steer-roping and bronc-busting are basic cowboy activities of the big Chilcotin and Cariboo ranches. But beyond that, it's an occasion where old friends (who may not have seen each other for months) gather to gossip, drink and discuss the business of living. And for three days in early June nearly everyone gets gloriously drunk in one big whoop-up, a concentrated and deliberate undoing of sobriety.

11 Sometimes, the Mountie corporal in charge of order tells me, there are knifings and robberies; fights are commonplace. "At the Williams Lake Stampede five people died this year." But, he hastens to add, "Three of the deaths were from natural causes."

12 The stampede ground roughly resembles a football field; it's a kind of oblong arena floored with floury grey dust, 150 yards long but not quite that wide, fenced with lodgepole pine. Spectators—tourists, Indians and local people—perch atop the fence or peer through rail-

ings. Mounties prowl the perimeter, deterrents, hopefully, to any trouble.

13 In a high tower above the cattle chutes, Slim Recknock, six feet and 200 pounds of 30-year-old cowboy, is the PA announcer. He sounds like a caller at a barn dance. When a calf is reluctant to leave the chute, Slim bellows: "Crank his tail a little."

14 A brown calf bursts from Chute No. 2, maybe 300 pounds of veal on the hoof. George Palmatier bursts after him. Grey dust explodes in a moving cloud. The big calf is ahead of him. The cowboy disappears entirely, then reemerges, his rope snaking out to snag the twisting terrified head. Rapidly securing one end of the rope to the saddle, he dismounts and follows the rope hand-over-hand to the brown calf.

15 Then it's a swift wrestling match. The idea is to get that calf down quickly, one arm around his neck, the other encircling his front leg. But the calf is reluctant. "That there's a strong calf," Slim says dryly. But George manages. Front and hind legs are roped together and Palmatier stands like an actor, arms thrown wide to take a bow from the first-day audience. The drama consumes only 18 seconds.

16 A fine grey dust begins to settle over everything. And everybody: Indians, whites, tourists, Mounties. The hot Chilcotin sun urges sweat under armpits and over foreheads, and the sweat streaks patterns in the dust. After a while you can taste dust.

17 Bareback riding looks most dangerous to me. Broncs are chosen on the basis of being the most cantankerous of the most cantankerous. The convulsing animal is supposed to be ridden for eight seconds. William Billy Boy doesn't last that long; he flies upward and downward at such speed that when he lands, the dust bomb obscures him for a period longer than the ride itself. I think: no wonder these broncs are slightly irritable, the way they're mounted in the chutes; they stand in this passageway narrow enough to keep them from turning to kick, or sink those strong yellow teeth into a rider. I did see one try to turn around in that passageway. He got stuck.

18 Dave Lewis comes from the launching pad of Chute No. 3 on a horse called Drifter, who doesn't drift much. He keeps trying to kick the sun with both hind legs; almost manages too. In a space of eight seconds Drifter scrapes his rider against the fence, rocks forward and backward, damn near stands on his head, bucks, fishtails, and does some upside-down spins for good measure. (I'm not sure what fishtailing means, but the horse knew.)

19 Lewis gets taken off by another mounted cowboy in full flight. He's done his eight long seconds. Drifter remains in orbit until he gets chased into the corral, where he stands trembling, and blessedly alone.

20 Cow milking is next: now there's something ridiculous about grown men trying to make a range cow stand still long enough to squeeze a few flying drops of milk into a beer bottle.

21 Calf-roping again: Wes Jasper misses lassoing the flying critter with his first cast, but produces a reserve rope and scores a ringer. His time is lousy, but there's some satisfaction in not failing completely, especially with your girl watching.

22 Chilcotins and whites, and maybe a few of the Sticks, drink beer in the Stockmen's Hall. The Indians tend to be in little groups off by themselves, but not entirely so. Some mix with the ranchers and cowboys: old friendships exclude racial prejudice. I drink beer with Tom Howe, some Kamloops tourists, a rancher and his wife, and an Indian named Marvin Paul. Marvin is an artist: he's just spent three weeks carving a small totem pole, for which he accepted four dollars. He is slightly drunk, and he shows me a pencil sketch of himself and I give him five bucks for it. I feel virtuous.

23 Returning from the privy, I notice an old Indian sleeping beside the steps. His face is carved black walnut and he might have posed for some of Paul Kane's 19th-century paintings. There's a western bluebird nesting in the roof's overhang, unbothered by all the noise, doing routine bluebird things. Inside the hall I say Hi Again to Marvin Paul (who is pretty far gone by now), chat with the riding's Social Credit MLA, and buy beer for Ben Belanger, one of the rodeo judges.

24 Only cowboys, sailors and a few others have a ready-made mythology with which to identify. They love the movies of John Wayne and Gary Cooper; they listen to country and western music, practically standing to attention when Wilf Carter sings *Oh, That Strawberry Roan*. But they are real-life cowboys and real-life cowboys work hard and long.

25 And the Indian cowboys have the additional picturesquity of being Indians. With a name like William Billy Boy or Sundayman Lashaway, you have a right. If it weren't for the take-home-pay, I'd much rather be Sundayman Lashaway than Al Purdy.

26 Panhandle Phillips, a local old-timer with bowed legs and beak nose, is something more than a colorful hometown boy. He figures prominently in all of Rich Hobson's three books, but mainly in *Grass*

Beyond The Mountains. He's 67, came here from the U.S. with Hobson in the mid-Thirties. The two men went out with packhorses in search of grasslands. Sixty miles north of Anahim, peering through binoculars at a small opening in the Algak Mountains, they saw the beginnings of grazing country that funneled out into an eventual ranch of four million acres. Those high grasslands belonged to the crown, and were then available at a dollar or so an acre. Four million dollars. But you didn't need to lay all that cash on the barrelhead. Anyway, the two men discovered the grass beyond the mountains, in high alpine country unknown to white men, surrounded by a dull-green jackpine world stretching more than 1,000 miles from the 52nd parallel to the Arctic tundra.

27 Talking with Panhandle Phillips is experiencing an echo from the Hobson book. I mention there are only three graves in the Anahim cemetery. Panhandle says: "People don't die up here very often." Then he looks at me out of his eye's corner to see how I'm reacting.

28 We have some trouble in finding the 10-foot-by-eight-foot cabin Panhandle and his partner built in the Thirties, then abandoned quickly when the stove smoke nearly asphyxiated them. It sits roofless and rotting in the altered landscape, and must have given him an odd feeling, this being the first time he's returned to the site. He says: "You don't get lost in this country, you just get kinda confused for two weeks." I am a bit wary at this point, anticipating another picturesque remark. He knows I'm waiting. He keeps me waiting.

29 On Saturday night Slim Recknock, the rodeo announcer, got something stuck in his throat while eating supper. His good friend, Ben Belanger, found him choking for his life near their camp. Ben whomped his friend on the back so hard Slim got mad and wanted to fight. But instead he went to the hospital, fuming a little but unable to express proper indignation. Ben took over the rodeo announcing job Sunday: the day 10-, 12- and 14-year-old cowboys replaced the adults. There was this little black dog that kept yapping after the arena livestock. After enduring the dog a few minutes, Ben announced coldly: "That dog ain't helping the cowboys at all. If he doesn't leave, I'm gonna cut his tail off—right behind the ears!"

30 Ben came to the Chilcotin from Barrie, Ontario, when he was 18, and worked as cowboy and lumberjack; he's a strapping, slim-hipped, wide-shouldered man. Several years ago Ben decided he wanted to be a writer, taught himself to string words together, then wrote for the Kamloops *Daily Sentinel.*

31 But writing's only one of his ambitions: the other is to find a green spread of high grasslands, the same way Panhandle Phillips and Rich Hobson did 40 years ago. But there isn't much good ranch country left now, what with the influx of people from outside. Ben has often taken a packtrain into the mountains over the past 12 years; he's lived on fish and bannock for up to three years. He wants to own a ranch: "You know, start small with a milk cow so she can look after her calves, and gradually build up a beef herd."

32 Despite Ben Belanger's capabilities, it seems doubtful he'll ever attain ownership of his dream ranch. In Victoria, the government has frozen sales of all crown land, reasoning that only 5% of BC's total area is arable land. It wants to take a good look even at cattle raising land, before it's sold cheaply. Several years ago on one of his packtrain expeditions Ben located 1,280 acres of promising land, and stayed two summers to investigate water and grass potential. When he applied to Victoria for the right to purchase, he was turned down. And this was long before the land freeze. Every time he has applied during the past 12 years, exactly the same thing has happened: not always a flat no, but no, nonetheless.

33 "I'm not the only one," he says grimly. "A friend of mine, Ken Karrens, leased 320 acres of crown land some time back. The government told him to go ahead with improvements, so he drained some meadows, built a cabin, bought a Cat, spent quite a chunk of money. Then they raised his lease fee 800%, and finally took the land away from him altogether. Ken went to Victoria raging mad, and got thrown out of the Parliament Buildings."

34 Ben is defiant about the whole situation. He is now squatting on some land near Redstone and doesn't care who knows it.

35 The rodeo's last day was Sunday, with Ben Belanger announcing, and the crowd slightly smaller. Jack Palmatier won the three-hundred dollar saddle as best all-around cowboy, the most important award. On Monday morning the stampede grounds were deserted, dust settled: Panhandle Phillips, Lester Dorsey and William Billy Boy gone back to upland meadows to cut their winter hay. It seems an almost empty world, bright sun shining, the distant Itcha and Algak ranges snow-capped and silent.

36 Up in those high mountains there are landslides sometimes as sun loosens the binding blanket of snow. In the 60-below Chilcotin winter trees freeze with loud explosions, lakes and rivers crack and roar. Things that happen there, small deaths and the birth of spring—these

are unknown unwritten local history in which the human animals are not participants. Moose and grizzlies play their deadly game of hide-and-seek in the high country. Great wolves run in packs farther north. As we're getting ready to drive out, Tom and I are silent. The land itself overshadows everything else, a cold empire of mountains.

Al Purdy, "Boozy Saddles," *Maclean's* (May, 1975), pp. 78-80. (With revisions made by the author for the present text.)

Questions

1. **Subject**
   Purdy's story can be seen not only as the narration of a particular series of incidents that he experienced at first hand but also as an attempt to capture in prose a particular way of life. Explain.
2. **Audience**
   Explain why a North-American audience would have an easier time understanding and appreciating this story than an English-speaking European audience.
3. **Purpose**
   Comment on the way of life that is being described and indicate how description aids the author in his purpose.
4. **Structure and Style**
   (a) Comment on the way in which Purdy's diction helps establish the atmosphere of the essay.
   (b) More specifically, comment on how the diction in paragraphs 15 to 22 helps create a sense of action.
   (c) Comment on the effectiveness of the last paragraph. How does it suggest that a particular world has passed out of existence?

5 *Description*

Introduction to the Mode

In general, in university or college writing, description, like narration, will come into play largely in the service of some other mode. Of course, this does not mean that description cannot stand on its own. Character sketches and technical descriptions are types of writing that need not form part of a larger context—though they normally do. Rarely is there such a thing as a descriptive passage that attains total objectivity. This is because every author will see the same scene with different eyes, will bring a different social, cultural, and sometimes even artistic background to bear on what is being described. Notice for example, the following description written by the Group of Seven artist A.Y. Jackson:

> A few days later, on 22nd August, we were four miles off Bathurst Island. It was snowing. Just before we rounded Cape Cockburn we ran for several miles alongside a floe of polar ice which we followed as though it were a canal bank. It was the largest ice floe Falke had ever seen. It was old, worn, and full of hollows filled with pools of fresh water which looked blue-green. We dubbed it the Harris ice pan. Up to that time we had not found anything named "Harris" in the Arctic. We got about halfway between Bathurst and Byam Martin Islands, where we were brought to a halt as there appeared to be no more open water. At midnight the landscape looked like an endless prairie covered with snow. Little pools of water here and there reflected the sun glow; to the east, the coast of Bathurst was blotted out by an approaching snow squall.

A.Y. Jackson, *A Painter's Country* (Toronto: Clarke Irwin, 1958), pp. 130-31.

On the surface, this passage looks very much like an objective description of part of an Arctic voyage. We may be tempted to think that Jackson describes this scene very much as anyone else might. But notice how the personal and subjective do, nevertheless, find a place in this otherwise quite neutral and unspectacular description. In the third sentence of the passage Jackson describes the polar ice as if "it were a canal bank." This simile is a striking one and certainly not one that would come to the mind of just anyone seeing the same scene as Jackson. The second example is even more personal. Near the end of the passage Jackson dares to wax poetical and describes the landscape as "an endless prairie, covered with snow." In this sentence Jackson brings his painter's eye to the frozen Arctic and through this very personal view of what he sees emphasizes the size and apparent relentlessness of the Arctic landscape. Neatly tucked into this ostensibly objective description, then, are two examples of highly personal "seeing."

One can, of course, find descriptive passages where description and authorial comment or meditation on it is more obviously highlighted. In the following passage, try to determine how Ludwig moves beyond Jackson not only in descriptive vividness, but also in the way in which he turns the scene over in his mind:

> Under canopies, in the few places one may sit and nurse a soft drink or beer without ransoming away an arm and a leg, the older folks stake claims to a seat, sip slowly, sagged and wilted. Arm in arm, leather-jacketed and blue-jeaned couples, parties, gangs, sweep through the crowd, in a great hurry to do it all before the chuckwagon horses change back to mice. Anyone dreaming of "one big break" must make his hit in the next few hours. So it's *hurry, hurry, hurry scurry,* the rhythm on the midway, *click shuffle, scrape curse* in the casino, while in easy contrast, the young people space themselves out in front of the Sun Tree, make one joint service a dozen unhurried smokers while tired rock music ekes out its wobbly decibels. From time to time a pot-fogged dreamer floats off in the direction of food and foodlines—lines and lines here as elsewhere, sullen lines, giggly lines, crying lines (where the children wait for their last Stampede ride). The masses mass to pay out what was saved from bread to spend on circuses.

Jack Ludwig, "Get an Outfit, Be a Cowboy," *Maclean's* (July, 1975), p. 24.

What one notices in this passage is not only a plethora of vivid and sometimes eccentric description, but an authorial commentary on the scene—an attitude if you like—issuing from the description itself. In other words, the author's careful choice of descriptive words lets us know how he responds to what he is describing.

The descriptive writer's greatest aid in achieving the desired end is an appeal to the reader's senses. Without this appeal, the notion of making a place or scene or event come to life on the page is meaningless. We live in and by our senses. Consider how often we use the following: "What does he/she/it look like?" "How does it taste?" "Does it feel good?" "What's that smell?" "Did you hear that?" These questions reflect how common primary sense experience is for us—to distance ourselves from the sensuous domain is to enter the realm of abstraction. Consequently, the writer who appeals to the reader's senses is appealing directly to the reader's experience. The writer of effective descriptions will involve as many or as few of the senses as are necessary to the impression being created.

Though we normally think of description as dealing with persons, places, or things external to us, we should not forget that we can also present our internal life—our feelings, emotions, thoughts—powerfully through description as well. Consider the following description of a train trip on Canada's "Rapido."

> ...4:45 p.m., sharp, the station moves away from us...leaving me exposed sudden to the body of my city...out the back corner of my eye that becalmed Beaux-Arts bulk, rising like a series of improved Buckingham Palaces piled atop each other—the Royal York, could only be she
>
> the long slit unended of Yonge Street—like all our streets—dissolved only by infinity
>
> with that wedding-cake turn-of-the-century prestige bank at the lower left-hand corner—Front Street corner: a kind of gaudy bodyguard for the longeststreetintheworldthatisYongestreet ending only in our Ontario Lake District. Bank of Montreal, at that!
>
> with its back square upon me, the squat cube of our beer baron's art centre: O'Keefe
>
> overtopping all these, the soft-nosed phallicity of Bank of Commerce—circumspect, uncircumcised—32 stories of Canadian self-satisfaction
>
> the new National Trust tower, well below
>
> & below again, prickly up these closed commercial shops, the spired incisions of the old City of Churches—Saint James & Michael & Metropole

Scott Symons, from *Place d'Armes* (Toronto: McClelland and Stewart, 1967), p. 8.

In this passage Symons brings the various scenes that pass him by to life. He does this by creating a sense of speed in his prose (simulating the movement of the train), and by using descriptive imagery that gives a visual excitement to the scene. The description is highly idiosyncratic; the images are unusual; the pace of the passage rapid. The description in this passage captures the author's feeling for what he sees; the emotional impact of the entire scene is strong for him as he passes by it bit by bit. Not only do we discover the author's feelings for what he sees, but we ourselves are treated to a "new" view of a relatively old city. In short, in this passage Symons removes the veil of familiarity for us while at the same time allowing us to experience and "feel" the scenes that he passes.

The three quoted passages are obviously very different and have different ends in view. It is of primary importance for writers of description to know where they stand at all times—both mentally, in terms of attitude, and physically, in terms of location. In the Jackson passage, the author's physical location is a boat in the Arctic. What he describes rather sparingly are the scenes of the Arctic landscape that he sees from his vantage point. And his mental attitude reflects this touring stance: he describes scenes clearly, and on two occasions quite vividly, but he neither dwells on them nor probes them for some hidden significance. His purpose is to give a brief description of a scene, and he remains securely on the surface of it. To present detailed descriptions of his own reactions and to launch into political and cultural meditations or diatribes would be to direct attention away from the scene and toward himself, the observer. We would have to question this confusion of attitude or stance.

The Symons passage goes to the other extreme. The author's physical location is a train. From his seat in a rapidly moving train he describes the scenes of Toronto life as he passes by them. But the nature of his description sets it apart from the largely "objective" stance that Jackson takes. Perhaps all of us have had the experience of sitting in a train observing the world. But none of us would describe it in the highly personal and eccentric way that Symons does. Clearly Symons wants us to "re-see" a site that might already be familiar to us; he also wants us to understand how he feels about it. The scene, then, becomes the occasion for allowing us to learn more about the author's attitudes; the description of the scene is not an end in itself.

Coming between these two passages is Ludwig's. Ludwig is obviously more interested than Jackson in letting us know how *he* feels about what he sees. But his description is clearly not as impressionistic as that of Symons. Like Jackson, he wants us to be aware of the scene; however, unlike Symons, he does not treat the scene simply as a point of departure for the presentation of his own highly personal reflections on it.

In light of what we have just said, it is important to note that many discussions of descriptive writing speak of a spectrum stretching from objective description at one end to subjective at the other. Regularly we are told that objective description leans toward the scientific mode, presenting only the facts about what is measurably there, while subjective description concerns itself with the emotions, with our personal perceptions and preferences. Yet the objectivity/subjectivity polarity begs questions. So-called objective descriptions cannot help but be selective. Authors must leave some things out, and their choices express personal judgments. Similarly, in the supposedly emotional/personal subjective description there is, in good prose at any rate, an attitude or stance presented which reflects substantial reasoning and so a certain authorial detachment.

For our purposes, a more useful distinction is between telling and showing, always keeping in mind that in most cases there is mingling and overlap. Descriptions that tell about, rather than show, the qualities of the subject in question are most useful in expository writing where explanation or overview is needed. The author keeps a certain distance from the item being described because there is usually a larger context of thought into which the description fits. The distance prevents the description from running away with the whole piece. In the following passage Ken Dryden describes the kind of heroism that is all too regularly imposed on the star hockey player. Dryden's point is that this heroic stature that many attain is the result of playing a game:

> It is the kind of special treatment we have grown accustomed to, and enjoy. We have been *special* for most of our lives. It began with hockey, with names and faces in local papers as teenagers, with hockey jackets that only the best players on the best teams wore, with parents who competed not so quietly on the side. It will end with hockey. But in between, the longer and better we play, the more all-encompassing the treatment becomes, the more hockey seems irrelevant to it. For we are special, *period*. Others understand that—*they know.* We know. They give, easily and naturally: slippers, sweaters, plant holders, mitts, baby blankets, baby clothes knit and sent in the mail; paintings, carvings, etchings, sculptures in clay, metal or papier mâché; shirts, slacks, coats, suits, ties, underwear; cars, carpets, sofas, chairs, refrigerators, beds, washers, dryers, stoves, TVs, stereos, at cost or no cost at all. A hundred letters a week, more than 3,000 letters a year—"You're the best," all but a few of them say. On the street, in restaurants and theaters, you are pointed out, pointed at, talked about like the weather. Your picture is hung from a boy's bedroom wall, appears in magazines and newspapers, on radio and TV; hockey cards, posters, T-shirts, and curios, everywhere, anywhere, name, face, thousands of times, flashed to an audience that waves into TV cameras, that writes to editors to have proud yellowed clippings in their wallets.

Ken Dryden, *The Game* (Toronto: Macmillan of Canada, 1983), pp. 158-159.

In this passage, Dryden is talking about hockey heroism and how it is attained. The passage, although important for the description of how heroism is in some measure forced on players, is nevertheless part of a larger case that Ken Dryden is making about the game of hockey itself. The movement of the piece is not toward the particular, but the general—Dryden is not discussing a specific hero but heroism in general as it applies to hockey.

Descriptions that *show* the qualities of their subject tend to move the other way, from the general to the particular. Call to mind again the Scott Symons passage quoted above. There we are not concerned with a general reaction to a scene by a representative human being; rather we are interested in the particular—some might even say peculiar—reaction of Symons himself. In this example, the author must get close to the scene to convey the details that will make this scene live. We get a greater range of diction and syntax in Symons' passage as he tries to convey the experience that *he* is having. The difference lies there: "telling" helps the author convey ideas (in Dryden's case, how hockey players come to think of themselves as heroes); "showing" helps the author convey experiences (in Symons's case, his "vision" of Toronto from a moving train).

Arrangement Strategies

Whatever else descriptive authors do, they must be sure to include only those features that contribute to the dominant impression the description is meant to achieve. All elements must work toward this impression, and until you know what impression you want to create, you do not know what your organization or arrangement should be; you do not know where you stand. Once you are sure of the impression you are after you have a number of possible principles of arrangement to choose from.

Deductive and Inductive Arrangement

As with narration, you may develop your descriptive paragraphs deductively or inductively. All of the passages quoted in this chapter proceed deductively, opening with a general statement which is then fleshed out with descriptive sentences. Both methods have much to recommend them and your choice of which to follow will depend largely on the effect you want to create. Deductive development is appropriate when you want to make the main point up front and flesh it out in what follows. Inductive development, by holding the main point or summary statement to the end, allows and, in fact, forces the reader to concentrate on the details as they are presented.

Spatial Arrangement

Spatial arrangement is a useful way to keep the reader oriented at all times. For example, you may describe an object from front to back, side to side, top to bottom, or background to foreground. You may go from wall to wall, room to room, or street to street in a spatial arrangement. Notice how in the Symons passage, the author moves from building to building.

Temporal Arrangement

A temporal arrangement allows you to describe something as it changes (or does not change) over time. Whether your span is seconds or eons, the passing of time provides a natural principle of organization. Take, for instance, the Dryden passage. Dryden focuses on when the special treatment accorded sports figures began, when it will end, and what comes in between. The manifestations of heroism described in the passage are ones that occur again and again. We get a sense that the ritual of hockey-hero worship, like all rituals, is repetitive and never-ending. The final phrase "thousands of times" captures the feeling of constant repetition.

Thematic Arrangement

Thematic organization emphasizes the dominant impression, often by means of repetition. In the Ludwig passage, notice how many expressions reiterate the impression created by words such as "sagged" and "wilted."

Comparative Arrangement

A final principle of arrangement that an author can take advantage of is arrangement by comparison. Symons, for example, as well as proceeding spatially, also makes use of metaphors and similes to enliven the description that he is writing. Figures of speech extend the range of experience a description covers and so increase the readership to which it can appeal. They also ignite our imagination and so help us to bring the subject to life.

Hands On: Reading

Exercise

Actively read the following passage paying particular attention to the subject, audience, and purpose of the piece. As you consider the essay, think about some of the aspects and strategies of description outlined in this chapter and relate them to the essay's subject, audience, and purpose. To refresh your memory, some of the main points made in this chapter were as follows:

1. The differences between subjective and objective description.
2. The differences between description as an end in itself and description in the service of other types of writing.
3. The types of descriptive organization.

Once you have actively read the essay, write a summary of it and response to it.

FARLEY MOWAT

THE COMING OF THE DEER

From our vantage point all of this achromatic world lay sombrely below us as we waited for the coming of the deer. We had not long to wait. Franz caught my arm and pointed to the convoluted slopes of the distant southern hills, and I could just discern a line of motion. It seemed to me that the slopes were sliding gently downward to the bay, as if the innumerable boulders that protruded from the hills had suddenly been set adrift to roll in slow motion down upon the ice. I watched intently, not certain whether the sun's glare had begun to affect my eyes so that they played fool tricks on me. Then the slow avalanches reached the far shore and debouched over the bay. I tried to count the little dots. Ten, fifty, a hundred, three hundred—and I gave up. In broken twisted lines, in bunches and beaded ropes, the deer streamed out on to the ice until they were moving north across a front of several miles.

From that distance they barely seemed to move, and yet in a few minutes they had reached the centre of the bay and had begun to take on shape. I had binoculars, but in my preoccupation with the spectacle below I had not thought to use them. Now I lifted the glasses to my eyes. The long skeins dissolved at once into endless rows of deer, each following upon the footsteps of the animals ahead. Here and there along the lines a yearling kept its place beside a mother who was swollen with the new fawn she carried. There were no bucks. All these animals were does, all pregnant, all driving inexorably towards the north and the flat plains where they would soon give birth.

The leaders reached our shore and began the ascent, but across the bay the avalanche continued and grew heavier. The surface of the bay, for six miles east and west, had become one undulating mass of animals, and still they came.

Without hurry, but without pause, unthinking, but directly driven, they filed down to the ice and, following the tracks of those who had crossed first, made for our shore. Highways began to grow. The black ice was pounded and shattered until it again became white with broken crystals. The broad roads stretched across the bay, multiplied, grew into one another until at length they disappeared and the whole sweep of ice was one great road.

The herds were swelling past our look-out now. Ten paces from us, five, then we were forced to stand and wave our arms to avoid being trampled on. The does gazed briefly and incuriously at us, swung a few feet away and passed on to the north without altering their gait.

Hours passed like minutes. The flow continued at an unbroken level until the sun stood poised on the horizon's rim. And I became slowly conscious of a great apathy. Life, my life and that of Franz, of all living things I knew, seemed to have become meaningless. For here was life on such a scale that it was beyond all comprehension. It numbed my mind and left me feeling as if the inanimate world had been saturated with a reckless prodigality in that sacred and precious thing called life. I thought of the twelve deer slaughtered on the banks of Windy River and I no longer felt horror or disgust. I felt nothing for the dead who were drowned beyond memory in this living flow of blood that swept across the plains.

It was nearly dusk when we roused ourselves. We walked silently to the sled and I felt a little sick. I began to doubt the reality of the vision I had seen. The ice had begun to freeze as the sun went down and the sled bumped so wickedly over the endless hoofprints that I was forced to run along behind it. A dozen times we passed close to a late herd of deer and each time the dogs, in defiance of Franz, lunged in pursuit and could be halted only when we overturned the sled to hold them back. There was no doubt about it—the vision had been real.

Farley Mowat, *People of the Deer* (Toronto: McClelland and Stewart Ltd., revised ed. 1975), pp. 70-72.

Hands On: Reading into Writing

The following assignment deals with writing in the descriptive mode. The subject is nostalgia.

Assignment

1. Actively read the following four descriptive essays on various aspects of nostalgia.
2. Answer the questions appended to each essay. Your careful responses to these questions should act as a spur to your thought and so should assist you when you complete the reading workbook entry.

3. Complete a reading workbook entry for each essay:
   (a) Comment on subject, audience, and purpose.
   (b) Identify thesis statement, topic sentence, or controlling idea.
   (c) Comment on developmental strategies.
   (d) Prepare an outline.
   (e) Write a summary.
   (f) Write a response, of at least one hundred words.
4. Once you have finished dealing with the readings on an individual basis, you will have at least four hundred words of informed response on the subject of nostalgia. This body of material will serve as the basis for your own *descriptive* essay on the subject, which should consist of three or four double-spaced typewritten pages. Remember what has been mentioned time and again in this book: the techniques that you learn as you actively read will be the ones that you put to good use when you write your own essay.
   (a) Examine your responses.
   (b) Develop a workable topic in view of your subject, audience, and purpose.
   (c) Determine effective developmental strategies.
   (d) Develop a thesis statement.
   (e) Develop an outline.
   (f) Write a first draft.
   (g) Revise.

ROBERT THOMAS ALLEN

WHERE WOMEN FEARED TO TREAD

1 Whenever I come across a magazine with a woman smiling at me confidently from the cover over some title like *Why I'll Soon Show Some Men Slobs That I Can Play Pro Hockey,* I wish her luck and head for one of the few places left where I know I won't run into her, like a barbershop I've gone to for 20 years where the only reminder of women is a 1949 calendar for AC spark plugs with a picture of a pink, plump girl in a veil sitting on the moon.

2 It's a warm and friendly cave with a green linoleum floor and a pleasant aroma of cigar smoke and hair tonic, where the men are all polite to one another and protect one another from unpleasant thoughts, like growing old. "You gotta lotsa dark hair yet," the barber

will say into the mirror to a customer, holding up maybe three hairs. The men never talk about women. They talk about other men, with admiration: "That guy, he's a got muscles on his neck bigger than my legs," the barber will say, a remark you wouldn't hear at a women's meeting in a hundred years. He's still a bit confused about the language, and apparently about Canadians, and pronounces "muscles" so that it sounds like "Molson's," which makes it even better. When some oldtimer gets up from the chair, the barber takes a step backwards to get a better view of this fine specimen of male magnificence, and the shoeshine man stops sweeping the floor and stands with his push broom at "Present Arms!" There's an atmosphere of kindness even from youths who occasionally get in there by mistake, thinking it's a hairstylist's. One time an old fellow got an awful kink in his back when he got up from having a shave and just kept saying cheerfully to the ceiling, "I'll be all right in a minute," while two customers helped him to a chair, holding him up by the elbows and saying things like, "You won't be able to play polo for a day or two," and a young guy called out encouragingly, "All you need is a good massage, pop." "By god, I think you're right, sonny," the old gent said, and five minutes later, his kink gone, he headed out the door into the sunshine of at least one more lovely day.

3 I've got favorite routes around an old part of town with pie-shaped buildings that were built by men for men when they were the only people working downtown, except for a few women whom, in my youth, men had just stopped calling "typewriters"—places with solid marble-topped counters and washrooms with urinals 6 feet high that a man can disappear into like a shy woodland creature, and restaurants where you usually find nothing but men who all agree with one another and listen to one another with fascination.

4 "That's an interesting point, Harry," a man will say, hands cupped around his pipe, peering at some speaker sideways through the smoke, clearly thinking the speaker is a fine fellow. They lean forward and ask one another how to spell their names. "Do you spell that with a "C," a man will say, waiting with real interest for the reply, and they exchange business cards. They've forgotten all about women, and if one comes in, they watch her suspiciously, like the day a woman in a red pantsuit came in with a baby in a basket. The men peered into the basket silently as she passed, as if suddenly reminded of something. Now and then when a newcomer, perhaps wearing a blue blazer and some medals for lawn bowling, comes in and doesn't

know the system of getting food, other men help him, and it's a common sight to see a man who may be president of an insurance company showing a stranger how to get the rolls or, pipe in one hand and bread tongs in the other, putting rolls on some new boy's plate, a nice gesture that you never see in mixed company. In a cafeteria I ate at the other day, I looked at a plate of beans and wieners and asked a woman if that was her order. She just glared at me as if she knew some Woman of the Year in Biochemistry would soon be making men out of soybeans, gave a little shake of her head and shunted my tray along the rails like a cue ball.

5 A lot of the old places have disappeared. The editorial offices of this magazine are over the site of one of them—McConkey's Lunch—where they used to serve what they called a businessmen's lunch of lamb stew for 35 cents and where at noon you could see two rows of men facing one another, all eating with their hats on, sitting in chairs that had surfaces about the size of a TV tray attached to them, like lecture-room desks.

6 Sometimes I look in the window of a copying-machine place that used to be a restaurant, where two or three times a week I'd sit at a big round table full of men I worked with, mostly advertising space salesmen, who all understood one another and knew one another so well they had almost eliminated speech. They'd allow long silences that in a group of women would have only meant they'd all had a fight, but here meant only that they were trying not to face the thought of going back to work. Some men sat sideways, holding their topcoats ready to go, coming out with no thought more profound than, "I wonder how long a man could live on fish." When anybody arrived, it was with a set little ritual, like a spear-sharpening ceremony. Nobody spoke to him and he didn't look at the other men. As he pulled up a chair he kept looking out the front window, as if at some unusual sight. He kept on looking over his friends' heads, rubbed his hands, then pressed his nose into his knuckles and finally looked sideways at some guy's vest and said something like, "Thought you were going to be in Winnipeg this week."

7 I can still hear conversations like this in an old-style hardware store near my place, where men can move quietly among axe handles and coils of rope, like grouse. A long speech in this place is, "Takes an 8-inch slag bolt," or "She'll take about a pound of tile grout." Or a clerk will say, "Finding what you want, Chief?" clinging to the tradition of men giving one another honorary titles, like "Colonel" or

"Governor" or "Captain." A clerk and a customer can stand side by side looking at something as if they could stand there all day—or all year—as free of vibes as two pieces of putty, the customer maybe picking tension screws out of the compartments of a metal tray, which he holds just below his chin, and dropping them back into the tray with a sound that reminds me of my pop's cellar workbench, where he used to disappear every night right after supper. One day a woman came into this store and called, "Is anybody here?" apparently thinking everyone had died, or gone fishing to Baffin Island, although there were men there behind shelves of nails, looking at saws and making gouging motions with Swedish chisels.

8 Another place I go is a men's tailoring shop that is still holding out, with everything but moats and drawbridges, against the times and the new men's stores with names like Ziggy's Let It All Hang Out Shop. It's oak-panelled and smells of shoe polish and tweed and the fitting rooms are behind a Gothic arch with a crest over it with one of those mottos in Latin like, "Trust Only in Sharp Points," and the salesmen take pride in little courtly graces no matter how long it is since you were last in. "Let me have that button sewn on before it falls off," a salesman will say, adding, "Our workroom couldn't have sewn that on properly," pretending he doesn't know you've worn the same suit since 1964. If you mention something about putting on a little weight when the fitter is looking at the tape measure, he will stand sideways and stick his stomach out and slap it just to show you everyone is sagging in the same place. I thought of him one day recently when I went into a big discount store and a woman came toward me in the men's suit department, gave me one quick unemotional look, said something like "44 short" or "stubby-legged fat" and began rummaging through some suits at the end of the rack.

9 I don't want women to have unequal rights in these places—I want them to keep out of them. They have enough places where they can go. A woman peered at me the other day out of a *poolroom.* I've run into this woman, or her sister, in a men's underwear department, and worse, in a drugstore owned by a man who's worn carpet slippers ever since I was a kid and who always, if there was a woman customer within earshot, came out from around the counter, listened to my problems, head bowed, the two of us looking as if we were in prayer, and said quietly he got the same thing himself when he'd been lifting stones at the cottage. He'd whisper, "Try these," and, like a pusher, hand me something down around knee level. The last time I

went there the place had changed hands and a woman of about 50 in a blue smock listened to me describe the agony I was going through as if her thoughts were far away, like on six different delivery rooms, and when I'd finished she kept on looking at me as if she thought I'd been kidding, then tossed me a tube and said, "What else?"

10 I know all this is the result of growing up in an age when there were sharp distinctions between the worlds of men and women, either of which to a kid could look better than the other at any given time. When I got into a school-yard fight and lost, spectacularly, I didn't want to see anyone for a week who didn't cook and crochet, but most times I wanted to be with the men of our neighborhood.

11 Now and then I had to go shopping with my mother. She used to take me with her into places like Madame Wurm's Ladies' Wear and I used to get inside those circular racks and run until the dresses all stood out straight. I remember one piece-goods store where the owner, a Mr. Byers, used to watch me spinning stools as if he'd like to stuff me down between a couple of bolts of buckram. But my pop used to take me to magnificent places where the men all wore dirty white canvas aprons darkened with iron filings and stained with the rouge they used for polishing spoons and where pulleys and drive belts whirred and the pale winter sun came through dirty glass windows reinforced with chicken wire, and men dipped things into vats of muriatic acid that hissed and made wonderful choking stinks. There were men's places on the street, too, like the bottom of the gardens down by the back fence where the fathers of the neighborhood gathered on Saturday mornings to carry out fascinating projects. The wooden garages were a sort of early motor-age equivalent of a waterfront, with Fords and Gray-Dorts being careened—barnacles of carbons scraped off them in preparation for voyages to strange far-off places, like Kingston. I could visit Mr. Middleton's stable in the lane, in which lived the only horse left in our district, a gelding that ordinarily was as quiet as a spaniel but occasionally went berserk from too much domesticity, an exhilarating event with women giving little screams and men shouting and wheels scraping sideways and the sound of thumping hooves and jingling harness when the horse swerved up on to front lawns with the whites of his eyes showing, driving his hooves into flower beds.

12 Regularly, once or twice every summer, my pop took my brother and me fishing. We'd go by train, about 40 miles, and come home sitting in the smoker, a lovely plush cubbyhole with spittoons, where

men with ashes on their vests sat knee to knee telling of their adventures in the great world that was waiting for you when you grew up and got your own show on the road, as the train rocked through the night past misty cedar swamps and snake fences and Holsteins. Every now and then the conductor would stop and lean into the smoker, his hands on top of the doorway, and hang there swaying and listening to the talk.

13 Some of these men's places were doomed by changing times, and probably most of them deserved it, like one restaurant I used to go to where the men all floated upward on the elevator one floor higher than where women were allowed to eat—to a place called the Men's Mezzanine. But whenever I read how "Wendy went to work and Bob stayed home and kept house," I think of places like that with pleasure. There's no doubt about it, they were closed clubs, and probably immoral on sociological grounds, like a club I still occasionally get invited to for lunch where the men sit in the sun in what used to be the living room of an old brick mansion, looking out on a sumac tree and weedy back yard, everything going to seed, the members pouring one another beers and making appointments. "I'd like to talk to you a minute when you get a chance, George," a man says, bending over and tapping some member's bony knee, like someone out of Galsworthy—say, a baronet wanting to talk to his lawyer about a slander suit. It's all a bit staged, but there's a kind of stuffy conviviality about the place all the same.

14 There's nothing wrong with some purely male qualities—a tendency to horseplay, for instance. A while ago I ran into a man named Harvey who I'd begun working with in an advertising office soon after leaving high school but hadn't seen for years. We stood on the curb, jingling the change in our pockets, looking across the street at a Chinese poultry store as if 25 or 30 years of our lives hadn't happened. At one point, after we'd made a few remarks about the heavy traffic, he said, "You know, I'm an extremely wealthy man." He stated it without pride, or apology, but just as an interesting fact, the way he would have said years ago that he'd found a place where he could eat for a quarter. It didn't matter; I was thinking of the day someone came into the layout room and said the boss, a man named Bedford, wanted him, and in a purely male moment of spontaneous clowning he stood up and yelled, "YOU GO BACK AND TELL CHARLIE BEDFORD I CAN LICK HIM," just as Mr. Bedford, a short, harrassed man with yellow hair, who had changed his mind and followed the

messenger to the layout room, came in through the swinging doors. "For God's sake, Harvey," he said, and just kept on going past Harvey with a long-suffering, yet somehow, understanding expression on his face that I wish now could have been preserved—along with a lot of other historic male landmarks.

Robert Thomas Allen, "Where Women Feared to Tread," *The Canadian*, 28 August, 1976, pp. 8, 10.

Questions

1. **Subject**
   In this essay, the author seems to be writing about the gradual and inevitable passing of an era. What era is he writing about and how do we know it is passing? Why is the word "nostalgic" appropriate to his treatment of this era?
2. **Audience**
   By referring specifically to passages within the essay, speculate on the audience to whom this piece is directed. Do you feel that the tone of the essay might anger or alienate a particular category of reader?
3. **Purpose**
   Comment on how vivid descriptions in this essay help the author attain his purpose, namely the calling up of a particular cultural mythology.
4. **Structure and Style**
   (a) This essay is divided into two parts. Where does part 2 begin? How does its content differ from part 1?
   (b) Comment on how the author's movements through various male haunts in part 1 help maintain the structural integrity of the essay.
   (c) Why is the use of the word "cave" to describe the barbershop (paragraph 2) appropriate? Cite other words and phrases in this essay that help give it its particular tone.

PIERRE BERTON

FLOATING DOWN THE YUKON

1 No words of mine could ever prepare my children for the magic of the Yukon River and no words on paper, or photographs, either, can really capture it. There is an allure here that defies description. The Yukon gets under your skin as no other part of this country can; it has been under mine for more than 50 years.

2 Part of the magic, I suppose, is the feeling that the river is eternal. I remember one particular sunlit day when we all sensed this. We had fastened the rafts together and were drifting at about five miles an hour beneath the wooded banks and between the islands, talking, singing, reading or simply watching the dark scroll of the forest unwind. Somebody spotted a bald eagle in the sky and then two cow moose appeared in a slough on our left. Later we happened upon two grizzlies scampering up a hillside. It was impressed upon us that this was the way the river had always been and, hopefully, always would be. I doubt at that moment if there was another human being within 50 miles. For the Yukon valley is almost as empty of life today as it was when the first explorers slipped down its channel from Lake Bennett to Norton Sound on the Bering Sea; it must look today just about as it did then. The high clay banks have been spared the ravages of civilization; the swallows still nest there by the tens of thousands. The forbidding cliffs of black basalt still run for miles on the right side of the river north of the Pelly's mouth; nobody has drilled into them or painted them or raped them with a rockcrusher. The green islands in the channels are devoid of billboards. The crystal streams that tumble down the wooded gulches are free of pollution. The few axe marks on the trees are half a century old; no one has bothered to log the Yukon valley. The blue hills roll off into the mists of the horizon, ridge upon ridge, unmarred and unscarred. The river cuts its serpentine pathway through them, sometimes squeezing narrowly between rocks of shattered conglomerate, sometimes spreading itself thinly over tawny meadows, changing from mile to mile yet never changing from decade to decade in its unrelenting journey to the sea.

3 It is ironic that when I was young and living on the banks of the Yukon, I hungered for cities I had never seen in the same way that today's youth hungers for a wilderness experience they have never known. Today our communion with the wild comes in fits and starts through a few square feet of cottage lakefront or a brief encounter with an untrammeled corner of a national park. But the Yukon experience is total. You can camp anywhere and be sure no one else will camp beside you. You can drift for days without encountering a soul. You can seize and keep an island for your own.

4 For 11 days we lived on the Yukon, protected from the intrusion of the world. We read no newspapers and heard no radio. We cooked fresh Yukon salmon over hot coals and fried grayling newly pulled

from the river. Our food was seasoned with wild onions and our liquor was mixed with the juice of cranberries gathered on the spot. On several occasions, at lunchtime, we picked our dessert from nearby raspberry bushes. Once we passed an Indian smoking salmon on a rack by the bank; the resultant hors d'oeuvre was better than any served by a three-star restaurant. So were the mushrooms gathered in our hats and deep fried instantly in the pan.

5 Yet, in the midst of this wilderness, we were always conscious of the passing of man and the presence of history. Wherever we camped we were made aware of the river's gaudy past and this served to enrich our journey; an old gangplank rotting in the weeds; the remains of a wood cart rusting in the willows; the hull of the old stern-wheeler Klondike, outlined beneath the ripples below a slide of black clay; the Evelyn, her paint long since peeled away, sitting on the ways at Shipyard Island near the Teslin's mouth; a skeletal gold dredge half submerged just past Dutch Bluff; pink insulators wired to the trees marking the original Dawson telegraph line; an abandoned church vestry crammed with missionary tracts from 1900; empty trading posts, police stations, telegraph offices, mission houses and schools; old cabins by the score, some of them tottering on the lip of the eroding riverbank; old stumps, old kettles, old frying pans, old picks and shovels and, of course, old graves. Men were here once; now they are gone; the river goes on.

6 The ghost villages—there are 16 of them between Whitehorse and Dawson—contribute to the feeling of timelessness. In many of these, delphinium and Arctic poppy have escaped the neat confines of long-forgotten gardens and run wild through patches of fireweed and yellow arnica. Abandoned bedsteads poke up through the waving foxtails. The bright berries and shiny leaves of kinnikinnick blur the edges of broken machinery. Junk has been transformed into artifacts.

7 But old memories haunt certain cabins; Joe Ladue's crumbling trading post can still be found on Ogilvie Island; it was from here that Robert Henderson embarked in 1896 on the journey that led to the Klondike strike. The orderly room of the Yukon Field Force has been preserved at Selkirk as a reminder of the time when Ottawa felt the need of troops in the Yukon to save the territory from the Americans. At Yukon Crossing we explored the remains of a roadhouse where my mother had stayed in 1910 during a memorable week-long journey in an open stage coach in the dead of winter. And opposite Kirkman Bar there was an abandoned cabin where a colorful French Canadian

named Laderoute once ran a river post office. He wore gold earrings and kept a herd of pet goats that followed him around like dogs and I can still remember a certain June day in 1926 when an earlier family of Bertons, making this same river journey, sat down at his table to a luncheon of porcupine stew. I was only six at the time but the flavor, hot and gamy, still comes back to me.

8 Thirty years after that first river trip, my mother wrote these words: "...the memory of those lazy days, drifting with the current through that silent, wild country, with my children young and my husband in his prime, has never left me and remains as vivid and as sharp as if it all happened a week ago. Wishing is futile, I know, but I would give a great deal to be able to do it all again."

9 And so would I, and so, I think, would my children. No doubt they will have that chance, as I had—unless we spoil the Yukon country, too, with hydro dams, pipelines and asphalt.

Pierre Berton, "Floating Down the Yukon," *Maclean's* (December, 1972), pp. 37, 39, 76.

Questions

1. **Subject**
   Comment on the way in which the author plays past against present—history against our own world—in this essay. In what way is Berton's trip a deeply spiritual odyssey for him?
2. **Audience**
   Some writers maintain that hidden within all people is a strong need to experience, if only vicariously, the beauties of the pastoral world. In what way does Pierre Berton appeal to this universal need in his audience?
3. **Purpose**
   In the second sentence of the essay, the author suggests that in some ways it is impossible to describe what he is about to describe ("There is an allure here that defies descripton."). If it is the author's purpose to try and capture this "allure" in his writing, do you think that his descriptive techniques help him in this endeavour?
4. **Structure and Style**
   (a) Comment on the relationship between the topic sentence and illustrative details in paragraph 5.
   (b) Explain how the connotations of the phrase "floating down" in the title of the essay help convey the tone of the essay.
   (c) Comment on the effectiveness of the final sentence in this essay.

BARRY BROADFOOT

GRAND BEACH, THEN AND NOW

Oh, show me the way to go home
I'm tired and I wanna go to bed
I had a glass of beer about an hour ago
And it's gone right to my head.
(The word "head" was sung as "he-e-e-ed!")

1 A song from my childhood, a song from the past, brings back the good old days when a family was closely knit and the Great Depression was a very tight belt around us all, and yet for two wonderful weeks every summer there was happiness in a small cottage among the pines. We spent long days on a mile-long beach of the finest sand, and at night we paraded along the boardwalk at Grand Beach as if it were a promenade in the south of France. Life was good.

2 I remember that song well. In that year, 1936, everyone was singing it as, in family groups, they strolled home to their cottages in the deepening dusk, each little house throwing out a warm rectangle of golden orange from the kerosene lamp, welcoming those who were coming home.

3 There we were, my father, my mother, my sister, seven, and myself, ten, strolling home, two by two. Each of us held a small cardboard box of chips, mine always awash in brown vinegar. We ate those long and slender chips slowly, savoring every one and hoping they would last until we got home. They never did. We didn't cast the boxes aside because people just did not litter in those days.

4 The price of the chips was five cents, and while it may seem extremely low compared to today's side of fries for eighty cents, many a canny mother thought them expensive, considering a hundred-pound sack of spuds could be bought for less than a dollar. It was said that the man who had won high bid on the chip concession stand from the Canadian National Railway, which owned Grand Beach resort, made enough in those two months of summer to own a fine house in Winnipeg, take a long luxury trip to Florida every winter, and—oh horrors!—play the ponies. That meant he was a gambling man, a person of sinister character, but he just looked like a man in a frenzy as he stood throwing panfuls of raw potatoes into his two huge kettles, tossing the heavy wire baskets to free the chips of the boiling

grease, and dumping them into trays presided over by his two daughters. At the end of each day his white apron was splattered with grease and his chef's hat drooped to starboard. There was a joke made endlessly by those waiting in the two lineups—chips, five cents, on the left, and fish and chips, ten cents, on the right. Every time a nickel or dime dropped into the cups that served as cash register, someone would say, "Another two cents for Mr. Reynold's Florida holiday," and someone else would add, "While we're freezing."

5 Mr. Reynolds never smiled at these brilliant sallies. Nobody laughed at two cents. It was a lot of money in the Dirty Thirties. Five cents would buy a bottle of Coca-Cola or a bottle of Stone Ginger Beer, and if anyone had had the wit or wisdom then to save those Stone bottles, they would fetch fifteen or twenty dollars today on the collectables market.

6 On the long boardwalk leading to the lagoon more than a mile away, a concessionaire sold a hamburger—known in Winnipeg as a nip—for five cents; an ice-cream cone was also a nickel, and a juicy hotdog was another nickel. Even at these prices, he made a profit.

7 At the large grocery, where everybody said prices were exorbitant and shook their fists to the sky cursing the C.N.R. for grinding the faces of the poor in the dust, one could buy a one-quart bottle of orange or cola Kik for eight cents and hamburger meat for eight cents a pound. (Goddam the C.N.R.—in Winnipeg it was seven cents.) Buns were ten cents a dozen and Dad's cookies five cents a dozen.

8 One by one, the families would turn off to their cottages, but before that mothers would say, as they passed the large public toilets scattered throughout the campsite, "Anyone want to go? If you do, go now. I won't have any of you tykes stumbling around out here in the middle of the night," adding ominously, "when you never know what might happen." I always wondered what might happen. I know now. It would happen now, but it was unthinkable then and no one would ever know anyway because the newspapers did not print details of crimes like that. In those days even the most vicious gang rape was called "an assault." Today, an assault can be hitting a neighbor with a spitball.

9 The cottages were small and square, following the guidelines laid down by the C.N.R.'s management department. Any resident could go into someone else's cottage blindfolded and move around quite easily, even to finding the kindling and firewood supplied by the company. None of the 312 cottages—the twenty-six letters of the

alphabet multiplied by twelve cottages to a block—were exactly the same, but essentially they were alike. If you met a friend on the boardwalk you would say you lived in R-9 and not Raspberry Rendezvous, which was the cottage we rented for years at twelve dollars a week. Each cottage had two or three bedrooms, but they were part of one large area because the walls were only seven feet high and the doors were heavy cloths hanging from crossbars. Each bedroom contained a Winnipeg couch, which folded out to double-size, and each had a chest of drawers. The main area was living-room-dining-room-kitchen-fighting-loving-card-playing-room, and it had a large table, several chairs, some old calendars on the walls, linoleum on the floor, and that was about it.

10 The part that served as kitchen had a big, black McCleery stove with four holes and a five-gallon heating reservoir. Dishes, pots, and pans went into cupboards as well as the groceries you lugged from Winnipeg or bought at that store with The! Exorbitant! Prices! Oh yes, there was the necessary icebox. The ice came in twenty-five-pound blocks, and they cost nothing because the C.N.R. provided each cottage with a book of ice tickets to last the summer—and woebetide the cottage tenant who could not come up with that book. Every cottage had a cart, a box fixed with tiny wheels and a handle to pull, and the ice was collected from a big barn that was filled every winter with two hundred-pound blocks, which the local Indians harvested from Lake Winnipeg. Many an Indian family of the Grand Marais Reserve could thank the C.N.R. and not the Department of Indian Affairs for their livelihood because of the ice-harvesting and maintenance work they did in the winter and spring.

11 During the summer months I never saw an Indian working for the C.N.R. The work was done by dozens of college students, and most must have come from families of some wealth who had influence. The jobs were never given to the thousands of destitute youths who found it impossible to get any kind of job, summer or winter. These coveted but low-paying jobs were passed on, down the years, from brother to brother, or friend to friend. It was believed that once a youth got an armlock on a job, his recommendation of a successor was always accepted. A recommendation, therefore, could mean money. Not much, perhaps, but a little went a very long way.

12 So we'd file into the room and my mother would light up another of the oil lamps and my father would settle down at the table with his copy of the *Winnipeg Free Press* that had come in on the "Moonlight

Special", which had arrived from the city that evening. The paper was only five cents, but you got five dollars' worth of news in it. No one had a portable radio—which was as big as an apple box in those days—and besides, who could afford batteries? Why, only the rich folk who had eleven-room cottages called "summer places" at Lake of the Woods and who would never think of renting a twelve-dollar-a-week cottage with the public toilet four hundred yards away.

13 My father would read out the headlines, making dry wit of the antics of an idiot called Hitler who was stirring up the peasantry in Germany, and commenting on Russia's announcement of a new five-year plan, saying, "If they couldn't make the last two work, how do they expect this one to work?" There was little news of the thousands dispossessed by the Great Depression, the long lines of hopeless and rejected men and youths at soup kitchens in every major city of our great and prosperous land while the banks foreclosed ruthlessly on prairie farmers right, left and center. Nothing ever appeared in the papers because the press, in an unofficial silent conspiracy, hid the true facts from a nation and a world in economic despair and disarray. But any good news made headlines. If a company announced plans to build a seventy-five-thousand-dollar addition to its warehouse on Higgins Avenue, thus giving ten men work for two months, it was worthy of front-page play. A story as inconsequential as the sale of twenty-thousand bushels of Annapolis Valley apples to some obscure Caribbean British colony was hailed as a great boost to the Nova Scotian economy.

14 My father would read "Mrs. Thomson Advises"—she was the Ann Landers of the day—and say, "That crazy woman. . . ." If we wanted to learn what that stern, socially correct, and liberated woman had to say about love, marriage, and The Great Beyond, we had to wait until he had finished. He never read the sports pages.

15 Sometimes, my sister and I, when we weren't at war, would play Snap and Old Maid and Rummy and Fish and Hearts and woebetide the person who failed to include a pack of cards in our luggage. Monopoly was the rage those days, a worldwide mania, but we couldn't afford the game. The owners of Monopoly knew they had the world by the tail on a downhill pull and charged $4.50 for it and made millions. I read later that the man who invented the game sold it to a company for a pittance and died penniless.

16 But Raspberry Rendezvous had one feature which made it elect above the rest. A gramophone. The big brute of a thing stood on four

shaky legs so that it wobbled when it was wound up. There was a stock of records, and night after night the reedy voice of Carson Robinson, the Willy Nelson of the thirties, would drift out into the night. I still remember the words to "I Learned About Women From 'Er" and "Abdul the Bulbul Ameer," two of our favorites.

17 There was also Cohan's "I'm a Yankee Doodle Dandy," the wailing "Brother Can You Spare a Dime," a dreadful tune with bad lyrics that became the marching song of the Depression, and many forgettable others. We sang the old favorites, "My Gal Sal," and "Swanee River," and the hit of that year, "Red Sails in the Sunset." If any record company wants to reissue "Red Sails" I can guarantee it will lose its corporate shirt, but we were young, innocent, and happy in those days and hadn't been introduced to the melodic tunes of the rock-and-roll age and the assault of a young man of nineteen with long hair earning hundreds of thousands of dollars pounding a guitar into matchwood while hollering 'I luvya, I wannya' over and over until the record was used up.

18 About ten o'clock my mother would ask, "Who wants cinnamon toast?" Before we could answer she'd be reaching for the box of Eddy's matches, and one would flare. The kindling would catch and within two minutes there would be a brave fire throwing dancing shadows on the ceiling. The hand-held wire toaster would be loaded with two slices, and by the time eight were done and buttered, the pot was boiling with water for cocoa. It was always cocoa because a smart advertising man had come up with a campaign saying cocoa had no caffeine in it, thus preventing the long sleepless nights caused by the caffeine in coffee and tea. Years later I read that cocoa had as much caffeine in it as coffee and tea, and I only knew because a firm selling carob told me so in their ads. Carob, naturally, has no caffeine.

19 My mother always let us put on our own cinnamon because some like a little, some like a lot, some wouldn't care if they had it or not. I'll always remember those evenings, the shifting firelight on the ceiling, the warm pool of the lantern light on the oilcloth on the table, the four cups, all different shapes and colors, the big plate of toast, and the munch, munch, munch, and the slurp, slurp, slurp. 'Firelight' and 'cocoa' are still buzz words of happiness to me.

20 And as Samuel Pepys used to end his daily entry in his diary, "And so to bed. . . ."

21 At 7:00 A.M. the call "Fresh fish, fresh fish" was heard in the land and my mother would take two quarters from the teacup on the shelf

above the stove and I'd run out to join the small crowd around Manuel, the half-breed—now they try and add dignity to their wretched state by calling them Métis. Manuel was a huge man, always dressed in black pants and orange sweater, and his hands were forever bleeding slightly from nicks caused by his flashing fileting knife.

22 I loved that knife and I once asked him where he had got it and he said "I got me this here bastard file and then I got me another that was harder and I filed down that bastard file and that's the knife you see me with." Then he said, "See that there knot on that old poplar tree there?" Casually, he fired the knife from thirty feet away and it thunked into the center of the small knot. I was sure he was superb at everything he did.

23 Once I went out fishing before dawn, and as his old one-lunger was putt-putting us back to the beach where he did his fileting, he told me about his life. He did not mention the harshness, the poverty, and the discrimination his people accepted as their punishment for being born Indian. He talked and laughed his way through a half-hour's account of the good things in his life, the big pickerel catches, the tricks he played on other breeds, the weddings and dances, his three little daughters, and offhandedly of his prowess—"Sure, there's a lot of husbands for miles around here that hate Manuel's guts." That one statement, accompanied by his booming laugh, stays with me as the strongest memory of him.

24 The filets were the biggest, thickest, juiciest, and bone-free I have ever tasted and they were two for a quarter. When I bought four he'd always throw in a fifth and wink and say, "For your pussy. Gotta pussy, ain't you?" The men would chuckle and the women would look at the ground, and it was a couple of years before I learned what Manuel's joke meant.

Barry Broadfoot, "Grand Beach, Then and Now," in *My Own Years* (Toronto: Doubleday, 1983), pp. 40-45.

Questions

1. Subject

In one sense the subject of the essay is summed up in its title, "Grand Beach, Then and Now." In another sense one might argue that the title does not truly capture the author's emphasis in the essay. Comment.

2. **Audience**
Although this is a highly personal account of a past long gone, the author makes the piece have a general audience appeal by emphasizing something we all understand, namely, money. Explain how this works in the essay.
3. **Purpose**
Is it necessary for a reader to know the scene as the author knows it to appreciate the picture that the author is trying to describe? How does the description enhance the author's purpose? Answer this question by focusing on one or two paragraphs in this essay.
4. **Structure and Style**
(a) Comment on the chronological sequence of this descriptive essay. Does the time factor contribute to the unity of the piece?
(b) One way of looking at the structure of this essay is to examine the way in which the author moves in his description from outside to inside. How does this work?

MARGARET LAURENCE

WHERE THE WORLD BEGAN

1 A strange place it was, that place where the world began. A place of incredible happenings, splendors and revelations, despairs like multitudinous pits of isolated hells. A place of shadow-spookiness, inhabited by the unknowable dead. A place of jubilation and of mourning, horrible and beautiful.

2 It was, in fact, a small prairie town.

3 Because that settlement and that land were my first and for many years my only real knowledge of this planet, in some profound way they remain my world, my way of viewing. My eyes were formed there. Towns like ours, set in a sea of land, have been described thousands of times as dull, bleak, flat, uninteresting. I have had it said to me that the railway trip across Canada is spectacular, except for the prairies, when it would be desirable to go to sleep for several days, until the ordeal is over. I am always unable to argue this point effectively. All I can say is—well, you really have to live there to know that country. The town of my childhood could be called bizarre, agonizingly repressive or cruel at times, and the land in which it grew could be called harsh in the violence of its seasonal changes. But never merely flat or uninteresting. Never dull.

4 In winter, we used to hitch rides on the back of the milk sleigh, our moccasins squeaking and slithering on the hard rutted snow of the roads, our hands in ice-bubbled mitts hanging onto the box edge of the sleigh for dear life, while Bert grinned at us through his great frosted moustache and shouted the horse into speed, daring us to stay put. Those mornings, rising, there would be the perpetual fascination of the frost feathers on windows, the ferns and flowers and eerie faces traced there during the night by unseen artists of the wind. Evenings, coming back from skating, the sky would be black but not dark, for you could see a cold glitter of stars from one side of the earth's rim to the other. And then the sometime astonishment when you saw the Northern Lights flaring in swift ice flames across the sky, like the scrawled signature of God. After a blizzard, when the snowploughs hadn't yet got through, school would be closed for the day, the assumption being that the town's young could not possibly flounder through five feet of snow in the pursuit of education. We would then gaily don snowshoes and flounder for miles out into the white dazzling deserts, in pursuit of a different kind of knowing. If you came back too close to night, through the woods at the foot of the town hill, the thin black branches of poplar and chokecherry now meringued with frost, sometimes you heard coyotes. Or maybe the banshee wolf-voices were really only inside your head.

5 Summers were scorching, and when no rain came and the wheat became bleached and dried before it headed, the faces of farmers and townspeople would not smile much, and you took for granted, because it never seemed to have been any different, the frequent knocking at the back door and the young men standing there, mumbling or thrusting defiantly their requests for a drink of water and a sandwich if you could spare it. They were riding the freights, and you never knew where they had come from, or where they might end up, if anywhere. The Drought and Depression were like evil deities which had been there always. You understood and did not understand.

6 Yet the outside world had its continuing marvels. The poplar bluffs and the small river were filled and surrounded with a zillion different grasses, stones and weed flowers. The meadowlarks sang undaunted from the twanging telephone wires along the gravel highway. Once we found an old flat-bottomed scow, and launched her, poling along the shallow brown waters, mending her with wodges of hastily chewed Spearmint, grounding her among the tangles of yellow marsh marigolds that grew succulently along the banks of the shrunken river, while the sun made our skins smell dusty-warm.

7 My best friend lived in an apartment above some stores on Main Street, an elegant apartment with royal-blue velvet curtains. The back roof, scarcely sloping at all, was corrugated tin, of a furnace-like warmth on a July afternoon, and we would sit there drinking lemonade and looking across the back lane at the Fire Hall. Sometimes our vigil would be rewarded. Oh joy! Somebody's house burning down! We had an almost-perfect callousness in some ways. Then the wooden tower's bronze bell would clonk and toll like a thousand speeded funerals in a time of plague, and in a few minutes the team of giant black horses would cannon forth, pulling the fire wagon like some scarlet chariot of the Goths, while the firemen clung with one hand, adjusting their helmets as they went.

8 The oddities of the place were endless. An elderly lady used to serve, as her afternoon tea offering to other ladies, soda biscuits spread with peanut butter and topped with a whole marshmallow. Some considered this slightly eccentric, when compared with chopped egg sandwiches, and admittedly talked about her behind her back, but no one ever refused these delicacies or indicated to her that they thought she had slipped a cog. Another lady dyed her hair a bright and cheery orange, by strangers often mistaken at 20 paces for a feather hat. My own beloved stepmother wore a silver fox neckpiece, a whole pelt, *with the embalmed(?) head still on.* My Ontario Irish grandfather said *sparrow grass,* a more interesting term for asparagus. The town dump was known as *the nuisance grounds,* a phrase fraught with weird connotations, as though the effluvia of our lives was beneath contempt but at the same time was subtly threatening to the determined and sometimes hysterical propriety of our ways.

9 Some oddities were, as idiom had it, "funny ha ha"; others were "funny peculiar." Some were not so very funny at all. An old man lived, deranged, in a shack in the valley. Perhaps he wasn't even all that old, but to us he seemed a wild Methuselah figure, shambling among the underbrush and the tall couch grass, muttering indecipherable curses or blessings, a prophet who had forgotten his prophecies. Everyone in town knew him, but no one knew him. He lived among us as though only occasionally and momentarily visible. The kids called him Andy Gump, and feared him. Some sought to prove their bravery by tormenting him. They were the medieval bear baiters, and he the lumbering bewildered bear, half blind, only rarely turning to snarl. Everything is to be found in a town like mine. Belsen, writ small but with the same ink.

10 All of us cast stones in one shape or another. In grade school,

among the vulnerable and violet girls we were, the feared and despised were those few older girls from what was charmingly called "the wrong side of the tracks." Tough in talk and tougher in muscle, they were said to be whores already. And probably were, that being about the only profession readily accessible to them, there.

11 The dead lived in that place, too. Not only the grandparents who had, in local parlance, "passed on" and who gloomed, bearded or bonneted, from the sepia photographs in old albums, but also the uncles, forever 18 or 19, whose names were carved on the granite family stones in the cemetery, but whose bones lay in France. My own young mother lay in that graveyard, beside other dead of our kin, and when I was 10, my father too, only 40, left the living town for the dead dwelling on the hill.

12 When I was 18, I couldn't wait to get out of that town, away from the prairies. I did not know then that I would carry the land and town all my life within my skull, that they would form the mainspring and source of the writing I was to do, wherever and however far away I might live.

13 This was my territory in the time of my youth, and in a sense my life since then has been an attempt to look at it, to come to terms with it. Stultifying to the mind it could certainly be, and sometimes was, but not to the imagination. It was many things, but it was never dull.

14 The same, I now see, could be said for Canada in general. Why on earth did generations of Canadians pretend to believe this country dull? We knew perfectly well it wasn't. Yet for so long we did not proclaim what we knew. If our upsurge of so-called nationalism seems odd or irrelevant now to outsiders, and even to some of our own people *(what's all the fuss about?)*, they might try to understand that for many years we valued ourselves insufficiently, living as we did under the huge shadows of those two dominating figures, Uncle Sam and Britannia. We have only just begun to value ourselves, our land, our abilities. We have only just begun to recognize our legends and to give shape to our myths.

15 There are, God knows, enough aspects to deplore about this country. When I see the killing of our lakes and rivers with industrial wastes, I feel rage and despair. When I see our industries and natural resources increasingly taken over by America, I feel an overwhelming discouragement, especially as I cannot simply say, "damn Yankees." It should never be forgotten that it is we ourselves who have sold such a large amount of our birthright for a mess of plastic Progress. When

I saw the War Measures Act being invoked, I lost forever the vestigial remains of the naïve wish-belief that repression could not happen here, or would not. And yet of course I had known all along in the deepest and often hidden cave of the heart that anything can happen anywhere, for the seeds both of man's freedom and of his captivity are found everywhere, even in the microcosm of a prairie town. But in raging against our injustices, our stupidities, I do so *as family,* as I did, and still do in writing, about those aspects of my town which I hated and which are always in some ways aspects of myself.

16 The land still draws me more than other lands. I have lived in Africa and in England, but splendid as both can be they do not have the power to move me in the same way as, for example, that part of southern Ontario where I spent four months last summer in a cedar cabin beside a river. "Scratch a Canadian and you find a phony pioneer," I used to say to myself, in warning. But all the same it is true, I think, that we are not yet totally alienated from physical earth, and let us only pray we do not become so. I once thought that my lifelong fear and mistrust of cities made me a kind of old-fashioned freak; now I see it differently.

17 The cabin has a long window across its front western wall, and sitting at the oak table there, in the mornings, I used to look out at the river and at the tall trees beyond, green-gold in the early light. The river was bronze; the sun caught it strangely, reflecting upon its surface the near-shore sand ripples underneath, making it seem momentarily as though a whole flotilla of gold flickerings sailed there. Suddenly, the silver crescenting of a fish, gone before the eye could clearly give image to it. The old man next door said these leaping fish were carp. Himself, he preferred muskie, for he was a real fisherman and the muskie gave him a fight. The wind most often blew from the south, and the river flowed toward the south, so when the water was wind-riffled and the current was strong, the river seemed to be flowing both ways. I liked this, and interpreted it as an omen, a natural symbol.

18 A few years ago, when I was back in Winnipeg, I gave a talk at my old college. It was open to the public, and afterward a very old man came up to me and asked me if my maiden name had been Wemyss. I said yes, thinking that he might have known my father or my grandfather. But no. "When I was a young lad," he said, "I once worked for your great-grandfather, Robert Wemyss, when he had the sheep ranch." I think that was the moment when I realized something of

great importance to me. My long-ago families came from Scotland and Ireland, but in a sense that no longer mattered so much. My true roots were here and would remain so, whatever happened.

19 I am not very patriotic, in the usual meaning of that word. I cannot say, "My country right or wrong" in any political, social or literary context. But one thing is inalterable, for better or worse.

20 This is not only where my world began. It is also the land of my ancestors.

Margaret Laurence, "Where the World Began," *Maclean's* (December, 1972), pp. 23, 80. Except from *Heart of a Stranger,* (Toronto: McClelland and Stewart, 1976).

Questions

1. **Subject**
   Looking back over the essay after reading it once, we can see how the opening paragraph moves beyond the particular reference of the prairie town. How do the descriptions of the subject in paragraph 1 also apply to the author's comments on the country?
2. **Audience**
   The author moves from a particular description in this essay to a general commentary on the nature of the country Canada. How might an audience feel at being pulled into the essay when the pronoun shifts from "I" to "we"?
3. **Purpose**
   This essay is divided into two sections. In what sense can the first be seen as an extended metaphor for the second? How do narration and description work together to create a unified impression for the reader?
4. **Structure and Style**
   (a) Comment on the relationship between topic sentence and illustrative detail in paragraph 8.
   (b) Explain what the author means by the final sentence of paragraph 9. How does it relate to the paragraph of which it is a part?
   (c) Speculate on why the second paragraph of the essay is a single line sentence.
   (d) What exactly does Margaret Laurence mean by "world," a word which is found both in the title of the essay and in its first sentence?

6 *Exposition*

Introduction to the Mode

Expository writing—along with argumentation, one of the two main types of writing in college and university—is writing primarily designed to inform or explain. Its basic purpose is to provide information to an audience wishing to broaden its knowledge on a particular topic, or to help the audience better understand information it already possesses. Whichever of these purposes is chosen, the expository writer is normally more knowledgeable about the subject than the audience. People read expository writing to be informed and to learn; expository writers write, presumably, because they have something to teach. Whether you are explaining something as simple as how to make bran muffins or as complex as the differences in political philosophy between the Liberal and Conservative parties, you need to be aware that clarity and precision in writing are especially important in the expository mode. Being aware of the nature of your audience is also particularly crucial in exposition. If you are writing an essay in which you are explaining a type of photographic technique to a group of photographers, the chances are you can take much more for granted about photography than you could if you were explaining the same process to people who had just bought their first camera. Similarly, writing about the effects of a Canadian winter on wildlife to a group of Canadian naturalists would present a different explanatory chore from that of an essay on the same topic to a group of Floridians with a vague interest in animals. Simply handing over information would be more important in the former case, while improving understanding would matter more in the latter instance. However, whatever your topic and whoever your audience, you can be certain to have less difficulty writing an expository essay if you take into account the various developmental strategies at your disposal.

Before we turn to an examination of these strategies as they apply to exposition, it is important to state that regularly we find a combination of these strategies in a single essay. To take an absurd example: suppose you were writing an essay in which you were trying to explain the process of changing a flat tire to an audience of Bedouin camel drivers; in order to make your essay comprehensible to an audience whose knowledge of your subject would be slight or even non-existent, you might have to *define* both a car and a tire; explain the *cause* of flat tires and the *effects* of sharp objects penetrating rubber; give *examples* of sharp objects that can penetrate rubber; make *comparisons* between the functions that tires serve and the functions that camels' legs serve. Only at this stage might you be able to turn to the *process* of changing a flat tire. Look, for example, at the following excerpt from an essay on the historian Donald Creighton:

> D.G. Creighton was the greatest Canadian historian since, and perhaps even including, F.X. Garneau. In shifting, uncertain times his art celebrated and sought to inspire the survival of his nation.
>
> But this will be homage, not historiography. Unlike Garneau, who was a notary and a civil servant, Creighton made a profession of history. Of the many fine eulogies published since his death, none has dealt with his primary vocation—a curious omission especially in view of some newspapers' loudly proclaimed interest in teaching as opposed to research and publication. For fifty years D.G. Creighton taught in the History Department at the University of Toronto. How he taught deserves some comment.
>
> I studied with him close to the end of his career when he might have been expected to slow down or coast on his reputation. Far from it. He continued writing at the same steady pace, producing four books and a collection of essays in recent years. He also continued to work at his teaching. I attended two of his seminars and for several years he supervised my thesis. I was constantly awed by his devotion to his calling, the conscious effort he put into teaching, and his fierce commitment to those he always referred to as *his* students. He was a great scholar and a great teacher.
>
> Once, somewhat thoughtlessly, I burst into his office to ask for help with something that seemed important at the time. "Are you busy?" I asked. There he sat in the wicker chair off in the corner of the room. The chair creaked as he shambled to his feet, a little impatient with me I sensed. "Well, I have a seminar in an hour," he replied, "and I'm just finishing the reading." But he dealt graciously with my intrusion and I sped off dumbfounded that someone who had been through the material as many times as he had, who knew the subject as intimately as he did, would still, as retirement approached, do the reading for an undergraduate seminar. Now, as a busy teacher myself, I am even more amazed. He always referred to himself as a professional historian. He was also a professional teacher. But he made his own rules.

There was nothing spontaneous, improvised or casual about his seminar. At times it was stiff and awkward. It was always formal and correct. He took great care laying out the question to be discussed and the readings; he gave the paper giver specific guidance, and he expected the rest of us to return having mastered the literature, prepared to conduct an intelligent discussion of the topic. We were never expected to tear up the paper being presented in any vindictive, "American," hyper-critical way. Thorough, dispassionate discussion was the object. Certain points were expected to emerge from the discussion, however, and Creighton took pains to make sure these essentials were grasped during our amateurish deliberations.

H.V. Nelles, "Creighton's Seminar," *The Canadian Forum,* Vol. 60, (No. 702), p. 5.

These few paragraphs about a famous Canadian are written largely in the expository mode. The author's subject is Donald Creighton; his thesis concerns Creighton's talent as a teacher. What the author intends to *show,* or *explain,* or *inform* us of is an aspect of Donald Creighton's life that he thinks has gone largely unacknowledged. Subject and purpose work together here as they must in all good writing; but what about audience? Presumably the audience that the author must have in mind is one that at least recognizes Donald Creighton's name, in other words an audience that knows something—however slight—about Creighton and might like to know something more—in this case his skill as a teacher.

It is interesting to note how various developmental strategies work together in these five paragraphs to help the author carry out his purpose. One could argue that the major developmental strategy is *definition;* after all, the author intends to provide further information about an already famous man, information that will make us more familiar with him. In a sense, then, he is defining a certain quality about Donald Creighton's life that many of us know nothing about. From one perspective, definition exemplifies the basic expository impulse—to make a thing clearer. In this case, Creighton's great teaching skills are highlighted. But notice also the importance of other developmental strategies. In paragraph 2, sentence 2 the author uses *contrast* to sharpen our sense of Creighton's personality as historian. The author also uses *illustration* or *example* to indicate Creighton's skill as a teacher. This is evident primarily in the fifth paragraph where he introduces the example of the seminar. Within the same paragraph we see the use of *process* development as Nelles outlines the steps by which Creighton created a successful seminar. Finally, perhaps to suggest the person behind the historian, Nelles introduces the *narrative mode* in paragraph 4; this little story is based on an exchange that the author once had with the great man himself. To create a sense of immediacy, the author recalls part of the exact conversation for us. As this example of expository writing makes abundantly clear, good writing is made up of a judicious mix of strategies and rarely ever just one. In your own writing you should use various developmental strategies to help you deal with questions such as subject, audience, and purpose; you should never get to the point where you feel straitjacketed or hemmed in by any one strategy even though one strategy normally predominates in each piece of writing.

Developmental Strategies

Process Analysis

Process writing is largely writing that tells people how to do something: how to change a tire; how to avoid paying income tax; how to lose twenty pounds; how to be successful at college or university. Each of the following examples of process writing deals with a different subject in a different way. The first is a simple recipe:

Oat Bran Cookies

175 mL (3/4 cup) butter or margarine
250 mL (1 cup) white sugar
125 mL (1/2 cup) brown sugar
1 egg (slightly beaten)
250 mL (1 cup) flour
50 mL (1/4 cup) oats
250 mL (1 cup) bran
175 mL (3/4 cup) coconut
5 mL (1 tsp) baking powder
5 mL (1 tsp) baking soda
250 mL (1 cup) raisins (optional)

Cream butter or margarine, sugar, and egg together. Combine all dry ingredients and stir in gradually to the butter/sugar/egg mixture. Mix until all ingredients are well incorporated. Drop by teaspoonful onto greased cookie sheet. Bake at 180° C (350° F) for 12-15 minutes. Makes approximately 4 dozen cookies.

Process writing doesn't get much simpler than this. In fact, recipes or instructions in general are about the most basic type of process writing one can find. Notice how the next example of process writing takes the recipe format and parodies it:

Recipe for a Canadian Novel

Ingredients: one Indian,
one Mountie, one Eskimo,
one Doukhobor.

Add: one small-town whore,
two thousand miles of wheat,
one farmer impotent and bent.

His fair-haired daughter too,
then a Laurentian mountain
and a Montreal Jew.

Include also, a young boy
with a dying pet
and a mortgage unmet.

Should this sour, sweeten
with maple syrup—
French-Canadian even,

but dilute, if foreign
to the taste.
Stir, until beaten.

Drop in exotic and tangy
place names—Toronto,
Saskatoon, Hudson Bay.

For distinctive flavour:
garnish with maple leaves.
Mix, then leave.

Dice in one Confederation poet
complete with verse
(remove mould first).

To prepare the sauce:
paragraphs of bad prose
that never seem to stop.

Bring to a simmer,
but avoid a boil.
Pour, place in oven, bake.

Slice or leave whole.
Serves twenty million all told—
when cold.

John Robert Colombo, "Recipe for a Canadian Novel," *Abracadabra* (Toronto: McClelland and Stewart Ltd., 1967), pp. 28-29.

Clearly here the author is using the familar and somewhat hackneyed recipe process form to satirize Canadian writing. He does not expect us to take seriously the "recipe" he gives us, for there is no possibility that anything edible could come from it. Rather, he is perhaps suggesting that all too often Canadian novels lack imagination, so much so that they can be written by simply inserting the ingredients he mentions in his poem.

The final example of process writing is based upon a writer's response to the question "How long a day do you put in?"

> It's not a matter of a big day. I work, say, till noon and sometimes in the afternoon, but the unconscious is working for you most of the time. I wake up in the middle of the night and do most of my thinking then, and set it up for the next morning. It's not the number of hours. People who actually turn out a great deal of work often seem to spend a very short time at the typewriter. I do a great deal of re-writing. With the beginning of a book, I will often re-write first paragraphs, and the first few pages, thirty and forty times, because another belief I have is that in that moment, in that fix, in those first crucial pages, all the reader's decisions are made. To trust or not to trust? And all stylistic decisions are really made at that point, especially nowadays.
>
> Brian Moore, in [Silver] Donald Cameron, *Conversations with Canadian Novelists, 2* (Toronto: Macmillan, 1973), p. 77.

Notice in his response how the writer begins in a fairly conventional process way by moving from one time period to the next ("I work, say, till noon and sometimes in the afternoon. . . ."). We soon realize that the chronological catalogue does not capture the essence of his method of writing. As a result we move into a description of process which is entirely personal and idiosyncratic, a method which works for the author but might not work for us. We have moved a long way in this process piece from the recipe format which, if religiously followed, will have the same results for all.

Cause and Effect

Cause and effect is that writing strategy that makes use of the relationships that actually *exist* between things or that can be *created* between things. Also, in one of its manifestations it studies the consequences of actions, events, or various phenomena. In this first excerpt of cause-and-effect writing we see a largely irrefutable relationship established between two things. And it is irrefutable because it is personal. In other words we have no right to question the effect that the author describes because it is solely *hers:*

> Always, when approaching London, a surge of sinking awfulness swept over me as we came to its outskirts, and the train began slithering through suburban manufacturing districts. Open country turned to human congestion, brick and mortar pressed close both sides of our way—ache of overcrowded space, murk, dullness stared from behind the glazed fronts and backs of brick houses. No matter how hard I tried, I could not take interest in manufacturing districts—they wilted me. Love of everything, that swamped me in the country, was congealed here, stuffed away like rotten lettuce. Nothing within me responded to the hum of machinery.
>
> Emily Carr, *Growing Pains: The Autobiography of Emily Carr* (Toronto: Clarke, Irwin, 1946), p. 182.

Although the author's attitude towards industrial cities may not be ours—although the *effects* she feels may or may not represent what we feel—we are prepared to respect her views since they are completely hers. She is not trying to suggest that her views should be anyone else's, nor is she trying to convince us that hers are the only proper views of industrial life. Compare the following expository passage on the effects of television on politics:

> The enormity of television's impact upon the institutions of society is immeasurable, if only because there is not yet an end to it, only a continuing, deepening process of cause and effect. How can one measure the impact of the medium which has made the afternoon, for example, a killing ground for newspapers? To say that television has made all politics presidential, or driven general magazines and afternoon papers to the wall, is so commonly accepted a fact as to have become trite. But television has done considerably more and is still doing so.
>
> Because it demanded increasingly heavy dollops of money, television "reformed" political financing to give the parties significantly greater resources to purchase not only television time but people and techniques, including computerized direct mail and public opinion research. As a result, while present-day party cadres are very well paid and highly professionalized, voluntarism is all but dead.
>
> The rank-and-file of the parties, once considered to represent an omnibus of interests, have become competing factions acting on behalf of special or regional interests. Their usefulness in the political process is rapidly decreasing. They too perceive the system as presidential; they too think of politics in the same simple or detached

> terms as do non-partisans. Politics, which once inspired group loyalty and avid commitment, now arouses a consuming interest in techniques and in endless critical evaluations of leadership suitability as deduced from television performance. Were it not for private ambition or patronage interests, anarchy would be certain.

Dalton Camp, *An Eclectic Eel* (Ottawa: Deneau, 1981), p. xvi.

Since this is a complex cause-and-effect passage, it might be valuable to test your understanding of this strategy by identifying all of the effects that Camp mentions in these paragraphs. Like the first passage, this one shows or informs us of certain effects, but unlike the first one it *assumes* a position about television that we might like to doubt or at least question. It is up to the author of this second passage to *prove* the validity of what he shows us. In other words, in order to win our support for his statements he must, sooner or later, move from the expository mode to the argumentative or persuasive one.

The final example of the cause-and-effect strategy is taken from a novel. It brings cause and effect together; the speaker begins to contemplate the past as a result of a scene he sees from his car window:

> I am on my way to Union Terrace in the Dart when I am strongly affected by a sense of the past: the early nineteen-forties, the war years in old Middlesburgh. It happens at the corner of Britannia Road and Prospect where I am stopped for a red light. Through my windshield I watch five teen-aged girls running. They have come down Prospect Street from Union Place Secondary School and now run across in front of me, stiff-hipped and pigeon-toed, holding their books to their chests. They are making for the restaurant next to the Pix Theatre. Watching them, I am overcome by haunted feelings, touched by fragments of the past. It is *déjà vu* for certain, but also something else, something deeper and stronger. Within me thrives the keenest sense of time and place. I seem able to reach out and feel the texture of those days: the high-school girls in their plaid skirts and bulky white sweaters, their ankle socks and brown and white saddle shoes. I have half a mind to abandon the Dart and follow them into the restaurant, ask if their mothers didn't once grow up in Middlesburgh, Ontario. It's all here at the corner of Britannia Road and Prospect at a quarter to five on a winter afternoon—this lost time, figured forth now in an *ambience* as resonant and palpable as an old sepia retrogravure. The sadness of it is suffocating.

Richard B. Wright, *The Weekend Man* (New York: Farrar, Straus, and Giroux, 1970), pp. 196-197.

In this passage, the sight of some young girls *causes* the speaker to think about the early nineteen-forties, the period of his own youth. The *effects* of this are numerous for him: he is "haunted" by certain "feelings"; he thinks of similar scenes during his own adolescence; he is tempted to abandon his car and follow the girls; he is overwhelmed by sadness. This passage in turn forces the reader to ask why the speaker feels this way; in other words the effects of this scene on the speaker force us as readers to ask what *caused* those effects; the answer might be that the speaker in this scene realizes his own mortality.

Comparison and Contrast

The comparison-and-contrast strategy looks at similarities and/or differences between various phenomena. When using this strategy care must be taken to ensure that there is some central and genuine comparative core shared by the items you choose to look at. The first example of this strategy stresses differences rather than similarity:

> I cannot, in other words, divorce questions about progress and technology from questions about the essence of America and Europe. The European character is as essentially bound up with eschatology and the messianic idea of progress as is the American character with the structure of technology, hedonism, pragmatism and so on. But I cannot honestly find any connection between Canada and such phenomena as progress, technology, hedonism, cynicism or anything else for that matter. Not even with "mediocrity" (a frequently-discussed issue in Canada). If Europeans and Americans are progress-oriented and hedonistic it has (as I understand it) everything to do with the fact of their being Europeans and Americans. If we Canadians are infected with any particular pathology, however, it does not strike me as having anything to do with our being Canadian. It suggests rather the influence of European and American culture on our lives. If anything, Canadianism would seem to be the absence rather than the presence of foreign influence, the suspension rather than the affirmation of ideological commitments to destiny, progress, mission and so on.
>
> Lionel Rubinoff, "National Purpose and Ideology," in *Notes for a Native Land,* ed. Andy Wainwright (Ottawa: Oberon, 1969), p. 45.

Although you might argue that this passage is about similarities as well as differences because the author compares American and European life, in fact what the author is trying to stress are the differences between Canadian life and American and European life. Therefore the accent in this passage is on the ways in which Canadian life is unlike life in the other cultures he mentions. It is extremely important to recognize this fact; to ignore it is to miss the important emphasis in the passage on Canadian distinctiveness.

The second example of comparison-and-contrast writing is a fine example of the way in which an author can combine and structure differences and similarities to highlight particular aspects of each:

> In Canada, neither circumstances nor tradition permitted the evolution of so ebullient and all-embracing a figure. Nevertheless, both English- and French-Canadian poetries in this period had been hard at work attempting to create myths—which may account for the fact that neither resulted in a useful "record of Canadian life." French Canadians, intent on creating a national consciousness that would survive British domination, had paid scant heed to "recording the facts," at least in poetry. English-Canadian poets, struggling to sustain the exaggerated ideals of "the Loyalist response," misrepresented the "facts" not only in the mother country, but to themselves. Both were handicapped by growing up as conservative societies in the shadow of a liberal and expanding United States. But French Canadians held an important advantage. A common religious and agrarian tradition, the cohesion of a folk culture and the presence of foreign overlords all acted as a continuing centripetal force, drawing them together and maintaining unity. In English Canada, circumstances were the exact opposite. The inhabitants, originating from England, Ireland, Scotland and the United States, differing in religion, cultural background and point of view, were dispersed in a strange, frequently harsh environment and disturbed by the proximity of "greener fields" to the south. These factors acted as a centrifugal force, separating English Canadians and preventing the fusion of a much-needed "national ideal."

T.E. Farley, *Exiles and Pioneers: Two Visions of Canada's Future, 1825-1975* (Ottawa: Borealis, 1976), p. 49.

Farley's passage is such a nicely balanced comparison-and-contrast paragraph that a brief analysis of its structure seems in order. In sentence 2 the author introduces a similarity between the two Canadian cultures that are the subjects of this paragraph. This similarity is signalled by the use of the word "both" in this second sentence. Quickly, however, sentences 3 and 4 introduce the first difference, nicely captured by the balanced phrases that open each sentence ("French Canadians, intent on creating. . . ." "English-Canadian poets, struggling to sustain. . . ."). Sentence 5 suggests the basic similarity lying behind the differences outlined in sentences 4 and 5. Once again the key signalling word here is "Both." Sentences 6 and 7 introduce the second major difference between the two cultures emphasized by the use of the antonyms "centripetal" (sentence 6) and "centrifugal" (sentence 7).

The final comparison-and-contrast example is interesting because of the number of items it includes in its sweep. Normally, when we think of comparison-and-contrast we think of comparison and contrast between two terms. In the following passage the two major terms are Anglophone and Francophone. But notice how categories within these two general terms are also compared and contrasted:

> A surprisingly high 86 per cent of all respondents agreed with the statement, "It would be a good thing if all Canadians could speak both English and French." Francophones were somewhat more likely to agree (97 per cent) than Anglophones (81 per cent); and university education and some fluency in speaking the second language also correlated highly to agreement with that statement. Years of second-language study and relative fluency in the second official language corresponded proportionally to disagreement with the notion that English should be Canada's only official language. In general, there were marked differences between the responses of Anglophones and Francophones and between those of young people and their elders. More Francophones of all ages gave answers we can categorize as "positive" towards the official languages. For most questions, there was also a clear pattern by age, with the 15-to-24 age group being the most positive. The older people were, the less likely they were to have a positive view on the matter. This age correlation showed up most strongly among Anglophones. Young Anglophones generally held much more positive views than older Anglophones. Young Francophones tended to share the positive views of their elders. Furthermore, when asked how useful a knowledge of the second official language was to them now and would be in 10 years, Francophones were much more likely to respond "very" or "quite" useful.

> Commissioner of Official Languages, *Annual Report, 1985* (Ottawa: Minister of Supply and Services Canada, 1986), pp. 166-167.

Definition

Using the definition strategy requires in the first instance that you be aware of what makes one thing different from another. Definitions must be precise and clear enough to convey exactly what you are trying to elucidate. For example, to define a dog as an animal is only the first step in what could be quite a long process of discrimination. Definitions may be very conventional or wildly impressionistic, but they must provide enough information within their terms to make clear the essence of what they are trying to define. The first example of definition is quite a conventional one that makes use of the strategy of process to define the technique of silk-screening:

> The silk screen is a stencil process, but instead of using cut-out stencils the design is outlined on a silk screen stretched tight in a steel frame; the colour is squeezed through the silk on stiff cards. After the first colour is applied every trace of it is printed over on the screen with a stop-out varnish; each successive colour is then pushed through the screen and stopped out. When the last colour is applied, it goes through the only part of the screen not stopped out. By this process up to a thousand impressions can be made.
>
> A.Y. Jackson, *A Painter's Country* (Toronto, Vancouver: Clarke, Irwin, 1958; reprinted, 1964), p. 168.

Though this is a relatively conventional definition, it is also clear that this definition through process is far more detailed than the definition of the term "silk screen" that you might find in an ordinary dictionary. And this is because the person defining the term—A.Y. Jackson—is an artist who has an intimate knowledge of the technique he is describing.

The second example of definition is made up of "fact" and "interpretation." As such, it is an interesting example of the way in which definition can sometimes escape the confines of the cold, uninvolved, and objective dictionary definition:

> The French Canadians (they number about a third of the population) are descended from 60,000 original *habitants* whose roots in France were cut off by the Conquest of 1759. Their involvement with English-speaking Canadians has been less a matter of choice than of necessity. Though French communities may be found scattered from the Atlantic to the Pacific, the St. Lawrence river valley is in the fullest sense the heartland of French Canada. The feeling of inwardness, of a shared (and tragic) history, of loyalty to a common faith and a geographical *patrie* or homeland is very strong among French Canadians. It has enabled them to maintain their unique identity in the face of the most formidable social and economic challenges.
>
> Neil Compton, "Broadcasting and Canadian Culture," *Commentary* 38, November 1964, p. 75.

Try to determine which of the above statements are objective and which are interpretive.

The next example of definition writing gives a good indication of how difficult it is to define the complexities of the human personality. This definition paragraph is interesting as well because it makes use of comparison and contrast to suggest the oftentimes conflicting definitions that various people will arrive at when they are looking at the same person:

> It is possible, on any given day, to hear him described by two equally reasonable persons as a ruthless, cold-blooded autocrat and as a man so soft-hearted that he cannot bring himself to get tough with inept ministers; as a dabbler in issues and as a man who insists with excessive tenacity on finishing anything he starts; as an arrogant, remote patrician and as a person of exceptional charm and sensitivity; as the only leader who can put Quebec in its place, and as a Quebecer who values the welfare of his own province above all else. As a Liberal insider once put it: "Somebody is going to say some day, 'Will the real Mr. Trudeau please stand up,' and about fifty-eight people will rise."
>
> George Radwanski, *Trudeau* (Toronto: Macmillan, 1978), pp. 25-26.

Classification and Division

Classifying and dividing are ways of sorting human experience or phenomena into orderly systems or categories. When we classify we group things into particular categories; when we divide we examine the components of the categories we have created. Notice, for instance, this first example. The author classifies trees into two types and then spends time examining one type in particular in order to divide it into various sorts of trees:

> To the traveller driving by them on the highway, most trees look fairly much alike, except in winter, when some remain green (the softwoods) and others lose their leaves (the hardwoods). To those who have lived in and by and with the forests, this distinction is only the beginning. For many reasons softwoods have been regarded as much more valuable than hardwoods in North America, and the Northern Ontario forests contain many important softwoods.
>
> In the southeast, between Sudbury and Sault Ste. Marie, and in the far west, between the head of Lake Superior and the Lake of the Woods, the majestic white and red pines were the first softwoods to be cut in great numbers. In the rest of the region, north as far as James Bay (where the forests become less dense because of poorer soils and a colder climate) the most important softwoods have been white and black spruce. Others such as jack pine, balsam, and hemlock, and

even some hardwoods such as white birch and poplar, have been of some importance, but the real prizes have been the white pine and white spruce.

Victor C. Smith, "Lumbering, Pulp and Paper, and Forestry," in *A Vast and Magnificent Land,* ed. Matt Bray and Ernie Epp (Thunder Bay: Lakehead University; Sudbury: Laurentian University, 1984), p. 75.

In the next example the author looks back at his fellow highschool graduates and classifies them according to their present occupations:

Among us, at FFHS, were future leaders of the community. Progressive parents. Reform-minded aldermen. Anti-fallout enthusiasts. Collectors of early French-Canadian furniture. Boys who would actually grow up to be doctors and lecture on early cancer warnings to ladies' clubs. Girls who would appear in the social pages of the Montreal *Star,* sponsoring concerts in aid of retarded children (regardless of race, color, or creed) and luncheon hour fashion shows, proceeds to the Hebrew University. Lawyers. Notaries. Professors and marvellously with-it rabbis, who could not only quote Rabbi Akiba but could also get a kick out of a hockey game.

Mordecai Richler, "Going Home," in *Notes on an Endangered Species* (New York: Alfred A. Knopf, 1974), p. 182.

Had Richler in this passage stopped to examine the types of lawyers who graduated from his high-school, he would have been engaged in the *division* process.

In the final example, the author examines estuaries and divides them into three types:

Estuaries, even of streams that are approximately the same size, differ enormously, and I think that common sense and personal preference, as well as those two fallibles, experience and local knowledge, should be allowed to enter into the choice of a fishing tide. Most of the small-stream estuaries I know fall into three main types. There are those which run over shallow gravel bars, often dividing into several small channels; those which enter cleanly at high tide over a fall or a rocky bed and cut a long channel through sand or mud flats covered by saltwater except at the lowest tides; and those that enter through saltwater meadows, cutting a long channel between high mudbanks.

Roderick Haig-Brown, "The Nature of Estuaries," *Fisherman's Fall* (Don Mills: William Collins Sons, 1964).

Example or Illustration

All essays worth their salt must provide a sufficient number of detailed statements to elucidate general assertions. One of the most prevalent and effective types of detailed statements is the one based on example or illustration. Sometimes one example is enough to illustrate the general point; more often, however, writers clarify their claims or general statements by providing a number of illustrations.

In this first passage the author gives examples of the way in which Canada can affect the poetic temperament:

> It is a country for poets in other ways too. When first I arrived in Victoria I was taken to a house on Ten-Mile Point, and I wept at the sheer beauty of the country to which I had come. Happiness flooded me like a wave. Travelling through the Rockies, and even riding that long straight road from Calgary to Edmonton, I am awed and dazed at the grandeur of the imagination which is Canada. I have found space here, the freedom to move and, moving, breathe deep. The mountains preserve their solitude. The rivers are copious with life, the shores generous with oysters, mussels, clams and the sinewy symbolism of driftwood.

Robin Skelton, "O Canada!" in *Notes for a Native Land*, ed. Andy Wainwright (Ottawa: Oberon, 1969), pp. 81-82.

In the following passage, the author tries to capture the elusiveness of a particular character by giving examples of how he defied precise categorization:

> But John Hornby eluded all the categories. He had no commercial or scientific ambitions, no will-o'-the-wisp dream of gold or fur. His past was not notably disreputable even though his own account of it had some intriguing gaps in it. He was said to be wealthy—and that at times was about half-true. He was well-educated, a Harrovian, spoke in a soft scholarly voice, was not much given to profane language, and was even by some suspected of being a learned man because he knew a few colloquial phrases of French, German, and Italian. Professionally, during the ten years before the Fort Norman photograph, he was not an explorer, a trapper, a prospector; he was something of all these, but a caricature of them all. By instinct and habit he was most like a trapper, and could have been a good trapper but for his love of animals and his hatred of steel traps. Unlike many Indians, he never killed except for food; and like many Indians, he was often in the mat-

ter of food notoriously improvident. He was not a particularly good shot with a rifle, and was even rather careless in looking after his weapons; yet he managed to keep himself alive.

George Whalley, *The Legend of John Hornby* (London: John Murray, 1962), p. 6.

Hands On: Reading

Exercise

Actively read the following expository essay paying particular attention to the subject, audience, and purpose of the piece. As you consider this essay, think about the many aspects and strategies of exposition outlined in this chapter and relate them to the essay's subject, audience and purpose. Once you have actively read the essay write a summary of it and a response to it.

The following clues may help you in your analysis of the passage. Among other things, you should be able to find the following in the essay:

1. Cause and effect strategy
2. Illustration strategy
3. A tripartite structure

G.B. SINCLAIR

GROUNDS FOR CONCERN

Caffeine is the most widely used drug in the world. Most North Americans begin using it in childhood and continue to use it into old age. Although "caffeine" and "coffee" are synonymous for many of us, coffee accounts for only about sixty per cent of the caffeine consumed in Canada. Tea is responsible for another thirty per cent, and the remaining ten per cent is found in chocolate, soft drinks, and a variety of prescription and over-the-counter medications.

Recent research conducted primarily in the United States and Canada has isolated a growing list of hazards associated with caffeine in general and coffee in particular. Large doses of caffeine can produce heartburn, stomach upset, increased urination, and irregular heartbeat. More than 250 milligrams of caffeine (about the amount contained in three to five cups of coffee) can cause caffeinism or "coffee nerves." The symptoms include anxiety, muscle twitching, increased pulse, irritability, and insomnia. Office and restaurant workers who have access to continuous supplies of freshly brewed coffee are prime candidates for this condition.

According to K.Z. Bezchlibnyk and J.J. Jeffries, caffeinism is in many instances indistinguishable from anxiety neurosis. (Medical journals report several cases of patients who have undergone long-term psychiatric treatment when all that was required was decaffeination.) Bezchlibnyk, director of pharmacy at the Clarke Institute of Psychiatry in Toronto, and Jeffries, associate professor of psychiatry and pharmacy at the University of Toronto, note that, in spite of the detrimental effects of caffeine, many psychiatric hospitals serve coffee as often as six times daily. A patient at almost any Canadian hospital may be given the opportunity to drink twelve cups of coffee or tea a day.

Bezchlibnyk and Jeffries point to a Montreal study in which schizophrenic patients were switched to decaffeinated coffee without their knowledge or that of their attendants. Psychological tests showed a substantial decrease in hostility, suspiciousness, anxiety, and irritability; the improvement was lost with the return to regular coffee. Since caffeine can aggravate symptoms and interfere with both diagnosis and treatment, Bezchlibnyk and Jeffries have urged that decaffeinated coffee be used in psychiatric wards. Institutions, however, often resist such suggestions. "In our experience," report the pharmacists, "it is the medical and professional staffs—not the patients—who oppose such changes."

Coffee, tea, or cola drinkers who decide to quit cold turkey usually discover another of caffeine's attributes: it's addictive. Heavy coffee drinkers may experience dramatic withdrawal symptoms—depression, lethargy, vomiting, and headaches—if they attempt to break the habit suddenly. Moreover, the past few decades have seen an enormous increase in the consumption of soft drinks, the major source of caffeine for most children and some adults. Although soft drink manufacturers claim they use caffeine only to enhance flavour, critics maintain that caffeine is deliberately added to get kids hooked on these products. A twelve-ounce can of cola contains about one-third as much caffeine as a cup of coffee. But, because a child weighs considerably less than an adult, one cola soft drink consumed by a child is roughly equivalent to a cup of coffee drunk by an adult.

Richard Gilbert, who combines his work at the Ontario Addiction Research Foundation with his duties as a Toronto alderman, points out that caffeine would probably be rejected if approval were sought for it as a food additive under present Canadian health criteria. He is also convinced that, if the usual drug safety precautions were enforced, coffee bags would carry a label warning pregnant women not to drink more than half a cup a day.

Quantities of caffeine in the body's organs and tissues are more or less in proportion to their water content. Because the ovaries, the testes, and the fetus in the womb may be regularly bathed in caffeine, the drug has great opportunity to cause genetic mutations or abnormal births. Several studies have shown that high doses of caffeine increase the risk of birth defects in lab animals. Others report that excessive coffee intake by pregnant women may increase the incidence of stillbirths, prematurity, miscarriage, or malformations in the fetus.

However, a number of other investigations (including a recent Harvard study of more than 12,000 women who gave birth between 1977 and 1980) suggest that coffee has no adverse effects on human pregnancy. The findings are inconclusive; in the meantime, government reminders against use of caffeine in pregnancy remain in effect.

Caffeine readily crosses the placenta from the mother to the fetus. Jacob Aranda, professor of pediatrics at McGill, tested blood samples from thirty babies and found all had caffeine in their bloodstream at birth. There is research to suggest that the reason caffeine is effective in the treatment of infant apnea, or non-breathing, is that caffeine withdrawal is responsible for this condition. Aranda and Tonris Turmen, a researcher at the Montreal Children's Hospital, are now investigating the role of caffeine in sudden infant death syndrome.

Trevor Smith, a nutritionist at the University of Guelph, argues that caffeine can lead to obesity: it stimulates contractions in the stomach which give rise to feelings of hunger. It also triggers a blood-sugar "spike"—a quick increase in the sugar concentration of the blood which accounts for the "pick-me-up" quality of a cup of coffee. Within ninety minutes, however, the body's insulin reaction causes the sugar levels to drop, the mood to slump, and the appetite to soar.

• • •

For all the controversy that surrounds it, caffeine has its uses. Coffee was introduced into Europe primarily as a medicine; in the seventeenth century it was used as a treatment for such ailments as roaring in the ears, swooning fits, head pains, rickets, and consumption.

According to a Swiss study, caffeine can cause a twelve per cent increase in the rate of metabolism. The Swiss researchers, unlike Trevor Smith, suggest that drinking coffee can help people *lose* weight through an increased oxidation of the body's fat deposits.

As a stimulant, caffeine can be beneficial: it's used frequently to stimulate breathing, especially in newborn infants suffering respiratory and circulatory problems. It's also effective in the treatment of certain hyperactive children, for whom it has a paradoxically calming effect. Its major therapeutic use is in headache pills. But according to Richard Gilbert, headache is often a symptom of caffeine withdrawal, and headache pills may work by relieving pain caused in the first place by lack of caffeine. In which case, he says, a cup of coffee would provide the same service at less cost.

Even in relatively low doses, caffeine can decrease fatigue and increase mental alertness. It also seems to increase muscle strength and reduce the boredom connected with dull or repetitive tasks. After two cups of coffee, driving skills improve and typing becomes faster and more accurate. It is no accident that workers are given coffee breaks at the two times in the day when mental alertness is likely to be low and fatigue high.

Caffeine's restorative effect has long been recognized—"When one drinks coffee, the ideas come marching in like armies," declared Honoré de Balzac, who drank vast quantities as he worked on his novels—but it wasn't until two years ago that scientists at the University of Saskatchewan identified the biochemical mechanism responsible for this effect. Working with lab animals, John Phillis and Peter Wu found that caffeine speeds up the firing of cells in the nervous system by blocking the effects of adenosine, a natural depressant in the body.

Current scientific reports suggest that caffeine may inhibit cancer. Researchers at the University of Minnesota recently announced that large amounts of green coffee beans have been found to enhance the body's defences against cancer-producing chemicals in animals. Moreover, caffeine appears to increase the effectiveness of radiation therapy and cancer-treating drugs. Because caffeine stimulates cells when they should be resting, it may work by preventing the radiated cells from shutting down for repairs, thereby impeding the spread of the disease.

Caffeine is also used by commercial stockbreeders to enhance sperm quality during artificial insemination. And in Tokyo, hot coffee baths are recommended for those who wish to lose weight, as well as those who suffer from stomach problems or rheumatism.

• • •

Caffeine consumption varies with age, sex, and geographic region. Daily intake generally increases until about age sixty, and then decreases as people turn from coffee to tea—which, cup for cup, usually contains less caffeine. According to a recent U.S. survey, men between the ages of forty and forty-nine are the biggest consumers of coffee. Overall, however, women tend to consume more caffeine than men; both sexes drink about the same amount of coffee, but women drink considerably more tea.

The effects of caffeine occur within thirty to sixty minutes after ingestion. For the average person, caffeine's half-life (the time it takes for half the amount to disappear from the body) is about three and a half hours. For smokers, however, the half-life is substantially reduced. This means that people who quit smoking may become jittery if they don't decrease their coffee intake at the same time. Because many heavy coffee drinkers are also smokers, it's often difficult to separate the health risks of tobacco and caffeine.

Even if they don't smoke, women who have a tendency to develop breast lumps are wise to eliminate caffeine from their diets. An Ohio State University study reported that cystic breast disease cleared up in more than seventy-five per cent of women who stopped using tea, coffee, chocolate, and cola.

Although caffeine consumption is higher per capita in the U.S. than in Canada, there is evidence that excessive use is greater among Canadians. According to Richard Gilbert, twenty-eight per cent of the adults in this country drink the caffeine equivalent of five or more cups of coffee a day. Coffee consumption, observes Gilbert, generally increases as you cross Canada from east to west. Tea consumption, on the other hand, increases as you go from west to east.

The equivalent of one or two cups of coffee a day is probably not harmful though some people should carefully restrict their caffeine intake. Because coffee stimulates the release of acids in the stomach, people with ulcers or other gastro-intestinal problems are advised to avoid drinking it. Patients suffering from fever, high blood pressure, or cardiovascular disease should also stay away from caffeine; it raises body temperature, heartbeat, and blood pressure.

One last bit of bad news. Despite what the TV commercials say, you can't wean yourself off caffeine by switching to large amounts of "decaffeinated" coffee. It, too, may contain considerable quantities of caffeine.

G.B. Sinclair, "Grounds for Concern," *Saturday Night* (September, 1982), pp. 9-11.

Hands On: Reading into Writing

The following assignment deals with writing in the expository mode. The subject is sports.

Assignment

1. Actively read the following six expository essays on various aspects of *sports.*
2. Answer the questions appended to each essay. Your careful responses to these questions should act as a spur to your thought and so should assist you when you complete the reading workbook entry.
3. Complete a reading workbook entry for each essay:
   (a) Comment on subject, audience, and purpose.
   (b) Identify thesis statement, topic sentence, or controlling idea.
   (c) Comment on developmental strategies.
   (d) Prepare an outline.
   (e) Write a summary.
   (f) Write a response, of at least one hundred words.
4. Once you have finished dealing with the readings on an individual basis, you will have at least six hundred words of informed response on the subject of sports. This body of material will serve as the basis for your own *expository* essay on the subject, which should consist of three or four double-spaced typewritten pages. Remember what has been mentioned time and again in this book: the techniques that you learn as you actively read will be the ones that you put to good use when you write your own essay.
   (a) Examine your responses.
   (b) Develop a workable topic in view of your subject, audience, and purpose.
   (c) Determine effective developmental strategies.
   (d) Develop a thesis statement.
   (e) Develop an outline.
   (f) Write a first draft.
   (g) Revise.

HARRY BRUCE
THE ALCHEMY OF SAILING

1 All the dark winter she's in our driveway, up on her trailer, dead as a boulder on the ocean floor, a pathetic reproof to the terrible season that keeps her there. We tore up an old yellow tent in November and lashed it around her but it didn't work. The blizzards off the ocean come screaming up the bay in a way you'd have to feel to believe, and they rip the tent and yank it around as though they had hands, and then they dump the wild snow in her, and it melts, and turns to ice in her fiber-glass belly.

2 By March, the bay that lies for miles below our eastern windows begins to break up and turn from white to blue, and move again, and the days lengthen and the sun comes at us from a better height, and I remember that she's not really as dead as a boulder, she's no more dead than the sleeping trees, or a winter bear. She's waiting, and so am I.

3 I begin to fiddle in the basement. I dust off her two small masts, touch things up with Pratt and Lambert Spar Varnish (Quick Drying), take her rusty brown mainsail downtown to get a tiny hole patched. I blow $1.50 on *Yachting* magazine, I go out to the driveway and run my hands along her teak gunwales, inspect her rose bottom, her white boot top, her sea-green topsides, her eager bow. I love her plump conformation for the seven hundredth time and I know that, one sweet day soon, she'll be back on the bay where she lives and, together, we'll storm the glittering ocean, and I'll be *alive* again in a way I've not known at any time since winter laid her low.

4 I'll not be alone in this resurrection. In Canada, the sailboat industry is booming now as it has never boomed before. Manufacturers' sales of sailboats have almost doubled in four years, sailboat imports more than tripled between 1966 and 1971, and God alone knows exactly how many amateur sailboat builders were at work this past winter in the garages, basements and backyards of the country.

5 City people are increasingly desperate for evidence that they can be alive in a natural world, and there's a connection in yearnings between the back-to-the-land movement we hear so much about these days and a back-to-the-water movement in sailing craft. Back to Nature. Back to something clean and simple. Back to a life in which the main worries are not other people and what they do to them-

selves and to us but, rather, the right time to sow and the right time to reap, the proper construction of a root cellar, rounding up a lost animal, how to sink a well...

6 Or the shape of the thunderheads over an empty horizon, how soon to run for harbor, whether you can lay the marker buoy on the tack you're on now, whether or not to reef the main, the fog off the starboard bow, the mysterious breakers off the port bow, the biting flies under the hot sky of a sweaty calm, finding a safe anchorage, what the wind does as the sun dies, and the weather the morning may bring. Sailing reminds millions of men and women that they are alive and, during our moments afloat, a small part of each one of us becomes a Captain Joshua Slocum.

7 Lovers of literature about seafarers will know that on November 14, 1909, the great Joshua Slocum, Nova Scotia-born, aged 65, left the New England port of Vineyard Haven in his famous and beloved little sloop the Spray, outward bound for what he'd told a friend were "some faraway places," and that no one ever again saw either the captain or a trace of his vessel. Eleven sad years had passed since he and the Spray, all by themselves, had made their immortal voyage around the world, and by 1909 they were both in tatters. No one will ever know exactly what was on his mind that morning.

8 Perhaps, somewhere in the williwaws of this strange man's head, there was an obsession blowing and it said the time had come for him to die at sea in the vessel he had come to know as well as any man had ever known anything. Perhaps not. But the thing that is clear—from his classic *Sailing Alone Around The World*—is that, throughout his middle age and maybe his whole life, he never experienced such fear and glory, such peace and high ecstasy, such visions and grace, such communion with the wild creatures of the seas of the spinning world or so deep and mystical an awareness of the fact of his *being,* as he did during the days and nights of his time alone with the Spray.

9 He loved her, and the meaning of his love is that sailing is not merely a sport; Slocum was not comparable to a Sunday golfer or a lunchtime handball nut; and sailing craft are never just sports paraphernalia. They do not belong to the family of baseball bats, lacrosse sticks, skates, shuttlecocks, Olympic pools and jockstraps.

10 Sailing is as old as riding horses. Men have been going down to the sea in ships to do business in great waters for as long as they've been building roads, raising cattle or writing words; but, despite thousands of years of accumulated sailing lore, no one will ever know all

that we need to know about the relationships among sails and seas and winds and the powers of the sun and moon above. No, sailing is not a sport. It's a life. . . .

11 Sailing is active worship, a sacrifice of what we usually are to the children of God we might once have been, a reunion with blowing forces and unknowable chemistries and whirling planetary laws that must surely have something to do with the beginning of everything. Asleep in the black heart of February nights, I have dreams in which I am aboard gargantuan sailboats of unearthly grace and unspeakable power, and they rush me over massive cushions of green ocean toward destinations I never discover.

12 Slocum, says his biographer Walter Teller, was "a kind of prophet of the value of insecurity" and, though yachting experts have described the Spray as an unseaworthy old tub, Slocum himself knew she was beautiful beyond words and on the day he launched her he wrote simply, "She sat on the water like a swan." We can't all sail around the world. We can't all own Sprays.

13 On the days we choose to sail, however, we can smell for a while just a breath of the value of insecurity. We can see the cat's-paw of change move toward us over the water and we can discover for ourselves, again and again, that no well-designed and usefully loved sailboat, no matter how small she may be, ever fails to sit on the water like a swan. (Except when the things none of us can control conspire against her.)

14 An eight-year-old girl, at the helm of a sawed-off seven-foot plywood pram with a pink sail that's smaller than her bedsheet, glides over a brown pond under city trees, through the shimmering reflections of skyscrapers, and across the park and down a long hot summer afternoon of her life. She is messing about with the same principles of propulsion that, each winter, drive tens of millions of dollars' worth of impossibly gleaming yachts crashing and sliding their way through hundreds of miles of tumbling southern seas in the month-long Southern Ocean Racing Conference.

15 The yachts have dazzling equipment, towering grace, great white cloud after cloud of swinging, billowing, thundering sails. But they are all sisters to the little girl's pram, and the little girl is sister to the hard-drinking rich men who battle one another in the SORC because all winds are variations of an eternal wind, and those men would have to sail the pram pretty much the way she sails it.

16 It's this same wind that brings to life hundreds of thousands of

other sailboats, out of thousands of ports and clubs, sailing in hundreds of racing classes, in more regattas than any yachting magazine has ever been able to list, over putrid canals, lifeless reservoirs, greasy harbors, a world of lakes, and among utterly trustworthy tides, currents of treachery, icebergs moving south, buoys, bells, lightships, horns, whistles, flags, markers, hail, warm plopping rain, and out, too, among the strange birds, flying fish, hallucinations and the long swells of the Pacific Ocean at the equator's line.

17 When the little girl hoists her sail, cleats her halyard, drops her centreboard, takes the mainsheet in one hand and the tiller in the other and starts across the park, she is not only joining a fraternity of experience that included Captain Slocum and everyone else who ever sailed a boat, she is not only offering herself to an infinity of possible adventures, she is also accepting the power of whatever laws govern the relationships between people, sails and hulls on the one hand and, on the other, moving water, the location of the stars, and the sun-driven wind. She will watch what she's doing this afternoon. She will consider the influences on the pond because, at the moment, the pond is exactly where she is alive.

18 Sailing restores your ability to hear things one at a time. The city may have wrecked for a while your ear's readiness to discriminate. There is a sound I'll know in my head even when I've lost all true hearing, and it is the gentle, ringing clap-clang of steel halyards slapping aluminum masts aboard boats at their moorings. If you're trying to sleep on one of those boats it can be maddening, but this sound of insomnia is also the sound of evening peace in a perfect world, like cowbells in the pastures of your childhood; and it is the sound, too, of a dew-wet sunny dawn in the fragrance of a port you've just awakened to see by daylight for the first time. It summons you to coffee you can count on tasting better than coffee has ever tasted before.

19 The halyards are a sound of port, like the clunk of ice cubes in plastic tumblers, the creak of rowlocks, or a greeting called across quiet water under the voluminous trees of a friendly shore. The seagoing sounds are more violent: the explosive *thwack* of a balloon spinnaker catching all the wind it can hold in a fantastic split second; the fluttering thunder of a luffing mainsail; the metallic rattle, the smooth, hard, ratcheting click of a jib-sheet winch. There is the sound, in our own boat, of the heavy centreboard vibrating in its trunk—a kind of dull, chattering, humming complaint against the pressures of the sea.

20 Every boat has her unique creaks, groans, rattles and noisemaking partnerships of things; and always, in addition to the wind's whistling affair with the standing rigging, there is the sound of the water rushing against the thin, curvaceous skin of the hull that separates you from the depths. (When our four-year-old was only two and three weeks out of his mother's womb he was a bilious cranky babe, and the one place where he'd sleep for hours on end was down among the gurgling, slapping, bubbling harmonies in the bows of our 24-footer.) If I were to go blind, I'd want people to take me sailing.

21 The sounds are a part of being at the very centre of something important, and aboard a powerboat you do not hear them. Not the ones I mean. You do not glide. You *shake* your way through the water and things that are alive would rather not have much to do with you. "Porpoises," Slocum observed, "always prefer sailing ships." And today, whale researchers out of Halifax track the great beasts of the sea by schooner.

22 Then there are the things you see. There is, of course, no end to them, which is another reason why I say sailing is not a sport but a life. You can't record all the visual experiences of a life, even when they're as moving, as astounding, as significant, as frightening and tranquilizing as they're bound to be aboard a moving sailboat. The things you see are part of a great distance, and all of them swing with the motion of your craft, which obeys the motion of the water, and you can see all of the sky a *complete* horizon, the dome above, the moving ceaseless plain below. Slocum knew.

23 Slocum was well off Nova Scotia, on the first leg of his circumnavigation of the globe, when he discovered the Spray's amazing ability to hold a course on her own and, on the night of July 5, 1895, she was making eight knots, and he was feeling just fine: "The fog lifting before night, I was afforded a look at the sun just as it was touching the sea. I watched it go down and out of sight. Then I turned my face eastward, and there, apparently at the very end of the bowsprit, was the smiling full moon rising out of the sea. Neptune himself coming over the bows could not have startled me more. 'Good morning, sir,' I cried, 'I'm glad to see you.'"

24 It pleases me to live in the province where Slocum was born, to share with the odd fishing boat (there are situations in which marine engines are forgivable) a stretch of the strange cruel shoreline and seagoing heritage of Nova Scotia. We live about four miles from the open ocean on a fjord near Halifax. Our current boat—the one in the

driveway—is a chunky, open 18-footer with three loose-footed sails, lots of freeboard and, for her size, marvelous abilities in heavy weather. She must be one of the world's smallest yawls and, though she looks like a converted fishing dory, she sails as an anetelope runs.

25 We moor her a few hundred yards from our house and, since the wind usually comes up the bay, she tugs at her float with her nose raised toward the open sea and, all day, she mutely begs us to let her set us free. We buck out to the ocean, tacking between the slowly widening shores of scrubby spruce and bright, bald, salt-scoured rock, and we're still close-hauled as we pass the ever barer islands and the midstream rocks that are deathtraps for vessels and heaven for cormorants . . . and then, beyond the farther islands on the long wave-corrugated skyline, we can see it all, blazing and gleaming under the summer sun, the whole, great, bouncing, marching, magnificent mess—the Atlantic Ocean—and just about then, the boat seems to slip up over one of the more gentle slopes on a roller coaster and we can feel the ride in our stomachs. Then she does it again. She slips up and over the ocean swell and moves on to the open sea, and the feeling is not quite like anything we ever knew in all the hours of happy sailing we spent during the years on Lake Ontario.

26 We reach back and forth along the coast, shuddering at the awful weight of ocean water on rock, watching it blam skyward like the cold bursts of white firecrackers, and considering uneasily the terrible suck of it as it slides home again.

27 We find secret islands, sweet anchorages in calm backwaters of such Caribbean clarity we can see the fish moving 10 or 12 feet below, and we unpack mountains of impossibly delicious sandwiches, grapes, oranges, soft cheese, and drinks that are exquisite under our own sun. Hawks sail, seagulls wheel and squawk, the ocean roars on the windward shore of the island, and we lie down on the hot sand here on the lee side, and watch our little vessel as she rides at anchor and sits on the water like a swan. Before dark, we run up the bay and home to supper.

28 Usually, we take our three kids on these southbound dashes to the ocean and, once, we all saw two slick black porpoises gamboling and arching and dancing through the cold rollers as though they were lovers in a field of grass, and the sight of them—the big, precious, utterly wild creatures out there exactly where they belonged—shocked us so that the memory is with us now, and for a long time.

29 There was a day, too, my wife and I left the kids at home because

the wind was gusting beyond 40, and we got out there a few hundred yards off the real shore, the outer shore, and we saw a sumptuous 40-foot cruising sloop reaching inshore through the long beams of the late sun, heading for quieter water, and the whole ocean sparkled crazily and threw up such a commotion that this big, prudent deep-sea racer flew only her jib.

30 All three of our little sails were drawing beautifully and our boat charged up one side of the waves and shot down the other with a zest and courage that I was sure could not help but astound the sloop's skipper. (How could he know we were too scared to lose way long enough to reef our main or, indeed, that for a while we were too scared even to try going about so we could go on home?)

31 But enough. You get a sailboat-lover reminiscing, and he'll go on all night. The point is only this: you learn from sailing that, although you must forever deal with forces of wind and weather that predate all memory and still defy our understanding, no two days of sailing are ever the same. If we were capable of measuring the changes, we'd find that no two *seconds* of sailing are ever the same either. Sailing is as infinitely various as the changing face of the sky, and once you begin to feel this you will be able to say with Captain Slocum, "The days passed happily with me wherever my ship sailed."

Harry Bruce, "The Alchemy of Sailing," *Maclean's* (July, 1973), pp. 24-25, 42-43.

Questions

1. **Subject**
   In the final paragraph of the essay the author introduces a long concluding passage with the phrase: "The point is only this." Then follows the point. How does the "point" that follows act as a summary of the subject of the essay?
2. **Audience**
   The author makes use of a number of particular terms associated with sailing that an audience unknowledgeable about this world might not understand. Identify one of these. Does the use of these terms turn the reader off the essay? Why or why not?
3. **Purpose**
   It is not enough to say that in this expository essay the author is defining sailing. He is, in fact, doing rather more than this. Of what does this "rather more" consist? Locate areas in the essay where the author makes use of narrative, argument, the developmental strategies of analogy and comparison. Are these devices used to good effect?

4. Structure and Style
   (a) In what sense is the word "alchemy" in the title of this essay appropriate to the author's purpose?
   (b) Comment on the appropriateness of the opening two paragraphs.
   (c) How is the final reference to Captain Slocum a fitting conclusion to this essay?

MORLEY CALLAGHAN

MORLEY CALLAGHAN REMEMBERS FOSTER HEWITT

1 Early in the 1920s, when I was at college and working in the summer months as a reporter on *The Toronto Daily Star,* I used to see occasionally a thin-faced, slightly built man about my own age who, whenever I saw him, seemed to be hurrying from one office to another. I never saw him at a desk in the news room. When I asked who he was I was told that he was Foster Hewitt, the son of the sports editor, W.A. Hewitt, and that he was fooling around with the idea of a hockey broadcast on radio. At that time the *Star,* across the road from Child's restaurant on King Street, had a remarkable crew of reporters. Gordon Sinclair was there, and for four months Ernest Hemingway was suffering and bleeding under the whip of the legendary city editor, Harry Hindmarsh. Hindmarsh later described us as a raffish crew, too big for our britches. But there was nothing raffish about Foster Hewitt.

2 If Hewitt had any boon companions, they were not on the editorial staff. I used to like going across to Child's for a coffee and long conversations, but I never saw Foster Hewitt—trim, dapper, pale—sitting around with the boys.If anyone had told me he was a boxer, I would have thought the idea absurd. Nor could I have dreamed that one day he would become a great actor, powerful enough to draw the people of his country together.

• • •

3 I had played hockey in the old Toronto Hockey League until I was seventeen. I liked watching hockey games. Only when I could not see them did I listen to a radio broadcast. When the 1930s came around Hewitt's Saturday night broadcasts had a huge and loyal audience, a

tribal family around a national hearth. I thought people listened to Hewitt on Saturday night because they couldn't get to the Gardens.

4 One night I called in on my father and mother at their home and found them sitting in the dark, near the radio, listening to Foster Hewitt. I turned on the light. My father had a happy smile and my mother's blue eyes were shining with excitement.

5 I was bemused—I had no idea either one of them had any interest in hockey. My father had had no interest in sport. Though I had played baseball in all the city leagues, I could never get him to come and watch me pitch. Yet there he was listening to Foster Hewitt with my mother, both of them breathless with pleasure. About a week later I phoned, expecting to have a long conversation with my mother. She told me rather hurriedly that the Leafs were losing three to two and she would call me back.

6 They had never seen a hockey game, so I got them two tickets for a Saturday night game at the Gardens. The next day I went to see them. How had they liked the game? It was confusing, they said apologetically, alomost upsetting and very strange. I said I'd get them tickets again. No, they said, looking at each other uneasily, they were more comfortable listening at home.

7 I thought the trip to the Gardens, the crowd, the traffic, must have been unfamiliar and tiring for them. But a year or so later a friend—Bertram Brooker, a painter and writer and later vice president of MacLaren Advertising—asked me if my wife and I would come to his home on Saturday night to hear the Hewitt broadcast of the hockey game. He had friends, cronies, painters, musicians, and writers, who came to his place every Saturday for the game and a party.

8 "I didn't know you liked hockey," I said. "But since you obviously do, then why don't we go to a game together?"

9 "I don't want to go to a game."

10 Baffled, I said bluntly, "Then you don't like hockey."

11 "So you say," he said curtly, and a silence fell between us, a kind of hostility. We dropped the subject, and I imagined that he and his intellectual friends were like my father and mother. A real game of hockey might have bewildered them.

• • •

12 Why so many people preferred to listen to Foster Hewitt rather than seeing a game continued to baffle me until the evening a neighbour asked me if I'd go with him to the Gardens to see a Canadiens-Leafs game.

13 His wife came to my house to visit with my wife and listen to the broadcast while we went off to the Gardens. Hockey is a peculiar game, a little like ballet. At its best it has a flash, a suspense, a grace, an elegance in the pattern of the playmaking. At its grinding worst it's dull, heavy, and monotonous. That night we found ourselves watching a dull game.

14 When we got home my wife said, "My, we were wishing we could have been with you. It must have been quite a game."

15 "It was a tedious game," I said sourly.

16 "What's the matter with you two?" my neighbour's wife asked. "Foster was so excited, and we got so excited too."

17 Now I thought I had got the hang of Foster Hewitt's powerful magic. With amused and satisfied cynicism, I thought that he was one of the world's greatest salesmen. He could take the most ordinary game—the product—and package it by selecting what he saw on the ice, so exciting himself that he could draw around him a million listeners—much of English-speaking Canada coming together under his spell. And I decided there and then that the National Hockey League owed him about $10-million for what he had done for the game.

• • •

18 In the 1940s, the National Film Board hired a director of documentaries to make a film about hockey. This director, a fellow from New York named Irving Jacoby, asked me if I would write some narration. Jacoby and I became friends, and he wanted to use my voice for the whole narration. But the film board guy said he wanted a voice that sounded more like that of a BBC announcer, an impersonal voice.

19 On the day we were doing the voice testing, Foster Hewitt joined us. He was to do a two-minute broadcast of a hockey game, for use in the film. He came in looking exactly as he had when I'd first seen him in the old *Star* building—just as slim and trim, just as inconspicuous. Wasting no time, knowing exactly what was expected of him, he went into the sound booth.

20 I could have believed I was at home and he was at Maple Leaf Gardens—that slightly high-pitched voice, the deliberate pauses, mounting tension, the sense of some fierce impending action on the ice when he said, "He dumps it in." Then the exultant cry, "He shoots, he scores!" I wanted to stand up and yell. I could have sworn he was at least watching a movie of a game. But there was no movie. There was no game. He didn't need a game. He was just as good

without one. Astonished, I realized what an extraordinary creative artist he was. In his own way Foster Hewitt was as good as Marlon Brando. He could give life to things!

21 When Hewitt had finished his job he came out of the sound booth. I walked to the door with him but he had no time for idle conversation. As I watched him get into his big grey Cadillac and drive away, I remember thinking, there goes the greatest dramatic artist in the whole country.

22 Remarkable as he was, though, he had his limitations. He was like a dramatist who had done only one play. What made him unique was that, for two generations of Canadians, he became bigger than his play. He became the play.

Morley Callaghan, "Morley Callaghan Remembers Foster Hewitt," *Saturday Night* (September, 1985), pp. 40, 42.

Questions

1. **Subject**
   At one point in this essay Morley Callaghan refers to Foster Hewitt as "a great actor"; at another he calls him "the world's greatest salesman." In what sense do these two terms capture the definition of the man who is the subject of Callaghan's essay?
2. **Audience**
   Those of us who never had the opportunity to hear a Foster Hewitt radio broadcast, who never, that is, were part of the "tribal family around a national hearth," might not feel what Callaghan feels for the man's power. How do the narrative examples help to draw us into the orbit of Hewitt's power?
3. **Purpose**
   Explain how the final narrative anecdote in this essay is the highest tribute the author pays to Hewitt.
4. **Structure and Style**
   (a) Explain how Hewitt as a man apart from other men is skillfully suggested throughout the essay.
   (b) Explain the meaning of the final sentence in the essay.
   (c) Explain how the author can call Hewitt "an extraordinary creative artist." Has his essay helped to make this description believable in the eyes of the reader?

TRENT FRAYNE

AS FRENCH CANADIAN AS BASEBALL

1 It is a tight tense moment. The bases are filled with Pittsburghs. The count is three and two on Roberto Clemente, a very tough Pirate. The Expos are in bad trouble. Some of their fans can't look.

2 Suddenly, in the boxes along the first-base side and in the reserved seats back of them, a tiny ripple of applause begins and slowly swells. People stand. They smile. They clap their hands. They are turned now to the entrance ramp back of the plate. The people in the lower boxes have their backs to the field and they, too, are smiling and clapping their hands. It is a standing ovation.

3 The nature of this divertissement? Two girls with long blond hair are walking from the entrance toward their seats back of first base. Their hair is halfway down their backs, pure gold. They are wearing black velvet hot pants and white blouses. They smile, very pleased by the applause and only a little embarrassed. When they reach their seats and sit down, the hand clapping drifts off, and the fans sit down, too.

4 "What is the count?" a man asks, turning back to the field. "Mon Dieu! Three-and-two!"

• • •

5 Sanity was barely preserved when Montreal sneaked through the back door into the National Baseball League three years ago. Now, in spite of two kidnappings, one national crisis, un uncounted number of blown mailboxes, and a murder that numbed the whole country, the Expos still cast their spell of pure magic over Jarry Park.

6 Lesser towns might falter under the weighty spotlight that chronically finds Montreal countenancing fiscal disaster or an international incident or some impenetrable strike, but yeasty old Paris-on-the-St. Lawrence goes right along skirting ruin and always, it seems, coming up smelling like eau de cologne. With broader slums, worse sewage and more per capita unemployment than any other city in the country, Montreal has more people enjoying themselves than any place twice its size—streaming into Expo 67 four years ago, exploding over an out-of-the-blue Grey Cup champion last November, ecstatic over yet another Stanley Cup last May, *oo-la-la*-ing over the summer

Olympics in 1976, or bubbling over in Jarry Park, the world's smallest big-league ball park and largest bilingual loony bin.

7 Last year, 1,424,683 admissions were recorded in this cosy city-owned playpen surrounded by a swimming pool and a soccer field and acres of deep grass and tall old maples. People flock here by subway or drive north and west, through the Greek district, two or three miles on St. Laurent Boulevard from the main streets in the midtown core, Ste. Catherine and Dorchester. This year, by the time the Chicago Cubs close out the Expos' home season on September 30, attendance may hit 1,500,000, close to twice the number who watched the Canadiens in the Forum last season (including the nine games of the Stanley Cup play-offs).

8 Unlike the Canadiens or the Alouettes, the Expos are not winners; they have not acquired their incredibly loyal and devoted following because they are the best. In their first season they lost 110 games, and that ain't easy. In one stretch, often grasping defeat from the very jaws of victory, they lost 20 in a row, close to a league record. But then, they are by no means the worst either. They don't have outfielders who catch fly balls on the top of the head, and their hitters never triple into double plays. They are a very respectable ball club, growing more so with time. They cut their defeats to 89 last year, and this year for three glorious days in April they were actually in first place. In short, the Expos are not to be mistaken for the New York Mets in *their* early days, when losers everywhere identified with *their* truly impressive futility.

9 Expo fans are knowledgeable baseball observers, not some Jacques-come-latelies suddenly adopting a new kind of self-expression unavailable to the rest of Canada and therefore to be cherished. There is a mistaken notion that when Expo fans applaud a foul ball they do it out of ignorance of the game. This is nonsense. They do it out of love. What happens night after night at Jarry Park is a love-in.

10 Quebec has been in love with baseball since at least 1903 when Montreal had a team in the Eastern League. Today there are 5,000 boys between nine and 12 playing Little League baseball in Quebec, and 75,000 boys under 20 are registered with the Quebec Amateur Baseball Federation. There are numerous leagues for older players, including the long-established Provincial League where big-leaguers Sal Maglie and Vic Power played when they were banned from baseball in the United States after jumping to a so-called outlaw league in Mexico.

11 Harry Simmons, a baseball historian, says that one Harry Wright, captain of the Boston Red Stockings, took a baseball team to Montreal in 1872 to play an exhibition game against the Montreal Cricket Club. Simmons, a gentle stocky man with a ready smile, now works in the office of the baseball commissioner, Bowie Kuhn, in New York, but maintains a home in Montreal. He moved there some 20 years ago with the late Frank (Shag) Shaughnessy, himself a transplanted American who was president of the International League. Shaughnessy decided to shift league headquarters to Montreal after two New York-area ball clubs, Jersey City and Newark, dropped out of the IL in the early 1950s.

12 "In those days Montreal had the highest attendance in the minor leagues for years on end," Simmons recalls. "The Montreal Royals were the top farm club of the old Brooklyn Dodgers, and crowds of 22,000 were not at all unusual at old Delorimier Stadium in Montreal's east end. When Jackie Robinson became the first black man to play in organized baseball in 1946, the Brooklyn owner, Branch Rickey, sent him to Montreal to hone his skills. Montreal saw great baseball in the years before television killed the minor leagues. Seasonal attendance of 400,000-plus was commonplace. In that period, promotion was local, not province wide and even international as it is now. A whole new group of outlanders came into the media, especially into radio and television, during the 1960s in Montreal; they thought baseball was a phenomenon when the Expos came along because they hadn't done their history lessons."

13 For generations, baseball has been the summertime diversion in Montreal that hockey is in winter. Summer camps and summer cottages do not abound in Quebec as they do in, say, Ontario. A kid plays ball all summer, and his old man follows the major-league standings. Even after the Royals folded in 1960 the game got a big play in the papers, especially the French papers which would recast their late editions in the small hours of the morning to include the box scores of big-league games in Los Angeles and San Francisco that wouldn't end until 2 a.m. Montreal time.

14 There are vast areas of Montreal where the streets are carbon copies of themselves—like Durocher Street, say, in a section called Park Extension, an endless narrow avenue of identical brick houses set tightly together, each with a tiny iron-grille balcony extending over the sidewalk on the second floor. On hot humid nights the tenants live in their neighbor's laps, sitting out in undershirts trying to cool

off. Breaking this residential pattern are occasional long streets of uninviting stores, cheap and weary, their paint peeling—second-hand stores, pizza joints, groceries with worn wooden floors, greasy-spoon restaurants, gas stations on the corner.

15 The people who live and work here rarely escape from the city, and to highlight their lives their bread-and-circuses Mayor Jean Drapeau hands them a galaxy of gaudy baubles—Man and His World, the Olympics, the Expos. Drapeau unflaggingly pursued a big-league baseball franchise, sending his executive assistant, a big affable handshaker named Gerry Snyder, to major-league offices and major-league meetings to spread the Montreal gospel and remind the moguls of the promotional success of Expo 67. To land the franchise, Drapeau not only promised the moon in the form of a domed stadium within three years but, as a stopgap until a dome could be built, turned over Jarry Park to the ball club and tossed three million dollars into the pot to enlarge it. No sod has been turned for a dome, of course, but who knows what will come out of an architect's dreams as he plans accommodation for the noble Olympics—with federal funding. Meanwhile, there's no chance whatever that the National League will hold Drapeau to his contract to produce a dome by 1972. In spite of its tiny seating capacity of 28,456 Jarry Park outdrew two thirds of the other 23 big-league clubs, including the world-champion Baltimore Orioles who have never matched Montreal's 1970 attendance in spite of a 55,000-capacity modern ball park.

16 The least surprised man in Montreal when Expomania swept the city—next, perhaps, to Drapeau himself—was Charles Bronfman, the principal owner who has put at least five million dollars into an operation that cost $10 million for franchise rights and runs close to half that in annual operating expenses.

17 "I grew up here," explains the heir to the Seagram Distillers fortune. "I knew from personal observation as a kid that French-speaking people loved baseball and I knew how they sat out on their balconies in their undershirts with nothing to do. I also know, and have always known, that they have a great capacity for joy."

• • •

18 Rusty Staub has hit another home run. He circles the bases, tall, erect, wearing a small smile of delight. Wild cries fill the night air. The crowd teems, standing and shouting. The lights on the scoreboard flash in happy disarray. The organ crashes a joyous staccato. As Rusty

crosses the plate and wheels toward the Montreal dugout on the third-base side, he touches the stubby peak of his blue batting helmet, his head lowered, responding to the uproar. He disappears down the dugout steps and the din subsides.

19 "Quack, quack."

20 Quack, *quack?* What is this quack, quack? People stand and strain their necks, turning toward the back of the stands. Where is the quack, quack?

21 High up, a man waves a duck, a white duck, *un canard blanc.* He waves it above his head, saluting Rusty Staub. "Quack, quack," says the duck again. The people laugh and point. And then they give the man with the white duck a standing ovation.

• • •

22 Bronfman turned 40 last June 27. He is a lean, dark, sharp-featured balding man who wears expensively tailored casual clothes and often talks with a kind of half grin on his face, an assured man. He is president of House of Seagram Ltd., the Canadian arm of Distillers Corporation-Seagrams Ltd., the parent company of the empire of which his 80-year-old father Samuel is the president. Charles' brother, Edgar Bronfman, is president of Joseph E. Seagram and Sons, Inc., in New York, the United States branch. But the Expos are Charles' baby; the ball club is not a Seagram promotion as, say, sponsorship of the Canadian Open golf championship used to be.

23 On weekdays Charles Bronfman sits in the House of Seagram building in downtown Montreal across Peel Street from the Mount Royal Hotel, a tiny Disneyland castle of turrets and venerable grey stone. He is on the second floor in a big comfortable office furnished in deep carpeting, soft lighting, deep brown leather chairs, and a curious mixture of whiskey bottles, baseball bats, two large Harold Towns, a color photograph of his father having a drink while playing solitaire, and a likeness of himself wearing an Expo uniform (his number is 83, as in Seagram's 83) painted by the former football star turned sports artist Tex Coulter. A photo of Bronfman with golfer Arnold Palmer lies on the floor in a corner, the discarded game.

24 "The success of the Expos is part conscious, part unconscious," Bronfman says, settling into one of the deep chairs around his copper coffee table, crossing one carefully pressed knee over the other. "What was unconscious was the layout of the park itself, the intimacy that put these famous players—Willie Mays, Hank Aaron, Bob Gib-

son, our own Rusty Staub—almost within touching distance of the fans. Why, in most parks the players just aren't real; they're toy figures off in the distance. You buy an expensive seat in Atlanta or in the Astrodome and you discover you're 100 feet and more behind the closest base. Baseball is an intimate game. The pitcher and the hitter are primitives; the guy with a stone and the guy with a club. To be close to this is terribly exciting. We got this as sort of a fluke; it was simply a question of doing the possible with the seating.

25 "But we did some things consciously, too. I remember when I used to watch the Royals in Delorimier. All the Jews sat on the first-base side, all the French Canadians on the third-base side, and the WASP guys anywhere. I didn't want that. I deliberately mixed up the season-ticket applicants so that Jewish names and French-Canadian names and WASP names were made neighbours. And we didn't want beer hawked in the stands. We wanted people to line up for it at booths under the stands so that presidents of companies and truck drivers would all be in there together. There was only one thing we wanted our customers to have in common: they were *Expo* fans. And we wanted everybody to know they were wanted. We even hired a guy whose sole job was to watch the ushers; if he caught anybody being rude to a fan that usher was out.

26 "We knew, having to start from scratch, that it'd take time to assemble a contending team. The miracle of the Mets took seven years, remember. But, philosophically, we didn't want clowns; we didn't want any Marvin Throneberrys with two left feet. We knew our fans would stay with us as long as the players tried, as long as they gave their best. The first guy who was ever booed at Jarry Park was our pitcher, Mudcat Grant, who didn't run out a sacrifice bunt one time. The fans thought he wasn't trying, so they booed him."

27 (The saddest man in baseball was Mudcat Grant the day the Expos traded him to St. Louis, a pennant contender. "I played in a lot of cities but this is the only one where being black *simply doesn't make any difference*," Grant said. "This is the only place I've ever felt free.")

28 "It is my personal opinion," says Charles Bronfman, "that our French-speaking fans see themselves in the Expos. Just as the Expos are an emerging team, the French are an emerging people in this country. That's what Quebec's all about. Suddenly they're coming on in the business world. It used to be that if they didn't become a doctor, lawyer, notary or priest, they'd be nothing. But now they know if they try they can make it. So they're patient with us as long as we try."

29 It is the bottom of the eighth. Los Angeles leads 6-0. They have this one all but wrapped up and it is a big night for Dodger pitcher Bill Singer. He has allowed two hits, completely in charge, monotonously setting down the Expos. He gets one man here in the eighth, then another. An error gives a life to an Expo. Then Singer walks a man. He's still in charge, but the park has come alive. The scoreboard, with creeping letters, spells out GO GO EXPO! The organist, Fernand Lapierre, crashes ominous chords. The atmosphere is tense, the crowd buzzing. The batter, John Bateman, knocks a routine two-hop bouncer to the third baseman who steps on the bag and ends the inning. Does the crowd jeer, hoot, boo its sudden frustration? *Mais non.* The crowd sighs a long sad "ah-h-h-h" of disappointment. The organ chirps *Whatever Will Be, Will Be,* and the people laugh and clap and buzz again. Usherettes in their miniskirts and swinging capes, some of them with platinum hair coiffed high as a pop fly, pat their pretty hands in encouragement. "Next in*ning,* we will get them," an usherette cries. But next inning, they don't. Singer preserves his two-hitter. It is over. "Tomor*row,*" the girl calls to the Expos disappearing into the dugout. "Tomor*row* you'll win, eh?"

• • •

30 Apart from the prices (all seats in the half-moon from first to third, more than 12,000 of them, are either $3.50 or five dollars; a pint of beer is 60 cents, a hamburger 60 cents, coffee 20 cents, the lowly hot dog 40 cents) the Expo management is highly considerate, even imaginative. In celebrating the club's first birthday John McHale, the president who happened to be attending a meeting in Seattle, was seized just before he retired for the night by an inspiration. It was 11 p.m. in Seattle, two in the morning back in Montreal when he telephoned Lou Martin, then stadium manager at Jarry Park.

31 "Lou, are you awake?"

32 "Yah, yah, I'm awake."

33 "Are you sober?"

34 "Yah, I'm sober."

35 "Are you stting down?"

36 "Sitting down? For crissakes, John, I'm *ly*ing down. It's two o'clock in the morning."

37 "Okay, I want 20,000 candles and 20,000 cupcakes for the fans at the ballpark for the birthday tonight."

38 "Twenty *thous*and!" cried Martin, "John, are *you* sober?"

39 So that night, with more than 15,000 people in the stands, the

floodlights went out, the fans lit their candles, and everybody sang "Happy Birthday, Dear Expos." And later that night, nearly 5,000 cupcakes were delivered to Montreal orphanages.

40 Last year, just before mid-season, the Expos dipped a speculative toe into uncharted waters: they won five straight games at home. By the fourth inning of that fifth game they were ahead 9-0, and a victory seemed certain.

41 "Barbara," an exultant Charles Bronfman said to his wife. "I'll be back in a minute. I've just had the greatest idea I've ever had in my life."

42 He left his box, found John McHale among the serfs in press row, and said calmly, "I've got me an idea."

43 McHale, a tall, lean Detroit-born career baseball man of 49 who some observers believed would be appointed the game's commissioner prior to his taking on the top executive job for Bronfman, retorted with a similar calm. "You want to give everybody in the ball park a free ticket."

44 Later, reconstructing the scene in his office, Bronfman said McHale often seems to read his mind. "It's like we were married," he observed.

45 Anyway, some 17,000 fans were given tickets good for a future game—roughly a $35,000 gesture—and season-ticket holders who already owned future-game tickets were allocated an extra seat for a guest.

• • •

46 John Robertson, the large bushy-browed columnist of the Montreal *Star,* attacks the hot buffet in the press lounge before a night game.

47 "This place is a Peter Sellers movie," he says, munching roast beef and escalloped potatoes. "Two people from out-of-town get a cab at their hotel, tell the guy they want to go to Expo. The guy brings them here. They come in, look around baffled, and ask where's the Hungarian exhibit. The usher is undismayed. 'Dere he is, No. 14, Marv Staehle, our only Hungarian.'

48 "The people here are different people than you find at the Forum for hockey. It's a lunch-bucket crowd here, a family crowd, and they get slaughtered with politeness. At the Forum you feel you ought to tiptoe like it was Buckingham Palace; you get the feeling they figure they're doing you a favor just letting you buy a ticket. Here? Well, let's just say they're glad to see you. The best time to come is a double

header on a Sunday afternoon in midsummer. Halfway through the second game they're full of beer and full of sun and they singalong with the organ. It's a happy joint."

• • •

49 The Mayans of the Yucatan Peninsula played ball games before ecstatic crowds in the sixth century at Chichen-Itza, and a century later at Uxmal, and the ruins of their ball courts are prowled today by all sorts of visitors rooting around in the Mexican rubble. Ball games were an obsession with these people, who had one tiny aberration: when the games ended they beheaded the captain of the losing side. These days, they vilify the umpires.

50 Of Expomania, Dr. Alastair MacLeod, a psychiatrist and the executive director of the Mental Hygiene Institute in Montreal, says: "I'm not sure of this, quite frankly, but it's conceivable that this is a ritualistic device whereby you can let off a lot of aggression without much damage to anybody. Like the Mayan ball games in the temples of the Yucatan, and like the Roman circus in a way, the people really come to be friendly with each other; it's a ritualistic handling of aggression in a way that turns it into competition and enjoyment without much damage. It's the type of thing one can get a great deal of enjoyment out of for a relatively small sum of money, bringing themselves together, and what you see is a group phenomenon, principally of the lower-income group."

51 It is a lovely Sunday and the Expos are handling the New York Mets. All through the sunny afternoon there is this fan behind the Expos' dugout playing his fiddle. Merry, happy tunes, polkas and French folk songs. He sways his shoulders as he sits there in the sun, and his arm pumps in frenzy as it rushes the bow across the strings. And then in the seventh inning there is a home run and the Expos leap farther ahead, and the man with the fiddle jumps to his feet and stands in the aisle, fairly bouncing his bow across the singing violin. He starts down the aisle, still playing, and everyone turns to watch and to smile and to cry out in laughter, and when he reaches the bottom of the steps he hops onto the roof of the Expo dugout and there he stands, doing a happy jig, bending and swooping as he plays.

52 And what do you suppose happens then? Why, the laughing people all rise to their feet and . . . of course! A standing ovation.

Trent Frayne, "As French Canadian as Baseball," *Macleans*, (August, 1971), pp. 26, 54-56.

Questions

1. **Subject**
   Explain how the title of this essay, although initially perplexing, is an absolutely accurate encapsulation of the subject of this essay.
2. **Audience**
   How does the author approach his subject so that it might appeal to an audience that has no interest in baseball?
3. **Purpose**
   Explain why the author shifts back and forth in his narrative from actual baseball scenes at the Park itself to scenes off the field. How does this shifting help the author attain his end?
4. **Structure and Style**
   (a) How important to the essay is the author's summary of the brief history of Montreal baseball? Comment on the appropriateness of the placement of this history segment.
   (b) How effective to the essay as a whole are the passages of dialogue and direct discourse found in the essay?
   (c) How does the author tie the end of the essay to its beginning?

ABBY HOFFMAN*

RUNNING FOR GOLD

1 It is one of those ambivalent fall afternoons in Toronto's High Park. The brisk air forebodes winter; the brilliant sunshine recalls summer. The park's nature trails are almost devoid of people, the only sounds those of rustling oak leaves underfoot. It's all quite idyllic, although the farther I run the less note I take of the scenery and the more I take of my legs. Up ahead, at the edge of Grenadier Pond, three kids are fishing. I've passed them twice already; and as I come into view again, the three turn their attention from fishing poles to me. They poke each other and hold a hasty conference. As I approach, the youngest (always the most brazen) shouts:

2 "Hey, mister, are you a lady jogger?"

*Abby Hoffman is a four-time Olympian and currently the Director General of the federal government's sport agency, Sport Canada. She is an outspoken advocate on behalf of Canadian sport with particular interests in athletes' rights and expanding opportunities for females in sport.

3 After a dozen or so years of training in public parks and streets, I'm used to some pretty strange comments. But this one really has me baffled. I'm mildly irked at being mistaken for a jogger—we runners go to great lengths to distinguish ourselves from the ignominious jogger, since the jogger image carries for us the trauma of premature retirement—but I give myself the benefit of the doubt and interpret their inquiry as to whether I am a lady as an exclamation, not a question. Cursing their impudence, I run on, increasing my tempo.

4 I am often asked if I race against men. I don't. But when I am asked—and this is invariably the *next* question—if I can beat men at my distance I take advantage of the question's ambiguity, and lying a little say, "Yes." I actually can beat the vast majority of men—99.9% of them. I cannot, however, defeat even a mediocre male who trains seriously to race the half-mile, my best event. Come the 1976 Olympics in Montreal, I may well have my problems with the other women running the half-mile, but at least I won't need to contend with any of the tiny fraction of men who would be sure to defeat me.

5 Somehow the legitimacy of women's sports is tied to their ability to be just as good as men. It is true that the men's Olympic sprint champion Valery Borzov will always beat the women's champion Renate Stecher and that Mark Spitz will outswim Shane Gould every time.

6 But, just for fun, let's ask why men don't perform the balance beam event in gymnastics. In this event, Russia's Olga Korbut usually exhausts her audience with her incredible poise and aesthetic dexterity. Why can an 82-pound girl do what no man can do? Simple—because women are different in a way that makes them superior athletes in this particular event. Women achieve a better balance because of a lower centre of gravity—rump, to the layman. It must be accepted that while both men and women are able to do sports well, they approach the task differently. Men are better at the quick, powerful movement—the end-to-end rush or slapshot in hockey, the knockout punch in boxing. Women, with their smaller stature, lack of large heavy muscles and consequently greater flexibility, have a degree of grace in physical movements that men are unable to equal.

7 The North American emphasis on sports is in terms of competition, where the goal is to dominate the opposition. And this serves to emphasize the "inferiority" of women's athletics. The European tradition starts with gymnastics and the development of the individual's coordination, balance, stamina and strength. It leads to a much healthier situation: equally stringent standards of achievement are

applied to boys and girls, and there is less tendency to associate prowess in sport with only one sex. In the North American manner of segregation by sex in physical education classes, boys are unable to share in the natural aesthetic qualities that girls bring to sport, and the girls fail to profit from the natural aggressiveness and strength of the boys.

8 Athletes themselves are aware of male superiority in terms of brute strength and raw power, but that kind of superiority is not the motivating force of the athlete. At the highest levels one learns how much more there is than simply winning and losing. All through my childhood I fantasized about breaking an Olympic record. And I finally did it in Munich—regrettably, there were seven others in front of me breaking that same record. There is a poignancy to reality that juvenile fantasy fails to consider. I am sure, however, that as Olympic finalists all eight of us fulfilled childhood ambitions that day.

9 We often like to think of our own era as the most progressive. In the case of women's sport this just isn't so. Admittedly, the mid-Fifties was a pretty trivial period, but when I was caught playing hockey on a boys' team the incident became headline copy. At the time I reveled in all the ballyhoo—I must have been the only player in the world with a private dressing room—but I could never figure out why a girl wanting to play hockey was such a sensation. I was more confused by the fact that none of my girl friends would admit that *they* wanted to play. People had forgotten that women's ice hockey teams were known in 1900 and that national championships were held in women's hockey in the 1930s.

10 The real heyday of women's sport in Canada was the mid-Twenties to mid-Thirties. The prosperity of the Twenties and the flood of women into the labor force opened up hitherto taboo activities to all classes of women, and athletics was undoubtedly one of these. Led by Myrtle Cook, we won an Olympic Track and Field title at the 1928 Amsterdam Olympics, and Canada's best-known team abroad—Percy Page's Edmonton Grads' Ladies Basketball Team—dominated the world.

11 But it was to be short-lived. In the early Thirties women's baseball was drawing 5,000 spectators a game to Toronto's Sunnyside Park; women's senior basketball games were carried live on the radio with the play-by-play commentary of Bobby Rosenfeld; and sports columnists Phyllis Griffiths, Alexandrine Gibb and Rosenfeld were reporting regularly on women's athletics. By 1934, however, the validity of

women's sports was under attack. Vancouver columnist Andy Lytle wrote a long article asking, "Girls, is sport good for you?" and offered a definitive "No." The bad times of the Depression years meant conservative attitudes toward women, and this in turn spelled a return to the old idea that rough, aggressive, competitive sport was bad for females.

12 Following the Second World War, this country and its newfound prosperity created a mood of middle-class values and affluence. And anything that smacked of lower-class habits, such as boisterous body contact and team games among females, was forsaken.

13 It wasn't only that women turned away from sport, but the 1950s also spawned a number of myths about athletics for women. Women were supposed to be too delicate to perform any but the most modest sports; women who engaged in body contact sports would damage their vital organs; athletic women would become masculinized in appearance and behavior; and women who took part in vigorous sport would later have difficulty bearing children.

14 I personally encountered the absurdity of several of these myths. After one of my very first races (at the then unheard-of distance of two miles) I was accosted by a matronly type who warned that hard training would impair my ability to have children. (I insolently told the old bag to patent her invention while plotting secretly how best to use this against my coach to have my training load reduced.) When I attended University of Toronto I attempted to train on what was the only indoor track in Toronto located in the university men's athletic building. I not only received a belligerent escort to the door but I was also admonished that "girls don't train."

15 Regrettably, the international governing bodies of sport have helped to perpetuate one myth: that some of those girls out there aren't quite girls. And their solution to this problem is the sex test. Every competitor must submit herself to this test. It used to involve an examination by a panel of medical judges, but thanks to modern science it's now a very proper affair. A chromosome count is taken based on the examination of a hair follicle. I have personally undergone the test seven times—surely worthy of a note in the Guinness Book of Records—and am pleased to say that I've passed every time. I actually took a few hairs belonging to my younger brother to Munich, hoping to slip them through and create a little comic relief. But the scions of the official body watching over the proceedings were not the least amused by my lightheartedness. Most of the women athletes, however, think the

test is a joke. Olga Connolly, the Olympic discus champion in 1956, and married with two children when she competed in Munich in 1972, announced: "If I fail the test, my husband Harold [also an Olympic champion] will have to have the children from now on." Anyway, along with thousands of other women athletes, I now have a certificate duly stamped, imprinted, signed and authorized proclaiming to the world that I am, if not wholly female, at least "sex-chromatin positive."

16 Some of the myths are not really damaging—merely frustrating. The women-don't-train myth simply means that many public facilities don't provide changing or shower facilities for women athletes. In Toronto, the same Department of Parks and Recreation that builds changing facilities for the exclusive use of boys runs a competitive program for girls and boys. But in these public recreation centres, the time allocation for girls' athletics is about one third less than boys, and often, to hide the disparity, cooking and sewing will appear on the sports-for-girls timetable. Disparities in funding are even worse. In many Canadian universities the budget for the men's football team is larger than that for the entire women's athletics program.

17 It is not a single thing that accounts for the lack of sports interest among women; rather it is many things which together create an environment that suggests to girls that sports are mainly for boys. I attended a school in Toronto noted for its excellent football teams. We were near the bottom academically but we had terrific traditions in sport. (I confess to helping sustain both traditions.) Five afternoons every fall we were let off school early so we could attend the Big Game. The morning before kickoff was devoted to a pep rally during which we were exhorted to hysterical frenzy by the principal, the coaches and the cheerleaders. The players looked on grimly from their seats on the stage. They were the prime objects of status and prestige in the school. The community spirit of the school depended on them, and they served also as an excuse for the physical indolence of the rest of the student body. Not only was it virtually demanded that we attend the Big Games, but every fall the girls were subjected in health classes to several weeks instruction in the rules of football. We weren't to play the game—where we might have gained some true idea about it—but we were to pick up enough knowledge to at least participate intelligently in the idolatry. The girls, meanwhile, played their games in the smaller *girls' gym* with no spectator facilities and no

team uniforms. And as for a girls' track meet—much too strenuous.

18 However, times do change. At my old school two years ago, the girls boycotted the usual male-dominated awards' assembly and staged their own instead to recognize the outstanding *female* athletes in the school. The unfortunate fact, though, is that the schools still do not succeed either in enhancing the fitness levels of the students or in providing good competitive opportunities. Most girls leave school in a physically autistic state and haven't the faintest idea how to get any pleasure from sport.

19 The school situation is bad enough, but other areas provide further evidence of the limited sports environment for women. The federal government's National Advisory Council on Fitness and Amateur Sport has never had more than five women on its 30-member board. Of the nearly 200 Canadian coaches sent to major international competitions since 1960, only 5% have been women. In all of professional sport, only one woman—figure-skating's Janet Lynn—commands a larger contract than the top male. And in most pro sports, where the interest level and spectator appeal for the men and women is comparable, as it is in tennis, say, the women still get considerably less prize money.

20 The sports media have helped to make the names of our greatest female athletes household words. Canadians have made glamorous national heroes of personalities such as Barbara Ann Scott, Marilyn Bell and Nancy Greene in a way usually reserved for NHL stars. Knowledge of our sports heroines has undoubtedly encouraged thousands of girls to take up sport, but the image of the female athlete created by the media has been an ambivalent one. On the one hand our successes are readily acknowledged, but on the other women still appear as intruders on the sports page. Frequently, physical appearance takes precedence over performance: women athletes are often depicted as either hideously grotesque or else beauties whose figures amply compensate for any lack of athletic talent.

21 A recent *Weekend* magazine article on the Vancouver Chimos volleyball team claimed that the women's aggressive playing style made them look "like lionesses in heat."

22 *Globe & Mail* columnist Dick Beddoes loves to comment that he prefers "nothing more strenuous than motherhood for the ladies." On one occasion he devoted an entire column to maligning pentathlon standout Debbie van Kiekebelt's shot putting—claiming that Cana-

dian males wouldn't have their hormones stirred by lady shot putters. Too bad for Dick—if Debbie van Kiekebelt can't stir his hormones, no woman can.

23 And where the print medium is merely chauvinistic, television sports can be totally neglectful. Except for the really major events, there is virtually no regular coverage of women's team games. Despite the fact that fully one third of the sports viewing audience is female, there are next to no women sportscasters in Canada. The idea of a woman reading the sports news or doing the color commentary of an event in which the contestants are male is apparently not to be tolerated.

24 It is often pointed out that our women athletes have a better record in international competition than the men, and many who assess our prospects for the 1976 Olympics look first to women. Canadian women have in fact produced 15 *fewer* gold medals than the men in Commonwealth, Pan-American and Olympic competition since 1960, but if we consider that men take part in more than twice as many sports the women do have a decided edge. And most recently, memories of the Canadian performances at the Christchurch Commonwealth Games turn to golds by Jane Haist, Wendy Cook, Glenda Reiser, Bev Boys and the team victory of the Canadian female swimmers over the Australians. All this despite the apparent conspiracy amongst the schools, the media, the recreation authorities and the Canadian culture itself to turn girls away from sport.

25 It makes you wonder what women might do with a little backing.

Abby Hoffman, "Running for Gold," *Maclean's* (February, 1975), pp. 31-33.

Questions

1. **Subject**
   Locate the sentence that best serves as the thesis statement of the essay. Would ''controlling idea'' be a better formulation?
2. **Audience**
   Speculate on how a male audience might respond to this essay. Is there anything in the essay to suggest that the female athletes' plight is the responsibility of the male world?

3. **Purpose**
   Hoffman makes use of narrative as well as exposition and argumentation in this essay. Does any one particular mode predominate? How do they all work together to help the author attain her purpose?
4. **Structure and Style**
   This essay provides an excellent example of a clearly structured piece of writing. Decide where each of the following sections begin, and comment on the importance of the order:
   I Personal anecdote and introduction.
   II History.
   III Myths
      a) school
      b) government
      c) media
   IV Conclusion.

MARCI McDONALD

OUT OF THE ROUGH

1 In the coffeeshop of a rambling Ramada Inn on Houston's no. 59 freeway, Sandra Post moved among the tables, chain-smoking nervously. Other women straggled in around her—big, square-jawed, rawboned women, freckled and rangy. Not your ordinary women, it was clear at a glance. Their faces were confidently naked of makeup, skin etched in squint lines and leathered by an unrelenting sun. Their haircuts were styled with one eye to the wind, and they walked with a lope from the hip in long, easy strides. Over the red vinyl booths and morning coffee, they congregated for the week's $100,000 tournament. They slapped each other on the back in greeting, took playful swipes at passing shoulders, traded loud twangy insults that passed for talk. "Hey Postie!" they called out, the restaurant transformed with instant locker-room fraternity, and Sandra Post hurtled across the room for some reunion heavy with its heartiness. "You know," she says, finally lighting over a paper place mat for breakfast, "it's always good to be back."

2 It is back after a two-week layoff from the Ladies Professional Golf Association circuit, but for Sandra Post it is even more. It is the comeback of a pro career that had swept off the tee nearly seven years

before full of promise and miracle putts when she set off at 19 from Oakville, Ontario, a giggling blond bubble gummer who took her hair down from its eternal rollers, dabbed Chanel No. 5 behind her ears and promptly went out to knock off the golfing Goliath, all-time money winner Kathy Whitworth, copping the prestigious LPGA championship in a play-off by a whopping seven strokes. But three years later the girl they'd predicted as the next star of the circuit woke up in hospital one morning on the brink of collapse, a bitter broken marriage on her hands, a listless broken career on the record books, written off at 22, a golf has-been. It is a comeback that has taken two long years etched in hurt and grim determination and served as living testament to the redeeming qualities of that great North American institution, divorce—perhaps the most remarkable comeback in all of women's golfing history. But it has been a journey that Sandra Post has measured out as shrewdly as an alien fairway, savoring every step along the course. "I really believe that I've been given a second chance," she says. "And I wasn't going to blow it this time. I was determined I was gonnna make it back or I was gonna die tryin'. I wanted to be a success again and I was willing to sacrifice anything, just anything. I was a desperate little girl."

3 A trace of that desperation has ebbed now. In December she wrapped up a 1974 season with $50,000 in winnings, more money than all the Canadian male golfers on the more lucrative men's tour combined. As the '75 circuit rolled into gear, she was already in second place in earnings and was counted enough of a contender again to land a coveted Colgate commercial which showed her grinning out of a bubblebath in the raw. But the biggest change of all was that Sandra Post had finally won the second tournament of her career, the plum Colgate Far East in Melbourne, Australia, and when she stood up in the wind there to accept her $14,000 cheque before the TV cameras and the clapping, tears had suddenly blistered in her eyes and she hadn't been able to get the words out that would say just what it all meant.

4 "I just couldn't get it all together, I was so emotional," she said. "I mean, I'd made my money over the last two years. I'd played well. I was layin' them in there. But I wanted to win, I had to win. It was a drive so strong I could taste it. And boy, when I tasted that victory it was sweet. I think I knew then that I'd finally made it again after all these years."

5 Under the cold fluorescent glare of the coffeeshop, Sandra Post looks little different than the teen-ager who started out seven years ago grinning from the sports pages, the first Canadian ever to make the pro tour. The face is a little rounder maybe, the legs a little more solid in her tight patchwork jeans, the tanned cleavage spilling out from her well-unbuttoned shirt a trifle more generous. "I'm the chunky one with the straight hair," she had warned the night before over the phone, self-conscious about the 128 pounds she was carrying on her five-foot-four frame. She doesn't like to talk about her weight and discusses it constantly, obsessively. At the very mention, she orders cold cereal and tea for breakfast. She runs her fingers through the short bleached blond thatch now left to the vagaries of nature, the constant battle of the curlers abandoned years ago. But at 27, she is still one of the tour's most attractive lures in a solid, spunky, cheerleader sort of way.

6 The real difference now is that Sandra Post ranks as a veteran. Nothing had pointed it up more than the Orange Blossom Classic a month before in St. Petersburg—the same tournament at which she'd once made her pro debut—when a pretty 19-year old rookie named Amy Alcott with barely a month's experience on the circuit snatched the $5,000 first-prize money from under her nose with a 20-foot putt on the eighteenth.

7 Later in the morning when Renee Powell, her former roommate, stops by to congratulate her on that fight, Sandra Post will shake her head philosophically. "History repeated itself," she says. "I mean, I beat Whitworth in my rookie year, then Alcott who's a rookie beat me. I knew how she must have felt, though she could probably cope with it better than I did. When I beat Whitworth it was like my tenth tournament. I mean, I didn't believe it. I was just a thrilled little kid. And even though you don't purposely do it, you don't practise as hard after. You get a little lazy. I wouldn't change anything now, but maybe if I'd handled it a little better it might not have taken me another seven years to win again."

• • •

8 Above the practice tee at Westwood Country Club on the concrete shopping centre fringes of Houston, the day hangs limp and dun-colored, the hint of a Texas thunderstorm thick and threatening in the air. It is an hour later and Sandra Post has pulled a loose white V-neck over her pants, pushed a white cotton porkpie hat low over her eyes

and there is a squat, more solid cast to her frame as she lines up in a row beside the others, eyeing the distant yardage markers that loom like white carny shooting gallery flags out in the field. Since she began her comeback she has not let a day go by without practising.

9 To watch her now, all sombre concentration, in-turned and grim, you can see the solemn fascination that molded the short sharp backswing, the quick hard down-drive, the perfect twisting arc as the driver head shocks the ball with a splitting crack and lifts it high and gentle out to the 200-yard mark. Her tour caddy Chuck, an emaciated looking wisp with a worn face like a tragic mask, stands by handing her clubs with unspoken understanding, but it is not to him that she talks but to the scarlet driver grasped in her scarlet golf glove. "Come on, Big Red," she says. She is lost in the ritual of years of that same motion, hours of standing in one spot knocking them out, a life measured out in buckets of practice balls. In a way it is the only life she has ever known.

10 A skinny little kid whose fruit farmer father had never quite accustomed himself to the fact that he hadn't had a son, she was dragged off one day on their yearly Florida winter vacation to watch the South Atlantic Ladies Open in Miami with him. "And I was captivated, just captivated," she says. "I went right back home and told them all that I was gonna be a lady golfer." She was five years old.

11 Not that Cliff Post was a man to take a five-year-old's fantasies lightly. The next year back in Florida she turned up in the LPGA gallery with her own little cut-down club. She took to the rhythm of standing there swinging at the tiny white pocked ball for hours as if she were born to it. She putted as if mesmerized. Years later one of the players she followed, Marilynn Smith, a gentle neatly hairsprayed lady who is still on the tour today, remembers "this wee little thing, so determined" and the letters penned in a painful childish scribble charting her playing course: at nine, winning her first tournament; shooting in the low seventies by the time she was 13; at 14, in the Ontario Junior scoring a 71.

12 School, friends, nothing came before golf. "In the summer everybody'd go up north to their cottages or swimming," she says, walking the course now in a practice round. "But I'd hit golf balls all day. My mother'd drop me off at 7 a.m. and I'd come home after dark." Then she would go to the driving range with her father and knock them out again under the eerie neon floodlights' glow. Until the day she turned pro, he was the only coach she'd ever known, a

man sometimes regarded as the stage father of the 18-hole set, and there are those who've seen them fighting tooth and club on a fairway over how to play the ball. But he remains probably her closest friend. She still plays with him almost every afternoon when she's home at her Boynton Beach, Fla., condominium and he's down at his winter vacation spot nearby, calls twice a week and after every tournament, and the first thing she did when she won the Colgate Far East was to phone him at 3 a.m. in Florida. Cliff Post was so emotional he couldn't say a word.

13 "My parents did everything in their power to help me become a lady golfer," she says. "Sure, it set me apart. But that was alright, see, 'cause this was what I was gonna do. I was workin' toward somethin' all the time."

14 Over the years she never once wavered from the dream. It was a steely determination that earned her the reputation of being cocky early. She was constantly at war with the entrenched Canadian women's golf establishment, always shooting off her mouth. In 1964, just weeks before her sixteenth birthday, they showed what they thought by leaving her off the Ontario junior team—a slap that, she says, "kinda took the sting outa me. Unless you're a real determined little kid, they'll beat you down." But Sandra Post was a real determined little kid. She talked her father into flying her out to Calgary to compete in the Canadian Junior and promptly walked off with it, beating the entire Ontario elect by eight strokes. She won it the next two years too. "My biggest sin was they thought I thought I was too good," she says, still resentful. "But I was 15. All I wanted to do was play golf."

15 Three years later when she turned pro, the veterans marveled at that same gritty fight. She never once flinched from nerves all through the wearing extra-day play-off with Whitworth; at the end there was no tear of relief in her eye. But afterward sportswriters would make the pilgrimage to the circuit for magazine stories on Sandra Post and come back quietly caustic. "The worst part of my game?" she would crow into their tape recorders. "There really isn't one." She expressed boredom with the circuit, said it was a tough life, no life for a girl, and after all, as she saw it, "I proved to everybody I could do it. I won, not just anything, but a major title; I was rookie of the year; made a lot of money. How many men make $25,000 a year?"

16 Even today diplomacy and tact are not among Sandra Post's strong points. At lunch that day I watch her get up in the middle of another

player's emotional anecdote about her childhood, announcing blithely, "Well, I gotta go practise now." But as she says in her brisk adopted Florida twang, "I think I've grown up a lot. When I was waitin' for my [divorce] decree, I got thinkin'. I realized that I could do better than I'd already done. That was just a scratch on the surface. So I came back. What alternative did I have? It's the only thing I know. It's my life. It's in my blood."

• • •

17 The LPGA tour is a tough life. It is a heady, harried wash 'n' wear grind, a tight 100-woman traveling road show where one day's winner may be the next day's loser and there's no time in between for introspection; but it's back into the next plane or rent-a-car for the next motel room on the edge of the next town you never get to see. It is a capsuled unreal existence played out in a searing public spotlight where each flick of the wrist can be seen under the scoreboard's relentless scrutiny, where an unseemly swearword or betrayal of unladylike fury can cost a $50 fine and a girl's only friends are her opponents. It is a life of such fishbowl vulnerability that those on the tour always refer to it as Out Here.

18 Out Here there is a camaraderie that betrays the loneliness of the long-distance golfer. Out Here, where once she didn't mix much, Sandra Post now visits with a vengeance, running between clumps of girls for quick, bright non-conversations, playing cards late into the night and talking about it like some school-age sorority girl. Now that she has chosen this life, she clings to it tenaciously. Friendships are staked out with a fierceness, cliques formed—and rivalries. Out Here where the prize money has more than doubled to $1.8 million since she started out seven years ago and a player's worth is measured as much in her press clippings as in her pars, there is a wary eye out for the newcomers such as lithe shapely 20-year-old Laura Baugh whose color-coordinated mini-skirts and vital statistics are paraded all over the sports pages above her scores. The rest of the mainstream may be struggling for a sense of womanhood based on something other than curls and curves, but in ladies golf the lookers are promoted and envied, a lure for the galleries and the take at the tournament gate. "Oh, we're not libbers," says Sandra Post, slightly defensive. "We're not into women's lib at all. I'm not even sure what it's about."

19 It is late the next night after a lack-lustre, sodden pro-am tournament and back in the Ramada Inn coffeeshop around a corner booth,

the talk turns to what color of blond to bleach to, who's pregnant and whose boyfriend is flying in for the weekend, who has managed to mix marriage and golf. Over a slice of lemon pie, Sandra Post suddenly grows uncharacteristically silent. The bounce of earlier that evening, when she'd rocked along the expressway in her rented Chevy with the Top 40 blaring on the car radio, is gone now. It isn't until the following morning, when she lies back on the bed in her motel room waiting out frigid temperatures and the announcement that the tournament would be canceled, that the story comes spilling out: the disastrous two-year marriage to a good-looking Florida golf pro named John Elliott two years after she turned pro and a month after he got sent home from army service in Vietnam; her virtual three-year disappearance from golf. She still winces at the memory.

20 "It was awful," she says. "I was havin' a terrible inner struggle mixin' a married life with golf. When I was out playin', I felt I should be home, and when I was home, I felt I should be out playin'. I got so I didn't hardly play at all. I was shooting bad. I lost my confidence. I'd just completely lost my will for golf."

21 In the three seasons of her marriage, she played only 39 events for a total of $12,000—less than half of what she'd made in her first year as a pro. She was constantly abandoning the LPGA circuit to fly off to his side. But the fairytale wedding of two kids who would swing down the fairways of life together was already running into the rough. John Elliott was always better known as Sandra Post's husband and there was no secret he resented it. "A lot of times John would be playing against Sandra's reputation more than against the other golfers," says a friend who played with him. When he failed to qualify for the PGA in the States and came up to join the Canadian summer circuit, he ended up in a series of tantrums with officials, ripping up his scorecard, screaming over rulings, once during the Canadian Open even chalking up a two-week suspension after a verbal set-to. It all blew up one day in Vancouver when she found herself hastily invited to leave his room—and his life. "He just said, 'Out,'" she says quietly. "Let's put it this way, he had to get rid of me real fast 'cause *she* was comin' in. See, you can only fight the girl friends so long. I couldn't believe this was happening to me."

22 In hysterics she called a 32-year-old wealthy Bostonian law-graduate-turned-entrepreneur named Leigh Kandar who'd known them both. He put her on the next plane for Boston, saw her through

the next harrowing six months and the two years since, both as business agent and the current love of her life. "I was such a mess," she says. "I went down to 112 pounds, I got real sick—oh God, was I sick. I was hemorrhagin' for eight days and they didn't know what it was. I had to go into the hospital. And comin' up out of the anesthetic, there's John beggin' to be taken back."

23 Leigh Kandar keeps a protective cordon around her now, invests her money, okays all interviews with a rhetorical flourish that would make Richard Nixon's former press secretary Ron Ziegler sound like a master of straightforward English. "I have spoken to Sandra about the matter to which you alluded pertaining to an interview," he had told a reporter over the phone a week earlier. "Sandra would be delighted to serve you in the capacity of interviewee, per se." He doesn't play golf—"doesn't know one end of a golf club from another," she says. But at the time it could hardly have been less of a problem. For six months Sandra Post just lay around her Florida apartment, listless, confused, never picked up a golf club.

24 "Then one day they called me to come play the Colgate Pro-Am in Miami," she says. "So I drove down, took a look at the prize money and I saw golf was gettin' to be a better place for a woman to make a livin'. I finished tenth and that night I couldn't sleep. I got in the car and drove home at 3 a.m." She drove straight to Leigh Kandar's Florida apartment and when she couldn't get in, she started hammering on the door. "Leigh, Leigh," she hollered. "I just had to tell you this. I'm going back into golf."

25 "I just felt so good," say says.

26 She was out practising the very next day. In her first tournament back she made $600—$20,000 by the end of that year. It has been uphill ever since, even if there have been hazards along the way. She spent the first six months back having to watch John Elliott hold hands with Marlene Hagge, the tour's 41-year-old well-preserved bombshell. "Maybe it was part spite," she says, "But it lasted six months and I was playin' every day in front of them, in front of everybody. I did alright Out There in the day, but boy, you shoulda seen me at night. I was a mess. I don't know how I got through that time." Ironically, she and Marlene Hagge are now inseparable. And Sandra Post looks back on it all as "a good experience. It's made me what I am and I'm glad I went through it. I'm a much happier person now. And all that—it seems like another life."

27 She lies back on the bed, estimating that she'll stay Out Here another five years but after that, whether the future holds the marriage and kids she once said she wanted more than anything else, more than golf itself...she is silent. "I don't know," she says, staring out the window, thoughtful. "My life now is right here. To do the best I can. I'm still very determined to win. And I can't be thinkin' of other things five years from now. I have to take one day at a time."

28 Suddenly, it seems only natural to ask Sandra Post what changed her mind that life Out Here wasn't the life for a girl. She pauses for a moment and then she smiles. "Maybe it isn't for a girl," she says. "Maybe it's for a woman."

Marci McDonald, "Out of the Rough," *Maclean's* (June, 1975), pp. 46, 48-50.

Questions

1. **Subject**
   Explain how the title of the essay is appropriate for the sport and the life being described. Find other examples in the essay of terms drawn from golf that also apply to Sandra Post's life.
2. **Audience**
   Is the audience to whom this essay is directed one that needs to know about the sport of golf in order to appreciate the author's point?
3. **Purpose**
   Explain how exposition and narrative work together in this essay.
4. **Structure and Style**
   (a) Comment on the style of Sandra Post's own comments on herself and her life. What impression does the reader receive about Post based on her way of speaking?
   (b) Critically examine the following sentence from this essay:
   "She still plays with him almost every afternoon when she's home at her Boynton Beach, Fla., condominium and he's down at his winter vacation spot nearby, calls twice a week and after every tournament, and the first thing she did when she won the Colgate Far East was to phone him at 3 a.m. in Florida."
   How might you improve the style of this sentence?
   (c) What does Post mean when in the final paragraph she says "Maybe it isn't for a girl," ... "Maybe it's for a woman"? How do these phrases capture the essential point about Post's life that the author tries to convey?

JACQUES PLANTE

HOW TO WATCH THE STANLEY CUP

1 By the time you read this I could be watching the Stanley Cup play-offs from the same position you are—in front of a television screen. But I don't think so. I think my club, the Toronto Maple Leafs, will be right in there, and I'll be in my usual place, in the goalie's net, which happens to be the best spot in any hockey rink for taking in a game and figuring out the play. Goalies are special people. If you look at the National Hockey League rule book, you'll see that the rules say each team must have "18 players and two goaltenders." That makes us different right there, and one of the differences is that we can, if we're smart, learn more about the science of the game—and more about how to watch hockey scientifically—than anyone in the arenas or on television.

2 To tell the truth, I feel a little sorry for you watching the play-offs on TV. You don't see enough of the play. All you get game after game is a close-up of some guy carrying the puck. That's wrong. The cameras should pull back and let you see a whole zone with all the players taking their different positions on the ice.

3 Let me give you an example. Johnny Bucyk of the Boston Bruins has been scoring an awful lot of goals this season, right? Well, if you've only seen him in television games then you don't know how he's managed to score so many. Probably all you've caught is quick glimpses of him whipping the puck into a net. But if you were given a zone view of the play, you'd learn Bucyk's secret. He's a floater. He moves away from the flow of the play, lagging behind while Johnny McKenzie, on his line, or sometimes their centre, Fred Stanfield, digs the puck from behind the opponent's net and gets it out to Bucyk. That's the Bruins' strategy. They make the opposition goalie and defensemen turn around and look behind them, while Bucyk is out front doing his floating act. You know he's there, but you can't see him, and by the time you look to the front it's too late. Bucyk doesn't touch the puck much, but when he does—whoosh—it's in the net.

4 How does Yvan Cournoyer score so many goals for Montreal Canadiens? Well, what you probably don't see on television is the way his centre, big Jean Béliveau, goes into the other team's corners and draws

in two and sometimes three defending players to check him. He's so strong that just one man can't contain him. The defensemen know they shouldn't all rush in at Béliveau, but they can't seem to help themselves. And that leaves little Cournoyer all alone ready for the pass. New York Rangers use the same system with Dave Balon and young Walt Tkaczuk. There goes Tkaczuk into the corner, a big aggressive guy, upsetting the balance of the defense, and there's Balon out front ready to pop in the pass. Just look how many goals he's scored this year—and see how many more he'll score in the playoffs. The question you want answered, watching him on TV, is how come? And television should tell you.

5 I think good TV commentary is especially important for young boys coming up in hockey. Kids need to be told how things are done; I should know—I get 200 letters a day from them asking for advice. And one of the big troubles is that hockey coaching is away behind the times, from the NHL on down. In pro football, they have a backfield coach, a defensive line coach, an offensive line coach, a pass-catchers' coach, all kinds of coaches. Every individual football player learns how to do his particular job. But in hockey, where every individual player is expected to know how to do his particular job *at top speed,* each team has only one coach. You can't tell me one single coach can teach all the specialized jobs in hockey. That's crazy.

6 The best coaches of all should work at the junior level. Ever since the NHL stopped direct sponsorship of junior teams, the calibre of coaching down there has dropped off. Too many junior coaches don't teach the game, and you can spot the results in the weaknesses in the play of the young players coming up to the NHL from junior.

7 For one thing, they haven't learned much about defensive hockey. That's why Cournoyer spent most of his first three years with Canadiens sitting on the bench. He scored 20 goals one season on the power play, but he didn't work a regular shift because nobody had taught him how to switch to defensive play when his team lost the puck. You watch thinking guys on our Toronto team like Dave Keon and Norm Ullman. They have a smooth knack for picking up their checks as the play changes suddenly from offensive to defensive, which is something that you're taught and that you work at for years. And the young forwards usually don't know anything about defensive zones. When the puck is in your own end of the ice, each of your forwards isn't supposed to check a specific man; he checks whoever is in the zone on his side from the blue line halfway into the net. He

has to decide which opposing player in his zone is most likely to get the puck and stick close to him, always ready to switch off if he has to. Donnie Marshall at Buffalo is a genius at this. He doesn't chase around like a madman the way the young players do. Instead, he's practically invisible until, suddenly, there he is, checking away the puck. That's a science.

8 Then there's the business of learning to talk on the ice. I always talk. During delays in play, for example, I like to tip off the young players on our team about face-offs in our end. Watch Danny O'Shea of Minnesota, I might remind them, because he cheats on face-offs by leaning forward before the referee drops the puck. Or I might warn our centres not to back away when they're facing off with Béliveau or Red Berenson of Detroit or Ralph Backstrom of Los Angeles, because once in a while they like to fire at the net right from the drop of the puck.

9 But, more than that, I call out warnings and instructions while play is actually going on. I learned the habit from Doug Harvey back in the 1950s with Montreal. When I had control of the puck at the side of the net, for instance, and Harvey was coming back to pick it up, he'd want me to warn him which way to turn after he took the puck. He couldn't see what the checkers were doing behind him, but I could, and I'd tell him whether to turn around the net and cut straight down the ice or take a wider detour into the corner. A small detail, maybe, but you bet it paid off.

10 There are all kinds of instructions you can holler to the players on your team. I wish the Leafs did it more. Paul Henderson is our best talker on the ice. If you've ever wondered how Paul gets so many breakaways, the answer is simple—he uses his mouth. Watch Paul when he's going down his wing, without the puck, toward the other team's defense. He'll put on his good speed to make a quick turn between the two defensemen, and at the right moment he'll yell and Normie Ullman, or whoever's carrying the puck, will lay it right on his stick. And the chances are that Paul is gone for a goal. Everybody should learn to talk it up the way he does.

11 Well, maybe you can't catch Paul's yells on TV and maybe there are some pieces of strategy you're bound to miss, but there's plenty you can see if you look sharp. Study Bobby Orr, for one guy. I mean, study the way he carries the puck. He doesn't keep it on the blade of his stick. Instead he always pushes it out in front of him. That style gives him a double advantage. First, it makes him almost impossible to check because if the checker hits Bobby's stick, he won't knock the

puck away. Orr still has it under control out there in front of him. And, second, the defense has no idea which way Bobby's going to move around them. When a guy handles the puck on his blade, you can almost always read which way he's going to commit himself. But not with Orr—he's practically unstoppable. J.C. Tremblay of Montreal is another master at throwing the puck up ahead, and among the younger players our own Jim McKenny is developing the same technique.

12 You can learn a lot about offensive hockey by examining the different ways players handle themselves when they break in on the net for a shot. I certainly watch those plays like an eagle. I'd get killed if I didn't. Most NHL players follow the same pattern: they'll come at the net with their forehand ready and then either fire the puck or hold off and go to their backhand. A goalie can adjust to them, go with their moves and try for the save. But there are maybe a dozen players in the league who can cross you up. They'll come in, wait until you think it's too late for them to use their forehand, and then in that split second while you, the goalie, are adjusting for a backhand, they'll give you a delayed forehand. It sounds simple, but it's really a difficult physical manoeuvre. Watch for it. Béliveau can do it, and so can Bob Nevin at New York and Dickie Duff of Buffalo and Keon on our team. And so can young Syl Apps at Pittsburgh. He used it on me for a goal in late January, and afterwards I asked myself, a kid like that? Am I losing my touch? But I found out that he'd been practising the shot for weeks.

13 Another trick is shooting off the wrong leg. A left-hand player will always shoot off his right leg, and vice versa. So when a left-hand guy comes at me and doesn't fire off his right, I automatically relax for a fraction of a second until he's taken a stride on his left leg and is back again to his right. But there are a few players who can take advantage of that momentary lapse and shoot off the wrong leg. It's a tough shot to master, but watch out for Berenson and Jean Ratelle of New York. They're the best at it. Claude Provost who used to be a right-winger with my old Montreal team could pull it off, too, but he always gave the trick away by hoisting his right leg up in the air. The guys kidded him about that all the time because he looked so weird.

14 The difference between the great scorers in the NHL and the average scorers is that the great ones can change their minds in the wink of an eye. They're like football runners, such as Gale Sayers or Leroy Kelly, who'll find one hole in the line plugged and then, instead of

trying to bull through, quickly switch to another opening. High scorers in hockey, if you'll watch them, operate the same way. They're always looking for new holes, testing you in new ways. That's Phil Esposito of Boston for you —he's forever trying new shooting tricks. There's no single shot you can watch for from him.

15 And like the other superstars, Esposito makes a point of remembering the habits and weaknesses of the players on the other teams, especially the goalies, and he plays to their weaknesses, not their strengths. That sounds only elementary, but, let me tell you, there are plenty of NHL players who don't know how to think these things through. In the league today, we play each team only six times in the regular season, not 14 as we did in the old days, and since each team uses two goalies, the players may go against a certain goaltender only a couple or three times a season. Well, most players will forget to make a note of a goalie's weak points, and they'll end up playing right into his hands. Glenn Hall of St. Louis, for instance, likes to flop on the ice, and you've got to shoot high on him if you want any hope at all of scoring. But, oh no, most players do the reflex thing and keep the puck low and hard, just off the ice the way they're taught. And Hall comes up with a bunch of spectacular saves. What the fans don't know when they give him all those ovations is that the shooters have gone to his strong point. But not Esposito and a few others. Watch them—they'll fire high on Glenn.

16 I find a big challenge in figuring out not just how to play established stars like Esposito but how to play the good young shooters who are new to the league. Gil Perrault of Buffalo Sabres, I've found, has all the moves of a veteran. He pushes the puck out front the way Orr does, and he doesn't give you a hint about his intentions when he comes in on the net. Bob Clarke of Philadelphia shows me the same kind of talent. So does Marc Tardif of Montreal, though he has a tendency to turn lazy now and then.

17 Another young player, Tom Webster of the Detroit Red Wings, gives you an example of the most obvious change that the younger generation has emphasized in hockey. Webster's strictly a slap shooter. Oh brother, that damned slap shot! It's the same in all sports of course—in tennis, the big serve; in baseball, the tape-measure home run; in football, the long bomb. You get brute stuff in every game these days and not so much finesse. Most of the slap-shot artists are on the older teams in the NHL, the original six, while the expansion clubs have

only a couple of slappers per team. A goalie can at least relax a little against the new teams.

18 You have no idea what an effect the slap shot has had on goalies. I get tight just thinking about the shot a couple of days before I go into a game against a team like Boston or Chicago. I'm certainly not saying that slap shots make up most of those teams' offenses. The Bruins are great because they can throw the puck around with those quick passes of theirs; everybody on the team always knows where the other guys will be positioned, and if nothing else works they always have the weight to bull through any situation. At Chicago, the Hawks have the most famous slap-shot man of them all, Bobby Hull, but even he relies on another talent for his goals. He's a player, like Bucyk, who lags in from behind to pick up passes in the clear. Still, with both teams, it's the slap shots that get me on edge before a game.

19 There are a lot of problems with the shot. The puck, you know, comes off a slap shot toward a goalie at a speed of 50 feet in half a second. Blink and you miss it. What's worse, since I don't blink, is that I still only have time to throw out an elbow or an unprotected part of a leg, instead of a glove or a pad, and I catch some painful bruises every game. Another problem is that the puck is black and the tape on the shooters' sticks is black, and this means that there's a quick moment when a goalie can't distinguish between the puck and the stick. Which is which? By the time you decide, the puck is half way to the net.

20 The arenas that we play in around the league are another factor that affects play, especially for goalies. They're all different and they all take getting used to. You'll find, if you watch the games closely, that more long shots go in for goals in Boston Garden than in other arenas. That's because the Garden allows smoking, and as the game goes on the playing surface grows darker with haze, making it tougher to pick out the puck. At Boston, too, the centre ice zone is shorter than in other rinks, and that cuts down on any team's long-passing game. The Bruins, you'll notice, specialize in a sharp short-passing style.

21 St. Louis has the best arena in the NHL for crowd atmosphere. I've never experienced anything like it in any other hockey city—the crowd in St. Louis cheers and chants and sings for the whole 60 minutes the way crowds in other places cheer and chant and sing only after the home team scores a goal. They give the Blues an

unbelievable lift, and the noise is accentuated because the arena has a high dome that seems to double the volume. Montreal Forum has a special atmosphere, too, but it's more a matter of the team's tradition. There's something about the Canadiens' bright-red sweaters and their long history of Stanley Cups and the insults and jokes from all those knowledgeable fans that lets you know you're really in for a game of hockey in the Forum. I remember, when I was with New York Rangers, the players would start worrying two weeks before a game in Montreal. We'd end up too tense to put up a strong show, and I think a lot of that feeling of tension is still sticking with some players.

22 Chicago Stadium is tough on a goalie for a couple of reasons. One is the 30 steps you have to take from the dressing room up to the ice surface. The climb drains some of the zip out of you before the game even starts. The double balconies that lean way out over the ice are another problem; you can never quite shake the feeling that some night a fan is going to land on your net. But at least the Chicago rink is built according to all the regulations, which is more than you can say for some other arenas. In Vancouver, the boards are so lively that a puck comes off them as if another player was drilling it back. And the Detroit Olympia has no corners. The queer shape of the boards behind the nets means that a puck shot at them will always rebound right out in front of the goalie. You should see Gordie Howe and Alex Delvecchio play the caroms. They're like two billiards champions at work.

• • •

23 One arena that suits me fine is Maple Leaf Gardens. I have always played well in it, even before I joined Toronto. It's brightly lit, which helps an old guy like me, and it's got all the facilities, including a hospital nearby—another essential for me. In fact, the whole Maple Leaf organization strikes me as first class, and I don't think some of the Leaf players realize how lucky they are. They've been spoiled.

24 But not so spoiled that they haven't played some excellent hockey during this past season—and, as far as I'm concerned, they'll play more great hockey in the play-offs. But you have to remember, speaking of the play-offs, that the kind of hockey you're going to be seeing from us and from all the teams in the Stanley Cup games will be a lot different from the style you get during the regular season, more cautious, more defense-minded. Part of the reason is obvious—it's just because none of the players wants to make a mistake that would blow away the winners' share of the Stanley Cup. But just as big a reason

lies in the fact that, in the play-offs, you go against the same team for a long series of games. The forwards know they'll be checking the same man each game, and they study him so closely that they get to know all his little moves. During the season, most players in the NHL just take each opponent and each game as they come along without really analyzing them. They figure the winter is long enough and tough enough without working on extra problems. But in the play-offs, even the big offensive stars suddenly learn how to play defensive hockey. They don't want to be the ones who let the other team score.

25 The players who stand out in the play-offs are often guys nobody has paid any particular attention to during the year. Floyd Curry was always coming through in the Stanley Cup finals for Montreal when I played with the Canadiens, and so was Dick Duff. The reason was simple: they were strong positional players who knew how to check and how to arrive at the right place at the right time.

26 The whole atmosphere of the play-offs makes for better team play. It's like a big family affair because all the players on each team usually go away to a motel together for a couple of weeks. There are no families around, no distractions, and all we can talk about is hockey. We tip each other off on little tricks we've noticed in the opposition players and we discuss hockey more than at any other time during the year. Things are completely unselfish. That's partly because nobody on the team is going for a bonus for scoring so many goals or getting so many shutouts the way they are in the regular season. Everybody plays for the team and not for himself. That makes it easier for the goalies in some ways. I know that I have always had a hell of a good record in play-offs, except for one series against Detroit a long time ago, and a lot of my success has been thanks to my teams' defensive teamwork. But I also know that I get more keyed up in play-offs, sharper, more alert, better in the goal. After all, I don't want to be the guy who blows the Stanley Cup either.

27 I don't, of course, see myself doing anything like that. From the time Toronto drafted me, I set out to do a job for them. I decided in June 1970 that I'd have to make up for my age—I'm 42—with more speed, and that to pick up speed, I'd have to be lighter. So I cut out my evening snack and the two or three bottles of beer I used to drink daily, and my weight dropped from 185 to 171. It paid off. I'm quicker at 171, a better goalie, and, with all the good young players on our team, the Maple Leafs have come through better than anyone expected. I'm really confident, even though I'm writing these words

before the end of the regular NHL season, that I'll be watching the Stanley Cup play-offs from the goalie's net. And I hope I look good—or at least smart—to you watching from back there in front of your television screens.

Jacques Plante, "How to Watch the Stanley Cup," *Maclean's* (May, 1971), pp. 25-26, 52-53.

Questions

1. **Subject**
   The title of this essay suggests there is a particular way of watching hockey and particular things to look for and expect. The essay outlines what many of these things are. What does the essay tell us about what television allows us to see? What does it tell us about the author's hockey eyes?
2. **Audience**
   Comment on the author's use of the second person ("you") in this essay. What effect does it have on the reader? Is the author altogether consistent in his pronoun references?
3. **Purpose**
   Comment on the author's use of illustration in this essay. Do the illustrations serve an expository or persuasive end or a combination of both?
4. **Structure and Style**
   Do you find a tension in the essay between its title, "How to Watch the Stanley Cup," and the author's statement in paragraph one that "Goalies are special people"? To what extent does the second statement serve the purpose of the first? How is this developed in this essay?

7 Argumentation

Introduction to the Mode

After narration, description, and exposition, we come to the fourth of the writing modes: argumentation and persuasion. Rather than telling a story, describing something, or explaining and informing, argumentation's primary aim is to convince. Of all of the modes of writing, argumentation is perhaps the most prevalent, and the one that you will make most use of in your own writing as a student. The prevalence and popularity of this mode can be explained in part by the very nature of the world in which we live: a strongly polemicized one. If we read or think at all, we are regularly asked—or must ask ourselves—about the various merits and demerits of positions, causes, and possible courses of action. Are we in favour of or opposed to nuclear disarmament? In large measure our answer will be based on arguments that we have heard or read, for or against the question. Are the Toronto Blue Jays a better or worse baseball team than the Montréal Expos? The answer to this question will be determined in part by an objective set of statistics. But statistics do not solve all contentious issues and skillful writers might even use the same figures as their opponent to try to prove the opposite. Should I buy a new car? You may be helped in your answer to this question by reading an article which points out the positive points in favour of buying a new car instead of a used one, but ultimately the decision you take in this very personal matter will also be based on the pros and cons you generate as you try to *convince* or *persuade* yourself of the rightness or wrongness of such an action. In short, as long as there is more than one side to an issue, argumentation or persuasion will continue to be an important mode of writing, not only at this stage of your career but throughout your life. A clear understanding of what is involved in this mode will help you determine the cogency of not only complex polemical matters, but also of shabby and shallow argumentation that is so much a part of the world of advertising and consumerism.

One way of looking at argumentation is to differentiate it from the expository mode. The main difference between exposition (explaining and informing) and argumentation and persuasion (convincing) involves the degree of acceptance the author's comments will have. If you were writing a newspaper article entitled "The Distinctiveness of Sudbury," its content and presentation would change depending on whether you were publishing in the Sudbury *Star* or the Toronto *Star.* In the first case you could probably assume that the inhabitants of Sudbury accepted your basic views and would read your article mainly for additional information. In the second case, however, you might be up against long-entrenched conceptions of Sudbury as moonscape and you might have to convince a largely sceptical audience of your views.

A second distinction that has to be drawn is the one between argumentation and persuasion. The main point here is that you should not, finally, distinguish between them. Although argumentation is often considered to be an intellectual appeal while persuasion is seen as emotional, we would surely have to say that an argument that is purely cerebral makes only a fraction of the appeal it could. Similarly, a persuasive piece that studiously avoids any appeal to the reader's mind is little more than a con job. Normally, then, argumentative writing is made up of a judicious combination of both emotion and argument.

Clearly the essence of argumentation is authorial opinion. In large measure it is the taking of a side or position that differentiates argumentation from all other modes of writing. Notice how the wording of the following general subjects can help separate one mode of writing from another:

1. Canadian Fashion in Clothing
2. A History of the Montréal Canadiens
3. Canadian Fiction Writers of the 1980s

As best we can tell, each of these three subject areas is non-controversial. Number 1 could be written primarily in the expository and descriptive modes. Number 2 could probably best be handled in an expository and narrative fashion, while number 3 could be clearly expository. Now notice how the following three related subjects suggest argumentation or persuasion:

1. Canadian Dependence on American Styles
2. The Montréal Canadiens: Canada's Only True Hockey Team
3. Contemporary Canadian Fiction: World Class

The wording of these subjects suggests that argumentation will be the most appropriate mode for demonstrating the validity of the various positions taken. Argumentation, then, is the mode of writing that expresses a contentious or debatable opinion with a view to convincing the reader.

The following opening paragraph of an essay leaves little doubt about the mode of writing that the author intends to employ:

> Our health care system, while supposed to remedy some of the human ills produced by industrial capitalism, is itself beset with difficulties. We no longer expect that more of the same in health care will produce healthier Canadians. Increasing the number of doctors,

nurses, hospital beds and advanced medical technologies has not brought either better cures or better care. Indeed we have discovered that the side effects of many medical techniques are worse than the diseases they are supposed to cure, that the excessive use of prescription and non-prescription drugs constitutes a public hazard, that our system of providing health services encourages the increasing proliferation of unnecessary procedures and an application of technology regardless of its efficacy and of the needs of the patient. Patient care is a forgotten word, lost in the new health technologies of CAT scanners, countless routine blood tests, and endless varieties of drugs.

David Coburn, "Patients Rights: A New Deal in Health Care," *Canadian Forum*, Vol. 60, No. 699 (May, 1980), p. 14.

It would be naive to think that the claims made in this paragraph would be universally acknowledged as valid and indisputable. Obviously the author of this passage wants to argue the point that "Patient care is a forgotten word." Although many patients who have had a disagreeable experience with the medical profession might agree with the opinion expressed in the opening paragraph, doubtless many others, including a large segment of the medical profession itself, would not. Having made his side of the issue clear in the opening paragraph, the author must now go on to win reader support for his position by convincing and persuading. Certainly, one of the ways to do this would be to marshall statistics, facts, and reasonable and verifiable data to his side. It is all very well to make general accusations against an established system; it is quite another thing to demonstrate the validity of the charges with specific facts and clear reasoning. Like all good opening paragraphs, this one makes a series of general claims and indicates the general shape of the essay to follow.

It is particularly important when using the argumentative mode to make clear from the beginning of the piece exactly what the limits of your position will be. Otherwise the reader may be expecting more from the argument than you are prepared or able to provide. In the above paragraph the author has set himself a formidable task: his job is to demonstrate the weaknesses in a highly traditional and generally highly regarded profession. In the process he challenges many of the things we have taken for granted about medicine in this country (see sentence 2 ff.). Although he uses the pronoun "we" when he criticizes medical practices, he has not, for all that, necessarily earned our support. Only at the end of the essay will we know whether the use of the word "we" is truly justified. For only then will we really know whether or not we agree with the author's opinion.

As was suggested in the opening chapter of this book, subject, audience, and purpose are central concerns of all good reading and writing. Using only the above opening paragraph, let us try to determine whether the author has provided us with any meaningful clues about these three important areas.

Subject. In broad terms it is quite clear from only a cursory reading of this paragraph that the general subject under discussion is medicine and medical care as it affects the patient. Initially we might feel that the author plans to write an expository essay on the difficulties that beset our health care system. Certainly one can see an expository posture being taken in the first sentence. However, when we arrive at the last sentence of the paragraph we encounter the paragraph's true topic sentence and presumably the essay's thesis statement. Clearly the one major difficulty that the author wants to focus on is the problem of patient care which has somehow got lost in the ever-increasing technological wonders that the world of medicine has at its disposal. This particular thesis statement is an interesting one because it uses a structure that is regularly found in argumentative writing and which can, in fact, serve as an important clue to whether a piece is written in the argumentative mode or not. Very often argumentative essays use a thesis statement with a stated or implied "although" clause within them. The "although" clause normally introduces and contains the position that the author wishes to attack; the principal clause of the thesis statement, on the other hand, expresses the position that the author wants to support. So, for instance, in this sentence the main clause is "Patient care is a forgotten word" and this represents the opinion that the author plans to support. The implied "although" clause is the rest of the sentence and represents the view that the author is opposed to or wishes to question. To paraphrase this thesis statement, the author is stating that *although* medicine now makes use of many new technologies, blood tests and many varieties of drugs, true patient care is lacking in the profession. One also might read into this final sentence, on the strength of what has come before it, that the author is seeing a cause-and-effect relationship between new technologies and the decline in patient care.

Audience. The author refers to "our" in the first sentence and to "we" at other points in the paragraph. Presumably he has all Canadians in mind in these designations, but would it be too much to suggest that he has in mind, in particular, all Canadians who avail themselves of medical services and who are not part of the medical profession itself? Although there is no good reason for us not to think of doctors and nurses as patients themselves, we regularly do not do so. The author, perhaps taking advantage of this particular way of seeing things, sets up an adversarial situation in his opening paragraph to the point where the "we" and "our" refer to all Canadians who at one time or another have had to put up with the fact that "Patient care is a forgotten word."

Purpose. Trying to convince or persuade the reader that "Patient care is a forgotten word" is the clear purpose of this essay, but in order to attain his main purpose, the author must also work to persuade the reader of other things. For instance, he must show the validity of the charges he brings against the profession. We must be convinced that "increasing the number of doctors, nurses, hospital beds and advanced medical technologies has not brought either better cures or better care" (sentence 2). Similarly, we must be shown the validity of the claim that he makes in sentence 4. In other words, the main aim depends very much on the author convincing us of a number of other bold statements that he makes prior to arriving at his thesis statement. From one point of view, we might say that the author has written the easiest part of his argumentative essay in composing his first paragraph. What now remains is the winning of audience support through cogent and clearly organized argumentation.

Inductive and Deductive Argumentation

Once you have determined your subject, audience, and purpose you can begin to organize your paper. Argumentative organization is usually a combination of induction and deduction. Induction reasons from examples to a conclusion. The writer first surveys a certain number of examples and then makes an "inductive leap" to the conclusion. It is as if everything falls into place all at once. You must, however, be sure you give your reader fair and representative examples to *induce* the desired leap to the conclusion. Otherwise you will simply appear to be "jumping to conclusions" from flimsy evidence. Notice the way in which the following passage builds towards the general conclusion:

> Lingering concerns about Nicaragua's future must be balanced by a realization of where our righteousness about the definition of a democratic government leads. Our own mistakes vis-à-vis the blots in our history of violence, injustice, and discrimination should never allow us to expect either perfection from others or the imitation of our goals born from eighteenth and nineteenth century experience. Nicaraguans and others struggle valiantly to overcome harsh twentieth century oppression. We must allow and sometimes celebrate the birth of new applications of classic democratic principles to redress modern circumstances. This is part of the essential meaning of national liberation to millions of people in the world today. And Canadians should certainly be familiar by now with the complexities involved in such efforts and with the need for consistent domestic and external policies. Foreign policy that does not abide by the same internal principles of freedom and right to self-determination will undermine the real and widespread practice of these doctrines at home.

Marcia Kircher, "Nicaragua: Revolution Plus One," *Canadian Forum*, Vol. 60, No. 703 (October, 1980), p. 8.

A reader might be forgiven for thinking that the first sentence in the paragraph is the topic sentence. After all, it is a general assertion that certainly requires proof before we can accept it as valid. But what follows are a number of sentences that exemplify the reasons why Canadians should react tolerantly to the attempts on the part of the Nicaraguans to free themselves from oppression. The final sentence of the paragraph is the one that makes the inductive leap from the examples cited before it. Finally, Canadians are exhorted to show some consistency between domestic and foreign policies in order to safeguard the very freedoms for which others outside Canadian borders are fighting. Seen in this way, the entire paragraph, including the rather general assertion made in the opening sentence, builds towards the conclusion.

Unlike induction, deduction reasons from premises to a conclusion. The backbone of deductive reasoning is the syllogism—a basic logical structure for verifying the truth of assertions. Aristotle offers a famous example:

Major premise. All men are mortal.
Minor premise. Socrates is a man.
Conclusion. Therefore Socrates is mortal.

Normally our deductive reasoning does not follow such a schematized pattern. Still, if we take time we can discern the syllogistic structures in much of our thought. We might, for example, come across the following headline in a national newspaper: "Prolonged chemical emissions from factories in Vancouver will cause birth defects." Hidden in this assertion is the following syllogism:

Major premise.	Long-term chemical emissions can cause birth defects in nearby populations.
Minor premise.	Factories in Vancouver have been emitting chemicals for decades.
Conclusion.	Vancouver residents will see an increase in birth defects.

Just as inductive reasoning must have good examples, so deductive reasoning needs sound premises. For the syllogism to work, its major premise must be accepted as true. Notice the organizational pattern in the following paragraph:

> Nature dreadful and infinite has inhibited the growth of the higher amenities in Canada. The living has never been easy. The need to wrestle a livelihood from a cruel land has put a premium on some of the sterner virtues—frugality and caution, discipline and endurance. Geography even more than religion has made us puritans, although ours is a puritanism tempered by orgy. Outnumbered by the trees and unable to lick them, a lot of Canadians look as though they had joined them—having gone all faceless or a bit pulp-and-papery, and

mournful as the evening jack-pine round the edges of the voice, as if (in Priestly's phrase) something long lost and dear were being endlessly regretted. Or there are those who run—by car, train or plane (flying more air miles per capita than any other people), lickety-split as if the spirit of the northern woods, the *Wendigo,* himself, were on their trails. Nature has not always been an enemy, but she has rarely been something to be tamed either. At best we have exploited her quickly and moved on. No wonder the atmosphere of our towns still often suggests that of a mining camp or the logging drive, the trading post or the sleeping compound. If transportation has been crucial for Canada, and our main-street towns attest to the worship of train and motor car, then communications (more telephone calls than anybody else), particularly radio and television (the world's longest networks), have been vital. It is no surprise when some of old Rawhide's Canadian characters become so addicted to the telegraph key that they can only talk in the dah-dah-dits of Morse code.

William Kilbourn, *Canada: A Guide to the Peaceable Kingdom* (Toronto: Macmillan, 1970), p. xiv.

The opening general assertion of the paragraph calls for corroboration and demonstration. The rest of the paragraph provides the details and examples that support the opening sentence. If, however, you do not accept the assertion that "Nature dreadful and infinite has inhibited the growth of the higher amenities in Canada," the rest of the argument is of little point. What would have to be done in order to provide proof would be to give examples of the validity of the major premise. The author of the syllogism would first have to argue this point inductively and then introduce the deductive argument. This mixed pattern is quite common.

Developmental Strategies

Another major organizational decision that you must make when you contemplate writing your argumentation paper is the developmental strategy or strategies that you will employ. For instance, if you want to write a paper arguing that the Toronto Blue Jays is a better baseball team than the Montréal Expos, your best developmental strategy might be *comparison*. If, however, you decide to write on the need for more creative uses of computers in Canadian society, you will probably have to spend a good deal of your argumentative essay *defining* what you mean by the term "creative uses." Clearly, the decision to use one developmental strategy in an argumentative essay does not preclude the use of others. For instance in the largely comparative Toronto Blue Jays/Montréal Expos paper you might want to use *cause and effect* to explain why the Blue Jays are a better team, *definition* to clarify the type of statistics you are using, and *example* to give specific details in order to gain reader support. Any number of possible developmental strategies can find their way into argumentative essays. Normally, however, one predominates and helps to give your essay a particular shape. What follows is a series of examples of developmental strategies used in various portions of argumentative essays. (Further commentary on these strategies can be found in appendix 1.) Notice in these examples how the use of a particular strategy acts as a structural guide for the author in introducing or developing the argument.

Comparison

> As monuments the parliament buildings in Ottawa and the Toronto City Hall have in common the need not just to house government, but to represent it, to create a distinctive presence marked by memorable forms. How this should be done was easily answered when the parliament buildings were rebuilt after the fire of 1916, not so easily by the 1950's when the new Toronto and Ottawa City Halls were built and 'modern' architecture was well established in Canada. The greater success of the Toronto building as presence and symbol has everything to do with its distance from the idea of modern architecture which the Ottawa City Hall represents.

Michael McCordie, "Modern Monuments," *Canadian Forum*, Vol. 58, No. 681 (May, 1978), p. 26.

The last sentence of this paragraph seems to indicate that in order to convey his position that one thing (in this case the Toronto City Hall) is better than something else (the Ottawa City Hall) the author is going to make use of *comparison*.

Analogy

> At present I am developing what I call a 'universal' feeling about being a woman. I am what I am because of what I say, how I act, and most importantly, how I think. I feel that a female, whether she is a housewife, mother, or career woman, must do the best she can at whatever she tries.
>
> It's something like Jackie Robinson breaking the colour barrier in baseball. As the first black playing in the major leagues, he had to be 'better than the rest' not only for himself, but for all other black sportsmen who would follow him.

Liz McKee, "A Woman's View of Liberation," *Canada and the World* 40 (December, 1974), p. 23.

In this passage McKee makes a comparison between a woman's plight and a well-known example of prejudice overcome, namely the case of Jackie Robinson. This *analogy* strengthens the author's intuitive point which, by itself, may lack the impact to move people to recognize its significance or importance: oppressed contemporary women must work as hard in their own way as Robinson did in his.

Cause and Effect

> Modern civilization makes all local cultures anachronistic. Where modern science has achieved its mastery, there is no place for local cultures. It has often been argued that geography and language caused Canada's defeat. But behind these is a necessity that is incomparably more powerful. Our culture floundered on the aspirations of the age of progress.
>
> George Grant, *Lament for a Nation* (Toronto: McClelland and Stewart, 1965), p. 54.

In this brief passage the author relies heavily on *cause and effect.* Notice how the first sentence boldly expresses a cause-and-effect relationship: modern civilization, the author argues, results in the displacement of local cultures. A similar cause-and-effect position is expressed in sentence 2. Sentences 3, 4, and 5 are rather interesting since they cast doubt on a traditional cause-and-effect relationship and introduce another to replace or supplement it.

Definition

> Then, you may ask, if my book does not survey, evaluate, provide histories or biographies or offer original and brilliant insights, what does it do? It attempts one simple thing. It outlines a number of key patterns which I hope will function like the field markings in bird-books: they will help you distinguish this species from all others, Canadian literature from the other literatures with which it is often compared or confused. Each key pattern must occur often enough in Canadian literature as a whole to make it significant. These key patterns, taken together, constitute the shape of Canadian literature insofar as it is *Canadian* literature, and that shape is also a reflection of a national habit of mind.
>
> Margaret Atwood, *Survival: A Thematic Guide to Canadian Literature,* (Toronto: House of Anansi Press, 1972), p. 13.

In this passage the author provides a precise *definition* of her book so as to arrive at an argumentative thesis statement, namely that Canadian literature is made up of certain "key patterns" that reflect "a national habit of mind." This thesis statement will, of course, be proven in the book that she has written.

Example

The best of novels are only scenarios, to be completed by the reader's own experience. They do not give us feeling: they draw out such feeling as we have. If fiction is going out of fashion (which is said from time to time but which I do not believe), it is not because fiction is any worse than it was: apart from the pepper and curry fiction already referred to, the general level of it is probably better. But great numbers of people find fault with fiction because they do not give themselves a chance to respond to it. It is the way they read which is at fault. The great success of Emlyn Williams in reading Dickens and Dylan Thomas to large audiences shows us where the trouble lies. I have seen Mr. Williams hold a large audience spellbound as he read, in two and a half hours, an abridgment of Dickens' *Bleak House.* He had their undivided attention, and he read with all the resources of a consummate actor.

. . . .

Sir John Gielgud moves audiences similarly by reading Shakespeare. Thomas's *Under Milk Wood* and Fry's *The Lady's Not for Burning* come to life on phonograph records, and the catalogues of large recording companies contain many examples of recorded plays and excerpts from books. Ah, you may say, but those are performances by actors. Yes, and if you want the best from reading, you must learn to give the best performances of which you are capable, sitting soundless in your chair, with your book before you.

Robertson Davies, *A Voice From the Attic* (Toronto: McClelland and Stewart, 1960; reissued, 1972), pp. 13-14.

Here the author uses *examples* to demonstrate the point that he wants to argue, namely that those who find fault with fiction do so because they have not cultivated the habit of careful reading.

To reiterate: whether your argument is primarily inductive, deductive, or a combination of the two, you will be able to develop it by employing any or all of the developmental strategies from narration through to classification and division. Although mention was made earlier of the mental and emotional appeals being together in good arguments, it is clear that certain of the strategies lend themselves more easily to logical appeals while others favour emotional ones. If your argument is heavily concerned with detailing the consequences of an action, then the cause-and-effect pattern will be appropriate for development. You may find that an analogy is helpful in clarifying a point; comparison and contrast would then be your choice.

And, of course, example and illustration will come into play whenever you are presenting examples, referring to authorities, quoting testimony, or giving statistics. On the other hand, narration and description will be your prime resources when you want to make emotional, ethical, or imaginative appeals. However, since a good writer will want to make *all* these appeals to some extent, most of the strategies of development will come into play in a well-constructed argument.

Argumentative Pitfalls

If the main purpose of argumentative writing is to win reader support for your position, you should do everything in your power to avoid anything that will detract from this goal. Many potentially good arguments have been lost because of sloppy argumentative practices and logical fallacies.

Begging the Question

This often-misused term actually refers to the practice of assuming the validity of what you want to demonstrate before you prove it. For example, if you were asked to write an essay arguing that there is violence in the game of hockey, you would be begging the question if you began your essay with a sentence such as the following: "It is high time that the government of Canada took steps to reduce the amount of violence in the game of hockey." It is your job to *prove* that hockey violence exists.

The *Post hoc, ergo propter hoc* Fallacy

This error in thinking is based on the assumption that because something happened after something else, the first event was the cause of the second. In other words this fallacy confuses sequence with consequence. Many superstitions are based on the *post hoc, ergo propter hoc* fallacy. The young man who believes that his sudden success with women is due to the new sweater he bought last week has fallen prey to the *post hoc* fallacy. Much advertising uses this fallacy to convince us that our lives will change for the better if we buy a certain product.

False analogy

Using analogies and comparisons are effective ways of arguing only if there is a valid connection between the two items being compared. The hospital chief administrator who insists that his hospital should be run on the same basis as a commercial hotel may soon find himself in trouble with the Canadian government and the Ministry of Health. It is indeed true that hotels and hospitals both have rooms and beds to house people, but the differences between the two institutions are far greater than their apparent similarities.

Generalization

Perhaps of all errors in argumentation, hasty generalizations are the ones most frequently made by students in their writing. Because students are taught that they must argue their positions strongly, they sometimes feel that using the most inclusive statements will help them attain this goal. In fact, inclusive statements are often damaging. Overstatements and generalizations encourage your readers to question your fair-mindedness and temperance. Imprudent and sweeping accusations or claims put your credibility as an author in doubt. Be cautious in your writing about using words like "all," "everyone," "always," "only," "never," "nobody," and "most." Notice how the following statement makes use of wildly unsubstantiated generalizations:

> Almost all university students in Canada support the New Democratic Party. This is so because students in general are free-thinkers and lean towards the left politically. However, when they leave school, most of these students will end up supporting the Conservative or Liberal parties.

The Either/Or Fallacy

Most issues in our complex world are neither black nor white; rather they are often a middling gray, less extreme than an "either-or" position suggests. In your writing, avoid this fallacy. Sentences such as the following do little to win reader sympathy:

> Canadians should either support free trade with the United States or openly admit their communist sympathies.

The Ad hominem Fallacy

An author who attacks a person rather than a position is often engaging in the *ad hominem* fallacy. For instance, if you were accused of stealing money from your company, your main job would be to disprove the charge rather than to attack those who brought the charge against you.

Further Comments on Organization

Sequencing

In writing your basic argument essay, organizing in ascending or climactic order is essential. Avoid at all costs the argument that throws its hardest punch first and then has nothing left. Psychology discusses a phenomenon called the "recency effect," in which people are most strongly influenced by the item in a series that they have seen most recently. The same applies to arguments. Certainly it is good to start forcefully, but then move to weaker points and gradually develop to your climax. If you have five points in five paragraphs, a possible structure would number them thus: 4, 1, 2, 3, 5 (with 1 being the weakest and 5 the strongest).

Dealing with the Opposition

Any argument worthy of the name faces its opposition squarely. To divert your audience's attention away from opposing views rather than to answer those views is to cheat your audience and certainly not to convince it. If a writer is not prepared to meet the opposition then the writer's argument cannot carry much weight. A sign of a writer's credibility is a willingness either to acknowledge the rightness of other viewpoints as well as their limitations (a concessive pattern) or to display their weaknesses in a thorough manner (a refutation pattern). In your arguments you will, of course, want to devote more time to your own view than to those of your opponents, and this is natural. Decide what the main opposing points are and counter those—preferably leaving the final quarter or third of your paper for your own points alone. A warning: don't chase down trivial points; doing so makes you trivial in your reader's eyes.

Common Transitional Signals for Argumentation

One of the signs that an essay is written in the argumentative mode is the transitional signals found within it. As has been stated, argumentative essays regularly contain your own opinion plus attempts on your part to counter the opposition. These two elements are often signalled by some or all of the following terms. What follows is the plan of an imaginary argumentative essay consisting of five paragraphs: one opening paragraph, a closing paragraph, and three middle paragraphs which make up the body of the essay. Notice how the transitional signals work.

Paragraph 1. Your opening paragraph introducing the subject and leading to the thesis statement: "Although many studies show . . . it is my view that . . ."

Paragraph 2. "Despite the claims made by many people that . . ."; your point: "Nevertheless . . ."; a further point: "Furthermore . . ."

Paragraph 3. A transitional link with paragraph 2: "Besides . . ."; concession to opposition: "Granted . . ."; your rebuttal: "However . . ."

Paragraph 4. Where you make three strong points: your first point: "Not only . . . but also . . ."; your second point: "Moreover . . ."; your third point: "Indeed . . ."

Concluding paragraph. "Therefore . . ." or "As a result . . ." or "We can see . . ."

Obviously the above scheme is merely one example of a whole range of possible organizational patterns and transitional signals. The important point to realize is that these signals can help keep your reader on track.

Hands On: Reading

Exercise

Actively read the following argumentative essay and relate the many aspects of argumentation outlined in this chapter to its subject, audience, and purpose. Look for instance at such organizational items as induction, deduction, and developmental strategy. Pay attention as well to the order in which the points of the argument are made. Once you have actively read the essay, write a summary of it and a response to it.

The following clues may help you in your analysis of the passage:

1. Narration
2. Example
3. Inductive reasoning
4. Deductive reasoning
5. Exposition
6. Evidence
7. Cause-and-effect argumentation

SAM SOLECKI

ANANSI, OBERON, PRESS PORCEPIC, LESTER & ORPEN DENNYS, HURTIG, TURNSTONE... THE STATE OF THE CANADIAN PUBLISHING INDUSTRY

Begin with a parable of and for the times.

A small Canadian press publishes a *literary* novel (Robbe-Grillet not Arthur Hailey) by a relatively unknown writer with a small but loyal following. The novel, *mirabile dictu,* receives an almost immediate rave review in *Maclean's* followed by almost equally enthusiastic notices in the Toronto *Star* and *The Globe and Mail.* Within three months it has also attracted the attention of an American publisher.

Now comes the *Canadian* part of the story: unless you have a very nationalistic book store in your area or a closet nationalist running your local W.H. Smith or Classics or Co--- (I can't say it), chances are you won't be able to find Helen Weinzweig's *Basic Black With Pearls* (Anansi). The reasons? An inadequate system of distribution, the unwillingness of certain book supermarkets (you can't call them bookstores) to handle small presses, and the predominance of American mass market paperbacks.

As a recent report from the Association of Canadian publishers (*An Industrial Strategy*) makes clear, these are just three of literally dozens of problems that not only prevent the majority of Canadians from seeing Canadian books but also threaten the existence of the entire English Canadian sector of the industry.

More Canadians than ever before are reading Canadian books published by Canadian publishers—yet the 15-year-old industry admits that Canadian owned companies are "in a state of crisis," having just gone through the worst spring season in the industry's recent history. These are the publishers who in the last two decades have produced the majority of the books dealing with Canadian issues. Within the last five years they have published 84 percent of Canadian fiction, 96 percent of Canadian poetry, 92 percent of books on Canadian history, 81 percent of books on Canadian politics, sociology and social conditions.

In contrast to most documents of this kind, the ACP Report offers both a detailed analysis of specific problems—distribution, foreign competition, the unprofitability of cultural publishing—as well as specific short term and long range recommendations for their solution—co-publishing with government agencies, the repatriation of the industry through the Foreign Investment Review Agency, a modern industry-wide distribution system, duties on imported books and so on. There is a healthy awareness throughout of what the industry can and cannot accomplish under the present circumstances. As well there is a realization that if the Canadian publishing industry is ever to be more than a number of under-capitalized companies it is going to need continuing and often massive assistance from provincial and federal governments.

All the other recommendations, from Canadian content in school curricula to library purchases of Canadian books and continuing aid to writers' organizations, are ultimately irrelevant unless ACP receives a favourable hearing for its two major proposals:

1. The immediate establishment of an arm's length mechanism at the federal level for the development of coherent policy for publishing as a cultural industry. This body should be empowered to act as a banker, to subsidize, to lobby other government departments, to regulate, and develop programs for market development.

2. The commitment at the federal and provincial levels to ongoing subsidy through arts councils of culturally significant publishing.

The alternative to greater government involvement in publishing is the possibility that within a decade, perhaps sooner, we will see the end of Canadian publishing as we have known it. Left will be several small presses producing poetry chapbooks and American branch-plants whose idea of a daring venture in Canadian content is a new novel by Arthur Hailey. As these statistics make more than obvious, we are all involved in the industry's success or failure. Without a strong Canadian publishing industry the idea of an economically, politically and culturally independent Canada will never be realized.

Sam Solecki, "Anansi, Oberon, Press Porcepic, Lester & Orpen Dennys, Hurtig, Turnstone . . . The State of the Canadian Publishing Industry," *The Canadian Forum*, Vol. 60, No. 703 (October, 1980), p. 4.

Hands On: Reading into Writing

The following assignment deals with argumentation. The subject is censorship.

Assignment

1. Actively read the following six argumentative essays (written over a period of three decades) on various aspects of *censorship.*
2. Answer the questions appended to each essay. Your careful responses to these questions should act as a spur to your thought and so should assist you when you complete the reading workbook entry.
3. Complete a reading workbook entry for each essay:
   (a) Comment on subject, audience, and purpose.
   (b) Identify thesis statement, topic sentence, or controlling idea.
   (c) Comment on development strategies.
   (d) Prepare an outline.
   (e) Write a summary.
   (f) Write a response, of at least one hundred words.
4. Once you have finished dealing with the readings on an individual basis, you will have at least six hundred words of informed response to the issue of censorship. This body of material will serve as the basis for your own three or four typewritten page *argumentative* essay on the

subject. Remember what has been mentioned time and again in this book: the techniques that you learn as you actively read will be the ones that you put to good use when you write your own essay.

(a) Examine your responses.
(b) Develop a workable topic in view of your subject, audience, and purpose.
(c) Determine effective developmental strategies.
(d) Develop a thesis statement.
(e) Develop an outline.
(f) Write a first draft.
(g) Revise.

BARBARA AMIEL

ANYONE WHO SUPPORTS CENSORSHIP, BE WARNED: THIS MAY MAKE YOU UPCHUCK

1 If I hadn't been listening carefully I might have missed the sentence and gone on thinking that MP Mark MacGuigan, mastermind behind the justice committee's Report on Pornography, just didn't like smut. I myself have never been able to see anything socially redeeming in photographs of acne-scarred, anemic young ladies straddling pigs, vibrators and one another. The ladies look so uncomfortable and the pigs understandably unenthusiastic about coupling with something that doesn't have a cloven hoof. But on CBC's *Radio Noon* MacGuigan gave a hint of higher motives behind his new censorship recommendations apart from his deeply felt belief that such photos besmirch *all* women and *all* pigs. Explained MacGuigan: "There's a small group making a large amount of money out of pornography and these people aren't even Canadians. They're mostly Americans. Almost all of our pornography is imported."

2 Well, there it is, folks. MacGuigan is a Trade Protectionist. If only we'd beef up the powers of customs officers and stop all that popular American filth maybe an indigenous porno industry will bloom. After all, why shouldn't Canadian pork get a chance too?

3 Like many Canadians I'd never actually been inside stores selling "marital aids" and dirty books. Last week in a flush of journalistic

integrity I dragged my reluctant husband on a tour of inspection warning him that we must be prepared for attacks of queasy stomach and waves of nausea. "It just makes me want to upchuck," said MP Simma Holt, a member of MacGuigan's committee after she had scrutinized an array of bondage outfits, rubber sex aids and magazines. After standing for some time looking at similar material I began to wonder about the ability of Mrs. Holt to cope with the vicissitudes of life on so delicate a tummy. Granted there is nothing arousing or artistic about most rubber penises. Still, a member of Parliament who "upchucks" in the face of one that has been *procured* for her inspection, having had days to prepare for the encounter rather than suddenly meeting one flashed in an alleyway, must have a rather highly strung system.

4 Which got me thinking that the reason I am adamantly opposed to censorship is (1) the sort of people who are drawn to the job and, what follows from this, (2) the material that inevitably ends up suppressed.

5 Even as I was graduating Simma-cum-lewde in Toronto's sex shops, the Ontario censor banned the highly acclaimed film *Pretty Baby* by French director Louis Malle. The film is the story of a 14-year old girl born in a New Orleans whorehouse at the turn of the century where she enters her mother's profession with some enthusiasm. It's a good and harmless film which was banned, as Ontario censor Donald Sims made clear, not because of pornography but because it was "exploitative of children." (Given that attitude Little Red Riding Hood is in for some tough sledding: violence, transvestism, and hints of bestial sexual practices. "My, grandmother, what big teeth you have." "All the better to eat you with, my dear.") The banning of *Pretty Baby* was a made-to-measure example of a pattern as old as censorship itself. Smut goes underground and continues to flourish commercially while works of art which have no commercial underground are banned. Sims explained that he had been influenced in his decision by a recent homosexual rape-murder of a young Toronto boy. This implied that he too was an advocate of the Mark MacGuigan school of social science which claims a direct relationship between looking at representations of sex-and-violence and subsequent deranged behavior. Just why Mrs. Holt, MacGuigan, Sims *et al* are immune to this and are not now frothing at the mouth, having been exposed to *Housewives in Bondage,* is something probably only their respective

spouses can explain. Still, if repressing representations of sex and violence had any effect on human behavior the Soviet Union ought to be the most non-violent society in the world and India, where on-screen kissing is banned, ought to have the smallest population. In fact, copulation and sadism seem to flourish independently.

6 It may be true, though it's never been demonstrated, that pornography stimulates a few people to harm others. But it's also true, and has been amply demonstrated, that some people are stimulated to mayhem through a reading (or misreading) of Marx, Nietzsche or the Bible. Should we ban them as well, Chairman MacGuigan? And if the possibility of harm is the only criterion, why not?

7 In the early '60s the press reported a law passed in Turkey under which anyone who publicly stated in speech or writing that Turkey was *not* a democracy was liable to two years' imprisonment. It took a decade or so for MacGuigan and his crew to discover the limitless possibilities of this sort of legislation, and we are now well on our way to Catching Up With Turkey.

8 Our society is based on "egalitarianism, consensuality and mutuality," says MacGuigan, so we are "clearly justified in controlling and prohibiting" the ideas of our coequals, whose mutual sensuality is different from ours. Sorry, no buy. You don't have to like violence or plastic penises to know that outlawing other people's tastes and ideas is the real obscenity.

Barbara Amiel, "Anyone Who Supports Censorship, Be Warned: This May Make You Upchuck," *Maclean's*, (May 1978), p. 78.

Questions

1. **Subject**
   Explain why Amiel argues against censorship and calls it "the real obscenity."
2. **Audience**
   The question of censorship, in and of itself, often gives rise to strong emotional responses. How is this particularly evident in this essay through the tone that Amiel uses?
3. **Purpose**
   Comment on the relationship between illustration and argument in this essay.

4. Structure and Style
- (a) Comment on the assumptions that lie behind Amiel's phrase in the sentence in paragraph 5: "It's a good and harmless film which was banned."
- (b) Explain why Amiel stresses the word *procured* in paragraph 3.
- (c) Explain the analogy in the last two paragraphs. In your opinion is it valid?

ROBERT FULFORD

BEWARE: THE CENSORS ARE MARCHING AGAIN

1 The sexual censors are always waiting, waiting in the shadows, waiting for their chance to pounce. The censors, when they appear among us, take various forms—sometimes they show themselves as politicians, sometimes as policemen or judges, sometimes as revivalist ministers, sometimes as "concerned parents." They all, however, speak and act from the same set of impulses. They are terrified of sexuality. They have been taught to fear their own sexuality, and they in turn fear the sexuality of their children. They wish to pass on their hideous repressions not only to their children but to the culture in which they live. They do not accept, as the rest of us do, a pluralist culture in which it is acknowledged that what dismays or appals me may delight you and should be free to do so. They believe that what dismays or appals *them* should simply cease to exist.

2 Now they are out among us again, fighting their old fight. In a nervous time, a period of economic and social strain, they are crawling out of the woodwork. Censorship, they sense, is an idea whose time—once more!—has come. In every section of Canada they have implored their MPs to "stamp out pornography," and the government has responded by introducing amendments to the Criminal Code that are terrifying in their implications—the definition of obscenity is to be so broadened that almost anything that offends anyone can be prosecuted. In many towns, teachers and school boards are under pressure to strip their libraries of every book, however innocent, that might endanger a parent's peace of mind.

3 For the censors, sex is sex, and even if it appears in the works of irreproachable authors like Margaret Laurence or Ernest Buckler it

must be eliminated. The censors like to say that they are really fighting against "the wave of pornography," but in community after community they disprove their own claims by attacking books that present sex in a context of decency and honour. Typically, they rip sexual passages out of context and present them at public hearings as evidence, thereby proving they care nothing for either literature or fairness. It is not *Penthouse* they hate; it is sex.

4 Well, I hate *Penthouse*, and everything it stands for, but as a pluralist I know that its existence—and the existence of a few dozen other magazines like it—is the price I pay for my own freedom to read Vladimir Nabokov, or for that matter Margaret Laurence. The censors, though, are not willing to pay that price, and for good reason: they aren't interested in Nabokov, Laurence, or any other serious writing. They don't read much, so if the freedom to read is denied them, they won't miss it. In the same way, those who censor movies—the chairman of the Ontario Board of Censors, Don Sims, who banned *Pretty Baby*, is a fine example—are almost inevitably persons who have never shown any dedication to the ideals of the cinema. If movies are once again driven back to the fairy tale level of the Bad Old Days, it won't bother *them*.

• • •

5 It's important to place the current wave of censorship in historical context. In the last two decades, freedom of expression has been enormously enlarged in all the Western democratic countries. We have vastly more freedom than we had, say, in the early 1950s. Even if the censors of today succeed in what they propose, they can cut back on only a small part of that freedom. The point is, however, that they won't stop there. If they ban *Penthouse* today they'll get to work on *Playboy* tomorrow; if they get Margaret Laurence out of the schools they'll go on to W.O. Mitchell. Their appetite will not be sated by a small meal. It will grow as we feed it, till it reaches the dimensions of totalitarianism.

6 The new freedoms that began in the 1950s—the freeing of *Lady Chatterley's Lover* in 1959 was perhaps the turning point—obviously have not had entirely beneficial results for our culture. Every honest civil libertarian would probably admit that pornography is an unpleasant by-product of the new freedom; but only a few wide-eyed optimists ever suggested that freedom would bring nothing but good. Just as free enterprise can bring us urban blight or pollution, just as free political speech can bring us John Diefenbaker, so freedom of sexual expression has made pornography widely available for the first

time. Those who fought for free expression in 1960 may be dismayed by the pornographers they have accidentally enriched. As the English writer John Wain has put it:

7 "...good people will be free in good ways, and nasty squalid little people will be free in nasty squalid little ways. Greasy men who are engaged in making money out of the degradation of the sexual instinct...will always claim to be encouraging freedom, and they will always have liberals backed into a corner so that no one who wants to be thought a liberal will ever support any form of censorship."

8 In the old days, the late Paul Goodman insisted that if legal restrictions were lifted from pornography, it would "ennoble all our art," "humanize sexuality," have "beautiful cultural advantages." Few were so naïve. Most of the civil libertarians simply wanted us all, as Wain put it, to be free in our good or if necessary our nasty squalid little ways, as we chose. We believed then in personal choice; we have to believe in it now, even if the personal choices of some of our contemporaries seem repellent to us.

9 But if freedom hasn't brought us the renaissance in human values that Goodman promised, it has brought us a great deal of value. Novels and movies can now describe life as we actually live it, and set down human speech as it actually is spoken. These seem to me enormous gains, both for the high arts and the popular arts. They are not to be given up without a struggle.

• • •

10 Many of the current censorship lobbies—the Ministerial Association in Saint John is one, Renaissance International in Toronto is another—focus their activities on the schools. This is a shrewd tactic. It calls to their support both our commonly shared anxieties about our children (who is not worried that his or her children will be somehow damaged in The World Out There?) but also whatever guilt we may have about our own inadequacy as parents. Furthermore, it attacks teachers and school librarians at a moment in history when they are most vulnerable. What teacher, in 1978, is not at least vaguely worried about his or her job? What librarian is not worried about whether, four or five years from now, there will even *be* school libraries? (Perhaps trustees, bothered by all the fuss, will decide libraries are frills.) These are years of crisis in the schools, and the censors—scenting blood—are closing in.

11 There is a sense in which liberals have brought at least some of this on themselves. Liberals traditionally have tried to use the schools for

their own purposes, to teach their own doctrines, to socialize children in the ways liberals believe proper. (Sex education, which began about twenty years ago in the schools, is essentially a liberal attempt to spread liberal values through tax-supported institutions, whether or not all parents want their children given sex education; it has caused enormous difficulties, and probably done more harm than good.) Now the active conservatives, who are no smaller a minority than the active liberals, want to use the schools to promote or at least protect *their* values. Their action throws into question the whole idea of the school as a tool for changing society, for the arbitrary sculpting of the next generation's outlook.

12 None of that, of course, justifies trying to limit the range of school libraries, or tying the hands of school librarians. They are, as a class, conservative enough, without the extra inhibition of parents and school boards looking over their shoulders.

• • •

13 For some of us, all this has the feeling of a re-run. Libertarians who contemplate the new wave of censorship feel as the Duke of Wellington would have felt if, on the day after Waterloo, he had been informed that Napoleon was once more marshalling his troops and the battle must be joined again. A feeling of ennui, naturally enough, overtakes us—which may explain why there has been no significant outcry against the new Criminal Code changes. We thought, perhaps subconsciously and certainly naïvely, that the struggle for freedom of expression was over. But it's not. It's never over.

Robert Fulford, "Beware: The Censors are Marching Again," *Saturday Night*, (September, 1978), pp. 12, 13.

Questions

1. **Subject**
   Fulford argues that the absence of censorship will permit people to be free. Does he see any negative consequences of a lack of censorship? How does he respond to them?
2. **Audience**
   Comment on the extent to which emotion and unverified claims mar the argumentative integrity of this essay (focus on paragraphs 1 to 4). To what extent does the emotional rhetoric help define the tone of the essay?

3. **Purpose**
   Does Fulford ever acknowledge that the forces against which he is arguing have a possible case to make? If not does this refusal to acknowledge another side to the argument affect his credibility?
4. **Structure and Style**
   (a) Explain the effectiveness of the repetition in sentences 3 to 7.
   (b) Comment on how the sentence "In a nervous time, a period of economic and social strain, they are crawling out of the woodwork," reflects a particular attitude on the author's part. How does the audience react to such terminology?
   (c) Find at least one example each of deductive and inductive argumentation in the essay.

RALPH HEINTZMAN
LIBERALISM AND CENSORSHIP

1 After a period of more than a decade in which it had seemed to fade from view, the issue of censorship has emerged again in the last year as a matter of public debate in Canada. The re-emergence of the issue suggests that certain questions many had thought settled were in fact only temporarily set aside. The assumption of a portion of the community—that the state has no right to restrict public expression—has proven to be less widely accepted than seemed for a time to be the case. The attempted reassertion of the state's right to control certain kinds of public expression—apparently with the support of a wide segment of opinion—has alarmed those who assumed such a right was already extinct, or on the point of becoming so.

2 The reaction of many within the intellectual and artistic community has been commendably energetic. The Book and Periodical Development Council has formed a special task force on censorship chaired by Timothy Findley. A recent broadcast of *Cross-Country Check-Up* was mobilized against censorship. Among many others, the editor of *Saturday Night* and the book columnist of the *Globe & Mail* have strongly deplored the reassertion of a right to censorship, the latter repeatedly and in sensational terms.

3 All of these voices are perfectly correct in diagnosing a problem of censorship, but the real problem is a rather different one than most of them seem to think: it is a failure to think clearly about the issue. The bulk of recent commentary on censorship in Canada has been a crude mixture of knee-jerk reactions, unexamined premises, and the wielding of bogeys. This is as true of those who oppose censorship as of

those who favour it, but it is perhaps more surprising and regrettable in the case of the former. The censorship debate has not been characterized by the careful thought and distinctions one would hope to find on such a sensitive and divisive issue, especially from the "intellectuals" whose special care it ought to be to make just such distinctions.

4 The result is a state of high confusion in which a number of separate issues have been mixed together and the real issue has been almost entirely obscured. One is scarcely justified, for example, in mixing up the right of parents and school boards to decide what the children in their care shall be required to read with the issue of censorship properly so-called. The exercise of this right does not interfere with what may be published and sold, or even with what young people may read, but only with what they may be *required* to read, which is a different matter altogether. Like all other rights, this one may be exercised with good judgment or bad—and, more often than not, with the latter—but the existence of the right itself cannot be questioned. Indeed, parents who failed to exercise it would probably be more open to censure than those who did.

5 Similarly, it is an abuse of common sense to confuse the well-meaning efforts of a city council to license and supervise—not ban—the sale of pornographic literature with a limitation, even a potential one, on political expression, as William French has done. The lack of proportion involved in this kind of judgment goes to the heart of the confusion surrounding the discussion of censorship and the refusal of those engaged in it to make the necessary distinctions.

6 It is essential to distinguish, for example, between the maintenance of a minimum level of public decorum and the censorship of political debate. Those who refuse to acknowledge this distinction and who argue, as Robert Fulford has, that any form of censorship leads inevitably to totalitarianism are just as guilty as if they were to attack liberals as communists or conservatives as fascists: they are indulging in a form of intellectual McCarthyism. It cannot be seriously maintained that insistence on a certain standard of public decorum is a threat to political life, any more than concern for a decent level of manners is a threat to social life. In fact the reverse is more probable in both cases: a high standard of public manners may well be the condition for a high standard of political and social life. In any event, the increasing license of our own time does not seem to have raised the level of political discourse noticeably, to say the least, above the standard achieved in another age by a Burke, a Marx, or a Mill.

7 One ought also to make a more careful distinction than is usually the case today between the practice of censorship and the level of artistic expression. It is by no means self-evident, as many today assume without adequate reflection, that the existence of censorship inevitably entails a loss of artistic power. As everyone knows, nineteenth-century Russia was subject to a high degree of political censorship (though not nearly as high as in the Soviet Union today), yet it also witnessed one of the greatest flowerings of literary creativity in the history of the world, thus perhaps confirming Northrop Frye's suggestion that literature actually flourishes in difficult circumstances. The facts are so striking that one is almost tempted to suggest that a measure of censorship might be a reasonable price to pay for a Pushkin, a Turgenev, or a Chekhov, let alone a Dostoevsky or a Tolstoy! Though utterly facetious, such a thought does underline the fact that those who oppose any form of censorship cannot do so on the ground that it inevitably means a lowering of artistic standards. Once again the reverse could be just as easily maintained. In fact, the celebrated critic George Steiner has done precisely that in his most recent book, *On Difficulty.*

8 That certainly does not mean, of course, that the case against censorship is without merit, but it suggests that those who argue it must give more sustained attention than they have yet done to their premises. All too often these remain unexplored, while the weight of their argument rests on a number of bogeys exploited to intimidate and silence their opponents. Since these bogeys will not withstand serious criticism, the opponents of censorship must strengthen and refine their case. In doing so, they will have to take a harder look at their own presuppositions.

9 One of the curious things is the inconsistency these presuppositions often involve. In my own experience—and it is worth emphasizing that the views expressed here are those of the editor alone and do not necessarily reflect those of any other persons or institutions associated with the *Journal*—virtually all those who oppose censorship on principle are equally strongly in favour of legislation against hate literature and various forms of racial abuse. Yet this too is a form of censorship. Thus the opposition is not really to censorship at all but only to certain forms of it. The right of the state to enact controls on public expression is admitted: only the objects of censorship remain in dispute.

10 This concession alters the nature of the debate fundamentally. It is

no longer a question of whether censorship should exist—this being now admitted—but of what should be censored, and how. Answers to these questions presuppose answers to others. Most of the recent controversy about censorship in Canada has been about censorship of pornography or of explicitly sexual material. If, as I have suggested, one cannot successfully argue that censorship in any form is necessarily a threat to political life or to artistic integrity, then in order to decide whether the state ought to exercise its right to censorship in relation to these matters one requires a coherent view of the place of sexuality in the human spirit and of the implications of this view for the development or preservation of a civil society.

11 Supplying answers to *these* questions is enormously complicated in our time by the role of liberalism as the prevailing ideology of the intellectually influential. In fact, the intellectual confusion surrounding the issue of censorship—the *real* problem of censorship defined above—is largely the consequence of both the strengths and weaknesses of the liberal mind.

12 As Lionel Trilling remarked in his suggestive review of the Kinsey report, later reprinted in *The Liberal Imagination,* the good side of liberalism in sexual matters is "its impulse toward acceptance and liberation, its broad and generous desire for others that they be not harshly judged." This generous side of liberalism is greatly to be cherished and admired, but when it has been given due credit "as a sign of something good and enlarging," Trilling wrote,

> we cannot help observing that it is often associated with an almost intentional intellectual weakness. It goes with a nearly conscious aversion from making intellectual distinctions, almost as if out of the belief that an intellectual distinction must lead to a social discrimination or exclusion. We might say that those who most explicitly assert and wish to practice the democratic virtues have taken it as their assumption that all social facts—with the exception of exclusion and economic hardship—must be *accepted,* not merely in the scientific sense but also in the social sense, in the sense, that is, that no judgment must be passed on them, that any conclusion drawn from them which perceives values and consequences will turn out to be 'undemocratic.'

13 The prevailing liberal view of sexuality is shaped by the behaviourist assumption that human acts can only be judged—if

indeed they can be judged at all—according to generalizations drawn from the observation of what people actually do. The liberal mind shrinks, therefore, from judging sexual behaviour

> except, presumably, in so far as it causes pain to others... the preponderant weight of its argument is that a fact is a physical fact, to be considered only in its physical aspect and apart from any idea or ideal that might make it a social fact, as having no ascertainable personal or cultural meaning and no possible consequences—as being, indeed, not available to social interpretation at all. In short, [liberalism]...by its primitive conception of the nature of fact quite negates the importance and even the existence of sexuality as a social fact.

14 Yet is is precisely the meaning of sexuality as a social fact with which one must grapple before the question of censorship can be satisfactorily resolved. This is a very large matter and no approach to it can be suggested here, but it is obvious that much will depend on one's notion of the human mind or spirit. It is not common nowadays to think of the mind in Platonic terms, that is, as requiring mental "guardians" to keep in order the potentially unruly energies and forces of which it is in large part composed. But since this view of mind has been held even longer than our modern one, perhaps it deserves more attention than it now receives.

15 In this view, the passions are conceived as being a vitally important element of mind, perhaps even its centre, but, by their very power, being also capable of great destruction and therefore in need of careful direction and control. The individual citizen's control over his own passions is, in fact, the foundation of social discipline and social order. The sexual passions in particular have almost always been regarded as forces of tremendous power for good or evil. An intuition of their awesome power explains why so many religions incorporate elements of sexuality into their own mythology and worship, yet also encircle them with a great variety of prohibitions and taboos. The purpose and origin of such prohibitions vary greatly but their fundamental source is the intuition that this power cannot safely be trifled with, that it should not be taken in hand lightly or frivolously, but reverently, discreetly....They are warning signs posted around the passions to caution the unwary: "Handle with care." Chastity, as Benedict Domdaniel remarks in *A Mixture of Frailties,* is having the body in the soul's keeping: just that and nothing more.

16 The modern or liberal frame of mind regards the passions in a very different light. For one thing, it approaches them with far less awe. In its classical mood, it is more sanguine about the power of naked rationality to control and direct them for good. In its romantic mood, it is inclined to look on every impulse of the human spirit as potentially creative and therefore not to be checked or disciplined without loss: the romantic hero is often one who by giving in to his passions and violating the taboos achieves a level of knowledge or experience denied to others. The view that almost every impulse is potentially creative is not wrong, of course. But it overlooks the complementary Platonic or Augustinian insight that there is a hierarchy in the realm of the good and that evil enters the world not through the triumph of bad over good, but through our own preference for a lesser good to the exclusion of a greater. Thus it gravely minimizes the potential for evil implicit in acts or impulses which may be, in their own terms, good.

17 For another thing, the liberal mind interprets sexuality in terms of certain analogies drawn from modern technology. The Freudian or twentieth-century notion of sexuality was shaped by the analogy of the steam engine. As pressure builds up within the steam boiler or the human psyche, it must be let off in some form if an explosion is to be avoided. Thus the liberal mind concludes that the basic sexual "drives" demand "release" if damage is not to be done to the personality. However, as Tom Wolfe has pointed out, the usefulness of this analogy appears increasingly doubtful. As both electronic technology and neurological research advance, we have learned that the mind is far more comparable to a computer than to a steam engine. If so, the conclusion to be drawn about human behaviour is exactly reversed. Far from providing a healthful "release," each successive act or thought actually "programmes" the mind for continued activity of the same kind, until, if the programming is sufficiently complete, the mind can dwell on little else. Obviously a theory of mind which took this contemporary analogy seriously would adopt a very different attitude to censorship than the prevailing one, especially censorship of material which might become available to children and so "programme" their imaginations.

18 If the assumptions of the liberal mind about human nature and sexuality are shown to be flawed or incomplete, then it may be wise to give correspondingly greater attention to that other tradition of thought which approaches the powers of the spirit with greater awe, which conceives the mind as requiring "guardians" and as having to

be kept in order, with no little difficulty. If the need is admitted, then influences which increase the difficulty can be rightfully considered anti-social, since tending to break down that inner self-control on which social order depends. In this view, the process of civilization, the process of establishing an ever-increasing degree of civility in social and political life, depends upon each member of the community establishing greater dominion over his or her own psyche and emotions. To the degree that self-control is inhibited by the deliberate arousal of passion or desire, to that degree a civil society becomes a more distant and elusive goal and society moves closer to a state of barbarism.

19 If so, the recent reassertion of the public's right to establish minimum standards of decorum may not be necessarily unwelcome. Now that we have enjoyed the fruits of forty years or so of liberalism in sexual matters as in political, there is perhaps room for the reassertion of another range of values and for a reexamination of the claims of excellence, in human behaviour and social conduct as in other things. The liberal impulse to tolerance and acceptance is wholly admirable, but it needs to be balanced and complemented by something else. If it leads to a paralysis of the faculty of judgment, it becomes one of those good things by which so much evil can be done. We need to transcend what Trilling called liberalism's "primitive conception of the nature of fact" and to learn again to make balanced judgments about the ultimate meaning and consequence of human behaviour.

20 If the apparent public concern with censorship expresses a confused groping toward a revival of critical judgment in sexual and social matters, then it may deserve more than contempt, however misguided or badly motivated some of the noisiest advocates of censorship may be. The role of the intellectual community should not be to thwart or deny the right to censorship—a denial which would not be sincere in any case—but rather to guide it and help it avoid the crude and harmful purposes to which it might be put. If certain works, films, or publications do not undermine civility as alleged but contribute instead to the process of civilization, then it should not be beyond the power of the intellectual community to say why. But it will have to do so with greater intellectual and moral rigour than in the recent past. The public is not as foolish as the *cognoscenti* often believe. It may sometimes fall into the error of thinking that a truly moral work of art cannot contain what it considers to be "immoral" scenes or characters, but it rarely makes the opposite mistake, to which so many artists and intellectuals are vulnerable, of thinking that art is

beyond good and evil, and should not be judged, in the final analysis, by moral standards as well as aesthetic ones.

21 The intellectual, artistic, and journalistic communities would perhaps do well to embrace the claims of civility and excellence and to work out their implications for the public depiction of sexuality in more satisfying terms than they have yet done, rather than fighting the principle of censorship itself. Above all, they should avoid basing opposition to censorship on the defence of civil liberties. For one thing, there is no opposition between them. In fact, the first may be a prerequisite for the second, since it is improbable that civil liberty would long survive in a society threatened by social decadence and disorder. For another thing, there can be little doubt which of the two the public would ultimately choose if forced to do so. That is why the choice should not be forced upon it. To suggest that civil liberties and censorship are not compatible is to call into question, in the long run, not censorship, as many assume, but liberty itself.

Ralph Heintzman, "Liberalism and Censorship," *The Journal of Canadian Studies*, Vol. 13 (Winter, 1978-1979), pp. 1-2, 120-122.

Questions

1. **Subject**
   Locate the thesis statement of this essay (hint: search the first three paragraphs) and show how the author argues this position in the essay.
2. **Audience**
   Do you find any evidence in the essay to suggest that the author is writing for an educated audience? If you do, say how the author takes pains to explain his sometimes arcane references to a less educated audience.
3. **Purpose**
   Give proof to show that Heintzman's argumentative purpose attempts to point to the values of both the libertarian point of view and the pro-censorship point of view.
4. **Structure and Style**
   (a) Explain what Heintzman means by the following sentence (paragraph 20): "If the apparent public concern with censorship expresses a confused groping toward a revival of critical judgment in sexual social matters, then it may deserve more than contempt, however misguided or badly motivated some of the noisiest advocates of censorship may be."
   (b) Explain the relationship between general statement and detail in paragraph 7.
   (c) How does the final sentence of the essay reiterate the thesis of the entire essay?

MARGARET LAURENCE
THE GREATER EVIL

1 I have a troubled feeling that I may be capable of doublethink, the ability to hold two opposing beliefs simultaneously. In the matter of censorship, doublethink seems, alas, appropriate. As a writer, my response to censorship of any kind is that I am totally opposed to it. But when I consider some of the vile material that is being peddled freely, I want to see some kind of control. I don't think I am being hypocritical. I have a sense of honest bewilderment. I have struggled with this inner problem for years, and now, with the spate of really bad video films and porn magazines flooding the market, my sense of ambiguity grows. I am certain of one thing, though. I cannot be alone in my uncertainty.

2 I have good reason to mistrust and fear censorship. I have been burned by the would-be book censors. Not burned in effigy, nor suffered my books being burned, not yet anyhow. But burned nonetheless, scorched mentally and emotionally. This has happened in more than one part of Canada, but the worst experience for me was in my own county of Peterborough a few years ago, when a group of people, sincere within their limited scope, no doubt, sought to have my novel, *The Diviners,* banned from the Grade 13 course and the school libraries. The book was attacked as obscene, pornographic, immoral and blasphemous. It is, I need hardly say, none of these things. Open meetings of the school board were held. Letters, pro and con, appeared in the local newspaper. Some awful things were said about the book and about me personally, mostly by people who had not read the book or met me. In retrospect, some of the comments seem pretty funny, but at the time I was hurt and furious. One person confidently stated that "Margaret Laurence's aim in life is to destroy the home and the family." In an interview, another person claimed that the novel contained a detailed account, calculated to titillate, of the sex life of the housefly. I couldn't recollect any such scene. Then I remembered that when Morag, as a child, is embarrassed by the sad, self-deprecating talk of her stepmother, the gentle, obese Prin, the girl seeks anything at all to focus on, so she need not listen. "She looked at two flies fucking, buzzing as they did it." Beginning and end of sensational scene. The reporter asked if the fundamentalist minister himself had found the scene sexually stimulating. "Oh

no," was the reply. "I'm a happily married man." At one open meeting, a man rose to condemn the novel and said that he spoke for a delegation of seven: himself, his wife, their four children—and God. In another county, a bachelor pharmacist accused me of adding to the rate of venereal disease in Canada by writing my books. He claimed that young people should not be given any information about sex until they are physically mature—"at about the age of 21." I hoped his knowledge of pharmacy was greater than his knowledge of biology.

3 Many readers, teachers and students did speak out for the novel, which was ultimately restored to the Grade 13 course. But the entire episode was enough to make me come down heavily against censorship, and especially against self-appointed groups of vigilantes. At the time I made a statement, which said, in part: "Surely it cannot do other than help in the growing toward a responsible maturity, for our young people to read novels in which many aspects of human life are dealt with, by writers whose basic faith is in the unique and irreplaceable value of the human individual."

4 I hold to that position. Artists of all kinds have been persecuted, imprisoned, tortured and killed, in many countries and at many times throughout history, for portraying life as they honestly saw it. Artistic suppression and political suppression go hand in hand, and always have. I would not advocate the banning of even such an evil and obscene book as Hitler's *Mein Kampf*. I think we must learn to recognize our enemies, to counter inhuman ranting with human and humane beliefs and practices. With censorship, the really bad stuff would tend to go underground and flourish covertly, while works of genuine artistic merit might get the axe (and yes, I know that "genuine artistic merit" is very difficult to define). I worry that censorship of any kind might lead to the suppression of anyone who speaks out against anything in our society, the suppression of artists, and the eventual clamping down on ideas, human perceptions, questionings. I think of our distinguished constitutional lawyer and poet F.R. Scott. In an essay written in 1933, he said: "'The time, it is to be hoped, has gone by,' wrote John Stuart Mill, 'when any defence would be necessary of the principle of freedom of speech.' His hope was vain. The time for defending freedom never goes by. Freedom is a habit that must be kept alive by use."

5 And yet—my ambiguity remains. The pornography industry is now enormous, and includes so-called "kiddie porn." Most of us do not look at this stuff, nor do we have any notion how widespread it is,

nor how degrading and brutal toward women and children, for it is they who are the chief victims in such magazines and films. Let me make one thing clear. I do not object to books or films or anything else that deals with sex, if those scenes are between two adults who are entering into this relationship of their own free will. (You may well say—what about *Lolita?* I hated the book, as a matter of fact, and no, I wouldn't advocate banning Nabokov. Ambiguity.) I do not object to the portrayal of social injustice, of terrible things done to one human by another or by governments or groups of whatever kind, as long as this is shown for what it is. But when we see films and photographs, *making use of real live women and children,* that portray horrifying violence, whether associated with sex or simply violence on its own, as being acceptable, on-turning, a thrill a minute, then I object.

6 The distinction must be made between erotic and pornographic. Eroticism is the portrayal of sexual expression between two people who desire each other and who have entered this relationship with mutual agreement. Pornography, on the other hand, is the portrayal of coercion and violence, usually with sexual connotations, and, like rape in real life, it has less to do with sex than with subjugation and cruelty. Pornography is not in any sense life-affirming. It is a denial of life. It is a repudiation of any feelings of love and tenderness and mutual passion. It is about hurting people, mainly women, and having that brutality seen as socially acceptable, even desirable.

7 As a woman, a mother, a writer, I cannot express adequately my feelings of fear, anger and outrage at this material. I have to say that I consider visual material to be more dangerous than any printed verbal material. Possibly I will be accused of being elitist and of favoring my own medium, the printed word, and possibly such a charge could be true. I just don't know. The reason I feel this way, however, is that these films and photographs make use of living women and children—not only a degradation of them, but also a strong suggestion to the viewer that violence against women and children, real persons, is acceptable. One of the most sinister aspects of these films and photographs is that they frequently communicate the idea that not only is violence against women OK—women actually *enjoy* being the subject of insanely brutal treatment, actually enjoy being chained, beaten, mutilated and even killed. This aspect of pornography, of course, reinforces and purports to excuse the behaviour of some men who do indeed hate women. I could weep in grief and rage when I think of this attitude. As for the use of children in pornography, this

is unspeakable and should be forbidden by law. The effect of this material is a matter of some dispute, and nothing can be proved either way, but many people believe that such scenes have been frighteningly re-enacted in real life in one way or another.

8 But is censorship, in any of the media involved, the answer? I think of John Milton's *Areopagitica; A Speech for the Liberty of Unlicensed Printing, to the Parliament of England,* in 1644, in which these words appear: "He that can apprehend and consider vice with all her baits and seeming pleasures, and yet abstain, and yet distinguish, and yet prefer that which is truly better, he is the true wayfaring Christian. I cannot praise a fugitive and cloistered virtue, unexercised and unbreathed, that never sallies out and sees her adversary, but slinks out of the race, where that immortal garland is to be run for, not without dust and heat." Obviously, Milton was not thinking of the sort of video films that anyone can now show at home, where any passing boy child can perhaps get the message that cruelty is OK and fun, and any passing girl child may wonder if that is what will be expected of her, to be a victim. All the same, we forget Milton's words at our peril.

9 The situation is not without its ironies. It has created some very strange comrades-in-arms. We find a number of feminists taking a strong stand *for* censorship, and being praised and applauded by people whose own stance is light-years away from feminism, the same people who would like my books, Alice Munro's books, W.O. Mitchell's books, banned from our high schools. We see civil libertarians who are *against* censorship and for free expression arguing that "anything goes," a view that must rejoice the hearts of purveyors of this inhumane material, but certainly distresses mine.

10 I consider myself to be both a feminist and a strong supporter of civil liberties and free speech, but there is no way I want to be on the same team as the would-be book-banning groups who claim that no contemporary novels should be taught or read in our schools. There is no way, either, that I want to be on the same team as the pornographers.

11 What position can a person like myself honestly take? The whole subject is enormously complex, but I must finally come down against a censorship board, whether for the visual media or for the printed word. I think that such boards tend to operate by vague and ill-defined standards. What can "acceptable community standards" possibly mean? It depends on which community you're talking about,

and within any one community, even the smallest village, there are always going to be wide differences. Censorship boards tend to be insufficiently accountable. I believe that in cases of obscenity, test cases have to be brought before the courts and tried openly in accordance with our federal obscenity laws. The long-term solution, of course, is to educate our children of both sexes to realize that violence against women and children, against anyone, is not acceptable, and to equalize the status of women in our society.

12 What about Section 159 of the Criminal Code, "Offences Tending to Corrupt Morals"? My impression of federal law in this area is that its intentions are certainly right, its aims are toward justice, and it is indeed in some ways woefully outdated and in need of clarification. Clarification and amendment have not been and will not be easy. The clause that is most widely known to the general public is Section 159(8): "For the purpose of this Act, any publication a dominant characteristic of which is the undue exploitation of sex, or of sex and any one or more of the following subjects, namely, crime, horror, cruelty and violence, shall be deemed to be obscene." I think the first use of the words "of sex" could be deleted. How much sex between consenting adults is too much? Are three scenes OK but ten excessive? Frankly, among the many things I worry about in my life, as a citizen and as a writer, this is not one of them. But how are we to enshrine in our laws the idea that the degradation and coercion of women and children, of anyone, is dreadful, without putting into jeopardy the portrayal of social injustice seen as injustice? How are we to formulate a law that says the use of real women and children in situations of demeanment and violence, shown as desirable fun stuff, is not acceptable, while at the same time not making it possible for people who don't like artists questioning the status quo to bring charges against those who must continue to speak out against the violation of the human person and spirit?

13 In one case cited in the Criminal Code, the judge declares: "The onus of proof upon the Crown may be discharged by simply producing the publication without expert opinion evidence. Furthermore, where, although the book has certain literary merit particularly for the more sophisticated reader, it was available for the general public to whom the book was neither symbolism nor a psychological study the accused cannot rely on the defence of public good." "Public good" is later defined as "necessary or advantageous to religion or morality, to the administration of justice, the pursuit of science, literature or art, or other objects of general interest." If this precedent means what it

appears to say, it alarms me. It appears to put works of "literary merit" into some jeopardy, especially as expert opinion evidence need not be heard. If a book of mine were on trial, I would certainly want expert opinion evidence. I do not always agree with the views of the literary critics, or of teachers, but at least, and reassuringly, many of them know how to read with informed skill.

14 Realizing the difficulty of accurate definitions, I think that violence itself, shown as desirable, must be dealt with in some way in this law. It is *not* all right for men to beat and torture women. *It is wrong.* I also think that the exploitation of real live children for "kiddie porn" should be dealt with as a separate issue in law and should not be allowed, ever.

15 The more I think about it, the more the whole question becomes disturbingly complicated. Yet I believe it is a question that citizens, Parliament and the legal profession must continue to grapple with. It is not enough for citizens to dismiss our obscenity laws as inadequate and outdated, and then turn the whole matter over to censorship boards. Our laws are not engraved on stone. They have been formulated carefully, although sometimes not well, but with a regard to a general justice. The law is not perfect, but it *is* public. It can be changed, but not upon the whim of a few. An informed and alert public is a necessary component of democracy. When laws need revision, we must seek to have them revised, not toward any narrowing down but toward a greater justice for all people, children, women and men, so that our lives may be lived without our being victimized, terrorized or exploited. Freedom is more fragile than any of us in Canada would like to believe. I think again of F.R. Scott's words: "Freedom is a habit that must be kept alive by use." Freedom, however, means responsibility and concern toward others. It does not mean that unscrupulous persons are permitted to exploit, demean and coerce others. It is said, correctly, that there is a demand for pornography. But should this demand be used to justify its unchallenged existence and distribution? Some men are said to "need" pornography. To me this is like saying some men "need" to beat up their wives or commit murder. Must women and children be victims in order to assuage the fears and insecurities of those men who want to feel they are totally powerful in a quite unreal way? I don't think so. If some men "need" pornography, then I as a woman will never be a party to it, not even by the tacit agreement of silence. We and they had better try together to control and redirect those needs. I think that citizens can and should protest in any nonviolent way possible against the

brutalities and callousness of pornography, including one area I haven't even been able to deal with here, the demeanment of women in many advertisements.

16 In the long run, it is all-important to raise our children to know the reality of others; to let them know that sex can and should be an expression of love and tenderness and mutual caring, not hatred and domination of the victor/victim kind; to communicate to our daughters and our sons that to be truly human is to try to be loving and responsible, strong not because of power but because of self-respect and respect for others.

17 In *Areopagitica,* Milton said: "That which purifies us is trial, and trial is by what is contrary." In the final analysis, we and our society will not stand or fall by what we are "permitted" to see or hear or read, but by what we ourselves choose. We must, however, have some societal agreement as to what is acceptable in the widest frame of reference possible, but still within the basic concept that *damaging people is wrong.* Murder is not acceptable, and neither is the abasement, demeanment and exploitation of human persons, whatever their race, religion, age or gender. Not all of this can be enshrined in law. Laws can never make people more understanding and compassionate toward one another. That is what individual people try to do, in our imperfect and familial ways. What the law *can* do is attempt to curb, by open process in public courts, the worst excesses of humankind's always-in-some-way-present inhumanity to humankind.

18 This is as close as I can get to formulating my own beliefs. It is an incomplete and in many ways a contradictory formulation, and I am well aware of that. Perhaps this isn't such a bad thing. I don't think we can or should ever get to a point where we feel we know, probably in a simplistic way, what all the answers are or that we ourselves hold them and no one else does. The struggle will probably always go on, as it always has in one way or another. The new technology has brought its own intricacies. I doubt that the human heart and conscience will ever be relieved of their burdens, and I certainly hope they are not. This particular struggle, *for* human freedom and *against* the awfulness that seeks to masquerade as freedom but is really slavery, will not ever be easy or simple, but it is a struggle that those of us who are concerned must never cease to enter into, even though it will continue to be, in Milton's words, "not without dust and heat."

Margaret Laurence, "The Greater Evil," *Toronto Life* (September, 1984), pp. 58-59, 92, 94, 96.

Questions

1. **Subject**
   (a) How does the title "The Greater Evil" reflect the subject of this essay? Focusing on the irony in the essay may help you with your answer to the question.
   (b) Explain the difference Laurence draws between eroticism and pornography.
2. **Audience**
   Indicate how the author tries to gain audience support through her example in paragraph 2.
3. **Purpose**
   Explain how the argumentative purpose of this essay not only makes a point, but also gives voice to difficult questions in the author's mind.
4. **Structure and Style**
   (a) Comment on how the final paragraph of the essay serves as an appropriate summary of Margaret Laurence's position.
   (b) Make clear how the "And yet—" phrase of the opening of paragraph 5 indicates a major change in thought in the essay.
   (c) Explain how the author's ambivalence helps determine the structure of this essay.

PAUL STUEWE

BETTER DEAD THAN READ?

1 There's a familiar bogey astir in the land. Cry "Censorship!" in a crowded theatre these days and you'll be trampled to death by liberals manning the battle stations of editorial opinion and engaged reportage. What's all the fuss about? Mainly it's about a few groups of concerned parents in mostly rural areas of Nova Scotia, New Brunswick, and Ontario who have begun to take an active interest in what their children are being encouraged to read in school. Furthermore, they have had the temerity to suggest that certain books are unsuitable for impressionable young minds.

2 The most recent censorship crisis has occurred in Huron County, Ont., an agricultural area about 120 miles west of Toronto. William French of the *Globe and Mail* has diagnosed a "strange mood" infecting the Huron County population with a desire to keep such books as *The Diviners, Catcher in the Rye,* and *Of Mice and Men* out of the hands

of local high-school students. Curious about the psychology of any group foolhardy enough to go up against both the teaching *and* the intellectual establishments, I paid a visit to Huron County and found that the realities are rather different from the picture presented by the national media.

3 After reading press coverage of the controversy, I had expected to be confronted by crazed bands of Bible-waving fanatics burning books in the town square and extracting oaths of moral purity from local high-school teachers. Instead I found that the pro-censorship forces are led by two capable spokesmen whose arguments have a high degree of logical and moral force and are firmly grounded in community traditions at least as old as the notion of Canada itself.

4 One of these spokesmen is Elmer Umbach, a pharmacist who operates his own drugstore on the main street of Lucknow, a town on the northern edge of Huron County. Umbach represents the more intransigent wing of the fundamentalist, evangelical Christian opposition to the books in question, and his first words to me are: "I want you to insist that what I'm saying is a *declaration of truth,* and I am not interested in discussing or dialoguing with you." A finger stabs at me in emphasis. "It's available to anyone else from the same place I got it—the Bible. It's the only source of successful moral living, and the only system that has ever proved to work for everyone's good."

5 This unpromising beginning has taken place in front of several customers and staff at Umbach's drugstore. But later over coffee in the secluded back room of a neighbouring restaurant he unbends a bit and expands on his involvement with the pro-censorship movement. Umbach is not married, and thus has no children in the local school system; but he is active in community religious groups, and when some of his fellow churchmen became upset about the kinds of books being taught to Huron County students, he was asked to be their spokesman.

6 For Umbach and his associates, the salient fact of the controversy is that children are involved, children for whom their parents are morally responsible until they reach adulthood and children who are in danger of corruption from those who are supposed to be setting them a sound moral example: "Teachers now believe that students won't be well-rounded unless they study books such as *The Diviners* and *Catcher in the Rye,* but we don't agree. We believe that a child is not mature until he is physically mature, at about the age of 21. Until then he is not able to handle things like sex, and should not be exposed to them." He stresses that it's the protection of children that

requires such strong action: "As far as adults are concerned, they can go ahead and destroy themselves any way they want to."

7 As a pharmacist, Umbach sees some of the nastier consequences of a decade of sexual revolution. The number and severity of cases of venereal disease is increasing rapidly in his hometown. Where a liberal would argue that this calls for more sexual education, he draws just the opposite conclusion: "Young people get venereal disease because they practise free love the way Margaret Laurence and such writers advocate. But when they get it they don't go to her for help—they come to me, which is what they should have done in the first place."

8 This raises, albeit obliquely, one of the thornier issues in the controversy over book censorship: Does the reading of books actually influence behaviour and what are the consequences of the possible answers? A common liberal response is some variation on, "There is no evidence that anyone ever did anything simply because they read about it in a book" This (a) is untrue, since there is some social-scientific evidence to the contrary, although it is by no means unequivocal, and (b) tends to diminish radically the significance of reading. If books don't influence behaviour, then there would be little point in preferring one book over another for classroom use and school boards could save money by using a book already in most student's homes—and in the case of Huron County, the Bible would certainly qualify.

9 The problem here is the double-edged nature of the liberal response. By denying that books encourage certain specific activities (sexual ones, usually), it lays itself open to the more serious charge that books are, at most, entertaining diversions. If the tactical reasons for this are understandable—no one in their right mind would want to have to tell a group of Huron County parents their children were reading a book containing sexual incidents, that these were presented in a positive way, and that their children were likely to take them to heart—the thorough-going spinelessness of the position is still unacceptable. Does anyone reading this doubt that there are connections between reading and our social behaviour? We may not know exactly what the connections are, and we certainly don't want to say that reading about something necessarily entails doing it; but within these common-sense limitations, I suspect that we can all bring to mind examples ranging from direct emulation (I know that reading Norman Mailer's "The Time of Her Time" led to my first important sexual experience) to more diffuse effects (I'm sure that reading Proust as a

teenager made me into something of an aesthete, although there's no way of proving it). To argue the contrary is to reduce reading to the level of twiddling thumbs and scratching itches, and if you've read this far I doubt that you're that sort of person.

10 And if it may be objected that proponents of book censorship don't argue at such a sophisticated intellectual level, let me introduce you to a Huron County man who proved quite able to do so when I talked to him. Lloyd Barth, a retired schoolteacher, moved six years ago into the small community of Blyth, where he does a bit of gentlemanly farming and keeps an eye on the passing scene. Barth is an intelligent and articulate spokesman for the local pro-censorship forces and his story sheds a great deal of light on the issues and circumstances involved.

11 Barth and his family, which includes two children who attend a local high school, moved to Blyth for certain specific reasons: "The people we met here impressed us as good people and good Christians, as being industrious, friendly, and of high moral standards." He experienced the kindliness and consideration of his neighbours when his home burned to the ground during the busy growing season a year after he arrived. Local farmers dropped what they were doing to help the Barths save what they could and begin to rebuild.

12 In a community imbued with such mutual concern and shared values, the position of school teacher is seen rather differently than it is in more fragmented urban societies. As Barth puts it: "We've always thought of teachers as *dedicated,* a spiritual word meaning that they offer themselves up for the good of the children. For us, teachers came right after God, ministers, and parents, and were always pure in thought and action; and teaching was a *profession,* which means to speak out the good that is in you."

13 Thus Barth is perturbed by some recent developments in the practice of teaching. The notion that teachers might strike, for example, is repugnant to him; it suggests that what was once a noble profession now has become merely a job. He sees his children coming home from school with an apparently endless series of fact-gathering projects and worries that they aren't learning anything about principles and morals. And when his children were required to read books he considered filled with blasphemy and obscenity, this naturally quiet and contemplative man felt compelled to become a social activist.

14 Two points must be emphasized here. First, much of the opposition to *The Diviners* and similar books is aroused because students are either required or encouraged to read them in school. Barth and fellow members of a group called "Concerned Citizens" know that there are many people who enjoy this kind of literature and while they are not happy about that fact, they have no plans to muzzle Margaret Laurence, boycott McClelland & Stewart, or even remove the 18 copies of the book in the Huron County library system. They just don't want it being forcibly injected into their homes, and that's quite different from advocating the sort of prior censorship exercised in totalitarian societies. Second, they are even more outraged by blasphemy than they are by obscenity—not least because many of them are farmers whose awareness of the sexual facts of life is rather more direct than that of most town-dwellers. Their concern with obscenity is largely a matter of context, and emerges only when what they would define as "immoral" sex (infidelity, prostitution, perversion) is being described. But Barth argues that "blasphemy is *never* in context." So the group is more concerned about God's name being taken in vain in such books as Steinbeck's *Of Mice and Men* than it is by the overt sexual content of *The Diviners*. Both these points should be kept in mind the next time you read something about the "sexually repressed fascist" many liberals identify as the typical proponent of censorship.

15 The strength of groups such as Concerned Citizens is grounded in a shared perception of a threat to the values of their community, and even to the sanctity of their very homes. There are no large funds, no outside agitators, no Canada Council grants inflating a minority gripe into a public issue. In his canvassing of area parents, Barth finds that he need only show them the books in question to arouse their energetic wrath. Where outsiders have been involved, as when the Writer's Union sent a delegation to Huron County in June to defend the books under attack, they have succeeded only in swelling the ranks of the local opposition. (Concerned Citizens was formed in July as a direct result of what was interpreted as an invasion by alien elements with no stake in the community and an obvious vested interest in promoting books such as *The Diviners*.) Let me repeat, if I haven't made it clear already, that people such as Lloyd Barth are not dummies, or hicks, or pathological mental cases. They believe that everything that is important to them is under attack and are fighting back

with all the power they can muster. And as long as their opponents continue to treat them with condescension, their numbers and influence will continue to increase and multiply.

16 Concerned Citizens achieved its initial success in late August when the Huron County Board of Education voted to remove *The Diviners* from the list of books approved for study in its five high schools. (It seems that the trustees are more upset by "obscenity" than blasphemy). Before this decision, Lloyd Barth had canvassed all 16 trustees, and had again found that, in most cases, he had only to show them certain passages from the books under fire to win support for his arguments. By that time Concerned Citizens had shaken down to a hard core of active members, following what Barth decribes as "Stalin's principle of decreasing the numbers and increasing the power," and was also able to bring pressure to bear on some of the trustees. It was a classic exercise in community organization tactics: define the issue; recruit those willing to commit themselves to it; and use every avenue of public and private influence available.

17 The word "community" keeps cropping up because it is essential to a proper understanding of what is going on in Huron County. There it connotes an integration of social and family life that just doesn't exist in big cities; urban residents accept a much higher degree of disjunction between their public and private selves. Many Huron County people have been aroused to the point where they intend to exercise control over what happens in their community in the same fashion that urban social activists proposed in the 1960s and early 1970s, and anyone planning on opposing them will have to operate in the same context and with the same methods as groups such as Concerned Citizens.

18 The moral issues involved here are not simple ones. If I ever have children, and they attend a school where they are required to read a book that is repugnant to my most deeply held beliefs, I hope that I will have the fortitude to not interfere with their experience of a world that I know to be composed of good, evil, and indifference. But if it were a book that glorified war, or advocated the right of the strong to exploit the weak, I am also sure that I would, at the very least, be tempted to have it proscribed. Those without convictions of any kind may cast the first stones.

19 But what about the significance of events in Huron County for the Canadian community as a whole? My view is that they have been blown out of meaningful proportion, and that there are the more seri-

ous threats to liberty than those discerned by liberal commentators looking for red-necks in the woodpile. Viewed objectively, the people who live in Huron County are for the most part on the receiving end of social forces over which they have no effective control. If they do succeed in removing certain books from their high schools, these books will still be available commercially and in public libraries; and if they should succeed in removing them from the community entirely—a position on which groups such as Concerned Citizens are unlikely to reach a consensus, from my observations—this would not affect the existence of the books; and would have only the most minimal impact upon the processes of their production and distribution. If a large number of such communities acted in concert, then the alarm might well have to be raised. But that isn't happening and isn't likely to happen, given the localized nature of the conflicts involved and the absence of anything resembling a national ban-the-books movement. No, as things stand the pro-censorship forces in Huron County have about as much chance of affecting Canadian literature as they do of converting the rest of us to their particular religious beliefs.

20 The real threat to freedom of expression in Canada will come, as such threats have always come, from those who wield centralized power without fear of check or control. The 1970 War Measures Act was the most effective censorship ever implemented in Canada; periodicals were seized, the press was muzzled, and it became impossible to exercise what we had come to think of as our natural political rights. Big government has big powers—and it still has them: at the moment the editor and publisher of the Toronto *Sun* are being prosecuted for printing secret RCMP documents; and amendments are being proposed to the Criminal Code that would broaden the legal definition of obscenity to the point where almost any serious work of literature could be judged obscene. The new definition would make obscene anything of which "the dominant characteristic of the matter or thing is the undue exploitation of sex, violence, crime, horror, cruelty or the undue degradation of the human person." If you consider the potential vagaries of interpreting "dominant" and "undue," not to mention "sex, violence, crime . . ." and so forth, I suspect you'll agree that this is one bogey that does call for protest on the widest possible scale.

21 Thus while the media have been diverting us with tales of attempted censorship in the boondocks, the people and institutions with real power have gone about their traditional tasks of making

laws and regulations conforming to the requirements of power, secure in the knowledge that what little opposition there is is laughably ineffective. If some of our national political and cultural leaders possessed the sort of moral conviction exemplified by Lloyd Barth and Elmer Umbach, they'd be righteously upset about that. They'd probably even try to do something about it. (I would like to thank Deanna Groetzinger for her help in the preparation of this article.)

Paul Stuewe, "Better Dead Than Read?", *Books in Canada*, (October, 1978), pp. 3-7.

Questions

1. **Subject**
   On the strength of your reading, would you say that the author is in favour of or opposed to censorship? Or would you choose to put the question in a different way?
2. **Audience**
   Comment on the effect the following sentence has on the reader: "To argue the contrary is to reduce reading to the level of twiddling thumbs and scratching itches, and if you've read this far I doubt that you're that sort of person."
3. **Purpose**
   Describe the relationship between the expository and argumentative mode in this essay.
4. **Structure and Style**
   (a) Explain how the second last paragraph of the essay demonstrates the author's abhorrence of censorship of a particular type. Does his view here contradict what he has said earlier about the subject?
   (b) Look up the following words in the dictionary: "red-neck," "fundamentalist," "fanatics." Explain how the connotations of these words as used in the essay are similar.

TIMOTHY FINDLEY
BETTER DEAD THAN READ? AN OPPOSING VIEW

1 Paul Stuewe's report ("Better Dead Than Read?") in the October issue of *Books in Canada,* though admirable in its concluding passages, is nonetheless sufficiently peppered with cant and inaccuracies to warrant a reply. Most of the inaccuracies and pretty well all of the cant appear in quotation marks. So far as the cant is concerned, that's entirely appropriate. But when it comes to facts, Stuewe has failed to probe the integrity of what he is quoting and, therefore, leaves his readers with a false impression of where matters stand with regard to the banning of books in this country. Throughout the course of his report he relies, for the most part, on the statements and opinions of two men. Only two. Based on what they have to say, however, he draws definitive conclusions that do not reflect the facts about what is happening. One of Stuewe's conclusions, for instance, is that the censorship problem is not at all widespread and that wherever it does appear it is not to be taken seriously. He confines his report to recent events in Huron County, Ont., where the local Board of Education has voted to remove Margaret Laurence's *The Diviners* from the list of books approved for study in high schools. Stuewe's conclusion? "If a large number of such communities acted in concert, then the alarm might well have to be raised. But that isn't happening and it isn't likely to happen. . . ." Wrong. It has happened before. It is still happening. And the more we slough it off as being of no consequence, the more it is going to happen in the future.

2 Mister Stuewe himself points out that book banners are currently hard at work in Nova Scotia and New Brunswick, although he dismisses them as living "mostly in rural areas." As if that didn't matter. He also says that those of us who are concerned about this problem are looking for "red-necks in the woodpile" and that we aren't going to find them. I agree. The woodpile is deserted. Whatever you want to call whoever was in there, they've come out. Some people come out of closets. Some come out of woodpiles. I wouldn't call them "redneck." I wouldn't call them anything. I only know that Huron County has set a precedent. So did Dade County, Florida, and the results of that single county precedent have been disastrous for

human rights all across the U.S. I don't want the same kind of disaster to happen here—either to people or to books. And if you look at the books that keep coming under fire in this campaign (and don't fool yourselves for one minute that it isn't a campaign), you will find they all have something in common: concern for people and compassion for the human condition. I find that very odd.

3 Stuewe's report is based, as I've said, on the statements and opinions of two men. Both are residents of Huron County and both represent a group that calls itself Concerned Citizens. The report states that "the strength of groups such as Concerned Citizens lies only in their shared perception of a threat to the values of their community," and that "there are no large funds, no outside agitators, no Canada Council grants inflating a minority gripe into a public issue." Every word of this is inaccurate. To begin with, the opinions reflected in the report are those of the leading spokesman for an evangelical association that calls itself Renaissance International. I refer to the Reverend Kenneth Campbell, a man who has mounted a major campaign against books and the education system of this country. He voiced these opinions almost word for word over CBC-Radio only a few months ago. Yet, though his words are parroted again and again by those directly quoted in Stuewe's report, his name is not even mentioned. Here, perhaps, is why:

4 While protesting that there are no large funds at their disposal, Renaissance International and its sister citizens' groups have been able to support their campaign in very high style indeed. Renaissance was established with a budget of $100,000. It is registered as a non-profit, charitable organization and publishes a magazine called *Encounter.* You can become a member for $10, $100, or $1,000. Membership fees and subscription fees to the magazine are all tax-deductible. Whenever Renaissance goes on the road it hires large and expensive arenas and public halls in which to sell its rhetoric. Posters and media advertising announce its presence.

5 For several months now Campbell has had a persistent American guest on his platform. But, of course, who would dare call Anita Bryant an "outside agitator"? And how many readers are aware that the Reverend Kenneth Campbell, using Ms. Bryant as his come-on, only this past summer set up his platform in London, Ont., from which place you can spit into Huron County? And Campbell's target on the literary front? You guessed it: *The Diviners.* Funny isn't it, that everywhere that Kenny goes, Margaret Laurence gets in trouble. Of course, it's the local citizens' groups who do the shooting.

6 Lastly, with regard to the phrase about "Canada Council grants inflating a minority gripe," I assume this refers to the fact that The Writers' Union of Canada, a recipient of such grants, has had the audacity to mouth off in opposition to the damage being done to books and writers by the pro-banning campaign. If my assumption is correct, then I can only say that an inflated minority soon becomes a majority. And more power to it. Financial and otherwise. Thornton Wilder wrote a marvellous thing about money in his play *The Matchmaker:* "Money, you should pardon the expression, is like manure. It should be spread around encouraging young things to grow!" However, the way Reverend Campbell is spreading money on this current campaign against books and the education system makes me think that what *he* has in mind is more like encouraging young things to *ossify*.

7 I come now to an insinuation in the report that has been repeated once too often: namely that in *The Diviners* Margaret Laurence advocates immoral behaviour. Kenneth Campbell has been on about this for long enough. That he has now spread his garbage into the mouths of his disciples is really very tiresome and childish. This time, the source of the insunuation is a pharmacist in Huron County by the name of Elmer Umbach, who states that "young people get venereal disease because they practise free love the way Margaret Laurence and such writers advocate."

8 To begin with, if I were Margaret Laurence I'd sue Elmer Umbach for that statement: flat out, no holds barred. Once and for all, let it be said that the only kind of "free love" advocated by Margaret Laurence is compassion. And that is not an opinion. That is a fact. Accusations of the kind levelled by Pharmacist Umbach and Evangelist Campbell are nothing less than tragic blunders of the intellect. In damning this book they have slandered and damaged a rare and moving document of human aspirations and a work of art, the sole aim of which is to express the spiritual reconciliation between human beings and life.

9 As for Pharmacist Umbach, if he were to read the whole of Margaret Laurence's work instead of excerpting only those passages that suit his needs he might find it in himself to stock a little of the compassion she advocates on his shelves. He might even discover that it averts more human ills than the whole amplitude of pharmaceutical prophylactics he now dispenses. When reading this man's blindly obtuse statements ("What I'm saying is a declaration of truth and I am not interested in discussing or dialoguing with you") I wondered if he had not perhaps misunderstood the terms of his profession. As a

pharmacist, he is only required to sell prophylactics: he is not required to become one.

10 The report states that "Concerned Citizens was formed [in Huron County] as a direct result of what was interpreted as an invasion of alien elements with no stake in the community and an obvious vested interest in promoting such books as *The Diviners*." This harks back to an earlier reference in the report to a time when "the Writers' Union sent a delegation to Huron County...to defend the books under attack." To begin with, the Writers' Union did not, willy-nilly, send a delegation. One of that union's members, Alice Munro, is a citizen of Huron County and consequently the Writers' Union was already a presence in that area. The truth is that a group of concerned teachers and students invited two other members of the union to bolster their fight against the book banning. And if Alice Munro cannot stand up in her own community (with or without fellow writers by her side) and defend Canadian books—including her own—against discrimination, then the final paragraphs of the report, in which Stuewe points out the dangers of censorship and people's innate responsibility to fight it, are meaningless. Furthermore, the whole accusatory stance that writers only go to bat for books because they have a "vested interest" is just as tiresomely innocent of intelligence as Reverend Campbell's other quotes dotted about the Huronian canon of stock phrases. The only vested interest one writer has in another's work is his investment *as a reader* in its integrity. Alice Munro doesn't make a cent out of Margaret Laurence's books. And do I really have to point out that Margaret Laurence did not set foot in Huron County during any of this debate? But Alice Munro did, and *she* had a vested interest in her own endangered books. Strange, aren't they, these writers: how they want it both ways? Wanting both to write and to be read. And to eat and live in houses and pay bills and stuff like that. Really strange. Stranger still that they believe in the value of their own work.

11 The whole of this current movement concerned with the censorship and banning of books—whether in schools or libraries or courts of law—is riddled with false moral indignation and fake concern for the hearts and minds of our children. It stems, in my opinion, from a truly evil manipulation of people's genuine fear and uncertainty about the world we live in. And the society we've created. And the children we've borne. The voices that inform the report and give it its tone speak often of their children and of hopes for their moral and spiritual character. Well, those are the same concerns of the books these people want to ban and of the men and women who wrote

them. Why are we so afraid of our own children that we want to close their hearts and minds to the fund of compassion they would find in these books? *Who Has Seen the Wind?, Lives of Girls and Women, The Diviners, One Day in the Life of Ivan Denisovitch, The Diary of Anne Frank, Huckleberry Finn.* The list goes on and on, and it grows and grows every year. It scares the hell out of me. The Reverend Campbell even speaks of bowdlerizing Shakespeare.

12 Do we really have to go through all this again? Has nothing been learned? Of course, it has been argued that these books have "only been banned in the high schools. Anyone can read them after that." Wrong. Once banned in schools books will always be read without respect for their true qualities. Even now children riffle the pages of these books—wherever they may find them—looking for "the dirty bits." This is not the book's fault. Nor the fault of its writer. It is the fault of those who have condemned the book as "obscene" or "pornographic" or "filled with profane language." Literature is being locked away with the truly obscene, as much as to imply that Margaret Laurence is an advocate of "child abuse." And this, of course, is nothing less than intellectual blasphemy.

13 It is an artist's privilege to see what others cannot see. Sometimes this is not a happy privilege. Sometimes what is seen is very hard to bear, and equally difficult to voice. But if it is the artist's privilege to see, it is also his job to tell what he sees. As W.H. Auden did, looking over his shoulder into Europe in 1939 and writing: "Intellectual disgrace stares from every human face, and the seas of pity lie locked and frozen in each eye."

14 These days, he wouldn't even have to look over his shoulder. But I don't want to close on that note, any more than Auden did. His poem, from which those lines are taken, was about the death of a poet—W.B. Yeats. Its last verse makes a far better epigraph for the idea I have tried to express here, which is the idea that a false issue is being raised by people who, for motives of their own, want to prevent certain books from reaching the minds that most require them, minds that can make the future better than the present and infinitely better than the past. What Auden wrote is as fine a definition of the desired effect of an artist's work as anyone will ever give. And, like it or not Huron County, it applies to Margaret Laurence's *The Diviners:*

In the deserts of the heart,
Let the healing fountain start,
In the prison of his days
Teach the free man how to praise.

Of course, Auden understood these things. He was censured, too. And banned. But he's still in print.

Timothy Findley, "Better Dead Than Read? An Opposing View," *Books in Canada*, (December, 1978), pp. 3-5.

Questions

1. **Subject**
   Findley's essay is a response to Stuewe's. Outline the major point in Stuewe's essay that Findley tries to answer. How successful is he?
2. **Audience**
   How is the reader meant to feel the dangers of groups who advocate book censorship? Much of Stuewe's point about their innocence is based on a quantitative argument. How does Findley counter this view?
3. **Purpose**
   Is Findley's response a purely objective rebuttal of Stuewe's position or does he allow emotion to enter his discussion? If he does, does it work for or against his argument?
4. **Structure and Style**
   (a) Locate two sentence fragments in Findley's essay and comment on their use.
   (b) Why might Findley find it necessary to quote W.H. Auden, an important British poet of the twentieth century?

8 *Supplementary Essays*

Contents and Analysis

1. Amiel, Barbara. "The Chaos of Criminal Justice in Canada. Or: In Defence of Vengeance," *(Saturday Night,* September, 1975).
   Subjects. Social behaviour, changing attitudes, morality
   Modes. Argumentation, exposition, narration

2. Callwood, June. "June Callwood's Canada: Crying Brokenhearted Over You," (*Maclean's,* January, 1972).
   Subjects. Social morality, Canadian culture, social behaviour
   Modes. Argumentation, exposition

3. Camp, Dalton. "The Decline in Public Morality," (*Saturday Night,* January, 1981).
   Subjects. Morality, social behaviour, changing attitudes
   Modes. Argumentation, exposition, narration

4. Charney, Ann. "The Monument," (*Saturday Night,* January, 1987).
   Subjects. Social behaviour, Canadian heroes
   Modes. Exposition, argumentation

5. Collins, Anne. "On Commitment," (*Toronto Life,* September, 1985).
   Subjects. Women's movement, social morality, social behaviour, changing attitudes
   Modes. Argumentation, exposition

6. Fotheringham, Allan. "Dan George's Last Stand," (*Maclean's,* July, 1971).
   Subjects. Ethnic groups, media
   Modes. Exposition, narration

7. Freeman, Barbara. "'Every Stroke Upward:' Women Journalists in Canada, 1880-1906," (*Canadian Women Studies,* 17,3 Fall, 1986).
   Subjects. Canadian culture, women's movement
   Modes. Narration, exposition

8. Fulford, Robert. "Charter of Wrongs," (*Saturday Night*, December, 1986).
Subjects. Canadian sovereignty
Modes. Argumentation, exposition

9. Gwyn, Sandra. "Over Home," (*Saturday Night*, January, 1987).
Subjects. Changing attitudes, Canadian identity, Canadian culture
Modes. Exposition, argumentation

10. Haynes, Robert H. "What is the Biological Revolution?," (*Canadian Forum*, August, 1975).
Subjects. Nature, changing attitudes, morality
Modes. Argumentation, exposition

11. Lévesque René. "Heartbreak," (from *Memoirs*, McClelland and Stewart, 1986).
Subjects. Canadian sovereignty, ethnic groups
Modes. Narration, exposition, description, argumentation

12. Macdonald, Sir John A. From "Speech in the Legislative Assembly, February 6, 1865," (in *Parliamentary Debates*...).
Subjects. Canadian sovereignty, Canadian culture
Modes. Argumentation, exposition

13. Maillet, Antonine. "Aunt Evangeline's Treasure," (*Saturday Night*, January, 1987).
Subjects. Nostalgia
Modes. Narration, exposition

14. McLuhan, Marshall. "The Violence of the Media," (*Canadian Forum*, September, 1976).
Subjects. Media, social behaviour
Modes. Argumentation, exposition

15. Roberts, Sir Charles G.D. "In the Deep of the Grass," (from *The Watchers of the Trails*, L.C. Page and Co., 1904).
Subjects. Nature
Modes. Narration, description

16. Ross, Colin. "The Story of Grey Owl," (*The Compass*, #5, Winter, 1979).
Subjects. Nature, Canadian culture, ethnic groups, Canadian sovereignty
Modes. Argumentation, exposition, narration

17. Schafer, R. Murray. "Canadian Culture: Colonial Culture," (*Canadian Forum*, March, 1984).
Subjects. Canadian culture
Modes. Argumentation, exposition

18. Suzuki, David T. "A Planet for the Taking," (*Canadian Forum*, February, 1985).
Subjects. Nature, morality
Modes. Argumentation, exposition

19. Whalley, George. "Introduction," (from George Whalley, ed., *Death in the Barren Ground: The Diary of Edgar Christian*, Oberon Press, 1980).
Subjects. Action/adventure, nature
Modes. Narration, description

BARBARA AMIEL

THE CHAOS OF CRIMINAL JUSTICE IN CANADA. OR: IN DEFENCE OF VENGEANCE

Last June in Torrance, California, a group of people threw a man over a cliff. The man had confessed to stealing two television sets and a stereo receiver. Later the sheriff explained, "You just don't steal a man's TV." The theft had been reported to the police but the executioners were impatient: the thief was a heroin addict, his haul was relatively small, in all likelihood he would get a suspended sentence. Maybe just a fine. His body was found at the bottom of a 200-foot cliff.

The incident was an eloquent plea in favour of society's institutionalizing of punishment. Criminal law was originally fashioned not only to punish thieves of television sets but to save them from angry mobs and to make sure the Biblical eye-for-an-eye approach to justice did not become an eye for a scratch. Vengeance and retribution were recognized as important threads in the social fabric, *not because they deterred or reformed the offender but because they reassured and satisfied the offended.*

This was not the satisfaction of some dark animal need. Citizens entered into the social contract with the understanding that society would guarantee—or at least put a premium on—their lives, dignity, and the right to enjoy their possessions. It was only when retribution followed injury that citizens could be reassured and satisfied that society really did place some value on their persons. This was—and is—a central need for any society. And, just as excessive or unjust punishment brutalizes the offender because it suggests that he is of no value, insufficient punishment brutalizes the victim for the same reason.

But in the recent decades modern society has turned away from punishment and retribution. Such goals have come to be considered barbaric and unenlightened, and have fallen into disrepute. The ultimate aims of criminal justice have become reform and rehabilitation. The Philadelphia Quakers started it all back in 1789 when they came up with the penitentiary sentence as a humane alternative to exile and an encouragement to reform. The social scientists of the twentieth century were more humane still, with their emphasis on social engineering to achieve similar goals of reform and rehabilitation. But in recent years a battered society has discovered that these goals are eluding enlightened law-makers and experts much as they eluded the Grand Inquisitors before them.

The fault probably lies in the nature of our institutions and possibly in the nature of man, but almost certainly in the nature of social scientists who seem committed to the belief that all crime has environmental causes. Today we are faced with a choice. We can cling to the idea that more of what we have unsuccessfully tried in the last century will work. Or we can go back to the theories of punishment and exile that existed before. There is no way we can pretend that those earlier solutions worked, if by "work" we mean that they either totally deterred or rehabilitated criminals. They did work, however, if by "work" we mean that they created a sense of reassurance and satisfaction in society at large and made it clear that certain actions were approved and others condemned.

• • •

Outside the courtroom in Toronto, six of Johnny's friends sprawled on the benches lining the corridor. Occasionally one of them would get up, his high-heeled platform shoes echoing clack-clack down the halls to the water fountain and then clack-clack back and silence. Sometimes one of the girls giggled. When they talked it was mainly guessing about what the judge would give Johnny for drug trafficking. "Four months," said one of them contemptuously. "It could be a year, two..." said Johnny's brother, and started crying again. Two years. No joke.

Inside the courtroom, sealed off from the hot June afternoon, sobered by the wood-panelling but most of all by the arrival of the judge, Johnny's friends squirmed on the wooden benches reserved for spectators. No more wisecracks, no more paper darts thrown across the courtroom. They sat on the wooden benches and squirmed because they were scared. Scared that their friend would be sent up for a year or more. Scared he wouldn't be around to organize a new hustle.

The pre-sentence report was read in snatches. Johnny had been previously convicted of theft and sentenced to four months and two years' probation. He'd been paroled after two months, had violated his probation, had left home to live in a hotel with friends. While on probation he was convicted of possession of LSD for purposes of trafficking. Johnny had refused to take vocational courses or improve his education. The judge paused at this and looked concerned. "It is the hope of this court," he said in a vague and distant way, "that you may some time after this next custodial period wish to further your education."

Johnny made no response. The sentence of the court was four months in reformatory and two years' probation. As the judge pronounced sentence the six friends loosened, smiled, and slapped one another. Score one. Afterwards the thin boy said to Johnny's brother: "What'd I tell you? Four months." As they walked to the escalator they were figuring what to do in September when Johnny would be out on parole.

• • •

Two hundred years ago Johnny would have had his hand cut off for stealing a loaf of bread. Whatever that lacked in justice and appropriateness, it did make subsequent thefts difficult. Fifty years ago Johnny, as a second offender, would have gone to prison for a term at least a little longer than that given for his first offence. But with the 1938 *Report of the Royal Commission to Investigate the Penal System,* chaired by Mr. Justice Joseph Archambault, Canada committed itself to the rehabilitative ideal. In the following years, platoons of social scientists formulated new methods to rehabilitate Johnny. Central to their thought was a belief that crime was directly related to poverty or social conditions. This did not explain why the overwhelming majority of poor Canadians did not commit crimes, nor why many well-off ones did. Neither did it explain why, during the 1950s, 1960s, and 1970s, when Canadians were enjoying rapidly improving standards of living and social services unequalled in any other period in Canadian history, the crime rates—instead of going down—were rapidly going up. What seemed unthinkable to social scientists was the common-sense notion that much crime may be committed because in the opinion of some people the risk is worth the pay-off.

Some criminals, on the other hand, were quite articulate about their motivation. One such man I knew, from a close and stable lower-middle-class family, had an impressive burglary and manslaughter record. One day in 1970 he took time out from planning an armed robbery in Toronto to explain himself. "Look," he told me, "I could work and work for what, $200 a week? It's a drag. This way I risk maybe a couple of years away, but maybe I get $100,000. Maybe more." A month later he was arrested in Toronto's Union Station on a charge of trafficking in heroin and released on bail. While on bail he went back to "small stuff"—working apartment buildings and selling his haul (wigs, jewellery, clothing, and accessories) to coffee waitresses and cocktail girls who were delighted to get a fur coat for $300.

But judges and juries were listening to social scientists, not to criminals, and were relieved to think they were sending the disadvantaged to a better world where they might be redeemed. This relief was short-lived. By the 1970s it was clear that the same faces were reappearing in court with startling regularity. Prisons, it seemed, in spite of all their new programmes, therapists, and increased community follow-up, were not rehabilitating offenders at all. Money spent on treatment programmes and facilities (including personnel and community programmes) increased substantially during the late 1960s and early 1970s. Though the crime rate and the number of persons convicted of criminal offences went up steadily each year, the number of people actually in prison remained stable over 1969-74 at about 20,000. Provincial institutions, led by Ontario and British Columbia, experimented with an array of alternatives to straight incarceration, including treatment-oriented programmes for addicts and special facilities for young offenders. The federal penitentiary system still had an absurdly small number of psychiatrists, psychologists, and social workers on call (just under 200 for an inmate population of about 7,800) but that was better than ratios in schools and institutions outside prison. The ratio was deplorable only if you subscribed to the viewpoint that those who committed a crime were *ipso facto* "sick" or "disturbed." Furthermore, in 1972 about forty-five per cent of all penitentiary inmates were taking educational and vocational classes, while day parole and temporary absences (which exceeded 35,000 in 1972) were used by inmates to attend community educational facilities.

If there's anything wrong with the penitentiary system it's not the lack of educational opportunities or treatment facilities but the lack of security for inmates from one another. Rape and intimidation do not constitute part of a prison sentence, and the society that incarcerates has an obligation to protect the people it punishes and, at the very least, be liable to them for any damages. Unfortunately, since it's unfashionable to suggest that some prisoners are truly wicked, there's little emphasis on ensuring that prisoners serve the sentences of the court and not of their fellow prisoners.

The emphasis is placed instead on the rehabilitation programmes of social scientists. But the uncomfortable truth is that nothing seems to make much difference: prisoners who get special treatment are as likely to be back in court on new charges as those who simply serve their time locked up.

A recent study of inmates at Guelph Correctional Centre in Ontario came up with some interesting figures. About sixty-four per cent of inmates who served their time in the regular facilities were later reconvicted. Inmates who were chosen for an adult training centre with major emphasis on educational upgrading had a reconviction rate of fifty-eight per cent. Those who got away from the institutional claustrophobia of Guelph to spend their time in a small mimimum security forestry project responded with a seventy-one per cent reconviction rate. (So much for the therapeutic value of the whole earth approach.) Inmates who needed special care and were channelled out of Guelph to psychiatric facilities under the Department of Health maintained a sixty-three per cent reconviction figure, while even those sent to specialized drug and alcohol treatment centres with high staff-to-patient ratios came back at the rate of forty-seven per cent. Since only those inmates with a decent chance of rehabilitation were chosen for the programmes in the first place (after prescreening by psychologists and social workers), it's difficult to escape the conclusion that locking up offenders was probably as effective as special programmes, and from a utilitarian point of view much cheaper.

Parole isn't much help either. In spite of the National Parole Service's successful noises to the contrary, a 1974 study of penitentiary paroles by the solicitor-general's office showed that 53.7 per cent of individuals released on parole were back in prison within five years of their release, and the proportion of total recidivism occurring during the parole period was steadily increasing. In addition, the number of paroles *forfeited* outnumbered by three to one paroles *revoked.* (Paroles can be revoked for minor offences or the breaking of parole regulations; they are automatically forfeited if a parolee is convicted of another indictable offense. Apologists for parole violators like to blame onerous parole rules for the failure of parole.) True, James Atack of the National Parole Service was reported in the Toronto *Globe and Mail* to be enthusiastically claiming that parole violations were down to 3.8 per cent in 1974, while a more sober William Outerbridge of the National Parole Board was claiming in the Toronto *Star* twenty per cent for the same year. But whatever the truth, the statistics are virtually useless without such information as length of sentence left to be served when parole was granted. Neither can the difficulty of finding employment be cited as a major factor if Solicitor-General Warren Allmand's claim that eighty per cent of parolees are constructively employed and paying taxes is to be believed.

Judges, faced with the failure of prisons to reform more than about a third of their inmates, have become increasingly reluctant to send people to prison. This seems to be based on a theory that prisons cause crime. In 1969, just under forty per cent of Canadians convicted of an *indictable* offence were sentenced to a prison term. Correction officials estimate that 1974 figures may be as low as thirty per cent. In a detailed study of the sentencing philosophy of magistrates, Professor John Hogarth of the University of Toronto Criminology Centre documents the ascendancy of "non-punitive" magistrates. Magistrates who cling to the idea that punishment and vengeance have something significant to do with sentencing are not only in the minority but seem socially isolated from their more progressive and humane colleagues. Meanwhile, social scientists faced with the failure of "treatment" to reform criminals blame not human nature but imprisonment.

The next step was predictable: bad prison conditions were cited not to get better prisons built but to justify *emptying* prisons. Since nothing inspires enthusiasm in the civil service like a new social science scheme (in spite of the signal failure of the old ones) committees were set up to study legal ways to empty prisons. The concept of ending imprisonment has a name: *diversion*. Diversion-oriented groups would work out alternatives to incarceration. In December, 1972, under the wing of the solicitor-general's department, a federal-provincial committee of deputy ministers commissioned a study on ways to implement diversion. By 1974 the Law Reform Commission was on to it, and by 1975 it was official: imprisonment, said the Law Reform Commission, is inhumane and inappropriate. Diversion was in.

Diversion keeps people out of prison by finding some other method of "reconciliation" between the "offender" and the "community." (Diversion also has its own special vocabulary.) Diversion can take place at various stages in the criminal justice system: before a charge is laid, before trial, or afterwards. Instead of going to prison, the offender comes to some arrangement that may involve doing a period of work for a community project and possibly reimbursing the community for his crime. Should he renege on this arrangement, his "diversion" would end and he would be sent back to court. Solicitor-General Allmand, a diversion enthusiast, explains: "The idea would be to keep a man in contact with his regular ties of family and job and reimburse the community."

Diversion supporters point to alcoholics, drug users, prostitutes, and vagrants as examples of people unnecessarily cluttering up prisons and rendering criminal justice ineffective. But in fact most rational Canadians would like to see these categories of offences not simply penalized under diversion, but no longer criminal offences at all. Neither is there, or should there be, much enthusiasm for chucking young first offenders into prison. And in fact they rarely are. Diversion has been a welcomed fact of life for years with police and community agencies working together to "clear" reported offences outside the courts. In many cases, by the time a youth is actually booked on a first offence he may have been through the community organizations several times. But diversion advocates use these sympathetic targets (alcoholics, first offenders) to cover up their true aim: the minimizing of all offences against property and indeed most violent offences as well.

The Law Reform Commission, set up by Ottawa under the Law Reform Commission Act of 1970 to recommend changes in Canadian law, has been the most visible advocate of dismantling or downgrading prisons. Some of its recommendations, issued in working papers, have been pretty radical. Among them: a *maximum* three year sentence for those violent criminals and murderers unlikely to repeat their crime; no imprisonment for most non-violent crime; no more life sentences. But the single most influential advocate of ending imprisonment is the man federally in charge of bringing criminals to justice—Solicitor-General Warren Allmand. Allmand claims that even now sixty per cent of those convicted of criminal offences are not sentenced to prison. They receive either fines, probation, suspended sentences, or complete and partial discharges. This percentage, taken together with those criminals never apprehended (estimates range as high as ninety per cent), or those who never come to trial, comes as no surprise to many Canadians who have long suspected that in cost/benefit terms, crime pays. What may surprise them is Allmand's determination to increase that percentage.

• • •

Warren Allmand is a man who agonizes over the psychological strain of imprisonment and shares the worry that the Law Reform Commission expressed about "the anxiety that can be induced" by incarceration. Curiously, he is less concerned about the psychological anxiety of society at large. While social scientists have been studying the psyches of convicts, a similar study of their victims and the most cursory look at Gallup polls and letters to the editor might indicate the far more dangerous psychological trauma of society.

"There's no place for vengeance," says Allmand. "I know how people feel... their concept of justice is an eye for an eye and it's very hard to change that approach.... They say we're ruining society with this kind of programme [diversion]. But I think that's completely false. If we have a lack of discipline and more crime in society, most of it starts with the family.... It's a cop-out to blame anything else."

Allmand the social engineer displays the same kind of easy confidence chemical engineers displayed until it was suddenly discovered that the environment was too complex to be changed at will by miracle sprays. All the unwanted bugs and weeds that cluttered up the physical landscape were discovered to have been there for a purpose, and our crude interference disturbed the delicate balance. In the far more complex landscape of the human mind it may be just as dangerous and futile to attack the unwanted weeds of vengeance with the DDT of diversion.

Allmand sees most offences and certainly all property crime (theft, fraud, breaking and entry, etc.) as crimes to be dealt with outside prison. He wants offenders to pay for their crimes through work programmes in the community and, if necessary, to receive psychiatric and social assistance in community-based centres. "There may come a time," he admits, "when we have to say: 'Look, you've done this five times, six times, this time you're going to jail. We're going to try something else. We'll have you examined by psychiatrists, psychologists. There's something wrong with you.'"

No one can doubt Allmand's integrity and sincerity, but he has an almost mystical belief in the social sciences and rehabilitation in spite of his own department's studies which have chronicled their failures.

He perceives most criminals as suffering from a lack of love early in life and acting out their deprived childhood through rebellious antisocial acts. He simply cannot believe that criminals are other than sick. These views have been increasingly discarded by criminologists, but, even if true, they hold out little hope for a favourable change in Canada's crime rate. Unless, of course, we decide to license prospective parents only after suitable (and infallible) psychological testing.

In a not untypical case in Toronto last year, a twenty-two-year-old man broke into several apartments and finally, in one of them, indecently assaulted the occupant. The man had a criminal record, had previously refused educational and employment assistance while on probation, and had what the Crown Attorney described as a general attitude of lawlessness. The judge indicated his concern about the accused's limited educational background and the importance of achieving his rehabilitation. His view was that the protection of the public would be best achieved by a suspended sentence and probation, which might bring about the man's reformation. The appeal court, being less progressive, felt that the public need for protection would be better reflected by a reformatory sentence of two years less a day. Even this would make him eligible for parole in about seven months.

Psychological needs aside, most Canadians would probably sacrifice their satisfaction in retribution and punishment if "rehabilitation" would, as its advocates claim, protect them from recidivism. But, as leading criminologists like Edwin H. Sutherland and Donald R. Cressey have reluctantly pointed out (and major studies in New York last year confirm), when results are compared between treatment programmes to "reform" criminals, and punishment programmes to "deter" them, there is no proof that either method is more successful than the other. Recidivism seems unaltered. All we do know, alas, is that as long as criminals are in jail they cannot add to the crime rate. With more than two-thirds of all known crime accounted for by repeat offenders (in 1973, seventy per cent of all Canadian correctional admissions were repeaters, the largest group of these having six or more previous commitments) more incarceration for even short periods of time may have a significant effect on the crime rate. Under Allmand's schemes we would have the very worst of two worlds: no protection through incapacitation and probably no decrease in recidivism. Criminals would get no better, only freer to injure us.

It is the eighth time Gloria has been charged. She has seven convictions stretching over about fourteen years. She is forty years old, very overweight, and bored stiff with waiting in the corridor for the judge to return from lunch. Next to her are a group of men and women in their early twenties charged with possession of marijuana for purposes of trafficking. They are listless and bored. One of the group has failed to show up today and the others are discussing with enviable legal know-how the appropriate responses to the bench warrant that will be issued. Gloria shifts her weight uncomfortably and listens to her lawyer. He's talking about what she should say when her case comes up.

Today Gloria is charged with possession of stolen goods. In the past she has been charged with fraud, shoplifting, possession of drugs for trafficking, and assault. Gloria is not particulary interested in the lawyer that the court insisted she have when she was remanded for this hearing. She knew the goods were stolen, paid sixty dollars for them, and plans to plead guilty. If the lawyer wants to speak about her sentence, that's fine. "I won't get much," she predicts to the quiet seventeen-year-old girl who has come down to the court with her. They talk about going down to Simpsons to lift a sweater Gloria wants.

Gloria is lucky today: she could easily have received a reformatory sentence. But the judge, noting Gloria's cooperation with the police in this most recent charge, and noting further that Gloria is on welfare, decides that a prison term or fine would be inappropriate. He gives her a suspended sentence of two years with the warning that should she be caught doing anything *while on the suspended sentence,* she will be sent to prison. Gloria smirks and waddles lazily out of court.

Gloria doesn't think her offences are particularly serious, perhaps because she rarely goes to prison. If she does, she rarely serves so much as a third of her sentence. What diversion theorists do not take into account is that people will act, to some extent, according to how they believe society views their actions. A fine or suspended sentence means the offence is small stuff. Recidivists like Gloria find that diversion simply means they can carry on as usual, stealing to pay off the fine from their last conviction. In fact, diversion reduces itself to a simple equation for the property offender: if he steals property, he may have to pay for it plus a fine. This reduces property crime to the dimensions of illegal parking.

While diversion advocates are lobbying to steer many crimes out of prison, the Law Reform Commission and Allmand are also lobbying to lighten the sentences of those imprisoned for *violent* crimes. Many Canadians suspect that the actual time served already for violent crimes may be too light. A combination of factors account for some relatively short prison terms now: at the courtroom level many murders get reduced to manslaughter because it's claimed some unpleasant remark made by the victim "provoked" the murderer. Provocation reduces murder to manslaughter and this defence is helped by the convenience of not having the victim around to testify. Manslaughter sentences may put offenders back on the streets fairly fast. In 1973, almost eighty-three per cent of the sentences given for murder-reduced-to-manslaughter were under ten years. Over half of those were under five years, which could mean parole in eighteen months (or day parole much earlier).

About thirty-five per cent of those acquitted for murder are found not guilty by reason of insanity. This way out of a murder conviction may be rising as the courts continue to interpret "insanity" more liberally. Though "temporary" insanity is not a defence in Canadian law, in fact it is not unusual for those acquitted on grounds of insanity to regain their equilibrium and freedom in a matter of months. One man acquitted of a *triple* murder charge on insanity grounds in 1971 was back at his mechanic's job in less than three years. This raised some eyebrows even in Toronto's progressive forensic community.

Of twenty-seven murderers discharged from prison in 1973 (actually thirty-seven were discharged but statistics are available on only twenty-seven), five served less than four years and twenty-one served between five and nine years; of manslaughter discharges, sixty-seven per cent had served less than three years; attempted murder discharges, seventy-seven per cent—less than four years; in rape convictions (an offence for which only the most brutal attacks generally get to court), ninety-four per cent of those released had served less than three years. Given the statistics, Canadians may be excused for thinking that the length of incarceration is often grotesquely out of proportion to the havoc and pain created by the criminal.

But Allmand sees no reason for fixing mandatory minimum sentences for a crime, no matter how brutal. This is in accord with his emphasis on the prisoner determining his prison sentence rather than society exercising retribution. Violent criminals should, he thinks, be moved in and out of prison according to their psychological state, with far less emphasis on the crime committed. "There is some good in everyone," he says and denounces mandatory life imprisonment as an admission that rehabilitation has failed. He concedes that it may be difficult to tell who is rehabilitated and who is not, but will not allow himself to be prejudiced in this judgement by the crimes the prisoner has committed.

Like most advocates of lighter prison sentences and more diversion from the criminal justice system, Allmand talks as though it were a proven fact that leniency aids in rehabilitation and protection of society. If only society could forgo its vengeful instincts and abandon such useless concepts as deterrence, the argument goes, we'd all be better protected. In fact, though it must be acknowledged that the evidence is far from extensive, scientific studies either indicate precisely the opposite or are inconclusive. Recent work done in the United States assessed whether the certainty of receiving a prison sentence (rather than probation or a fine) and the severity of the sentence would deter crime. All studies indicated that the certainty of going to prison has a significant deterrent effect. (Severity seemed to affect only murder rates, though one University of Chicago study went further and concluded that severity also affected general crime rates.) The news of these studies does not seem to have reached Ottawa. But common sense ought to have told us long before the scientists did. Some social scientists would have us believe that criminals are a breed apart, but in fact it's more reasonable to assume that some criminals, like the rest of us, weigh the risks and consequences of their actions and act accordingly.

• • •

One of our major problems today is that politicians and people in general divide roughly into two groups: liberals and conservatives. Liberals, as a general rule, want to do a great deal about improving the social environment and see little merit in punishment. Conservatives, as a general rule, see immense merit in punishment and care little about improving the environment. Whichever group happens to be in vogue or in power, it is clear that only half of the problem is being tackled by either.

It is quite evident that enlightened self-interest governs the action of some criminals, and these people could be effectively deterred by raising the penalties involved in crime and the opportunities and rewards offered by a non-criminal existence. There is another group that commits crime in an impulsive, unpredictable, and "sick" fashion. This is the group most often cited by liberals when they talk about the futility of long prison terms as a deterrent. The liberals, of course, are right: psycopaths and sociopaths will not measure their actions against their reasonable consequences. But even such people can be effectively incapacitated and society has every conceivable moral right to demand that they should be. At the same time, of course, insofar as sociopaths may be cured medically or may not even become sociopaths in the first place if they are permitted to grow up in a better environment, we should make every effort to achieve that better world *concurrently* with their incapacitation.

What society has a right to demand is that its members should not serve as guinea pigs for the laboratory experiments of forensic scientists and sociologists any more than they should be the guinea pigs for the experiments of pharmaceutical companies.

• • •

A society in which crime goes without real punishment and victims receive no satisfaction for their injury is a society that may turn to vigilante justice. Men may be thrown off cliffs for stealing a television set. The frightful cost of aping our Victorian ancestors and sweeping not sex but retribution under the carpet is beginning to show. Many Canadians are angry, resentful, and (as Gallup poll statistics on capital punishment show) increasingly bloodthirsty. Cynicism and a callous indifference to good and evil are the products of a society that, like ours, is less concerned with the needs of those who observe its rules than with those who break them.

Regardless of whether punishment deters or rehabilitates, it is necessary for justice. When Warren Allmand was asked whether vengeance was an element of justice he was shocked: "No, no, of course not," he replied. But of course vengeance is as much a part of justice as mercy. Without either, society would have only passionless sanctions of utility, the most dehumanizing approach of all, the approach of scientists to rats in a Skinner maze.

Ultimately, in such a dispassionate paradise of bureaucrats, there would be neither love nor hate, neither vengeance nor mercy, only preventive regulations. Any society that denies the concept of individual responsibility must either perish in a chaos of criminal and vigilante lawlessness or end up denying all of its citizens any individual freedom.

Barbara Amiel, "The Chaos of Criminal Justice in Canada. Or: In Defence of Vengeance," *Saturday Night* (September, 1975), pp. 19-25.

JUNE CALLWOOD

JUNE CALLWOOD'S CANADA: CRYING BROKENHEARTED OVER YOU

I wish I knew where my Canada is, or if it is. Since October, 1970, I've been trying to adjust myself to the realization that what I believed all my life was Canada—a land somehow more noble than any other, more tolerant, brave, and even true, whatever true means—never existed at all except in my head, where its sole function was to enlarge my vision of me, the typical Canadian, noble, tolerant, brave and, especially, true.

I'm feeling wretched these days for what, at bottom, is the wrong reason: I weep for me. What collapsed when my countrymen loved the War Measures Act, *loved it,* was my conceit that I was something special because I am a Canadian, irreducibly Canadian, a Canadian moreover who can trace lineage back to what Canadian history textbooks graciously call savages.

It has dawned on me after all these years of being thrilled by parades, Prairies, the flag fluttering at the top of the pole, twilight in Muskoka, a glittering day after an ice storm, and assorted seacoasts where the waves and rocks behave erotically with one another, that Canadians are a nasty lot, have been thoroughly, confidently, serenely rotten throughout their history, and that the War Measures Act just put the ongoing, established, lusty, truly Canadian folk festival of Hate Your Neighbour on a firmer legal basis.

Reality is giving me pain, and it would be Canadian of me to be glad of it. Canadians believe in pain; it's good for people; there is nothing more Canadian than that concept. We strap five-year-olds in our kindergartens for the offense of being restless—*stop being five!* We hire police and prison guards who know 50 ways to hurt an underweight teen-ager without leaving a mark on him. We lock up the poor in mental hospitals and prisons to teach them a good lesson—*stop being poor!* We elevate as judges, mayors, premiers, police chiefs and prime ministers those who declare that the people will stop starving, or being young, or being Indian, or being old, or being angry, if you just punch them in the head.

There is no evidence that they are right; human beings do not seem to respond positively to being hurt and humiliated. This simple truth can be demonstrated with any small laboratory animal, if you have the heart for it. Just isolate him, keep him half-hungry, half-scared, and frustrated; or merely ask him, repeatedly, to do something which is impossible for him. In a surprisingly short time he will either become suicidal, which will take the form of total apathy or self-mutilation, or he will become murderous and attack everything that comes near him.

You can prove the same experiment another way if you happen to like small laboratory animals. Give him the diet that he requires to thrive, a varied environment that permits him to explore and develop, and some affection. What you will then have on your hands is a perky, healthy, confident small animal.

Canadians may know all about the small laboratory animals, but they don't apply the knowledge to their relationships, and particularly their relationships with young human beings, because they simply can't. Trusting and loving are skills people pick up from being trusted and loved, and that's an experience that isn't common. What lies in the heart of everyone is fear and those who have more fear than they can bear (which is just about everybody) protect themselves by being wrathful and righteous; by giving pain, they are safer.

A member of a motorcycle gang taught me that. He was describing how he once kicked a man unconscious and I said Why? and he was amazed that I didn't know. So he wouldn't hurt me, he explained.

Canadians are very frightened of one another, which makes them lonely, which makes them dangerous to their own kind. We put more people in prison, per capita, than any other Western society in the world. Our prisons duplicate the conditions for making small laboratory animals insane—they are full of the destruction of young lives.

The schools are perhaps the most Canadian aspect of the entire country. They have a strong resemblance to the jails, in that incarceration in them is also involuntary and joyless and the program encourages stupidity and insensitivity. Schools don't use a method of instruction that corresponds to the natural way people learn, and thus are assured of a bumper harvest of children who can't figure out the school game well enough to stimulate learning. They therefore are designated as failures. That's what school seems to be all about: *Find the winners.* The losers fall out of the boat, half-literate non-swimmers full of despair, while the winners sit there for years rowing away, robots who have been half-dead since they were eight years old.

That's how you turn out a real Canadian, you break his heart and punish his élan. It does have its drawbacks. A few years ago Statistics

Canada estimated that one out of every 10 Canadians born in 1965 would spend part of his life in a mental hospital. *A mental hospital.* Three years ago SC revised its estimate and reported that one in every eight Canadians born that year would be treated in a psychiatric institution. In 1970 it had to be changed again, to one in every six Canadians born in 1965 will be in a psychiatric institution some day.

It isn't easy to distinguish mental hospitals from jails, since both likely were built about 100 years ago, both stink, and both are full of the poor. Well-to-do people don't become insane, lucky them; instead they have a praiseworthy disorder known as a breakdown from overwork, and they are attended gently in comfort and privacy in the psychiatric wings of general hospitals.

What we're really proficient at in this country, besides knowing what's good for other people (which unfailingly is something unpleasant), is driving ourselves insane. Maybe the one has something to do with the other.

A careful, conservative survey of Canadian children was done over a three-year period by a distinguished group called CELDIC, the Commission on Emotional and Learning Disorders in Children. It was reported in 1970, to a massively disinterested nation, that we have more than one million children under the age of 19 in need of immediate help if they are to become functioning adults, and that they aren't getting it. The Prime Minister wrote me that he was shocked. "One million children!" he mused. The Leader of the Opposition was also shocked, but got the name of the organization wrong.

Canadians ignore a million children in distress because they simply don't believe it. One of the myths of the country, as entrenched as the myth about western hospitality, is that Canadians love their children. They don't.

Back when I had this fantasy about the inherent goodness of Canadians, I thought we were coming out of the muck. I started meeting these marvelous people all over the country, great teachers, exhausted doctors, social workers even, nutty idealists who sometimes were little old ladies in tennis shoes, sometimes were impeccably groomed and scented Junior Leaguers, sometimes were bearded young guys who brought their babies. They talked of concern and change and making institutions humane, and it looked to me as though they were beginning to succeed.

So I wasn't prepared for what happened with the War Measures

Act, that it was a hit. I didn't expect that the country would be so delighted, enthusiastic, grateful for a ruthless deed based on hatred and mistrust. I really thought we had it figured out, at last, that the cost of devaluing any man's life is that your own life becomes a crock of junk.

The students demonstrated, of course. Being Canadian, they demonstrated—a few thousand of them at York University—*for* the War Measures Act. The protest against it at Toronto City Hall was poorly attended; the police took pictures of those who came.

I would have liked it on the night of October 16 if the Prime Minister had used that televised speech to say hold steady, these are black days but believe in the strength and goodness of the country, trust in the law, which is adequate, more than adequate, to round up the criminals. I wouldn't have minded a simple prayer; the sense of God, if you can feel it, is enlarging. Maybe he could have asked Canadians to shake hands with everyone they meet for a day. That's not naïve, that's not bleeding heart: traditionally, the handshake is to show that you don't hold a weapon; it is a simple, effective way to reduce fear between individuals. It works. Ask the little laboratory animals.

Instead, the great Canadian malaise, persecution of the different, has been exacerbated. On the beautiful Prairies this summer, a police car drove straight at a hitchhiker. His leap into the ditch saved his life but he was cut and bruised. While the United States was excited at the suppression of the New York *Times'* reports of the Vietnam investigation, a Canadian judge stopped the CBC from airing an account of the Vallières trial, a straightforward recital of the transcripts, and it was a note in an entertainment column.

In the wash of vengeance that has followed the War Measures Act, Canadians have an opportunity to excel on a world basis at what we do best, which is to hurt people. An international organization, the respected League for the Rights of Man, inspected a Quebec prison and reports that it is "scandalous and inhuman." The investigator claims that it is worse than the infamous jails of Algiers, where the torture was spectacular. So Canada *is* making a mark for itself, after all.

It's somebody's Canada, I suppose. Maybe it's almost everybody's Canada. My problem is I still can't believe it.

June Callwood, "June Callwood's Canada: Crying Brokenhearted Over You," *Maclean's* (January, 1972), pp. 18, 67.

DALTON CAMP

THE DECLINE IN PUBLIC MORALITY

The Canadian Tire outlet in a shopping mall in Fredericton, New Brunswick, is the closest place I can find a good selection of battery-powered lamps. It is also a place where certain lessons may be learned. Living in the country, I am not always aware of the prevalence of shoplifters in the city, but apparently they are everywhere. The stores, and the mall itself, were plastered with warnings to potential thieves. As I entered Canadian Tire I sensed I was among the criminal element.

The lamp of my choice was foreign-made, compact, and powered by dry-cell batteries, priced at $19.89, plus tax, batteries additional. Like the Queen—although for different reasons—I do not carry money. I deal in personal cheques and corporate plastic. Gathering up my lamp and batteries, I proceeded to the check-out counter, innocent of the ordeal that awaited.

Canadian Tire does not accept out-of-town cheques. Furthermore, among the array of credit cards I offered as a substitute, none was acceptable. Canadian Tire accepts only Canadian Tire credit cards.

Not to worry: you can qualify almost instantly for a Canadian Tire credit card by going to another counter and filling out a form. But what appeared to be a ready and congenial solution to the impasse was not. The second question asked on the form was the name of my present employer—difficult to answer, since I have none. The third question—how long employed with present employer?—was impossible. Further questions were outrageous: what was my wife's name, that of *her* employer, and for how long had she been employed by him? I asked to see the manager.

The youth appearing before me in the guise of the manager plainly was not: evidence of acne, a stock-room coat beneath an inscrutable smirk. Detecting trouble, he asked what mine was.

"What possible business is it of Canadian Tire where my wife works?"

By way of reply, a shrug. Then: "If you don't wanna fill out the form, don't fill it out. Sup to you." But, obviously, no form, no plastic; no lamp either.

I departed the premises. Any hardware store would do as well. Indeed, the hardware store, an old family firm, had the same lamp, the same batteries, at a comparable price. No inhibitions about credit cards either—all were welcome. The transaction was swiftly completed—almost.

"What's your telephone number?" asked the salesperson.

"I don't give it out."

Though I have seldom been more serious, this produced only a distracted smile.

"That's okay," she said, brightly. "Could I see your driver's licence for identification?"

"I don't have a driver's licence," I told her. "I travel on horseback. Would you like to know the name of my horse?"

"C'mon," she pleaded, "just your telephone number will do."

So I lied. "The number is 488"—that much was true—"9992." That much wasn't. But it satisfied her. And I got my lamp.

The moral of the story is, of course, never leave home without your identity, the minimal proof of it being your licence, telephone, and SIN numbers. Veterans of the last war will remember their catechism: if captured by the enemy, give only your name, rank, and number. In the jungle warfare of the plazas, who needs a name?

A journalist I know, assigned to write a story on the operations of the credit bureau in his community, telephoned to arrange an interview with the manager. He was immediately asked for his social insurance number, which he declined to give. Arriving for the interview, he asked the manager the reason for his request.

"So I could look up your credit rating," the man said, laughing, "and see what kind of guy you are."

I suspect some correlation between the burgeoning traffic in numbers, files and data banks, and the collapse of public morality. Such is not, of course, endemic to the marketplace, but it is where the corruption of interpersonal relations has become common to the most ordinary of transactions. Testimony to the state of public morality is evidenced daily on the pedestrian rounds of the shopping public. There isn't any.

When the subject of morality comes up—which is not often these days—people tend to invert the word to immorality, leading to thoughts of sexual promiscuity. Since it is impossible to quantify promiscuity in an age of avid permissiveness, there is really not much to think about, other than to marvel that celibacy and virginity were once considered importantly virtuous.

But there *was* a public morality, one that governed our conduct at least as much as did the law of the land. The wonder of it was that we largely subscribed to it, as did everyone else we knew or would want to know. It allowed us to live in a state resembling harmony by accepting a set of assumptions about one another that were mutually reassuring: that a man's word was his bond, that another's property and privacy were inviolate, that there existed a vast majority of fellow citizens who prized their reputations as highly as we valued our own. There were concomitant norms for social conduct, speech, dress, and general decorum which, taken together, made the behaviour of most of us comfortably predictable.

Perhaps the essential ingredient of that public morality was a compelling need for respectability. It now seems quaint, and somehow touching. Still, it encouraged a society, in which trust was pervasive, to function with a certitude that can only be regarded as admirable. Anyway, it is lost. A man's word is no longer enough; disregard for property varies from indifference to wantonness, while the intrusion upon privacy has become relentless. Public morality, as some of us knew it, has gone the way of iambic pentameter and the Ten Commandments.

The problem of contemporary society is not that it is so relentlessly impersonal (in a peculiar way, it isn't), but that all members of it are suspect. Day after day, in uncounted, numbing, trivial incidents, we are confronted by the presumption of guilt—as potential forger, bankrupt, thief, counterfeiter, spendthrift, or credit risk—and, day after day, we are obliged to produce evidence of our innocence. To be dealt with routinely as untrustworthy or unreliable is immediately insulting and inevitably demeaning. It would be more tolerable if we were programmed to produce dossier material at the push of a button, like bloodless robots.

What has been lost is considerably greater than anything gained, which cannot be much more than the peace of mind of American Express or Visa. The common view that governed society for so long—the presumption that most people were reliable, honest, trustworthy, sharing a common moral earnest of right and wrong—has been succeeded by the revised presumption that there are simply too many untrustworthy people about to trust anyone. Of all the values we have lost, perhaps the greatest has been face value.

Face value is still enjoyed by celebrities; and yet, recollection persists of life in a community in which everyone must either have been a celebrity of sorts—unlikely—or possessed face value sufficient to obtain credit and to negotiate countless other transactions supported only by one's persona and one's word. I once attended a social function at which a woman friend of mine arrived on the arm of a man who had recently been paroled after serving a sentence for murder. She and I discussed at some length the considerable difficulties encountered by her friend in finding suitable employment, a predicament as regrettable to me as it was comprehensible. What remains incomprehensible are the enormous numbers of blameless, law-abiding people whose personal integrity and honesty are routinely discounted for the lack of prima facie evidence of both.

If one is not to be recognized on sight as being worthy of trust—or even given the benefit of doubt—how is it possible that most of us could ever become deserving? The truth is that a reputation for responsibility, which was formerly publicly acknowledged, is now a matter of secrecy, something stapled to one's social insurance number in a credit bureau. As a consequence, many of us truly do not give a damn about how we are regarded, leaving such personal credentials as reliability and responsibility to the mysteries of unseen computers. A generation ago, people considered such intangibles vital.

• • •

Perhaps the recognition of a public morality existed merely as part of a simpler, smaller universe. Perhaps the absence of it is part of our world's gathering size and complexity. We could, then, concede any possibility of a revised public morality, and yield to the prospect of living in a darkening world of infinite scepticism devoid of conscience.

The grounds for suspicion and caution are confirmed in the grim discrepancies between sales and inventory; in those long tables, resembling logarithms, recording credit cards stolen, strayed, or withdrawn; in the burgeoning business of collection agencies; in the rising numbers of repossessions, and in the accumulation of cheques marked n.s.f. Unquestionably, one's views of human nature, and of such niceties as public morality, are not impervious to the influence of direct experience.

Money, having lost its value, may no longer be the root of all evil: credit has taken its place. The impulse to buy now and pay later admits to a belief that whatever we deny ourselves today will surely cost more tomorrow. Those who still believe in the homely wisdom of living within measurable means can only be regarded as eccentrics. It is not greed or rampant materialism that motivates so many to irresponsibility; it is the realization that money is now the least durable of life's material possessions.

Many years ago, as a young Liberal, I led the fight against a resolution, moved at a party conference, advocating legalized lotteries. My strongest debating point was to cite in parts of the world where lotteries were legal—Italy, France, South America, Cuba—a certain manifestation of economic injustice, an unstable currency, and a hopelessly depressed lower class. The motion was defeated, though not nearly so overwhelmingly as it would carry were it moved today. The argument against is no longer valid: in a recent essay on neo-conservatism Lewis Lapham, the editor of *Harper's,* put it very well: America (like Canada) is changing from an investor society to a speculator society. The only good buck is the fast one, free of tax.

Carl Beigie, president of the C.D. Howe Institute, has pleaded for reduced consumption: "The main reason we have to decrease consumption," he says, "is that it's necessary to increase investment, which determines tomorrow's output." Fat chance. As Lapham pointed out, when inflation reaches a rate of fifteen per cent—a prospect not far distant—you will need to double your income in four years to remain as solvent as you were in the first year—an achievement, for most, that is scarcely realistic. Instead, for the average consumer-taxpayer-citizen, a lottery ticket looks to be ultimately the best hope against terminal overdraft.

Public morality may be impossible to sustain in a world that has lost its sense of posterity. Since so many of us live as though there were no tomorrow, the notion of posterity becomes too painful to contemplate—even though, without it, we are left simply in hock, and without plan or purpose. The cruellest deprivation created by inflation has been the loss of posterity as a fundamental consideration in public policy and private life.

In the past, the generally accepted relationship between citizen and government was based on the rule-of-thumb objective of the greater good for the greatest number. In the gravity flow between taxes paid and benefits received, there was for many years the illusion of a perfect symbiosis. But with the government now spending some forty per cent of the nation's productivity, and much of that outlay invisible, the relationship seems to have become outrageously parasitic. To add injury to insult, any who manage to save, or who invest in government paper, end up losers, their principal withered by inflation, the yield nicked by the tax-collector.

The traditional allegiance of citizen to government has vanished; trust and confidence have been replaced by a brooding suspicion and growing hostility. And as between government and governed, the feeling appears mutual: the mistrust that is the ethos of the marketplace flourishes nowhere more than at Revenue Canada.

• • •

In 1967-68, Revenue Canada investigated 289 cases of suspected tax evasion, recovering $13-million in unpaid tax as the result of its exertions. In 1979-80, Revenue Canada investigated 949 suspected cases of tax evasion; the yield in tax recovery, fines, and penalties amounted to about $37-million. Along the way, the department's investigative staff has grown from 200 to more than 500—further evidence to sustain the widespread belief that crime increases in direct proportion to the numbers employed to detect it.

These figures may not seem remarkable, bearing in mind that there are 12.5-million Canadian taxpayers whose voluntary tax payments total $26-billion a year. But, as a genial spokesman for Revenue Canada told an enquirer, the department's investigative branch "is only scratching the surface."

Last year, scratching the surface produced a total of $488-million for all tax recoveries, including those resulting from fraud, evasion, and human error. A tax investigator for the department reckons that it loses $2-billion each year in revenues from those either smart and lucky enough to cheat the system successfully, or from those blissfully unaware they are doing so.

At Revenue Canada, the difference between fraud and human error is blurred. The majority of tax evasion investigations don't go to court because there isn't enough evidence to prove fraud. Or enough courts, either. Where discovered, the tax due gets paid, along with the appropriate penalty. The emboldened cheater and the merely confused usually enjoy the same summary justice. In the eyes of the beholder, there is no difference.

The perception of government as adversary, familiar enough to tyrannies, is novel to democracy, just as an unspoken, casual anarchy is peculiar to a society supposedly governed by the rule of law. But when the currency is debased and mistrust is made a way of life, what is left of public morality must be enforced in law, by statute, ordinance, and regulation—so many of them that no citizen could be aware of them all.

This helps explain why law-abiding people are wary of the police and terrified of the courts. For most, acquaintance with law enforcement extends only to the Motor Vehicle Safety Act and not much beyond. But it is enough: one need only blunder into a speed trap, be ambushed by a ghost car, or pulled over at a check-point, to comprehend the real limits to such illusory rights as protection against entrapment, self-incrimination, search, seizure, and arbitrary judgement. (My God, one wonders, what must it be like for some wretch apprehended for a serious offence?)

We are being nudged toward a greater compliance with the law by the strategy of encouraging the stark fear of it. We have become accustomed to living in the shadow of surveillance: routinely interrogated, monitored, detained, searched. Considerations of personal integrity, public morality, right and wrong, become ephemeral. Importantly, we need no longer think for ourselves: a sense of what is right or wrong is no longer a matter of private conscience or broadly accepted public covenant, but the endless business of legislators, magistrates, attorneys, censors, and the police. What is right is whatever is lawful; what is lawful is whatever goes unnoticed.

The citizen who won my vote as 1980 man of the year was a fellow in Telkwa, B.C., who refused to accept a piece of certified mail at the post office because his name had been spelled wrong. He then failed to respond to an order to appear in court, being otherwise occupied owing to the pressure of business. He was subsequently waited upon by six officers of the RCMP, each dressed in riot gear, plus two sheriffs, a conservation officer, and a police dog. They removed him from his home in handcuffs and jailed him for two hours, after which a judge fined him $400.

The registered letter had been a call for jury duty. He said he told the sheriff he would be happy to serve if they'd only spell his name right. The judge said he was making a mockery of the law by using a technicality. It provides an example of our condition: we are all only approximately who we think we are; the distinction between someone named Camp and one named Cmpr is a technicality, and ought to be as trifling to both of them as to the sheriff.

• • •

It could be said that we are not as moral as we used to be, but then we never were. More than a hundred years ago, George Eliot's tormented hero of *Middlemarch* discovered the ambiguities of morality:

Our deeds still travel with us from afar,
And what we have been makes us what we are.

Homily it is, but now not exactly true—no one who has known this country for what it was would easily recognize it for what it has become. We have not become the sum of our history; we resemble something like the denial of it. Compassion, the willingness to share, tolerance and trust, respect for people and their property, the belief that ends and means are ethically compatible—none of these remembered parts of our public morality has survived.

Once, one of the strongest words in the language was "liar." To cover the human capacity for dissembling, we recognized the social necessity of "white" lies. But lying, like cheating, was anathema to the public morality, and perhaps the most conclusive evidence of morality's decline is that lying has become global, epic, persistent, pervasive. A charge that would have been a fighting word a generation ago—that of liar—has been defused of meaning by the generally accepted view that truth has become irrelevant. Apart from surviving as a biblical injunction, truth has become debatable, subjective, multisided, a matter of opinion, unnecessary, and more often than not dangerous. The Gulf of Tonkin resolution, which gave Lyndon Johnson a free hand in Vietnam, was inspired by a lie; Richard Nixon's covert invasion of Cambodia was covered by lies; the chances are good that Canadians will never know the truth about the "apprehended insurrection" in 1970, an event surrounded by lies.

The shock to one's value system by the legitimizing of untruths depends on one's age; preference for the truth may be a generational phenomenon. Those raised by television come to know early in life how far removed its illusion is from truth. No one who has reached the primary grades believes "Mean Joe" Greene would give his shirt for a bottle of pop, any more than they would expect to meet Joe Namath and find him reeking of Brut. But it doesn't matter whether they believe it or not; we are not dealing any longer with home truths but with palatable ones. Viewers may watch *the fifth estate,* Oral Roberts, or the prime minister of this country and decide for themselves how much, if anything, they see or hear they need accept as gospel.

Some of us, raised by the makers of Camel cigarettes in the belief there was "not a cough in a carload," continue to resist the earnest if awkward blandishment of revisionist opinion that "danger to health increases with amount smoked." We remain ruefully chagrined even though the possibility exists that what would now be irresponsibly dishonest was, in its day, nothing more than puffery.

The youthful television generation has acquired a scepticism beyond its years. And while it can be manipulated even as its elders, it is truly not deceived. What our children know, which we happily did not, is that they live in a world of deception and illusion. For them, the TV pitchman's crafts are a part of life. With the added inheritance of our disillusionment, they will not be a generation easily given to trust or moved to revive a public morality.

Our public morality declined with the change of both perspective and perception. As to perspective, we no longer look up to anyone; as to perception, we no longer value the role and function of so many who once warranted our respect because of what they did. A generation ago, there *were* those we considered pillars of society, a term in present disuse. They included teachers, physicians, clergymen, politicians, members of the military, the police—even the postman!—and others whose responsibilities bore upon our needs. It now seems so long ago as to be Dickensian, but there were many who evoked a respect not untinged with gratitude. At the root of it, I suppose, was the recognition of selflessness and sacrifice. We trusted teachers to train our children; we knew that doctors not only made house calls but also frequently went unpaid; we felt reassured seeing the cop on his beat, and we were convinced that all of them were motivated by an altruism fundamental to the existence of a public morality.

In that altruism there was more than a little injustice, and many were as exploited as they were venerated. Recently, I looked out from an office window at Queen's Park, Toronto, upon a crowd of striking teachers, howling down the minister of education while the police stood by awaiting contingency. It struck me that each of those forces gathered below in the obligatory acting out of their respective roles had improved their lot in everything but public esteem. Presumably, if the price of such esteem is insecurity and a reduced income, then a great majority would say to hell with it. And yet, the understood presence of human pillars in the structure of society once truly held it together: they were a presence beyond price, beyond anything any of us could afford.

I have left the politician to the last, as would anyone. Unlike that of their constituents, the lot of politicians has steadily improved over the past decade. They have continued to earn more, accrue more, and gather more perquisites unto themselves than any other class or kind of Canadian, save professional hockey players. Elected politicians have established themselves as a brahmin caste. It cost today's taxpayers almost $100-million a year merely to attend to the administrative needs of 282 members of the House of Commons. Politics, which used to be considered a form of public service with recognized uncertainties and slight material benefits, is now a full-time job, and its rewards are being scaled to the premise that it's a life's work.

Years ago, after the war and the election of a Labour government in Britain, I listened to Beverley Baxter lamenting the fact that members' indemnities had just been increased to £1,000 a year. A Canadian expatriate and professional journalist, himself a member of parliament in Westminster, Baxter expressed the fear that people would inevitably be drawn to politics "because there was money in it." Bloated with idealism, I expressed vigorous disagreement.

Years later, however, during a leadership struggle in the Progressive Conservative Party, a Tory MP came to me in tears, saying that if John Diefenbaker were deposed as the party's leader, he himself would lose his seat—his premise being that only Diefenbaker had elected him. "And then what are you going to do for me?" he asked. "Can you find me another job paying $12,000 a year?" He is still in the House.

Among the considerations a prime minister or premier must now give to the exercise of his prerogative of dissolution is its possible effect on the morale of his caucus. He will know that foremost in the minds of many of his supporters is the impact an election might have on their pensions. More than one quiet election campaign has been waged for an incumbent based on an appeal for support because, if defeated, he would not qualify for pension benefits.

Perhaps the ultimate wisdom was that of Robert Manion, who advised "no man should go into politics unless independently rich or independently poor." But it remains surely one of the anomalies of the welfare state that none have benefitted so much from its generous impulses as the architects of it. Behind the public spectacle of ritual partisan controversy, notably in the federal parliament, there has developed a broad and agreeable consensus to strengthen and improve upon the prospects of incumbency of all honourable members. There cannot be much left for them to achieve in that respect, other than tenure.

None of this matters much these days to a citizenry drained of its capacity for righteous indignation. There are other distractions than politics—which have become, anyway, an abstraction. While the world shrinks, the distance from Ottawa grows more distant. Alienation is not quite the word for the prevailing public mood—incredulity might be better. Paradoxically, Ottawa was closer to us when it seemed more remote. When it was a mystery, we believed in its ameliorating powers. Our allegiance required our trust, and at the heart of our trust was our need for order, stability, justice, and security. For these, really, there is still nowhere else to turn.

Canadians long enjoyed the politics of great adventures and grand designs. Our early politicians were nation-builders, the later ones ambitious to create a new liberal society; even Diefenbaker proclaimed a vision. Canadians went to the polls to reconfirm a moral obligation as their brother's keeper in elections that were celebrations of yet another harvest of shared abundance.

• • •

Now that it's over, and the politics of scarcity has begun, few know or remember how much has been lost. Without trust, allegiance is gone: there are neither followers nor leaders, but government and governed. Present-day politics lack the once-familiar dimension of either adventure or grand design, bearing merely the imprint of the strategems of underlings in a coarse struggle for purposeless power. (We are currently led by a man who became the first leader to be muzzled in a national campaign by his retainers—"We low-bridged him," as one of his key advisers put it. Imagine Jack Pickersgill saying that of Mackenzie King. Or Allister Grosart of John Diefenbaker.)

During 1979-80, in less than a year, our political parties spent $21.5-million in two election campaigns, about seventy per cent of that for advertising, mostly television. Seventeen years earlier, the expenditure of $600,000 for campaign advertising would have been considered adequate and, in my experience, all there was to be had anyway. In each of the two most recent elections, the party that spent the most lost: there is no substantive evidence that any of this lavish outlay had any influence upon the result. Indeed, the common public reaction was one of disbelief, since the bulk of the advertising was negative, destructive, and degrading.

A public morality presumed self-imposed limits to public behaviour, acknowledging the requirement of restraint as a moderating influence in partisan politics. We have learned from experience—or thought we had—that the risk of excess increases with the scale of the enterprise and size of the stake. In the increasing frenzy that marks the present wars among Canada's political parties, in which incivility and insult are packaged by professionals for home delivery, a bemused citizen must wonder what the struggle has come to be about and what the prize could be.

The citizen will not see in the struggle any reflection of his own interests and concerns. If he is aware that all this artful manipulation and tugging at his fears and apprehensions is meant to influence his opinion (perhaps to reinforce it), he will be right, but no wiser. Like government itself, the business of politics is beyond him or, if not that, beneath him.

We no longer vote for what we get, but for whom; it has been more than twenty years since a major political party produced a serious statement of its policy intentions and, being elected, acted upon it. I am not so naïve as to believe that politics ever was or will be the activity of solely virtuous people, that promises made must be promises kept. But what sustained our confidence in political parties and in public men was the belief that the contest was not merely between them, but about us.

What has been will likely never be again; anyway, nostalgia may well exaggerate the past, as it concedes the present and resigns the future. Alvin Toffler, the futurist, pleads for recognition of "new realities," urging that we redesign our political institutions. Seeing what remains of them, we might as well.

"I really believe," Toffler has said, "that unless each of us now begins thinking about and imagining alternatives to present political structures, we will land in something far worse than runaway inflation or an economic depression." The "something far worse" could be to continue to live in a society in which there is neither mutual trust nor shared values, and no public morality to maintain them.

Much of our present troubles are of our own doing: a despairing passivity; an insensitivity to insult and arrogance, almost as though we had been immunized against them; and a growing capacity for cynicism to fill the void of a lapsed capacity for indignation.

"In the meantime," as Albert Camus wrote of France in its post-war moral depression, "we must live, we must create in the storm... we must now stop commenting on our time in order to give it form."

Our own history indicates that we as a society have been at our best when so much else seemed at its worst. For a brief while, during the anxious suspence of the Québec referendum, one sensed the disciplined restraint and tempered resolve of which we are capable. That it swiftly passed is less important than its rediscovery: we can respond to challenge.

It is possible to say, without recrimination, that the failure of our political institutions to inspire either trust or respect has been in large measure induced by the inadequacy of our leadership. If we have left too much to the politicians—and to journalism—and assumed nothing of the burden ourselves, it is fair to say that so long as our leaders appeal to our opinions, rather than to our values, we will have little to say, and less to do. But it is ironic that while politics has been practised in an echo-chamber—politicians repeating majority opinion as their own—the public opinion of politics has plummeted.

Toffler proposes we rethink our position, which might be, for us, a first act of creation in our storm. The evidence is ample that the nation cannot be led unless it is inspired to follow, and it will not be inspired to follow until trust and confidence have been resumed in its leadership. Our leadership is exhausted of its moral credit. Only new leadership is sufficient to the task of restoring a sense of moral authority to government, without which there can be no public morality. In the meantime, our society will remain bereft.

Dalton Camp, "The Decline in Public Morality," *Saturday Night,* (January, 1981), pp. 26, 28-31.

ANN CHARNEY
THE MONUMENT

The world's most expensive stadium—a diamond bigger than the Ritz—is located at the modest east end of Sherbrooke Street, some five kilometres from downtown Montreal and the elegant Ritz-Carlton itself. The unfinished stadium may be the world's most expensive structure, except that no-one has yet priced the Pyramids. On clear nights, its unmistakable futuristic profile is clearly visible from the lookout points on Mount Royal, sailing through the darkness like a brightly lit spaceship. At close range, its vast, empty hulk, dwarfed by giant construction cranes that loom over the edge of the open dome, suggests some herculean task that has defeated the Titans themselves. Most of the time, however, you can't really see the place for the numbers. And no wonder. The fantasy, the excess, the extravagance, the pure wondrous waste of it, are dazzling. So far, the cost of the Olympic Stadium runs to something like a billion dollars, and it keeps rising.

To put this astronomic sum in perspective, a Montreal newspaper asked an accounting firm to translate the price of North America's eight other domed stadiums into 1984 Canadian dollars. The results showed that together these eight stadiums—the Houston Astrodome ($124.9-million), the New Orleans Superdome ($357-million), the Pontiac Silverdome ($118.9-million), the Seattle Kingdome ($132.4-million), the Syracuse Carrier Dome ($44.2-million), the Minneapolis Metrodome ($78.6-million), B.C. Place ($132.2-million), and the Indianapolis Hoosier Dome ($101.2-million)—cost in total just $97.3-million more than Montreal's one stadium. Quebec has every chance in the world, however, of bridging this gap and surpassing the combined total as it proceeds with plans to complete the original design.

One detail alone will suffice to illustrate how the spirit of grandeur flourishes undiminished by time and changing political administrations: specially designed sewing machines, weighing two tons, have been imported from Japan for the purpose of assembling the immense rolls of canvas destined to become the roof. The canvas itself has been preserved in climatically controlled conditions beneath the stadium, with all the care appropriate to maintaining a piece of the Holy Shroud in some sacred crypt.

• • •

How did Montrealers achieve this singular distinction? Credit must be given to the city's indomitable mayor for a quarter of a century, Jean Drapeau, whose small physical stature belies the breadth of his visions. As Flaubert said of his masterpiece, "Mme Bovary, c'est moi," so Drapeau can truthfully say of "le stade olympique."

According to people close to him, the dream of creating a monument graced with a tower from which one could see the entire city was with him back when he was first elected mayor, in 1954. It surfaced during Expo '67, when he manoeuvred to have the Eiffel Tower dismantled and reassembled in Montreal for the duration of the world's fair. As negotiations stalled, the mayor commissioned a French architect, J. Robert Dalb, to design a new tower that would combine the most notable features of the Eiffel Tower and the Leaning Tower of Pisa. It was not built, owing to lack of funds, but the dream survived to appear again in 1970 when the mayor, in a spectacular feat of diplomacy, secured the Olympic Summer Games of 1976 for Montreal. He assured Olympic officials that the games would be "modest" and self-financing, and that their cost would not exceed $125-million.

The mayor's visionary schemes, however, were not to be hampered by such practical concessions. With supreme confidence he selected the French architect, Roger Taillibert, known for his complex and extravagant creations, to design the Olympic facilities. "We [French Canadians] can only survive if we accept the challenge of quality. That is why I chose Roger Taillibert... He is one of the five greatest architects in the world—and I don't know the other four, if they exist." Undisturbed by the fact that Canada thus became the only country in the history of the modern Olympics to have chosen a foreign architect, Drapeau explained with serenity, "Art transcends nationalism." When the Quebec association of architects accused the mayor of planning the Olympics in an atmosphere of "lies and secrecy," he responded that he was the only person competent to decide when and to what extent citizens would be informed. The man was rising to the scale of the monument he envisioned.

On April 6, 1972, in a lavish "son et lumière" presentation, the mayor introduced a model of Taillibert's scheme to a select audience of invited guests and foreign journalists. At the heart of the sports complex was the spectacular stadium flanked by a massive, inclined tower which would rise to the height of a fifty-storey building and which would support a suspended, retractable roof. The mayor's eloquent performance stressed the magnificence of Taillibert's design and avoided all crass considerations of dollars and cents.

A handful of demonstrators representing anti-poverty groups slightly marred the occasion, but they were easily contained. During a question-and-answer period following the presentation, the mayor assured his audience that the whole enterprise would not cost taxpayers anything since revenues would be derived from "extraordinary sources" such as an Olympic lottery, the sale of special commemorative stamps, coins, and so on. Later, the mayor went further in his assurances when he promised, in his usual vivid style, "The Olympics can no more have a deficit than a man can have a baby."

In the weeks following the press conference, the few figures obtained by persistent journalists from close-mouthed city and Olympic officials seemed to confirm the mayor's seductive optimism. For the following year, a kind of self-satisfied lull of anticipation settled over the entire issue. The city basked in the expectant glory of the celebration to come. Actual construction of the stadium was not to begin until 1974 for the simple reason, it was later revealed, that detailed plans were not available. Taillibert, who saw himself primarily as an artist, was in no hurry, apparently, to provide the construction drawings and specifications necessary for the realization of his grand design. Meanwhile, the mayor supported his architect with a fervour any artist might well envy.

When work finally began on the stadium, less than two years before its official opening, it went less than smoothly. There was the problem of time—the Superdome in New Orleans, then under construction, took five years to build—and the difficulties posed by the complexity of the design which, to make matters worse, continued to evolve according to the creator's whim. Instead of rising upwards, the stadium seemed to be sinking into a financial and technological morass.

The mayor, however, never lost faith. While his critics spoke of a lunatic obsession, he evoked the Pyramids, the Sphinx, the Eiffel Tower, and wondered if *they* had been appreciated in their time. He extolled the pride of creating a monument that would last through the ages and draw people from around the world. Speaking to the Montreal Board of Trade, he recalled that Pericles had been rebuked for building the Acropolis instead of warships. "I prefer," said the mayor, "to be chastised now and understood later."

During these hard times, only Roger Taillibert seemed to defend the vision that had united the two men: "That's all Canadians and North Americans think about, money, money, money. It doesn't interest me at all. When you look at the Eiffel Tower, what remains...? The honorarium Eiffel received or the structure?" Taillibert's indifference to money seemed to vanish rapidly in the following years. In 1978, he sued the Olympic Installation Board and the city of Montreal for $32.6-million, above and beyond the $6.8-million settlement offered by the Quebec government. The Quebec Superior Court awarded him another $3.4-million.

While the importance of the mayor's role in the creation of the stadium is paramount, credit must also be given to his loyal electorate. Not only did the voters remain faithful to the man and his dream during the years of toil and sacrifice exacted by the elliptical maw of the headless idol, they stuck by him in the unpleasant aftermath of the Olympics.

The whole extent of the Olympic folly was detailed by the Malouf Commission, set up in 1977 by the Quebec government and headed by Mr. Justice Albert Malouf of the Quebec Superior Court, which tried to determine how the cost of the games had rocketed from an estimated $120-million to well over $1-billion. The inquiry revealed a sordid tale of graft and incompetence, and concluded that "the choice [of the stadium] was dictated by considerations of esthetics and grandeur without any serious study of costs and feasibility beforehand."

The inquiry came and went and the people of Montreal continued to elect Jean Drapeau. More than that, a survey in 1984 indicated that three-quarters of the city's French-speaking voters were in favour of completing the tower and the stadium according to the original design, thus proving the wisdom of a pensée from the writer Antoine de Saint-Exupéry which the mayor is said to be fond of quoting: "Force men to build a tower together and they will become brothers; throw them some grain and they will be at one another's throats."

In 1985, the Quebec government agreed to complete the stadium, citing among other reasons the fact that, unfinished, the stadium remained "an embarrassing monument to incompetence." The cost of finishing it is expected to run around $120-million, but a certain understandable scepticism has already been expressed about the firmness of that sum. The government's decision ignored serious doubts about the feasibility of the original design—in 1979, part of a roof of a similar stadium in Paris designed by Taillibert collapsed, crushing thirty then unoccupied seats—as well as less expensive and more proven solutions for covering the stadium.

With a roof or without, the stadium leaves something to be desired as a place to watch sports. Designed for track and field, it supposedly had the much-vaunted advantage of being a multi-purpose facility. The stadium does boast a hydraulic pitcher's mound (which rises and descends discreetly) and rolls of astroturf (which can be unzipped as easily as a stripper's costume), but spectators remain so far from the field that, as one sports writer put it, you need a detective to find the ball.

Banal common sense and an affinity for the utilitarian have never been characteristic of Quebec society. Quebeckers have usually left such considerations to their thriftier and duller English-speaking neighbours, preferring to affirm their existence in grandiose dreams that exalt the collective spirit.

• • •

The Olympic stadium is not the first extravagant Quebec monument dedicated to this spirit. Jean-Claude Marsan, an architectural historian, cites several other telling examples. At the beginning of the nineteenth century, while the English were busy developing the economy, French Canadians were building Notre Dame, the largest church north of Mexico at the time. A century later, in the midst of the Depression, Marsan points out, they built Saint Joseph's Oratory, the fourth-largest sanctuary in the world. During the same period, the University of Montreal, while lacking funds to pay its professors' salaries, was nevertheless creating a lavish campus which Marsan calls "the monument that most resembles Versailles."

More recently, there was the celebrated case of Mirabel International Airport. One of the largest airports in the world, Mirabel is used to only thirteen per cent of its capacity, and handles less traffic than the airport at Moose Jaw.

Seen in this context, the stadium fits neatly into the psychic landscape of Montreal. Even its billion-dollar aura falls into place. The fabulous figure becomes the essential element of sacrifice that replaces the live offering and renders the place sacred, distinct from the ordinary and the commonplace. As befits a monument created in the image of man, this modern Pharaonic dream has shown that it is not immune to the ravages of time. For all the solidity of this concrete and steel, it seems strangely perishable. Already, after only a decade of exposure to the elements, it bears unmistakable signs of decay.

In the not-too-distant future, in its stripped and ruined state, the Olympic Stadium will finally achieve the grandeur of its original conception. Long after Jean Drapeau has gone to his final reward, the Big O—like the Parthenon, or the Colosseum, or the Mayan temples—will draw the curious of the world whom he so presciently awaited.

Ann Charney, "The Monument," *Saturday Night*, (January, 1987), pp. 122-124, 126.

ANNE COLLINS
ON COMMITMENT

There was no doubting the woman's commitment. She was active in the pro-choice and women's health movements, a birth-control counsellor, a single mother—a feminist by her own and anyone's definition. Yet, sitting in the sunny office of the clinic where she worked, she told me pointedly, "I wish there was another word for it." We had been talking about the politics of abortion when we struck the rock of feminism. I had just finished saying that many of the anti-abortion women I met had an accurate analysis of where women fit in the big picture, but turned their anger into a stick with which to beat feminists. She had been beaten with that stick too, to the point where she was beginning to regard the word as a hindrance to her work: "I make great strides with so-called ordinary women as long as they don't think they're talking to a feminist. They might feel exactly the way I do about how society discriminates against them, they might be struggling to come into their own. But if the *word* slips in, they stop talking or tell me emphatically that they are not *feminists*."

I know that when I first saw myself described in print as a feminist I winced. It felt both like being forced out of a closet about beliefs I certainly held, and an incredible limitation on me. What has happened in fifteen years of feminist activism in Canada to make me wince at the term? In her contribution to the recent feminist anthology, *Sisterhood is Global,* Simone de Beauvoir writes that in the last few years people have become two-faced about feminism. Still eager to accept the rewards of activism—its slow but steady transformations of workplace, family, medicine, religion, politics and law—women have grown increasingly reluctant to bear the label. The feminist movement has turned in on itself, protectively preaching to the converted in a language that seems deliberately exclusive; the feminist community in Toronto sometimes feels like a hot-house boarding school in which intimate cliques war over issues barely comprehensible to outsiders. More important, the business of feminism has broken down into a series of individual projects. Women work for choice in abortion, or legal protection under the new Charter of Rights and Freedoms, or against pornography and violence against women, or against censorship, or for daycare, equal pay and better health care. But moving in a larger community, these activists hesitate to bring up any overarching idea of a feminist agenda. Perhaps it's because to a certain extent single-issue activism works. Whereas the Feminist Party of Canada made no headway.

But the word that slips most often into condemnations of feminism is neither unwieldy nor unworkable, but selfish. This word is not only thrown about by the Phyllis Schlaflys of the world (on CBC radio she proclaimed, "Feminism teaches the woman to put her own self-satisfaction ahead of every other goal"), but by women who by every yardstick of sympathy and achievement are feminists. "Feminist" conjures in many people's minds the picture of a lone agent, a solitary woman cut off from the "normal" pursuits of womanhood, out for herself because she doesn't have the opportunity to care for others. A woman with nothing better to do, as a friend of mine put it. Despite the fact that all feminist issues are about redefining community, about breaking down the barriers between public and private life—and that feminism intensely offers connection, not separation—the image of a feminist as a scarily selfish female persists.

And de Beauvoir, who accuses us of duplicity, has to bear some responsibility for the selfish face of feminism. Her book *The Second Sex,* published in English in 1952, set much of the theoretical stage for twentieth-century-brand feminism—written in revulsion against the nineteenth-century vision of idealized womanhood. Elizabeth Cady Stanton may have warned her Victorian colleagues that "self-development is a higher duty than self-sacrifice. The thing which most retards and militates against women's self-development is self-sacrifice." But her voice was lost in her times. The first wave of feminism, in suffrage, education, social purity and temperance movements, in the end played to the vision of woman as self-sacrificer. The social transformations of that century had made middle-class women queens of the private realm and keepers of their husbands' consciences; the pragmatic arguments for the improvement of women's lot were not for their own sakes but because they were mothers. Children (the future) were almost exclusively in the female hands.

De Beauvoir resented the definition of woman as born to care for others; to her it made women passive hostages to nature, trapped by the side-effects of heterosexual love. What women had to do to liberate themselves was to free themselves from nature, and explode the engulfing myth of transcendent motherhood. The problem was that de Beauvoir, and her inheritors, threw the baby out with the bath water, denying, as feminist theorist Mary O'Brien points out in her brilliant *The Politics of Reproduction,* the creativity of childbearing. *The Second Sex* cast women out onto a lonely existentialist, androgynous plain where they were faced with the task of inventing themselves. De Beauvoir in that book appeared repelled by the actual process of pregnancy, and she still derides any strain of feminism "which celebrates women's cycles, rhythms, and bodily fluids" and any feminist who suggests that there might be any such thing as a female consciousness. As O'Brien puts it, for de Beauvoir "Freedom for women is finally an act which imitates men."

The early thinkers of second-wave feminism turned the things that women do (bear children, take care of relationships) into extra baggage hauled on the quest for self-fulfillment. Throughout the 200 years of the movement toward women's liberation, a pendulum swings: women fight either for equality with men *or* for the bolstering and protection of their female difference. That struggle is encapsulated right now in the controvery over abortion rights. The pro-choice vision is of women as individuals who need freedom of choice to maintain control over their lives, to compete and survive in a male-defined world. The anti-abortion movement pleads for the special status of women and wants to reinstate the outgrown protectionism of the nuclear family.

The either/or decision modern feminism has asked women to make is to choose between themselves and their sex. Former *City Woman* editor Dawn MacDonald expressed the dilemma choosing "self" caused for a generation of female achievers in a controversial editorial for the magazine: "We broke with the past, saying it had nothing to teach us except more of the same. We broke with the future, saying we had only one life to live and it is happening now. Some of us even broke with the species, saying biology is not our destiny, we had no *need* to procreate while we did have a need to discover our true selves." She looked at the ultimate idealized woman, Mother Teresa, who insists that we are born to sacrifice, and concluded that the nun was a "reminder in the flesh that sometimes there is a kind of pathology at work when the individual is always placed ahead of the health of the family, the community, and the species." The subtext was that women weren't meant to be lonely atoms of humanity but intimately connected to community.

The elusive but necessary trick is to understand that what feminism should demand is not putting self *above* others but considering self *with* others. For a few years, in a flush of rebellion against everything everyone always said we should be, we may have gone overboard on our definition of individual fulfillment. Simply, I think, because coming to any sort of grips with "self" has always been a tough task for women. I remember my teenage list of qualities I thought unbecoming to my sex: aggression, assertion, ambition. I remember (vividly) the disgust and guilt I heaped on myself when I "selfishly" exited from an early relationship that was lovingly edging me toward marriage and children. And then the two years of growing pains when the next man I loved called my bluff and insisted that I both had, and should live up to, ambition. At the time I thought my condition was purely personal; later, small threads began to weave themselves together. Though I read the early feminist texts (de Beauvoir, Germaine Greer, Shulamith Firestone and company) and became almost ill with anger and recognition, I rejected the feminist movement's most often projected picture of women as powerless victims. The clues I needed I found most often in the musings of female artists, who were trying to be both creative and responsible to others. Mary Pratt, for instance, had four children in quick succession and at 30 found herself still not the painter she had dreamed of becoming. Then she realized it wasn't motherhood that kept her under, but "my inability to take myself, my life and my work seriously."

American psychologist Carol Gilligan has found that taking oneself seriously is in fact the major crisis of female maturity. Drawing on the work of gender theorist Nancy Chodorow and her own ten-year-long studies of male and female moral development, Gilligan concluded that because children are largely cared for by women, boys define themselves as different and separate from their mothers, while girls see themselves as like—and so feel no urgent need to draw individual boundaries. Women soon understand the ebbs and flows of relationships, but not necessarily what they owe to themselves. Writes Gilligan in her book *In a Different Voice:* "The conflict between self and other thus constitutes the central moral problem for women, posing a dilemma whose resolution requires a reconciliation between feminity and adulthood. In the absence of such a reconciliation, the moral problem cannot be resolved. The 'good woman' masks assertion in evasion, denying responsibility by claiming only to meet the needs of others, while the 'bad woman' forgoes or renounces the commitments that bind her in self-deception and betrayal."

"Good women" love others; "bad women" love themselves. This is the thought that still taints the image of feminism, since feminists are obviously "bad women." But creeping slowly into the picture are thinkers such as Gilligan, who show the bad side-effects of the either/or, who recognize that women don't really grow up (will stay victims, stay powerless) until they realize that they themselves are worthy objects of care. And the contraceptive revolution, twenty-five years old this year, has also forced the issue. Even though the pill and the IUD are flawed methods, and our access to abortion as a back-up protection is still uneven to say the least, women—feminists or otherwise—are faced with a new freedom. Children are chosen.

Granted, society places limitations on choosing children freely, but women can't consider themselves any more as accident victims of heterosexual sex, hijacked by children. This new wave of female freedom is scary: I heard the fear in both male and female voices while talking about abortion, an issue that brings self into conflict with other like no other. If women were no longer forced into self-sacrifice, would they continue to be the glue that binds, the maintenance workers on relationships? With women "free," how could men guarantee they would still have the chance to become fathers? Feminism, especially feminism of the "pseudo-man," as Mary O'Brien calls it, fed fears that women might turn out to be men in sheep's clothing.

Selfish, marginal, passé, balkanized. All these words contribute to the present popular description of feminism. But the description is a thorough misunderstanding of the cutting edge of feminist thought today. Women such as O'Brien and Gilligan are at the forefront of a radical attempt to break down the female either/or—aided and abetted by a fundamental change in the female condition that neither nineteenth-century feminists nor Simone de Beauvoir anticipated. Motherhood is no longer either a "mere" biological imperative or a sainted and self-sacrificing path, but a chosen role—and increasingly chosen by both men and women, as they attempt that new twentieth-century pursuit, "parenting."

The feminist movement has lost a bit of its footing, but at the same time, women (and men) have been slowly building confidence in and acceptance of female experience. This is true in the most obvious sense; working women make fewer apologies for pregnancy; men take paternity leave; lip service at least is paid to the notion that both men and women should take part in early child care—which, if you consider Gilligan's work, could utterly change human nature. And there is the subtler sense—in the arts and in the relations between the sexes, in biography and history—that our culture is slowly opening its ears to women's voices.

In some ways, the women's movement has been paradoxically personal, waylaid by visions of individual freedoms rather than true social transformation. I think this is because we have been living in a divided psychic house, trying to strip away parts of ourselves to succeed (or survive) within existing structures. The new feminism puts ourselves and our understanding of relationships back together again, and asks that the world change to fit us.

Anne Collins, "On Commitment," *Toronto Life*, (September, 1985), pp. 34, 48-9, 51-2.

ALLAN FOTHERINGHAM

DAN GEORGE'S LAST STAND

The flame from the refinery stack on the south bluff of Burrard Inlet casts a moving reflection across the waters of the fjord that reaches into the innards of Vancouver. Day and night, that wavering flame from the Standard Oil refinery reflects all the way over the mile of water to the north shore of the inlet, where the faded wooden houses of the Burrard Reserve are scattered. Thirty yards up the slope there is a small white cottage, a front door awaiting unbuilt steps. As you struggle up the incline with puppy dogs at foot, past the Coke bottles and abandoned car, there appears in the window above a face like a copper moon. The face is the face of a man paying obeisance to *his* section of earth, *his* view, the portion of the realm that belongs to *his* eyes. Dan George has lived 71 years on this slope, 100 yards covering the distance between the house where he was born, the house he built, and in which he raised his family, and the house where he now lives. Two cultures face each other across the mile of water—linked by the constancy of the flame. There is a similar consistency to the life of Dan George. He is a portage across time.

Burrard Reserve No. 3 forms a tattered buffer between the boxes of a North Vancouver subdivision and the summer homes and cabin cruisers of Deep Cove farther up the inlet. It is just along the shore here, some six miles from downtown Vancouver, that the tormented novelist Malcolm Lowry lived in a squatter's shack and fueled his genius with fatal quantities of alcohol. The feel of Dan George can best be appreciated by imagining him on this slope for 71 years, looking across the water and watching his world change. "The government came through Canada and measured out a piece of land for us and called it our 'reserve.' We did not have the freedom to roam as we were used to do," he says. He could see the housing march out from the city, decade by decade, reducing the thick timber to subdivision squares. Now, peeking from the tip of Burnaby Mountain at left are the stark towers of Simon Fraser University, which will serve this summer as the site for the eight-million-dollar filming of Aldous Huxley's novel *Brave New World*.

In the house a dark-eyed grandchild in diapers paws at Dan's knee. His pretty daughter, Marie George, lives with him in the house with her three children. Dan George is a short man, just five-foot-six. But it is as if his body had come from two separate men. All the weight of those 165 pounds is in massive shoulders and chest, the product of 27 years as a longshoreman. The powerful arms hang to tiny hips, the flat belly of a teen-ager and to short, bowed legs. His triangular form is that of a trapeze artist. And from that thick chest is rationed out, in spaced intervals, the soft fog of his voice. It is impossible to translate into print the husky whisper of Dan George's voice, or the measured cadence of his speech. And there is that face, like a bronzed catcher's mitt. It is full of canyons and gullies and arroyos, the soft folds of hills—erosions of time and spirit that in fact have made it more beautiful. When he begins to smile, there is a slow-motion telegraphing. The seams begin to soften. The face unfolds like a wrinkled brown shopping bag, the lines and creases taking new shapes and directions. It is both timeless and one of the magnificent faces of our time. He points out the window and across the river to the oil refineries which have come to defile the bluff. "They wanted to build them on this shore. My father stopped them."

It is unnerving to talk to a man with such a face and voice who muses over the possibility of touching three different centuries. He was born in 1899 and conceivably could reach the year 2000, since his uncle lived until 110 and his mother to 95. He takes quiet satisfaction in the idea. There is a personal object lesson in history to sit down with a man, still active, who loaded lumber by hand onto full-rigged sailing ships from foreign ports. European stock came to this country to put down roots. With Dan George it is the other way; he seems to flow from the earth. He is a fixed position in a world of impermanence.

His mother was a full-blooded descendant of the warrior Wautsauk, who walked with a wolf. Wautsauk kept a wolf as a constant companion and went aboard Captain George Vancouver's ship when it explored Burrard Inlet in 1792. He can remember a great-great-uncle who could tell stories of the dark-colored men who came even before Captain Vancouver—the Spanish explorers with their Moorish slaves.

Just below where Dan's little house sits there was once an enormous fort which the tribe built for protection from raiding parties of war canoes. Not far away is the spot where the first Mass in that part of Canada was conducted over a century ago. Queen Victoria gave the tribe three apple trees to commemorate the event. Two perished and the third died when Dan's mother did.

Today the Dollarton Highway cuts through, speeding motorists to the new housing beyond on streets named Beachview and Baycrest and Seashell Lane. Burrard Reserve No. 3 and the George family remain, some of the 32,000 of BC's 48,000 Indians who still live on reserves. In the old house Dan built is son Bob, his wife and their 14 children. Beside it is the $12,000 aluminum house trailer of son Lenny, the moody, talented youngster who seems to have a promising acting future if he wants it.

For Dan, the only time away from the reserve were the 12 years at the residential school run by the Oblate Fathers in a clearing of timber in North Vancouver. At 19 he married Amy Jack, a beautiful and strong-willed woman. "I made up my mind to try to get her when I was 16," Dan remembers. Amy, from another reserve, was 15 when her mother told her she was to marry a young man from the Burrard Reserve. She cried all night and her parents let her wait a year before the marriage. Amy died a lingering death of cancer just weeks before Dan had to undergo his Academy Award ordeal.

When a bit player in the Los Angeles Music Centre called out the name of veteran British actor John Mills as the Best Supporting Actor for his role as the village idiot in *Ryan's Daughter,* Dan, nominated for his role in *Little Big Man,* turned and said, "I feel as if someone's just pulled a wet blanket off me."

"I'm glad in a way that he didn't get it," broadcaster Hilda Mortimer said later. She was one of the friends who accompanied him to Hollywood and who broke into tears when the result was announced. "You could just feel the trapdoor closing on all those people down there who wanted to *use* him. We sat in a room together the next day and waited for all those promised people who never came. The magazines. The agents. The studio people. The trapdoor simply closed."

The makers of *Little Big Man* first sought Sir Laurence Olivier for the role of Old Lodge Skins. Then they sought the brilliant Paul Scofield. Richard Boone was offered $300,000 for the part. Dan George received $16,000 for the same role. There is little of it left.

"The only thing Dan has ever bought for himself," says a friend, "was a secondhand 1964 Acadian with the money from his first movie. He'd never even had a car. That's gone. Someone smashed it up." Another part of the money went to natives in Peru and to Father Joseph Kane, who helped Dan before leaving BC for South America as a missionary.

• • •

Dan has never had much money. Mostly Indians and half-breeds were used in lumber handling when he went to work on the docks in

1920. Forty cents an hour, 10 hours a day. Four men packing 40-foot lengths of four-by-12s. ("I liked to sit and listen to him talk," remembers Sam Engler, a retired longshoreman who worked the same ships. "He seemed so cultured.")

Dan stayed at it for 27 years until a swinging timber, 24 inches square, crashed into him and tossed him 30 feet. It smashed all the muscles in his hip ("my bones were too strong to break") and brought on complications that caused one leg to shrink. He failed to get compensation and has never received any pension benefits from the now powerful International Longshoremen's and Warehousemen's Union.

"I could have fought the compensation people," he now says, "but it is the nature of our ancestors. We don't have the staying power of the white man. If we get a bad deal, we don't go back."

At a banquet not long ago, Dan told the story of the drunk staggering home late at night to find a sardonic wife who gently removed his shoes, slipped a pillow under his shaky head on the sofa and asked if he wanted to make love. "Oh we might as well," mumbled the drunk. "I'm going to get hell when I get home anyway."

The old man with the long white hair waited for the laughter to subside, then said, "That story's true, 'cause I was the man." They laughed at that, too, but while the story may have been apocryphal the message wasn't. There was a younger time on the docks when drink was a problem.

"We were Gang 44," remembers Dan, fondling the child at his knee. "I can remember when our number went up on the board at the hiring hall. Eleven men—you learn to know each other. We quit at three so there was always the beer parlor. We had pride in Gang 44. They called us the Wolf Pack." The interviewer recalls Wautsauk.

There were also those longshoring accidents that happened when a cargo of rum or whiskey arrived. A case dropped was a case that must be disposed of. "One of the reasons I quit the docks. Drink was getting into a habit. We raise our children by example. Not a good example coming home every night half-cut."

It was during these times that the problems of the succession to band leadership arose. Dan and the eldest brother Henry were enjoying life, perhaps too much so for the liking of old Chief Slaholte George. He surprised everyone by bypassing them and reaching 20 years down the family scale, naming 15-year-old son John as the next chief.

The responsibilities of the role were obviously heavy on a teen-age boy and eventually John George left to live in the United States. Dan was elected to succeed him and by the time he was voted out of office in 1963, after serving 12 years, he had begun his television appearances in the Cariboo series scripted by Vancouver journalist Paul St. Pierre, now the Liberal MP for Coast Chilcotin. The title "chief" naturally adhered to his publicity, but by this time his younger brother was back from the U.S. and affirmed by band vote as their leader.

"He thinks I don't like him," Dan says softly, gazing out the window toward the house where Chief John George lives. He turns away sadly. "How can you hate someone who's your brother?"

Dan has since been named "honorary chief" of both the Shuswap and Squamish tribes but the resentment from his brother runs deep. "Chief John L. George" is defiantly emblazoned on his mailbox down the road and from that position he must watch the steady procession of TV crews and reporters climbing the slope to Dan's house. It is not a pleasant situation. "You've got to understand," says someone close to the George family, "that there is internecine warfare on every reserve. You have people cooped up within a restricted space. It's bound to happen. It's just that there is practically no one but Georges on this reserve so they have to fight with one another." The apparent anger led to a vote which barred on of Dan's own daughters from reserve status. The vote was a product of the alienation between the brothers. Many of the band resent the hip world of Dan's son Lenny, who has brought some of the temptations of the young to the reserve and has married a white girl. Through all this contempt, the old man has been a bridge over troubled waters.

Slumped under a tree in front of his house is an old blue cart with "Dan George and his Indian Entertainers" printed on the side. The time is past when, with his children, he hauled that around to small rodeos, when his rickety-tick band played legion hall dances, Dan solemnly slapping the double bass and twirling it around as comic relief during the two-bar breaks.

• • •

Earlier this year 800 guests packed a Hotel Vancouver ballroom to see him accept the Canadian Council of Christians and Jews' prestigious Human Relations Award. As the TV cameras edged in, Dan slipped off his glasses and told of how his father, Chief Slaholte George, took him hunting as a boy for the first and last time. "He taught me to love animals," said Dan. "And for the next 19 years he taught me to love human beings. It is a proud feeling to be a man. We Indians have been luckier than most."

"A proud feeling to be a man." The words sat there and hung above that banquet room of dinner jackets, inhabited by businessmen who would go to office towers next morning to dispatch bits of paper to other office towers. "Luckier than most." It is a remarkable statement to come from an Indian and it comes from a man who has been acclaimed for adding dignity to his people while leveling bitter accusations at the white man.

"We used to talk of the 'noble red man,'" says Father Bert Dunlop, an Oblate who is a close adviser. "It became a cliché. But really, that's what Dan is. Noble."

A buoyant birthday crowd of 32,000 in Vancouver's Empire Stadium on July 1, 1967, was silenced by Dan George's speech, a noble figure on the field reciting his bitter soliloquy of how his people had been treated. A "Lament for Confederation" Dan called it:

"How long have I known you, O Canada? A hundred years. And many many *seelanum* more. And today, when you celebrate your hundred years, O Canada, I am sad for all the Indian people throughout the land.

"For I have known you when your forests were mine; when they gave me my meat and my clothing. I have known you in your streams and rivers where your fish flashed and danced in the sun, where the waters said come, come and eat of my abundance. I have known you in the freedom of your winds. And my spirit, like the winds, once roamed your good lands.

"But in the long hundred years since the white man came, I have seen my freedom disappear like the salmon going mysteriously out to sea. The white man's strange customs which I could not understand pressed down upon me until I could no longer breathe.

"When I fought to protect my land and my home, I was called a savage. When I neither understood nor welcomed this way of life, I was called lazy. When I tried to rule my people, I was stripped of my authority...

"O Canada, how can I celebrate with you this Centenary, this hundred years? Shall I thank you for the reserves that are left me of my beautiful forests For the canned fish of my rivers? For the loss of my pride and authority, even among my own people? For the lack of my will to fight back?"

His moving performance in George Ryga's play *The Ecstasy of Rita Joe* was not so much a role as a personal statement on the skid-road treatment of Indian women. It was not acting, but an acting out of himself, his own experience. I remember when the Playhouse Theatre took *Rita Joe* to the National Arts Centre and, the word of his performance seeping over to Parliament Hill, Prime Minister Trudeau and Justice Minister John Turner sought him out one night backstage, shaking his hand and peering into his eyes as if expecting to find therein the answers to a new government's guilt for past treatment of the native people. Afterward we went to a party at the home of an Ottawa millionaire, and, while the actresses frolicked in the pool and squealed in the sauna, Dan sat there, an island in a sea of theatrical kisses and celebrations. He wanted his slope.

It is Father Dunlop who helps him work out his speeches and soliloquies, the two of them working rather as a composer and a lyricist, sensing each other's moods and developing a theme.

• • •

He has become conscious of his power as a celebrity and often uses it to help his people. He is now a culture hero soliciting applause on entering any room. Aware of the power his presence has given him, he recently appeared as an expert witness at an inquest into the skid-road death of another Indian woman. A charge of discrimination involved daughter Marie, who trained as a hairdresser but couldn't get a job because "some of the white ladies didn't like an Indian touching them."

Then there was that fine moment in television when Dick Cavett asked him, "Is it any different being an Indian in Canada?"

"No," said Dan George.

Dan George's sense of being an Indian is a great distance from that of Red Power advocate Harold Cardinal, who takes fact-finding tours of New York's Bedford-Stuyvesant poor people's corporation and who talks of touring Israel's kibbutzim.

Dan George transcends Red Power, equaling its advocates in bitterness (they quote his speeches, while dropping the positive endings) but going beyond to the Indian roots of natural harmony and communion with the land and the living things on it.

It has been explained that *our* sense of time can be expressed in a series of tight circles—the boundaries of weekend to weekend, month to month, or year to year that govern our activities. The Indian has no such concept. Time for him is expressed as one long straight line, stretching off into the distance. It is why, Dan explains, the Indian has such trouble adapting to the white man's rigorous concern for fixed hours of work. "It is hard for others to understand. We keep things inside. Our sense of humor, everything. It's all inside."

"What Dan has taught me is the language of silence," says Kay Cronin, a gentle woman who is director of the Oblate Fathers communications centre. "Indian boys come into my office and may not speak for the first 10 minutes. You have to learn to empty your heart so that it can be a receptacle. Indians concentrate on perfecting human relationships. That's what Dan is so good at. *We* concentrate on acquiring material things."

She tells of conferences at the University of British Columbia, with all the experts delivering their papers on solutions to the Indian problem, "when suddenly they'll remember that perhaps they might ask the Indians. They turn to Dan and say, 'Now what do you think?' There is about 12 seconds of dead air. When he finally *does* speak, they're ready to listen.

"He's the only man I've seen who uses timing as well as Jack Benny. He uses the silence to communicate."

Phil Keatley, a Vancouver CBC producer, has guided his career and tried to protect him against those who would use him. It was Keatley who first recognized the acting potential inherent in the old man's natural dignity and soft expressiveness. It is Keatley who advises him on movie roles and it is Keatley who would like to see Dan cast in the role of a cardinal. On reflection, an interesting idea, not inappropriate.

• • •

Dan George's skill is not overly exploiting his role as a "chief" but in the meantime using the prestige it gives him to work for his people. It's a narrow trail to tread. He picks his spots and occasions, and with that remarkable timing and those electric spaces of silence leads us to a few insights into a man "luckier than most."

"I think we need to listen to him," says Kay Cronin, "not for what he can tell us about Indians but what he can tell us about ourselves." He's the portage over time.

Behind Dan's little house is the scraggly second growth that will no longer support game. As we walk down the hill away from the house, an ungainly freighter slides over the water, headed for the loading dock at the end of the inlet that will fill it with coal. A clothesline sags under the weight of the laundry of Bob George's 14 children. Across on the opposite bluff the Standard Oil refinery plans an expansion that would double its output.

"Eight years ago I dedicated myself to try to do something that would give a name to the Indian people," says Dan in his whisper. He pauses. "I feel I've attained my goal. Moving off the reserve is for another generation."

The puppy dogs yelp playfully around the aluminum trailer of Lenny George. We shake hands and I leave him on the slope—*his* slope—the copper moon of his face watching the water.

Allan Fotheringham, "Dan George's Last Stand," *Maclean's* (July, 1971), pp. 28-29, 50-52.

BARBARA FREEMAN

"EVERY STROKE UPWARD": WOMEN JOURNALISTS IN CANADA, 1880-1906

One morning, in the spring of 1904, Margaret Graham, a nineteen-year-old newspaper writer, marched into the Canadian Pacific Railways office in Montreal looking for publicity director George Ham. Her goal was to persuade him to take a group of newspaper women to the St. Louis World Exposition. He had earlier escorted a party of male journalists there, but had never offered the same trip to women writers. The angry Graham, Ham later wrote, felt that "women had altogether been ignobly ignored and she demonstratively demanded to know why poor downtrodden females should thus be so shabbily treated." He promised her that, if she could find a dozen press women, he would be happy to oblige her. She came up with fourteen and, true to his promise, Ham took them to St. Louis, in two private railway cars, free of charge.

Women who were working as journalists in Canada at the time were used to being disregarded by the men in the profession. Like women entering other fields, such as medicine and law, they found that they had to struggle to make their presence felt.

Some of the women on the St. Louis excursion were new to the newspaper world; others had been writing for years. Some wrote only for their home-town newspapers, while others moved all over

Canada during their journalism careers. There were francophones as well as anglophones, Easterners as well as women from the West.

Together, they were representative of those who had been entering a new profession for women—journalism—since the late 1800s. Their ranks included the "dean" of female literary journalists in Canada, Agnes Maule Machar of Kingston, Ontario; journalist-turned-novelist, Sara Jeannette Duncan; the popular women's page writer, "Kit" Coleman of the Toronto *Mail and Empire;* the Agriculture editor of the *Manitoba Free Press,* E. Cora Hind, who was one of the very few women in a senior editorial position; and the unconventional Maritimer, Kate Simpson Hayes, who eventually brought them all together as members of the Canadian Women's Press Club.

Their reasons for becoming journalists varied. Some had always wanted to write; others entered the field because they suddenly found themselves without financial support and needed to make a living. They were single, married, separated and widowed, with and without children. All were, however, educated, middle-class women who were doing something quite untypical for many women of their generation—pursuing a career.

Like many pioneers, these women often found the going rough. Before the mid-1880s, women were not allowed into newspaper offices at all, with their gruff male inhabitants banging away at typewriters beneath clouds of tobacco smoke. Newsrooms were dirty, noisy places and considered quite unsuitable for respectable middle-class women. According to newspaperman Hector Charlesworth, men wrote the scattered bits of "women's news" until the 1880s when newspapers became more compartmentalized—partly to appeal to advertisers—and the women's pages were created. The few women who were already working for newspapers as short story writers, literary journalists or society editors, did so at home and sent their items in by messenger.

In the nineteenth century, there was no firm division between creative writing and journalism. Newspapers often published short stories, poetry, book reviews, opinion columns and editorials, all written by the same people.

One of the most prolific was Agnes Maule Machar (1837-1927); she wrote novels, poetry and opinion pieces on issues close to her heart (such as temperance, education for women, and improvements to the squalid living conditions endured by working-class people). Her work appeared mainly in periodicals such as *Rose-Bedford's Canadian*

Monthly and National Review and *The Week*, during the 1870s, '80s and '90s. She also contributed to the Toronto *Globe* and other daily newspapers, and continued to write well into the 1920s.

Machar was a rarity among women of her generation. She was well educated by her father, who was the second principal of Queen's College in Kingston, decades before girls in Canada were given equal education with boys. It was a time when women writers often disguised their presence on the literary scene by using male *nom-de-plumes* or by remaining anonymous—ploys that allowed them some success while upholding the Victorian code of female modesty. It was considered unseemly for a middle-class woman to "go public" about anything.

Machar was an early "social gospel" advocate in Canada who felt that practical application of the lessons from the Sermon on the Mount did more good in this world than piety without action. Much of her writing dealt with this theme.

For a long time, apparently to please her conservative mother, Machar did not sign her name to her articles. Upon reaching middle age, she finally began to use a pen-name, "Fidelis," a reflection of her strong Christian faith. The use of pen-names such as hers was a common practice among journalists of both sexes, but particularly for women, who often took on a male persona. For example, Sara Jeannette Duncan (1861-1922) enjoyed a meteoric early career as "Garth Grafton" before she finally began to sign her own name to her work.

Duncan was a young career woman of the 1880s—a member of the generation that succeeded Agnes Maule Machar's. She started at the Brantford *Expositor*, her Ontario hometown newspaper, moved to Washington where she wrote editorials for the *Post*, and later returned to Canada as women's page editor of the *Globe* and then as Ottawa correspondent for the *Montreal Star* and *The Week*.

This was an amazing record of journalistic accomplishment for a woman who was still in her twenties. But despite this success, she was still cautious about her vulnerability as a woman writer. One way to circumvent unfair criticism, she once explained, was to use a male *nom-de-plume:*

> *. . . in the case of a distinctively masculine pen-name as George Eliot or Charles Egbert Craddock, I believe the selection is due to a dread of that instinctive bias in criticism which a woman's acknowledged literary effort invariably suffers* (Toronto *Globe*, May 27, 1885).

Duncan had her own biases about what women could accomplish in journalism. She believed women could write literary criticism, political and social commentary, advice columns and travel features. But she drew the line at day-to-day news reporting with its strict deadlines: she did not believe that women could think and work fast enough for that kind of assignment. Her bias was consistent with her middle-of-the-road approach (for the time) on other issues: she believed, for example, that women should have the vote but that they did not know enough about the law to be Members of Parliament.

Duncan herself had been the victim of some prejudice in the journalism field. As a rookie, she once approached a Toronto newspaper editor, E.E. Sheppard, and asked him for a job. He turned her down, explaining that the last woman he had hired had not done a good job. Years later, he rued that day in print, devoting much of his column to praise of Duncan's writing ability and literary success. Certainly, Duncan can be given much credit for opening the eyes of male editors to the potential of female journalists. She represents a transition point between the somewhat elite intellectual journalist and the everyday women's page editor: she was both in her time.

The women's page offered the most opportunity for ambitious female writers because it was the only editorial department of a newspaper in which women were generally welcome. Of course, they were not treated the same as the men. Their male editors often refused to take them seriously because they wrote "women's" news—and indeed, whatever their ambitions, they were relegated to the women's pages from the start. Very few managed to slip over the gender border into the "male" reporting areas of politics, business and crime. Those who did—like Duncan, Cora Hind and occasionally "Kit" Coleman—received greater recognition than most of their female colleagues.

Kathleen Blake Coleman, "Kit" of the Toronto *Mail*, was the most popular woman's page writer of late nineteenth century Canada. Her Saturday page, "Women's Kingdom," appealed to both sexes, thereby helping to boost the *Mail's* circulation. Coleman (1864-1915) was a tall, spirited red-head, of aristocratic Irish connections, with a bright, lively and sometimes irreverent style. She did not confine her writing to fashion notes and recipes, but commented on most of the political and social events of her day.

In fact, it is a mistake to assume that the women's pages were less than serious journalistic efforts. Coleman, like Duncan and other female colleagues, was very much interested in federal politics; Canada's relations with Britain; international events and many social concerns (such as the movement of women into the workforce, female suffrage, street urchins, poverty, prostitution, and temperance).

"Kit," a small-l liberal with conservative leanings, had her opinions on all of these issues, as did the other writers. Her politics were not always consistent, but they did reflect the experiences of a woman brought up in a genteel environment who never expected to have to earn her own living.

Kathleen Blake was born near Galway in western Ireland and had a privileged upbringing, during which she received a good education. At sixteen, her parents persuaded her to marry a local squire who was forty years her senior—apparently their attempt to keep the family finances in order. But when her husband died four years later, he left her destitute.

The young widow emigrated to Canada, worked as a secretary in Toronto, married her boss, E.J. Watkins, and moved to Winnipeg, where she had two children, a girl and a boy. When her second husband died suddenly, she moved back to Toronto where she did freelance writing to support herself and her children. When she was hired by the *Mail* in 1889, she became an immediate success and was a leading figure in journalism for the next twenty-five years. She was, in fact, a self-made woman and proud of it.

This is not to say that she bacame a rich woman. The pay for both sexes in journalism was poor and it was usually worse for women, because their work was not considered as important as the men's. There were no paid holidays, or unions, or other advantages for the newspaper writer of either sex. When Coleman first started in the business, she made $20 a month—not much more than a domestic servant—and had to do light housekeeping overtime to make ends meet. Even after she became a successful writer, she complained of long hours, few holidays and inadequate pay. One source has it that she received $35 a week from the day she was hired—a generous sum for the time. It is more likely that she was earning that much by the time she quit the *Mail* in 1911 and began syndicating her columns at $5 each.

Her popularity did mean that her editors gave her certain privileges. Unlike most women's page writers, "Kit" was occasionally allowed to escape in order to cover events in other parts of the world.

In 1898, after much wrangling with the United States Army, she managed to make her way to Cuba to write about the grim conditions being suffered by young soldiers fighting in the Spanish-American war. On another occasion, in Cleveland, she smuggled herself into the cell of a notorious female fraud artist, Cassie Chadwick, and got an exclusive story.

It cannot be said that "Kit" was typical of women's page writers. Few were as sophisticated, as bright or wrote as well as she did. But she was the acknowledged leader in her field at the time and, by all accounts, well-loved by most of her sister-journalists, especially the young "cubs," who looked to her for encouragement and advice.

"Kit" would tell them that a woman must serve her apprenticeship, as hard and discouraging as rejection letters from editors could be, if she expected to be successful. But an awareness of one's image as a woman was also important in journalism:

> *...and if she would try to infuse a little of her charming femininity into her writings—then, indeed, she will be a great success. Her individuality will shine out strongly, and she will charm, intoxicate and allure you in dull, cold type just as much, perhaps more, than if you were sitting beside her, looking into the depths of her soft eyes* (Toronto *Mail*, November 16, 1889).

It is clear that writing was becoming acceptable as a profession for women—as long as the writers in question maintained a certain propriety in print. Female pen-names were now preferred and were commonly used from the time the women's pages were established. There were, of course, exceptions to the rule: there were mavericks among the women journalists in Canada who, for one reason or another, did not conform to social expectations.

One was E. Cora Hind, the Agriculture and Commercial Editor of the *Manitoba Free Press*. When she first applied there for a newspaper job in 1882, she was turned down because she was a woman. She set up a typewriting service, got to know the farmers and businessmen who were her clients, and started writing freelance articles about the agricultural market. When newspaper editors urged her to use E.C. Hind as her byline, she refused, insisting on E. Cora Hind because she wanted her readers to know she was a woman.

By the time she was finally hired by the *Free Press* in 1902, Hind had established a reputation as an agricultural expert, one she maintained for the next forty years. She became world-renowned for the accuracy of her crop forecasts—and the acidity of her tongue in the face of male disapproval.

But maintaining a feminine image was important to her as well. Because Hind brooked no nonsense, did a "man's job" and never married, it was easy for her detractors to question her femininity. Probably the best-known photograph of her shows her standing in a field, dressed in what was considered masculine attire—riding britches, boots and a scout's hat—examining a sheaf of wheat. This particular image of the woman on the job appears to have made some of her more protective women friends uneasy. They were quick to point out that when Hind was not out on her rural rounds, she wore dresses, large feminine hats, and always had her knitting basket by her side. She was, one younger contemporary recalls today, a very "womanly" woman, who loved to crochet lacey underwear for her female friends!

There were other women who maintained a proper outward image, but who were not typical of their generation. One of the more interesting women in journalism was Kate Simpson Hayes, who worked in a number of Canadian cities and was well-respected by her peers, despite a very unconventional private life.

Hayes started her career in 1873 at the age of sixteen, writing a children's column under the byline "Ivy" for the *St. Croix Courier* in St. Stephen, New Brunswick, for the sum of one dollar a year. As an adult she taught school for a while, and then married a senator. But the marriage failed and, despite her Roman Catholic upbringing, Hayes left her husband and struck out on her own. During her career, she worked as George Ham's assistant in the CPR offices in Montreal and, as "Mary Markwell," first women's page editor of the *Manitoba Free Press*. Eventually she moved to Ottawa to work as a journalist and, not incidentally, to be with her married lover, Nicholas Flood Davin, a journalist-turned-Member of Parliament.

Her private life probably did raise eyebrows among her sister-journalists, but Hayes filled a prominent role among them as the organizer of the Canadian Women's Press Club. The club had been "Kit" Coleman's idea, an offspring of George Ham's trip to the St. Louis Exposition, and Coleman was its first president. But it wasn't until 1906, when Hayes organized its first national conference in Winnipeg, that the fifty-member club became firmly established and branches started to spring up across Canada.

From its beginning the CWPC deliberately cultivated a professional, patriotic image—but an intriguing clause referring to its members' proper "social and moral connections" was discreetly dropped from its constitution at that first conference. The club's records do not explain what happened, but it appears that the women agreed not to judge each other's private circumstances, but to emphasize professional qualifications. It is likely that Hayes, who took over as president, had something to do with the change.

The press club's members were prominent and not-so-prominent women who had been working in various capacities on newspapers and other publications across Canada for years, but who had never before banded together for mutual professional and personal support. The members included Agnes Maule Machar, Sara Jeannette Duncan (married by then and writing novels in India), "Kit" Coleman, E. Cora Hind, and Kate Simpson Hayes. Other names that appeared on the membership list were: Lucy Maud Montgomery, former society editor of the Halifax *Echo* and future novelist; Robertine ("Francoise") Barry, who had her own women's weekly, *Le Journal de Francoise* in Montreal and who led the francophone contingent of the press club; Sara McLagan, the first female newspaper publisher in Canada, who took over the Vancouver *World* from her late husband; Agnes Deans Cameron, who explored the Canadian North and made her living by writing and lecturing about her adventures; and small-town newspaper journalists such as Gertrude Balmer Watt, the cub reporter "Peggy" of the Woodstock, Ontario, *Sentinel Review.*

Full of optimism, they adopted a motto for their club—"Every Stroke Upward"—and vowed to work together to advance journalism as a career for women—women who wanted to write in their own names, do whatever job in journalism they wanted to do, and be considered the professional equals of the men with whom they worked. In 1906, after more than twenty years in the profession, they wanted women journalists to be given the recognition they so rightly felt they deserved.

Barbara Freeman, "'Every Stroke Upward:' Women Journalists in Canada, 1880-1906," *Canadian Women Studies,* Vol. 17, No. 3 (Fall, 1986), pp. 43-46.

ROBERT FULFORD

CHARTER OF WRONGS

The Constitution is what the judges say it is.
—U.S. CHIEF JUSTICE CHARLES EVANS HUGHES

Nobody ever called Pierre Trudeau a supporter of the American way of life, but it has recently become clear that in a strange and unexpected way he presided over the Americanization of Canada. It has been commonplace for a long time to say that our major political institutions have been growing steadily closer to those of the United States: the concentration of power in the person of the prime minister has often and justly been called "presidential," and our political parties—with their flamboyant and expensive leadership conventions, their opinion polling, and their TV advertising—have slavishly copied the American models, often bringing in hired American experts to tell them how to do it. It might be argued, however, that these are simply modern practices and techniques, made inevitable by the growth of government and mass communications. But the principle that Trudeau brought us with the Canadian Charter of Rights and Freedoms is absolutely and intrinsically American and reaches back to the roots of the U.S. Constitution in the eighteenth century. It is the principle that judges know better than politicians what is good for everyone.

Trudeau, of course, is the main author of the Charter, and many a future history book will cite it as his main legacy; but his two predecessors, John Diefenbaker and Lester Pearson, will deserve mention as collaborators. During all his years in opposition Diefenbaker campaigned for a bill of rights, and as prime minister he put one through Parliament. That wasn't "entrenched," however—it was a bill like all others and could be erased by Parliament as easily as it was passed. Diefenbaker wanted a permanent and relatively untouchable bill, but couldn't get it. Pearson, when Trudeau was his justice minister, proposed to follow through on Diefenbaker's earlier idea—a bill that would be agreed on by the provinces, would be written in the constitution, and could not easily be breached by Parliament or a provincial legislature. Pearson failed too, but Trudeau took up the idea and tirelessly pursued it through meeting after meeting with the provincial premiers. In general, they didn't like it—at times they vehemently opposed it—but Trudeau wore them down. His Charter became a crusade, and as he and his ministers pushed the idea it grew popular. After a while entrenched rights seemed necessary, and then they seemed inevitable. Some Canadians must have begun to wonder how in the world we had ever managed so long without them. Voices opposing the idea grew steadily weaker. When Premier Sterling Lyon of Manitoba said in 1980 that an entrenched charter of rights would be inconsistent with democratic theory or even with the principles of parliamentary government, he was easily dismissed as a reactionary Tory standing in the way of national progress. So in 1982, along with patriation, the Charter of Rights and Freedoms became constitutional. All of us, overnight, were freer.

Or were we? Did we, before 1982, suffer under some form of tyranny? Our democracy was surely imperfect, our governments made mistakes and infringed our rights—as all governments, even the best, sometimes do. But were we any less free than the citizens of those democracies, such as the United States, with constitutionally entrenched rights? I never heard anyone say we were, except during the autumn of 1970, when the Trudeau government used the arbitrary powers of the War Measures Act to deal with the October Crisis (whether the Charter would prevent a recurrence of that, we may never know). And yet our governments agreed that we needed *guaranteed* freedoms, not just the (perhaps) temporary freedoms under which we had been living for generations, first as British subjects and then as Canadians with the British tradition of parliamentary supremacy. Parliament, and the people we had sent to it, were till 1982 the main guarantee of our rights. Now we had rights that were written down, and would be enforced by court orders. Parliament and the legislatures might pass laws limiting or threatening our freedom; but we would have recourse to the judges, who would then make certain that our rights were not abridged. In future the politicians could override these rights only with difficulty—and would in the process be publicly perceived as being guilty of breaching the Charter, now a sacred document.

• • •

When Chief Justice Earl Warren wrote the U.S. Supreme Court's unanimous decision in *Brown v. Board of Education of Topeka, Kansas,* in 1954, he changed the course of American life. This was perhaps the most important single judgment of a court anywhere in the world in modern times. With a stroke the Warren Court made the pernicious practice of segregated public education illegal and started the process of broadening civil rights for blacks. Everywhere, people of liberal views rejoiced. The U.S. Constitution, speaking through Warren and his brethren, had beaten down the racism of state legislatures and local school boards.

It would be hard to argue that the Warren Court was wrong that day, but the judicial events that followed were not in all cases so clearly beneficial. The U.S. Supreme Court became "activist," and began handing down rulings on every aspect of American public life. Lower courts swiftly followed in the Supreme Court's wake. The United States became, to a degree it had not been before, a court-driven society. The citizens became more litigious than at any previous time or place in the history of civilization. It came to be assumed that rights of almost every kind were defined in court. Soon it was routine for U.S. city governments, state legislatures, Congress, and even the president to defer to the courts. Should white students from the suburbs of Boston be sent by bus to school in downtown Boston, and black students from the slums in the city core sent to the suburbs? The court would decide. Then how many students should be bused, from exactly where to exactly where? The court would decide that, too.

When Chief Justice Hughes said, half a century ago, that the Constitution is what the judges say it is, he was talking about the broad principles of the Constitution. He didn't mean that judges should be expected to dictate every detail of public policy; but that is what eventually came to pass. Not everyone agreed that this was ideal democratic practice, or even an improvement over rule by politicians. Inevitably, many Americans have grown restive under the power of the courts. Certain presidents, most recently Ronald Reagan, have tried to curb that power by appointing judges with more modest views of judicial discretion. So far, these appointments have not made a notable change. In 1967 the great American legal philosopher, Sidney Hook, wrote: "One recent and not uninfluential view maintains that no law can be properly regarded as the law of democratic American society until it has been validated by the United States Supreme Court." At the time Hook meant it almost satirically; he raised the point only to denounce it. Today that quotation would be close to a description of reality. American law is now judge-made law.

And so, increasingly, is Canadian law. Before 1982, Canadian law rested on the principle of parliamentary supremacy. Then, the courts could do little more than interpret Parliament's will; now they can say that Parliament is wrong. As D.D. Carter of the Queen's University law faculty recently put it, "The Charter now allows our courts to overrule legislation... This shift of authority is nothing less than a fundamental alteration of our constitutional arrangements." Carter admitted that in 1982 he expected nothing of the kind. After all, the Charter said that the guarantees of fundamental freedoms were to be qualified by the limits that could reasonably be justified in a free society. Moreover, Canadian judges had traditionally been cautious about dealing with political and economic issues. As Carter then saw it, the Charter would certainly apply to criminal justice and to language rights; but it would not, surely, affect in any serious way those areas where ground rules were already settled.

Carter, like many others, was wrong. Emboldened by their new powers, judges have decided that every arrangement that comes before them can be tested against the Charter. More important, they have apparently determined that anyone who defends established practices must accept the responsibility of demonstrating that these practices are consistent with the Charter. In Carter's specialty, industrial relations, the result may be chaos. Challenges that are now moving through the judicial system threaten labour laws that unions took generations to win. Is the certification process, a key element in orderly labour relations, consistent with the Charter? No-one knows for sure. Is collective bargaining itself protected by the Charter? That's unclear too. For decades Canadian law has tended to favour collective rights over individual rights; the Charter may reverse that preference. Carter's conclusion: "The Charter now creates the potential for virtually every labour relations issue to be outfitted in constitutional clothing, handing over to constitutional lawyers and judges a wide discretion to re-shape the Canadian labour law system."

That is not what the Charter's most fervent supporters intended. Tommy Douglas, the first national leader of the New Democrats, was an early advocate of an entrenched bill of rights; David Lewis, the second national leader, was equally enthusiastic. Were they alive today, would they be delighted to see that the Charter is now threatening the future of the labour movement? How would they greet the news that the right of labour unions to donate money to political parties—a right that makes the NDP possible—is now in jeopardy because of a challenge under the Charter sponsored by the National Citizens' Coalition?

• • •

Many a lawyer, it now seems clear, will be made wealthy by the Charter. A major constitutional challenge, running right up to the Supreme Court, can consume hundreds of thousands of dollars. Only those who can pay exhorbitant lawyers' fees will pursue such a challenge; the logical inference is that the Charter will, in the long term, favour the rich. Corporations have happily fastened on the idea that a corporation, in law, can have the same status as a person; a corporation, therefore, can use the Charter as easily as a person can, and with less financial pain. Last spring the *Globe and Mail's* Report on Business told its readers: "The jury is still out on exactly how widely the courts will apply Charter rights to business. But the early trends are favorable to corporate interests." It should be no surprise that judges, most of them drawn from the same class that produces managers and owners, will listen carefully to the complaints of corporations.

Almost anything done by Parliament or a legislature can be challenged. The doctors of Ontario, by making their dispute over extra-billing into a Charter case, may defeat the government and win the right to charge whatever their patients can pay. Those of us who happen to support the doctors may be momentarily pleased. But will we be happy that the majority decision of the Ontario legislature, enthusiastically supported by the electorate, has been overturned? Will we be as anxious to defer to judicial review when a government measure we support is under attack?

American constitutional theorists have often argued that judicial supremacy is a check on the irrational impulses of the mob, that judges can be relied upon to overturn those laws that are pushed through the democratic process by the passions of the moment. But judges may be as susceptible as anyone else to fashions in ideology; and, unlike politicians, they cannot easily be unseated when their views prove unpalatable to the citizens. Sidney Hook, in *The Paradoxes of Freedom,* asked: "If the Court is to serve as the keeper of the community's conscience, who is to keep the Court's conscience?" Canadians know very little about their judges (far less than Americans know). For all of our history, until now, judges have been distant figures who applied—for the most part uncontroversially—the laws. Now we have asked the same people not only to apply but to reshape and even (when they please) overturn the laws. They are plunged deeply into what we normally think of as the political process—defining who can do what, balancing this need against that right, determining which cause deserves society's sympathetic attention and which does not. And yet they remain above that process. Who dares to picket a judge? Who (the contempt-of-court rules being what they are) will dare to scrutinize and criticize the judges as we normally scrutinize and criticize the politicians? Since so many broad business issues will be decided by the courts, will it soon be necessary to examine the financial holdings of judges, as we now examine those of cabinet ministers?

Trudeau recognized, rightly, that there are elected politicians who can—out of stupidity or lust for power—turn into dictators. He set out to save us from them. Instead, he created a whole new class of potential dictators. The Charter was the great legal project of Trudeau's generation; undoing it may turn out to be the great legal project of the generation following him.

Robert Fulford, "Charter of Wrongs," *Saturday Night*, (December, 1986), pp. 7-9.

SANDRA GWYN

OVER HOME

The Union Jack flew over my childhood: Newfoundland, in the 1930s and 1940s, was still "Britain's oldest colony," and proud of it. On July 1, we mourned rather than celebrated, for this was the anniversary of the day in 1916 when the Royal Newfoundland Regiment went over the top at Beaumont-Hamel, as gallantly and as disastrously as the Light Brigade. Victoria, where I entered my teens, was still, circa 1949, a colony in spirit, ruled by elderly colonels with salmon flies in their hats. (At the Oak Bay theatre, behind a façade that resembled Anne Hathaway's cottage, my best friend, Janet, and I watched transfixed as James Mason peered down Margaret Lockwood's cleavage in *The Wicked Lady*.)

In the 1950s Dalhousie University in Halifax liked to think of itself as Canada's equivalent to Edinburgh University. Being a pseudo-Scot meant reading, *really* reading, English literature. The benefit of this was that when I went off to London in 1956, the season of Suez, to become cultured and sophisticated (but really to grow up), I could find my way round without a map. Upon Westminster Bridge I stood with William Wordsworth and agreed that earth had not anything to show more fair. Up Bond Street I streamed, with Virginia Woolf's Mrs. Dalloway; down King William Street I flowed with T.S. Eliot, listening, in front of Saint Mary Woolnoth, for the "dead sound on the final stroke of nine."

There was another reason for my happy haze in London, though it didn't occur to me until much later. Being Canadian was a plus—not an A-plus, but a solid B. Being Canadian may even have got me my first job, as a glorified gofer at the Institute of Contemporary Arts, where the deputy director, Lawrence Alloway (he minted the phrase "Pop Art"), kept talking about this "incredible Canadian" whose name I'd never heard—Marshall McLuhan. In the newspapers, Lester Pearson's name kept cropping up for having done something worthy at the U.N. The Brits I met were always asking about Canada because, "Well, I'm thinking about hopping across the pond myself." We'd done well in the war, and in the 1950s we were doing extraordinarily well: Kitimat, Laborador iron ore, the St. Lawrence Seaway.

Time passed. I came home, married one of those Brits who'd jumped over the pond a few years earlier, and became a Canadian in my marrow—not just because Joey Smallwood and Mackenzie King had conspired to make me one by act of parliament. I even became an Ottawa-phile. More time passed and then came a chance my husband could not pass up: a posting to London to look out from there at the world. My own leave-taking was ambivalent. Not only was I rooted deep in my own country, I was becoming obsessed with its history. But it meant going back to a city that has always filled a large space in my imagination, a city in which I had been young.

I knew London, thirty years on, would no longer be the city I'd fallen in love with. It would be grubbier, poorer, manifestly no longer the capital of a great power. And I was now approaching it not from a quasi-colony but from a pretty sophisticated middle power. What I hadn't counted on discovering was that London had retained no space in its imagination for me—which is to say, for my country.

The moment of truth arrived early, when a British journalist invited us over for drinks. I was delighted—it meant we'd left the security blanket of other expatriate Canadians—to realize that everyone else in the room was a Brit. I was standing by the fireplace absorbing the sociology of it all—people were much more casually dressed than at comparable get-togethers in Cabbagetown or New Edinburgh, but the Brie and Soave and stripped pine were much the same—when a BBC type came over, muttered his name in the incomprehensible British way, and remarked that the host had told him I was a Canadian writer. I nodded, and got all set to be interesting. "Frankly," he continued, "I wasn't aware there were any writers in Canada."

Two other moments followed in quick succession. "I've got some cousins in Canada," remarked a literary agent. "They're the dreariest people I know." Then a snatch of conversation overheard while en route to refill my glass: "Such a boring game, Trivial Pursuit. You might know it was invented by Canadians."

Except that our hosts couldn't have been nicer, and that my husband was somewhere out there making contacts, I'd probably have got into a shouting match. A sense of proportion—a Canadian sense, that is—soon overcame my hurt and fury. These Brits, I had to recognize, were neither upper-class twits nor rough-edged yobs. They were nice talky literary types who probably voted Social Democratic and ran round Hyde Park for SportAid. They hadn't even realized they were being rude. They were—this hit me going home in the taxi—exactly like the people I'd known in Ottawa and Toronto who'd been gratuitously rude about Newfoundland and then puzzled when I'd raged at their jokes. The Brits view Canada nowadays much as Canadians used to view Newfoundland—and, to a degree, still do. An easy joke. A target that doesn't fight back. A place about which it has become socially acceptable to be contemptuous.

• • •

"Below is the list of the six words most commonly associated with Canada, in descending order: 1. Mounties 2. Forests/Lakes/Mountains/Rocks/Trees 3. Snow/Cold weather 4. Niagara Falls 5. Log Cabins 6. Ice Hockey." Tom Ferns, a bright eighteen-year old from Hamilton, Ontario, doing an exchange year at a college in Warwickshire, assembled this list by polling his forty-three classmates. He also collected these teenage comments about his country. "I know there's a French part, and I know there's a cold part and some mountains"; "It's governed by the Queen"; "Lots of lumberjacks"; "They eat maple syrup." The comment I like best was, "The people there are crazy about the Queen and they can't talk properly."

The striking thing about Ferns's findings is that the grandparents, maybe even the great-grandparents of his respondents would have answered his questions about Canada in the same way. But for that brief blip in the late 1950s (which I'd happened to witness), Canada is stuck with a set of perceptions that were fixed, immutably, about the time that *Saturday Night* was born.

The first purveyors of the Canadian image to the British public were the late-Victorian governors general: Dufferin, Lorne, Lansdowne, Stanley, Aberdeen, Minto. These proconsuls were both gatekeepers—British opinion-makers such as Rudyard Kipling and the young Winston Churchill always made Rideau Hall their first stop—and mythmakers. The Canada they invented was shaped by the two governing principles of late-Victorian aristocrats: the dream of empire and the ideal of chivalry.

They had their work cut out for them. Up until about the mid-1870s, the prevailing image of Canada had been established by Susanna Moodie, the author in 1852 of *Roughing It in the Bush:* cold, inhospitable, uncouth. But once Disraeli was in office and imperialism in flower, Canada, as the northern star in the crown, had to be made interesting. For Dufferin, the answer was to turn coldness and inhospitality to advantage, to make Canada both exotic and feminine, a kind of *princesse lointaine* living in an ice palace, the perfect foil for his manly virtue. Dufferin embraced the cold, challenged it, wooed it with torch-lit skating parties and imperial progressions on snowshoe. "Thermometer 20° below zero.... D. wears less than he used to do in May at home, and scarcely seems to feel the cold at all," his countess marvelled. The magic worked. Canada, in Kipling's phrase, became "Our Lady of the Snows," "Daughter am I in my mother's house, but mistress in my own."

For Dufferin's most energetic successor, the fourth Earl of Minto, it was Canada's vast emptiness that brought out the imperial gusto. In 1885 he fought in the North West Rebellion. In 1901, as governor general, he revisited the old battlefields by covered wagon. Westerners, he wrote, were "splendid people, one finds them refined, full of energy, and one sighs to think of the stupid duchesses to be found in the old country." It was Minto who organized the team of voyageurs sent out to relieve Gordon at Khartoum in 1884; it was also Minto who, in 1900, assisted the government in sending mounted horsemen to help Kitchener chase Boers across the veld. In the British imagination, Our Lady of the Snows now had a companion, the gallant Canuck in his scarlet tunic. Before long, the North West Mounted Police became the RCMP.

By the first decade of the new century, the image of Canada as a kind of *Boy's Own Magazine* version of Camelot—less seductive than India or Africa yet attractive because it was manly, straightforward, and healthy—had taken root. Out came thousands of young squires to start ranches in the Alberta foothills or to plant fruit trees in the Okanagan, the "gentlemen emigrants" as Patrick Dunae called them in his 1981 social history. Out to inspect, on a CPR freebie, came the most celebrated lady novelist of the day, Mrs. Humphry Ward. "In Canada, the jaded will still has room to work," she burbled in her 1910 romance, *Canadian Born.* "Where in Europe can you match the sense of... boundless space, boundless opportunity?"

The First World War put an end to most of that. Boundlessness, it developed, had limitations. In the trenches, Canadians discovered they had more in common with Yankee soldiers than with British ones. The Brits stopped looking westward after the Armistice. They yearned for hot countries, wanted to be jaded again, turned to rubber plantations in Malaya or dusky maidens in Tahiti as depicted by Somerset Maugham. Despite the best efforts of Grey Owl and John Buchan, who as governor general in the late 1930s set his novel *Sick Heart River* in the Arctic, Canada slipped out of fashion. Grey Owl was exposed as a fraud. *Sick Heart River* was a flop. "Being here is much the same as if one were in Baffin Land," Wyndham Lewis wrote from Toronto in 1942. He described Toronto as a "sanctimonious icebox."

Only once, in the 1950s, when Pearsonian charm and postwar boom made us seem an attractive alternative to British austerity, has attention returned. Otherwise, nothing that's happened in Canada has made much difference. Not bilingualism. Not multiculturalism. Not Toronto, the city that works. Not Stratford, the Montreal Symphony, Roy Thomson Hall, or the CBC, even though the BBC hasn't a single interviewer who can hold a candle to Gzowski or Gabereau (in the opinion of the British novelist and playwright John Mortimer). "It's very, very difficult to budge the preconceptions," says Margaret Horsfield, a British Columbian who is one of the BBC's top radio freelancers and has managed to get about ten programmes about Canada on air—from Susanna Moodie to life on an oil rig. "You have to go over the ground that they know—the Mounties, Grey Owl, and so on—and then maybe, just maybe, you can surprise them."

The best illustration of what we're up against can be found in a piece by Jean Rook in the *Daily Express* in 1984. The Queen was in Toronto and Canadian reporters had made some faintly lese-majesty comments about her clothes. Rook blasted back. "Of all wet, wooden places at the end of the earth, Canada has a nerve to criticize.... Canada is a bore—all three-and-a-half million square miles of it. In winter, it's a great white waste of time. The rest of the year it's under water, or leaves.... You can't see what few people there are for trees."

To be seen that way is irritating, even though—struggling to be fair and balanced and *Canadian*—I rather admire the resolute vigour of her attack. But read Rook's statement closely and you realize she's the Susanna Moodie of the 1980s. To Rook, and to most of her readers, Canada today is exactly what it was to Moodie: a great white waste of time.

This led me on to another moment of truth. The reason why the nicest people, like the BBC type at the party, say the rudest things straight to your face is that they don't realize you're there. We are an invisible people. "He came from nowhere and accomplished great things," reads the inscription on the memorial plaque to Roy Thomson in St. Paul's Cathedral. Except for the *Financial Times,* no British newspaper or television network has a full-time reporter in Canada. They don't believe there's anyone there to write about—and in this age of media, not to be written about or video-taped is not to exist.

• • •

"Respondents were asked to jot down what sprang to their mind when they thought of North America for a holiday destination." Thus reads the introductory section of an analysis of interviews with Brits, aged twenty-five to forty-five, recently conducted on behalf of Tourism Canada. "For many," the report continued, "'America' seemed to be the operative word, and the picture that emerged was of the U.S.A. The stereotype... was one of excitement, variety, a faster life-style.... Most people had quite vivid images of the U.S.A. gleaned from films and TV series.... Even the violence... portrayed on film and TV does not seem to be off-putting—indeed, may even add some excitement to the idea of visiting the U.S.A."

When discussion at last got round to Canada—was "forced" to get round to it, as the report writer noted with a hint of asperity—respondents conceded that "it must have some decent weather for some of the time but they seemed generally uncertain.... As one woman commented, 'I've never heard of anyone just going to Canada for a holiday.'"

Simply because it was so monochromatic and understated, the Tourism Canada report reinforced my own subjective findings—the chorus of taxi drivers, greengrocers, hairdressers, dishwasher-installers all asking the same old question: "What part of the States d'you come from, luv?" One of our problems, clearly, is that we aren't troublesome. "It is hard to love a country if it doesn't also awaken a measure of awe and fear," Michael Ignatieff, the Canadian writer now living in London, remarked in an essay. "I love Canada, but the trouble is, there's no sense of danger," the Ottawa-born novelist and poet Elizabeth Smart said to me not long before she died. The Brits may fear and at times hate the U.S., but they also love it. We, the nice guys, get noticed last.

There's a related problem. Once upon a time we were the North American gatekeepers for the Brits, a familiar and welcoming point of entry into the continent. Now, they go directly to the U.S. Mortimer, the day I interviewed him, was in between trips to New York and Los

Angeles. An old Dalhousie friend, the playwright Simon (*Butley*) Gray, has just got back from three months in New York; my downstairs neighbour, a merchant banker, hops over to Houston regularly. British culture has become Anglo-American culture. The links are political, financial, economic, cultural, artistic, journalistic. Today's gentlemen emigrants don't need Canada any more. They go directly to the North American heartland. So they don't notice us.

That the British should find the U.S. more exciting and more profitable than Canada isn't surprising. We're used to being overshadowed. But as my time here had made painfully clear, a much smaller planet is pushing us into the shadows. "Australia," said my sister-in-law, "is such a vivid kind of country."

• • •

Those bloody Australians. Almost all of my interviews—"Tell me honestly, what d'you think of us?"—turned at around midpoint into a one-sided conversation about Australians. This really drove me foolish, because my memories of British opinion about Australians go back to the late 1950s. Then, Aussies hung out in digs round the Earl's Court tube station and sallied out only in groups. Mostly, they drank beer and got into arguments and, as a blessed relief from those two activities, launched into off-key choruses of "Tie Me Kangaroo Down, Sport." They were, as everyone knew, uncultured and crude, and defensive-aggressive because they knew they were uncultured and crude.

Since then the Australians have produced *Gallipoli, Breaker Morant,* and *My Brilliant Career.* Plus a Nobel Prize winner in Patrick White, and a blockbuster novelist in Colleen McCullough. Not to mention Germaine Greer and Dr. Helen Caldicott. The bloody New Zealanders, for that matter, have produced a Booker Prize winner in Keri Hulme, and a splendid singer in Dame Kiri Te Kanawa.

The Aussies, and the Kiwis, have circumstantial advantages over us. They play the same sports as the Brits, cricket and rugger, and tennis. (The one local sport that we're good at is snooker. Cliff Thorburn is probably the best-known Canadian in England.) They also have that distinctive, "Stri'an" style of speech, so that the Aussie-ness of Rupert Murdoch, of *The Times* and of union-smashing fame, gets noticed in a way that the Canadian-ness of Conrad Black of *The Daily Telegraph* doesn't.

But what the Aussies have that really moves them out from the crowd is the quality that the Brits describe as "fizz." They aren't easy to like. But they're impossible not to notice. There's a chippy, defiant, working-class edge that both attracts the British and slightly intimidates them. ("Poms," the Aussies in turn like to sneer at the effete English.) We by contrast allow ourselves to be intimidated by the Brits, psyched out by that effortless air of superiority that's the last echo of empire, overawed by institutions like the BBC, *The Times Literary Supplement,* and the Royal Shakespeare Company. Worse, we're so desperate not to be mistaken for Yanks that we spend a lot of our time hanging round on the fringes, mumbling.

John Mortimer is as good a judge as any of the comparative attractions of "Oz" and of us. He's talked up his books from Halifax to Victoria; one of his plays had its world premiere in Ottawa. "I really enjoy Canada," he told me. "The people are nice, the bookstores are good, the restaurants are excellent." But he went on. "There are two characteristics of Australians that you notice and are impressed by. First, they aren't afraid to caricature themselves. Second, they don't defer to authority. That's why you remember them."

• • •

"We're in an almost psychotic state as a country," Adrienne Clarkson, Ontario's agent general in Paris, remarked in a recent interview. "It's not a question of identity: the problem is that we don't know how to show it to other people." Henry Wrong, the Toronto-born arts administrator who runs London's highly successful Barbican Centre, says almost the same thing. "We've got no edge. We don't seem able to market our ideas at all. There's a greyness that's incomprehensible." "Everyone is terribly polite but they're all so terribly earnest," remarks Ann Barr, features editor of *The Observer.* The cultural centre at Canada House, ranked back in Ottawa as a shining example of its kind, is a case in point. It's a relentless hive of activity: there's a gallery with a new exhibition every couple of months; there are play readings, book launchings, recitals two or three times a week, film festivals celebrating everyone from Norman McLaren to David Cronenberg. The missing ingredient is fizz. "Our belief is that credibility comes from the professional arts community," explains David Peacock, cultural counsellor from 1981 until last September, "not from the general British public." That's another way of saying that if you never take a risk you'll never get egg on your face.

Perhaps it was inevitable that we've failed to interest the Brits. We're just not exotic. That segment of the population that reads *The Guardian,* and still seeks hopefully for a newer world, finds it not just in the Antipodes but also in India and Africa: the novels of Salman Rushdie, the essays of V.S. Naipaul, the Market Theatre of Johannesburg. Mostly, though, British eyes have turned inward. An influential cultural figure today is the "Young Fogey." He goes in for heavy tweeds and bicycle clips. His other enthusiasms, as Mortimer notes in *Paradise Postponed*, are "the Church of England, English watercolours, and Victorian animal paintings." It's a retreat from Empire Lost to a little England that never was.

Just time and distance are fraying away the transatlantic links between us. During the 1970s, what with Quebec nationalism and regionalism and the rest of it, we switched off the world and stared at our own navels. As Charles Ritchie, high commissioner in London from 1967 to 1971, noted, severing our links with Britain was unofficial official policy in Ottawa. "There is no interest in Canada in tightening relations with the United Kingdom or in reporting home on British policies," he wrote in his diary on April 15, 1969. "Dispatches from Paris are read because French politics affect our future as a nation.... The 'British connection' seems to be receding out of view." The consequence of that downgrading of the connection became glaringly obvious during the 1981-82 fracas over patriating the constitution. The Brits, it was evident, had forgotten that Canada was a confederation. Canadians—Pierre Trudeau in particular—had forgotten that backbench M.P.s at Westminister are genuinely independent and if told to do something "holding their noses" will do exactly the opposite.

The monarchy of course remains. But for how long, once the Queen departs? Canada is no longer thought of here as a place one might emigrate to: just 5,000 Brits went in 1984, as against 63,000 in 1966. We're both members of the Commonwealth, of course, but at Commonwealth Conferences we are very often on opposite sides of issues: Rhodesia in the 1970s, South Africa today.

We have the language of Chaucer and of Shakespeare in common, or most of us do. We have historical, cultural, and institutional connections. Put simply, it was natural for Black to buy *The Telegraph* while it would have been unnatural for him to have bought *La Stampa* or *Die Zeit*. Even so, my own theory is that we now have more in common with the Scandinavians than with the Brits: the same northernness, the same introversion, the same topographical rawness, the same egalitarianism. This notion first dawned on me after a comment from my next-door neighbour in Little Venice, the writer David

Leitch. "You Canadians remind me of the Danes," he said, "and I mean that as a compliment." I found more support in a remark by Robertson Davies. "We are a northern people living in the northern reach of North America. Our writing is more like the writing of Scandinavian people than American or English."

Yet it *matters* that we've become invisible in Britain. The equation is straightforward. If we can't make it in Britain, then we can't make it anywhere in Europe. If we can't make it in Europe, then we have no counterweight—a *psychological* counterweight mattering more than a political or an economic one—to the U.S. Roy McMurtry, now that he's worked his way into his new career as high commissioner in London, seems to understand that a new beginning has to be made. He's talking up with his opposite number in Ottawa, Sir Derek Day, the idea of a new Canada-U.K. society to replace absurd old institutions such as the Canada Club of London, the 176-year-old businessmen's forum that still refuses to admit women as members. The best definition of the new approach came from a mole at the British Foreign Office. "We've got to get out from under that dead weight of nostalgia: the mother country, the former colony, and all the rest of the rubbish. We have to start looking at each other as we really are, a couple of middle-sized powers with quite a few interests in common."

But if we're going to make it in Britain—or remake it—we're going to have to work at it. No longer can we expect to be liked—even though, as Canadians, we *always* expect to be liked. We've become too rich, too secure, we've had things much too easy to be liked any more than the Swiss or the Swedes are liked. Nor, given the ascendancy of the Australians, can we take refuge in the easy explanation for British indifference: they're just being snobbish towards an ex-colony.

Lastly—this final message from the pulpit is the roughest—we have to come to terms with the fact that the Brits may not be entirely wrong about us. Recently a couple of observations jolted me, and may jolt you. The first came from Belle Shenkman. She's the queen bee of Canadian culture in London and, to a degree, in Europe. Among other ventures, she organized the Toronto Symphony's major European tour last autumn. "The real trouble with Canadians," she said, "is that *we aren't curious.* We don't seem to want to make the effort to find out what makes other societies tick."

Ouch. Shenkman's observation popped back in mind later, when some Canadian friends dropped round three days after touching down at Heathrow and commented, at length, upon how this part of

London resembled that part of Toronto, how another part looked like Vancouver, and yet another part resembled, for God's sake, the road into Montreal from Dorval.

A sharper jolt was provided by Becky Bryan. She's twenty-six, coltish and rangy and mouthy, a kind of up-market Sheila Copps, a stock-market analyst who as a candidate for the Liberal-SDP Alliance in the 1983 election was the youngest candidate of any party and ran second, and will run in the next election, this time in a seat where she may well win. (She also turns up a lot on TV.)

The point about Becky Bryan is that she's one of us, or used to be. Her father emigrated to Toronto, married a Canadian, and moved back to Britain for business reasons shortly before Becky entered her teens. All through the London School of Economics, and into politics, she kept on thinking of herself as a Canadian. After her election defeat—"It's the kind of thing that makes you reflect, what do you really want to do with your life?"—she went back to Toronto, perhaps to stay. It was the summer of 1984. During it, she discovered, "I wasn't a Canadian any more." The reason was that season's election campaign. "I couldn't believe the puerile level of the debate," Bryan told me. "God knows we've got terrible problems here, but people are talking about them, debating them, thinking about them."

Back home, when I raged about Newfie jokes, I hadn't the least doubt about the rightness of my cause. But I couldn't think of a single argument to make to Becky Bryan.

• • •

I intended to end this article there, and hated to have to do so. But then, as a good deed in a naughty world, came an invitation to Canada Day festivities at Canada House. Dutifully, I put on a maple-leaf pin and took the tube down. Inside the lobby, everything seemed terribly polite and earnest. The ladies from the Canadian Women's Club were passing round coffee and sandwiches. Politely. Roy McMurtry and the agents general of the provinces were holding a levee. Earnestly. In the recital room, the kids who belong to the Pacific Mennonite Children's Choir were singing "Over the Rainbow" politely, followed by a much-too-earnest rendition of "I'se the B'y" by the neatly blazered boys of the Ridley College choir.

But what happened next wasn't earnest at all. Nor was it all that polite. Roy McMurtry came charging downstairs. "Let's go!" he exhorted, less a diplomat than a former captain of the University of Toronto football squad. We—me and my husband and several hundred other expatriate Canadians including, of all people, Mel Watkins—streamed out into the bright sunlight of Trafalgar Square. As tourists looked on in amazement, the Mennonite Choir, and the one from Ridley, plus the Edmonton Youth Orchestra and the Winona Senior Public School Brass Quintet, all with instruments at the ready, raced for the base of Nelson's monument. "Hoo boy!" one kid shouted to another. "We're going to stand up there and we're all going to sing 'O Canada'!"

And sing it we all did, oblivious for once to the fact that people were staring. On cue, as the last "stand on guard" died away, someone up on the roof of Canada House let fly a bunch of balloons. This was not a discreet and understated little bunch of balloons. This was *two thousand balloons,* red ones and white ones, in joyous profusion. On the soft summer breeze, they drifted over the National Gallery, over the spire of St. Martin's-in-the-Fields, and we all watched until the last one had gone out of sight.

Sandra Gwyn, "Over Home," *Saturday Night,* (January, 1987), pp. 93-96, 98-100.

ROBERT H. HAYNES

WHAT IS THE BIOLOGICAL REVOLUTION?

We seem to be assaulted daily with cries of political, cultural, sexual, and even theatrical revolutions. While most of us are capable of quiet adaptation to changing circumstances, we soon acquire immunity against the cries of hucksters for whom anything, however mildly novel, must be 'revolutionary', if it is to be sold to others. So biologists talking revolution may appear a pathetic lot, trying merely to raise their voices above the noise of the intellectual marketplace. Still, there is a revolution in biology. Its ideology was established over a century ago with the publication of the *Origin of the Species* in 1859 but the technological base for its implementation is being laid only now in contemporary developments in molecular genetics, neurophysiology, ecology, and medicine.

Much nonsense has been written on this subject by scientists and journalists alike. For example, the April 19, 1971, cover story of *Time* magazine contained the following statements:

> Indeed, only the development of an artificial womb capable of supporting life stands in the way of routine ectogenesis, or gestation outside the uterus, and now even this problem may yield to soluton.... Once their...device is perfected, the baby hatchery of Aldous Huxley's *Brave New World* will be a reality and life without birth a problem rather than a prophecy.

or, as another 'prospect',

> It might be possible to develop 'knowledge pills' that would impart instant skill in French, tennis, music or math. Some scientists fantasize that supergeniuses will someday be produced by increasing brain size, through either genetic manipulation or through transplantation of brain cells to newborn infants or to the fetus in the womb.

Some readers of *Time* magazine surely would have been amused but otherwise unimpressed by such exuberant fantasy. However, these and other less obvious pieces of nonsense were set cheek by jowl in the same article with quite sober and balanced assessments of current biomedical research, and no criteria were offered to enable readers to distinguish the real science from the science fiction. No wonder that many people are worried at the thought of further experimental enquiry into the nature, origin, and behaviour of living organisms. Even scientists of the greatest eminence have responded in kind to the sensationalist questions of journalists. Exaggerated portents of ecological disaster, space-age plagues, world-wide famine, even forthcoming ice ages now emanate from many 'authoritative sources'. The cost of such hyperbole is to spread alarm among the naive and to lose credibility with the wise. (It may well be that the increasing interest in astrology, mysticism, and introspective cults, the citizen backlash against many forms of urban and technological development, and the erosion of government support for scientific research are in part reactions against these scientistic nightmares that are as remote as they are odious.)

Revolutions have two essential elements: a distinctive ideology and some practical means for producing change. From such fertile unions of ideology and instrumentality there emerge changes in public standards, shifting social values and ethical conflicts of many kinds. To pursue this theme for biology one must compare the generally prevailing philosophical conceptions as to man's place in nature, as well as the technical capabilities of biomedical science, in the pre-Darwinian and contemporary periods. Such comparison should help us to understand how the biological revolution has excited the kind of ethical conflict that may ultimately lead to institutionalized changes in personal and social values.

The two elements of revolution are in some ways analogous to the theoretical and technological edges of the scientists' sword. We hear a great deal about technical developments in the life sciences, for example, the isolation and synthesis of genes, prenatal diagnosis of genetic disorders, organ transplants, behaviour control by telemetric stimulaton of the brain, and the detection of potential carcinogens in commonly used foods, cosmetics, and drugs. However, much less is said of the basic ideological shift that occurred subsequent to the demonstration by Darwin, Huxley, and their followers that man is a part and product of the evolution of plant and animal species on this planet. It is this change in world-view that is our primary concern in this essay.

In 1691, John Ray, an early Fellow of the Royal Society who is regarded as the father of British natural history, published his most popular and influential work, entitled *The Wisdom of God manifested in the Works of the Creation.* In this book Ray describes the multitudinous variety and perfection of living organisms, the beauty and minuteness of their parts, and many now classic examples of the adaptation of biological structure to function; all of this is taken by Ray as the manifestation of God's design and creativity in nature.

During the eighteenth century ideas in biology changed so slowly that over one hundred years later, in 1829, the eighth Earl of Bridgewater, a Fellow of the Royal Society and of All Souls College, Oxford, bequeathed eight thousand pounds to the president of the Royal Society to underwrite the publication of a series of books designed to demonstrate 'the Power, Wisdom and Goodness of God, as manifested in the Creation'. The nine 'Bridgewater Treatises' appeared during the years 1833-1840 and were reissued in many subsequent editions. Their titles alone tell much about prevailing views of the world among the intellectual élite of the time: John Kidd, first Aldrichian professor of chemistry and later Regius professor of medicine at Oxford, wrote *On the adaptation of external nature to the physical condition of man—principally with reference to the supply of his wants and the exercise of his intellectual faculties;* William Buckland, Oxford's first reader in geology, twice president of the Geological Society and author of *Reliquiae Diluvianae,* a popular work which argued that fossils of extinct animals found in Yorkshire caves attested to the action of the Biblical flood, also wrote the Bridgewater treatise *Geology and mineralogy considered with reference to natural theology;* and Thomas Chalmers, the eminent Scottish mathematician and divine, wrote *On the power, wisdom, and goodness of God as manifested in the adaptation of external nature to the moral and intellectual constitution of man.*

These and many similar works belong to the tradition of William Paley's *Natural theology, or evidences of the existence and attributes of the Deity collected from the appearances of nature* (1802); this book, next to the Bible one of the more widely studied in the Victorian age, was later annotated and illustrated by Sir Charles Bell and the Lord Chancellor Brougham in 1836. (An examination based on Paley's *Evidences of Christianity* remained, even into the twentieth century, among the basic requirements for the bachelor's degree at a number of well-known universities.) Much nineteenth century biology was cast within the framework of natural theology, the aim of which was to make plausible the existence of God by the argument from design and to give a systematic view of what can be learned of theological truth in the light of nature. For Paley this enterprise would provide strong foundation for the belief that 'God Almighty wills and wishes the happiness of his creatures' and that 'adequate motive must be supplied to virtue by a system of future rewards and punishment'.

In the foregoing paragraph perhaps I have belaboured the issue, but my impression is that in this secular age modern students find it hard to believe that the views of Paley and the authors of the Bridgewater Treatises were held, not only by the simple and pious, but by the majority of the best educated people in nineteenth century Europe and America; and surveys suggest that similar views persist today in the hearts or minds of many. Some of the essential elements of this widespread pre-Darwinian view of life were the beliefs that the earth was created by God as a home for man; that all species were individually perfected by God at the time of their creation and have remained ever unchanged and immutable; that man is set in dominion over all other forms of life and that we are to be fruitful, to multiply, and to replenish the earth; that the resources of the earth are essentially limitless, regardless of the rate of human 'replenishment'; that the inevitable misery and vice of the fecund masses as described by Malthus constitute grounds for setting aside proposals to ameliorate the economic condition of the poor, since any general increase in comfort would lead only to further increase in their numbers and hence to even greater misery; that our individual physical and moral endowments at birth and our general state of health, wealth, and happiness—even the length of our lives and mode of death—reflect but the will of God; and, finally, that man possesses not only an imponderable mind—the ghost of the machine—but also an immortal soul. Weighted down with such metaphysical baggage it's a miracle that anyone ever arrived in the twentieth century!

If one doubts that views such as those recited above were held—and held dearly by many—consider the treatment accorded Ludwig Büchner, professor in medicine at Tübingen, who in 1855 published his book, *Kraft und Stoff,* in which he argued that the world as we know it is a product of the evolution of matter under the action of discernible physical forces; that life is a particular and specific combination of matter which, in favourable circumstances, can be spontaneously generated; that there is no 'vital principle'; that evolution has proceeded from life to consciousness; that it is foolish for man to believe that the earth was made for him in the face of the difficulties he encounters in inhabiting it; that there is no God, no final cause, no immortality, no substance of the soul; that human freedom of will is limited by physiological and environmental factors that we have yet to understand; that mind is a collective word for the 'highest' activities or functions of the brain, the study of which poses the greatest challenge for future physiological research; and, finally, that nature works and evolves in accord with physical law but that it has no purpose, no will, no laws imposed by extraneous authority and no supernatural ethical sanction. The views expressed in this work, published four years before Darwin's *Origin of the Species,* excited such fierce opposition that Büchner was compelled to give up his post at Tübingen and to retire to his home in Darmstadt as a physician in private practice. In retrospect many of Büchner's ideas, especially in physics, were naive (being limited by the science of his time), but his general perceptions were close to the mark. Perhaps he received some consolation for his heresy as he watched his book pass through seventeen German and twenty-two foreign editions.

It is still popular to dismiss the sometimes dogmatic views of nineteenth-century free-thinkers as being immoral, shallow, or unkind. Certainly the agnostic position of a Huxley or Darwin is more defensible in principle than the atheist stance of a Büchner or Engels. Indeed it is essential for scientists to be open-minded, tentative, and self-correcting through observation and experiment; for no one can predict what remains to be discovered in the ultimate interactions of matter and energy, the farthest reaches of space or the dimly appreciated complexities of the brain. But history does seem to show that as science takes one step forward, hobgoblins take one step back. This is not to say that contemporary science has risen above metaphysical dispute, or that scientists are innocent of cherished presuppositions of their own. But one can hope that some line of common sense always separates experimental science from the quicksand of subjective speculation.

Modern views of the nature, origin, and evolution of the earth, and current hypotheses on the neural basis of mental phenomena, are much more subtle and complex than those of even the most advanced nineteenth-century thinkers. However, if we make bold for a moment and try to abstract something like a contemporary world view from the vast proliferation of modern science, it is surprising to see how close we are to a Büchner or Huxley and how far from a Paley or Ray. It is this contrast in outlook that constitutes the ideological base of the biological revolution.

The word 'evolution' suggests to most people the idea that plant and animal species are not immutable but rather have developed slowly, over long periods of geologic time, from simpler ancestral species. This was a revolutionary concept one hundred years ago, but today scientists consider biological evolution to be only one aspect of much vaster processes of evolutionary change in the universe as a whole. For not only have plants and animals evolved from simpler ancestors, but the very atoms of physics, the molecules of chemistry and the stars and planets of astronomy have 'evolved' through time as well—though by very different mechanisms.

Matter and energy are the two fundamental, and since Einstein interconvertible, components of the physical world. The history of this world, as understood by scientists today, consists in the gradual organization of matter (utilizing appropriate forms of energy) into structures such as atoms, molecules, stars, and planets under the influence of nuclear, electromagnetic, and gravitational fields of force. Furthermore, astrophysical and geochemical evidence indicates that we inhabit an expanding universe which has been subject to evolutionary change at each of several (hierarchical) levels of material organization.[1] Following the burst of a primordial 'fireball' of matter-

[1]Metaphysical extrapolation of these facts to an ultimate 'cosmic evolutionary process' is neither justified nor intended here.

energy (11 to 15 billion years ago) stars and galactic systems began to form in which changing conditions of temperature and pressure permitted the stepwise build-up of the various atomic elements and the formation of the simplest gaseous molecules. These processes of *atomic evolution* continue in stars today throughout the universe.

The origin of the primordial 'fireball' is, of course, unknown. It may have been created in some unfathomable way by the 'Creator' of the great myths of mankind. But equally fascinating to the imagination, and tantalizingly consistent with physical theory and cosmological data, is a current speculation that the original fireball appeared by chance, 'out of nowhere' as a sudden fluctuation of the vacuum of some larger space in which our four-dimensional space-time world is embedded. As the physicist E.P. Tryon wryly remarked[2] this theory 'offers the modest proposal that our universe is simply one of those things which happen from time to time'!

The solar system seems to have arisen from the accretion (4.5 billion years ago) of vast clouds of interplanetary gas and dust (ejected by stars and supernovae) in the vicinity of the sun. In the cooling atmosphere and seas of the primitive earth, conditions became appropriate for further stages of chemical or *molecular evolution.*

During the first billion years of earth history these latter processes, driven photochemically by solar radiation, gradually gave rise to the complex organic materials necessary for the assembly of the first primitive microorganisms and the onset of *biological evolution* of the primitive global ecosystem. Two and one-half billion years passed between the appearance of the first known fossil microorganisms and the luxuriant expansion of primitive invertebrates in the inland seas of the Cambrian era some six hundred million years ago. Biological evolution then seems to have quickened and only five hundred million years elapsed before our earliest prosimian ancestors diverged from their insectivorous precursors in the cretaceous forests.

Very recently on the scale of geologic time—certainly less than one million years ago—*Homo erectus* and subsequently *Homo sapiens* learned to use tools and to communicate these highly adaptive skills from one generation to the next through the rapid and efficient method of syntactic speech, rather than the slow and chancy method of genetic inheritance. Thus we see the beginnings of human *cultural*

[2]*Nature 246,* 396 (1973).

evolution, and perhaps as family and tribal groups learned the advantages of cooperation and division of labour among their members, the beginnings of social and ethical value systems as well.

These various evolutionary regimes, though taking place through very different mechanisms, all depend upon a supply of the appropriate materials and a suitable flow of energy. For example, biological evolution proceeds within the thin interfaces of ocean, land, and air. This surface region of our planet is part of a system that is open with respect to the flux of solar radiation in that the incident energy from the sun is balanced by an equivalent energy loss from the earth to the cold sink of outer space. Thus, the sun-earth-outer space system is in a steady state with respect to energy flow. However, the system is closed with respect to the materials comprising the earth: only trivial amounts of matter arrive upon, or are lost from, most planets (usually meteorites but now also space vehicles). It has been shown, principally by Harold Morowitz at Yale University, that in such energetically open, but materially closed, steady-state systems, cycles of matter will occur, the precise character of which depends on the initial chemical composition of the system. Reasoning in this way it can be shown that the energy responsible not only for the meteorological cycles of wind, rain, and ocean currents, but also for the evolution and maintenance of the global ecosystem, derives from the constant flux of light from the sun. The materials thereby cycled through the 'biosphere' come only from the earth's crust, the oceans, and the atmosphere. Because our planet is closed to the importation of new materials and because the practical availability of certain essential materials is declining as a result of man's activities, there are limits to the amount of material that can be produced and used by living organisms. Indeed, for a generation that has viewed the entire planet from outer space on the television screen it should be obvious that the materials and productivity of the earth are finite, and quite incapable of supporting an indefinitely expanding human population at a level of nourishment and material comfort equivalent even to that regarded as the 'poverty line' in North America. For both ecological and economic reasons, global management of natural resources and human fertility must be achieved. Clearly this is no easy task in the unfortunate context of a world divided by nation states, ethnic groups, and social strata whose relations are governed primarily by the 'law of the jungle', rather than by any clear recognition of the necessity for cooperation in a closed system with very definite limits to growth.

It was the patient, reflective Charles Darwin, who often saw reason in his study of evolution to quote the naturalists' aphorism, *natura non facit saltum* (nature does not take leaps), who declined the proffered honour of Karl Marx's dedication for *Das Kapital,* but who nonetheless triggered a revolution that continues to this day. From the research of his contemporaries and successors we have come to realize that the earth is a small planet on which life arose gradually, but spontaneously, from inorganic matter; that the enormous variety and diversity of organisms is perhaps less remarkable than their basic similarities and interdependence; that the common features and interdependence of organisms are manifest in many ways—in evolutionary and ecological relations, in analogous patterns of cellular architecture and development, in remarkable similarities in biochemical pathways and processes, and, finally, in the universality of the genetic code itself; that animal behaviour and mental phenomena are emergent properties of brains and nervous systems, the proper development and functioning of which depend crucially on the variety and intensity of early sensory stimulation; and, finally, that man's birth, death, and state of health are determined by the interplay of genetic, physiological, and environmental factors that can be modified or controlled within the limits of available biomedical technology.

• • •

Even if a latter-day Theodosius the Great were to decree that all the world was to embrace the ideology of the biological revolution, it would be of small consequence for our daily labours, our social behaviour, or any other aspect of everyday life. Rather it is the second, instrumental, element of the biological revolution that is the proximal cause of present concerns in this area. Whether one seeks to prove or disprove a theorist's conjecture, to find the cause of a disease, to cure a patient's ailment, or to enhance a farmer's product, experiments must be performed, tools and techniques must be developed. Ideas are the catalysts of science, medicine, industry, and agriculture—but they are not the final product nor do they provide the means for carrying out in practice the options and enterprises that may be theoretically possible. Advances in biomedical technology, especially since the end of the Second World War, now allow us to monitor and to intervene in a wide range of biological processes—from heredity to consciousness, and from the diseases of organisms to the pathology of ecosystems—and it is these practical powers that make it imperative to consider the biological revolution, its ethical implications, and their consequences for society.

In the *Descent of Man,* Darwin showed that *Homo sapiens* is an animal, a product of evolution; molecular biology, neurophysiology, medicine, and ecology are now providing the means to implement the consequences of man's being a part of nature and subject to increasingly well-understood physical and biological laws. But during the very time that we have come clearly to perceive and even to manipulate the laws that govern our physical nature, we seem unable to find evidence for the existence of any absolute ethical principles; and our vaunted 'moral nature', believed since time immemorial to be the crowning glory of man, is now seen by scientists and philosophers alike to be as much of a mirage as most of our other tender presumptions about the nature of man. Still, doctors must decide from whom and to whom to transplant an organ; when and under what circumstances they should carry out an abortion; and after what measures have failed they should pronounce a terminal patient dead. Biologists and social scientists must decide whether the knowledge to be gained is worth the cost, hazard, or indignity of certain types of experimental study involving human subjects. Citizens of wealthy countries must decide where and how to allocate their limited reserves of food, minerals, and energy among the hungry nations of the world. Such decisions, both small and great, are being made, and must be made virtually every day in laboratories and hospitals, in board rooms and legislatures. We say that moral considerations enter into such questions, but anyone who has ever been involved in making decisions, either for himself or on behalf of others, knows how readily ethical conflicts arise, and, even when the die is cast, how uncertain we remain, whether we have relied in coming to our judgement on the standards of Socrates or of Christ, the opinion of a jury or the cost-benefit analysis of the Rand Corporation.

No one has ever succeeded in showing how moral guidelines or ethical norms can be derived logically from either intuition or authority, philosophy or science: perhaps there is no reason why anyone *ought* to do anything; perhaps in the long run, moral conflicts are as well resolved by the toss of a coin as by agonizing appraisal. On the other hand, some biologists have argued that altruism and other modes of 'ethical' behaviour are innate or instinctual in man, products of group selection in evolution. But alas, as social and political history so clearly demonstrates, altruism rarely extends beyond the relatively intimate groups to which the individual perceives himself as belonging. Still, we can hope that as more and more people become aware of the biological basis of the human predicament, the old group barriers will gradually erode and the invidious process of pseudospeciation among men will come to an end. Then we may see that the only group membership of ultimate concern is that of survivor on 'lifeboat earth'. And hard though it may be, we will probably find it necessary to reset our ethical compass as each new storm waxes and wanes—but even such a compass seems better than none at all.

• • •

In summary, a brief response to our original question might go something like this: the biological revolution entails a change in world view from that of natural theology with its specially created, immutable species and its dualistic view of man as a moral being with an immortal soul, to one of evolutionary materialism with its mutable, phylogenetically related species embedded in a global ecosystem of photochemical origin, and its essentially monistic view of man possessed of no ineffable substances that distinguish him qualitatively from other parts of nature. More importantly, the biological revolution has been realized in the development of an elaborate technology that increasingly enobles us to implement the consequences of our being a product and a part of natural processes which can be observed, analyzed, and modified in hitherto undreamed of ways. The interdependent growth of a revolutionary world view and modern biomedical and ecological technique increasingly confronts us with ethical dilemmas and challenges to our values the like of which we have never met before. The absolute moral imperatives and explicit rules of behaviour of the old religions are being slowly replaced—for pragmatic reasons if none other—by an ethic whose single basic norm of reasoned goodwill and altruistic behaviour within self-recognizing human groups may be innate in *Homo sapiens*. The challenge is how to extend the altruism within existing groups to ever larger cooperative ensembles of people in the hope of reducing the ground of self-destructive competition among men and nations; for it is sobering to reflect that under the 'laws of the jungle', natural selection leads not only to the formation of species, but also to their extinction.

Robert H. Haynes, "What Is the Biological Revolution?" *Man and the Biological Revolution*, ed. Robert H. Haynes. The Gerstein Lectures 1973-74 (Toronto: York University, 1976), pp. 3-17. (Published as "Biological Revolution?" in *Canadian Forum*, August 1975, pp. 15-18.)

RENÉ LÉVESQUE
HEARTBREAK

> The government of Quebec has made public its proposal to negotiate a new agreement with the rest of Canada, based on the equality of nations;
>
> this agreement would enable Quebec to acquire the exclusive power to make its laws, levy its taxes and establish relations abroad—in other words, sovereignty—and at the same time to maintain with Canada an economic association including a common currency;
>
> no change in political status resulting from these negotiations will be effected without approval by the people through another referendum; on these terms do you give the Government of Quebec the mandate to negotiate the proposed agreement between Quebec and Canada?

It was rather long and heavy but, to use a word that is fashionable today, it was perfectly "transparent." In three short paragraphs and some hundred words the essence was there for anyone who knew how to read.

The holiday season [Christmas, 1979] gave all a chance to talk it over in their families, and seeing that on the whole the question was pretty well received, we began to look forward confidently to the debate that would mark the real opening of the campaign in February.

A first leitmotif would naturally be a critical analysis of the federal regime. But the most important theme, one that everyone would have to explore according to his or her own feelings and experience, was the promise sovereignty-association held for the future. On this score what was required of our elected members was nothing short of the best performance of their careers. I never saw such discipline in our ranks nor such willingness to work. With the help of a battalion of research assistants we had mobilized, even the least articulate MNAs strove like slaves, absolutely determined to surpass themselves. And they succeeded. We had really thought of everything, right down to crash courses for those who didn't "come across" on TV. From delivery to dress, everything was impeccable, for everyone knew how crucial the issue was, and for once there was no absenteeism.

Nor was there the least false note. Day after day on our side one could witness the most extraordinary performances. An unprecedented flood of tight arguments backed by stunning examples soon began to flow from this marvellous teamwork, contributing to an atmosphere that was emotional and almost euphoric. Claude Charron, who had replaced Robert Burns as parliamentary chief, patrolled the ranks handing out advice and encouragement, an administrative task that did not prevent him from turning in one of his most unforgettable speeches. Emulation constantly improved our output.

What a contrast to the disarray in the opposite camp. Elected party leader in 1978, and just recently MNA for Argenteuil, Claude Ryan was as awkward as a debutante and, worse still, showed sure signs of inebriation at being close to the goal of political power. Since his party had been winning by-elections handily, he was beginning to see himself as head of government already. But although he was sure of himself, he was skimpily and poorly prepared for the debate. Content to harp away that the referendum question was dishonest and must surely hide sinister intentions, from the start he took the path of pure and simple demagoguery. There is nothing old veterans of the House like better, accustomed as they are to playing with clichés rather than ideas, so his Liberal cohorts followed his example with relish. In reply to dense and passionate statements on our side, they sat back and croaked "séparatisses, séparatisses." Our determination to situate ourselves on a level worthy of the subject was met by mean-minded, repetitive, and most often childish refrains. The merciless eye of the camera revealed a Claude Ryan staring about vacantly while the rest of the herd, floored by the steady broadside we directed at them, no longer managed to conceal their confusion.

The public could see very well what was going on. Rarely has a political debate been anticipated so impatiently and then followed so closely by so many Québécois, and they got our message all the better because our adversaries could only conjure up the most trivial contradictions.

The polls were not slow to confirm that we had won this first round hands down....

Keyed up by the clear victory we had won in the National Assembly, "Committees for the Oui" spread throughout the country like wildfire. There was at least one in every riding. In many businesses employees had their own groups, too. One after another we saw "Economists for the Oui," "Lawyers for the Oui," "Scientists for the Oui." Crowning the pyramid, the "Regroupement National" could boast spectacular members: senior civil servants like Thérèse Baron, military heroes like General Allard, writers and artists like Marie-Claire Blais and Fabienne Thibault, an important collection of former ministers and members of both the federal and provincial parliaments, front-line combatants like the Association des Gens de l'Air, well-known university figures like the Rector of Sherbrooke, Yves Martin, and the Vice-Dean of Laval, Christine Piette, and a good number of the most respected spokesmen for rural Quebec. Painting a moving picture of the future he hoped to assure his children by his option, the leader of the Union Nationale, Rodrigue Biron, also joined our ranks.

The eminent businessman and veteran indépendantiste Fernand Paré was in charge of the "Foundation for the Oui" that was to collect more than three and a half million dollars. Its vice-president was Madeleine Ferron, wife of the late Robert Cliche, who shortly before his death had written these prophetic words: "In my view, one of the gravest dangers would be a Non in the referendum. English Canada would believe that the crisis was over and would slip back into its lethargy."

And what precisely was happening in English Canada? Forget for the time being the Quebec branch of the Anglo establishment where the halt, the sick, the lame, and the dead were being conscripted for the "Non" and where the exceptionally rare dissidents, huddled together in their CASA (Comité Anglophone pour la Souveraineté-Association), risked the same fate as that meted out to former Liberal minister Kevin Drummond, whose "Oui" had cost him the loss of friends and a rift in his family.

Outside Quebec, on the contrary, opinion was less entrenched. The situation appeared to be still quite fluid. Bill Davis and his Ontario government might refuse in advance to negotiate as much as they liked, but they were far from reflecting the opinion of people most directly concerned. Since they had always been the principal beneficiaries of the federal regime, the leaders of Ontario society obviously preferred to retain the status quo, but if Quebec said "Oui," wouldn't they come to terms to maintain a hold on the common market of association? This, at any rate, was the conclusion a team of researchers from York University came to when a solid majority of decision-makers chosen from every sector of society admitted that in the event of a victory for the "Oui" they would opt for accommodation. In the Atlantic Provinces there wasn't the least hesitation. Quoting a study made for the Task Force on Canadian Unity, the *Globe and Mail* noted that they "would be favourable to economic union between their region and an independent Quebec. In the same breath 65% of those polled said that if a 'free and democratic' vote went in this direction, Quebec should be authorized to quit the Canadian federation."

Economist Abraham Rotstein provided figures that eloquently describe the economic interdependence that binds a great number of Canadians: "In Ontario no less than 105,800 jobs depend directly on the Quebec market. Ontario enterprises annually export 4.6 billion dollars worth of manufactured goods to Quebec.... [Rotstein] estimates that there are 9,000 workers in the Maritimes whose salaries depend on sales to Quebec. The Prairies sell $432,000,000 in consumer goods to Quebec (particularly beef they are unable to sell elsewhere in America) which supports some 10,000 jobs. Finally, 3,000 persons in B.C. have jobs related to exports to Quebec. In the reverse direction the number of jobs is approximately identical."[1]

Could Québécois have been right, then, when at the end of March they replied 71 per cent "Oui" and only 16 per cent "Non" to the question: Will Canada negotiate? Perhaps they were, as long as one kept in mind, applying it to the present context, the judgement Mazzini passed on the British in the last century, a view that has been constantly confirmed by history since: "From time immemorial it has been English policy [read Anglo-Canadian] to put obstacles in the path of any factor that might seem to introduce a new element into the European [Canadian] picture, and then to accept it as soon as it has been solemnly accomplished...."

As could be expected, we, too, were to be presented with every kind of obstacle imaginable. But just the same, we felt that a great many of our people, perhaps even that small majority the polls indicated, expected to see the "Oui" succeed and, though they did not always show it openly, had actually come to hope it would.

This was all the more so because in Ottawa, as among provincial federalists, the situation remained fluid. When the multi-billion-dollar decision came up whether to build the F-16 fighter plane, the economic benefits of which would go principally to Quebec, or the F-18, with 80 or 90 per cent of contracts going to Ontario, Trudeau's government was faced with turbulence in its Quebec caucus. Claude Ryan's cohorts, meanwhile, continued in the depression caused by their parliamentary discomfiture. The "Non" were feverishly seeking a strike force but, failing to discover a trigger mechanism, seemed incapable of inventing one.

It was we, alas, who were going to give them the booster they needed. One day in March in a modest meeting that would normally have sunk quietly beneath the sands of time, Lise Payette got caught

[1]*Le Devoir*, December 19, 1979

up in one of those feminist declarations prompted by her job as Minister of the Status of Women. In the most logical way imaginable she had set about exposing a school text presenting two great incarnations of traditional sexism—little Guy, future champion and perfect macho, and little Yvette, model miniature housewife, broken in to be perfectly submissive. So far so good. But carried away by her subject and "pushed by some devil," our colleague dropped a remark to the effect that Quebec women would have to learn to sit up and sit still if ever Claude Ryan took power because he was married to a protracted "Yvette." This was not only in poor taste but untrue and Lise Payette soon heard about it, for several journalists made a point of enumerating Madame Ryan's exceptional accomplishments and made it a duty to execute the guilty party in the public square.

This deplorable slip was a small enough cause, but it was destined to have resounding effects. Toward the end of March, well supported by Liberals, several hundred "Yvettes" met in Quebec City. And when, on April 7, thousands more filled the Montreal Forum waving the Canadian flag in one hand and the fleur-de-lys in the other, having quickly forgotten the incident that had served as a pretext to launch their reinvigorated "Non," we understood that the opposition machine had finally got off the ground.

The next forty days that took us up to May 20 deserve to be described in detail, hour by hour, for the edification of future generations, if not for those who were steamrolled by them.

It was an unqualifiable deluge of lies, threats, and blackmail. The federal Minister of Energy, Marc Lalonde, promised a sovereign Quebec an energy deficit of exactly $16.6 billion. His colleague in social affairs, Monique Bégin, predicted a phenomenally high level of taxation just to be able to maintain old age pensions and family allowances. Taking what could be called the "low road" and hitting shamelessly below the belt, unscrupulous terrorists infiltrated the weakest sectors of society, for example, an old folks home where one of them, seeing some oranges in a bowl, had the gall to tell the senior citizens sitting around: "Watch out now, if the separatists win, you'll never see any more oranges in Quebec." No one knew how to evoke this pitiful, down-at-heel Quebec with more verve than Jean Chrétien, belching out in conclusion his caricature of Claude Morin, promoted ambassador of some equally under-developed country driving around in a Cadillac "avec le flag su'l'hood."

Despite rules that we had legitimately established but that had been rapidly trampled underfoot, the "Non" camp had no scruples about floating their campaign on floods of money, the exact total of which, unless I am mistaken, will never be known. The tribunals we addressed prudently sidestepped the issue with a few remarks that amounted to placing federal public funds beyond the reach of any Quebec law. How many millions were swallowed up in Ottawa back offices where all the "Non" propaganda was prepared, including material used by the provincial Liberals? How much more to paper the media and every corner of the country with "Me? I'm staying in... for my own good," and that "NON merci" that even cropped up in anti-alcoholic advertising from Honourable Madame Bégin's Ministry of Health and Welfare?

Nerves and stomach pinched and pummelled by such savage blows, public resolution began to falter. In the most fragile strata, among seniors and "floaters," who are always like a feather in the wind, the hurricane of "Non" propaganda wreaked havoc. It seemed to be irresistable and dealt in fear. From West to East, from Blakeney in Saskatchewan to Hatfield in New Brunswick, came the heralds of the Anglo-Canadian refusal. Sniffing their victory to be, they felt free now to write us off in the most callous tones. By the end of April everyone knew, in Ottawa as in Quebec, that we would not reach our 62 per cent and that even a straight majority was no longer a sure thing in French Quebec.

It was at this point that Trudeau, who had become prime minister again the month before, decided to step on stage and participate without risk in the last act. First on May 2, 1980, presenting himself before the receptive audience of the Chamber of Commerce, he began by indulging in heavy irony, citing our cowardice, saying we hadn't dared to go straight to the goal, machine gun in hand... like Zimbabwe or Algeria. Seeing that he was on the wrong track he fell back on another analogy, less explosive though just as misplaced. "Suppose," he said, "that Cuba or Haiti came proposing to associate with us, because down there they like Canadian prosperity, the Canadian countryside, Canadian women... So they vote on it and agree, massively, yes, we want association with Canada. Would we, in the name of democracy, be obliged to accept them? Would our only choice, in the name of fair play, be to consent: 'Well, yes, they voted for it, so we don't have anything to say in the matter'? (*Much laughter and sustained applause.*)" Finally, betraying both his peevishness and his relief, our improviser imagined the care with which a Castro or a Duvalier would have felt out the ground in order to avoid simply being told "Go and get lost!"

To my mind such remarks deserve a choice place in a little manual entitled "The Way to Insult People Without Risk Who Don't Think the Way You Do." It would be a very thin volume, for history doesn't record many who have treated their fellows so grossly. As for the anthology of political duplicity that would fill several fat volumes, the historic encounter of the following week certainly deserves to be enshrined there.

On May 14, one week before the vote, here, in résumé, is how Trudeau, before thousands of Montrealers and addressing the whole of Quebec, proclaimed that he and his were ready to put their heads on the block: "We, MPs from Quebec, as Québécois to vote Non, and at the same time we warn Canadians in other provinces that this Non should not be interpreted as proof that all is well here, or that there are not changes to be made. On the contrary, it is with the aim of getting things changed that we re putting our seats on the line."

Change, okay. But what change? That remained a mystery. Considering the past and so many claims so often reiterated, any right-minded person couldn't help thinking that nothing less than greater autonomy and better guarantees for Quebec were in question. If not, it was just an airy promise, or else something no democratic politician could permit himself at this moment—sheer deceit.

Every chance we had to speak in public over the next days we demanded specifics. In vain. The sphinx kept his secret, knowing full well that if he revealed the true nature of his thought, innumerable Québécois would turn away in disgust. He was biding his time while we spent our last strength trying to reach that vital minimum of a strong majority French vote. Describing the instinctive and perfectly comprehensible solidarity Anglophones showed in throwing their support massively to the other side, I went around begging our people to show the same solidarity for once in our history. But it was too late. Or perhaps it wasn't yet time...

To this day no one knows if our two-fifths vote for the "Oui" represented 49 or 51 per cent of French Quebec that night. On the other hand, the three-fifths vote for the "Non" was sadly incontestable. And hard to swallow, I had to add when speaking to some 5,000 partisans who had gathered at the Paul Sauvé Arena just the same. At the back of the platform, side by side, stood Corinne holding back her tears and Lise Payette dressed in black like a penitent; before me swam a sea of faces that no other defeat had thrown into such dejection.

"The day will come, however," I said, trying to convince myself, "and we will be here to greet it. But I must admit that tonight I would be hard pressed to tell you when or how. In the meantime we must live together. . . ." To cut words short I struck up the Vigneault song that had practically become our anthem, "Gens du pays," off-key, as usual. Then I took my leave with "A la prochaine!"—a sentiment that was also a bit off-key but might at least help forget the present a little.

In Ottawa Trudeau lost no time in transforming himself into the wheedling healer full of solicitude for the downtrodden, pretending to spread balm on our wounds by praising our sense of democracy, a perfect Tartufe as we would soon discover, once again.

René Lévesque, "Heartbreak," from *Memoirs*, trans. by Philip Stratford (Toronto: McClelland and Stewart, 1986), pp. 301-309.

SIR JOHN A. MACDONALD

SPEECH IN THE LEGISLATIVE ASSEMBLY, FEBRUARY 6, 1865

The whole scheme of Confederation, as propounded by the Conference, as agreed to and sanctioned by the Canadian Government, and as now presented for the consideration of the people, and the Legislature, bears upon its face the marks of compromise.

Of necessity there must have been a great deal of mutual concession. When we think of the representatives of five colonies, all supposed to have different interests, meeting together, charged with the duty of protecting those interests and of pressing the views of their own localities and sections, it must be admitted that had we not met in a spirit of conciliation, and with an anxious desire to promote this union; if we had not been impressed with the idea contained in the words of the resolution—"That the best interests and present and future prosperity of British North America would be promoted by a Federal Union under the Crown of Great Britain,"—all our efforts might have proved to be of no avail. If we had not felt that, after coming to this conclusion, we were bound to set aside our private opinions on matters of detail, if we had not felt ourselves bound to look at what was practicable, not obstinately rejecting the opinions of others nor adhering to our own; if we had not met, I say, in a spirit of conciliation, and with an anxious, overruling desire to form one people under one government, we never would have succeeded. With these views, we press the question on this House and the country.

I say to this House, if you do not believe that the union of the colonies is for the advantage of the country, that the joining of these five peoples into one nation, under one sovereign, is for the benefit of all, then reject the scheme. Reject it if you do not believe it to be for the present advantage and future prosperity of yourselves and your children. But if, after a calm and full consideration of this scheme, it is believed, as a whole, to be for the advantage of this province—if the House and country believe this union to be one which will ensure for us British laws, British connection, and British freedom—and increase and develop the social, political and material prosperity of the country, then I implore this House and the country to lay aside all prejudices, and accept the scheme which we offer. I ask this House to meet the question in the same spirit in which the delegates met it. I ask each member of this House to lay aside his own opinions as to particular details, and to accept the scheme as a whole if he think it beneficial as a whole.

As I stated in the preliminary discussion, we must consider this scheme in the light of a treaty. By a happy coincidence of circumstances, just when an Administration had been formed in Canada for the purpose of attempting a solution of the difficulties under which we laboured, at the same time the Lower Provinces, actuated by a similar feeling, appointed a Conference with a view to a union among themselves, without being cognizant of the position the government was taking in Canada. If it had not been for this fortunate coincidence of events, never, perhaps, for a long series of years would we have been able to bring this scheme to a practical conclusion.

But we did succeed. We made the arrangement, agreed upon the scheme, and the deputations from the several governments represented at the Conference went back pledged to lay it before their governments, and to ask the legislatures and people of their respective provinces to assent to it. I trust the scheme will be assented to as a whole. I am sure this House will not seek to alter it in its unimportant details: and, if altered in any important provisions, the result must be that the whole will be set aside, and we must begin *de novo.* If any important changes are made, every one of the colonies will feel itself absolved from the implied obligation to deal with it as a Treaty, each province will feel itself at liberty to amend it *ad libitum* so as to suit its own views and interests; in fact, the whole of our labours will have been for nought, and we will have to renew our negotiations with all the colonies for the purpose of establishing some new scheme.

I hope the House will not adopt any such a course as will postpone, perhaps for ever, or at all events for a long period, all chances of union. All the statesmen and the public men who have written or spoken on the subject admit the advantages of a union, if it were practicable: and now when it is proved to be practicable, if we do not embrace this opportunity the present favorable time will pass away, and we may never have it again. Because, just so surely as this scheme is defeated, will be revived the original proposition for a union of the Maritime Provinces, irrespective of Canada: they will not remain as they are now, powerless, scattered, helpless communities; they will form themselves into a power, which, though not so strong as if united with Canada, will, nevertheless, be a powerful and considerable community, and it will be then too late for us to attempt to strengthen ourselves by this scheme, which, in the words of the resolution, "is for the best interests, and present and future prosperity of British North America."

If we are not blind to our present position, we must see the hazardous situation in which all the great interests of Canada stand in respect to the United States. I am no alarmist. I do not believe in the prospect of immediate war. I believe that the common sense of the two nations will prevent a war: still we cannot trust to probabilities. The Government and Legislature would be wanting in their duty to the people if they ran any risk. We know that the United States at this moment are engaged in a war of enormous dimensions—that the occasion of a war with Great Britain has again and again arisen, and may at any time in the future again arise. We cannot foresee what may be the result; we cannot say but that the two nations may drift into a war as other nations have done before. It would then be too late when war had commenced to think of measures for strengthening ourselves, or to begin negotiations for a union with the sister provinces.

At this moment, in consequence of the ill-feeling which has arisen between England and the United States—a feeling of which Canada was not the cause—in consequence of the irritation which now exists, owing to the unhappy state of affairs on this continent, the Reciprocity Treaty, it seems probable, is about to be brought to an end—our trade is hampered by the passport system, and at any moment we may be deprived of permission to carry our goods through United States channels—the bonded goods system may be done away with, and the winter trade through the United States put an end to. Our merchants may be obliged to return to the old system of bringing in during the summer months the supplies for the whole year. Ourselves already threatened, our trade interrupted, our intercourse, political and commercial, destroyed, if we do not take warning now when we have the opportunity, and while one avenue is threatened to be closed, open another by taking advantage of the present arrangement and the desire of the Lower Provinces to draw closer the alliance between us, we may suffer commercial and political disadvantages it may take long for us to overcome.

The Conference having come to the conclusion that a legislative union, pure and simple, was impracticable, our next attempt was to form a government upon federal principles, which would give to the General Government the strength of a legislative and administrative union, while at the same time it preserved that liberty of action for the different sections which is allowed by a Federal Union. And I am strong in the belief—that we have hit upon the happy medium in these resolutions, and that we have formed a scheme of government which unites the advantages of both, giving us the strength of a legislative union and the sectional freedom of a federal union, with protection to local interests.

In doing so we had the advantage of the experience of the United States. It is the fashion now to enlarge on the defects of the Constitution of the United States, but I am not one of those who look upon it as a failure. (Hear, hear.) I think and believe that it is one of the most skillful works which human intelligence ever created; is one of the most perfect organizations that ever governed a free people. To say that it has some defects is but to say that it is not the work of Omniscience, but of human intellects. We are happily situated in having had the opportunity of watching its operation, seeing its working from its infancy till now. It was in the main formed on the model of the Constitution of Great Britain, adapted to the circumstances of a new country, and was perhaps the only practicable system that could have been adopted under the circumstances existing at the time of its formation. We can now take advantage of the experience of the last seventy-eight years, during which that Constitution has existed, and I am strongly of the belief that we have, in a great measure, avoided in this system which we propose for the adoption of the people of Canada, the defects which time and events have shown to exist in the American Constitution.

In the first place, by a resolution which meets with the universal approval of the people of this country, we have provided that for all time to come, so far as we can legislate for the future, we shall have as the head of the executive power, the Sovereign of Great Britain. (Hear, hear.) No one can look into futurity and say what will be the destiny of this country. Changes come over nations and peoples in the course of ages. But, so far as we can legislate, we provide that, for all time to come, the Sovereign of Great Britain shall be the Sovereign of British North America.

By adhering to the monarchical principle, we avoid one defect inherent in the Constitution of the United States. By the election of the President by a majority and for a short period, he never is the sovereign and chief of the nation. He is never looked up to by the whole people as the head and front of the nation. He is at best but the successful leader of a party. This defect is all the greater on account of the practice of re-election. During his first term of office, he is employed in taking steps to secure his own re-election, and for his party a continuance of power. We avoid this by adhering to the monarchical principle—the Sovereign whom you respect and love. I believe that it is of the utmost importance to have that principle recognized, so that we shall have a Sovereign who is placed above the region of party—to whom all parties look up—who is not elevated by the action of one party nor depressed by the action of another, who is the common head and sovereign of all. (Hear, hear and cheers.)

In the Constitution we propose to continue the system of Responsible Government, which has existed in this province since 1841, and which has long obtained in the Mother Country. This is a feature of our Constitution as we have it now, and as we shall have it in the Federation, in which, I think, we avoid one of the great defects in the Constitution of the United States. There the President, during his term of office, is in a great measure a despot, a one-man power, with the command of the naval and military forces—with an immense amount of patronage as head of the Executive, and with the veto power as a branch of the legislature, perfectly uncontrolled by responsible advisers, his cabinet being departmental officers merely, whom he is not obliged by the Constitution to consult with, unless he chooses to do so. With us the Sovereign, or in this country the Representative of the Sovereign, can act only on the advice of his ministers, those ministers being responsible to the people through Parliament.

Prior to the formation of the American Union, as we all know, the different states which entered into it were separate colonies. They had no connection with each other further than that of having a common sovereign, just as with us at present. Their constitutions and their laws were different. They might and did legislate against each other, and when they revolted against the Mother Country they acted as separate sovereignties, and carried on the war by a kind of treaty of alliance against the common enemy. Ever since the union was formed the difficulty of what is called "State Rights" has existed, and this had much to do in bringing on the present unhappy war in the United States.

They commenced, in fact, at the wrong end. They declared by their Constitution that each state was a sovereignty in itself, and that all the powers incident to a sovereignty belonged to each state, except those powers which, by the Constitution, were conferred upon the General Government and Congress. Here we have adopted a different system. We have strengthened the General Government. We have given the General Legislature all the great subjects of legislation. We have conferred on them, not only specifically and in detail, all the powers which are incident to sovereignty, but we have expressly declared that all subjects of general interest not distinctly and exclusively conferred upon the local governments and local legislatures, shall be conferred upon the General Government and Legislature.

We have thus avoided that great source of weakness which has been the cause of the disruption of the United States. We have avoided all conflict of jurisdiction and authority, and if this constitution is carried out, as it will be in full detail in the Imperial Act to be passed if the colonies adopt the scheme, we will have in fact, as I said before, all the advantages of a legislative union under one administration, with, at the same time the guarantees for local institutions and for local laws, which are insisted upon by so many in the provinces now, I hope, to be united.

Sir John A. Macdonald, from "Speech in the Legislative Assembly, February 6, 1865," in *Parliamentary Debates on the Subject of the Confederation of the British North American Provinces*, 3rd Session, 8th Provincial Parliament of Canada.

ANTONINE MAILLET

AUNT EVANGELINE'S TREASURE

For once, the cat had got Aunt Evangeline's tongue. Imagine! Her own niece on her husband's side, the one who left ten years ago to go selling her stories in Montreal, and had herself polished up in all those fancy schools, and went traipsing all over the world—well, if she hasn't come back here and paid a small fortune for the tiniest tip of a sand dune that will most likely get swallowed by the sea with the first good tide in October. That young whippersnapper! What does she know about all the treasures hoarded up and buried by our ancestors over the past three hundred years?

"That's just the point, Aunt Evangeline. It's precisely to be better able to dig up those hidden treasures that I've come back; and to get a grander view of the whole country, I've driven piles into my dune of white sand with the firm intention of building myself a lighthouse—"

"What? A lighthouse, you say?"

This time Aunt Evangeline even forgot to swallow. She turned away without a word, looking like the wife of Moses who had just seen her husband drop the tablets containing the Ten Commandments. Then she muttered to herself so low that only the sea gulls could hear her:

"Now I've seen everything!"

And she had seen everything: two world wars, the Spanish flu, the Great Depression. And she had sailed bravely through into her eighties, trailing behind her a progeny running into three figures, not counting sons-in-law and daughters-in-law. She knew the century and the country better than anyone; why she would even pretend to be shocked, especially by a harebrained fool like myself who wanted to build a lighthouse on the sand and fill it up with a lot of moth-eaten old furniture, was a mystery to me.

Surely nothing could surprise a descendant of ten generations of pioneers, sod breakers, founders, a people who had spent half their history building and the other half defending what they had built. And yet, invaded on the flank by a niece who, armed with maps, compasses, T-squares, and a stack of yellowed, rat-chewed manuscripts, had confessed to having come to transcribe the oral chronicles of the country, my octogenarian aunt found herself for the first time in her life without a word to say.

In the end, though, she found her voice: the habit of a lifetime was too strong in her. She was descended from the survivors of three centuries of wars and deportations throughout America, of countless tossings on the wide, wide ocean. She took hold of herself, forgave me my lighthouse and the folly that made me want to write down her stories, and let her mind wander back through a family history so multilimbed and tangled that, intending to tell me only about Bouctouche, she ended up by presenting to me, like a golden loaf of bread fresh from the oven, the whole of Acadia—which that year, 1979, happened to be celebrating its 375th anniversary.

• • •

No longer is Acadia a country with its own government, its own capital, and its own laws. No longer is it a colony, or even a province. It was once all of those things, back when Europeans first came to transplant their roots into the soil of North America. Then the various Louis of France and Georges of England launched their Channel Wars, revised their charts, and corrected their maps, and in the end deleted Acadia from their world map and reduced the whole north Atlantic to only three provinces.

• • •

The Maritime Provinces of Canada.

Bouctouche was nestled into the lap of one of those provinces: New Brunswick. A big, chubby, well-fed baby of a village, surrounded by rolling hills, nursed by five or six rivers and fifty-six streams, freshened by the perfume of the forest on three sides and by the salt of the ocean on the fourth; a pearl of a village that, on June 24, 1985, the day of its bicentennial—which Aunt Evangeline, God rest her soul, did not live to see—hung an armorial chain around its mayor's neck and proclaimed itself a town.

As a town of fewer than 3,000 souls, it had slashed new roads and boulevards through the forest, dug itself an underground drainage system, sent its mayor to preside with his peers on the municipal council, and yet managed to remain the very model of a fair-sized coastal Acadian village—all of which was recounted, relived, and treated with the utmost scorn and resentment by Aunt Evangeline "The worst country in the world!" she would say, her voice trembling with nostalgic tenderness.

By 'country,' of course, she meant Bouctouche, the county, all the lands up and down the Atlantic coast where her people alone came to live when they returned from exile, from what it amused them to call the Great Unsettlement: a euphemism, you understand, and a term of derision.

"To be exiled, you know, it *unsettles* a person," she would say, without appearing to blame anyone. "No offence," she might add, to make sure she was properly understood.

I understood. I understood even more, perhaps, than she intended me to. The easy way she said "the others" when she referred to people from outside "the country" told me a lot about the mentality of her generation, which was also my father's and mother's generation. There was "us" and there were "the others." The others included all of you who did not disembark with Champlain in 1604 in what is now Nova Scotia; who were not beaten and abused at the hands of the British; who were not forced to return by foot through the backwoods of Georgia and the Carolinas and New England to reclaim a lost land; who did not speak French or, more accurately, that version of the language known as Acadian, the roots of which go back to the sixteenth and seventeenth centuries and even, with certain words, to the Middle Ages.

An old language then, plucked out of France and preserved almost intact throughout all the intervening generations. How Aunt Evangeline would cluck with pleasure when she spoke it, embellishing her stories with beautifully archaic turns of phrase. A language that had yet to be codified by the academies, dissected in language laboratories, reduced by purists, and augmented by cultural exchanges with the outside world. What Aunt Evangeline did not know, but what I could have told her, was that between the time of Rabelais, who made use in his books of a vocabulary of 100,000 words, and Racine, who only a century later had to make do with 5,000 words, the French language had been "purified" by a succession of grammarians intent on weeding out their cultural garden. And what happened to those 95,000 expurgated and forgotten words?

They're right here in Acadia, Aunt Evangeline, tucked away in your own unconscious, ancestral memory.

And what is more, this language once spoken in France but found there today only in antiquarian books and glossaries, is still alive in us: we could return it unscathed to our transatlantic cousins. And, because we have preserved it in our throats as well as in our loins, we could return it in its original accent.

But this brings a smile to the corners of Aunt Evangeline's lips, because there is nothing this fiery she-devil would like more than to open wide her linguistic and cultural treasure-trove—on condition that she be allowed to call a cat a cat and no beating about the bush. The Middle Ages, the Renaissance, Rabelais, Racine, syntax, the academies—the devil take the whole boiling, as far as she was concerned. She talked about life, about traditions, about a heritage transmitted in a direct line straight from the horse's mouth. Not about culture. I suppose I could have explained to her that it all amounted to more or less the same thing, that culture, for all its grand airs, was really just the sum of all those other things. But she would just have given me another of her reproving clucks.

"The things of life don't need all that literary mumbo jumbo," I could hear her saying. "They don't need to be stuffed into learned considerations of three points... big A, little b, little c. Life can't be defined. It's like a tree that is so much more than a tree; or like time, which drags us imperceptibly along in its wake." She knew a lot about time, having fought it and resisted it for eighty years knowing full well that it would have her skin in the end. She knew that a tree is made up of fruit and leaves and shade and breeze, flower, nut, nest. She was a storyteller, a pioneer, a chronicler, and she could tell you all about her country's brief history. And she could do it without so much as raising her voice, and with no literary additives.

And yet, without knowing it, she *did* add to the language, sprinkling it with rare words, ancient sayings, images fired in its very crucible. Like all Acadians of her generation, she delighted in hyperbole, double meaning, insinuations. History had taught them to be suspicious, these victims of other people's wars: suspicion, caution, patience, and the subtle art of querning their words to squeeze every ounce of juice out of them, without seeming to.

Some of that they inherited from their ancestors, from the depths of the French Middle Ages. The blood of Aunt Evangeline had already coursed through the veins of those wild and turbulent gluttons, the troubadours who created the *Roman de Renart,* the farces and the *fabliaux.* In the Acadia I knew, growing up at the flash point of oral and written traditions, the soul of the Middle Ages was still very much alive. It had the same kind of humour, at once acerbic and hail-fellow-well-met; the same infallible sense of timing, which always allowed us to get out of a ticklish scrape at the last possible moment; the same false air of resignation, with which we tiptoed through the centuries without waking up the sleeping bear; the same love of paradox, which makes the Acadian the most hospitable and the most mistrustful, the most modest and the most obscene, the most bashful and the most audacious fellow on earth. In short, he has inherited the fine old populist traditions of the Latin and Celtic cultures, which stretch far, far back into the abysses of time.

All of which, of course, Aunt Evangeline would quickly and loudly deny, shouting it from the top of my lighthouse tower. No use shoving my Latin down that woman's throat. Bouctouche is stuck in the very heart of Acadia; Acadia sits on the Atlantic coast; the Atlantic has nurtured her fishermen and sailors for three-and-a-half centuries; and the history of the country began in Port-Royal, which is now called Annapolis, with a certain Jacques à Antoine Maillet, the ancestor of her husband's family. The rest is no concern of hers. This woman, who gave birth to fifteen children–alone, and without losing a single one of them—absolutely refused to acknowledge that she had inherited anything from anyone other than the pioneers who had risked their lives to put down roots in the New World. Her own history began then, the day when a second Noah drew up his Ark alongside Sainte-Croix Island, floating in Baie Françoise, also known as Baie du Fond, which eventually became the Bay of Fundy. The country they saw was so beautiful, the land so rich, that this second Noah, in imitation of the first, popped the corks on a few wine bottles and celebrated his discovery—then ran his ship aground on a sand spit. He ended up spending the winter there, and that's how Acadia first saw the light of day—founded by an explorer named Champlain who had had too much to drink and had made too much good cheer.

As she told me this story, Aunt Evangeline laughed till her sides ached. That's the school she had been polished in. History, for a storyteller, is nothing more or less than a rollicking good story, a sparkling tale whose roots are planted firmly in real ground, whose facts have been solemnly authenticated by ten or fifteen generations of professional liars. And, true or false, her version was far more passionate, and much more humorous, than any official account; and as her niece I couldn't very well find fault with it anyway.

"And it was that same drunkard," she added, "who gave this name to the country: Arcadia, named in memory of another country that existed in the olden days, apparently, and which they say was a paradise on earth."

She lapsed into a thoughtful silence, then continued with utter conviction:

"Arcadia . . . it was too beautiful. I think they must have dropped the 'r' during the crossing, because they felt that any paradise they found on this side of the ocean would be a tiny bit smaller than the original."

• • •

I finished building my lighthouse that same summer, ten years ago, under the astonished gaze of the sea gulls and the suspicious eye of Aunt Evangeline, who'd seen a thing or two in her time, my girl! Since then I've scoured the four horizons and rummaged through the sand and the dunes and the seaweed, and I've yet to find a treasure more precious than the one I found buried under my feet when I laid the foundations for my lighthouse. It was a treasure that ten generations of my ancestors had jealously guarded, and which, unknown to her, Aunt Evangeline had delivered to me that day on a silver platter.

Antonine Maillet, "Aunt Evangeline's Treasure," trans. Wayne Grady, *Saturday Night*, (January, 1987), pp. 50-52. Excerpt from PAR DERRIÈRE CHEZ MON PÈRE, Leméac, 1987

MARSHALL McLUHAN
THE VIOLENCE OF THE MEDIA

"The Kingdom of Heaven suffereth violence." Violence against the Kingdom of Heaven proceeds by prayer and petition, prayer being one of the more extreme forms of violence, since it is conducted by superhuman force. It should not be surprising, therefore, that the ages of the utmost physical violence have also produced the greatest exemplars of heroic sanctity, as in the sixteenth century, and also today. Violence means the violation of territories, whether political or psychic, physical or moral. *The Listener* (December 75/January 76) records a dicussion on pornographic violence under the head "No victim, no pornography":

> *...How, in the age of Marxism, socialism, liberation, have we all come to be landed with de Sade? There's another very important thing to say here. To you and me, sexual meaning is meeting and entering the body of another person in the closest creative intimacy. The pervert—that is, the person to whom this has no meaning, who needs pornography—doesn't understand the meaning of sexuality. He needs to penetrate the body of the other person in order to find whether there is any meaning in there, just like a child sticking its needle in a teddy bear.*

To invade the private person, or to invade a group with teaching, with doctrines, with entertainment, all these are alike forms of violence. To assume the right to program the sensibilities or thoughts and fantasies of individuals or groups, has long been taken for granted as a viable form of personal or social action. The private educator as much as the college of propaganda in Rome, assumes a mandate to shape individuals and societies in any age.

Today, however, there is a new dimension in all of these activities. Electric media move information and people at the speed of light. It is this instant and total quality that constitutes the condition of mass man and the mass society, an effect that occurs not so much by virtue of size as speed of involvement and inclusiveness. Moreover, the hidden dimension in all electric media, whether the telephone, TV, or radio, is that *the sender is sent*. When you are on the phone, or on the air, you can be anywhere and everywhere at the same moment.

The violence that all electric media inflict on their users is that they are instantly invaded and deprived of their physical bodies and are merged in a network of extensions of their own nervous systems. As if this were not sufficient violence or invasion of individual rights, the elimination of the physical bodies of the electric media users also deprives them of the means of relating the program experience to their private individual selves, even as instant involvement suppresses private identity.

The loss of individual and personal meaning via the electronic media ensures a corresponding and reciprocal violence from those so deprived of their identities; for violence, whether spiritual or physical, is a quest for identity and the meaningful. The less identity, the more violence. Violence exerted by private individuals tends to have limited results, whereas the violence exerted by groups knows no bounds. Media are always and necessarily corporate or group activities, whether they are the mother tongues or the father images of big corporations. With the proliferation of multi-media in our time, there is a new consensus that some manner of media ecology and control be put into action; but against this proposal there is a negative and hidden factor in the Western world. Edward Hall, the anthropologist, has drawn attention to this negative attitude in the Western world in a recent study, *The Fourth Dimension in Architecture: The Impact of Building on Man's Behavior:*

> *The most pervasive and important assumption, a cornerstone in the edifice of Western thought, is one that lies hidden from our consciousness and has to do with man's relationship to his environment. Quite simply the Western view is that human processes, particularly behavior, are independent of environmental controls and influence.*

The obsessional concern of Western man with "content" and the correlative indifference to hidden environmental or side effects, stems from the very character of Western literacy. This is easy to observe by contrasting our scepticism about general or environmental effects with the attitudes of preliterate or non-literate societies of the Third World. In his *The Savage Mind* Levi-Strauss discusses the pervasive feeling of non-visual cultures that every kind of change effects everything else, adding that this kind of awareness is pure paranoia. Literate, or visual man, in contrast, has to be *shown* every kind of relationship. Visuality favours quantification and exact measurement and is not inclined to listen to the protests of the Chinese that telephone poles deeply disturb their entire psychic balance. It is true that Plato at the end of *The Republic* mentions that any change in musical rhythms could cause a political revolution: but jazz and Rock and jets are accepted as natural phenomena which could not disturb the psyche or sanity of a literate man. The "content" of any work, philosophical or physical, is the *efficient* cause in the situation. The *formal* cause concerns the effects proceeding from the total structure of the situation, which includes the public and the users. It is the *formal* cause which constitutes the environmental violence, the side effects of the media.

Harold Innis was one of the very few people since Plato to show serious interest in formal causes and the effects that result from the formal structures of total situations. The numerous commissions on violence that have marked our violent time have, without exception, paid attention only to the *efficient* cause, the program content of the media. The effects of the media themselves represent a form of violence so vast as to be unnoticed. It is a situation not unlike that in the old rhyme:

You hang the thief
Who steals the goose
from off the common,
But leave the larger felon loose
Who steals the common
from the goose.

In *Identity, Youth and Crisis* Erik H. Erikson observes:

In Jung's "persona" a weak ego seems to sell out to a compelling social prototype. A fake ego identity is established which suppresses rather than synthesizes those experiences and functions, which endanger the "front".

In *The Nuremberg Mind,* F.R. Miale and Michael Selzer, in search of understanding how the Nazi leaders could seem to be ordinary, well-intentioned people, encountered the fact that:

. . . values, and behavior of individuals are shaped by social forces beyond our control—and often, indeed, beyond our recognition.

The forces which are typically "beyond our recognition" are the environmental or diffused forces, what we ordinarily take for granted as the existing social services of the media, whether they be highways or airways. Since visual, rational man can find no "connection" between such forces and their victims, he throws up his hands in mystification. Radio had a fantastic and profound effect in retrieving the ordinary tribal consciousness of Germany in the 1920s and 1930s. TV, which is an addictive inner trip (regardless of program), sent American youth in pursuit of the occult and group awareness. Since there are no visual or quantifiable *connections* between radio and TV and their effects, Western man humbly and dumbly submits to their magic. What Miale and Selzer found by way of analogue for the monstrous behaviour of the Nazi leaders relates to the case of the psychological study at Yale undertaken by Stanley Milgram who "sought to discover the extent to which human beings will obey commands which come increasingly into conflict with their consciences." The teachers chosen for the job proceeded to demonstrate experimental shocks to subjects as part of a memory test:

> *Sweating, trembling, and in other ways indicating their extreme reluctance to continue administering the punishments,* 65 percent of the teachers nevertheless obeyed orders all the way to the end of the scale on the shock generator! *Not a single teacher disobeyed the experimenter's orders before reaching 300 volts—marked INTENSE SHOCK—and only 12.5 percent of them stopped at this point.*

Milgram concluded:

> *When the individual* is on his own, *conscience is brought into play. But when he functions in an organized mode, directions that come from the higher level component are not assessed against the internal standards of moral judgment. . . . The psychology of obedience does not depend on the placement within the larger hierarchy. . . . The social psychology of this century reveals a major lesson: often, it is not so much the kind of person a man is as the kind of situation in which he finds himself that determines how he will act.*

Since the kind of situations in which 20th century man exists are almost entirely products of the mass media, we have to face the further fact that these situations are beyond the ken of Western awareness. Western literate man is easily inclined to make moral protests, but is seemingly incapable of recognizing the *formal* or "acoustic" structure of situations which are disturbing and destroying him.

The group, or the crowd, has minimal identity and exists in a state of paranoic anxiety about any threats to its precarious pattern. In his classic work *Crowds and Power* Elias Canetti explains that all kinds of crowds experience a need to get bigger, and also fear that they are getting smaller. This passion can extend to money (one kind of crowd), as much as to the mindless group. The formal effects of the electric media in invading individuals and groups are in no way limited by the content or the programs so purveyed. The effects of the car are felt in the highways, factories and oil companies, or the service environment. The service environment constituted by electric networks acts as a kind of *formal* cause, or hidden *ground.* That which appears or is noticed is only the efficient cause. The Greeks gave no heed to the effects of the phonetic alphabet which transformed their inner and outer lives, ending the bardic colleges which had long served as their educational establishment. Like ourselves, the Greeks had a strong visual bias toward efficient causality and ethics and applied knowledge. Efficient causality is the world of logic and connectedness, and of specific goals and directions. In a word, it is the province of visual man. Until visual man, or alphabetic man, the pre-Socratics lived and thought in the acoustic or multi-directional world.

Today, the Third World, which is eager to resemble and to surpass the First World, is still in the elder province of intuitive experience which precedes the advent of phonetically literate or visual man. From his beginnings, phonetically literate man assumed it was his right to invade other cultures and to impose his discoveries wherever possible. Whereas the Graeco/Roman world, constituted by the phonetic alphabet and by techniques of visually applied knowledge, assumed a mission to extend itself and its institutions to the "lesser breeds," electronic man, on the other hand, has re-entered the world of acoustic experience, thereby losing all confidence in his right to impose the old visual culture of the West on people who have not yet been invaded by the phonetic alphabet. From the first, identified with the Graeco/Roman culture, Christianity had at the same time brought the hidden Word and the new visual culture to the "lesser breeds." Today, a crisis in Christianity emerges with the possibility of propagating the hidden Word directly without the benefit of the written word, or Graeco/Roman culture. The patterns of Western civilization are as incompatible with simultaneous or acoustic culture as the pre-Socratic Logos was incompatible with the alphabetic innovation.

The violence of dominant culture consists in the assumption of the right to invade and to shape groups and individuals with the preferred norms of one's choice. In the electronic world we now take for granted the co-existence of all cultures and their immediacy of access, while sheer diversity and range of cultural choice daily brings into doubt the rights of any one culture to impose itself on another. We have begun to doubt our own rights to mould and shape our own children. Women's Lib is by comparison a side issue, yet one that is essentially electronic in offering power to all participants.

Without exception, then, the activity of media, old and new, as invaders of both public and private space, raises the question and image of violence at every turn. At the speed of light, American political institutions are trembling and quailing in this bi-centennial year. Writing on "Pre-election blues" in the *Globe and Mail* on March 16, 1976, James Reston observed:

> *The more this capital fusses and agonizes over the election, the more it seems to long for fundamental change. It would never admit as much in public, but the truth comes out in private: from the top of the Administration and the Congress to the critical levels of the civil service, it is*

> *almost yearning for new faces and new beginnings. This may not be logical or even rational, for all the devilishly complicated problems will remain after the election, but there it is—an intuitive feeling that something is deeply wrong here and probably won't be corrected by the old cast of characters or the old ideological arguments of either party.*

He adds that:

> *This is not a partisan but a general feeling that Washington is not at the beginning of something but at the end of something.*

In the February issue of *Atlantic,* David Halberstam has some observations on TV and politics:

> *Television not only changed the balance of power, but it became a vital part of the new balance of power. Presidents knew the advantage they had in gaining access to the air and the difficulties any competing politician or institution had. Presidents had used or suffered press conferences for a variety of reasons, including a chance to listen to the country. Kennedy seized on live television as an opportunity for political theatre. He used reporters as pawns to help make him look better, smarter, shrewder, more capable, and in control. Indeed, mastery of the press conference became a kind of substitute for mastery of the political scene.*

He continues:

> *In that sense John Kennedy changed the presidency more than any recent predecessor with the exception of Franklin Roosevelt, who had slipped so naturally into the radio presidency. Kennedy's ascendancy, like Roosevelt's, was a confluence of a man and a technology, of a new political force and a politician with the skills and instincts to exploit it. The television audiences were acutely aware of style now. The President came not just into their towns but into their homes.*

The last sentence points to the violent invasive character of radio and television. Representative government had belonged to a period of communication by rail, when the representatives were at a considerable distance from the home. Both radio and TV restored the character of the tribal chieftain:

> *At the same time that television was granting immense and almost unchallenged power to the President, it was granting less and less power to anyone else, particularly its own people. The role of reporter and commentator was diminishing. There was less time for serious*

analysis, and fewer explanations of complicated stories. As the role of the reporter diminished, the role of technology grew.

As the primacy of the image increases, the role of parties and policies recedes, as is the case with all media "content." This is not to say that content and program have no function on TV. Indeed, their function is to assure that TV will be turned on so that it can perform its work of obliterating all individuality and all privacy. Mr. Eliot observed long ago that the chief use of the content of a poem is "to satisfy one habit of the reader, to keep his mind diverted and quiet, while the poem does its work upon him: much as the imaginary burglar is always provided with a bit of nice meat for the house-dog." Likewise, the function of a program is to keep the users occupied by some diversion while the medium itself does its work upon him.

Marshall McLuhan, "The Violence of the Media," *The Canadian Forum*, (September, 1976), pp. 9-12.

SIR CHARLES G.D. ROBERTS
IN THE DEEP OF THE GRASS

Misty gray green, washed with tints of the palest violet, spotted with red clover-blooms, white oxeyes, and hot orange Canada lilies, the deep-grassed levels basked under the July sun. A drowsy hum of bees and flies seemed to distil, with warm aromatic scents, from the sun-steeped blooms and grass-tops. The broad, blooming, tranquil expanse, shimmering and softly radiant in the heat, seemed the very epitome of summer. Now and again a small cloud-shadow sailed across it. Now and again a little wind, swooping down upon it gently, bent the grass-tops all one way, and spread a sudden silvery pallor. Save for the droning bees and flies there seemed to be but one live creature astir between the grass and the blue. A solitary marsh-hawk, far over by the rail fence, was winnowing slowly, slowly, hither and thither, lazily hunting.

All this was in the world above the grass-tops. But below the grass-tops was a very different world—a dense, tangled world of dim green shade, shot with piercing shafts of sun, and populous with small, furtive life. Here, among the brown and white roots, the crowded green stems, and the mottled stalks, the little earth kindreds went busily about their affairs and their desires, giving scant thought to the aerial world above them. All that made life significant to them was here in the warm green gloom; and when anything chanced to part the grass to its depths they would scurry away in unanimous indignation.

On a small stone, over which the green closed so thickly that, when he chanced to look upward, he caught but the scantiest shreds of sky, sat a half-grown field-mouse, washing his whiskers with his dainty claws. His tiny, bead-like eyes kept ceaseless watch, peering through the shadowy tangle for whatever might come near in the shape of foe or prey. Presently two or three stems above his head were beaten down, and a big green grasshopper, alighting clumsily from one of his blind leaps, fell sprawling on the stone. Before he could struggle to his long legs and climb back to the safer region of the grass-tops, the little mouse was upon him. Sharp, white teeth pierced his green mail, his legs kicked convulsively twice or thrice, and the faint iridescence faded out of his big, blank, foolish eyes. The mouse made his meal with relish, daintily discarding the dry legs and wing-cases. Then amid the green debris scattered upon the stone, he sat up, and once more went through his fastidious toilet.

But life for the little mouse in his grass-world was not quite all watching and hunting. When his toilet was complete, and he had amiably let a large black cricket crawl by unmolested, he suddenly began to whirl round on the stone, chasing his own tail. As he was amusing himself with this foolish play, another mouse, about the same size as himself, and probably of the same litter, jumped upon the stone, and knocked him off. He promptly retorted in kind; and for several minutes, as if the game were a well-understood one, the two kept it up, squeaking soft merriment, and apparently forgetful of all peril. The grass-tops above this play rocked and rustled in a way that would certainly have attracted attention had there been any eyes to see. But the marsh-hawk was still hunting lazily at the other side of the field, and no tragedy followed the childishness.

Both seemed to tire of the sport at the same instant; for suddenly they stopped, and hurried away through the grass on opposite sides of the stone, as if remembered business had just called to them. Whatever the business was, the first mouse seemed to forget it very speedily, for in half a minute he was back upon the stone again, combing his fine whiskers and scratching his ears. This done to his satisfaction, he dropped like a flash from his seat, and disappeared into a small hollow beneath it. As he did so, a hairy black spider darted out, and ran away among the roots.

A minute or two after the disappearance of the mouse, a creature came along which appeared gigantic in the diminutive world of the grass folk. It was nearly three feet long, and of the thickness of a man's finger. Of a steely gray-black, striped and reticulated in a mysterious pattern with a clear whitish yellow, it was an ominous shape indeed, as it glided smoothly and swiftly, in graceful curves, through the close green tangle. The cool shadows and thin lights touched it flickeringly as it went, and never a grass-top stirred to mark its sinister approach. Without a sound of warning it came straight up to the stone, and darted its narrow, cruel head into the hole.

There was a sharp squeak, and instantly the narrow head came out again, ejected by the force of the mouse's agonized spring. But the snake's teeth were fastened in the little animal's neck. The doom of the green world had come upon him while he slept.

But doomed though he was, the mouse was game. He knew there was no poison in those fangs that gripped him, and he struggled desperately to break free. His powerful hind legs kicked the ground with a force which the snake, hampered at first by the fact of its length being partly trailed out through the tangle, was unable to quite control. With unerring instinct—though this was the first snake he had ever encountered—the mouse strove to reach its enemy's back and sever the bone with the fine chisels of this teeth. But it was just this that the snake was watchful to prevent. Three times in his convulsive leaps the mouse succeeded in touching the snake's body—but with his feet only, never once with those destructive little teeth. The snake held him inexorably, with a steady, elastic pressure which yielded just so far, and never quite far enough. And in a minute or two the mouse's brave struggles grew more feeble.

All this, however,—the lashing and the wriggling and the jumping—had not gone on without much disturbance to the grass-tops. Timothy head and clover-bloom, oxeye, and feathery plume-grass, they had bowed and swayed and shivered till the commotion, very conspicuous to one looking down upon the tranquil, flowery sea of green, caught the attention of the marsh-hawk, which at that moment chanced to be perching on a high fence stake. The lean-headed, fierce-eyed, trim-feathered bird shot from his perch, and sailed on long wings over the grass to see what was happening. As the swift shadow hovered over the grass-tops, the snake looked up.

Well he understood the significance of that sudden shade. Jerking back his fangs with difficulty from the mouse's neck, he started to glide off under the thickest matting of the roots. But lightning-quick though he was, he was not quite quick enough. Just as his narrow head darted under the roots, the hawk, with wings held straight up, and talons reaching down, dropped upon him, and clutched the middle of his back in a grip of steel. The next moment he was jerked into the air, writhing and coiling, and striking in vain frenzy at his captor's mail of hard feathers. The hawk flew off with him over the sea of green to the top of the fence stake, there to devour him at leisure. The mouse, sore wounded but not past recovery, dragged himself back to the hollow under the stone. And over the stone the grass-tops, once more still, hummed with flies, and breathed warm perfumes in the distilling heat.

Sir Charles G.D. Roberts, "In the Deep of the Grass," from *The Watchers of the Trails*, (Boston: L.C. Page and Co., 1904), pp. 247-253.

COLIN ROSS

THE STORY OF GREY OWL

Once upon a time there was a pervert called Grey Owl, who lived in the Canadian woods. He is famous because he came to Canada and learned how to imitate the Indians—he wore a disguise and grew his hair long. The white people in Canada know so little about Indians, and about their own woods, that Grey Owl fooled them all for a long time. But even after they found out that the famous Indian was really only Archie Belaney from England, even then they still respected him. Canadians have so few heroes that they decided to have Archie Belaney for a hero—they said to themselves, "Old Archie sure fooled us, didn't he? What a great man he was, to be able to fool us all, and live like an Indian."

Archie was only like an Indian on the outside though. That's why the Canadians liked him, and made him a hero. They wanted to have a hero who played little boy's games in the woods, and made friends with the animals just like in a story book. Canadians don't like Indians, on the outside or on the inside. That's why they liked Archie so well, and still do—they know that he's just a pleasant Englishman on the inside, just like them. When they know that, then they can love his Indian clothes and his Indian canoe, and even think that maybe his Indian life is very beautiful. When it's only harmless old Archie Belaney inside that Indian costume, then the Canadian ladies have nothing to be afraid of. Why *there's* an Indian who would just *love* to talk to them, and tell them about his friendly animal pets in the woods.

The Canadian ladies may live in Canada, but they don't like Canada—they don't like the cold, they don't like the bears, they don't like the lonely prairies, they don't like the forest. They're afraid of all those things and places. They don't have to be afraid of Archie Belaney—he writes nice books for them, that sound just like Henry Williamson, and other nice Englishmen who love nature. Archie Belaney had a very big heart, not like Indians—if the Canadian ladies ever tried to talk to an Indian, that Indian's heart wouldn't like them. They wouldn't like the Indian either.

All the Canadians are very grateful to Archie Belaney. His books are such a relief for them. When they read his books then they're not afraid of nature anymore—Archie makes them feel that nature is tame and friendly and safe. The only difference between Archie's life in the woods and Mrs. Smith's life in the city is that Archie has beavers for pets. Mrs. Smith, and her neighbour Mrs. MacKenzie, both keep budgies. The Canadian ladies are *very* grateful to Archie for keeping beavers for pets. Beavers seem like the best symbol Canada could have, when you think of Archie Belaney's friendly pets. All those Indians care about is killing the poor beavers, and selling their skins.

"Yes sir, those Indians are awful," says Mrs. MacKenzie. "Why if they came to our city they'd probably eat my budgies. Those poor friendly beavers and rabbits that live in our beautiful forests, the Indians hunt them and kill them. And Indians never write lovely books like Grey Owl does. Isn't it a shame that they never learned how to write!"

"Quite a shame", says one of the ladies.

"Yes", says Mrs. Smith. "You know, we should form a club to help those poor Indians. They have no books and no shoes, and all they ever eat is rabbits and wild things. We should help them. It's a shame. They're people too you know, just like us. Let's gather up some money and give it to the Indians to buy food and clothes. It would be *such* a good thing to do."

"Very good", says another one of the ladies.

The bridge party was at Mrs. MacKenzie's house that day. Mr. MacKenzie wasn't feeling well so he was at home. Mr. MacKenzie is a fireman. Mr. MacKenzie was serving the ladies tea and cakes—he had gotten up too early to bake them.

Mr. MacKenzie is very proud of being a Canadian man. He's very tough. He fights fires in the city, and in the fall he takes his holidays and goes hunting just like an Indian. Just like Grey Owl. Mr. MacKenzie spoke up and said, "The Indians were good people. They only killed the friendly animals in the woods because they needed them for food and clothes. They couldn't let their children go hungry. The Indians were good people, and very good hunters. They just weren't very smart, that's all—they weren't quite as high up as we are in the family tree of man." Mr. MacKenzie was talking to his wife, explaining about Indians to her. All the other ladies were listening.

"As a matter of fact", continued Mr. MacKenzie, "we're at the top. Yes, ladies, it's true. Now if the Indians had been able to build cars and houses like us, then I'm sure they wouldn't have killed so many of the poor animals in nature. They would have loved them just like you love your budgies."

The ladies knew Mr. MacKenzie was a very good fireman, and they listened to what he said with a great deal of respect. Mrs. MacKenzie knew her husband went hunting in the fall though. She didn't like the poor dead wild animals he brought back, and she wondered how he could ever bring himself to pull the trigger. But Mr. MacKenzie is so tough and strong that he still has hunting instincts just like a real Indian. Just like Grey Owl. You can't expect him to stop hunting just because of the Canadian ladies. After all Mr. MacKenzie loves nature in his own way, and who is Mrs. MacKenzie to say his way is wrong?

The Canadian ladies are *very* grateful to Archie Belaney. They had some bad feelings about nature, and about Indians, but after they read his books they felt all right. The bad feelings went away. After the Canadian ladies read Archie's books they felt that the woods and the Indians were safe and friendly after all. And Archie Belaney was so concerned about his animal friends he went *all* the way to England, just to talk about them. Wasn't that a great thing for Canada!

Mr. MacKenzie doesn't have much time for books. But his wife and the other ladies have said such nice things about Grey Owl that *he* admires Grey Owl too. Mr. MacKenzie would never call Grey Owl just old Archie Belaney. If he did that then his wife's bad feelings about Indians might come back. That wouldn't be nice.

Mr. MacKenzie and his friends were so grateful to Archie for making the bad feelings go away that they got together. They made Archie into a hero, and promised never to call him anything but Grey Owl. If they called him just old Archie Belaney, then he might seem like just another Englishman.

Yes, it was a good day for Canada when Archie Belaney came over here and started pretending to be an Indian. There was quite a mystery to his life you know, not like the Indians, who just sneak around in the woods in a bad mood killing things. Let me show you what a nice guy Archie was—here's some of his writing. This is from his wonderful book which he called *Tales From an Empty Cabin:*

> There was a wood-chuck, a special chum of mine, who year after year made her home under the upper cabin, where she had every Spring a brood of wood-chucklets, or whatever they are called. She was an amiable old lady, who used often to watch me at my work and allowed me a number of privileges, including the rare one of handling her young ones. But if a stranger came, she would spread herself out so as to quite fill the entrance to her domicile, to keep the youngsters in, and when the stranger left she would emit a shrill whistling sound at his retreating back, very sure that she had frightened him away. She too has gone, her time fulfilled, and another has taken over her old home; a well-built, very trim young matron who stands up straight and very soldierly before her doorway, and tries to look in windows.

Old Archie sure was a tame Indian wasn't he. *Isn't* Mrs. Smith grateful for that! When Archie Belaney left his three aunts in England and came over to Canada Mrs. Smith really felt good. She loved nature then. "Good!" she thought to herself. Mr. Smith and Mr. MacKenzie were so grateful they gave Archie a place to live in a special park, and paid him for the rest of his life just to keep on playing games with animals. They never paid any real Indians.

When Archie writes a book, he writes just like an Englishman. That's the nicest way. He makes the woodchucks sound just like the ladies who read his books. Archie Belaney dressed up like an Indian and pretended to be one himself. The Canadian ladies loved him for that. But inside Archie was all the time an Englishman who called the woodchucks his chums. Archie had lots of friends. Some had feathers. Some had fur. Some wore hats to church. They were all one big happy family, Archie and Mr. Smith, and Mrs. Smith, and Mr.

MacKenzie, and his wife, and Mrs. Woodchuck and her woodchucklets. Archie sure had a nice time in nature. Wouldn't it be beautiful to live like an Indian too?

Indians are really very lovable people. If Mr. MacKenzie was an Indian he would be able to say wonderful things about nature too. Just like Archie and Geronimo. Archie Belaney was brought up by his three aunts in England. This was bad for little Archie—there were too many ladies around all the time. So when Archie got the chance he decided he'd *really* show his aunts he didn't need them. He'd go over to Canada and be a wild Indian, and no aunties would tell *him* what to do. Archie Belaney was one guy who sure was tough. He didn't need a bunch of aunties to take care of *him*. He was a wild Indian who lived by himself in nature and showed everybody. After he showed them real good, he came back to England.

Yes, Archie came back to England as an Indian, and gave speeches and went to dinners. He even went to dinner with that white man the King, and he sure didn't show *him* any respect. How could you expect a wild Indian to stand up when the King walked in the room? Boy, Archie really showed his aunts that time, when he went back to England.

Even when Archie was a little boy living in England he used to play at being an Indian. But he couldn't play Indians in England and still live with his aunts when he was thirty or forty. Everyone would laugh at him. Archie was smart. He went over to Canada and played at being an Indian over there. No one laughed at him in Canada; in fact he fooled them all and played the game for the rest of his life. Trouble was, he wasn't really an Indian on the inside. Inside Archie Belaney was an Englishman who got lonely for his aunts. What do you think he did? Well, he made friends with all the animals, then he never got lonely again, not for the rest of his life. When he wrote about his animal friends, in his books, he used words like "domicile", "chum", "youngsters", "matron" and maybe even "auntie".

The Canadian ladies are *very* grateful. They were worried about living in this country. But Archie helped them. He wrote books, and in his books he showed the Canadian ladies that all the wild animals are really just as warm and friendly as an aunt or a grandma. Wasn't that wonderful! Mr. MacKenzie and Mrs. Smith were grateful too. All the Canadian people loved Archie Belaney for doing this great thing, and promised *never* to call him anything but Grey Owl. And that's just what they did.

Colin Ross, "The Story of Grey Owl," *The Compass*, No. 5 (Winter, 1979), pp. 79-83.

R. MURRAY SCHAFER

CANADIAN CULTURE: COLONIAL CULTURE

I am going to speak the words of this lecture loudly. I want people to hear them. They are not very far away, these people. They are cultured, or want to be; but this does not mean they are very intelligent or inquisitive, and in fact their indifference to the cultural topic I have elected to discuss tonight is really quite astounding. I can hear them snickering already; but I also hear their teeth chattering as I prepare to cut into their favourite prejudice.

The job of the artist is to tell the truth. It is one of the few honest professions left. Once it has been formulated the truth is quite simple (it always is) but it is never easy to formulate. To raise a dimly-perceived intuition to the level of consciousness and action needs sharply chiselled words. This is how I must focus my thinking if I am going to pierce the minds and senses of the people I want to reach.

Our subject is Canadian culture. Both the adjective and the noun are emotional, and so they should be. They can't be objectified; they are under our fingernails, under our skin, fed by the heart. And yet they are not, like our blood, a part of us, but are artificial concepts which someone else prepared for us to inhabit. I am a Canadian by accident; but I did not receive my birthright like a telephone number; I inherited with it a complex nucleus of habits and sensations that trigger mixed emotions. I love my country, but I despise it also. I love its natural beauty, but I weep for the destruction of it. I recognize the molds that have shaped it but I agonize to reshape them. And I know that this is possible, even though I often wonder just what effect my efforts are having.

Culture is the *prima materia* for shaping societies. It is a strong weapon, a terrible weapon sometimes, but it is always at hand. The moment you pick up a fork you have it. It can be used to civilize and to barbarize. It is quite amoral. It can be used to strengthen pride and self-confidence or it can be used to weaken these qualities. What I have to say here is as much concerned with how culture can weaken as with how it can strengthen: hence the second part of the title. A colonial regime strengthens itself by pushing out from centre to margin. It makes raw materials from the extremities and ejects finished products from the centre. It would be wrong to think that this is a balanced exchange, for as the economic historian Harold Innis showed, the central producer always attempts to maintain control over his suppliers by paying cheaply for raw goods and in an exchange medium that will guarantee dependence. The same is true for culture. A colonial regime can never adjust its sights to recognize valuable cultural assets in the margins of the empire. Either the margin is a wasteland, or it is full of impediments that must be exterminated—as the Indians were exterminated in North America by the European colonialists. To the extent that culture in Canada is still colonial, we are concerned with the position of victim. To the extent that the victim is still alive, things can change.

When I mentioned to an American that I was now more interested in the development of Canadian culture than I was in his, and that I intended to write something about it, he said: "What are you a goddamned fascist?"—which shows how the cultural invader can be as paranoid about this subject as the threatened. The only way I can justify nationalism is to see it as a way of regulating what goes in and what goes out. I would like to see a balance in this exchange, nothing more. But it is a sign of how in control foreign interests are in Canada—I mean *mentally* in control—that every time we call for an accounting they accuse us of tribalism pointing towards another holocaust.

What I am concerned to express is an attitude that leads to maturity, not immaturity. I will put my contention quite simply: unless you let your culture mature, *you* will never mature; you will always remain someone else's clone. By failing to resist the inflow of foreign influence in Canada we have prevented this growth, which is natural and necessary for any human community. Maturity works from the inside out and cannot be plastered in like glitter on a ceiling. Yet this is precisely what the custodians of culture all across Canada are attempting to do. This activity is carried on in the highest places. I intend to name names and give examples as far as my personal fact-finding energies have permitted.

A note: This personal investigation is partly the odyssey of my own thinking on this subject over the years. If I speak of music it is because this is the field I know best. But what I shall say applies *mutatis mutandis* to the other arts too; and I know that there are many artists in other fields who feel the same way as I do.

About 20 years ago I was asked in an interview: "Is there or ought there to be a distinctively Canadian music?" I responded: "There isn't and there oughtn't." I was reminded of this recently by another interviewer who detected that I'd changed my mind. There is no inconsistency here, merely the lapse of twenty years. Let me tell you how I felt then so that you can understand the precise inclination of my thoughts today.

Thirty years ago we young composers were very conscious of the desire to move out internationally. It was the great era of the United Nations, the unity of the world and the harmony of all peoples. We were also more than vaguely aware of the dummy culture which then burdened this country, with a British organist in every cuckoo-nest. We wanted to seek our own level in an expanded world order. It was more a question of getting "away from here" than of going to any place in particular. We left home and the years of *wanderlust* commenced. Most of us went to Europe, a few to the States. The international *esprit* that was then in the air seemed most detectable in those places, specifically in New York, Paris or London, which is where most of us ended up. We found our mentors in those places; they taught us how to create in an acceptably international idiom. We took heart in the fact that artists in Madrid and Buenos Aires and Stockholm and Tokyo were also working in recognizable languages. We believed that soon the whole world would turn this way. McLuhan's global village concept later gave a boost to these expectations.

It was a pardonable sin. It took us half a lifetime to learn that what we had perceived as internationalism was really a new parochialism, spawned and carefully guarded by a few large centres in which the cultural industries were most highly developed. It would have been nearly impossible to rise to the top in these centres without certain advantages which we innocently lacked. What was wanted was copies, not originals. Our duty which was implicitly laid in our heads by our teachers was to extend the international style to the peripheries, centre to margin, that is, from New York to Toronto, Paris to Montreal, London to Vancouver. This is a role we willingly played without thinking of it in those terms any more than patrons at the National Arts Centre or listeners to the CBC think about it today. Nor probably have many of my colleagues of those years begun to think about it yet. They returned to satisfying jobs in universities or in other ways barricaded themselves from certain realities.

I began to think of this seriously for the first time when I moved to the country in 1975. That is when I wrote *Music in the Cold,* a little allegory about authentic and counterfeit Canadian culture, which I sent out to numerous friends as a Christmas present in 1977. The best response I received was from a Swede, who translated and published it in Scandinavia where there seemed to be a greater understanding of what I was talking about. Canadians seemed indifferent to it; only about 100 copies of it have been sold since.

The basic argument of *Music in the Cold,* is that culture is shaped by climate and geography, that as the product of a northern territory Canadian art has a wildness and vigour not evident in the hot-house effusions of more civilized centres. I tried to show that the essential difference between Canadian and European landscapes is that ours are not peoplescapes and that the viewpoint (i.e. the painter's position) of a Canadian landscape suggests hardship (cold, rough terrain, black flies, etc.) I tried to show how the real culture of the North is tough in this way, and that to appreciate it takes special techniques which are unknown to the aesthetes and hearties of hotter tropicalities.

I wanted Canadian music to develop in ways that recognized what some of our best writers and painters have known for some time. I did not want this to be its exclusive feature but rather to emerge as a trait against which other identities could be measured. Eventually the speculations of *Music in the Cold* took form in *Music for Wilderness Lake* and ultimately in *The Princess of the Stars,* which are the two most authentically Canadian pieces I've written. Typically, each of them has only been performed once, though I know that they touched a sensitive spot in many people, particularly those who witnessed the dawn performance of *The Princess of the Stars* on Heart Lake in 1981. With musicians positioned around the water and spectacularly costumed actors and dancers in canoes in the centre, an autumn ritual was enacted in which real birds intersected with singers and dancers imitating them, the sun-god appeared at the precise moment of sunrise, and the legendary substance of the plot sought in every way to unite the fate of characters in the drama with environmental changes in and around the water on a late-September morning.

This was not a piece which could be performed in New York or Paris or Vienna and that is precisely why I wrote it that way. To witness it one would have to make a pilgrimage to a Canadian lake—which reverses the rule that art can only be transmitted from the centre. The relationship with Indian mythology was neither consciously sought nor avoided. Both the music and the text were my own; but the setting and to some extent the context related this quite new work atavistically to something from the collective tribal history of all humans.

Now that I've given you some idea of the passage of my thinking over the years, let me return to the question of Canadian music. Is there a distinctively Canadian music? The questions dissolves into its own answer when we begin to see products that could best be described that way. Time is always turning interrogatives into affirmatives with the accumulation of data. We do not ask whether there is a distinctively German or French or Japanese music; we acknowledge these matters as demonstrated. Yet when we go deeper into the subject, we see that distinctively German music is nothing but a miscellany of many pieces in many different styles by many different composers. Yet the impression of coherence is confirmed because we keep hearing these pieces over and over. A recent survey of the 15 top orchestras in Canada showed that Beethoven was performed by every orchestra and that Mozart's music accounted for nearly 10% of the total programming of all orchestras combined. If the Canadian musical style is not evident it is because it is not allowed to countervail. I shall demonstrate the extent of its neglect in a moment; on the basis of these facts it would seem strange that anyone, *anno* 1983, could have *any* opinion on Canadian music whatever. When a piece of mine is performed it is fairly certain that the conductor is doing it for the first time, the orchestra has never played it before, the audience has never heard it, and the programme annotator knows nothing about it. From this adumbration of an event the critic is supposed to extract some vital truth for the national newspapers.

We are rather in the position of the Polish, Czech and Hungarian composers of the 19th century, who also had to fight to establish their identity. If you regard Dvorak—just to pick a figure—from the point of view of the 19th century Germany musical hegemony, he comes off as an inferior Brahms; but if you put that question aside and ask what he accomplished that Brahms didn't accomplish, he becomes a Czech hero. Now you could listen to Canadian music this way. You might detect English or Scandinavian influences in the music of Harry Somers or claim that Serge Garant orchestrates like Boulez; but if you consider how their music *differs* from these models, you perceive something quite new. That newness is Canadian—it can't be anything else; and if we had any musicologists in this country who weren't trained in Princeton or Oxford, they would now be busy pointing this out.

I am reminded of a story Istvan Anhalt told me about how he first became aware of the Canadian style of music. When he arrived from Hungary he wanted to see the country, so he took a train from Halifax to Montreal. All day he travelled through the woods of New Brunswick, seeing nothing but trees. Here and there he passed a grubby clearing with perhaps a sawmill or a gas station and a few squat houses, then more trees. When he first heard the music of John Beckwith his mind connected back to that experience. Here were bars of repetitious *ostinatti* followed by a sudden wild modulation, then the relentless repetitions again. The music and the forest were companions; they intensified one another.

A very civilized Japanese lady came to visit me in Bancroft. When I took her back to the bus station, it was crowded with local men, dressed traditionally: red hunting caps, open tan-coloured boots, tied halfway up, with jeans so low on the hips that the crotch was somewhere around the knees. "They're a bit rough," I said. "Yes," she replied, "I like."

Perhaps only the foreigners can appreciate the Canadian artifact or animal without prejudice, though it requires a particular mental attitude to do this. Such curiosity is seldom mustered by the post-colonial set whose models are always in another country.

To get back to Istvan Anhalt: when he wrote *La Tourangelle,* a scenic cantata based on the life of the immigrant nun, Marie de l'Incarnation, partly in his new home in Kingston, which looks out on a giant and ancient stone church, his own work became beautifully Canadian in the expression of a subject which probably only an immigrant could handle.

I am mentioning these things as inevitabilities. The list of authentic Canadian works is growing. But will you hear them in the National Arts Centre or on the CBC? Not for 50 years unless a lightning bolt hits the heads of the programmers for these institutions. So what fills their programmes at the moment? We shift into the analytical mode to find out.

First of all, CBC radio. By way of preface let me mention that all Canadian performers and composers of serious music who have been in the business for 10 or 30 years know that little by little CBC has reduced their employment possibilities. Gone are the house orchestras, gone are the commissions for composers, gone for the most part are the recitals for solo performers. In the survey I am about to present, which covers the first month of a new season, the CBC did not initiate a single musical programme; the few that are live were picked up as remote broadcasts of events under other sponsorship.

What I did was take the *CBC Radio Guide* for September 1983 and list all the names of musicians for the programmes on the stereo network (the main music network) by nationality. There are 630 foreign composers and performers listed compared to 82 Canadians. If we were to include those programmes which do not list their contents (*Stereo Morning, Off the Record,* etc.) the Canadian presence shrinks to near invisibility. For instance, a week-long (September 12-16) survey of all the music played during the 20 hours *Stereo Morning* is on the air showed these results:

Canadian composers 0
Canadian performers 4
Foreign composers and performers 140

A week-long (October 3-7) survey of *Off the Record* produced these results:

Canadian composers 0
Canadian performers 0
Foreign composers and performers 114

These are the results for 30 hours of actual broadcasting, from which it must be clear that Canadian musicians are being slapped off the air in those meandering programmes of recorded music, while announcers lick the boots and polish the halos of their foreign favourites. A sampling of remarks:

"Nifty Neville, one of the busiest men in the world"—after playing six recordings of Pommy ace Neville Marriner.

"The towering, basic essential classics"—in reference to the Mendelssohn Violin Concerto.

"Let's return to that marvellous Swedish baritone"—reference to Hagen Hagegard.

"We have some delightful English Baroque today."

Returning to the printed listings we should now see where the foreigners come from. We discover that the largest block of composers by far is German/Austrian (94) followed by French (46) Italian (25) British (25) and Russian (21). There are 13 Canadian composers in the listings. Almost all of these can be credited to one programme, *Two*

New Hours, but since this programme is especially designed to present unfamiliar music by young and unknown composers, the Canadian group is not particularly representative. Of the more established figures, only the name of Harry Somers appears. No Weinzweig, Freedman, Beckwith, Garant, Anhalt, Tremblay, Prevost, Papineau-Couture, Pentland, Willan, Champagne or MacMillan for the month of September.

Among the performers, the largest single contingent is British (111) followed by American (79). Only then come Canadians at 69 then German/Austrian (53) French (23) and others (33).

There is a cliché going around that music is international. Of course it isn't, but, like all culture products, is the expression of a particular people at a particular time. As such it may or may not be intelligible to other peoples at other times. If the CBC was really trying to educate us internationally we would be hearing music from Rajasthan or Iraq or Manchuria or the Tuamotu Archipelago. We don't, so we assume that *détente* is not their business. What is it? To endorse colonial loyalty by demonstrating that this smart music, which socially upward-bound Canadians should learn to appreciate, did not originate here, but comes to us from the eight or ten great lands of our forefathers (i.e., some of them). As a recent policy paper from the National Arts Centre put it: "We yearn for our Mozarts, our Shakespeares and our Picassos. Nation-building is a matter of establishing links; and to the extent that the Great Artist is lacking, Canadians face the problem of a missing link." In other words, if God had intended Canada to have music, Mozart would have been born in Regina. The fact that he was born in Salzburg is supposed to be incidental. As a matter of fact, Mozart wore a perfumed wig and lace panties and his music sounds like it. I am not raising issue with this any more than I do with Beethoven, whose music often reminds me of Vienna sausage; I am merely pointing out that any art exudes a variety of regional smells which are unavoidably packaged along with the product; and that when your *Stereo Morning* host opens up his programme with another piece of Mozart a little unvented miasma from Austria reaches our nostrils.

As John Weinzweig said, "Mozart is a pop composer." This makes him a perfect candidate for any station specializing in classical Mooze, which is what CBC stereo has become, as a survey of the repertoire could easily demonstrate. Not only do we have here a concentration of music from six or eight favoured countries, but we also have a shrunken repertoire in which the same peewee classics (viz.

Respighi's *Ancient Aires and Dances*) are played a dozen times a week in the manner of all pop stations. Pieces are broken apart and thrown together by announcers and producers who have little care for integrity, form or gracefulness in programme building. This is all in keeping with "abbreviation radio," a characteristic of most contemporary broadcasting. I don't want to get into the question of what radio could accomplish if it became in itself an art form (I've dealt with this in my article *Radical Radio, CF,* Dec/Jan. '82, 83), but I will say a few words about how it could assist in centring Canadian musical culture without drastic changes or additional expenses.

There is quite a lot of Canadian music. We even have dead composers. Heaven knows we have enough of undisputed innocuousness. There is also a good deal of interesting material from the 19th and early 20th centuries which no one knows about. Years ago for *10 Centuries Concerts* we revived a quite satisfactory 18th century opera. "Colas et Colinette," by Louis Quesnel, the equal of a good many European products of its type, John Beckwith has extended this work in the reconstructions he has made of old pieces for the festival at Sharon. There is a prejudice that Canadian music consists exclusively of unpleasant noises made by misfits like Schafer, which needs readjustment. The annals of Canadian music history are strewn with works which should be heard again, if only in order to make a final evaluation of them. I am speaking now of works by Leo Smith, W.O. Forsyth, Guillaume Couture, Rudolphe Mathieu, Herbert L. Clarke, Claude Champagne and Sir Ernest MacMillan. When I look at the 25 British composers (as compared with 13 Canadian) in the CBC stereo listings for September and see the names of Arnold Bax, E.J. Morean, Roger Quilter, Eric Coates, Arthur Benjamin, *inter alia,* I do not consider that group in any way superior to the Canadians I have mentioned.

The CBC has never attempted to record any of this material. A longstanding policy of recording some contemporary music seems to have been abandoned in favour of recording major Canadian orchestras in exclusively European repertoire. What I am trying to say is that the spectrum of Canadian material is exceedingly broad and makes numerous appeals, some of which may not be inconsistent with present offerings. Of course I would like to see a policy that goes well beyond this, but since the CBC may not be able to appreciate my wilder enthusiasms, I will for the moment not press them forward. In any country but Canada, this kind of material would have been recorded long ago and presented frequently enough to have worked its way into the marrow of national consciousness. It is unbelievable that a public broadcasting service that plays such a large role in the recording industry should be able to avoid it. When it is instituted there will be two important residual effects: the DJs will be forced to purr as thrillingly about "us" as they do about "them," and the performing rights money for these works will stay in Canada.

Every time a copyright work by a foreign composer is played in Canada, money is collected and shipped out of the country to the country in which the work originated. Can you imagine, on the basis of the figures I have presented, how much performing rights money is being sent out of Canada—for instance to Britain—as a result of the policies of our public broacasting system? Haven't we a right to demand that more of it should remain here to assist those who are building our own culture, and especially to demand it of a public corporation which has avowedly the same intention?

The discouragement of Canadian music on Canadian radio had been intentional and systematic. The aspirations of Canadian composers and performers have been blocked by a colonial administration that is blind and gutless and which, like all things colonial will have a temporary evanescence before it is overturned, perchance violently. I have given you some facts and thoughts on one aspect of the CBC service. You can think about what is happening on the other services. If you do, or rather when you do, you may feel like standing up and making some demands of your own.

I could go on to show how the patterning of all large organizations is similarly colonial without in any way impeding their abilities to grasp by far the largest share of public money made available for the arts—how, for instance, the Canadian Opera Company (which I indiscreetly point out is directed and managed by Americans) has not produced an original Canadian opera since they did Harry Somers' *Riel* in 1967,—how in 1984 they will be given $1,250,000 to produce an opera by an Englishman while Comus Music Theatre was given $60,000 to produce a Canadian work of infinitely greater complexity,—how the Toronto International Festival turned down both *Ra* and *Apocalypsis* and God knows how many other Canadian offerings to bring the Met to Canada,—how the Stratford Festival spends its millions on plummy British plays and squirts its music budget into Gilbert and Sullivan,—yes, I could go on for quite a while about all this but you know the tune as well as I do.

The dimensions of the monster who has been set up to devour us are of great magnitude. He appears very benign; he is on a decorated leash held by fistfuls of government administrators and doting heiresses; he speaks all the mittel-European languages; he knows how to purr when petted and he has beautiful well-kept fingers. But if you're a Canadian artist, he's out to strangle you and his mistresses will kick your carcass into the gutter as they parade him joyously across the country to the applause of punch-drunk audiences for whom he has become the Redeemer of Boredom and a narcosis for their lazy lives.

I've described the problem and I've given enough facts to release it from the charge of personal idiosyncrasy. I've limited my analysis to the field of music, because I know it best, but I also know it is not unique to this field. What we are really concerned with is a mental attitude which I have called colonial because that seems to be the most appropriate way to describe the insecurity which downgrades the local and elevates the alien without seriously evaluating either. This is a Canadian habit and while it may be weakening in some areas, in the aristocratic field of classical music it is hardening into a canker. If we can't lose this habit our culture will remain sick, and despite all establishment smugness, will look sick next to the presentations of independent people anywhere, whether black, white, yellow or red. How do we achieve independence from the scourge of colonialism? Radical changes of thinking are necessary and these are what now must be discussed.

Task number one: forget where you came from; only then will you find out where you are. Ask an Englishman where he came from and he'll say England; ask a Frenchman and he'll say France; ask a Canadian and he'll say Buffalo, or my mother came from Poland, or my grandfather sold rugs in Armenia. I told you that in *Music in the Cold* I tried to describe the Canadian experience from the point of view of one who was in harmony with the climate and the land. That is when I finally forgot where I came from and found out where I was. It was a good feeling: a feeling of strength and confidence. When you finally realize you come from Canada (with no strings attached) you find yourself brother and sister of the Indians and the Inuit. All your life you had denied this possibility on ethnic grounds—it's what our teachers taught us; now you discover that it is right and inevitable.

You must know that I am not merely speaking here of the rehabilitation of native culture. But if you are going to define Canadian culture, that is where you must start. Then the revolution will follow from a plenum, rather than a wasteland—the colonial contention. But if we don't do this, everything will always be out of alignment.

I mentioned at the beginning that a colonial regime was one with a strong centre and weak margins, or rather that this is the centralist perspective on it. Therefore if we are going to rid ourselves of colonial attitudes, our second task must be to abandon the centre-margin view of culture. And this should apply nationally as well as internationally. Culture in New York is no more significant than that in Toronto any more than that in Toronto surpasses in interest that in Kitchener or Bancroft. It is a matter of appropriateness. What makes central culture *apparently* more interesting is the way it is fanned about by the culture industries. This is the Maya of our age, the illusion, and we must learn to see through it. The warnings Schumaker gave in *Small is Beautiful* apply to culture as well as to economics.

I have dealt here with the subject of serious music because it concerns me most; my life depends on it. The situation is particularly serious because the whole system is exogenous and has been imported for the amusement of the social elite. Perhaps if I'd taken theatre or dance or film I would have had to retouch my arguments; but my friends in these professions assure me they are confronted with the same opposition.

It is time to sum up. I could follow academic practice and conclude that everything has now been said but since no one paid attention I'll say it all over again. But this would be doing you a disservice, because I think you have heard quite clearly what I have been saying and recognize truths in it despite whatever might have irritated you in the delivery.

And so my second last line is to you who have listened. I feel the pulse in your fingers and on your throats and I know that at last you are ready to come with us into the future, ready to listen to our songs and poems and look at our pictures and read our stories, because they are about you, and through them you will know yourselves, and behind them are the trees and the lakes and the snows of Canada, and behind them are the Indians, your ancestors, and behind them are the animals, and behind them is the myth, and without a myth the nation dies.

At the opening concert in Thomson Hall, sandwiched between the inevitable major compositions by an Englishman and a Frenchman, were two short Canadian works.

I was told to keep mine to 8 minutes. One piece on the concert got bravos. "They're cheering Canada," my wife said, and she was right.

My final line is to my fellow artists. Continue to weave your magic spells, on street corners, in the little theatres and houses of creation, on the empty roads and in the quiet of the night. They are getting sick of the old diet. The country belongs to us now. Tell them so.

R. Murray Schafer, "Canadian Culture: Colonial Culture," *Canadian Forum*, (March, 1984), pp. 14-19.

DAVID T. SUZUKI

A PLANET FOR THE TAKING

Canadians live under the remarkable illusion that we are technologically advanced people. Everything around us denies that assumption. We are, in many ways, a Third World country, selling our natural resources in exchange for the high technology of the industrialized world. Try going through your home and looking at the country of origin of your clothes, electrical appliances, books, car. The rare technological product that does have Canada stamped on it is usually from a branch plant of a multinational company centred in another country. But we differ from traditional Third World countries. We have a majority population of Caucasians and a very high level of literacy and affluence. And we have been able to maintain our seemingly advanced social state by virtue of an incredible bounty of natural resources.

Within the Canadian mystique there is also a sense of the vastness of this land. The prairies, the Arctic, the oceans, the mountains are ever present in our art and literature. This nation is built on our sense of the seeming endlessness of the expanse of wilderness and the output of nature and we have behaved as if this endlessness were real. Today we speak of renewable resources but our "harvest" procedures are more like a mining operation. We extract raw resources in the crudest of ways, gouging the land to get at its inner core, spewing our raw wastes into the air, water and soil in massive amounts while taking fish, birds, animals and trees in vast quantities without regard to the future. So we operate under a strange duality of mind: we have both a sense of the importance of the wilderness and space in our culture and an attitude that it is limitless and therefore we needn't worry.

Native cultures of the past may have been no more conservation-minded than we are but they lacked the technology to make the kind of impact that we do today. Canadians and Americans share one of the great natural wonders, the Great Lakes, which contain 20 percent of the world's fresh water, yet today even this massive body of water is terribly polluted and the populations of fish completely mixed-up by human activity. We speak of "managing" our resources but do it in a way that resembles the sledgehammer-on-the-head cure for a headache. On the west coast of Canada, Natives lived for millenia on the incredible abundance of five species of salmon. Today, the massive runs are gone and many biologists fear that the fish may be in mortal jeopardy because of both our fishing and management policies. Having improved fishing techniques this century to the point of endangering runs yet still knowing very little of the biology of the fish, we have assumed that we could build up the yield by simply dumping more back. But it wasn't known that sockeye salmon fry, for example, spend a year in a freshwater lake before going to sea. Millions of sockeye fry were dumped directly into the Fraser River where they died soon after. In Oregon, over-fishing and hydroelectric dams had decimated coho populations in the Columbia River. In one year, over 8 million fry were released of which only seven were ever caught. No one knows what's happening to the rest.

We act as if a fish were a fish, a duck a duck or a tree a tree. If we "harvest" one, we renew it by simply adding one or two back. But what we have learned is that all animals and plants are not equivalent. Each organism reflects the evolutionary history of its progenitors; in the case of salmon, each race and subrace of fish has been exquisitely honed by nature to return to a very specific part of the Pacific watershed. Similarly, in the enormous area of prairie pothole country in the centre of the continent, migratory birds do not just space themselves out according to the potholes that are empty. Scientists have discovered that the birds have been selected to return to a very restricted part of that area. And of course, our entire forestry policy is predicated on the ridiculous idea that a virgin stand of fir or cedar which has taken millenia to form and clings to a thin layer of topsoil can be replaced after clear-cut logging simply by sticking seedlings into the ground. How can anyone with even the most rudimentary understanding of biology and evolution ignore the realities of the complex interaction between organisms and the environment and attempt to manipulate wild populations as if they were tomato plants or chickens?

I believe that in large part our problems rest on our faith in the power of science and technology. At the beginning of this century, science, when applied by industry and medicine, promised a life immeasurably better and there is no doubt that society, indeed the planet, has been transformed by the impact of new ideas and inventions of science. Within my lifetime, I've seen the beginning of television, oral contraception, organ transplants, space travel, computers, jets, nuclear weapons, satellite communication, and polio vaccine. Each has changed society forever and made the world of my youth recede into the pages of history. But we have not achieved a technological utopia. The problems facing us today are immense and many are a direct consequence of science and technology. What has gone wrong?

I believe that the core of our 20th century dilemma lies in a fundamental limitation of science that most scientists, especially those in the life sciences, fail to recognize. Most of my colleagues take it for granted that our studies will ultimately be applicable to the "big picture," that our research will have beneficial payoffs to society eventually. That is because the thrust of modern science has been predicated on the Newtonian idea that the universe is like an enormous machine whose entire system will be reconstructed on the basis of our understanding of the parts. This is the fundamental reductionist faith in science: the whole is equal to the sum of its parts. It does make a lot of sense—what distinguishes science from other activities that purport to provide a comprehensive "world view" is its requirement that we focus on a part of nature isolated to as great an extent as possible from the rest of the system of which it is a part. This has provided enormous insights into that fragment of nature, often accompanied by power to manipulate it. But when we attempt to tinker with what lies in the field of our view, the effects ripple far beyond the barrel of the microscope. And so we are constantly surprised at the unexpected consequences of our interference. Scientists only know nature in "bits and pieces" and assume that higher levels of organization are simply the expression of the component parts. This is what impels neurobiologists to study the chemical and electrical behaviour of single neurons in the faith that it will ultimately lead to an understanding of what creativity and imgination are, a faith that I don't for a moment think will ever be fulfilled (although a lot of useful information will accrue).

Physicists, who originally set this view in motion, have this century, with the arrival of relativity and quantum theory, put to rest the notion that we will ever be able to reconstruct the entire universe from fundamental principles. Chemists know that a complete physical description of atoms of oxygen and hydrogen is of little value in predicting the behaviour of a water molecule. But biologists scream that any sense that there are properties of organization that don't exist at lower levels is "vitalism," a belief that there is some mystical life force in living organisms. And so biochemists and molecular biologists are intent on understanding the workings of organisms by learning all they can about sub-cellular organization.

Ironically, ecology, long scorned by molecular biologists as an inexact science, is now corroborating physics. In studying ecosystems, we are learning that a simple breakdown into components and their behaviour does not provide insight into how an entire collection of organisms in a natural setting will work. While many ecologists do continue to "model" ecosystems in computers in the hope that they will eventually derive a predictive tool, their science warns of the hazards of treating it too simply in management programs.

At present, our very terminology suggests that we think we can manage wild plants and animals as though they were domesticated organisms. We speak of "herds" of seals, of "culling," "harvesting," "stocks." The ultimate expression of our narrow view (and self-interested rationalizations) is seen in how we overlook the enormous environmental impact of our pollution, habitat destruction and extraction and blame seals and whales for the decline in fish populations or wolves for the decrease in moose—and then propose bounties as a solution!

But Canadians do value the spiritual importance of nature and want to see it survive for future generations. We also believe in the power of science to sustain a high quality of life. And while the current understanding of science's power is, I believe, misplaced, in fact the leading edges of physics and ecology may provide the insights that can get us off the current track. We need a very profound perceptual shift and soon.

David T. Suzuki, "A Planet for the Taking," *The Canadian Forum*, (February, 1985), pp. 6-8.

GEORGE WHALLEY

"INTRODUCTION" for DEATH IN THE BARREN GROUND: THE DIARY OF EDGAR CHRISTIAN

When Edgar Christian died on or about Wednesday 1 June, 1927 he was only five days away from his nineteenth birthday. Even if he had lived until his birthday he would have spent the day alone; for the last of his companions had died four weeks earlier. The place where Edgar lay down in his bunk for the last time and pulled a red Hudson's Bay blanket over his head was a small log cabin that he and his friends had built that fall on the north bank of the Thelon River in a small patch of sizeable spruce several miles north of the Northern Limit of Trees, abut 350 miles from any habitation on Great Slave Lake to the west or on Hudson Bay to the east.

The leader of the three-man party was John Hornby, Edgar's cousin, not yet 50 years' old, a man with nearly twenty years' experience of living and travelling in the Arctic and sub-Arctic. The other man was Harold Adlard, an Englishman like Edgar and Hornby; since 1923 he had been working on farms north of Edmonton with the idea of homesteading on his own account. He had joined the group almost by accident just as they were setting out for the North. He became 28 in October when the cabin was being built and the winter settling in.

The three men had left Edmonton in May 1926 in order to get into Great Slave Lake as soon as the break-up of the ice would allow. By the middle of June they were at the east end of Great Slave Lake, on Fairchild Point where the ruins of George Back's old Fort Reliance had been reduced to a couple of tall stone chimneys standing in an open terraced glade at the edge of a secluded bay. Hornby knew this country well—he had spent two winters near Fort Reliance—and he knew the country they were going into, for he had travelled down the Thelon with a companion only the year before and on the way had discovered the place where he hoped to build a cabin and pass a winter. As Hornby's party approached Reliance by canoe they met various trappers beginning to make their way out westerly to Fort Resolution at the mouth of the Great Slave River; all these were known to Hornby, some of them had been associates of his on Artillery Lake. At Fairchild Point, ice prevented them from making their next move into

Artillery Lake. It was probably well past the beginning of July when they left Fairchild Point and travelled south to the beginning of Pike's Portage to make the 700-foot climb and the long traverse into Artillery Lake where there were now no trappers, and to the Barren Ground where in those days neither Indians nor Eskimos lived or travelled.

Since the party had left Fort Resolution in June 1926 they had not been able to send any letters or messages outside. Hornby had been vague about his plans, but both Edgar and Harold in their last letters home had told their parents not to expect word until the early summer of 1928. But people who knew Hornby well were surprised that he had not come out to Resolution or to Baker Lake and Chesterfield Inlet at the end of the summer of 1927. By the spring of 1928, at the urging of Hornby's friends, the Mounted Police began to make inquiries among the people who worked near Reliance and Artillery Lake, and from Chesterfield Inlet they began to watch out for signs of Hornby whenever they were on patrol. Anxiety deepened through the summer, and by late July the Director of the North West Territories and Yukon Branch was sure that Hornby and his companions had perished somewhere east of Artillery Lake in the area established in the previous September as the Thelon Game Sanctuary. Already in June the RCMP at Fort Smith had asked a young geologist named H.S. Wilson, who was setting out with three companions to prospect on the Thelon and along the west coast of Hudson Bay, to look out for Hornby who (they said) had "disappeared east of Artillery Lake summer of 1926...accompanied by two young nephews"; he had "intended to erect a cabin near Junction of Hanbury & Thelon Rivers." Six weeks later, on the afternoon of 21 July, one of the Wilson party noticed "fairly recent cutting on left bank of [Thelon] river," and "almost at once observed small cabin and landed to investigate." They shouted from the shore; there was no answer and no signs of life. They climbed up the bank to the cabin and noticed outside the door two rifles leaning against the wall, and found that they were fully loaded. The cabin door was secured from inside; they broke it open and found a third loaded rifle standing against the wall inside the door. After examining the cabin and its contents they paddled quickly downstream for another two hours before camping for the night, "glad to get a little nearer civilization." They arrived at Chesterfield Inlet on the evening of 7 August, and that night the Sergeant in charge of the RCMP detachment there telegraphed to the Commissioner in Ottawa:

> H.S. Wilson here from Great Slave Lake. Reports finding bodies of Hornby party of three men at Cabin north bank Thelon River about 60 miles below junction of Hanbury. Death apparently due to starvation. Nothing disturbed. Full report on Nascopie which leaves here on 11th.

An attempt was made to get an RCMP patrol to the cabin by seaplane from Baker Lake, but the aircraft was damaged on the way to Baker Lake and the winter began to close in before it could be repaired. A winter patrol with dogs was considered then abandoned; but in the late winter, patrols from Fort Reliance laid out caches to support a patrol that would come in from the west in the spring. The patrol, led by Inspector Trundle, reached the cabin on 25 July, four days after the anniversary of Wilson's discovery of the cabin. Trundle had Wilson's detailed report and expected no surprises. But when he came into the house he found on the top of the stove in the middle of the cabin a piece of paper, the inscription scarcely legible:

WHO
LOOK IN
STOVE

In the cold and sodden ashes of the stove, perfectly preserved from the wet that had invaded and destroyed practically everything else in the cabin that was not made of wood or metal, he found—together with various letters, a few small notebooks, and some other papers—Edgar Christian's diary.

As soon as the police brought out the papers from the Thelon cabin and turned them over first to the Public Administrator, and then to the solicitor acting for the Hornby and Christian families, those who were allowed to read the diary recognized the quality of it. Extracts from the diary were printed in December 1929 along with the RCMP report in newspapers in Edmonton and in London. Edgar Christian, as writer of the diary, immediately became the central figure in a story that gripped the imagination of those who read about it at the time, a story that has become a permanent element in the Northern imagination ever since the whole diary was published eight years later.

In Edgar's diary however, the central figure is John Hornby—"Jack," "dear Jack"—as leader , provider, the centre of affection, the hero, the ideal, "the finest Man I have Ever known," "a foundation to build my Life upon." But in Edgar's diary John Hornby stands with his back to the light, in the elusive way that is at once typical of him and typical of all the records we have of him. None of the photographs they took on the journey in to the Thelon or at the cabin survived the invasions of frost and water. By July 1929 all that was left to recall what had happened in that desolate, storm-swept, merciless place was the pattern of Edgar's words, set down day by day in a book bound in red leather and labelled in gold letters "Records"—the adolescent voice speaking with strong simplicity and unwavering expectation out of the heart of a slow and inexorable disaster that need never have occurred.

Ever since the diary was published more than 40 years ago, the imprint of that voice has proved indelible to anybody who has listened to it. Very few people travel through that country even now; but nobody passes down the Thelon without putting ashore there, at the double bend in the river now named Hornby Point, and scrambling through the willow slash at the water's edge and up the steep gravel bank to the scattered tumble of logs that was once for three men (and one of them a boy) their stay for a time against death. To stand there is to taste the ambient solitude, the squalor of impotence, the terrible enclosedness of the cabin from inside, the daily menace of the coming down of night, almost total so close to the Arctic Circle, but at times with a sky clear enough for the stars, the aurora, and the moon to make a mysterious, even enchanting, mock-day. But even then, there was often the overcast of cloud or drift, the wind snarling at the fringe of spruce strangely rooted and sustained so far north of the treeline, the trunks twisted in their infinitely slow growth through three or four centuries.

In the stand of timber north of the cabin the stumps of the felled trees are pathetically beavered off, much too far above ground for competent axemanship. Here in the summer season that Edgar did not live to see, the ground squelches underfoot in the ground-cover that nourishes life in a shallow zone above the permafrost, and the tiny short-stemmed Alpine flowers—hosts of them, hosts of varieties of them—crowd the ground, criss-crossed by dingy-coloured butterflies. On the top of the hill to the north-west of the cabin Hornby built a windbreak of stones for a look-out and watched alone there by the hour. The three crosses on the graves to the east of the cabin are sometimes knocked down by animals, but somebody always sets them to rights again, as guardians to reprove anybody who would dare desecrate that place, haunted not so much by the three deaths as by the voice that tells of the living that went before the dying: a voice uttered in a firm round hand, the spelling insecure, the punctuation uncertain; the voice of a not-very-accomplished schoolboy, yet steady, generous in its admiration and in its sense of wonder for the man who had brought him to this, eloquent in its silences, confident in life right to the end.

George Whalley, "Introduction," from George Whalley, ed., *Death in the Barren Ground: The Diary of Edgar Christian*, (Ottawa: Oberon Press, 1980), pp. 15-20.

Anthology Pieces by Themes

Action/adventure

Berton, Pierre. "Floating Down the Yukon." (Chapter 5, Description)

Berton, Pierre. "Legends in the Rough." (Chapter 4, Narration)

Bruce, Harry. "The Alchemy of Sailing." (Chapter 6, Exposition)

Gzowski, Peter. From *The Morningside Papers.* (Chapter 4, Narration)

Onley, Toni. "The Longest Night." (Chapter 4, Narration)

Purdy, Al. "Boozy Saddles." (Chapter 4, Narration)

Whalley, George. "Introduction" from *Death in the Barren Ground: The Diary of Edgar Christian.* (Chapter 8, Supplementary)

Morality

Amiel, Barbara. "Anyone Who Supports Censorship, Be Warned: This May Make You Upchuck." (Chapter 7, Argumentation)

Callwood, June. "June Callwood's Canada: Crying Brokenhearted Over You." (Chapter 8, Supplementary)

Camp, Dalton. "The Decline in Public Morality." (Chapter 8, Supplementary)

Collins, Anne. "On Commitment." (Chapter 8, Supplementary)

Findley, Timothy. "Better Dead Than Read? An Opposing View." (Chapter 7, Argumentation)

Fulford, Robert. "Beware: The Censors Are Marching Again." (Chapter 7, Argumentation)

Haynes, Robert H. "What is the Biological Revolution?" (Chapter 8, Supplementary)

Heintzman, Ralph. "Liberalism and Censorship." (Chapter 7, Argumentation)

Laurence, Margaret. "The Greater Evil." (Chapter 7, Argumentation)

Stuewe, Paul. "Better Dead Than Read?" (Chapter 7, Argumentation)

Suzuki, David T. "A Planet For the Taking." (Chapter 8, Supplementary)

Censorship

Amiel, Barbara. "Anyone Who Supports Censorship, Be Warned: This May Make You Upchuck." (Chapter 7, Argumentation)

Findley, Timothy. "Better Dead Than Read? An Opposing View." (Chapter 7, Argumentation)

Fulford, Robert. "Beware: The Censors Are Marching Again." (Chapter 7, Argumentation)

Heintzman, Ralph. "Liberalism and Censorship." (Chapter 7, Argumentation)

Laurence, Margaret. "The Greater Evil." (Chapter 7, Argumentation)

Stuewe, Paul. "Better Dead Than Read?" (Chapter 7, Argumentation)

Changing attitudes

Collins, Anne. "On Commitment." (Chapter 8, Supplementary)

Gwyn, Sandra. "Over Home." (Chapter 8, Supplementary)

Gzowski, Peter. From *The Morningside Papers.* (Chapter 4, Narration)

Haynes, Robert H. "What is the Biological Revolution?" (Chapter 8, Supplementary)

Hoffman, Abby. "Running For Gold." (Chapter 6, Exposition)

Maillet, Antonine. "Aunt Evangeline's Treasure." (Chapter 8, Supplementary)

McDonald, Marci. "Out of the Rough." (Chapter 6, Exposition)

Canadian heroes

Berton, Pierre. "Legends in the Rough." (Chapter 4, Narration)

Callaghan, Morley. "Morley Callaghan Remembers Foster Hewitt." (Chapter 6, Exposition)

Charney, Ann. "The Monument." (Chapter 8, Supplementary)

Fotheringham, Allan. "Dan George's Last Stand." (Chapter 8, Supplementary)

Freeman, Barbara. "'Every Stroke Upward': Women Journalists in Canada 1880-1906." (Chapter 8, Supplementary)

Ross, Colin. "The Story of Grey Owl." (Chapter 8, Supplementary)

Canadian culture

Berton, Pierre. "Legends in the Rough." (Chapter 4, Narration)

Findley, Timothy. "Better Dead Than Read? An Opposing View." (Chapter 7, Argumentation)

Freeman, Barbara. "'Every Stroke Upward': Women Journalists in Canada 1880-1906." (Chapter 8, Supplementary)

Gwyn, Sandra. "Over Home." (Chapter 8, Supplementary)

Macdonald, John A. (Sir). "Speech in the Legislative Assembly, February 6, 1865." (Chapter 8, Supplementary)

Purdy, Al. "Boozy Saddles." (Chapter 4, Narration)

Ross, Colin. "The Story of Grey Owl." (Chapter 8, Supplementary)

Schafer, R. Murray. "Canadian Culture: Colonial Culture." (Chapter 8, Supplementary)

The environment and nature

Berton, Pierre. "Floating Down the Yukon." (Chapter 5, Description)

Haynes, Robert H. "What is the Biological Revolution?" (Chapter 8, Supplementary)

Roberts, Charles G.D. (Sir). "In the Deep of the Grass." (Chapter 8, Supplementary)

Ross, Colin. "The Story of Grey Owl." (Chapter 8, Supplementary)

Suzuki, David T. "A Planet For the Taking." (Chapter 8, Supplementary)

Whalley, George. "Introduction" from *Death in the Barren Ground: The Diary of Edgar Christian.* (Chapter 8, Supplementary)

Canadian sovereignty

Fulford, Robert. "Charter of Wrongs." (Chapter 8, Supplementary)

Lévesque, René. "Heartbreak." (Chapter 8, Supplementary)

Macdonald, John A. (Sir). "Speech in the Legislative Assembly, February 6, 1865." (Chapter 8, Supplementary)

Ross, Colin. "The Story of Grey Owl." (Chapter 8, Supplementary)

Women's movement

Collins, Anne. "On Commitment." (Chapter 8, Supplementary)

Freeman, Barbara. "'Every Stroke Upward': Women Journalists in Canada 1880-1906." (Chapter 8, Supplementary)

Haynes, Robert H. "What is the Biological Revolution?" (Chapter 8, Supplementary)

Hoffman, Abby. "Running For Gold." (Chapter 6, Exposition)

Laurence, Margaret. "The Greater Evil." (Chapter 7, Argumentation)

McDonald, Marci. "Out of the Rough." (Chapter 6, Exposition)

Nostalgia

Allen, Robert Thomas. "Where Women Feared To Tread." (Chapter 5, Description)

Berton, Pierre. "Floating Down the Yukon." (Chapter 5, Description)

Broadfoot, Barry. "Grand Beach, Then and Now." (Chapter 5, Description)

Callaghan, Morley. "Morley Callaghan Remembers Foster Hewitt." (Chapter 6, Exposition)

Laurence, Margaret. "Where the World Began." (Chapter 5, Description)

Maillet, Antonine. "Aunt Evangeline's Treasure." (Chapter 8, Supplementary)

Sports

Bruce, Harry. "The Alchemy of Sailing." (Chapter 6, Exposition)

Callaghan, Morley. "Morley Callaghan Remembers Foster Hewitt." (Chapter 6, Exposition)

Frayne, Trent. "As French Canadian as Baseball." (Chapter 6, Exposition)

Hoffman, Abby. "Running For Gold." (Chapter 6, Exposition)

McDonald, Marci. "Out of the Rough." (Chapter 6, Exposition)

Plante, Jacques. "How to Watch the Stanley Cup." (Chapter 6, Exposition)

Canadian identity

Berton, Pierre. "Legends in the Rough." (Chapter 4, Narration)

Fraser, Graham. "A Sense of Being." (Chapter 4, Narration)

Frayne, Trent. "As French Canadian as Baseball." (Chapter 6, Exposition)

Gwyn, Sandra. "Over Home." (Chapter 8, Supplementary)

Laurence, Margaret. "Where the World Began." (Chapter 5, Description)

Lévesque, René. "Heartbreak." (Chapter 8, Supplementary)

Maillet, Antonine. "Aunt Evangeline's Treasure." (Chapter 8, Supplementary)

Social behaviour

Amiel, Barbara. "The Chaos of Criminal Justice in Canada. Or: In Defence of Vengeance." (Chapter 8, Supplementary)

Callwood, June. "June Callwood's Canada: Crying Brokenhearted Over You." (Chapter 8, Supplementary)

Camp, Dalton. "The Decline in Public Morality." (Chapter 8, Supplementary)

Charney, Ann. "The Monument." (Chapter 8, Supplementary)

Collins, Anne. "On Commitment." (Chapter 8, Supplementary)

Fulford, Robert. "Beware: The Censors Are Marching Again." (Chapter 7, Argumentation)

Heintzman, Ralph. "Liberalism and Censorship." (Chapter 7, Argumentation)

Laurence, Margaret. "The Greater Evil." (Chapter 7, Argumentation)

McDonald, Marci. "Out of the Rough." (Chapter 6, Exposition)

McLuhan, Marshall. "The Violence of the Media." (Chapter 8, Supplementary)

PART THREE

THE RESEARCH PAPER

9 *Researching the Paper*

Introduction

At one time or another during your university or college career, you can expect to produce a library research paper. The research project is a relatively long and complex task but a rewarding one. Each stage of the project is important and not merely the long essay that completes it. If the stages are haphazardly or carelessly done, the end result will suffer. A large part of the project centres on the skillful use of library resources; as the project evolves you will become more familiar with what a library has to offer, so that you gradually become an independent researcher, familiar and comfortable enough with the library and how it works to ferret out previously unknown sources on your own.

The principles that you have learned in preceding chapters about active reading and written responses to your reading should stand you in good stead when you come to work on your research paper. Your careful attention to selected readings helped you both to generate ideas about what you read and, more importantly perhaps, to respond critically to those ideas. These ideas and responses in turn served as the raw material upon which you based your own written views.

The material that you search out in your university or college library for your research paper is analogous to the readings to which you responded in earlier chapters. You should read and treat the library material in the same way as those earlier readings: read it actively, being aware of subjects, audiences, and purposes; learn to determine the success that an author has in attaining the desired purpose; decide how you feel about what is being said and how it is being conveyed. Your responses to this research should serve as the raw material of your own research paper, helping you generate and shape your own ideas on the same subject.

Handling your research in this way represents the creative use of resource material. Accepting what others say and using it in an unthinking manner is being enslaved to your sources. Active reading of research material will help you determine the following: (1) what material is relevant to your topic; (2) what relevant material is actually useful; (3) how relevant and useful material is going to be employed in your paper.

Essentially, research requires that you conceive of a problem and that you put together a variety of research materials to help solve the problem or cast new light on it. You must deal with not knowing enough about the topic. Indeed, it is both necessary and helpful that this be so. The project will not be meaningful to you if you know at the beginning as much as you know at the end about your topic; there would have been no searching. Further, the acquisition of new information will help provide you with a strategy for writing to a general audience. If you choose a topic about which you know something but not enough to satisfy your curiosity, then by the end of the project you should know what needs to be said to an audience of readers who likewise know relatively little. Let your readers see that many of them do not know enough about the topic being discussed and in the course of the paper bring enough new information to bear to satisfy their curiosity.

Another feature of the problem must be one of understanding: something about your topic must be relatively hard to grasp. It will not be enough that you note one fact after another; to some degree facts must be made to serve ideas. A paper filled with mere pieces of new information would have no distinct purpose. To be adequately meaningful the facts have to be related to some point—normally the thesis of the research paper itself. What is called for beyond an increase in factual knowledge is increased understanding, on your part and the reader's part.

In all, we can conclude that the basic requirement for a successful research paper is a lively play of mind in and around data that you discover in the course of your investigation.

Originality

Students often wonder about how they can be original when it comes to preparing and writing a research paper. Often the question arises as the result of an instructor's comments about appropriate documentation on a research paper. If, for instance, an instructor asks a student to identify the sources used, the student is likely to respond that the whole paper is indebted to other people's ideas and that if all the sources were scrupulously identified the paper would be comprised of one footnote after another. The student's perplexity about what to document and what not to document often arises because of a failure to understand the meaning of the term *research* itself.

First of all, let it be said that when you are asked to write a research paper, your instructor knows that the paper will be made up largely of other people's opinions. That is self-evident and built into the nature of library research. A student's originality in writing a research paper need not reside in offering original ideas alongside ideas culled from other sources. Rather, originality in the library research paper most often resides in the skill with which the student *searches out* the ideas of others and *structures* and *organizes* these ideas in a meaningful and well-ordered paper. Consider an analogy: if you planned to build a family room in your house, you would first of all design the room, decide upon the materials you would need, purchase them and, finally, use them in the construction of your new room. When you finished the room, you could be proud of the fact that you built it. No one would argue that you used materials constructed and manufactured by others and therefore that you did not build the room yourself. So it is with research: the researcher selects from the raw materials that the library provides and then proceeds to build the essay by making use of those materials. The design, organization, and structure of the essay are the researcher's tasks. The researcher must decide how best to *use* the raw materials and how many of them to use. The finished project belongs unquestionably to the researcher.

This is not to say that there is no place for originality in the sense of a new idea. Often the interplay of data gives rise to a new idea that the researcher is entitled to use in the essay. But originality in this sense is relatively rare; when we use the term originality in connection with the research paper, normally we mean the skill that the student shows in *finding* data from a wide variety of sources and *using* that data in an organized fashion so that it corroborates the thesis of the paper itself.

The Subject

It may very well be that your instructor will provide you with your research paper subject. If this happens, a good deal of initial brainstorming has been done for you, for which you should be thankful. If, however, you are left totally on your own to find your own subject, there are a couple of tips that you might take to make your job easier. First of all, *try to find a subject in which you are truly interested.* Do not decide to write on the first thing that comes into your mind just because you cannot be bothered to think deeply. Remember, you will probably be working on your research paper for a lengthy period of time and your energy will no doubt flag from time to time. If you have chosen a subject in which you have very little interest, the chances of becoming bored by it and disheartened when you experience a set back are greater than they might be with a subject in which you have a true interest.

You might like to choose a subject for any of the following reasons: (1) you already have some knowledge of the subject but would like to acquire more; (2) you have an interest in the subject but very little knowledge of it; (3) you think you might like to pursue the subject in a formal way at some later stage, perhaps by taking a course.

The second tip regarding your choice of subject has to do with the availability of sources. *Before you finally decide on your subject, check the library in which you will be doing most of your hunting.* There is not much point deciding on a particular subject only to discover that your research library has very little material on that subject. Scout around your library with your potential subject in mind. If it is unresearchable in your library, abandon it for another that meets the demands of the assignment. Normally, students doing research papers are expected to make major use of the libraries within their institutions. Do not suppose that your interests will allow you to use whatever sources you can find in whatever locations. It is impractical to think that you can be registered in a university in one province and yet send home to another for research materials.

Once you have decided on a subject, the next step is to narrow it to a workable topic. Here you should follow the advice that you received earlier in this book in the chapters specifically devoted to active reading and active writing. Remember, as with your earlier, smaller writing assignments, so with your research paper: you must be aware of your subject, your audience, and your purpose and you must pay the same attention to your research source material as you did to the essays that you read in earlier chapters of this text. Those essays were in a sense small examples of research material: you had to comment on it, summarize it, and finally respond to it. You should perform the same tasks with the research material that you will locate for yourself as you set about working on your research paper.

Research Steps

In the following eight steps we present a brief summary of what you should be doing as your research paper progresses. These pages also serve as a guide to format. We include exercises that we have found useful in our classes and that incorporate standard formatting procedures for bibliography cards and note cards. In step 8, "Final Version," we reproduce a research paper on Down's Syndrome written by Melanie Beach, whose work we used as examples in chapters 2 and 3. Beach prepared the paper according to the 1984 guidelines of the Modern Language Association. As a check on format we have included her revised outline after the paper as a whole.

Step 1: Library Tour and Basic Reference Guides

In preparation for your research paper you should familiarize yourself with your institution's library and some of its important sources of general information. You can either make your own way through the library and ask questions when you have them or, more helpful perhaps, you can ask the reference librarian to show you the basic tools that all researchers in your subject need to know. Some writing classes have formal library tours. These tours should not be skipped or regarded as unimportant: getting to know your library will be an important first step in the research process.

When searching for books in your area, begin by consulting the library card catalogue or, if your library has one, the microfiche catalogue. Card (and microfiche) catalogues are normally organized according to author, title, and subject. When you begin your research, there is a good chance that you may not know any authors on your subject or any book titles. If this is the case, the best place to start is the subject index, which will guide you to titles and authors. Once you are familiar with some individual authors and titles of books you can make good use of the bibliographies that appear at the back of many books to find further written material on your topic. Remember: getting started is the hard part. However, once you make initial contact with a written source, often that source can lead you to others which, in turn, can continue the process.

As we have already suggested, books are not the only source of information. Equally important, and in many cases more important, is material contained within government documents, magazines, encyclopedias, dictionaries, and the like. Normally, finding material in government documents is easier than you might expect. Most libraries have a separate section or floor devoted to government documents, and there is usually one librarian who is an expert in this area. Making use of this person and familiarizing yourself with the Key Word Out of Context catalogue (KWOC) can help you find your way through the large amount of material published by the federal and provincial governments.

When we think of dictionaries we normally think of books that give us the meaning of words. Although this is the type of dictionary with which most of us are familiar, there are many other sorts of very specialized dictionaries. There are for instance, dictionaries of slang, of religion, of psychological terms, of quotations, of foreign phrases, of classical subjects, of fables, and so on. Although dictionaries do not provide detailed information on subjects (normally the same holds for encyclopedias), they are often a good point of departure because they provide an overview of a subject. Sometimes, as well, they list brief bibliographies in their subjects.

By far the most important resource to use in research is periodical literature. Periodical literature or serials is a general term that covers a wide range of material that is published periodically: weekly, biweekly, monthly, quarterly, or annually. Works of periodical literature differ widely. Some are very popular (*Maclean's, Canadian Living*); others are more esoteric (*Canadian Forum, Equinox*); and still others are scholarly (*Canadian Literature, Canadian Journal of Political Science*). Magazines that are not scholarly usually appeal to a general audience. Popular and semi-popular periodicals are easily identifiable: often they contain advertisements and pictures, most of them in colour. Scholarly journals rarely have pictures or advertisements for popular products although they very often have graphs or charts. Their most outstanding characteristic is their use of footnotes or endnotes.

Scholarly periodical literature is important to the researcher for several reasons. It is highly particularized and specific: usually a periodical article is on a single aspect of a particular topic and deals in depth with that aspect. You can often learn much from a journal article not only because of the detailed information it provides but also because it can teach you how to narrow a subject to manageable topics. When it touches on your topic, it can provide you with information of a detailed sort that can add depth and sophistication to your writing. Normally, you will find the most up-to-date information in journals rather than books. Periodical literature is also important for the bibliographic information it provides. Its notes or footnotes can often lead you to other important studies on your topic.

But how can you find your way through the vast amount of periodical literature that most libraries hold? One way, as suggested above, is to check the bibliographies published at the end of most scholarly books; such bibliographies can lead you to important journals and articles in your area. But another way is to make yourself familiar with what are known as periodical indexes. These indexes record the major periodical literature published from year to year. Usually they are organized according to author and title, and sometimes subject. A brief list of the major periodical indexes follows. Once again, talk to your reference librarian if you have any doubts about where to find them or how to use them.

Canadian Periodical Index
The Education Index
Essay and General Literature Index
French Periodical Index
Humanities Index
Poole's Index to Periodical Literature to 1887 replaced by the more current *Reader's Guide to Periodical Literature*
Social Sciences and Humanities Index
Social Sciences Index
Ulrich's International Periodical Directory

The following exercise will give you hands-on practice in using your library.

Library Exercise for ____________________

PART I: BOOKS

Name: ____________________ Date Due: ____________

1. Pick a topic ____________________

2. Using the Library of Congress *List of Subject Headings,* find the subject heading(s) you look under to find something on your topic. Then list them below.

   1. ____________ 2. ____________
   3. ____________ 4. ____________

3. Go to the Subject Catalogue and find an appropriate book on your topic. Now, supply the following information:

   Title of book________________________________

   Author of book________________________________

   Place of Publication____________Date of Publication____________

   Edition (if any)____________Pages____________

   Publisher____________Call No.____________

   Subject Tracings under which this book may be found

   1.____________2.____________
   3.____________4.____________

   Special features of book, if any (e.g. contains bibliography, illustrations, etc.)

   ____

4. In what part of the library system may this book be found?

   ____

5. Find the book on the shelves (or at least its location if it has been signed out). Now, look at the book to the immediate *right* of the one you are seeking and write down its

   1. Call No.____________2. Author____________

PART II: JOURNAL ARTICLES

1. Pick one of the following periodical indexes: find a periodical article *that is in this library* on your topic:

   Art Index
   Business Periodicals Index
   Canadian Business Periodicals Index
   Canadian Education Index
   Canadian Periodical Index

Cumulative Index to Nursing and Allied Health Literature
Education Index
Humanities Index
Index Medicus
Index to Canadian Legal Periodical Literature
International Nursing Index
P.A.I.S.
Readers Guide to Periodical Literature
Social Sciences Index

2. What index did you use to find this article?

   Name____

   Year____________________Volume (if any)____________________

   Page__________________________________(attach photocopy)

3. Now, provide the following information about the article you have found:

   Title of journal that your article appears in (NO ABBREVIATIONS)

   ____

   Date of journal________________Author of article________________

   Title of article____

   Volume No. of journal________Pages on which article appears________

   Issue of journal (if indicated)______________________________

   Special features of article (e.g. illustrated)

   ____

4. Locate your article in the library. Now, photocopy the title pages of *both* issue *and* article and attach before submitting.

Step 2: Subject, Audience, and Purpose, into Topic

Before you go to the library to begin searching for material for your paper, you need to have some idea of what you are looking for. Often an instructor will give you a topic to research, but just as often you will have to establish one yourself in a general subject area. In either case you need to generate enough preliminary material to indicate to you the areas you need to research and the questions you need to answer. The following questions will help you generate this material. Remember that the resulting topic is preliminary; you can only be sure of your topic after you have done some significant reading.

Step 2 (a): Subject

Do your best to find a subject that interests you. Frame specific questions about it and attempt to answer them to determine what your interest actually is. Do this questioning *in writing;* your thought will be more thorough this way. Do not be too concerned about finding complete answers. The important thing at this stage is finding the *questions*—finding thorough answers *is* your research.

1. Why are you interested in your subject?
2. What facts do you already have? What theories? Where did you get this information?
3. Use the basic journalist's questions to explore your subject. Ask as many *who* questions about your subject as you can think of. For example, if your subject is schizophrenia, you might ask *who* gets it, *who* is affected by it, etc. Now write down as many *what* questions as you can. Now *when, where, why.*
4. Look inside your subject: What characteristics does it have? What are its parts?
5. Look around your subject: What is it part of? What can it be compared to? What is its opposite?
6. Look at your subject in action: How does it work? What stages does it involve? What changes are involved? What causes these changes? What results from them? What if your subject did not exist?
7. Take a *who says so* view of your subject: Who are the authorities on your subject? What do they say? What is the popular view? How does your view differ from either the popular or authoritative view?
8. Take a metaphorical view: Complete the following sentence: My subject is like a ____.
   When you think about your subject, what images do you see?

Step 2 (b): Audience

Do not be satisfied by vaguely saying "general audience." Again, frame and answer specific questions.

1. What different groups of people might need to know about your subject?
2. For each group, what is its biggest concern with regard to your subject?

3. For each possible audience, what is your role as a writer?
4. Where are these audiences located?

Step 2 (c): Purpose

Do not be satisfied by saying "to convince" or "to inform." Do more detailed thinking. Again, frame and answer specific questions.

1. What do you want to achieve?
2. Do you want to explain? If so, what?
3. Do you want to convince? If so, why?
4. Who are your supporters; your opposers?
5. Who needs to learn something from you?

Step 2 (d): Topic

Taking all of these questions—and your preliminary responses to them—into account, determine a topic and set practical parameters.

1. Does it meet length requirements?
2. Is it researchable at your institution?

Step 3: The Preliminary Bibliography

When you are satisfied that you have a topic that will guide you into your research and that you have some defined questions to answer, you need to prepare a preliminary bibliography. In our course, we ask students for a ten-page double-spaced, typewritten paper. To ensure that they have sufficient material to work from, we require a preliminary bibliography of twenty items, allowing two items per page as a rough guide. Though students often think the requirement is excessive, we must repeat that the broader your base is the solider your paper will be. The final bibliography may only contain six to ten items, but they will be items chosen for their appropriateness, not simply the first ones you stumbled upon.

Use bibliography cards for this work. By putting complete information on cards at the outset you will save yourself frustrating return trips to the library later on. The cards will also allow you to prepare your alphabetical bibliographical list (of works cited) with ease because new items can be slotted into place painlessly. Putting all the items on one or two pages inevitably leads to cutting and pasting, or to confusion.

Below we have reproduced two cards 75 mm x 125 mm in proper format: one for a book, the other for an article. You will notice that each has an extremely brief annotation. A note such as this serves to remind you of the item's significance to your topic. Remember that at this stage you are not reading the material in any depth: skimming is enough. You are concerned here with finding material that might be worth a closer look. It is certain that some of the resources you find now will turn out to be useless to you—this is why you need to find plenty.

Sample card for a book

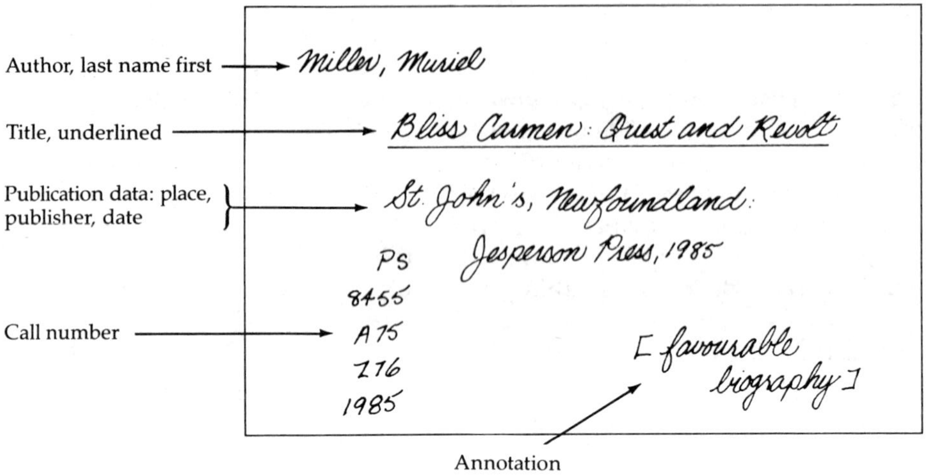

Sample card for a journal article

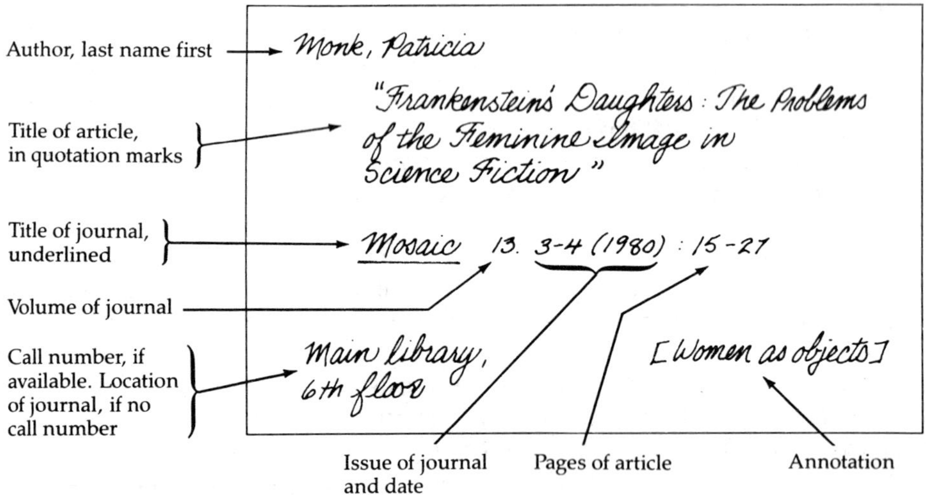

Step 4: Note Taking

If you have done your work on subject, audience, and purpose thoroughly, your note-taking stage becomes a matter of finding actual pieces of information to support your case. If, however, you have not determined your rhetorical context adequately, you will not recognize whether an item is particularly appropriate or not. In fact, most material on your broad subject will look useful. If this happens, you are in danger of losing control of your essay to your sources. Without a clear purpose, you will end up creating a patchwork of quotations tied together with weak transitions. With a clear purpose, on the other hand, you remain in control, *choosing* what *you* need to make an effective presentation.

Your notes, assuming that you are in control of your paper, will be largely of three kinds: direct quotations, paraphrases, and summaries. Do them on cards (100 mm x 150 mm) to enable you to shuffle them and try different ways of ordering your material. Numerous notes on sheets of paper prevent creative freedom in the planning stage. Keep *one* note per card. Attach a brief annotation to remind you what the note is about.

Here are three cards using a passage from W.L. Morton which we discuss more thoroughly in the section entitled "Using Quotation, Paraphrase, and Summary" (pp. 484 - 488).

Direct quotation

Full publication details will be on your bibliography card

Be sure to include the quotation marks and to quote *accurately.*

Morton 84

Canadian apprehension about the United States

"What Canada really fears is not the old America, but America in its new role of world power. It fears that America in seeking to maintain its world power will make demand after demand on Canada, each reasonable in itself, until the substance of independence is modified out of existence. More than that, it fears that the United States, in some sudden convulsion of the world balance, will simply occupy Canada. It fears also, out of its knowledge of the American temperament in action, that such an occupation could be made needlessly, or that once made, would not be unmade."

Paraphrases

Morton 84

Canadian apprehension about the United States

Morton lists a number of reasons why Canadians fear and resent American neighbourliness. The first reason he gives has to do with the United States' relatively new place of power in the world, and, as a result, its power over Canada. Canada resents American power because it fears that the altogether reasonable demands that the latter makes on the former on a day-to-day basis may, when they are accumulated, turn us into slaves of the United States. Furthermore, there are those, he argues, who worry about what a sudden shift in world affairs will do to our present friendly, if dependent, relationship with the United States. What they fear is invasion and, worse, permanent occupation, the latter the result of the American characteristic to not give back what it once has won.

Summary

> Morton 84 — Canadian apprehension about the United States
>
> Morton explains Canada's fear of the United States by commenting on the possibly unrestrained power of the States created as a result of changing world conditions; its predilection for occupying other countries; and its lack of understanding of and respect for national sovereignty other than its own.

Step 5: Thesis Statement and Outline

With your topic in mind you have been going through the material in your preliminary bibliography, identifying books and articles that will be worth close reading. You have also been taking these more important items and actively reading the pertinent sections. Of course, you will not do as detailed active reading for a book as you will for a paragraph, but you should still adhere to the format as much as possible—it will guide you to what is central and help you ignore what is peripheral. As well as completing some some version of the reading workbook entry for the research materials you have found, you have also been taking notes on passages you want to quote, paraphrase, or summarize. All in all, by the time you arrive at step 5 you should have amassed a substantial amount of material. Now you need to give it form.

Your thesis statement will act as a catalyst for the rather amorphous mass of material you have assembled. Once you make a claim, assert a position, or take a stance regarding your topic, some material will leap into prominence while other material will fade into the background. As we said in chapter 3, your thesis will often incorporate the developmental strategies suggested by your inventing and researching. And these strategies will also to some extent determine the shape of your outline. Review the appropriate section in appendix 1 once you have determined your developmental strategies. There you will find suggestions for organization.

Make your cards work for you at this stage. Lay them out in various patterns. Try strong points first; then place them last. Which placement gives the best effect? Your cards are building blocks that you can pile in many different ways. Do not settle for the first organization you try. Keep options open for a while; let your paper realize its full potential.

Step 6: First Draft

First of all, complete the planning checklist (pp. 76 - 77). When you are ready to proceed, follow the guidance provided in chapter 3 (pp. 77 - 78). One important point should be made here: when incorporating your quotations, be sure they are accurate. If you do not verify accuracy now, you will probably end up with undetectable errors in the final version. Also, put in your citations immediately, and *completely.* Too often we neglect what seem to be trifling aspects as we are pushing through a draft. Believe us, you will be grateful later on if you do your citing properly now. There is nothing more frustrating than having to go through a paper deciphering cryptic codes you were sure you would never forget.

Writing the draft is largely a matter of fleshing out and linking material you already have well in hand. Again we say it: if you've done conscientious planning your work now will be far more manageable.

Step 7: Revision

Sufficient guidance on revision is available in Chapter 3 on pages 84 to 100 and page 118. You should also review any entries in the glossary (appendix 2) pertaining to problems that show up in the draft.

Step 8: The Final Version

The research paper that follows can serve as an illustration of proper presentation, documentation format, quoting, paraphrasing, and summarizing. Read it in conjunction with the scholarly format section of this text (Chapter 10). Often principles do not come clear until readers see them in a living context. Beach's solid paper provides such a context.

Essay on Down's Syndrome by Melanie Beach

Melanie A. Beach

Dr. L. Steven

Engl. 1500EB

April 10, 1987

Down's Syndrome: What We Need to Know

Throughout our society there are a significant number of individuals who are born with a disorder that manifests itself in distinguishing physical characteristics and that can be immediately recognized. Once called Mongolism, and now referred to as Down's syndrome, "this disorder occurs...in approximately one in six-hundred births"(Hanson 2). A fairly small ratio, and yet many people do not know much about the disorder. Some of these people express sympathy saying, "Oh those poor diseased individuals"; others may say, "They are only mongolian idiots"(Pueschel 39); and others still may know the proper name of the disorder, but that may be all. To have a better understanding of the meaning of Down's syndrome and all that this anomaly entails, a study of its causes, its effects on personality, and its effect on physical, behavioural, and social development is necessary. These Down's syndrome afflicted individuals do not have any sort of disease, nor do they have a disorder that warrants institutionalization and isolation from society. These misconceptions, along with several others that have been formed about Down's syndrome individuals, must be rectified to allow for a full understanding of the disorder.

To begin to understand Down's syndrome, one must know about the cause. Down's syndrome is a chromosomal disorder that retards the physical and mental development of the individual afflicted with this abnormality. It has its effect at the time of conception, when genetic material is transferred from the parents to the newly formed being, in packages called chromosomes. Chromosomes are, in effect, genetically controlled entities that are present in every cell of the human body. Their purpose is to release messages or a "genetic code"(Cunningham 67) that will result in the expression of physical, mental, and emotional traits, and that are unique to each individual.

Each cell in the human body normally contains forty-six of these chromosomes. These chromosomes vary in shape and are numerically labelled from largest to smallest. The first twenty-two pairs of chromosomes are autosomes, while the twenty-third pair contains the genes that will determine gender. They are called sex chromosomes. For females the sex chromosome is assigned XX and for males it is XY(De La Cruz & Muller 2).

The female ovum or egg cell contains 23 chromosomes as does the male sperm cell. When they unite in conception, the forty-four autosomes pair up, each with its counterpart chromosome. The two remaining sex chromosomes also pair off together. One of the two X's from the mother will join with either the X or the Y from the father, depending on which one he donates to the new life. At the moment of conception the die is cast. Every genetically determined trait that that being will express within his or her lifetime is marked, unchangeable, in a new set of genes.

Frequently, however, there are genetic abnormalities that occur. An abnormality of the twenty-first chromosome evokes a disorder known as Down's syndrome. With this disorder, additional genetic material attaches itself to a twenty-first chromosome(De La Cruz & Muller 3). Thus, Down's syndrome is also referred to as Trisomy-21 "(tri-meaning 'three', soma meaning 'of the body'[of chromosome 21])"(Cunningham 74). This category of the disorder can be divided into three subsequent groups according to the configurations of the twenty-first chromosome.

The most frequently encountered type is Standard Trisomy-21. It accounts for approximately 90-95% of all Down's cases. The additional twenty-first chromosome is transferred to the zygote (or fertilized ovum) by its presence in the sperm or ovum of the parent, or by an abnormal first division of the fertilized cell(Cunningham 77). As a result, all of the cells of the developing zygote have an abnormal 47 chromosomes, three on chromosome 21.

About 4% of cases of Down's syndrome are of the type Translocation Trisomy-21. Here, a fragment of the extra twenty-first chromosome locates itself on another chromosome while the remainder fixates to the pair of twenty-first chromosomes. With this additional genetic material on chromosome 21, Down's syndrome results(Smith & Wilson 12). It is also interesting to note that in a rare number of cases, Translocation Trisomy-21 is carried by a parent who is of normal physical and mental development. This person has an extra twenty-first chromosome that is attached to a chromosome pair other than the twenty-first. Therefore, Down's syndrome is carried in this person's genes though the person shows no signs or ill effects of its presence. However, that parent may transfer the extra chromosome 21, through his or her reproductive cell, to result in the expression of Down's syndrome by the offspring(Smith & Wilson 13).

The third type of Down's syndrome is known as Mosaic Trisomy-21. It is even more rare than Translocation Trisomy-21 and occurs in approximately one percent of all cases(Pueschel 50). In Mosaicism, "the affected persons have cells of different chromosomal counts(for example, 46 in some cells and 47 in others)... [resulting] from an error in cell division of fertilized eggs"(De La Cruz & Muller 3).

Many people seem to be well aware that the risk of giving birth to a Down's syndrome child increases with the age of the mother. Awareness of the reasons for this, and insight into other factors that lead to Down's syndrome, must be sought. Statistics given by Cliff Cunningham indicate a strong relationship between the age of a mother and the number of births of Down's infants. Table 1 illustrates this.

Table 1: Statistics supporting the theory that maternal age is related to Down's syndrome births

Maternal Age	*No. of D.S. Births per Total No. of Live Births*
under 20	less than 1 in 2000
20-30	less than 1 in 1500
30-34	about 1 in 750-880
35-40	about 1 in 280-290
41-44	about 1 in 130-150
over 45	about 1 in 20-65

(Cunningham 86)

The lesser ability of older mothers to birth normal babies results from a deterioration of her reproductive system over the woman's lifetime. In the ovaries, the female egg cells(ova) are produced and partially matured until they, one by one, break free of the ovary at the woman's ovulatory period. In older women, these "oocytes"(De La Cruz & Muller 3), or partially matured ova, degenerate with age as do all other body systems. Thus, abnormalities are more likely to occur with the transfer of faulty cells(De La Cruz & Muller 3).

This fact about older mothers, though a well-supported one, seems to mask the fact that younger mothers, too, are susceptible to pregnancies involving a Down's syndrome fetus. In reality, there are a large number of infants born to women under 30 years of age that have this chromosomal abnormality(Cunningham 87).

Recent studies have indicated the father as a link to the Down's syndrome anomaly. Increased age of fathers seems to increase the likelihood of Down's syndrome in offspring in a small number of cases. There has been some evidence supporting the hypothesis that males over the age of 55 contribute to the production of this disorder as Cunningham has found in his research(87). Because male sperm are produced by a much different process, as compared with female ova production, the degenerative process is not the same. There may be other factors that lead to paternal origination of the Down's disorder however. According to Dr. Debra Bakker, 30% of the sperm produced by the testes of a male are structurally or biologically malformed and are, therefore, a possible cause for Down's syndrome.

Down's syndrome individuals are almost immediately recognizable. They have distinguishing physical traits that are shared by other Down's persons. Cunningham agrees that each Down's individual is unique and varies in the characteristics of the syndrome that he or she expresses. He states that "the child with Down's syndrome will not have all the signs or characteristics associated with the condition, and some characteristics will be more obvious in some children than in others(95)."

The most outstanding physical feature of any person would have to be the facial features. As a whole, the faces of Down's sufferers are somewhat smaller than normal due to the smaller head size. This might result in the greater attention given to other anatomical features of the face. Early naming of the disorder arose from the resemblance of the eyes of Down's syndrome individuals to those of Mongolians. The eyes are slanted upwards and most often are encircled by folds of skin. White speckles, called Brusfield's spots (Magalini & Scrascia 233), are commonly found in the iris of the eyes(Pueschel 58). The nose is characteristically somewhat flattened due to a "depressed nasal bone"(Pueschel 58). This gives the face an elongated appearance. Poor muscle tone around the mouth area and of the tongue of Down's syndrome individuals results in a continuously slack jaw and a "slightly protruding tongue"(Pueschel 58). With this inability to keep the jaw closed, breathing must regularly take place through oral, as opposed to nasal, respiratory means. This may account for the frequently dried lips of Down's individuals.

The hearing of such people is sometimes adversely affected by the configuration of the ears. Positioning of the ears lower than normal accounts for differences in inner ear structure. External ear conformation, such as their smaller size or the accentuated fold of the upper edge of the ear, may cause a lesser impairment of hearing(Pueschel 58).

There is a slightly underdeveloped bone growth of the extremities of people with Down's anomaly. The hands and feet are often short, as is the neck of these individuals(De La Cruz & Muller 3).

Secondary physical characteristics, such as hair and teeth, show similar patterns of development amongst the Down's syndrome population. Their hair tends to be rather thin and straight. Their teeth are often slow to develop and frequently of odd shape, or are missing(Smith & Wilson 30). Retarded development of external physical features are characteristic of people with Down's syndrome(Smith & Wilson 31).

Abnormalities of body structure are readily noticed by people, yet individuals with the Down's disorder show typical patterns of internal body development that are not so easily recognized. As well, they exhibit a similar course of mental growth that takes time to show its capacity.

Disorders of the internal body systems manifest themselves in Down's syndrome persons, though these anomalies may not be immediately detected. One significant area of concern is that of the functioning of the heart. According to the *Dictionary of Medical Syndromes*, congenital heart defects occur in approximately 50% of the cases of Down's syndrome(Magalini & Scrascia 233). This is the leading cause of death of Down's syndrome infants within their first year of life. However, improved medical techniques and the results of research have offered relief for these abnormalities in many cases. It is in this first year of life that problems resulting from the chromosomal abnormality must be noticed and corrected since this is a critical period in the development of the health of Down's syndrome infants(De La Cruz & Muller 4). Other physiological problems frequently encountered by Down's individuals include respiratory problems, and "[enlargement of the] liver and spleen"(De La Cruz & Muller 3).

One of the most debilitating characteristics experienced by Down's syndrome individuals is their slow mental development. De La Cruz and Muller reported that in 99% of the cases of this chromosome disorder there was mental retardation involved and that it varied in degree, from mild to severe(3). This mental deficiency has a significant affect on the lives of those so afflicted. It requires that these people have constant and controlled facilities in which to attain their highest developmental level.

These people face obstacles often greater than those experienced by normal individuals. Because of their physical appearance and mental abilities, Down's syndrome individuals are subjected to negative societal reactions, such as labelling. Frequently they are alienated from societal groups by society itself or by ignorant caretakers. As a result they do not become familiar with, and are unable to integrate into, the normally functioning sphere. Opportunities for learning experiences from which they can benefit may never arise.

A result of ignorance of people is the formation of misconceptions about disorders such as Down's syndrome and about the people who suffer from the disorder. Stereotyping has had a strong influence over the non-retarded public. Though not always incorrect it tends to be somewhat exaggerated in certain aspects.

The personalities of people with Down's disorder have fallen prey to stereotyping. If asked to describe what one thought the personality of a Down's syndrome individual to be, the answer would likely contain adjectives such as "affectionate, placid, or docile..." (Cunningham 120). These misconceptions stem from the fact that these people have delayed mental and physical growth. For example, smiling is a reflex that is innate and so it is the first response that an infant is capable of eliciting. Since Down's syndrome infants are at par, developmentally, with normal infants in the first few months of life, this response will occur at relatively the same time. However, laughter and other expressions of feeling such as anger and fear, develop later. With the developmental delays of Down's syndrome infants, the expression of these later emotions may be withheld slightly(Bigelow). As a result, these children may be labelled inappropriately.

These people live and grow in the same environments as everyone else (although this is a more recent development from previous institutionalization of Down's individuals). They too are susceptible to environmental influences on their personalities(Cunningham 121). A rearing situation that offers only ridicule, distant family relationships, and little support, might result in withdrawal, aggression, or rebelliousness by the child. Any number of behavioural disorders may be manifested in addition to the present chromosomal one. In an optimal teaching and stimulating environment, on the other hand, where parents show concern, understanding, and affection for their Down's child, the rewards will likely be a child with an agreeable personality and temperament(Cunningham 121).

Stereotypes of the personality of Down's syndrome children indicate "...an implicit assumption that these children are more easily directed by others and that caregiver-child interactions...involve fewer negative emotions..."(Gunn & Berry 842). This can be misleading since these people can be as temperamentally difficult as any child, if not more so. Parental handling of these children, to a large extent, influences their personality. If reared in a stable, structured home environment, with all the care and attention provided constantly, it is likely that an even-tempered, pleasant child will result. These children, since they don't have the mental capacity to control the expression of personality or temperament, must rely on others to guide them. In families where parents are permissive or neglectful, or where there is lack of affection and encouragement of the child, that child may be temperamentally difficult.

Arising from personality are the behavioural characteristics of Down's syndrome children. These qualities, too, are manipulated and controlled in the same ways that personality is. Again, these individuals are human. Though they tend to be easily contented, they have bouts of anger, aggression, and moodiness. They can be very possessive as well.

As a result of the physical and mental manifestations originating from their disorder, Down's syndrome children have a more difficult time with their socialization. It begins in infancy. Due to their developmental delays they are hindered in this process of socialization. Uncoordinated movements, especially in early infancy, inhibit the interaction of these children with other people and objects. De La Cruz and Muller support this idea. They refer to the importance of early stimulation of these children saying that, "because of their weak motor development...self-initiated activities [are reduced]"(5).

This delays the development of play activities in early childhood. Late onset of crawling and walking due to slow muscle development also delays their joining into the activities with children of their own age group. Not only does their motor development fall behind that of their peers, but they are not able to progress substantially in communication skill either.

Often there are delays of verbal ability due to the large tongues and/or mental deficiency. Sometimes it results from hearing disorders suffered by these individuals. If they cannot understand their peers, or their peers have difficulty communicating with them, each has a hard time relating. An inability to communicate leads to rejection of the Down's children and adds to their confusion and frustration(Gibson 233).

But, physical and mental disabilities alone do not account for all of the socialization delays. Again we revert back to the effects of stereotyping and human ignorance. According to Hetherington and Parke, who wrote the text *Child Psychology*, one of the things that children consider heavily when accepting their age-mates is appearance or attractiveness(554). Peers reject these children because they are different. Down's children are often not given the chance for adequate social growth outside of their homes or families. The "social isolation"(De La Cruz & Muller 6) may result in insufficient physical exercise. Not only does this adversely affect muscle tone, motor development, and social growth, but it allows for weight gain over and above a weight that these children can maintain. Specifically, this adds to the problems existent in congenital heart defects.

Since social interaction is so vital to the development of Down's syndrome children, there has been research done to allow for the incorporation of these children into a normal sphere. Down's syndrome imposes characteristic facial configurations on those affected by the disorder and these abnormalities may cause physical impairment, impairment of the ability to communicate, and often social alienation. Dr. Ian Munro of Toronto's Hospital for Sick Children has tried to rectify these problems. He performs plastic surgery on the faces of these children in the hopes of making them more readily accepted by society, and allowing them a more equal chance for adequate development(Shapiro 38). But, there is still some question about the morality of altering the facial features of Down's children. Some parents disagree with the surgical techniques and want society to accept Down's syndrome individuals as they are(Shapiro 38). Of course, if we could get rid of stereotypes and discrimination, this could be so. Humans are very critical. It takes a fair amount of coaxing to accept abnormalities.

Down's syndrome is a common disorder that few people know much about. Insight into the causes of this genetic anomaly, and study of the personality and the behaviours exhibited by these individuals, may result in a better understanding of the disorder. As well, with increased awareness of the plight of people with Down's syndrome, we can offer an optimal social environment for their adequate development.

Works Cited

Bakker, Dr. Debra. "Biological Aspects of Human Sexuality." Lecture at Laurentian University, Sudbury, March 2, 1987.

Bigelow, Dr. B. "Developmental Psychology." Lecture at Laurentian University, Sudbury, October 31, 1986.

Cunningham, Cliff. *Down's Syndrome: An Introduction for Parents.* Great Britain: Souvenir Press(E&A) Limited, 1986.

De La Cruz, F.F., J.Z. Muller. "Facts About Down's Syndrome." *Children Today,* 12(November/December 1983): 2-7.

Gibson, David. *Down's Syndrome.* Great Britain: Cambridge University Press, 1978.

Gunn, Pat, P. Berry. "Down's Syndrome Temperament and Maternal Response to Descriptions of Child Behavior." *Developmental Psychology*, 21(September 1985): 842-847.

Hanson, Marci J. *Teaching Your Down's Syndrome Infant: A Guide for Parents.* Baltimore: University Park Press, 1977.

Hetherington, E.M., R.D. Parke. *Child Psychology.* New York: McGraw-Hill Inc., 1986.

Magalini, Sergio I., Euclide Scrascia. "Down's." *Dictionary of Medical Syndromes.* Philadelphia: J.B. Lippincott Co., 1981.

Pueschel, Siegfried M. *Down's Syndrome: Growing and Learning.* Kansas City: Andrews and McMeel, 1982.

Shapiro, J. "New Faces for Down's Kids." *Maclean's*, 27 December 1982:38.

Smith, David W., A.A. Wilson. *The Child With Down's Syndrome.* Philadelphia: W.B. Saunders Co. Press, 1973.

A sample revised outline

Beach's revised outline (reproduced below) for the research paper you have just read is a very good example of format. Do not think, though, that yours must be as finely honed. Beach went through her paper after it was written using the outline as a check to see that she had delivered what she promised. You might want to do the same to your own paper.

Outline: Down's Syndrome:
What We Need to Know

Thesis Statement

To have a better understanding of the meaning of Down's syndrome and all that this anomaly entails, a study of its causes, its effects on personality, and its effects on physical, behavioural, and social development is necessary.

I. Introduction to the topic
   A. Incidence of Down's syndrome
   B. Thesis statement

II. The Cause of Down's syndrome
   A. A chromosomal disorder
   B. Configuration of the human chromosomes
      1. In normal individuals
      2. In Down's syndrome individuals
   C. Types of Down's syndrome
      1. Standard trisomy-21
      2. Translocation trisomy-21
      3. Mosaic trisomy-21
   D. Maternal age
   E. Paternal age

III. The physical traits exhibited by Down's syndrome individuals
   A. Facial features of these individuals
   B. Extremities and bone growth
   C. Secondary features such as hair and teeth
   D. Abnormalities of internal body structures
      1. Heart defects
      2. Abnormalities of the liver and spleen

IV. Mental development of Down's syndrome children

V. The reaction of society to Down's sufferers

A. Often the reaction is negative

B. Misconceptions formed concerning the personalities of Down's syndrome individuals

1. The root of the misconception

2. Reason for these views (reflex responses)

3. Environmental influences on personality: family relationships with the Down's syndrome child

4. Temperament and family stability

VI. Behaviour exhibited by Down's syndrome individuals

VII. Socialization of Children with the Down's anomaly

A. They are often delayed in socialization

B. Reasons for socialization delays in Down's children

1. Motor (physical) delays

2. Delays of, or lack of, the ability to communicate

3. Acceptance of Down's children

VIII. A proposed intervention program to facilitate the integration of children with Down's syndrome into the normally functioning society: plastic surgery

A. A major breakthrough

B. A question of ethics

IX. Conclusion

Guidelines for Dealing with Research Material

Guideline 1: Choosing with Variety in Mind

Use a variety of research materials. Do not become enslaved to one type of source; look for the following types of resources: books, collections of essays, scholarly articles in journals, newspapers, popular magazines, government documents, etc. It is also permissible to use non-written items such as taped items or recordings but only in a modest way. While such materials may constitute the main elements for certain projects (a sociological study, for example, that depends on recorded interviews), our project requires focusing attention on the basic literature of our libraries.

Guideline 2: Evaluating

Look at the material you find with a careful eye before you decide to use it. Unless you are trying to provide a historical perspective, it makes good sense to prefer what is up-to-date. Check for a scholarly basis. Does your source contain notes and a bibliography? What kind of journal does it come from? Is it scholarly or popular? Does it proclaim a particular bias? Can it be trusted to deal with the subject fairly? Check the bibliographies of other books on the subject. Do they mention your book? If not, it may be because the author is not reputable.

Guideline 3: Mixing

When writing your research paper, make sure to provide an appropriate mix of your sources. Do not, for instance, use one source for a sustained period of time in your essay. Organize in such a way that you move adroitly from source to source. Let us take an example: if you were using six sources in you paper, you would want to use all six in a way which indicated that you were not enslaved to any one of them for any particular part of your essay. Enslavement might mean using one source for your first six references, and then abandoning it and using another source for your next eight, using a third for your next five, and so on. This is a poor method of proceeding and it gives the impression that you have squeezed one source dry, abandoned it, moved on to another and done the same. It will certainly not convince your reader that you are in control of your research material or that you have a firm grip on the structure of your paper.

Guideline 4: Using Quotation, Paraphrase and Summary

At various stages in the development of a research paper, you will want to incorporate material from other sources which will state clearly and concisely the point or points that you are arguing or that will serve to illuminate or substantiate your more general statements. The three main methods of incorporating this information into the research paper are through the direct quotation (word-for-word, or *verbatim* quotations), the paraphrase (a re-phrasing *in your own words* of the material you wish to incorporate in the paper), and the summary (a boiling down of the essential points of the original to a much shorter version in your own words).

For good reasons, paraphrase and summary rather than direct quotation should play the largest part in your research paper. A skillful paraphrase is a sure sign that you have clearly understood the source from which you have taken the idea or ideas. Furthermore, it is a sure sign that you can also clearly communicate these ideas to your reader. And paraphrase allows you to use your own style in your essay while borrowing someone else's ideas. An essay that is made up of a large number of direct quotations from various sources is also, by necessity, composed of a wider variety of different authorial styles, many of which may not be compatible with your own. The result of using quotation when paraphrase would do is often a patchwork quilt of an essay made up of a variety of different prose styles.

Quotations

If you find that the clearest way of offering justification for some argument you have made is to quote some authority's views on the matter, then do so, but keep these points in mind:

1. Make sure that the excerpt is quoted accurately and that it does not misrepresent the author's intentions.
2. Use quotations sparingly. Too often papers suffer from "quotation congestion."
3. *Do not* list one quotation after another in your paper without some intervening commentary of your own. In other words, do not "grocery list" quotations. Transitional elements are sometimes formula phrases such as the following:

    On the other hand, Berton has argued in a recent study analyzing the effects of the building of the railway on Canadian identity that [quotation] [documentation here].

Or another variation:

> While Berton may be correct in his assessment of the matter, other critics have suggested alternative interpretations which are rather interesting. Cook, for instance, has noted that [quotation] and also that [quotation] [documentation].

4. Unless your context makes clear whom you are quoting, name your source when introducing a quotation. Here is an excerpt from an essay which uses a quotation awkwardly:

> Many observations have been made about the symbolic role of the knife in Margaret Laurence's *The Diviners.* "The knife is passed down from generation to generation, from Lazarus Tonnerre to...."

The following form is both clear and smooth:

> Though many observations have been made about the symbolic role of the knife in Margaret Laurence's *The Diviners*, D.G. Jones perhaps expressed it most clearly: "The knife is passed down from generation to generation, from Lazarus Tonnerre to...."

5. Most importantly, make sure that you provide a grammatical context for the quotation, that your introductory or transitional sentence meshes smoothly with the syntax of the quotation itself.

   Here is an example that switches from a plural form in the writer's introduction, to a singular form in the quotation:

> The Harper Handbook of Literary Terms defines dialects as "A variety of language belonging to a particular time, place or social group...."

In the following version, the syntax meshes smoothly—and grammatically—because both forms are now singular:

> The Harper Handbook of Literary Terms defines a dialect as "A variety of language belonging to a particular time, place or social group...."

Paraphrase

A paraphrase is basically a restatement of critical and other sources in your own words. Sometimes a paraphrase is equal in length to the original sources; more often a paraphrase will be a somewhat reduced version of those sources (but not as short as a summary).

Resist the urge to run one paraphrase after another with no intervening analysis or commentary of your own (as with direct quotations). Too often students will allow secondary or other sources to take over their paper, so much so that the paper basically becomes an anthology of paraphrases and/or quotations.

Since students often have a difficult time understanding how paraphrase in particular works, what follows are examples of various types of reshaping of source material. The first passage is the source itself; next is a reasonable paraphrase of the source followed by an example of paraphrase and direct quotation. The final example is an example of bad paraphrase which some would call plagiarism.

Source

> If then Canada's destiny is in its own hands, why is it disturbed by fear and resentment of America? The answer is plain. What Canada really fears is not the old America, but America in its new role of world power. It fears that America in seeking to maintain its world power will make demand after demand on Canada, each reasonable in itself, until the substance of independence is modified out of existence. More than that, it fears that the United States, in some sudden convulsion of the world balance, will simply occupy Canada. Circumstances may easily arise in which the United States would have no more choice than Canada. It fears also, out of its knowledge of the American temperament in action, that such an occupation could be made needlessly, or that once made, would not be unmade. For, the government and people of the United States, while they have come to accept Canadian nationhood, do not understand it and therefore do not value it. Canadian concern with this fact arises from a mature awareness that while Americans in their friendly way accept Canada as a neighbour, they are not in their heart of hearts convinced that Canadian nationhood is possessed of a moral significance comparable with that of their own great nation.

W.L. Morton, *The Canadian Identity* (Toronto: University of Toronto Press, 1961), p. 84.

Paraphrase

In his essay on "Canadian Nationhood and American World Power," W.L. Morton speculates on the relationship between the two neighbours who share the North American continent. In one paragraph of this essay, Morton lists a number of reasons why Canadians fear and resent American neighbourliness. The first reason he gives has to do

> with the United States' relatively new place of power in the world, and, as a result, its power over Canada. Canada resents American power because it fears that the altogether reasonable demands that the latter makes on the former on a day-to-day basis may, when they are accumulated, turn us into slaves of the United States. Furthermore, there are those, he argues, who worry about what a sudden shift in world affairs will do to our present friendly, if dependent, relationship with the United States. What they fear is invasion and, worse, permanent occupation, the latter the result of the American characteristic to not give back what it once has won. He concludes by pointing out that although Americans are prepared to accept Canada as a friendly and a sovereign country, at the same time they do not really understand or appreciate Canadian sovereignty largely because they do not believe that Canadian sovereignty is as significant or as important or as God-given as American nationhood (84).

This example is acceptable paraphrase. Even though one can find some words used here that are found in the original, they represent only a very small proportion of the total. More important, these words are incorporated into the paraphraser's own style and are made a part of the structure of the new paragraph. What this paraphrase shows is that the author has understood the sense of the original. The paraphraser is clearly indebted to the original for the ideas, and that point is made clear throughout the paraphrase with the various references to Morton. Needless to say, this paraphrase, like all paraphrases, needed documentation of some sort so that the reader would be aware of the original from which it had been taken.

Paraphrase and direct quotation

The author wanting to include some of the author's striking language in the paraphrase might begin in the following manner:

> In a paragraph from his essay "Canadian Nationhood and American World Power," W.L. Morton discusses why Canada "is disturbed by fear and resentment of America." He concludes that Canadians fear American power and that the legitimate demands that the United States makes on Canada on a day-to-day basis may, taken together, affect Canada's present "independence" to the point where it "is modified out of existence" (84).

In this combination of paraphrase and direct quotation the paraphraser is still in control of the material and has simply used (and acknowledged) certain key words and phrases from the original to give the paraphrase a flavour of the original.

Poor paraphrase

The following is an example of a bad paraphrase from the beginning of Morton's essay:

> Morton explains Canada's *fear and resentment of America* as a result of a number of factors. Canada doesn't fear *the old America*, but rather a new America in its *role of world power.* Canada fears that the United States in trying to hold onto *its world power* will make demands on Canada, *each reasonable in itself,* until Canadian independence is altered *out of existence* (84).

In this passage the paraphraser is slavishly indebted to the structure and language of the original to the point where we cannot decide whether he or she really understands the meaning of the original. *Notice the unacknowledged direct word and phrase borrowings.* Notice as well how when alterations to the original are attempted only a word or two is changed. In short, this is a bad paraphrase. It clings perilously to the original's language and organization and does not show any sense of initiative or individual style.

Summary

A summary can be thought of as a paraphrase that captures the main ideas of the original in markedly fewer words. The following is a summary of the W.L. Morton passage used in the paraphrase section.

> Morton explains Canada's fear of the United States by commenting on the possibly unrestrained power of the States created as a result of changing world conditions; its predilection for occupying other countries; and its lack of understanding of and respect for national sovereignty other than its own (84).

Guideline 5: Avoiding Plagiarism

Plagiarism, which is basically the use, without acknowledgement, of material (phrases, sentences, ideas, etc.) not one's own, is one of the most serious forms of academic dishonesty and clearly one you want to avoid. Plagiarism can take many forms; some of the most common are as follows:

1. Submitting work in which important words, phrases, or ideas are taken from another source without reference to that source

2. Submitting work that was actually written, in whole or in part, by someone other than the person submitting the work
3. Submitting work that was actually copied from another source
4. Submitting substantially unchanged work for one course that had already been submitted for another course

Since most often plagiarism is committed unconsciously or in ignorance, we plan to focus on (1) above. Items (2), (3), and (4) are more obviously dishonest and most students who commit one or other of these forms of academic dishonesty know from the beginning that they are cheating. Form (1), when it occurs and is detected, often comes as a tremendous surprise to the student who has unwittingly fallen into bad research and documentation habits.

A simple rule of thumb to avoid plagiarism is to make certain that you document *everything* in your paper that does not originate with you. Most obviously this means direct quotations that are clearly marked off as coming from another source through the use of quotation marks. But it also means documenting paraphrases and summaries of ideas that you have borrowed from another source. Some students mistakenly believe that as long as material is not directly quoted it need not be documented. Nothing could be further from the truth. Document not only word-for-word quotations, but also *ideas* that belong to others. In other words, even though paraphrases and summaries express ideas in your own words, the ideas they express were not originally yours and as such they require documentation just as much as direct quotations do. Look at your essay from the point of view of your reader and follow this simple rule: as a reader you have a right to know which words and/or ideas originate with the author and which do not. As a writer you have a responsibility to let your reader know which words and ideas are entirely yours and which are not. Documentation allows you to make these discriminations clear and it is your responsibility to make them. Acknowledgement of your sources is not only basic honesty but essential scholarly practice. It shows your readers that you are aware of the professional literature on your subject and it also allows your readers to follow up on the subject themselves by providing them with an indication of the material available in the field. In order, then, for these two ends to be met, you will want to make your documentation thorough and accurate.

Some students may wonder whether every sentence must be documented on grounds that the whole paper depends on borrowed ideas. The answer is that a viable essay cannot depend solely on borrowed ideas, and, further, that among ideas borrowed, some may not require documentation. Reviewing our earlier discussion of originality will help students overcome the despairing notion that they make no contribution of their own when they do research. A few words can be added concerning the not always simple problem of which ideas must be documented.

It is not necessary to document material that is generally recognized to be in the public domain. No documentation is required these days for such familiar scientific measurements as the speed of light. Nor do you need to cite a particular authority for the claim that Alexander Graham Bell invented the telephone. Further, you need not document or acknowledge adages such as "a rolling stone gathers no moss." Where ideas are not in dispute and common knowledge can be assumed, specific citations are not required.

On the other hand, there are good pedagogical reasons for asking students to take relatively little for granted. All of us must document special findings that we borrow to buttress claims we make. Although established experts on any topic (such as the circulation of the blood or photographic techniques) may treat some matters as common knowledge among themselves, those of us who are coming to a subject seriously for the first time must keep very careful track of where we found each concept or bit of information. Besides, keeping your own perspective as a student who is moving toward expertise and not confusing your own knowledge with that of the sources you use is necessary for thinking through what you have to say. An over-willingness to substitute a claim of common knowledge for a careful account of how you accumulated information leads to inadequate understanding. Finally, you should think of being generous in guiding your readers to sources that you found useful for your own purposes. The rule of thumb here is simply this: whenever you are uncertain about whether to accept an idea as common knowledge, document it. It is much better to be accused of overdocumentation than of underrepresenting your source and thereby committing plagiarism.

10 *Presenting the Paper*

Scholarly Format

For our purposes, two major methods of documenting sources predominate in the areas of the humanities and the social sciences. For the former we make use of the method found in what is known in an abbreviated form as the *MLA Handbook,* [Joseph Gibaldi and Walter S. Achtert, *MLA Handbook for Writers of Research Papers,* 2nd edition (New York: The Modern Language Association/America, 1984)]. For the latter we use the APA method based on guidelines found in the *Publication Manual of the American Psychological Association,* 3rd ed. (Menasha, Wisconsin: George Banta Co., 1983). There are, of course, a myriad of other methods of documentation available. However, since MLA and APA are widely acknowledged, we recommend that you learn one of these two methods and stick to it.

Parenthetical Citations

Parenthetical documentation (documentation within the text of the essay) relies on the listings in the bibliography given at the end of the research paper. The principle is that a parenthetical reference to the source is given in the text and full details of the source are given in the bibliography. Here is a simple example: suppose you were making your position felt on a particular topic and wanted to make clear that some other authority had made your point as well. You might say: This point has been mentioned before. Using the MLA method you would place immediately after the word "before" the author's last name in brackets and the page reference. Using the APA method you would place immediately after the word "before" the author's last name in brackets and the date of publication. (In APA these two items are separated by commas.)

MLA: (Frye 239)

APA: (Frye, 1978)

With direct quotations the MLA uses the same method as just mentioned, whereas APA includes the page reference plus the abbreviated form for page or pages.

MLA: (Smith 28)

APA: (Smith, 1976, p. 28)

If you want to make a general reference to a book or article as a whole and not to particular pages or sections, the best method is to mention the author's name in your text without parenthetical reference, for example:

But Pierre Berton has offered another view.

Full publishing details are provided in the bibliography.

The general methods given above can be applied in various other situations as well. The abbreviated list below indicates some of these possibilities for both the MLA and APA methods:

More than one author

MLA: (Messenger and Taylor 64)

APA: direct quotation (Messenger and Taylor, 1982, p. 64)

general reference (Messenger and Taylor, 1982)

Information from different places in one source

MLA: (Mowat 95-98, 275-276)

APA: direct quotation (Mowat, pp. 95-98, pp. 275-276)

general reference (Mowat, 1977)

Work cited has more than one volume

MLA: (Cameron 2:16-17)

APA: no indication: suggested method for direct quotation (Cameron, vol. 2, 1978, pp. 16-17)

general reference (Cameron, vol. 2, 1978)

Two or more works by the same author

For MLA include the author's name, followed by a comma, the title in shortened version of the title and the page reference. APA lists no specific method. The example cited is a suggested one.

APA uses letters following the date to differentiate multiple works published by the same author *in the same year.*

MLA: (Frye, *The Bush Garden* 16)

APA: direct quotation (Frye, The Bush Garden, 1978b, p. 16)

general reference (Frye, *The Bush Garden* 1978b)

Since the material with which social sciences and humanities students deal sometimes differs substantially, each type of student should consult the *MLA Handbook* or *APA Manual* for particular information that does not fit any of the models listed above.

Footnotes/Endnotes

In the new MLA system, footnotes and endnotes are reserved for comments, explanations, or other forms of amplifying on a point given in the text, when that additional information might interrupt the flow of argument but may nevertheless be of use to the reader. Footnotes are numbered in sequence, the number appearing in superscript (a half line above the normal line) immediately after the work or phrase requiring further information.

Footnotes appear at the foot of the page on which the reference occurs and are numbered in sequence. Footnotes have recently been replaced almost entirely by endnotes. Endnotes appear on a separate page at the end of the text of the essay, but before the bibliography. Endnotes are numbered sequentially and are double-spaced. Here is an example.

Text:

> Mordecai Richler, among others,[1] has been quick to analyze the overwhelming Canadian compulsion to denigrate our accomplishments.

Note:

> [1]Many of Richler's novels (see, for example, *The Apprenticeship of Duddy Kravitz*) present some analysis of Canadian self-consciousness. But see also the fiction of Margaret Laurence (e.g. *The Diviners*) and the poetry of Margaret Atwood (e.g. *Progressive Insanities of a Pioneer*). Pierre Berton, Canada's most renowned historical popularizer, has spent much of his writing life drawing our attention to our unknown but genuine Canadian heroes (e.g. *The National Dream*).

Note also that full publishing information is still provided in the bibliography.

APA Footnotes

As with the MLA system, footnotes, if used, should provide additional relevant information. If anything, APA discourages use of footnotes, arguing that greater integrity in an author's writing is served by incorporating all important material into the text. If footnotes *are* used, they are numbered consecutively throughout with superscript arabic numerals, as in the MLA system. APA does not place the notes at the foot of the page, but only on a separate page following the article but before the bibliography.

Quotation Forms

There are two main forms of quoted material used within the research paper: the shorter "in-text" quotation (see the examples used in the preceding points), and the "block" quotation. The general rules-of-thumb that govern the use of one type or the other are summed up in the following points.

Prose: Less Than Five Lines

If the quoted material is less than five lines in the source, incorporate it *within quotation marks* in the text of the essay.

If you are faced with the problem of using quotations within quotations, remember the outer quotation is set off with *double* quotation marks, and the inner quotation is set off with *single* quotation marks. Thus, for example, the following:

> Northrop Frye, commenting on the presence of the pastoral in early Canadian literature, states that "One writer speaks of the eighteenth-century Loyalist as looking 'to a past that had never existed for comfort and illumination,' which suggests that the pastoral myth had been around for some time."

This indicates to the reader that Frye is quoting a passage from another writer to support his own contention about the prevalence of the pastoral in Canadian writing. The passage within single quotations is from the unnamed source that Frye cites. The passage in double quotation marks is Frye himself.

Prose: Five Lines or More

If the quoted material is five lines or more, it should be presented in block form: indented ten spaces from the left margin, double-spaced, but *not* enclosed in quotation marks. However, *if* you are quoting dialogue, or have included dialogue excerpts within a prose text, then *do* set off the dialogue with quotation marks. For example:

A particular brand of novelistic humour is exemplified in the following passage:

> Harry, in a playful mood, invited the enormous Sister Pinsky to lunch, trying not to imagine how many pleats there were in her stomach and what agony it must be to support such pie-size breasts. "Come away with me, Sandra, we'll pool our vouchers and have us an orgy."

Poetry: Two Lines or Less

If the quoted material is two lines of poetry or less, incorporate it into the text of your essay, enclose it in double quotation marks, and indicate division between lines with a slash (/). Here is an example:

> Leonard Cohen opens his poem "Disguises" by saying "I am sorry that the rich man must go/and his house become a hospital."

Poetry: More Than Two Lines

If the quoted material is more than two lines of poetry, set it off in block format, use proper verse form—*one* line of poetry per line of type; do not use slashes; do not use quotation marks. For example:

> Leonard Cohen opens his poem "Disguises" by saying
>
> I am sorry that the rich man must go
> and his house become a hospital.
> I love his wine, his contemptuous servants,
> his ten-year-old ceremonies.

Omissions From Quoted Material

When portions of a quotation are omitted, the ellipsis is indicated by three spaced periods (. . .). If the omission comes at the end of a passage you are incorporating into your own sentence, indicate the omission with three spaced periods and then add your terminal punctuation. For example:

> Northrop Frye, commenting on the presence of the pastoral in early Canadian writing, states that "One writer speaks of the eighteenth-century Loyalist. . . ."

If you are using the parenthetical citation form of documentation and the end of the quotation is replaced by ellipsis marks, place the terminal punctuation *outside* the parentheses. For example:

> Northrop Frye, commenting on the presence of the pastoral in early Canadian writing, states that "One writer speaks of the eighteenth-century Loyalist . . ." (239).

Paraphrase Forms

Paraphrases are *not* enclosed in quotation marks but, like direct quotations, *are* documented by parenthetical citation (or by footnotes). Paraphrases are considered part of the text of the essay and are not indented.

It is important to remember, when paraphrasing, that you indicate to the reader where the paraphrase starts. This is usually done by using an introductory phrase or sentence in the text of your essay. The following samples suggest possible openings.

> Farley Mowat has suggested that for a variety of reasons we do not know exactly when our ancestors began to cross the Atlantic Ocean and explore the North American continent (3).

> A semi-factual account of the Viking explorers indicates that for a variety of reasons we do not know exactly when our ancestors began to cross the Atlantic Ocean and explore the North American continent (Mowat 3).

> In his book *West Viking*, Farley Mowat indicates that for a variety of reasons we do not know exactly when our ancestors began to cross the Atlantic Ocean and explore the North American continent (3).

It is also important to indicate where the paraphrase ends. The citation shown in these examples is an obvious clue.

Summary Forms

Summaries are treated in the same fashion as paraphrases. They should be introduced and documented so that the reader can clearly see their beginning and end. For example:

> In his most recent report on the state of bilingualism in Canada, the Commissioner of Official Languages implies that Canadian universities are not doing all that they can to promote bilingualism (189).

> A 1985 StatsCan study indicates quite clearly that the rich are getting richer, and the poor poorer (Cabal and Cliché 15-25).

James Eayrs' comments on the early years of the Royal Canadian Air Force (185-223) will probably serve as the basis for all further studies of the subject.

Bibliography/Works Cited

Under the title "Works Cited" or "Bibliography" you must list, on a separate page or pages to be placed at the end of the paper, all the works that have contributed ideas and information to your text.

Books

The following list of sample entries provides an indication of some of the major forms likely to be encountered.

Book by a single author

MLA: Lee, Betty. *Love and Whisky: The Story of the Dominion Drama Festival.* Toronto: McClelland and Stewart, 1973.

APA: Lee, Betty. (1973). *Love and Whisky: The Story of the Dominion Drama Festival.* Toronto: McClelland and Stewart.

Book by two or more persons

MLA: Hustein, H.H., L.J. Hughes, R.C. Kubysm. *Challenge and Survival: The History of Canada.* Scarborough: Prentice Hall, 1970.

Note: MLA uses the latin abbreviation *et al* (and others) for books by more than three authors.

APA: Hustein, H.H., Hughes, L.J., & Kubysm, R.C. (1970). *Challenge and survival: the history of Canada.* Scarborough: Prentice Hall.

An Anthology or Compilation

MLA: Gustafson, Ralph, ed. *The Penguin Book of Canadian Verse.* Harmondsworth: Penguin 1958, reprinted 1972.

APA: Gustafson, Ralph (1972) *The Penguin book of Canadian verse.* (reprint). Harmondsworth: Penguin.

A work in an anthology

MLA: Atwood, Margaret. "Paradoxes and Dilemmas: The Woman as Writer." *Writing Prose: Techniques and Purposes.* Ed. Thomas S. Kane et al. Canadian edition. Toronto: Oxford University Press, 1981, 203-04.

APA: Atwood, Margaret. (1981). Paradoxes and dilemmas: the woman as writer. In Thomas S. Kane et al (Eds.), *Writing prose: techniques and purposes.* (Canadian ed.). (pp. 203-04). Toronto: Oxford University Press.

An introduction, preface, foreword, or afterword

MLA: McPherson, Hugo. Introduction. *Barometer Rising.* By Hugh MacLennan. Toronto: McClelland and Stewart, 1958. IX-XV.

APA: McPherson, Hugo. (1958). Introduction. In Hugh MacLennan, *Barometer rising.* (pp. IX-XV). Toronto: McClelland and Stewart.

Article in reference book (encyclopedia, dictionary, etc.)

MLA: Barman, Jean. "Child Labour." *The Canadian Encyclopedia.* 1985 ed.

APA: Barman, Jean (1985). Child labour. In *The Canadian Encyclopedia.* (Vol. 1, pp.329-330). Edmonton, Alberta: Hurtig.

Government publications: no author

MLA: United Nations. Centre for National Resources. *State Petroleum Enterprises in Developing Countries.* Elmsford: Pergamon, 1980.

APA: United Nations. Centre for National Resources. (1980). *State petroleum enterprises in developing countries.* Elmsford: Pergamon.

Note: with APA, if the report has a report number, it should appear in brackets immediately after the title.

Government publications: author given

MLA: Cretin, Joe. *Porkbarrelling as Public Policy.* Ottawa: Queen's Printer, 1976.

APA: Cretin, Joe (1976). *Porkbarrelling as public policy.* Ottawa: Queen's Printer.

Articles

The following list covers examples that are most likely to be encountered by the student during the course of research.

An article in a journal with continuous pagination

MLA: Krasa, Eva M., "The Income Tax Treatment of Legal Expenses." *Canadian Tax Journal* 34 (1986): 757-800.

APA: Krasa, Eva M. (1986). The income tax treatment of legal expenses. *Canadian Tax Journal, 34,* 757-800.

An article in a journal that pages each issue separately or uses only issue numbers

MLA: Monk, Patricia. "Frankenstein's Daughters: The Problems of the Feminine Image in Science Fiction." *Mosaic* 13.3-4 (1980): 15-27.

Note: 13.3-4 means Volume 13, Issues 3 and 4 combined.

APA: Monk, Patricia. (1980). Frankenstein's daughters: theproblems of the feminine image in science fiction. *Mosaic, 13* (3-4), 15-27.

An article from a weekly or biweekly periodical

MLA: Quinn, Hal. "Drugs in Sports." *Maclean's* 17 June 1985: 40-43.

APA: Quinn, Hal. (1985, 17 June). Drugs in sports. *Maclean's,* pp. 40-43.

An article from a monthly or bimonthly periodical

MLA: Mowat, Robert J. "Stan Rogers: An Ontario Boy Sings of the Sea." *Atlantic Insight* Apr. 1985: 41-42.

APA: Mowat, Robert J. (1985, April). Stan Rogers: an Ontario boy sings of the sea. *Atlantic Insight,* pp. 41-42.

An article from a daily paper

MLA: MacDonald, Don. "Region Receives Compensation for Lost Interest." *Sudbury Star* 30 December 1986:1.

APA: MacDonald, Don. (1986, December 30). Region receives compensation for lost interest. *Sudbury Star,* p. 1.

An editorial

MLA: Doyle, Kevin. "The Epitome of Evil." Editorial. *Maclean's* 17 June 1985: 7.

APA: Doyle, Kevin. (1985, June 17). The epitome of evil [Editorial]. *Maclean's,* p. 7.

An anonymous article

MLA: "Tewksberry Eyes Record." *Globe and Mail* 2 February 1987: A13.

APA: Tewksberry eyes record. (1987, February 2). *Globe and Mail,* p. A13.

Essay Format

Paper

Always use white paper (normally 8½″ x 11″).

Margins

MLA: Leave 25 mm margins at the bottom and top of the page and on both sides.

APA: Leave 30 mm margins at the bottom and top of the page and on both sides.

Pagination

MLA: All pages must be numbered in the upper right-hand corner, 10 mm from the top. Do not use the abbreviation "p" for page.

APA: Use the same method, but do not number figure pages (i.e. graphs, charts, etc.).

Spacing

Double-spacing is essential in all essays or research papers.

Heading and title

MLA: A title page is not required for a research paper. Starting 25 mm from the top of your first page and allowing for the 25 mm margin, write on separate (double-spaced) lines your name, your professor's name, the course number, and the date. Again double-space and centre the title on the same page. Leave four spaces between the title of your paper and the first line of the essay. Do not use a period after the heading or title.

APA: Devise a title page on which should appear the title of the paper plus the author's name and institution. For a paper written for a course it would also be wise to include the date and the course number. The title should be typed in upper case and lower case letters. It should also be centred on the page. If the title is more than one line, double-space between lines. The author's name should be typed in upper case and lower case letters, centred and one double-spaced line below the title. Type the name of the institution, centred under the author's name, on the next double-spaced line.

PART FOUR

SUPPORTING MATERIAL

APPENDIX 1
Developmental Strategies

Comparison and Contrast

Whether they are conscious of it or not, people compare and contrast as a part of their daily activities. Those of us who watch Pepsi and Coke television commercials are watching commercials based essentially on comparison. Those of us who read *Canadian Consumer* are reading a magazine whose purpose is to let consumers know what the best buy is by comparing and contrasting commodities one with another. As part of a large consumer society, we are constantly being told to comparison shop. Sometimes this is extremely good advice, especially when a large outlay of money is at risk. It would be an unwise consumer indeed who bought a car without judging it against other cars and looking at such things as cost, gas mileage, size, and even colour. Even in less obvious areas of life, comparison and contrast play an important part. We regularly think of ourselves and what we possess in terms of other people and their possessions and make adjustments accordingly. For example, the facile philosophy of "keeping up with the Jones's" is based largely on the importance that some people place on emulating or outdoing others after comparing their lifestyles with someone else's. Regularly, though most often not consciously, we compare our sense of who we are with the view that others have of us and sometimes try to adjust ourselves to the image that we feel is most pleasing to others. No person is an island, not only because we need the company of others to survive, but also because we need to be sure that others are around to satisfy that compulsion to compare. In short, comparing and contrasting in everyday life is as natural, and sometimes as unconscious, as breathing.

But writing essays employing comparison and contrast is not as second-nature to us as thinking in a comparison-and-contrast way. Rather, like other types of writing, comparison-and-contrast writing requires a good deal of thought and planning. As well as paying attention to such matters as subject, audience, purpose, tone, and organization, you will have to be certain that the items you decide to compare and contrast are valid ones that belong to the same general class. For example, a valid subject for a comparison and contrast essay might be the relative merits of a waterbed and a spring mattress. Both of these items are from the same general class;

both can be meaningfully compared for softness or firmness, general comfort, durability, and cost, to name only a few categories. There would not be, however, much sense in comparing a waterbed with an elephant (unless you decided to treat the subject humorously) since there is no *basic similarity* between these two items.

Comparison and contrast are two aspects of the same exercise. The one sees similarities between things, the other differences. Although we can talk about comparison and contrast separately, normally in your writing (and in all writing of this type) these two elements are combined. In other words, when you write comparison-and-contrast essays you should normally show both similarities and differences between items, although you probably will try to stress one over the other depending on the nature of the items being assessed and your purpose in writing. For example, if you were writing a comparison-and-contrast essay on the spring mattress and the waterbed mattress, you would probably want to stress the differences between the two because you might want to point out to your reader that all bed mattresses, despite their simple function, are not the same. However, to speak only of the differences would be to ignore their similarities. Hence, you might want to begin your essay by briefly mentioning their similarities—perhaps to reinforce in your reader's mind that these are genuine items to compare because they belong in the same general class—and then move on to explain their differences in detail. So, you might want to open with a sentence that states that although these two types of mattresses perform the same function and come in the same bed sizes they are, nevertheless, very different in terms of their durability, comfort, appearance, and cost. The rest of the essay would then go on to point out the detailed differences between the two. If your *purpose* in this essay were to demonstrate that the waterbed mattress was generally the better of the two, you would be using comparison and contrast in the service of another mode of writing, namely, persuasion. This latter point—one type of writing serving another—is important to remember because it suggests the interdependence of types of writing, and makes clear that though we can talk about different modes of writing, we should not regard them as existing in isolation from each other.

Let us now turn to an example of comparison-and-contrast writing. What follows is an excerpt from an essay by Stephen Leacock called "The Rival Churches of St. Asaph and St. Osoph":

> The church of St. Asaph, more properly called St. Asaph's in the Fields, stands among the elm trees of Plutoria Avenue opposite the university, its tall spire pointing to the blue sky. Its rector is fond of saying that it seems to him to point, as it were, a warning against the sins of a commercial age. More particularly does he say this in his Lenten services at noonday, when the businessmen sit in front of him in rows, their bald heads uncovered and their faces stamped with

contrition as they think of mergers that they should have made, and real estate that they failed to buy for lack of faith.

The ground on which St. Asaph's stands is worth seven dollars and a half a foot. The mortgagees, as they kneel in prayer in their long frock-coats, feel that they have built upon a rock. It is a beautifully appointed church. There are windows with priceless stained glass that were imported from Normandy, the rector himself swearing out the invoices to save the congregation the grievous burden of the customs duty. There is a pipe organ in the transept that cost ten thousand dollars to instal. The debenture-holders, as they join in the morning anthem, love to hear the dulcet notes of the great organ and to reflect that it is as good as new. Just behind the church is St. Asaph's Sunday School, with a ten-thousand dollar mortgage of its own. And below that again, on the side street, is the building of the Young Men's Guild, with a bowling-alley and a swimming-bath deep enough to drown two young men at a time, and a billiard-room with seven tables. It is the rector's boast that with a Guild House such as that there is no need for any young man of the congregation to frequent a saloon. Nor is there.

And on Sunday mornings, when the great organ plays, and the mortgagees and the bond-holders and the debenture-holders and the Sunday school teachers and the billiard-markers all lift up their voices together, there is emitted from St. Asaph's a volume of praise that is practically as fine and effective as paid professional work.

St. Asaph's is episcopal. As a consequence it has in it and about it all those things which go to make up the episcopal church—brass tablets let into its walls, blackbirds singing in its elm trees, parishioners who dine at eight o'clock, and a rector who wears a little crucifix and dances the tango.

On the other hand, there stands upon the same street, not a hundred yards away, the rival church of St. Osoph—presbyterian down to its very foundations in bed-rock, thirty feet below the level of the avenue. It has a short, squat tower—and a low roof, and its narrow windows are glazed with frosted glass. It has dark spruce trees instead of elms, crows instead of blackbirds, and a gloomy minister with a shovel hat who lectures on philosophy on week-days at the university. He loves to think that his congregation are made of the lowly and the meek in spirit, and to reflect that, lowly and meek as they are, there are men among them that could buy out half the congregation of St. Asaph's.

St. Osoph's is only presbyterian in a special sense. It is, in fact, too presbyterian to be any longer connected with any other body whatsoever. It seceded some forty years ago from the original body to which it belonged, and later on, with three other churches, it seceded from the group of seceding congregations. Still later it fell into a difference with the three other churches on the question of eternal punishment, the word "eternal" not appearing to the elders of St. Osoph's to designate a sufficiently long period. The dispute ended in a secession which left the church of St. Osoph practically isolated in a world of sin whose approaching fate is neither denied nor deplored.

In one respect the rival churches of Plutoria Avenue had had a similar history. Each of them had moved up by successive stages from the lower and poorer parts of the city. Forty years ago St. Asaph's had been nothing more than a little frame church with a tin spire, away in the west of the slums, and St. Osoph's a square, diminutive building away in the east. But the site of St. Asaph's had been bought by a brewing company, and the trustees, shrewd men of business, themselves rising into wealth, had rebuilt it right in the track of the advancing tide of a real estate boom. The elders of St. Osoph, quiet men, but illumined by an inner light, had followed suit and moved their church right against the side of an expanding distillery. Thus both the churches, as decade followed decade, made their way up the slope of the City till St. Asaph's was presently gloriously expropriated by the street railway company, and planted its spire in triumph on Plutoria Avenue itself. But St. Osoph's followed. With each change of site it moved nearer and nearer to St. Asaph's. Its elders were shrewd men. With each move of their church they took careful thought in the rebuilding. In the manufacturing district it was built with sixteen windows on each side and was converted at a huge profit into a bicycle factory. On the residential street it was made long and deep and was sold to a moving picture company without the alteration of so much as a pew. As a last step a syndicate, formed among the members of the congregation themselves, bought ground on Plutoria Avenue, and sublet it to themselves as a site for the church, at a nominal interest of five per cent per annum, payable nominally every three months and secured by a nominal mortgage.

Stephen Leacock, "The Rival Churches of St. Asaph and St. Osoph," in *Arcadian Adventures With the Idle Rich* (Toronto: McClelland & Stewart, 1959 [New Canadian Library]), pp. 101-103.

The very title of this essay suggests that comparison and contrast is going to be central to the development of the main idea. In order for the author to make clear the nature of the rivalry between the two churches, he is going to have to tell us something about them. What we know from the title is that the subject of the essay will be two churches. And it is immediately apparent that there is the possibility of an appropriate comparison-and-contrast essay because of this subject. Obviously churches belong to the same general category (as do spring mattresses and waterbeds) and because of this they lend themselves to being seen in terms of each other.

The opening four paragraphs focus on the first of the two churches, St. Asaph's. In the first paragraph we learn about where it is located and also something about its rector's attitude towards the business world and the business people who make up a large segment of its congregation. Paragraphs 2 and 3 continue with the description. Once again what seems to be highlighted is the "business" and "material" component of the church. In paragraph 4 the denomination of the church is mentioned for the first time. However, so strong has the emphasis been in the first three paragraphs of the essay on the world of trade, commerce, and ostentatious wealth as it pertains to the establishment of St. Asaph's that when we reach the point in the essay where the denomination is finally named, we almost automatically associate the denomination with a particular kind of "devotion," namely, the devotion to money, possessions, real estate—the joys of wealth. In the first four paragraphs of this essay, Leacock makes very good use of the literary technique called irony.

Paragraph 5 introduces the other half of the comparison, the church of St. Osoph. Notice how the description of the first church serves as the basis for the description of the second: tower reminds us of spire, glazed windows of stained glass ones, spruce trees of elms, crows of blackbirds. Obviously the second church is a far less ostentatious establishment than the first. Leacock emphasizes that point by focusing on different aspects of the same item. But in case we begin to think that the sombre appearance of St. Osoph's denotes a poorer congregation, Leacock informs us that their rector loves to think that among his flock, "lowly and meek as they are, there are men . . . that could buy out half the congregation of St. Asaph's." But then comes the most revealing contrast, that is to say, revealing for the *ironic effect* that Leacock is trying to create here. As St. Asaph's is episcopalian, so St. Osoph's is presbyterian. In the sombre description of the second church, combined with indications that its members are distinctly well off, Leacock leads us to conclude something about the financial and economic status of presbyterianism: obviously it is not as concerned with displaying and enjoying its wealth as the espicopalian church down the *same* street: Plutoria Avenue (check your dictionary if you're not sure of the meaning of "plutocrat").

After highlighting external *differences* between the two *similar* items (rich churches), in paragraph 7 Leacock mentions another significant similarity: their history. Both churches have obviously improved their status, since both "had moved up by successive stages from the lower and poorer parts of the city." The irony lies in the fact that their outward differences mask an essential sameness, which Leacock captures masterfully in the almost identical names.

This skillful piece of comparison-and-contrast writing with its dextrous use of irony is a masterpiece. What is important to remember, however, is that Leacock is able to produce a skillful ironic piece only because he has maintained control over his comparison-and-contrast method of development.

Structuring a comparison-and-contrast essay can sometimes present problems. Should you deal with one half of the comparative whole altogether, and then use that material as the basis of the discussion of the second (as Leacock does), or should you compare one item at a time in each half as in the following excerpt from the same essay?

> There could be no greater contrast with Mr. Fareforth Furlong than the minister of St. Osoph's, the Rev. Dr. McTeague, who was also honorary professor of philosophy at the university. The one was young, the other was old; the one could dance, the other could not; the one moved about at church picnics and lawn teas among a bevy of disciples in pink and blue sashes; the other moped around under the trees of the university campus, with blinking eyes that saw nothing and an abstracted mind that had spent fifty years in trying to reconcile Hegel with St. Paul, and was still busy with it. Mr. Furlong went forward with the times; Dr. McTeague slid quietly backwards with the centuries.

Leacock, pp. 186-87 .

There is, of course no hard and fast rule about the method of development. Clearly, however, if you were to build an entire essay upon the latter method you might find yourself with little room for developing the comparisons and contrasts you are trying to establish. Perhaps the best advice is to use a judicious mixture of both methods, determining which to use by deciding upon the pace you want to create in the essay or paragraph.

Special Types of Comparison

Simile

A simile is a comparison that an author forces upon our consciousness by pointing to a not-always-obvious similarity between two things through the use of the linking words *like* or *as*. Notice the following example of a simile drawn from the Leacock passage cited above:

> And on Sunday mornings, when the great organ plays, and the mortgagees and the bond-holders and the debenture-holders and the Sunday school teachers and the billiard-markers all lift up their voices together, there is emitted from St. Asaph's a volume of praise that is practically as fine and effective as paid professional work.

The final four words of this sentence introduce the not-altogether-expected simile. What we see in this simile is how Leacock can emphasize the mercantile concerns of this particular church by comparing it to the world of business and commerce which, ideally at least, is not supposed to be part of a church's concern.

The fact that we have had to use a number of words to explain or unravel the simile suggests one of its natural strengths: it can say so much merely by using two well-chosen comparative items.

Metaphor

Simile becomes metaphor when the linking words *like* or *as* are omitted and, as a result, the comparison becomes identity. Metaphor can be an extremely descriptive and apt type of comparison, but, from the point of view of reason, it is, finally, illogical. Two different things cannot be the same thing and yet remain themselves, as seems to happen with metaphor. Although often most effective within the context of poetry, metaphor, if used judiciously, can be effective in expository and persuasive writing as well. Notice, for instance, how well it is used in the following excerpt from a Morley Callaghan essay:

> Above all, Paris was the good address. It was the one grand display window for international talent, and if you were at all interested in the way the intellectual cloth of the time was being cut you had to be there, even if you couldn't do more than press your nose against the window.

Morley Callaghan, *That Summer in Paris* (Toronto: Macmillan, 1963), p. 114.

Notice the use Callaghan makes of the metaphor of the window to describe Paris. Furthermore, pay attention to the use of a second metaphor in the passage to describe a particular way of thinking, a particular philosophy of the time. Finally, notice how this metaphor briefly and neatly encapsulates all of the lengthy explanation that would be needed to unravel it fully.

Analogy

Another type of special comparative technique is analogy. Analogy can be regarded as extended metaphor through which some one thing is explained in terms of another. Notice the following extended comparison between two very dissimilar things:

> The tent and the igloo are really only auxiliary shelters. The real home of the Ihalmiut is much like that of the turtle, for it is what he carries about on his back. In truth it is the only house that can enable men to survive on the merciless plains of the Barrens. It has central heating from the fat furnace of the body, its walls are insulated to a degree of perfection that we white men have not been able to surpass, or even emulate. It is complete, light in weight, easy to make and easy to keep

in repair. It costs nothing, for it is a gift of the land, through the deer. When I consider that house, my opinion of the astuteness of the Ihalmiut is no longer clouded.

Farley Mowat, *The People of the Deer* (Toronto: McClelland and Stewart, revised ed. 1975), p. 127.

As with simile and metaphor, analogy tries to convince you to see one thing in terms of another in order, usually, to make a feeling, a notion, or an explanation clear. Analogy is a particularly difficult type of comparison writing because of the need to hold onto the comparison and sustain it; therefore, you should not attempt it until you have mastered the more common type of comparison-and-contrast paper. But you can still admire it, and the excerpt from Mowat is an extremely good example of the type.

Steps and Guidelines

1. Limit comparison and contrast to two items

In order to avoid organizational and structural problems by trying to juggle too many things at once, limit your comparative essay to two items. By doing this you will not have to worry about complex permutations and combination problems. Comparing A and B is infinitely easier than comparing A and B and C. In the former case you have only two terms to deal with, each being seen in terms of the other; in the latter case you must not only talk about A in terms of B, but also B in terms of C, and A in terms of C. Normally, such an essay is a tangled mess and usually one of the items gets incomplete treatment. Remember you are trying to write a clear comparison paper, not to work out a complex mathematical problem.

2. Remember that to compare means to show both similarities and differences

This point was mentioned earlier. Suffice it to say that even though you may emphasize comparison over contrast or vice versa, you should deal with both in any comparison essay you write. Dealing with both may mean as little as acknowledging in a sentence or two—in an essay showing differences—that there are certain similarities between two items.

3. Emphasize the main point of the comparison

Normally you will be forced to do this because of length restrictions. Depending on what you are comparing, trying to talk about *all* similarities or differences between your chosen items might result in a very general presentation more in the form of a list than an essay. Dealing with too many points of comparison and contrast will result in an inadequately detailed presentation. Remember you must provide detail in all of the essays you write. Make sure that in comparison-and-contrast papers you restrict yourself to the main points so that you have space left to flesh them out.

4. Choose a topic that lends itself to comparison

Make sure that the things you want to compare and contrast lend themselves to this type of writing. You might want to compare items that belong to the same general class (waterbeds and spring mattresses, or two types of churches) or compare things by degree (the difficulty in scaling two mountains; whether teenagers today are better or worse than teenagers were twenty years ago).

5. Plan your essay by lining up the comparisons and contrasts and deciding upon the order of presentation

Make certain that you know the points you want to develop and the order you want to present them in. Notice the Leacock excerpt again. The author does not try to tell us everything about the two churches. Rather he is very selective, giving us only specific details and focusing in large measure upon attitudes. Obviously, Leacock planned his essay and did not list comparisons and contrasts in the order in which they first occurred to him.

6. Be sure you follow a method of presentation

You must decide how best to present your material in order to highlight the points you want to make. Should you proceed by discussing the items one at a time (the so-called "chunk" method) or feature-by-feature (the "slice" method)? Each method has its own merits depending on the end you have in mind. Most essays, however, are made up of a judicious combination of each method so as to avoid boredom.

Cause and Effect

Cause-and-effect thinking appeals to humanity's deepest instincts; in a profoundly mysterious world human beings want to know the answer or answers to the question *why.* Scientists in their search for causes live by the question *why.* Even the casual reader often judges the merits of a particular piece of fiction on whether it establishes appropriate and comprehensible causal relationships in its plot. Medical researchers quest for the causes of diseases; sociologists and psychologists try to understand how terrorists are born; mechanics are trained to tell us why our car will not start on wet mornings; historians tell us about the causes of the Peloponnesian war. Searching for causes, it seems, is a vital part of humanity's inquisitive nature.

Effects are no less important in our lives; if causes give us *reasons for,* effects provide us with *results of.* Scientists and social scientists try to predict the effects of certain phenomena or happenings. Normally scientists are on safer ground with their determinations; because they deal with people, social scientists can never be certain that the same action performed on different groups of people will have the same effect time and time again. And this uncertainty about the effects of any particular action tells us something of great importance about effects. Normally they are complex and manifold; often our attempts to determine or describe effects run the gamut from wild and irresponsible speculation to educated guesswork. Rarely are the causes and effects of anything simple, non-controversial, or singular.

Consider an example of the complexity of causes first: suppose we tried to determine why an individual takes hard drugs. We could gather a whole series of causes based upon the different types of people we asked. Drug takers themselves might say that they take drugs in order to feel relaxed and at peace with the world and themselves; their parents might claim that their offspring take drugs because they want to rebel against parental authority; a psychologist might claim that drug takers are succumbing to peer pressure; a sociologist might argue that the drugtakers take drugs because drugs are a way of escaping a success-motivated and rat-race society; the drug takers' minister might argue that they take them because they are not sufficiently God-fearing. With these responses, these varied experts feel that they hold the key to the problem; but standing back from the issue, we can see how the problem to which each is responding is more involved than an individual cause suggests. In fact, we might argue that each of them has come to the "solution" that reflects their own particular biases. Indeed, perhaps the drug takers take drugs for all of the reasons given or possibly for none of them.

Now let us turn to some examples that reflect the complexity of effects. Some effects, like some causes, are simple and straightforward. There is no question of what will happen if we drop a large piece of potassium into a beaker of water; without doubt there will be an explosion. Similarly, if you choose not to put gasoline in your car, one effect of this action is absolutely predictable. But usually effects are far more complex and controversial than this. What are the effects of jogging on the human body? Some cardiologists claim that it is good for cardio-pulmonary fitness; others, equally well qualified to comment, strongly disagree. What is particularly distressing and perplexing is that each side can produce "evidence" to support its case. Such complexity frustrates humankind in general in its search for certainty. Another example: what are the effects of introducing free trade in Canada? Higher unemployment, lower inflation, unhappy dependency on American goods, an increase in our gross national product or the reverse of all or some of these? When we move away from something as simple as predicting what will happen when we drop a piece of potassium into water, we are often into an area of controversy, bias, guesswork, and quasi-scientific speculation. Causes and effects, although a central concern in all areas of life, are as maddeningly perplexing and complex as they are ubiquitous.

Like process analysis, causal analysis deals with actions and events occurring during a period of time. Process analysis generally focuses on and emphasizes sequence: you must perform action A before you perform B for the process to be carried out effectively. For example, you cannot change your flat tire until you have removed the wheel nuts. Sequence, then, is normally central to process analysis. In causal analysis what is central is the *relationship* between events. B not only follows A, but is the direct result of A. Without A happening, B could not possibly occur. For example, if I place a piece of potassium in a beaker of water the result will be an explosion. Placing the piece of potassium in the water *causes* the explosion; this action results in a particular *effect*. The effect could not occur without the cause; B not only happens after A, but depends upon A.

The centrality of relationships between elements in causal analysis can lead to some wrong-headed causal links. One of the most prevalent is known as the *post hoc ergo propter hoc* fallacy, which means, literally, "after this, therefore because of this." This fallacy in relationships occurs when you assume that because something follows immediately after some other action or event, that action or event is the direct cause of the happening. For example, if you slam your finger in a door immediately after you have had a fight with a loved one, you might be tempted to see that person as the cause of your sore finger. Here the thinking is based on faulty logic because it confuses sequence with causality. (See page 271.)

Generally, it is easier to write a convincing and irrefutable cause-and-effect paper—either expository, argumentative, or a combination of both—if the subject you choose is impressionistic and subjective rather than scientific or polemical. People are less likely to quibble with your causes or effects if the experience you are detailing has a highly personal element built into it. Notice, for instance, the following whimsical and highly subjective analysis of English and Scottish food. The author's purpose is not to give a scientific analysis of causes or effects. Rather his purpose is to provide an altogether fictitious and humorous causal relationship between food and natural history and personality:

> Of all the foods I know, the most fascinating is the English, for like everything else English, it cannot be considered apart from history, nor is its message in any sense as simple as it seems. While the empire was a-building, Englishmen ate massive meals of protein and starch, but once the empire was built, the English ruling classes tried to come to terms with a dilemma their knowledge of history told them was critical for their national existence. If they enjoyed the pleasures of the table too much (and now they could utilize all the diets known to man) they would lose their empire for the same reason the Romans lost theirs. Yet what was the use of the empire if it condemned them to living permanently on Brussels sprouts?
>
> The ruling class of England thereupon came to a typically English compromise. Indifferent to the lower classes, themselves accustomed to spending at least a month of every year on the Continent where they could eat the delicious foods of decadence, they decided to outdo Sparta within the home island, nor was any law necessary to

guarantee the moral salubrity of English restaurant food. By that extrasensory perception which enables the island to survive, English cooks saw their duty and did it. Hence the boiled meats and fish, the cabbages and sprouts dripping with lukewarm water, the incredible gooseberry fools, the one all-purpose sauce that looks like ground caterpillars and is used to lubricate everything erroneously called a sweet. But those foreigners who believe the English drink the kind of coffee they do because they lack the wit to make it any other way, have as much understanding of the English mentality as the German admiral who believed the Grand Fleet held the seas after Jutland only because the British were too stupid to know they had been beaten.

If a wise maturity accounts for the food of England, masochism must be held responsible for what the Scotch eat. Believe no Scotchman who tells you that his countrymen can afford no better. When Lord Strathcona was a millionaire many times over, oatmeal porridge, so I am told, remained his favourite dish. Believe no Scotchman who attributes the national diet to the barrenness of Scottish soil. Scotland is surrounded by billions of the finest food fish in the world, and the Scotch are skilled fishermen. If they boil their salmon and halibut till no taste remains, if they bake out of their haddock the last drop of moisture, if they serve these ruined fish with a dry, grey potato and (for variation) boiled turnips and sprouts, if they offer for dessert soggy rice pudding with bloated raisins bulging out of it, if they equate a distaste for haggis with disloyalty to Scotland herself—let nobody pity them or wonder why they eat as they do. They prefer this diet because it gives them the pleasure of being miserable.

Hugh MacLennan, "By Their Foods . . ." in *Scotchman's Return and Other Essays* (Toronto: Macmillan, 1960), pp. 18-19.

This excerpt is essentially trying to explain the causes of English and Scottish eating habits; the first paragraph and a half explains in lengthy and pseudo-historical terms how and why the English came to develop their dreadful cooking habits. The last half of paragraph 2 details the results of their decision to "outdo Sparta." Paragraph 3 explains the reason why Scottish food is so dreadful. The middle section of the paragraph gives graphic examples of the results of Scottish masochism, and the final sentence reiterates the opening general assertion by equating the "masochism" reference of sentence 1 with the "miserable" reference of the final one. What is important to recognize in these paragraphs is the relationship between cause and effect. Although the author's main job is to outline the causes, he also recognizes the need to mention a limited number of effects in order to put life into his causal analysis.

Steps and Guidelines

1. Limit your discussion to causes or effects

What this guideline indicates is that you should limit your subject and understand your own method of proceeding. In an essay of about five hundred words, you want to make certain that you do not try to exhaust an entire subject. For instance, it would be unwise to try to explain the effects of abortion without limiting your discussion to, say, the psychological effects of abortion on women over forty or some such narrower topic of discussion. Without this limiting, your essay will read like very little more than an undeveloped list of causes or effects.

2. Start with an effect and try to explain its causes or start with a cause and try to determine or predict its effects

Early in your essay you must let your reader know how you intend to organize your paper. Following the advice above gives you a good start on the procedure. If you want to try to determine why smog is prevalent in Hamilton, Ontario, you are moving from cause to effect. It sometimes happens that the original pattern you establish—moving from cause to effect or vice versa—proceeds in the opposite direction from the one first intended. For instance, if you were speculating on why people drink you might first discover that you have to state that people drink because they feel relaxed when they do so. Notice that this statement is a cause of why people drink based upon the *effects* alcohol has on them. There is nothing wrong with this movement from cause to effect or effect to cause as long as you remember that your original pattern determines the general shape and direction of your paper.

3. Make certain that causes and effects are true and legitimate

You need to proceed cautiously when writing cause-and-effect papers, especially when you are speculating in them. What causes inflation? Do we know for certain? If you do not know for certain, avoid sounding dogmatic or you will lose the confidence of your reader. What are the effects of smoking? Obviously, there are some very evident ones: yellow-stained fingers and teeth, and bad breath to name only two. But does smoking cause cancer? At this stage, there is only a statistical link. One imprudent dogmatic speculation in a cause-and-effect paper can destroy the bond with your audience you should be trying to establish.

4. Acknowledge the possibility of several possible explanations

If such a situation obtains, be honest with your reader and acknowledge the existence of several possible causes. It may be that you want to deal with only a few related ones because you regard some as more important than others. If this is the case, it is still important to let your reader know that you are being selective and are aware that your causes or effects do not make up the whole picture.

5. Establish a large enough sample group in cause-and-effect papers that argue a point or establish a hypothesis

If you are trying to prove that juvenile delinquency is caused by broken homes, you would be unwise to base such a claim on two delinquents you know who have come from broken homes. Clearly a paper based on such a hypothesis must have a strong quantitative base to support it. Such a theory would require you to go beyond your own limited personal experiences.

Classification and Division

What courses are you taking? Just English. One other? If you are attending full-time on campus you might tell me you are taking English, psychology, history, political science, and math. And in doing so you would be classifying your university studies. The courses you take at university or college look at various aspects of their particular disciplines. These disciplines, in turn, are broad categories of human activity. We categorize—or classify—something as belonging to the discipline of psychology rather than English because it has *similarities* with other things in the psychological field. Categorizing, or classifying, or sorting, helps us deal with the plethora of activities, experiences, and information to which life exposes us every day. Without a way to organize the phenomena of our lives we would be, to borrow an illustration from Northrop Frye, "in the cultural situation of savages who have words for ash and willow and no word for tree" (*Anatomy of Criticism,* Princeton U.P., 1957, p. 13). Classifying allows us to organize items in terms of a larger whole. Through classification we are able to abstract from our experiences rather than deal with the primary phenomena all the time. A language, and the cultural traditions spawned by it, could not develop without our ability to classify.

Suppose, however, that after you told me your selection of courses I asked for more information about your English course. You might very well say that the course has three parts: graded compositions, a research project, and an examination. Here you would be working from the larger whole—the English course itself—down to its component parts; you would be dividing the course in order to look more closely at its *different* aspects. Division is as important as classification in our understanding of our world: categories help us sort phenomena, but division lets us examine—or analyze—those phenomena once they are sorted.

As you can easily see, division and classification often go hand in hand. Let us look at an example of the relationship between the two. Suppose you were interested in purchasing a children's swing set that could be installed in the backyard of your house. The first step would be to look through the catalogues to see what was available. The *classification*—according to size, features, and price—might be as follows: the "Low-priced four-legged swing set"; the "H-Frame fitness centre"; the "Care Bears six-legged swing set"; the "Deluxe Non-Rust Galvanized swing set"; the "Athletic Swing Centre"; the "Gym Dandy Whirl Wind Swing Set"; and the "Fire House Super Gym". Suppose you purchased the "Low-priced four-legged swing set". What you would discover when you got it home would be a number of parts and a set of instructions. By following the instructions you would see that the first thing to do would be carefully to *divide* the metallic pile into its parts: 2 swings, 1 sky-scooter, 4 legs, 2 chinning bars, 4 lengths of chain, 1 cross-beam, and a plastic bag containing an indefinite number of nuts and bolts. Before beginning to assemble, however, you would have to complete another task: *classifying* the bolts according to size. Among the bolts you might find 20 mm, 30 mm, 35 mm, 50 mm, and 80 mm varieties.

In the swing-set illustration, then, we have two examples of classification and one example of division. Each of the examples, though, has something in common: an element according to which the classification or division is organized. We said our swing sets were classified according to size, features, and price—these elements are the bases of classification. But what about the division into parts? We didn't mention a specific principle of division, but clearly the parts are divided according to function—what they *do* in the operation of the set as a whole. This may seem obvious, but we could have divided the parts according to colours, or length, or weight, though such principles of division would not have got us very far in assembling the swing set.

In both classifying and dividing you need to be sure that the organizing elements are logical and worthwhile. If the principle of division does not reveal anything of use—which would have been the case had we divided the parts of our swing set according to colour—then it should be abandoned and something more suitable found. Always work in conjunction with your topic sentence or thesis: if you keep your dominant purpose firmly in view it should act as a safeguard against quirky principles of division. With classification as well you need to take care to avoid mixing the organizing elements or overlapping them. If Canadian Tire had classified its swing sets according to (1) low price, (2) high price, and (3) sky-scooter equipped, it would have been mixing bases of classification (price and features) and overlapping them (sky-scooters can come in both expensive and inexpensive sets).

Division and classification are primarily used to inform or explain—they are standard expository strategies. We want to spend some time illustrating how the mixed approach can gain different effects, depending on whether you move from division to classification or vice versa. Often the distinctions between the approaches are less than clear. Possibly approaching the same subject, first from one avenue and then from the other, will focus the strategies more helpfully.

Imagine you are involved in writing a pamphlet entitled *The Student's Guide to University Survival*. The subject of your fourth chapter is "Problem

Professors." How do you approach the subject? One way is by dividing it into its various aspects. These could include the *history* of the problem, its present *significance*, its *extent*, and so on. Almost certainly one of the aspects would be the *types* of professors involved or the *types* of problems encountered. Here your strategy would change from division to classification as you outlined the problems of incompetence, or sexual harassment, or dogmatism; or as you briefly introduced "the sleeper" or "the power tripper." In this essay the classifications would only be one aspect of the larger organization by division.

You might, on the other hand, choose classification as the way to organize your subject. In this case "the absent-minded professor," "the sleeper," "the power tripper," "the trendy professor," and "the hobby-horse rider" would follow one another in separate sections of the essay. To examine the various types you would have to switch into division. Your discussion of "the trendy professor," for example, might be divided according to (1) clothing, (2) deportment, (3) characteristic activity, and (4) self-image. In this essay the divisions would serve to flesh out the larger classifications.

Though classification and division are largely expository strategies they are often successfully put to work in the argumentative mode. The issue essay, for example, may strive to divide arguments evenly into pros and cons in order to present an overview of the issue, but frequently the writer is partisan and concerned only to advance one particular cause. Then classification and division become powerful aids in exposing an opponent's weaknesses. When attacking that opponent's argumentative style, for example, you might divide it in two, saying it erred in thought and delivery. Then you could classify the thought in terms of how it erred: through obfuscation; through illogicality (for example, the *post hoc ergo propter hoc* fallacy); through sheer stupidity (as in the argument against translating the King James Version of the Bible into contemporary English because it was "the Bible St. Paul used"). Likewise, you could classify the delivery according to its various guises, from the Sunday-morning-TV-evangelist sublime to the used-car-salesman ridiculous. Pay attention to the following passage, written as an attack upon various types of fraudulent writing:

> Like most "literary theories," my ideas on the short story form are less "theories" than they are simple reactions—on the one hand—and "working principles"—on the other. And although they may have some relationship to that great grey Thing known as "Literature," they are first and foremost (as far as I am concerned) the tools of my own individual trade. If I am called upon to justify them in the Grand Arena of Criticism (as I am here doing) I think that I can do so, but I must issue the warning that I am doing something "after the fact." That is, having committed the crime of passion (as it were), I am now trying to explain how rational I was all the time.

In this paragraph the technique of classification is at work, although it is based upon an implicit assumption made by the author. The subject of the author's concern (which we will see developed in the following paragraphs) is the short story. This form—this classification as it were—is a genre of what the author calls "that great grey Thing known as 'Literature.'" In order to understand the particular class of literature which the author is going to talk about, we must recognize it as part of a much larger category containing many other classes. The category is literature, and some of the classes include the novel, poetry, drama, and the short story. In other words, in the opening sentence of this paragraph the author has introduced a classification; he has assumed that we know enough about literature to recognize its various classifications; the one he is particularly interested in is the short story. There is, however, a more obvious example of classification at work in this paragraph as well. In the first sentence the author introduces the notion of "literary theories" and classifies his ideas—his own personal "theories"—into two types: "simple reactions," and "working principles." The essay continues in the following vein:

> But most theories I believe, are developed in reaction to something or other—perhaps something even so vague as "the way things are." But the fact is that in the past ten years, as writer, teacher, and editor (of *The Fiddlehead*, for four years), I have found myself growing more and more dissatisfied with the stories I have been reading.
>
> This does not mean that I have much sympathy with what passes for "avant-garde." What is usually meant by that term is the use of typographical techniques which were developed fifty years ago (half a century!) and are now used in an attempt to finesse the writer into the future course of the "Development of Literature," or whatever. Most "avant-garde" is all flash and no substance. Worse, it is ridiculously easy to imitate and fake. Worse yet, it is imitative of the fresh fashion of the 1920's. Nothing could be more provincial than the aping of a fashion of fifty years ago; nothing is more futile, and nothing is done more often.
>
> In another way, however, I have reacted against some of the writing which was submitted to me when I was the editor of *The Fiddlehead*. This was quite often the symbol-sodden maundering parable of the beginning writer, and when I worked my way through it I thought to myself, "O ho somebody's been reading Coleridge and Kafka on the same afternoon." Mind you, I was less dissatisfied with this kind of attempt than I might have been. I began writing symbol-sodden parables when I was young and reading Coleridge and Kafka on the same afternoon. My friends said it was "pretty impressive stuff," although somehow it was never accepted for publication. Yes, and it was pretty

pretentious stuff, too—a papering-over of an insufficient conception with a flowered wall-paper of prose. One thinks one can disguise one's weakness—or one's youth—with great gobs of obscure prose. Its chief characteristic is that it is only obscure, and not worth the effort of disentangling it.

But I think that the writing which I have reacted most strongly against is what I call the "Academy" work—that is, the successful story of fifty years ago which I now teach three or four days a week, and the contemporary imitation of it. When this work is done by one of the masters, I am full of admiration for it. When it is a lesser imitation, it seems like pretty weak stuff.

Kent Thompson, "Academy Stuff," in *The Narrative Voice,* ed. John Metcalf (Toronto: McGraw-Hill, 1972), pp. 233-34.

In paragraphs 2, 3, 4, and 5 of this essay the author further classifies the short story into three types based upon his own experience as a writer, teacher, and editor. One thing to notice about these further classifications is that they are highly personal and impressionistic. He creates his types—"avant garde," "symbol-sodden maundering parable," and "Academy work"—by using his earlier mentioned and highly personal classifications of his own ideas into "simple reactions" and "working principles." Yet, within these classifications, division is also hard at work. Thompson's cursory treatment of the "avant garde" short story, for example, distinguishes it from the other classifications by dividing it into various characteristics: its use of "typographical techniques"; its flashiness and lack of substance; the fact that it is easily imitated; and its "aping" of the "fresh fashion of the 1920's." Another important element in these paragraphs is the way in which the author brings classification and division—a developmental strategy—to the aid of another developmental strategy, namely, definition. Classification and division help the author create categories into which he can then place distinct items that require definition: in this case, the three types of short stories that he finds objectionable.

Steps and guidelines

1. Classification focuses on similarities within a common field

Think of classification as the many different colour television sets that General Electric makes.

2. Division focuses on differences within a common field

Think of division as the many different components within a particular General Electric television model.

3. Normally classification and division work together

Review the Kent Thompson excerpt to see this principle in action.

Illustration

Communicating with illustrations is such a commonplace occurrence that we may have to prod ourselves to bring techniques for using them skillfully into conscious awareness. One shopper may tell another that a certain store has good bargains that day and name a few of them. Or a television watcher may complain that there are no good programmes in summer and list a few typical cases to drive the point home. A watchful parent, not content with a vague answer, may insist that a child give an illustration of activities planned for an evening's outing with friends. If we were to keep a diary of illustrations we encountered during each day's conversation, we would have many entries. Giving and taking illustrations or examples is simply a natural and usual conversational activity.

When it comes to writing, employing illustrations is no less frequent. We can expect illustrations in any pattern of writing. If we want to be effective in asserting that second-hand smoke is harmful, we need strong illustrations to make the case.

So usual is it to use illustrations that we may sharpen our understanding by seeking out instances in which illustrations are *not* appropriate. Unique events are a prime example. They must be narrated specifically. For example, the description of a particular traffic accident will give pertinent facts: this car and that collided at an intersection at such and such a time and with such and such results in personal or property damage. On the other hand a newspaper editorial which denounces mayhem on the roads will have illustrations or will lack effect.

Illustrations are tied to generalizations. When we make a general point, examples or illustrations become relevant. Assert that there is more than one way to skin a cat and you may be called upon to name at least two. State that walking can be a healthful exercise and you will be expected to cite one or more specific ways in which it is so. And the illustration needs the generalization for its significance. A list including sherbet, washing powder, paper towels, oranges, and turkey takes on one appearance when given in the context of "I want you to pick up a few things at the grocery store this afternoon," and quite a different appearance in the context of "I want you to practise spelling miscellaneous words."

For developing essays that employ illustrations as the dominant pattern, we need to consider carefully overall structural and rhetorical features.

In terms of structure, it is important to note the close relationship between exemplification essays, which use illustrations, and so-called *standard essay form*. At its most abstract, the form is simply that of introduction, middle or body, and conclusion—a scheme that is not confined to one strategy. But the association between illustration and the standard form is a close one because of the frequency with which students are asked to take a stand or to make a finding and to show the reasonableness of their beliefs by the evidence of illustrations, and because of the naturalness of the movement of thought from generalization to illustration.

Moreover, the relationship between generalization and illustration is suited to the standard form in a special way. Either the generalization sets us off on a hunt for examples, or a number of examples induces us to reach for a generalization to explain them. It should be said that the first alternative is normally to be preferred. Ordinarily, and perhaps especially in essay examinations, you will benefit from starting your essay with a strong assertion rather than waiting until the end to produce an explanatory one. In either case, however, it would be natural to make the most general of your statements at the beginning and end and to fill the middle with details, thus yielding the introduction, body, and conclusion of standard form. In the following paragraph the author tries to exemplify how Americans, generally ignorant of things Canadian, can nevertheless understand the importance of Canada to the US when certain economic relations are articulated. The paragraph is a good example of strong assertion coming first and being supported by a number of subsequent examples:

> In trade and economic relations, however, we see a clearer and surer pattern. Here it is easiest for the American to grasp the importance of Canada to his own country, for it can be done by absorbing a few simple yet gigantic facts. In this field the interaction between the two nations has reached an unprecedented magnitude. They exchange the world's greatest volume of bilateral trade. Canadian natural resources and sources of energy have also begun to figure prominently in American economic calculations. Americans have more capital invested in Canada than in any other foreign country, with the result that strategic sectors of the northern economy are controlled or heavily influenced from the United States. (Conversely, per capita Canadian investment in the American economy is even larger.) Canadian railroads, highways, air lines, and pipelines are intimately linked with their American counterparts: in the realm of transportation and communications the border is crossed by a traffic of enormous size and complexity. The majority of Canada's unionized workers belong to organizations that have their international headquarters in the United States. There is literally no equivalent anywhere in the world, no economic and financial interrelationship between two national states that is so vast and so intricate.
>
> Gerald M. Craig, "Northern Miracle?" in *The United States and Canada* (Cambridge: Harvard University Press, 1968), p. 6.

As well as noting the way in which this paragraph follows the more usual pattern of moving from generalization to example, notice also how the final sentence reiterates the opening, general assertion. The point to be made must be made twice, lest the illustrations between beginning and end make the reader forget what the list is designed to illustrate. Making the general point both at the beginning and the end is especially important in long paragraphs whose central sections often are filled with numerous illustrations.

Such a brief account necessarily oversimplifies the scheme; most notably it should be added that there is an interplay throughout an essay—within the introduction, within the body, and within the conclusion—between relatively general statements and relatively specific ones. And a given topic may well require more than examples for adequate development. Clarifying sentences may also be in order. The basic point remains, however, that illustration can be thought of as the standard essay and that it exhibits the scheme of introduction, body, and conclusion in an especially clear way.

Your rhetorical appraisal of illustration should always deal with author, subject, and audience. Are you a detached observer of cases that exemplify a general principle—as you might be when writing on the subject of mixed salads, noting, for instance, that one may use greens only and another may add chicken for substance? Or do you feel moved by an urgent need of your own—as you might be if you were discussing insidious ways in which our society promotes the use of hard liquor and recalled front-page reports on David Peterson, Frank Miller, and Lieutenant-Governor John Black Aird who were seen drinking brandy on the occasion of Peterson's winning the right to take over as Ontario's premier? How can you do justice to your subject? Especially you might ask whether the instances you have chosen are sufficiently representative; allowance for a tax-free $1000 of interest and dividends would not be a good example of how some provisions of the tax system benefit all of us.

Perhaps most important of all for illustrative essays is your relationship to the reader. Which examples will be clear and how many are needed is a question that can be answered only when you keep needs of your audience firmly in mind. To assure an unknowledgeable audience that in a pinch one can survive on food available in forests will probably require a fairly long string of instances; to those skilled in the ways of nature, however, probably a single strong case would be enough of a reminder to establish the point.

Steps and Guidelines

1. Be certain that you provide sufficient illustrations to support a general assertion

One of the most common criticisms made in essays of any sort is the one that concerns the validation of general statements. Students do not normally err by writing overly-specific or detailed essays. Rather the error lies in the opposite direction: the lack of detail to support general assertions. You must not only provide the details that the general assertion calls for, but you must also ensure that you provide *enough* of them.

2. Make your illustrations comprehensible

There is no point in trying to prove a general assertion by using illustrations that are beyond the comprehension of your reader. For instance, if you are trying to illustrate how the human eye works, and decide to use the camera as an example, don't tie your reader up in knots by using specialized photographic terminology. Illustrations are meant to support or elucidate; do not use them to obfuscate.

3. Do not feel the need to support every assertion that you make

Overkill as far as illustrations are concerned may overwhelm your reader. Usually one or two strong examples will serve to illustrate a position. Certainly one strong example is far better than a number of weak or questionable ones.

4. Do not allow the illustration to take on a life of its own

Remember that the illustration is to be used *in the service of* the general assertion. Do not make it compete with the assertion by giving it equal billing or dealing with it at such length that the original point is lost in the discussion of the example.

Definition

The dictionary is what most people think of when definition is mentioned, and certainly a well-worn dictionary is a good friend. Most of us, however, if we think about it, will acknowledge that dictionary definitions only go a short way toward defining the meaning that things have for us *in our lives.* How many of us, for example, feel at home with the following definition: "A solid-hoofed, perissodactyl quadruped (*Equus caballus*), having a flowing mane and tail, whose voice is a neigh" (*Oxford English Dictionary*)? Most of us would agree that the neigh is the important clue. Without that detail, and without a knowledge of Latin, would we recognize the horse? But a horse neighs; nothing else does, so we are sure of ourselves when we hear the word neigh. But what is a neigh? Let us turn again to the *Oxford English Dictionary:* "Of a horse: To utter its characteristic sound or cry." Now we are sent back to horse. The definition is circular; we will never find out what a neigh is—and probably will have trouble identifying a horse—from that passage of the *Oxford English Dictionary* alone.

But we know what horses and neighs are—from life, from the various encounters we have had with horses, or from cultural records. And the *Oxford English Dictionary* knows this too. It is generally acknowledged as the greatest English dictionary because it doesn't stop with the formal definition, but adds to it by putting it in a practical context that most people would understand. The definition of horse continues: "It is well known in the domestic state as a beast of burden and draught, and especially as used for riding upon." Further, the *Oxford English Dictionary* then quotes sentences employing the word "horse" which span the period of time from the earliest available written record of the word in the language up to its present use. In this way the dictionary attempts to compensate for its otherwise obvious lack of lived, human, *contextual* meaning.

Formal Definitions

The *Oxford English Dictionary* uses what are commonly called *formal definitions,* where the thing to be defined is placed in a class (quadruped) and followed by a list of characteristics that distinguish it from other members of that class (solid hoofs, neigh, etc.). Formal definitions, like division into parts and process analysis, tend to break things down into their components as a way to understand or identify the larger whole. The method is analytical, and it can help us to see features more clearly and accurately. Accuracy, however, may not be enough. Analytical method—and formal definitions—are limited when it comes to challenging an accepted definition, when the subject to be defined becomes controversial, or when, although normally familiar, the subject has to be seen in a special way.

Extended Definitions

When analysis will not suffice to define something adequately we can turn to synthesis. Instead of breaking something down into its component parts, we define it by presenting it in a context, as part of a larger whole. We are all aware that the relationships a person enters into can help to characterize that person; we need to recognize that these defining relationships are the basic means we have of conferring meaning on the people and things in the world around us. Even the *Oxford English Dictionary* moves into the relational sphere when it says that horses are well known "especially as used for riding upon." Riding is a fundamental relationship between humans and horses; yet a formal definition need not even mention it.

Formal definitions, then, are limited; to make them come to life we need to extend them. Extended definitions can be developed a number of ways. Five of the most basic are example, comparison, etymology, narrative, and negative definition.

Example

An example helps your readers to orient themselves by offering familiar reference points. If you are discussing paternalism, for instance, you might point to the doctors who wave away their patients' fears, the lawyers who skim over the fine print with a suggestion that they have everything under control, the professors who intimate that the problems you are having with your assignment aren't *really* all that bad, or the parents who avoid taking their child's problems seriously by attributing them to a "phase" the child is going through.

Comparison

Comparison can help you develop your definition in a number of ways: through figures of speech which widen the frame of reference for your readers, as might a simile: "A paternalistic government is like a father who leaves the training wheels on long after the child learns to ride the bike"; through comparisons: you might compare a paternalistic person to someone who is "condescending" or "patronizing"; or through synonyms, such as "fatherliness."

Etymology

An etymology, or the history of a word, can be useful, especially if the term's meaning is in a state of flux. If you have a dictionary that lists etymologies you can see how the word has developed. A little research into the times at which the various meanings were prevalent can potentially produce material for an essay. The *OED* is particularly helpful in providing this sort of information.

Narrative

Narrative anecdotes, of course, can liven up your project. If you are defining paternalism, an account of an episode in which you were forced into the role of a child by a probably kind-hearted but unthinking professional can win your reader's sympathy far more easily and effectively than an abstract discussion of the term.

Negative Definition

The last strategy we will mention here is negative definition. The above-mentioned methods of developing definition are essentially self-explanatory; negative definition, however, is less clear. We offer the following example of it by using an American illustration of paternalism that has received significant exposure on our Canadian television stations:

> As an actor Robert Young has made his living by being paternalistic. From "Father Knows Best" through "Marcus Welby, M.D." to coffee commercials, Young has epitomized the caring father figure who invites us to let him solve our problems. It's tempting, isn't it, to let the old family doctor, with his wealth of experience, sort out the knots we have tied ourselves in, and reassure us that all those new-fangled methods are just that, and of no account. It's tempting, yes, but more and more we are seeing that we should resist that temptation. Try asking that fatherly family doctor some hard questions about your treatment. Try taking some of the responsibility for your case into your own hands, and you may very likely see an aspect of paternalism that is not so cozy.

Negative definitions define by telling what something is not; in the above example the traditional view of paternal figures is clearly *not* how the author sees paternalism.

Extended definitions can use any or all of the possibilities glanced at here; whatever technique you choose, however, there is a very good chance that you will find yourself employing other developmental strategies as you develop your essay. Do not worry about this; overlap is natural. Do not be afraid to use the resources that are available. Remember that whether you are setting out to inform, to persuade, to challenge, or even to anger, it is *your* definition that you are championing, and you need to bring all your powers to bear in making it effective.

In the following example, notice how the definition of Canada's "absurdity" is altogether personal and idiosyncratic. You would never find Canada defined in this way in any dictionary or encyclopedia you cared to look into. Clearly what the author is attempting to show is *his personal* vision of the country—his personal definition—if you will:

> Canada, of course, is a geographical absurdity—a country of nearly 4,000,000 square miles, where eighty per cent of the population lives within a strip 3,000 miles long and 150 miles wide along the American border. The strip is not even continuous; the regions of Canada are cut off from one another by formidable natural barriers such as the Great Lakes, the Laurentian Shield, and the Rocky Mountains. By contrast, much of the boundary with the United States is purely arbitrary and theoretical.

Neil Compton, "Broadcasting and Canadian Culture," in *Canadian Writing Today*, ed. Mordecai Richler (Markham: Penguin, 1970), pp. 25-26.

The following excerpt from a book entitled *Mind Tricks for Parents* is a good example of the way in which the writers recognize the difference between the cold and objective analytical definition of a word that one finds in a dictionary and the living, vital, and, in a very real sense, legitimate meaning of the same word within a human, living context:

> "I'm a parent!" you exclaim as you look at the small, helpless creature that has been given over to you. But just what is a parent? *The Shorter Oxford English Dictionary* (if you have a child in one arm, you cannot possibly lift the full-size *Oxford English Dictionary*) defines a parent as "A person who has begotten or borne a child... a protector, a guardian, etc." Watch out! That etcetera means a lot! As a parent you are an object of love and affection, a teacher, a provider, a protector, a policeman, a lawmaker, a cook, a chauffeur, a maid, a butler, a

hairdresser, a nurse, and last but not least, a person in your own right.

Hélène Hoffman with Janet Rosenstock, *Mind Tricks for Parents* (Markham: Paperjacks, 1982), p. 9.

Steps and Guidelines

1. Dictionary definitions provide formal, analytical definitions not personal, contextually based ones

Remember that, depending on your purpose, the best definition of a word may not come from a dictionary. For instance, your *own* definition of the word "hobby" might be far more meaningful for your reader if you are trying to convey your passionate attraction towards photography.

2. Be aware of the existence of specialist dictionaries

There are many specialist and subject dictionaries now on the market. Make use of these if you are dealing with a particular subject. For instance, you will have a better chance of conveying the psychological meaning of the word "sublimation" if you examine a dictionary of psychology rather than an ordinary dictionary.

3. Make certain that the word you define has a specific enough focus to make the meaning clear and relevant

Trying to define a concept that is as broad as the concept of love, for example, is a counterproductive task. The dictionary will be very limited in use since the term is too vast to provide a specific meaning. If you are writing an essay on love you might be better advised to give examples of it based on your own experiences rather than to search a dictionary for its meaning and try to force your experience into the general definition. This point works together with number 1.

Process Analysis

If you have ever made bran muffins by following a recipe or assembled a bicycle by following a set of instructions or tried to lose twenty pounds by reading one of the many diet books on the market, you have, in one way or another, already been introduced to process writing. Process writing, like comparison and contrast, cause and effect, definition, illustration, and classification and division, is often used in the service of exposition. First and foremost, expository writing explains or shows or presents something to a reader. Process writing, more particularly, explains or shows or presents by showing *how to:* for example, how to do, find, discover, learn, examine, understand, build, work out, elucidate, decipher, improve, change, or perform something. Returning to our original three examples in the opening sentence, we can see how a recipe tells you *how to* make bran muffins, a set of instructions *how to* construct a bicycle, a diet book *how to* lose weight. Process writing, then, is, from one point of view, writing that instructs. Perhaps one of the most famous and popular examples of process writing is Dale Carnegie's book *How to Win Friends and Influence People.* In this book Carnegie points out the steps that one should take in order to be more popular with others and influence their lives, decisions, actions, etc. Because learning and self-improvement seem to be an innate human need (all of us, at one time or another, think we are too fat or too ineffectual or too little in control of our lives) "how to" books based on the process model of writing are extremely popular.

As well as instructing, however, process writing can also *inform* by providing the details that indicate how a certain end was attained. For instance, an essay that outlines the steps that former Prime Minister Trudeau took to achieve political power would be an informational process essay. So would a piece of writing that detailed the various stages in Samuel de Champlain's historic voyages culminating in his founding of Québec City.

In one sense, trying to distinguish between process writing that instructs and process writing that informs is futile, since all writing that informs also instructs and vice versa. However, the distinction between instructional and informational process writing is real, albeit subtle. Instructional process writing is more practical. Usually we read our automobile manual not for pleasure but rather to discover how to change a tire or to find out where the fuses are housed. We buy cookbooks not to read, as we might read a detective novel, but rather to find out how to make a particular dish. We buy a diet book to find out how to lose twenty pounds. Informational process writing is less practical; it is of no immediate usable value for us. We read about the stages culminating in Einstein's theory of relativity not because we want to use the theory ourselves but because of our interest in Einstein's mind, his thought processes, his genius. We read about Prime Minister Trudeau's rise to power not because we too want to be Prime Minister, but because of what it tells us about human motives, aspirations, and goals.

Although our bran muffin recipe, bicycle assembly instructions, and diet book are examples of instructional process writing, they do not get us very far when it comes to explaining the nature of a *process essay.* These very simple types of process writing are meant to do nothing but provide information in a certain order so that a particular practical end is achieved—good muffins, a bike that works, the loss of twenty pounds. Consider the following process piece detailing how you might best get from Québec City to Jonquière:

1. Cross the Pierre Laporte bridge. Keep going on Henry IV Boulevard. *Do not drive through the city.*
2. Drive 5 km on Henry IV Boulevard.

3. Take exit Ste-Anne de Beaupré-Chicoutimi (to your right).
4. Keep going for 4 to 5 km and take exit Chicoutimi (to your right).
5. Take Route #175 to go through the Laurentian Park. Allow 2½ to 3 h to go from Québec City to Jonquière.
6. The Laurentian Park is a provincial park and there is only one restaurant located halfway through the park.
7. Coming out of the park, you are still on Talbot Boulevard.
8. *First traffic light.* Turn left on Route 170 to Jonquière.

In these instructions the goal is to give a simple set of directions on how to get from one place to another in the most convenient way. Notice these features: (1) the instructions are in a certain order without which they would be impossible to decipher (the notion of order is important in *all* process writing and will be dealt with below); (2) the instructions are given in point form, each item clearly distinguished from the rest by a numeral, and particularly important information is in italic type; (3) the instructions are in the imperative form (do this, drive here, etc.) and the tone is cold and impersonal; (4) the language of the instructions does not call attention to itself as graceful, beautiful, or generally pleasing. Each statement is stark and unadorned and sharply separated from its neighbour. In short, there is no attempt here to do more than give someone precise instructions. Because this piece of process writing serves an entirely practical end, it has no particular aesthetic qualities in it.

These considerations bring us to the difference between process writing and the process essay. First consider an example:

> In Canada there are approximately 980 taxidermists, including those who work in laboratories. My mother, Pam McIlroy, is one of Canada's and perhaps the whole world's few licensed *women* taxidermists.
>
> My Mom says she has been catching, cleaning and cooking fish ever since she was big enough to carry her own fishing pole. Everyone laughed when she decided to learn how to mount our biggest fish for trophies. Mom is only five feet three inches tall and weighs about a hundred pounds, but when she wants anything done right, she learns how to do it herself. That is why she became a taxidermist.
>
> Mom says taxidermy as she does it dates back only about three hundred years, but long before that animals and birds were "stuffed" with straw or sawdust and kept for ornaments. Canadian Indians preserved the heads of porcupines, foxes, racoons, and birds to decorate their clothing. Mom went to London two nights a week for over six months to learn the trade. Then she tried examinations and became a licensed taxidermist. Mom had studied art at Queen's University, before I was born, and she says her art training helps her

now. She also studied animal anatomy, so that she knows all about the bodies of the trophies, the bones and other parts.

Mom has a big freezer where she stores specimens until she can work on them. After she skins an animal, she puts a preservative powder on the skin and wraps it in damp cloths.

I like to watch her prepare a fish. She lays the fish on paper and draws around the body, writing down how thick it is at various places on the body and tail. Before she skins it she washes it, mouth and all, with a solution to remove the mucous which covers all fish. Then she decides which side will show. Cutting it open on the other side, she removes the entrails, stuffs the opening with sand or cornmeal and sews it up. Keeping the fish damp with a special solution while she works, she poses the fish on a newspaper in a box of sand. She spreads the fins and tail, holding them with big pins. Then she pours a plaster over the fish and lets it set until the plaster hardens. Next she carefully lifts the fish out, watching so the scales don't curl.

Mom sharpens her knives, scissors and scalpel on whetstone, and starts to skin the fish, from the back of the head, cutting through the scales and skin only. With a dull knife she removes bits of flesh from the skin.

After she treats the skin, it is put in the plaster mold and shaped to fit. Next she puts a little square block of balsa wood in the cavity and fills the rest with papier-mâché which I help her make by shredding newspaper and mixing it to a pulp in hot water. I like beating it until there are no lumps, then Mom adds a paste to it that she makes herself.

When the papier-màché has set she takes the fish out of the mold and fastens it to a panel of wood by putting screws into the block of wood inside the fish. She curves the fins and tail so they look like a live fish with pieces of cardboard and pins. She fills the cheek muscles with papier-màché, through the mouth. When it looks perfect she hangs it on the wall to set. It takes about three hours of work to prepare the fish and then it has to set for two or three weeks.

When it has dried, Mom removes the wires and pins and the wood back and reinforces the fins and tail with tissue paper. Then she opens one of the little drawers in a chest and picks out the right coloured glass eyes. I am learning to pick the right eyes. Once I chose a duck's eye for a moose!

Mom has a lot of tools besides her knives, pins and big needles and floss for mending tears. She has small scales for weighing chemicals and pinchers, and she uses all her artist's equipment and brushes. She has a lot of electric tools too—a saw, a drill, a sander and a router. She uses the latter to shape the plaques which she designs for the trophies. My Mom would rather get a tool for her birthday than chocolates or a new dress.

Mom tells sportsmen to carry a camera with them to photograph their fish in colour, because a fish loses its colour as soon as it is out of the water. Or they can draw a picture of the fish and put the right colours in with crayons. Mom can then restore the right colours with enamels and lacquers which she mixes herself.

Mounting moose and deer heads is another of my Mom's specialities. The hide from a deer's head and shoulders is called a cape. Mom uses a salt cure which dries the cape stiff and hard. She soaks it until it is soft, ready to be put on the form which she made using a wooden frame, wire mesh and papier-màché.

Mom anchors the form on a working stand which was built to her specifications. She uses a special molding clay (like plasticine) to add the eyes, tear ducts and nose. The eyes that Mom uses are museum eyes. The antlers, which have been treated with a solution so the horns won't go soft, are polished and glazed, and then bolted to the head. She then molds the head with clay until it looks natural.

My Mom finishes a lot of bear rugs. They are commercially tanned, and then she makes the head form, inserts the eyes and molds and shapes the mouth, which comes in three pieces—huge teeth, red tongue and gums. Using her artist brushes she paints the nose and mouth.

Mom doesn't like to mount pets but she did mount Pinky, our albino clarise fish. Pinky didn't know he was a fish, he'd jump out of the aquarium and wiggle and bounce on the floor. One day he jumped out when no one was home and he died. Mom said a brave jumper should be rewarded. So she made a nice shiny plaque so Pinky could hang on our living room wall.

Mom would rather mount fish or animals than birds, because feathers make her sneeze.

Some people would be frightened in our living room because fish, rabbits and ducks sit on furniture or hang on the walls in frozen poses. They are "setting." Mom says it looks like a zoo, only the animals don't move.

Mom and I spend a lot of time in the woods and at zoos, studying live animals and birds. She says it is important to know what they look like when they are alive in their natural poses, so she can make them look natural when they are mounted.

I'm glad Mom is a taxidermist. She teaches me a lot about birds and fish and mammals.

Brant McIlroy, as told to Belva Kalbfleisch, "My Mother is a Taxidermist," in *Canadian Children's Annual* (1977), pp. 85-86.

Notice how in this essay the author works to establish a human context for her process by establishing contact with the reader and sparking his or her interest. The essay, to be sure, has a large process component to it. We learn about how fishes are stuffed, how instruments are sharpened, how moose and deer heads are prepared. But there is far more to the essay than a detailing of these steps. We learn a good deal about Mom's personality, when she became interested in taxidermy, something about the history of taxidermy, and so on. In other words, the author creates an interesting context for the process in this essay. We have moved a long way from the cold and impersonal set of instructions on how to make bran muffins or how to get from one place to another. The author of this essay is clearly interested in doing more than outlining a method; she is infusing a personality into her writing and taking into account the subject, audience, and purpose of the piece.

It is now time to turn to the actual means you can use to guide yourself in your process writing. Let us examine those means by working with an example: changing a car tire.

Steps and Guidelines

1. Find a topic appropriate to the required length of the paper

If you are asked to write a five hundred word process essay, it would probably be unwise to consider a topic such as the steps Pierre Trudeau took to become Prime Minister, or how to build a house, because such topics would result in very little more than a series of general statements which would probably raise more questions than they would answer. Remember that for all essays that you write, you must narrow your topic so that it can be *developed* within the word limit set for it. However, five hundred words is fine for describing how to change a car tire.

2. Be certain of all of the steps in the process

If you want your reader to understand the process you are trying to detail, you must make certain that you provide all of the central steps in the process. In our example, it would be useless to tell our readers that you have to remove the flat tire from the car if you failed to tell them about the importance of the jack in the process. Jotting down the steps that you think are central to the process is a good place to begin. In this jotting you are simulating the method of outlining a process found, for instance, on the bicycle instruction sheet.

3. Be certain that you put all of the steps in the correct order

You can't expect your reader to understand your process fully if one or more of your steps are out of order. In some process essays order may not be particularly important (we have experimented and found that when you are making bran muffins it does not matter if you add the milk before the eggs or vice versa), but in most processes, order is crucial. In our example, if you told the reader to remove the flat tire before also mentioning that the wheel nuts have to be removed you could be confusing your reader.

4. Do not get side-tracked on parts of the process

Remember, if your essay is about the steps one must follow in order to change a tire successfully, you should talk about the details within individual steps only insofar as they help clarify the process. Let's say that you get to the step where you mention the jack. You may want to make clear to your reader that there are different types of jacks—hand-crank jacks, hydraulic jacks, and air-bag jacks—and you may want to explain briefly how each one works; but you should probably not do more with this step, especially if your essay has a rather small word limit. To begin talking in detail about various components of the jack or to weigh the merits of one type against another may very well be an unnecessary digression. Further, you risk not getting back to the process as such.

5. Organize the material into paragraphs

Now that you have got reasonable control of the material that will go into your essay, you should consider what to do with it. One of the first things you should do is organize this material into paragraphs. Suppose you decide that there are six central steps in changing a tire: (1) preparing to remove the tire; (2) jacking up the car; (3) removing the flat tire; (4) putting on the new tire; (5) letting the car off the jack; (6) tightening the wheel nuts. If you think about it for a moment, you can see that the organization of your paper is actually found in these particular steps. Perhaps you can devote a paragraph to each of these central points, fleshing out the paragraph with *details* that make up each main point. For instance, point 1—preparing to remove the tire: under this main point you might want to discuss (1) how you first discovered that you had a flat tire; (2) the proper method of blocking the wheels of the car and why this is important; (3) removing the hubcap; (4) removing the wheel nuts with a tire-iron. All of these particular steps are part of the initial general point and could go together in a single paragraph. And so it would go with each of the other general points. Your paragraphs in this essay—six in all not counting the opening and closing paragraphs—would proceed in a linear fashion moving from the mention of the flat tire itself through to the end of the process.

6. Be aware of your audience

Remember, when you are writing an essay you are always writing it for someone. Awareness of your audience will determine how you approach your topic and your attitude toward it. Suppose you were being asked to write an essay on how to change a flat tire for a group of students in a driving instruction course. You would have to be meticulous in detailing the steps involved, and probably your tone (i.e., the attitude you have towards your subject) would be serious. If, however, you were writing the same essay for a group of automobile mechanics, your tone might be humorous and your presentation not objective but personal and anecdotal. In this latter case you might be interested in entertaining your readers in your process essay; in the former case, instructing them.

7. Create a context for your discussion

Refer again to the process essay reprinted above. Notice how the author manages to create a meaningful and interesting context for the discussion of the process of taxidermy. In short we can say that the essay seems to have been written by a real person and addressed to a real audience. It makes contact with the people whom it wants to reach. You should do your best to emulate this technique in process writing. It may mean starting your paper with a short anecdote or perhaps including some comparison. For instance, when you come to discuss removing the nuts from your flat tire, you might want to mention the wisdom of choosing the proper tire-iron for the job and briefly compare various types one with another. In other words, though you are being asked to write a process essay, do not feel that you cannot introduce other ways of writing into your paper. Almost all writing is made up of a variety of types. You are being asked to write a process essay *primarily.* Do not become enslaved to the type so that your essay reads like a traditional bran muffin recipe.

APPENDIX 2
Glossary of Usage and Guide to Revision

Your writing task is to develop ideas worth attending to. Your basic obligations are to carve out a subject, to think carefully about it, to provide evidence or relevant specific details to substantiate claims you make, to take account of audience reactions, and to write clearly. This appendix is subordinate to your basic project. You should not begin with the thought of making subjects and verbs agree or choosing between commas and dashes or even of spelling words correctly. Begin with the thought that communication is something worthwhile. That said, at some stage you will have to ensure that your writing meets expectations for college and university essays on such particular points as spelling, punctuation, grammar, and style. For that purpose, you should turn to the appendix as needed for help in improving the effectiveness of your communication. Use it when your instructor has objected not to your intentions but to your words or phrases or any of the other matters covered by the correction symbols on the inside cover of the text. Or look into it beforehand for revising your essays before you submit them. Learn something of the intricacies of choosing between *who* and *whom* or remind yourself of the pitfalls in relating modifiers to words they describe or limit.

Whenever it is reasonable to do so, the appendix will offer you firm guidance. You must not, however, expect it to relieve you of making careful choices. English is not a static thing, nor is it all of a piece. It changes over time, and at any given time it is subject to a good many variations—of educational level, of the particular discipline for which you are writing, of degrees of formality, of the medium used (whether the spoken or written word), and of still other circumstances that linguists continue to study. Certainly there are variations by region, with respect to individual words or favourite phrases; and, extremely important for our purposes, there are questions of variations—of Canadian English in relation to American and British English. Normally, the Canadian variant will coincide with one or the other, sometimes with an American variant and sometimes with a British one; but there are times when the Canadian national standard will not match the national standards in either of the other two countries. Furthermore, none of the variations is governed by legislation, and all of the types mentioned have legitimate uses on one occasion or another. Finally, it is natural for us to mix variations to some extent, moving for instance, among levels of formality within a single essay. However we examine the issue, then, we cannot escape the need for making choices among the possibilities offered to us by a changing and complex language system.

Too often, handbooks of English offer guidance by announcing conclusions without discussion, as if questions had already been settled and students need not trouble to think about them—only obey. That approach, which no doubt is not intended to be as arrogant as it sometimes seems, has the merit of a certain clarity and succinctness. But the cost is a misleading understanding of the way language works—as if English were forever closed to the input of its users. The approach also has the unfortunate potentiality of encouraging passivity when students should be encouraged to remain active.

Instead, we work on the assumption that in the long run all users of English contribute in some way to making the language what it is, and we want entries in the appendix—brief though they are—to keep alive the sense that how we use the language can be investigated and can be discussed. Just as we ask you to read attentively as a means of developing ideas for essays of your own, we ask you to observe carefully the practices of spelling, punctuation, grammar, and style that you find in the essays. Use your observations of actual practice as one kind of aid in increasing your command of English; and be prepared to make informed choices of practices that you find clear and useful, eschewing an occasional idiosyncrasy on the part of the writers you study and thinking over how your choices may affect your treatment of audience, subject, and purpose in your essays.

In line with that approach, we have, whenever possible, used actual sentences from printed sources for both examples and exercises in the appendix entries, instead of making up artificial ones. Canadian newspapers, especially *The Globe and Mail* and the Toronto *Star,* provide a good many examples, and we have often used sentences directly from the essays included in our text. Our discussions, themselves more brief than we might prefer, take some account of options. And in many cases, we provide a brief exercise.

We have attempted to inform our own choices by consulting handbooks of English, dictionaries, style sheets, and linguistic and grammatical studies as well as by our general reading and by observing the practices of our colleagues, our students, and ourselves. We continue to learn about the fascinating ways of English as we go, regarding the study as a pleasurable life-long challenge. We invite you to do the same.

Among sources especially helpful to us in preparing the appendix have been *A Comprehensive Grammar of the English Language* by Randolph Quirk and others (Longman, 1985); *The Canadian Style: A Guide to Writing and Editing* (The Department of the Secretary of State of Canada, 1985); and *Gage Canadian Dictionary* (1983).

abb Abbreviations

Clarify the abbreviation or make it conform to conventions

In college and university writing, abbreviations should be used sparingly and in accordance with principles of intelligibility and conventionality. MP and MLA (with or without periods) will be understood by Canadian audiences in the context of a discussion of politics. Only a much narrower audience would immediately understand ACP, even in a context of discussing publishing; it should be spelled out (Association of Canadian Publishers) the first time before the initials appear.

Beware of variations. The British seem to favour *Mr* and *Dr* without periods while Canadians seem to prefer those abbreviations with periods. For appropriate forms consult dictionaries and examples in essays and books relevant to your subject.

Exercise

List ten abbreviations from essays in this text and write out in full the words they stand for.

agr Agreement of Subject and Verb

Change the subject or verb as necessary to make the two agree in number

When reading and writing we are expected to understand that, normally, a singular subject takes a singular verb and a plural subject takes a plural verb. Sometimes, however, we are in doubt about the number of the subject or about where it is located, and it is not hard to find examples in print of what would be regarded as faults in the usual scholarly essay. Advice concerning some typical difficulties follows:

1. While certain plurals from the Latin—most notably *data* and *media*—are often treated as singular in English, formally they still are respected as plurals. When in doubt about whether your reader will accept such subjects in the singular, treat them as plural:

   > Electric media move information and people at the speed of light.
   >
   > Marshall McLuhan, "The Violence of the Media," *Canadian Forum*.

2. Because *none* is singular in form, use a singular verb with it as long as you are able to think of its meaning as singular.

   Furthermore, among the array of credit cards I offered as a substitute, none was acceptable.

   Dalton Camp, "The Decline in Public Morality," *Saturday Night.*

   A plural verb can be justified, however, when the context establishes a plural meaning for *none.*

   None of the 312 cottages—the twenty-six letters of the alphabet multiplied by twelve cottages to a block—were exactly the same, but essentially they were alike.

   Barry Broadfoot, from *My Own Years.*

3. After the phrase *one of those who,* use a plural whenever attention is drawn to the plurality of people involved.

   To this day I am one of those people who never feel guilty about doing nothing, and who don't get anxious after the first week of a three-week holiday.

   Larry Solway, "School Days, School Days," *The Canadian.*

4. With a linking verb, the subject before the verb, and not the noun complement following it, should determine the number:

   They have no books and no shoes, and all they ever eat is rabbits and wild things.

   Colin Ross, "The Story of Grey Owl," *The Compass.*

5. When a singular noun is the subject, do not allow a nearby plural noun in a modifying prepositional phrase to interfere with subject-verb agreement:

   Just over half (57 per cent) of all viewing is of Canadian programs, and viewing of dubbed and undubbed American programs has increased steadily over the last decade.

   Sandra Gathercole, "Changing Channels," *Canadian Forum*

6. Formally, when a relative pronoun is the subject, its antecedent determines whether the verb is singular or plural:

   And many French Canadians, who now profess to be baffled by the lack of support for the separatist cause among Québec-born Jews, were then out painting *À bas les Juifs* on the Laurentian highway.

   Mordecai Richler, "Home Thoughts," *The Canadian.*

7. For the most part, clause structures as subjects take singular verbs:

> What was certainly Irish, in both its teachings and its sheer bulk, was the church.
>
> Patrick O'Flaherty, "Caught in the Nets: Growing up Irish Catholic in Newfoundland," *Canadian Forum.*

For another problem of agreement, see *Collective Nouns.*

Exercise

For further guidance in general, pay careful attention to usage in the essays you read. For specific information, check dictionary treatments (including usage notes if they are given). Using a dictionary, write a sentence for any two of the following entries: (1) each; (2) number; (3) tactics; (4) there; (5) together with.

The *Gage Canadian Dictionary* provides good information for each word.

apos Apostrophe

Insert or delete an apostrophe as appropriate

Dictionaries do a good job of explaining the three traditional uses of the apostrophe. A word must be added about when not to use it.

1. A common mistake with certain pronouns seems to depend on mixing up the first two traditional functions of the apostrophe: to show possession and to mark contractions. We sometimes write *it's,* the contraction for *it is,* when we mean *its,* the possessive form of *it.* A similar mistake is to write *who's* when *whose* is intended.
2. The third traditional function of the apostrophe is to mark plurals of letters and numbers. In articles on hockey, we may read about the junior A's, or in discussion of the depression we may read about the 1930's. While that use is not wrong, an alternative now has wide acceptance. The practice favoured by essays in our text is to omit the apostrophe while retaining the *s:*

> Duncan was a young career woman of the 1880s—a member of the generation that succeeded Agnes Maule Marchar's.
>
> Barbara Freeman, "'Every Stroke Upward:' Women Journalists in Canada, 1880-1906," *Canadian Women Studies.*

app Appositive

Add or delete commas as required by context

Dictionaries explain that appositives are noun or noun substitutes that further explain other nouns. What needs to be added concerns punctuation.

Like a relative clause, an appositive can either provide required limitation or identification, or it can add information that is not essential to understanding. Commas are omitted when the appositive restricts its noun in an essential way, but commas are called for when the appositive adds non-essential information.

1. Restrictive
   (a) "Mack the Knife" is a familiar type: a restrictive appositive after a personal name. In the example below, a profession is used in the same restrictive way:

   > I've gathered some of them into a book (including the saga of Bill Johnston the pirate).
   >
   > Pierre Berton, "Legends in the Rough," *The Canadian.*

   (b) A second type of common restrictive appositive involves the phrasing "the fact that." *Fact* is given its restricted content by a "that" clause:

   > The fact that Canadians spend hours a day, from infancy, watching someone else's world go by in glossy dramatic images is not unrelated to both our cultural immaturity and our political dependence on the United States.
   >
   > Sandra Gathercole, "Changing Channels," *Canadian Forum.*

2. Non-restrictive
   In this case, a personal name is taken as providing essential identification and a by-the-way fact about that person is set apart by commas:

   > Carl, the grocer at nearby Nimpo Lake, has 300 cases of beer.
   >
   > Al Purdy, "Boozy Saddles," *Maclean's.*

c Comma

Add or delete a comma as required

The comma, the most frequent mark of punctuation, is used flexibly, so that it is easier to say where it may appear than where it must or must not appear. Despite the flexibility, care is needed, for much of the time the presence or absence of a comma affects emphasis or clarity.

1. Compound elements (two members)
   (a) Routinely use a comma between two independent clauses joined by a coordinating conjunction (including *and, but, or, for*):

   > Canadians have never formed a mass or a mass society, and we remain totally antipathetic to the psychology of the mass.
   >
   > Hugh Hood, "Moral Imagination: Canadian Thing," in William Kilbourn, ed., *Canada: A Guide to the Peaceable Kingdom* (Toronto: Macmillan, 1970)

   Writers sometimes omit the comma when they feel ideas will still be clear, especially when the clauses are short and closely related:

> Once it has been formulated the truth is quite simple (it always is) but it is never easy to formulate.
>
> R. Murray Schafer, "Canadian Culture: Colonial Culture," *Canadian Forum.*

(b) Use a comma between parts of a compound predicate only when you want to give the second element special emphasis:

> Archie was only like an Indian on the outside though. That's why the Canadians liked him, and made him a hero.
>
> Colin Ross, "The Story of Grey Owl," *The Compass.*

2. Series (three or more members)
Note that whether a comma should precede the coordinator before the last member of a series is an unresolved issue. Roughly, handbooks of English call for the comma to prevent a sometimes awkward pairing of the last two terms, while stylebooks used in newspaper and government offices reject the final comma because it may cast undue emphasis on the last member of the series. There is room for both practices. Our advice is to include the final comma whenever you are in doubt.

(a) Commas may be used instead of semicolons to separate a series of independent clauses as long as clarity is maintained:

> My impression of federal law in this area is that its intentions are certainly right, its aims are toward justice, and it is indeed in some ways woefully outdated and in need of clarification.
>
> Margaret Laurence, "The Greater Evil," *Toronto Life.*

(b) Commas are usual for separating phrases and individual words in a series:

> Within my lifetime, I've seen the beginning of television, oral contraception, organ transplants, space travel, computers, jets, nuclear weapons, satellite communication, and polio vaccine.
>
> David Suzuki, "A Planet for the Taking," *Canadian Forum.*

When the words are adjectives, take account of relationships. In the following example, commas appear as usual between three adjectives that separately and equally modify the same thing: "small animal." "Small" is not a member of that series because it forms a special unit with the noun; consequently no comma stands between "confident" and "small":

> What you will then have on your hands is a perky, healthy, confident small animal.
>
> June Callwood, "June Callwood's Canada: Crying Brokenhearted Over You," *Maclean's.*

(c) In the absence of a coordinating conjunction, use a comma before each member of the series:

> Try going through your home and looking at the country of origin of your clothes, electrical appliances, books, car.
>
> David Suzuki, "A Planet for the Taking," *Canadian Forum*.

3. Adverbial Clauses

(a) Normally, place a comma after an introductory adverbial clause (a clause beginning with a subordinating conjunction such as *although, if, when*), especially if the clause is relatively long.

> If the apparent public concern with censorship expresses a confused groping toward a revival of critical judgement in sexual and social matters, then it may deserve more than contempt, however misguided or badly motivated by some of the noisiest advocates of censorship may be.
>
> Ralph Heintzman, "Liberalism and Censorship," *The Journal of Canadian Studies*.

(b) An adverbial clause that follows the main clause is separated by a comma only if it is loosely related, providing supplementary information or an afterthought.

> Mr. Stuewe himself points out that book banners are currently hard at work in Nova Scotia and New Brunswick, although he dismisses them as living "mostly in rural areas."
>
> Timothy Findley, "Better Dead than Read? An Opposing View," *Books in Canada*.

4. Introductory words and phrases

(a) Commas are frequent after relatively long introductory phrases:

> On the long boardwalk leading to the lagoon more than a mile away, a concessionaire sold a hamburger—known in Winnipeg as a nip—for five cents. . . .
>
> Barry Broadfoot, from *My Own Years*.

(b) Commas are often used after individual introductory words that are felt to stand apart from the sentence as a whole:

> Once, one of the strongest words in the language was "liar."
>
> Dalton Camp, "The Decline in Public Morality," *Saturday Night*.

5. Words and phrases that interrupt sentence flow

Words of transition, contrast, and qualification as well as miscellaneous expressions that add information or help show the writer's thought processes may be set apart by commas:

> [Deanna Durbin's] birthplace, if mentioned, was a footnote that didn't matter.
>
> Robert Fulford, "The Super-Americans," *Saturday Night.*

Lawren, for example, looked like a Bay Street stockbroker in his suits.

> A.J. Casson, "Group Portrait," *Saturday Night.*

6. Concluding phrases
   Commas often precede participial structures that come after the main clause adding further commentary or information:

   > The silence enveloped me, punctuated by the sound of a distant waterfall or the rumble of a far-off avalanche.
   >
   > Toni Onley, "The Longest Night," *Saturday Night.*

7. Quotations
   Commas are often used to separate short quotations from the rest of the sentence:

   > Andy Lytle wrote a long article asking, "Girls, is sport good for you?" and offered a definitive "No."
   >
   > Abby Hoffman, "Running for Gold," *Maclean's.*

8. Main sentence elements
   Normally, commas should not break the contact between subjects and their verbs or verbs and their objects. For that reason few English teachers would accept the comma in the following sentence despite the prestige of its author:

   > To assume the right to program the sensibilities or thoughts and fantasies of individuals or groups, has long been taken for granted as a viable form of personal action.
   >
   > Marshall McLuhan, "The Violence of the Media," *Canadian Forum.*

coll Collective Nouns

Change one or the other element to make the verb and the pronoun that go with a collective noun agree in number

Collective nouns are singular in form, but they stand for groups. Consequently, they present a challenge with respect to choosing a verb to go with them and, when required, a pronoun to refer to them: should the verb and pronoun be singular or plural? Linguists tell us that the British more often treat collective nouns as plural than Americans do. Canadian preferences probably are closer to the Americans on this point, but the question needs further study. All are agreed, however, that most collective nouns can be thought of as either singular or plural under the pressure of specific contexts.

In these circumstances, consistency of treatment is especially important; if the verb shows you are thinking of the noun as singular, the pronoun referring to it should show the same thought:

> The group, or the crowd, has minimal identity and exists in a state of paranoic anxiety about any threats to its precarious pattern.
>
> Marshall McLuhan, "The Violence of the Media," *Canadian Forum*.

Exercise

Revise the following sentence for the sake of consistency: The couple was in Toronto yesterday to promote a ten-city tour of Canada next month with their dance performance, which they devised after their recent success on the London stage.

colon Colon

Delete the unnecessary colon, add one where no punctuation exists, or change the present punctuation to a colon

Characteristic uses of the colon are less likely to be a problem than where to place it. The following examples show how the colon announces that something is coming that explains what has already been said.

1. A single word

> The concept of ending imprisonment has a name: *diversion*.
>
> Barbara Amiel, "The Chaos of Criminal Justice in Canada: Or: In Defense of Vengeance," *Saturday Night*.

2. A series or list

> At one open meeting, a man rose to condemn the novel and said that he spoke for a delegation of seven: himself, his wife, their four children—and God.
>
> Margaret Laurence, "The Greater Evil," *Toronto Life*.

3. An independent clause

> Frequently, physical appearance takes precedence over performance: women athletes are often depicted as either hideously grotesque or else beauties whose figures amply compensate for any lack of athletic talent.
>
> Abby Hoffman, "Running for Gold," *Maclean's*.

Additionally, it may set off quotations (usually lengthy ones) or do such conventional tasks as set off minutes from hours.

For all but conventional functions, the correct position for the colon—so all the handbooks agree—is at the end of an otherwise complete sentence (as shown in the examples above). Unfortunately, the handbooks have not been able to convince all writers of that requirement; often in newspapers and magazines and occasionally in scholarly writing, one sees a colon after a verb before the predicate is complete or after the word *that* when it starts a subordinate clause. For college and university essays add words such as *this* or *as follows* to complete predicates before colons and simply omit colons after subordinating *that.*

Exercise

Revise the following sentence to conform with formal practice.

> Umbach represents the more intransigent wing of the fundamentalist, evangelical Christian opposition to the books in question, and his first words to me are: "I want you to insist that what I'm saying is a *declaration of truth,* and I am not interested in discussing or dialoguing with you."
>
> Paul Stuewe, "Better Dead than Read?" *Books in Canada.*

comp Comparing the Comparable

Change one or the other item of comparison or contrast so that the two items belong to the same rank

When you announce a comparison or contrast, careful readers expect comments on two things that go together in fundamental ways:

> The style of *First Blood,* like the style of many action novels, owes a good deal to Ernest Hemingway and of course John Rambo himself is the tough, lonely Hemingway hero carried to the point of parody.
>
> Robert Fulford, "The Super-Americans", *Saturday Night.*

Style here and style there is Fulford's choice. He might, of course, have spoken of how a movie compares with a novel (developing particular grounds for the comparison later); those items share a fundamental reality as artistic products. What needs to be avoided is saying that a style is like a novel or that a movie is like a style. Suggesting the worst, handbooks often call such a fault "illogical comparison." But even if we decide the fault stems from weak attention rather than weak logic, there seems to be no good reason to accept it.

Exercise

Straighten out the following passage after reviewing Frayne's essay to find out what is in fact being compared with Mayan ball games:

> Like the Mayan ball games in the temples of the Yucatan, and like the Roman circus in a way, the people really come to be friendly with each other; its a ritualistic handling of aggression in a way that turns it into competition and enjoyment without much damage.
>
> Trent Frayne, "As French Canadian as Baseball," *Maclean's.*

cs Comma Splice

Repunctuate or rewrite to avoid the problem

When two units that could stand as sentences come together without end punctuation, only certain means of uniting them are generally accepted. Comma splice is the name given to uniting two sentence units by means of a comma alone (without an accompanying coordinating conjunction).

Handbooks routinely call the comma splice a fault. Some leave it at that, others find certain instances permissible. All agree not to encourage rampant use. (A major danger is that a writer may use it by accident because of inattentiveness to clause structures.) A defence can sometimes be offered, however: the comma splice may point up the close relationship of ideas, affect emphasis, or add (when it is appropriate) a sense of speed or excitement. Occasional use of the comma splice by reputable writers (including several in our text) convinces us that it cannot always represent a mistake; it is sometimes a legitimate stylistic choice.

Our advice is that you avoid the comma splice in your own writing unless you can show a stylistic motive at a particular point. When your instructor does find that you have used the comma splice improperly, make sure you know how to correct it. Use any of the methods discussed in the entry *Fused or Run-on Sentence.*

Exercise

For practice in finding alternatives to the comma splice, revise the following sentences. (You are, of course, to keep the vocabulary and the intention of the original.)

> Some of us even broke with the species, saying biology is not our destiny, we had no *need* to procreate while we did have a need to discover our true selves.
>
> Dawn MacDonald, quoted by Anne Collins, "On Commitment," *Toronto Life.*

dash Dash

Use the dash or change it to another mark of punctuation as appropriate
Handbooks of English caution against overuse of the dash, and for good reason. The mark, a dynamic one often associated with informal writing, is extremely versatile; it is capable of replacing commas, colons, parentheses, and even semicolons or periods. Its availability can lead to an unhealthy neglect of the other, somewhat more formal marks, inducing careless thought and obscuring sometimes subtle but important distinctions.

The mere fact that the dash is dangerous, however, by no means condemns it. In the following sentence (which quotes a statement by Montréal Expos owner Charles Bronfman) a colon might seem awkward for introducing a list in the middle of a sentence, and dashes separate the names more clearly—and certainly more emphatically—than commas would do:

> What was unconscious was the layout of the park itself, the intimacy that put these famous players—Willie Mays, Hank Aaron, Bob Gibson, our own Rusty Staub—almost within touching distance of the fans.
>
> Trent Frayne, "As French Canadian as Baseball," *Maclean's*.

By all means use the dash on occasion (for summary as above, or for marking abrupt change or giving an element extra emphasis); just do not neglect alternatives.

Exercise

For practice in understanding the dash and its alternatives, change the punctuation in either one of the following sentences:

1. I was bemused—I had no idea either one of them had any interest in hockey.

   Morley Callaghan, "Morley Callaghan Remembers Foster Hewitt," *Saturday Night*.

2. There is the sound, in our own boat, of the heavy centreboard vibrating in its trunk—a kind of dull, chattering, humming complaint against the pressures of the sea.

   Harry Bruce, "The Alchemy of Sailing," *Maclean's*.

frag Fragmentary Sentences

Revise to eliminate the unacceptable fragment
Broadly, fragments are verbal units that lack some element essential to standard sentences but that are, nevertheless, punctuated as sentences. While

advertisers like them as a means of getting attention and simplifying messages and while we use them routinely in speech ("Not now!" "On with the show!" "What, me worry?" are all examples), we should be wary of fragments in essays. They may seem excessively casual and may prompt your instructor to suppose that you do not know the difference between a full sentence and a piece that is broken off of one.

Despite the dangers, fragments can sometimes be effective in writing; and, in fact, a good many essays in our collection use them. Fragments may help establish a personal voice, and they may focus attention effectively. In certain ways, the following contains a model fragment:

> This century is a weak and decadent parasite on a great expansive movement in human culture. The movement began about the time of the American revolution and continued with almost undiminished force until the Russian revolution a hundred and forty years later, the great age of the romantic imagination. We never got in on any of that.
>
> No political thinker like Burke or Coleridge or Marx; no painter like Delacroix or Goya; no spokesman for the language of democracy in literature like Wordsworth or Whitman.
>
> Hugh Hood, "Moral Imagination: Canadian Thing," in William Kilbourn, ed., *Canada: A Guide to the Peaceable Kingdom.*

Its learned content helps us understand that it is not a careless statement, and its contrast with a point in the preceding paragraph gives it a valid rhetorical purpose. Moreover, its structure is not that of the most objectionable fragments: it is not a piece that could readily have been integrated into the preceding or following sentence (see the exercise below). If we add what is missing in it (the subject and verb "We had" in parallel with the sentence that follows) we see that it belongs on its own.

Not all effective fragments behave the way Hood's does, but all good fragments should be motivated. For instance, they may help mark a transition or add needed emphasis. If you have no special purpose in mind, avoid them.

Exercise

Fragments most likely to be objectionable are those that can fit readily into another sentence with punctuation added, but without rewriting. While the authors of the following sentences might want to claim that a need for special emphasis justifies their fragments, both uses are more risky than the instance of Hood's article. For practice in understanding the alternatives, integrate the fragments into the sentences that precede them:

1. But if it is the artist's privilege to see, it is also his job to tell what he sees. As W.H. Auden did, looking over his shoulder into Europe in 1939 and writing: "Intellectual disgrace stares from every human face, and the seas of pity lie locked and frozen in each eye."

   Timothy Findley, "Better Dead Than Read? An Opposing View," *Books in Canada.*

2. You may want to add to what I've discovered. Or argue with my conclusions.

   Peter Gzowski, from *The Morningside Papers.*

fused **Fused or Run-on Sentence**

Revise to make two conventional sentences or a single larger one

As we all know, we begin each sentence with a capital letter and we end each sentence with end punctuation (period, question mark, or exclamation mark). A fused sentence or run-on occurs when we fail to signal the end of one sentence and the beginning of the next; we simply have two units capable of being sentences jammed together without any means of connection. The error most likely results from oversight rather than intention and is hard to find in print. Perhaps for printed sources some editor catches and eliminates the occasional oversight of that kind. Students, however, must do their own careful editing.

To correct a fused sentence, you may want to do no more than end the first sentence and give the second sentence its initial capital letter. You may find, however, that the two units would make a good larger sentence if you joined them properly. If they are short and closely related, a coordinating conjunction by itself may suffice ("and" or "but," for instance). More likely, you will need punctuation: a semicolon alone or a comma together with a coordinating conjunction work in most cases. When the second clause explains the first, a colon is appropriate. Finally, the presence of the fused sentence may cause you to rethink your intention and rewrite so that you no longer have two independent units. For that change, a ready solution is to start one unit with a subordinating conjunction (such as *though, because, if, when*) to replace an independent clause with a dependent one.

Exercise

For practice, correct the fused sentence by any of the methods discussed:

> Sports is a big and lucrative business it is very commercialized and even though there is a lot of money involved many athletes and teams are facing financial problems.

ital Italics

Add or delete italics as appropriate

In handwriting and typing, underlining is the equivalent of italics. Major uses of italics are to mark certain titles (look for examples in the essays in our text), to distinguish words as belonging to other languages, to set off words being considered as words (a task sometimes performed by quotation marks), and to add emphasis to a word. This last use is dealt with here.

Almost any word can be singled out for emphasis, and therein lies a danger: we may allow italics to do for us what might be accomplished by more careful phrasing or structuring (saying things more clearly and using main clauses, as well as beginning and concluding positions to convey our intention). Italics cannot, however, be forbidden altogether as their frequent use in our texts shows. Further, we should be alert to various relatively subtle effects that may accompany emphasis—the effect of belittlement, for instance, in the following passage:

> Thornton Wilder wrote a marvellous thing about money in his play *The Matchmaker:* "Money, you should pardon the expression, is like manure. It should be spread around encouraging young things to grow!" However, the way Reverend Campbell is spreading money on this current campaign against books and the education system makes me think that what *he* has in mind is more like encouraging young things to *ossify.*
>
> Timothy Findley, "Better Dead Than Read? An Opposing View," *Books in Canada.*

Exercise

To help you understand italics for emphasis, we have abbreviated a paragraph to two sentences: the first with the antecedent, the second with a pronoun referring to it. In addition, the second sentence has been altered to omit italics originally placed there. Add italics where you think the author might have put them; then check the original for yourself:

> The sexual censors are always waiting, waiting in the shadows, waiting for their chance to pounce... They believe that what dismays or appals them should simply cease to exist.
>
> Robert Fulford, "Beware: The Censors are Marching Again," *Saturday Night.*

mod Misused Modifiers

Move the modifier, or rewrite the sentence to avoid a misleading or absurd relationship

Broadly speaking, a modifier is misused if it is either unclear or unreasonable. Admittedly, there are some grey areas in determining which practices will offend readers; you will, however, want to be sure you understand major pitfalls and how to avoid them.

1. Sometimes we inadvertently force a modifer to apply to either of two words or two constructions. The effect is sometimes frustrating, sometimes merely amusing:

   > He's been caught apparently napping, his campaign staff have been accused of doubling as government employees and he made a serious slip by saying he would fire Bank of Canada governor Gerald Bouey during a commercial break in a television interview.
   >
   > A newspaper report on campaigning leading to the 1984 Liberal Party convention to choose a leader.

   Moving the modifer is the essential change required in such circumstances, although a bit of punctuation or rephrasing may also be appropriate: "he made a serious error during a commercial break by saying that he would fire . . . Bouey" or "by saying, during a commercial break, that he would fire. . . ."

2. Sometimes as well—instances with participles are typical—we may succeed in applying the modifier to only one thing but find we have attached it to the wrong one:

   > A recount has given him back his controller's seat on Etobicoke council, after losing it by 45 votes election night, Nov. 12.
   >
   > A newspaper report.

   It looks as if the recount, rather than the candidate, had done the losing. Merely moving the modifier around will not solve this problem; some rewriting is required.

   The modifier in cases of this sort is understood to modify whatever is the subject of the main clause. One solution to the problem then is to keep the modifier but rewrite so that it properly applies to the subject: "After a recount the controller regained his seat on Etobicoke council after losing it by 45 votes election night, Nov. 12." Alternatively, one can get rid of the modifier, normally by changing the modifying phrase into a subordinate clause: "A recount has given him back his controller's seat on Etobicoke council after he lost it by 45 votes election night, Nov. 12."

   What has been illustrated with the *-ing* participle applies also to infinitive phrases as modifiers. We are aware, however, that tolerance toward what we call misused modifiers varies, not just by individuals but even by disciplines. Thus, *A Comprehensive Grammar of the English Language* reports that scientific writers regularly accept such sentences as the following: "*To check on the reliability of the first experiment,* the experiment was replicated with a second set of subjects" (italics in the original). It was of course not "the experiment" that had the motive of checking on reliability; it was the experimenter: "To check on its reliability, the experimenter replicated the first experiment with a second set of subjects." Still, it seems, not everyone would see the need for the revision proposed.

Furthermore, there are some common expressions that are exempt outside the sciences from the requirement to modify the main subject. We would expect no objection to "Judging by this movie, the director is a master." We understand that the speaker is doing the judging.

Because of grey areas you may be uncertain about a modifier from time to time. When you are, keep strictly to the guideline provided. In the meantime keep watching for examples in your reading and judge which expressions seem to be clear and effective.

Exercise

Rewrite the following sentence to avoid a problematic modifier.

> Although often used sloppily as a synonym for *uninterested, not interested,* the distinction between the two should be retained...
>
> An excerpt on the meaning of *disinterested* from a handbook (a generally good one) currently in use in Canadian universities.

paral **Parallelism**

Revise the sentence to achieve parallelism

Parallelism, likeness in grammatical form, can be important both for basic clarity and general effectiveness wherever it is used. An outline, for instance, with no two headings that match in pattern would likely be too disorderly to guide your composition. And repetition of a pattern from sentence to sentence is often an aid to coherence of ideas. Treated here are instances within individual sentences where parallelism can be a stylistic requirement.

1. Coordinating conjunctions link equivalent items or structures; one would not say "Early to bed and I get up early." The following sentence provides several illustrations:

   > In the cold and sodden ashes of the stove, perfectly preserved from the wet that had invaded and destroyed practically everything else in the cabin that was not made of wood or metal, he found—together with various letters, a few small notebooks, and some other papers—Edgar Christian's diary.
   >
   > George Whalley, "Introduction," from George Whalley, ed., *Death in the Barren Ground: The Diary of Edgar Christian.*

2. All items in a series should be coordinated whether or not a coordinating conjunction is used:

> Canadians (like Canute) command the waves of Soviet superiority to be still, recite magic tautologies of self-vindication, dream of apocalyptic triumph, gloss over every defeat, celebrate every victory.
>
> Keith Garebian, "The Mythology of Hockey," *Canadian Forum.*

Exercise

Revise the following sentence for parallelism:

> Greater care must be taken to avoid infection, blood loss, and to control stress.
>
> A dentist's column in a newspaper.

parens **Parentheses**

Use parentheses as appropriate

Parentheses, like dashes, are used to set aside words, phrases, or clauses. They are, however, more formal than dashes; they suggest less attachment to the momentary movement of thought and more planning ahead.

When parentheses enclose an entire statement, capitalization and punctuation follow normal rules:

> (I do not mean that they never would be admitted to influence; they would, but mostly as junior partners, distributors of patronage, and functionaries.)
>
> Patrick O'Flaherty, writing about Irish Catholics in "Caught in the Nets," *Canadian Forum.*

An independent clause set apart by parentheses inside a larger sentence begins with a lower case letter and ends without a period, although it may take a question mark or exclamation mark:

> If our upsurge of so-called nationalism seems odd or irrelevant now to outsiders, and even to some of our own people (*what's all the fuss about?*), they might try to understand that for many years we valued ourselves insufficiently, living as we did under the huge shadows of those two dominating figures, Uncle Sam and Britannia.
>
> Margaret Laurence, "Where the World Began," *Maclean's.*

quot Quotation Marks

Add or delete quotation marks as appropriate

Apart from marking direct quotations and certain titles, (see chapter 9), quotation marks may be useful in calling special attention to words in a variety of ways (a function shared to some extent by the more formal italics). They can signal a shift in style, for instance to introduce an informal word or, perhaps, a technical term; they can suggest that a word is being used in an unexpected way. They can also be used to set apart words being considered as words. Handbooks rightly warn against reliance on quotation marks when the purpose is other than direct quotation; as much as possible, careful words in skillful arrangements should take care of points you want to make. Still, something (either quotation marks or italics) is required when words are treated as words, and, as our essayists show us, quotation marks are occasionally effective apart from quotation.

The following sentence makes double use of quotation marks, first in treating one word as a word and then in making us question the meaning of a second one (showing that the author has reservations about it):

> "Feminist" conjures in many people's minds the picture of a lone agent, a solitary woman cut off from the "normal" pursuits of womanhood, out for herself because she doesn't have the opportunity to care for others.
>
> Anne Collins, "On Commitment," *Toronto Life.*

In the sentence below, quotation marks signal that a word has a technical sense (which is then spelled out):

> It also triggers a blood-sugar "spike"—a quick increase in the sugar concentration of the blood which accounts for the "pick-me-up" quality of a cup of coffee.
>
> G.B. Sinclair, "Grounds for Concern," *Saturday Night.*

ref Pronoun Reference to Indefinite Antecedents

Change the antecedent or the pronoun to achieve agreement in number while avoiding sexism

Normally you will be expected to maintain formal agreement between antecedents and the pronouns that refer to them despite widespread and long-standing practice against the agreement in certain cases. The problem arises typically when the antecedent, although singular in form, appears in a context which creates a plural idea: A person may have several careers in __________ working years; Each of the children looked for __________ parents.

The temptation is great to fill in with "their" in both cases, and indeed the *Oxford English Dictionary* reports examples over centuries of *their* in reference to indefinite singulars. Nevertheless, formal guidelines call for a singular pronoun.

Such examples raise the question of agreement in number between pronoun and antecedent; they also raise the question of sexual bias. One way to satisfy the formal requirement of agreement in number is to use the singular masculine pronoun in each case: "his working years," "his parents." That solution also has a long tradition, but it is now, for many of us, offensive to the sense of fair play. Do only males have careers? Are all of the children in this group in fact boys? Some writers have decided to counterbalance the traditional bias by using the possessive "her" in such circumstances: "her working years," "her parents." Our advice is to use the singular masculine or singular feminine pronoun alone only when context gives the antecedent a definite identification with one or the other sex. (If all of the children are boys, write "his parents"; if they are all girls, write "her parents.") Otherwise, we believe, there are better solutions than either masculine or feminine bias pronouns.

A developing consensus on sexual bias, in which this text joins, is well represented by *The Canadian Style,* a publication by the Department of Secretary of State of Canada in 1983 designed first of all to guide public servants but also to contribute to promoting standards in Canadian English generally. In effect, the advice is to avoid phrasing that creates the problem of choosing between "he" and "she," but to use both pronouns—"he or she" (not always in the same order)—when necessary to avoid sexual bias. Often the best way to avoid the problem is to use the plural throughout: People may have to change jobs several times in their careers; All of the children looked for their parents. That solution takes care of agreement in number at the same time that it removes sexual bias. (One could also remove the need for a pronoun reference at all: Several careers are now commonplace during the working years.)

The solution of using some variant of the combination "he or she" is felt by some to be a bit awkward, especially if the phrase must be repeated within a brief space. It is probably that sense of awkwardness that accounts for a shift from the singular to the plural in the following sentence:

> First, a therapist will check the patient's heart condition, then fully inform him or her of what's about to happen, making sure they fully understand and consent.
>
> A psychology column in a newspaper.

Even if awkward, however, *she or he* is to be preferred to the masculine pronoun when both sexes are in question, and it satisfies the demand for matching a singular form with a singular form.

Exercise

Revise the following sentence in accordance with the guidelines discussed:

> Rid of the colonial mentality, the Canadian has a social and cultural opportunity without parallel in modern life. He can create the first modern state. . . .
>
> Hugh Hood, "Moral Imagination: Canadian Thing," in William Kilbourn, ed., *Canada: A Guide to the Peaceable Kingdom.*

refl Reflexive Pronouns

Replace the reflexive pronoun with the subject or object form of the personal pronoun as required by context

On occasion we find a reflexive pronoun (*myself* is typical) taking the place of the subject or object form of the personal pronoun. Grammarians have suggested that writers sometimes make the substitution in order to avoid choosing between forms. (See the entry *Subjects and Objects.*) Perhaps, too, the reflexive form may seem less aggressive than the simple personal forms. However that may be, a pronoun ending in *self* should normally appear in university essays only in the presence of a personal pronoun to which it refers:

> I consider myself to be both a feminist and a strong supporter of civil liberties and free speech, but there is no way I want to be on the same team as the would-be book-banning groups who claim that no contemporary novels should be taught or read in our schools.
>
> Margaret Laurence, "The Greater Evil," *Toronto Life.*

Exercise

In this sentence replace *myself* with the appropriate personal pronoun:

> There we were, my father, my mother, my sister, seven, and myself, ten, strolling home, two by two.
>
> Barry Broadfoot, from *My Own Years.*

rest Restrictive and Non-Restrictive Relative Clauses

Add or delete commas as required to mark the clause as restrictive or non-restrictive

Restrictive clauses, as the name suggests, restrict something; that is, they set limits on whatever is modified, permitting us to identify a person or define a thing as distinguished from others. Non-restrictive clauses do not;

they modify by providing additional information, which may be quite interesting or important but which is not essential to the meaning of the thing modified. (See *Appositives.*)

By a useful convention, we set non-restrictive clauses aside by commas; they are, after all, expendable. But we do not set restrictive ones aside; they are necessary to the meaning of what we are talking about. Because of the convention, punctuation becomes a powerful instrument for clarifying meaning.

1. When we omit commas, we tell our readers that the modifying clause makes our subject distinct from others.

   > Everyone who has cared to comment on the matter has pointed out that John J. Rambo—Vietnam war veteran, U.S. patriot, mass killer—is the great popular American hero of 1985.
   >
   > Robert Fulford, "The Super-Americans," in *Saturday Night.*

   At the same time that Fulford concentrates on what was said by those who have commented on Rambo, his restrictive clause lets us know that not everyone has "cared to comment."

2. When we include commas, we tell our readers that identification of the subject is to be sought outside of the modifier (either in other parts of the same sentence or in surrounding context) and that the information enclosed is in addition to what is essential.

   > Once upon a time there was a pervert called Grey Owl, who lived in the Canadian woods.
   >
   > Colin Ross, "The Story of Grey Owl," *The Compass.*

   In Ross's unfriendly treatment, the man in question has been sufficiently identified by being called "a pervert named Gray Owl"; the fact of living in the Canadian woods is interesting information but is not used to distinguish Grey Owl from anyone else.

Exercise

In the news story about a car bombing, the following sentence contained a non-restrictive clause. To practise your understanding, make up an explanation to justify using a non-restrictive clause; then make up an explanation for removing the commas and treating the same modifier as a restrictive one.

> The chief, who was unharmed, suspected disgruntled officers, but no arrests were made.

sp Spelling

Rewrite the word to conform with standard spelling in one or another of the dictionaries widely used in Canadian universities

To deal adequately with spelling, we need more categories than just correct and incorrect. Consider the following list of words, many gathered from the essays in our text: alright, centre, color, license, program, greyness, reknowned, sceptical, teenage, and travelled.

1. Most of these words have alternative (or variant) spellings, one coinciding with American use and the other coinciding with British use. That is true of center/centre; color/colour; program/programme; grayness/greyness; skeptical/sceptical; and traveled/travelled. Now and again someone will feel that only one of the alternatives is acceptable for Canadian use, but you can expect your instructor to accept either spelling (as long as you do not switch from one to the other in the same essay). The handbooks that comment at all on the issue agree on accepting either, and dictionaries alert to Canadian practice list and accept both (although they give them an order of preference based on their understanding of which dominates usage).

   The Canadian Style recommends *Gage Canadian Dictionary* as a guide for such words, with this exception: because of a still-standing order-in-council of 1890, *Canadian Style* advises preferring *-our* endings to *-or* ones.

2. Whether you treat *licence/license* as alternative spellings again depends on whether your practice coincides with American or British practice, but there is an extra feature to consider. When the word functions as a noun, the British prefer to spell it *licence;* and when it is a verb, to spell it *license.* American preference is to use *licence* for both parts of speech. *Gage Canadian Dictionary* finds that the Canadian preference is to make the distinction.
3. *Teenage* has the variant spelling *teen-age,* associated not with national preferences but with differing editorial policies on the use of the hyphen. Your instructor can be expected to accept either alternative as long as it appears in one or another reputable dictionary.
4. *Alright* is a somewhat odd case. It can be found in dictionaries as a standard variant of *all right,* but more often, dictionaries add a note explaining that it is substandard or at least questionable. Time will tell whether it will gain wider acceptance; just now it seems safer to avoid the spelling in scholarly essays.
5. *Reknowned* is simply a misspelling, not recorded in dictionaries.

Students for whom spelling in general is a problem probably would do well to choose just one dictionary as a guide. (For word meanings, usage notes, and the like, however, you should make use of as many dictionaries as you can handle.)

The *Gage Canadian Dictionary* has the approval of *The Canadian Style* and is certainly very useful for Canadian spelling. Other dictionaries with good attention to Canadian usage include *Funk and Wagnall's Standard College Dictionary,* Canadian Edition (Toronto: Fitzhenry & Whiteside) and the *Houghton Mifflin Canadian Dictionary of the English Language* (Markham, Ontario: Houghton Mifflin Canada, 1980).

sub/obj Subject Forms and Object Forms

Change the form of the pronoun as required by its function

In English, only certain personal pronouns and *wh*-pronouns (used in questions and relative clauses) have distinguishable forms that could be used the way a traditional "rule" requires: use subject forms as subjects and as complements after linking verbs and object forms as objects of verbs and prepositions. While the guidelines below conform to the requirement, discussion touches on its limited applicability. Our focus is on difficult cases.

Personal Pronouns: I/me; he/him; she/her; they/them

Grammarians tell us that the influence of sentence positions sometimes conflicts with the traditional demand based on function: roughly, positions in front of verbs belong to subjects and positions after verbs and prepositions belong to objects. We have no trouble saying "I'm okay" or "An idea struck me"; the subject form is in front of its verb and the object form after it. But if the function calls for one form and the position calls for another, we can expect uncertainty. We can expect some uncertainty as well if a pronoun is paired with another word as subject or object.

1. Use the subject form for complements after linking verbs:

> Mr. Kopyto told the court yesterday that he and others feel "It is not I, but the judicial system itself and the courts of this country that have really been on trial."
>
> A newspaper article quoting a lawyer who was accused of undue criticism of a Canadian court.

"I" accords with the guideline but is not in its usual place; most of us most of the time would say "It's not me." Because we write most effectively when we feel as comfortable as possible with our language, it is sometimes worth looking for a middle way between the formal requirement and the natural tendency. A good alternative here would be, "I have not really been on trial; it is the courts of this country that. . . ."

2. Use the subject form or the object form as required by the function the pronoun has, even when it is coordinated with another word:

> To you and me, sexual meaning is meeting and entering the body of another person in the closest creative intimacy.
>
> A quotation from a journal article in Marshall McLuhan, "The Violence of the Media," *Canadian Forum.*

"To you and me" accords with the formal guideline and pattern of putting objects after prepositions. It can be used as a model to avoid what has been identified as a mistake of overcorrectness (reaching for rules but misapplying them). "Between you and I," with the subject form after the preposition, is a familiar example, and, we note, a long-standing one. The *Oxford English Dictionary* explains that a subject sometimes replaces the object form "esp. when [it is] separated from the governing word by other words" (by the coordinated word in this case).

***Wh*-pronouns: who, whom, whoever, whomever**

Not everyone uses both forms of these pronouns: some people use only who. (The *Oxford English Dictionary* remarked of *whom* long ago, "no longer current in natural colloquial speech.") And even in writing we can be uncomfortable unless *whom* comes right after a preposition as in "it was available for the general public to whom the book was neither symbolism nor a psychological study," (from a legal decision quoted by Margaret Laurence in "The Greater Evil"). We all find it easy to use *who* as a subject in front of a verb, but following the guideline can become difficult in complex sentences in which uncertainty about the pronoun's position or function may arise.

1. Use *who* or *whoever* when it is the subject of a relative clause even when it is separated from its verb by an intervening clause:

   > The man who industry sources say was pegged to become head of the world's largest public firm, Burson-Marsteller, was stabbed to death on Sunday in a five-star West End hotel in London, England.
   >
   > From a newspaper report.

   In sentences of two or more clause structures, it is helpful to sort out all subject-verb relationships. Here, "man" is the subject of "was stabbed"; "sources" of "say," "who" of "was pegged." "Sources say" takes the whole "who" clause as its object, while "who" remains a subject within its clause.

2. Use *who* or *whoever* when it is the subject of a relative clause even if it comes after a verb or preposition.

   > Whatever you want to call whoever was in there, they've come out.
   >
   > Timothy Findley, "Better Dead Than Read: An Opposing View," *Books in Canada.*

3. Use *whom* when it is an object even if it comes before the verb or preposition that governs it:

   > And we find Bonapartism in Louis Napoleon... and perhaps a chastened and corrected version in a certain long-nosed general whom most Canadians, French and English, resent for his intervention in Canadian affairs.
   >
   > Hugh Hood, "Moral Imagination: Canadian Thing," in William Kilbourn, ed., *Canada: A Guide to the Peaceable Kingdom.*

   Sometimes a writer will risk greater informality:

   > A while ago I ran into a man named Harvey who I'd begun working with in an advertising office soon after leaving high school but hadn't seen for several years.
   >
   > Robert Thomas Allen, "Where Women Feared to Tread," *The Canadian.*

Whether a reader will object that "with" requires "whom" depends in part on the level of formality a particular essay requires.

Exercise

For a further look at subjects and verbs, take advantage of the *Oxford English Dictionary's* rich treatment (it will be in your university library). Under *who* and under *whom,* find one example for each that is introduced as "Used ungrammatically" (there are two such entries for each word), and revise the example in accordance with the formal guideline.

tense Verb Tenses

Change the verb tense as context requires

Our first thought about verb tenses may be that they go with time periods. They are not, however, fixed in roles that the names we give them indicate. Spoken by an announcer during a hockey game, "He shoots, he scores!" uses a present tense for a present event, but for the most part we use the present tense without simultaneous contact with what we are talking about. We use it regularly (as this discussion does) to explain things that transcend specific times. We also, frequently, use the present tense to repeat points made in books or articles regardless of the time of publication. "George Grant says" does not depend on his talking at this moment; we discuss his books that way. With another word in the sentence that indicates time, the present tense may announce the future: "The plane arrives at 10 a.m." The past tense normally marks events that ended in the past. Toni Onley explains that he "won the dispute" with Revenue Canada, showing that that particular struggle is over with ("The Longest Night").

But sometimes (especially if we include *could* and *would*) the past is used politely for a present event: "Did you have a question?" "Would you please put out that cigarette?"

Still, we use the tenses as one means of showing that two things occur at the same time or that one occurs before or after another. In that way they help us keep track of relationships in time. "He shoots, he scored!" would be odd. As you move through your essay (which will normally be dominated by either present or past tense) remain aware of how one event relates to another and change tenses only as specific circumstances require.

Exercise

In writing a report we are permitted to use the present tense: the report *says* this or that. That possibility, however, can be overridden for the sake of a verb sequence in which events occurring at the same time have the same tense. Make the appropriate change in this sentence:

> An international organization, the respected League for the Rights of Man, inspected a Quebec prison and reports that it is "scandalous and inhuman."
>
> June Callwood, "June Callwood's Canada: Crying Brokenhearted Over You," *Maclean's*.

term Grammatical Terminology

Refer to dictionaries to improve your understanding of grammatical terms and relationships

All good dictionaries provide grammatical information in main entries and in explanatory material in their introductions, although they differ in the details and in the number of prescriptions for usage that they offer. Sure to be included in what they say will be some treatment of the traditional terms of grammar that appear in handbooks and in this Glossary. If you need to refresh your understanding of what is meant by *appositive* or by *relative clause,* see what the dictionaries will do for you.

Further, instead of waiting to meet a term before you look it up, you may wish to do a quick general survey of grammatical terminology at the outset. For that purpose, you might try starting with the entry "part of speech" and playing the game of moving from term to term. By looking up *verb* in the *Gage Canadian Dictionary,* for example, you will find notes on transitive, intransitive, and linking verbs. Those words in turn will lead you to *object* and *complement*. Another word useful as a starting point is *inflection*.

Use your library as necessary for access to a variety of dictionaries. If you are diligent in searching through them, you can find not only basic definitions but subcategorization and examples to help you better understand what goes with what in the sentences you read and write. Further, you will find a number of rules, in the sense of what is regular in English (how plurals of nouns are formed, for instance) and, sometimes, prescriptions for what some writers think ought to be used or avoided on certain occasions. Under *quotation mark,* the *Gage Canadian Dictionary* will tell you where to place punctuation marks in relation to quotation marks, and under *exclamation mark,* it will add the stylistic advice not to use the mark very often.

than Comparisons Using *Than*

Use the subject form after the conjunction when one subject is being compared to another subject

Good dictionaries adequately introduce the issues of whether to think of *than* as a preposition (in which case the noun or pronoun following it would always be an object) or as a conjunction (in which case context would determine whether a subject or object follows). From us what you need perhaps is a word or two of advice.

Although there is nothing despicable about *than* as a preposition, routinely in university essays you should treat it as a conjunction.

In using it as a conjunction, think through what you mean and let your reader clearly understand you. "Robert's mother loved his older sister more than ______________" is open to two possibilities: "than [she did] him" or "than he [did]."

Exercise

To show you understand the more formal approach, revise sentence 2 to conform to the pattern of sentence 1:

1. Andy was exactly one foot taller than I was.

   Larry Solway, "School Days, School Days," *The Canadian.*

2. Kids would come from many blocks away to play, mostly "the big guys," friends of my brother, a year or two older than him, seven or eight years older than me.

   Ken Dryden, from *The Game.*

unacc Word Unacceptable in its Context

Choose a more acceptable word

Your instructor might find your use of a word unacceptable for any of a number of reasons: the word is so new that it may simply be a passing fad; the meaning you have in mind is no longer current; the word is overused so that it loses its impact; the word is too informal to be appropriate. Further it is possible (although fortunately with only a quite small percentage of our vocabulary) that the objection will be based on a conflict of views: your instructor may mistakenly suppose that the word does not at all have the meaning you give it, or may insist that careful writers should not use it that way even if its meaning can be found.

In our brief discussion, we lump the possibilities together under just two headings in order to emphasize the role of dictionaries and of other evidence of practice in guiding your word choices.

1. Wrong word
   For a clear cut category, we can stipulate that a word is wrong if dictionaries do not record the meaning the sentence demands. A physician once wrote to the *Globe and Mail* to complain that *decalitre* and *decilitre* had been confused in a story about blood cholesterol levels (quite a difference in how many milligrams of cholesterol per unit could be regarded as acceptable). *Affect* and *effect* are a more familiar pair of words often confused with each other. We may have trouble remembering which is which, but when we turn to dictionaries, we can tell which one we meant to use. In that sense, the use of a wrong word is not an intentional act; when we see the evidence, we change the word.
2. Divided usage
   Less clear cut are cases of divided usage in which some people use a word one way and other people another. Sometimes an objector thinks a word is wrong in the way that *decalitre* is wrong for *decilitre* only to discover that it is instead controversial. Letters to the editor in the *Globe and Mail* provide a rich source of examples. A leading Canadian novelist complained that CBC announcers, among others, were misusing the word *momentarily* to mean "in a moment" when, in fact, the word only means "for a moment." Several readers pointed out that dictionaries, North American ones at least, have recorded the meaning "in a moment" for years; whereupon the novelist replied that the word should nevertheless not be used that way, and no agreement was reached.

   In recent years, *hopefully* in the sense of "it is to be hoped" (as opposed to "in a hopeful manner") has been a major example of controversial usage. Writers illustrate both the controversial and the non-controversial use of the word:

   > Next year, hopefully, the Canada Council will pay novelists **not** to write.
   >
   > Mordecai Richler, "Endure, Endure: The Man from St. Urbain's Discovers the West," *Maclean's.*

   > That segment of the population that reads the *Guardian,* and still seeks hopefully for a newer world, finds it not just in the Antipodes but also in India and Africa: the novels of Salman Rushdie, the essays of V.S. Naipaul, the Market Theatre of Johannesburg.
   >
   > Sandra Gwyn, "Over Home," *Saturday Night.*

Objectors approve of Gwyn's usage on grounds that the adverb *hopefully* directly modifies a verb *seeks*. They are uncomfortable with Richler's sentence in which *hopefully* is not attached to any single element of the sentence. Defenders of *hopefully* point out that it is a sentence modifier in the way *mercifully* sometimes is, or *frankly*, as in the following:

> "Frankly," he continued, "I wasn't aware there were any writers in Canada."
>
> A passage in "Over Home" in which Sandra Gwyn quotes a British acquaintance.

Our advice is that you remain flexible when an instructor challenges a word usage. Since your instructor normally knows more about writing effectively than you do, you should welcome the opportunity to revise your work any time you have no independent grounds for questioning the objection. But since nobody knows it all, talk it over with your instructor when you find evidence on your side. See whether the meaning you have in mind is recorded as standard in reputable dictionaries (recorded without notes that say the word is restricted in use in some way—by being out of date, by being informal, and so on). Given dictionary support, look for further evidence available to us all without special training: how writers in books and periodicals you read use the word. Instructors can be expected to honour choices you have made with such care even when they personally reject the usage.

X Edit

Correct the problem

Your instructor may use this mark for anything that looks like a careless mistake or that is too badly expressed to take time with.

Often the problem will be a simple typographical error such as a missed or transposed letter. Sometimes, however, what is wrong can be explained in more than one way. The most economical explanation for the next sentence is that the author omitted a comma before "and":

> Mandel is a poet and a literary critic who is also a poet presents something of a special case.
>
> From a newspaper review of Eli Mandel's *The Family Romance*

Conceivably, however, "as" was typed as "is" and some extra words were left in from an earlier version, so that the intended sentence was as follows: "Mandel as a poet and a literary critic presents something of a special case."

A busy instructor should not be asked to work out the hypothetical alternatives faulty sentence by faulty sentence. Nor should the instructor be required to *guess* what causes a mistake. Assuming that a comma was missing above, is that because of an oversight or because the author did not understand the need for a comma?

Moral to the student: make sure you understand your own intentions, and proofread carefully to avoid X's. Your instructor may, understandably, guess that you know less than you do.

✓ Good Work!

From time to time your instructor may use a checkmark of approval because some element of your essay stands out. We especially recommend it to acknowledge evidence of improvement in a student's handling of any of the problems discussed in the Glossary.

Index